SACRED SITES OF ANCIENT EGYPT

SACRED SITES OF ANCIENT EGYPT

AN ILLUSTRATED GUIDE TO THE TEMPLES, TOMBS AND PYRAMIDS

LORNA OAKES

LORENZ BOOKS

For my husband John and all our many friends in Egypt

This edition is published by Lorenz Books, an imprint of Anness Publishing Ltd, Blaby Road, Wigston, Leicestershire LE18 4SE; info@anness.com

www.lorenzbooks.com; www.annesspublishing.com

A CIP catalogue record for this book is available from the British Library

Publisher: Joanna Lorenz
Project Editor: Claire Folkard
Designer: Jez MacBean
Illustrator: Chris Orr
Picture Researcher: Veneta Bullen
Production Controller: Mai-Ling Collyer

Page 1 *A detail from the so-called coronation chair of Tutankhamun.*

Page 2 *The majestic Sphinx before the pyramid of Khafre at Giza.*

Page 3 *Queen Tuya's jewel box from the tomb she shared with her husband, Yuya.*

Page 4 *The goddess Hathor welcomes Seti I into the Afterlife.*

Page 5 *Treasures from the tomb of King Psusennes of the 21st Dynasty.*

CONTENTS

Ancient Egypt in Context

The fourth millennium BC was a time of great importance to the ancient Egyptians. It was the main formative period, when the individual cultures of different areas were gradually replaced by that of Naqada, an important Predynastic centre in the south. The archaeological record has revealed the spread of the culture known as Naqada II, characterized by attractive buff-coloured pottery decorated with lively scenes of ships, animals and dancing women, throughout the Nile Valley and the Delta.

Political centralization seems to have followed in the wake of cultural unity and is encapsulated in the Narmer Palette, a famous ceremonial object now in the Cairo Museum, which was found at Hierakonpolis, another great, early southern centre. This depicts the early king Narmer (c.3100 BC), wearing the crown of Upper Egypt, subduing people of the Delta, and shows him a second time wearing the crown of Lower Egypt. The point at which unification took place is still a matter of discussion, although it is now thought that the Narmer Palette reflects an established situation, with a sole king already in control of the 'Two Lands', rather than recording the conquest of the north by a southern king, as was once proposed. Ongoing excavations at Abydos have brought to light the graves of kings of the Predynastic Period, who are now referred to as Dynasty Zero. Signs scratched on labels once attached to the grave goods of these rulers also attest to the development of writing at an earlier period than was previously thought.

From c.3100 BC, there is evidence for the existence of a capital city at Memphis. Finds from the related cemetery sites of Saqqara and Abydos show that at this time Egypt enjoyed a high level of artistic achievement, was engaged in far-flung trading relations and was administered by a highly organized and structured bureaucracy.

Although little is known of political events during the Old Kingdom (c.2686–c.2181 BC) which followed, the period is famous for its monumental architecture. The pyramids of Giza are testimony to the status of the kings and their control over resources of materials and labour, and not least the ability of the administration to organize such colossal enterprises.

This period of strength was followed by well over a century of insecurity, when the rule of Egypt was divided during the First Intermediate Period (c.2181–c.2055 BC). However, towards 2000 BC the kings who ruled from Thebes managed to establish control over the whole country. Mentuhotep II (c.2055–c.2004 BC), who reunited Egypt at the

▼ *During the 4th Dynasty, the kings of Egypt were buried in the famous pyramids at Giza in northern Egypt.*

▲ *In the New Kingdom, the royal tombs were situated in southern Egypt, in the remote area now known as the Valley of the Kings.*

beginning of the Middle Kingdom (c.2055–c.1650 BC), was always regarded with great reverence by later kings. In spite of the fact that Amenemhat I (c.1985–c.1955 BC) may have been a usurper and was probably assassinated, the Twelfth Dynasty kings were strong rulers who established control not only over the whole of Egypt but also over Nubia, where several fortresses near the Second Cataract were built to protect Egyptian trading interests.

The ensuing Second Intermediate Period (c.1650–c.1550 BC) was again a time of divided rule. The Hyksos kings, probably originating in the Syria–Palestine area, took over the Nile Delta, and the rule of the Egyptian kings was confined to the south. The texts known as The Story of Seqenenre and Apepi, as well as the Kamose Stela erected in the Temple of Amun at Karnak, tell of the attempts of the Egyptian kings to drive out the Hyksos, while the autobiography of Ahmose (a soldier in the army of King Ahmose) records their eventual success.

Many of the sites visited by tourists today belong to the New Kingdom (c.1550–c.1069 BC). The temples of Luxor and Karnak, the mortuary temples of the West Bank and the royal tombs of the Valley of the Kings are witness to the power and prosperity of Egypt at this time, as are the Tombs of the Nobles, the final resting places of the officials who served the kings of the Eighteenth, Nineteenth and Twentieth Dynasties. During this period, Egypt also controlled many of the petty states of Syria–Palestine and Nubia.

However, from the end of the Twentieth Dynasty, Egypt entered a period of comparative weakness, when the kings ruled the north and the high priests of Amun at Karnak ruled the south, although relations between the two seem to have been friendly. Egypt appears to have lost her former status in Syria–Palestine, while Nubia became independent, with a Kushite ruling family based in the city of Napata in the Sudan, to the south of the Fourth Cataract. These Kushite kings invaded Egypt in the mid-eighth century BC, and were later acknowledged as the Twenty-fifth Dynasty. In 701 BC, the Kushite king, Taharqo (690–664 BC), went to the aid of King Hezekiah of Jerusalem, who was threatened by Sennacherib of Assyria. Taharqo's temerity in supporting a rebellious vassal provoked Assyrian wrath: Egypt was subdued and became part of the Assyrian Empire for a time during the reign of Sennacherib's grandson, Ashurbanipal.

The governors of the Delta city of Sais at first ruled with Assyrian backing but were later to reign as the independent kings of the Twenty-sixth Dynasty. The Saite Period (664–525 BC) is regarded as an era of renaissance: culturally, there was a great deal of interest in the art and architecture of the past, which was consciously copied, but the period was also marked by a new realism in both sculpture and literature. Egypt was once again a united country under a firm central authority and became a power to be reckoned with on the world stage. Military campaigns were mounted to regain control of Nubia, and the Greek historian, Herodotus, describes an expedition sent by Nekau II (610–595 BC) to circumnavigate Africa.

Thereafter, the history of ancient Egypt is one of conquest by foreign powers: the Persians, Alexander the Great and finally Rome. ◆

Chronology and Geography

Predynastic Period **before c.3100**

Early settlements of various cultures
Development of farming
Pottery and copper smelting
Northward spread of Naqada II culture
Evidence of kings at Abydos
Earliest writing

Early Dynastic Period **c.3100–c.2686**

FIRST DYNASTY c.3100–c.2890
Capital at Memphis
Royal graves at Abydos
Narmer Palette
Bracelets from tomb of King Djer *c.3000*
Labels of King Den *c.2950*
SECOND DYNASTY c.2890–c.2686
Peribsen c.2700
Khasekhemwy c.2686

Old Kingdom **c.2686–c.2181**

THIRD DYNASTY c.2686–c.2613
Step Pyramid of Djoser (Netjerikhet)
FOURTH DYNASTY c.2613–c.2494
Sneferu's pyramids at Meidum and Dahshur
Great Pyramid of Khufu (Cheops)
Pyramid of Khafre (Chephren)
Pyramid of Menkaure (Mycerinus)
FIFTH DYNASTY c.2494–c.2345
Abusir pyramids of Sahure, Neferirkare and Niuserre
Sun temples at Abu Gurab
Saqqara Pyramid of Unas (Wenis): first Pyramid Texts
Tomb of Ti
SIXTH DYNASTY c.2345–c.2181
Pyramid of Teti at Saqqara
Pyramid of Pepi I (Meryre) at South Saqqara
Pepi II (Neferkare) c.2278–c.2184
Long reign of Pepi II
Autobiography of Harkhuf from tomb at Aswan
Tomb of Sabni and Mekhu

First Intermediate Period **c.2181–c.2055**

SEVENTH AND EIGHTH DYNASTIES c.2181–c.2125
NINTH AND TENTH DYNASTIES c.2160–c.2025
HERAKLEOPOLITAN RULERS:
Khety (Meryibre)
Khety (Wahkare)
Merykare
Ity
ELEVENTH DYNASTY (pre-conquest) c.2125–c.2055
THEBAN RULERS:
Mentuhotep I
Intef I, II and III

Middle Kingdom **c.2055–c.1650**

ELEVENTH DYNASTY (post-conquest) c.2055–c.1985
Egypt reunited by Mentuhotep II
TWELFTH DYNASTY c.1985–c.1795
Amenemhat I (Sehetepibre) c.1985–c.1955
King possibly a usurper, perhaps assassinated; capital at Itjtawy
Senusret I (Kheperkare) c.1965–c.1920
Period of joint rule (c.1965–c.1955) with his father
White chapel at Karnak
Amenemhat II (Nubkaure) c.1922–c.1878
Tomb of Sarenput II at Aswan
Senusret III (Khakaure) c.1874–c.1855
Egyptian control of Nubia strengthened
Amenemhat III (Nimaatre) c.1855–c.1808
Interest in land reclamation in the Faiyum
Queen Sobekneferu (Sobekkare) c.1799–c.1795
THIRTEENTH AND FOURTEENTH DYNASTIES c.1795–c.1650

Second Intermediate Period **c.1650–c.1550**

FIFTEENTH DYNASTY c.1650–c.1550
Delta ruled by Hyksos kings
SIXTEENTH DYNASTY c.1650–c.1550
Numerous 'kings', perhaps tribal chiefs and vassals of the Hyksos
SEVENTEENTH DYNASTY c.1650–c.1550
Egyptian kings ruling in south
The Story of Seqenenre and Apepi
Kamose Stela; Kamose's attempt to drive out Hyksos

New Kingdom **c.1550–c.1069**

EIGHTEENTH DYNASTY c.1550–c.1295
Ahmose (Nebpehtyre) c.1550–c.1525
Hyksos expelled
Autobiography of Ahmose son of Ebana at el-Kab
Amenhotep I (Djeserkare) c.1525–c.1504
Alabaster shrine at Karnak
Tuthmosis I (Aakheperkare) c.1504–c.1492
First royal tomb in Valley of the Kings
Foundation of tomb builders' village at Deir el-Medina
Queen Hatshepsut (Maatkare) c.1473–c.1458
Joint rule with Tuthmosis III
Funerary temple at Deir el-Bahri
Expedition to Punt
Obelisks at Karnak
Sole reign of Tuthmosis III (Menkheperre) c.1458–c.1425
Consolidation of Egyptian empire
Hall of Records and Festival Hall at Karnak
Tomb of Rekhmire at Thebes

Amenhotep II (Aakheperure) c.1427–c.1400
Tomb of Sennefer
Tuthmosis IV (Menkheperure) c.1400–c.1390
Tombs of Menna and Nakht at Thebes
Amenhotep III (Nebmaatre) c.1390–c.1352
Prosperous period marked by temple building
Luxor temple
Colossi of Memnon
Tomb of Ramose
Amenhotep IV/Akhenaten (Neferkheperurawaenre) c.1352–c.1336
Capital moved to Akhetaten (Tell el-Amarna)
Worship of the Aten
Distinctive artistic style
Tutankhamun (Nebkheperure) c.1336–c.1327
Capital moved back to Thebes
Restoration of traditional religion, funerary practices and beliefs
Ay (Kheperkheperure) c.1327–c.1323
Tomb in Western Valley
Horemheb (Djeserkheperure) c.1323–c.1295
Building at Karnak and Luxor
Tombs at Saqqara and Valley of the Kings
NINETEENTH DYNASTY c.1295–c.1186
Ramesses I (Menpehtyre) c.1295–c.1294
Throne inherited from Horemheb by army commander
Seti I (Menmaatre) c.1294–c.1279
Temple of Osiris at Abydos
Hypostyle Hall at Karnak
Ramesses II (Usermaatre Setepenre) c.1279–c.1213
Battle of Qadesh against Hittites; peace treaty and marriage to Hittite princess
Capital moved to Per-Ramesses in Delta
Ramesseum and Abydos temple
Building and embellishment at Luxor and Karnak Temples at Beit el-Wali, Derr, Wadi es-Sebua and Abu Simbel in Nubia
TWENTIETH DYNASTY c.1186–c.1069
Ramesses III (Usermaatre Meryamun) c.1184–c.1153
Medinet Habu

Third Intermediate Period **c.1069–c.747**

TWENTY-FIRST TO TWENTY-FOURTH DYNASTIES c.1069–c.747
North ruled by kings from Delta; South governed by High Priests from Thebes and local rulers

Late Period **c.747–332**

TWENTY-FIFTH DYNASTY c.747–656
Kushite Dynasty
Assyrian Conquest *671*
Assyrian destruction of Thebes *664*
TWENTY-SIXTH DYNASTY 664–525
Saite Dynasty
TWENTY-SEVENTH TO THIRTIETH DYNASTIES 525–332
Persian Conquest *525*
LAST EGYPTIAN DYNASTY 380–343
Conquest of Alexander *332*

Ptolemaic Period **332–30**

Ptolemy I *305–282*
Defeat of Antony and Cleopatra *30*

[All dates are BC]

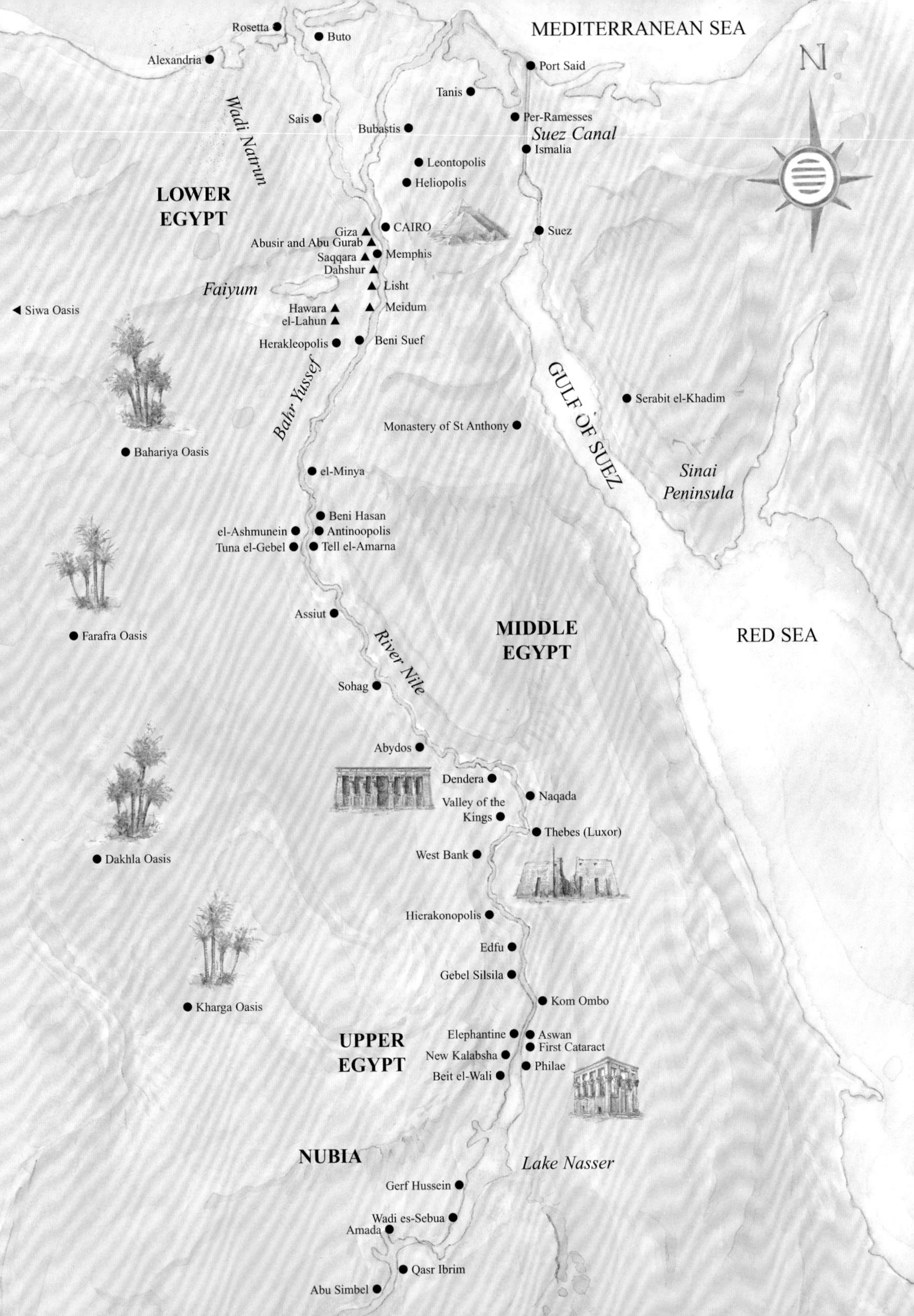
MEDITERRANEAN SEA
N
Rosetta
Buto
Alexandria
Port Said
Tanis
Wadi Natrun
Sais
Bubastis
Per-Ramesses
Suez Canal
Ismalia
Leontopolis
Heliopolis
LOWER EGYPT
Giza
CAIRO
Suez
Abusir and Abu Gurab
Saqqara
Memphis
Dahshur
Lisht
Faiyum
Siwa Oasis
Hawara
Meidum
el-Lahun
Herakleopolis
Beni Suef
GULF OF SUEZ
Serabit el-Khadim
Bahr Yussef
Monastery of St Anthony
Bahariya Oasis
el-Minya
Sinai Peninsula
Beni Hasan
el-Ashmunein
Antinoopolis
Tuna el-Gebel
Tell el-Amarna
Assiut
MIDDLE EGYPT
RED SEA
Farafra Oasis
River Nile
Sohag
Abydos
Dendera
Naqada
Valley of the Kings
Thebes (Luxor)
West Bank
Dakhla Oasis
Hierakonopolis
Edfu
Gebel Silsila
Kom Ombo
Kharga Oasis
Elephantine
Aswan
UPPER EGYPT
First Cataract
New Kalabsha
Philae
Beit el-Wali
NUBIA
Lake Nasser
Gerf Hussein
Wadi es-Sebua
Amada
Qasr Ibrim
Abu Simbel

Part One: Burial Places

From the dawn of history to the coming of Christianity, the ancient Egyptians seem to have cherished hope of eternal life. Even the most simple of graves from the Predynastic period to the end of the Pharaonic era contained grave goods, which appear to have been placed beside the body to provide for the needs of the deceased in the Afterlife.

Death was regarded as a welcome passage from this life to the next. In a Middle Kingdom text, 'The Dispute of a Man with his Ba', death is likened to a sick man's recovery, going out after confinement, a man's coming home after warfare, a man's longing for home after long years in captivity, or sitting under a sail on a breezy day.

All those who could afford it, therefore, spent much of their adult lives preparing an appropriate burial place. Many Old and Middle Kingdom officials built splendid tombs in the Memphite necropolis near to the pyramids of the kings they served, while the New Kingdom administrators made ready rock-cut tombs on the west bank of the Nile, not far from the royal tombs in the Valley of the Kings.

The Rediscovery of Ancient Egypt

Egypt has always been a source of fascination for the traveller. The romantic landscape of the River Nile, with its magnificent antiquities set among the palms of the fertile valley, and the allure of the barren desert stretching away to the horizon never fail to capture the hearts and minds of visitors. But one visit is never enough. The first acquaintance makes such an impact that we are left totally speechless with wonder. With the second and third visits we start to believe our eyes, and the great antiquity and achievements of this ancient civilization begin to sink in. Add to this the charm of the people, their friendliness and unfailing good humour, courtesy and hospitality, and we are permanently hooked.

From the time of Herodotus onwards, Greek and Roman visitors to Egypt were fascinated by the pyramids and the Valley of the Kings. European interest was awakened in the seventeenth century, when the first attempts were made to record the monuments. This eventually led to rivalry between European nations and the race began to build up the Egyptian collections in the great museums of the world.

◀ *A watercolour painted in 1923 by Douglas Macpherson shows a statue of Tutankhamun guarding the entrance to his burial chamber, which was entirely filled by a nest of four gilded wooden shrines placed over the sarcophagus.*

Early Travellers to Egypt

The earliest traveller known to have fallen under the spell of Egypt was the Greek historian Herodotus (c.490–c.420 BC). He visited Egypt in the mid-fifth century BC, and later recorded his travels in Book Two of his great work *The Histories*. This work is primarily about the war between Greece and Persia in the earlier part of that century, but it is much more than a blow-by-blow account of events. Herodotus is often called the 'Father of History' because of his breadth of vision and the far-ranging scope of his work. He was interested in the deep-rooted causes of the war, the previous history of the powers involved, and the achievements and customs of their peoples. Because Egypt was part of the Persian Empire at the time of the war, he included a section on Egypt. Nobody had ever written anything like it before.

The travels of Herodotus

Concerning his trip to Egypt, Herodotus wrote: 'I went and saw for myself as far as Elephantine, but further information is from hearsay'. The truth of his account is sometimes doubted. Writing about the building of the Giza pyramids, for instance, he was referring to a period 2,000 years before his own time, and he had to rely on what he was told by the Egyptian priests. He often provided two or more versions of an event, leaving his readers to make up their own minds. However, on the history of the Twenty-sixth Dynasty (664–525 BC), he is the best ancient source. Modern archaeology continues to prove that much of what he said about this period was true.

Strabo

The Greek historian and geographer Strabo (c.63 BC–c.AD 21) spent several years in Alexandria, the capital planned by Alexander the Great, though he did not live to see it built, on the Mediterranean coast. It was extended and embellished with additional buildings by the Ptolemies, who ruled Egypt after him. Strabo's description is one of the main sources of information about it:

> *The city has magnificent public precincts and royal palaces, which cover a fourth or even a third of the entire area. For just as each of the kings would from a love of splendour add some ornament to the public monuments, so he would provide himself at his own expense with a residence in addition to those already standing.*

Alexandria's public buildings included the great Museum, with its covered walk and dining hall for the convenience of scholars studying at the nearby Library. The two harbours and the lighthouse are also mentioned by Strabo, as well as the Theatre, the Gymnasium and the Temple of Serapis.

The whole city was criss-crossed with streets at right angles to each other, wide enough to take large numbers of horses and carriages. Strabo's description is particularly useful because much of the ancient city has disappeared under later building or now lies below the sea. It is exceptionally valuable to the teams of modern archaeologists who are now bringing parts of the old city to light.

Strabo also visited Upper Egypt, and described the tourist attractions of the day, such as the Colossi of Memnon and the royal tombs in the Valley of the Kings. About the latter he wrote: 'Above the Memnonium [the Ramesseum], are the tombs of the kings, which are hewn in stone, are about 40 in number, are marvellously constructed, and a spectacle worth seeing'.

▼ *At his Tivoli residence, Hadrian encapsulated the places and works of art he had seen on his travels in Greece and Egypt.*

▲ *Although recent excavation has revealed more of the site, the two gigantic statues of Amenhotep III are all the tourist usually gets to see of this once enormous mortuary temple, which served the cult of the deceased king.*

The Colossi of Memnon

Strabo was rather scathing on the subject of these two massive statues, which represent Amenhotep III (c.1390–c.1352 BC) and mark the site of his once great funerary temple. In Strabo's day, however, they were identified with the mythical King Memnon of Ethiopia, said to be the son of the Dawn, a hero who had gone to the aid of the Trojans against the Greeks.

The statues had been damaged by an earthquake in 27 BC, and one of them was reputed to give out weird noises. Most tourists were greatly impressed and gathered daily to hear the statue speak. Strabo cynically put the mystery down to the machinations of the local priests.

Hadrian saw the same statue in AD 130, but it did not 'speak' until the second day of his visit. A poetess in the imperial retinue, Julia Balbilla, carved on the statue a verse in praise of Memnon and Hadrian. The inscription can still be read today.

Hadrian

When the Roman emperor Hadrian (AD 117–138) arrived in Egypt in AD 130, he went first to Alexandria. There he spent some time in learned discussions with the scholars in the Museum. He then sailed up the Nile accompanied by his favourite, Antinous, who was accidentally drowned during the trip. In memory of his friend, Hadrian founded a new city, Antinoopolis, which was laid out on a grid along Greek lines, with two colonnaded main streets crossing at right angles and embellished with baths, temples and a theatre.

Graffiti inscribed by the tourists of antiquity bear witness to the interest aroused by Egypt's buildings and monuments during the Roman Period. Paramount among these were the obelisks inscribed with hieroglyphs, which the Romans could not decipher. Several emperors had obelisks taken to Rome, where they still stand today. The Roman naturalist Pliny the Elder wrote that the Emperor Augustus (27 BC–AD 14) used the obelisk set up in the Campus Martius in Rome as a sort of calendar, based on measurements of its shadow at various times throughout the year. Apparently it did not work. Emperor Constantine (AD 312–337) removed an obelisk of Tuthmosis III from its original site at Thebes and took it to Alexandria to await shipment to his new capital of Constantinople. Constantine died before the obelisk reached its destination, but Theodosius I finally set it up in the Hippodrome in AD 390.

Hadrian took an even more personal interest in the antiquities, and had some of them taken home to Italy to enhance his villa at Tivoli. It does not seem to be true, however, as scholars once thought, that he tried to recreate complete buildings. The building known today as the Serapaeum at Tivoli was once widely considered to be a 'replica' of the Temple of Serapis at Canopus near Alexandria, but is now identified as a triclinium (dining room). ◆

► *Portrait bust of the Emperor Hadrian who spent much of his reign travelling around the Empire, visiting Greece in AD 125 and 128 and Egypt in AD 130.*

The Reawakening of European Interest

After the fall of the Roman Empire, Europe forgot about Egypt for a time. Egypt became a Muslim country, and it was in any case difficult for Europeans to travel beyond Cairo and the Nile Delta. During the Middle Ages, most interest was focused on Egypt's links – real or otherwise – with the Bible. The pyramids at Giza, for instance, were fancifully identified as 'Joseph's granaries'. For the most part, Egypt was merely a staging post on the well-worn pilgrim route to Jerusalem during this time. Any European interest in Egypt lay in its associations with early Christianity rather than in the land of the pharaohs.

Religious missions

It was only in the seventeenth century that European expeditions to Egypt began again, and these were undertaken mainly for religious reasons. Monks went to Cairo to preach the gospel, but some of them took the opportunity to travel further afield. In 1672, the Dominican priest Father Vansleb was instructed by Jean Baptiste Colbert, chief minister of Louis XIV of France, to collect coins and ancient manuscripts while in the country. He visited the Red and White Monasteries at Sohag and the Monastery of St Anthony on the Red Sea. He also took an interest in the antiquities, particularly the mummies. On opening a pit at Saqqara, he came upon a room full of mummified birds and took some examples back to Europe. Travelling further south, he was the first European to describe Antinoopolis.

Slightly later, between 1714 and 26, another French priest, Claude Sicard, went on to explore the rest of the country. Father Sicard was the leader of the first Jesuit mission to Cairo and eventually he drew up the first scientific map of Egypt. This showed the precise locations of Memphis and Thebes, and

▼ *An early 19th-century watercolour engraving by Louis François Cassas shows the Sphinx and the pyramid of Khafre at Giza.*

▲ *Richard Pococke's 'map' of the Valley of the Kings. Although not accurate in the modern sense, archaeologists have been able to identify the tombs Pococke visited from the accompanying plans.*

all the main temple sites. He also pinpointed ten open tombs in the Valley of the Kings.

Early descriptions

The best account to survive from this early period, however, was written by Richard Pococke, Bishop of Ossory in Ireland, who visited Egypt in the late 1730s. His description of the Valley of the Kings, where he found 18 tombs (although only nine were open), was published in 1743 under the title *Observations on Egypt*. He also produced a map of the Giza pyramids, but this is schematic in the extreme and his description of the site does not agree with what is found on the ground.

Pococke's contemporary, the Danish traveller Friderik Norden, also visited the pyramids. He was a naval marine architect, and in 1755 he published a much more accurate account than Pococke's in his *Travels in Egypt and Nubia*. He had been commissioned by King Christian VI of Denmark to collect information of antiquarian interest; he travelled the length of Egypt and eventually penetrated Nubia. Frustrated in his attempt to reach the Second Cataract, he got as far as Derr, where he wrote an account of the temple of Tuthmosis III (c.1479–1425 BC).

During his travels, Norden recorded a huge amount of information on the monuments of ancient Egypt. His book was widely read by scholars and laymen alike, and its importance in providing accurate plans and drawings cannot be exaggerated. He was also interested in contemporary life. He warned that the local people were suspicious of foreign travellers, being convinced that they were all treasure seekers and practitioners of black magic, and crowds gathered to see them. In order to allay any such suspicions, Norden advised prospective travellers not to try to touch the antiquities, but to adopt Turkish dress, 'a pair of mustachios' and 'a grave and solemn air'. The first picture of a scene in a tomb in the Valley of the Kings was published in 1790 by the Scottish traveller, James Bruce. During his visit to the tomb of Ramesses III (c.1184–1153 BC) he was fascinated by a scene in a small side chamber, depicting harpists playing before some of the gods. Bruce's drawing is now lost but seems to have been elaborated by the plate-engraver who took many liberties with the original. Having never seen any ancient Egyptian art, he interpreted it according to contemporary taste in the neo-classical style. Although his illustration of the harpists affords some amusement today, the tomb of Ramesses III has ever since been known as 'Bruce's tomb'. ◆

Napoleon's Expedition to Egypt

In 1798, Napoleon Bonaparte of France mounted a great expedition to Egypt with the dual purpose of reducing the power of his chief adversary, England, and exploring a lost civilization. His military expedition was a failure, but his survey of Egypt brought the wonders of the ancient land to the attention of the whole of Europe.

Before leaving for Egypt, Napoleon ordered leading French scholars to assemble teams of professional surveyors, engineers, mathematicians, astronomers, chemists and botanists, as well as artists, architects and archaeologists. These experts were to survey and record all aspects of Egyptian life, past and present. The French soon made themselves masters of Cairo, after defeating the Mameluke rulers, but were beaten at sea by Nelson's English fleet at the Battle of Abukir Bay. Finding themselves stranded in Egypt, the French Commission on Arts and Sciences spent the next three years mapping the whole country, recording archaeological sites and monuments, and studying the flora and fauna and contemporary life of the Egyptian people.

Description de l'Egypte

The result was a massive work, the *Description de l'Egypte,* published in 20 volumes between 1809 and 1828. This monumental, lavishly illustrated work caused a tremendous sensation among the scholars and cognoscenti of Europe, depicting as it did the splendours of ancient Egypt as they had never been seen before. The Commission's artists had drawn precise views of many of the pyramids. Khufu's Great Pyramid and the Sphinx had been carefully measured and studied.

Further south, the Commission explored the Valley of the Kings, where 16 tombs were located. The map of the valley, drawn for the expedition by Jollois and de Villiers, two young engineers, was the first accurate map of the area ever to be made. They also discovered a secondary valley, the Western Valley, and in it the tomb of Amenhotep III (c.1390–1352), whose existence had not previously been known.

▲ *Napoleon Bonaparte who, in 1798, mounted an expedition aimed at the conquest of Egypt. This was accompanied by a special commission that recorded the flora, fauna and contemporary culture of Egypt and surveyed the antiquities.*

▲ *The Commissioners engaged in their survey. The results were published in* Description de l'Egypte, *which reawakened interest in the area.*

▲ *Members of Napoleon's expedition measure the Sphinx, as depicted in a drawing by Vivant Denon from* Voyages dans le Basse et la Haute Egypte.

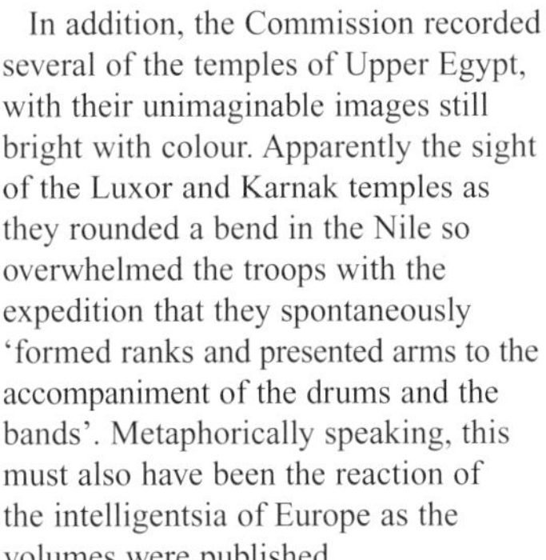

In addition, the Commission recorded several of the temples of Upper Egypt, with their unimaginable images still bright with colour. Apparently the sight of the Luxor and Karnak temples as they rounded a bend in the Nile so overwhelmed the troops with the expedition that they spontaneously 'formed ranks and presented arms to the accompaniment of the drums and the bands'. Metaphorically speaking, this must also have been the reaction of the intelligentsia of Europe as the volumes were published.

A popular version of the *Description,* the work of Vivant Denon, was published in 1802. This book, the *Voyages dans la Basse et la Haute Egypte,* became a great success. It ran to 40 editions and was also translated into English and German. The book brought the discoveries made in Egypt to a much wider readership and, together with the *Description de l'Egypte,* led to a wave of Egyptomania that swept across Europe. However, this renewed interest also sadly led to the unscrupulous looting of antiquities by private collectors and museums alike.

Vivant Denon

Egyptology owes a great deal to Baron Dominique Vivant Denon (1747–1825). He had served at court under Louis XV and also as ambassador of France at St Petersburg and Naples under Louis XVI and, despite his distinguished career, he managed to survive the French Revolution unscathed. The Empress Josephine, who found him a place on Napoleon's expedition to Egypt, later befriended him.

Denon proved himself to be a talented artist and undertook much of the Commission's illustrative work, albeit sometimes in very difficult conditions, surrounded by Mamelukes and Arabs taking potshots at him. He also complained at the little time he had at his disposal in the Valley of the Kings. Allowed only three hours to record six tombs, he exclaimed:

> *How was it possible to leave such precious curiosities, without taking a drawing of them? How to return without having at least a sketch to show? I earnestly demanded a quarter of an hour's grace: I was allowed twenty minutes; one person lighted me, while another held a taper to every object I pointed out to him, and I completed my task in the time prescribed with spirit and correctness.*

On his return from Egypt, Denon was appointed Director General of Museums, and he went on later to found the Musée Napoléon, now the Louvre, in Paris. ◆

▼ *Vivant Denon, whose discourse and publications made a great contribution to the rise of Egyptology.*

European Rivalry: Champollion and Young

One of the most important antiquities to be studied as a result of Napoleon's expedition was the Rosetta Stone. This slab of black basalt was discovered in 1799, incorporated into an old wall, by a French officer inspecting the building of Fort Julien, near Rosetta in the Delta. After the French defeat, the British seized the stone and today it is in the British Museum, London.

The stone was inscribed in three different kinds of writing. One section was in Greek, which could be read, one was in Egyptian hieroglyphs and the other was in a cursive script. The race was soon on to decipher it. The main contestants were the French linguist Jean-François Champollion (1790–1832), his compatriot Sylvestre de Sacy (1758–1832), the English scientist Dr Thomas Young (1773–1829) and the Swedish diplomat Johan David Akerblad (1763–1819). Both Champollion and Young had been child prodigies and were conversant with Greek, Latin, Hebrew, Arabic and Aramaic, as well as several European languages.

Deciphering the hieroglyphs

All four scholars recognized the importance of the Rosetta Stone as the key to a modern understanding of the history and culture of ancient Egypt. Each had a copy of the three texts, but it was 20 years before any real progress was made. The Greek text proved to be a decree celebrating the anniversary of the coronation of Ptolemy V (205–180 BC). It was guessed that the other two sections of the inscription were versions of the same text. The first clue came in the name of Ptolemy. This could be read in Greek and was found in the hieroglyphic version inside a cartouche, the oval outline that, it was also guessed, enclosed the names of a king. Young compared this cartouche with two others inscribed on an obelisk that had been brought to England from Philae and is now in Kingston Lacy, Dorset. On this he was able to recognize the names of both Ptolemy and Cleopatra, since they have several letters in common. However, he failed to crack the code because he refused to believe that, apart from use in foreign names (the Ptolemies were Macedonian), the hieroglyphs could have an alphabetic or phonetic value. He firmly believed that the hieroglyphs were symbols that conveyed the sense of a whole word. The breakthrough came when Champollion, aided by his knowledge of Coptic (the last written form of the ancient Egyptian

▲ *Jean-François Champollion did most to decipher Egyptian hieroglyphs by realizing that a sign could represent both an idea and a sound.*

language, which employed mostly Greek characters), realized that hieroglyphs could convey both an idea and a sound value. In 1822, he was able to study some copies of texts from the temples of Tuthmosis III (c.1479–c.1425 BC) and Ramesses II (c.1279–1213 BC) in Nubia. Again, the royal names were identifiable because they were written in cartouches. These kings were also known from the classical authors, and Champollion was able to refer to Coptic to confirm his intuition about their identities and the way in which the language worked. He knew that *ra* means 'sun' in Coptic, and in the cartouche he saw a sun disc that not only expressed the idea of 'sun' but the sound *ra* in Egyptian. He already knew the letter 's' from the Greek form of the name of Ptolemy (Ptolemaios). Guessing that the middle symbol was *mes*, he arrived at the name 'Ramesses'.

▼ *Written in Greek and ancient Egyptian, using three scripts (Greek, Egyptian hieroglyphs and demotic), the Rosetta Stone held the key to the decipherment of the ancient Egyptian texts.*

▶ *In 1828, Champollion travelled through Egypt and Nubia reading inscriptions. In this book he proved the accuracy of his decipherment.*

MONUMENTS DE L'EGYPTE ET DE LA NUBIE PAR CHAMPOLLION LE JEUNE

Champollion made his discoveries known in September 1822 in a lecture to the Paris Académie des Inscriptions et Belles Lettres, now famous as the *Lettre à M. Dacier.* He then went on to study as many texts as he could lay his hands on in Turin, Aix and Livorno, and at last fulfilled his ambition to visit Egypt. During his 15-month trip, he travelled from Alexandria to Abu Simbel and beyond, reading the ancient texts along the way. Each one confirmed the views he had expressed in his lecture. Writing to Dacier, he said:

Now that I have followed the course of the Nile from its mouth to the Second Cataract, I am in a position to tell you we need change nothing in our Alphabet of the Hieroglyphs, our alphabet is correct: it applies equally well to the Egyptian monuments built during the time of the Romans and the Ptolemies and – what is of much greater interest – to the inscriptions in all the temples, palaces and tombs dating from the time of the pharaohs.

Champollion was, however, scathing about the efforts of his rivals. Akerblad, he reckoned, could not read 'three words of an Egyptian inscription'. Although Young had made a valuable contribution to the decipherment of the Rosetta Stone, had correctly asserted that the second of the scripts was a cursive form of hieroglyphs and had published an article in the Encyclopaedia Britannica on the subject, Champollion dismissed his efforts as 'mere bragging'. For his part, Young refused to believe that Champollion had accurately cracked the code. ◆

The Race for the Antiquities

The discoveries that were made during Napoleon's expedition gave rise to a passion for all things Egyptian throughout Europe, and led to a lucrative trade in ancient artefacts, eagerly sought by both private collectors and public institutions. There were large fortunes to be made by the major collectors of the antiquities, and such was the competition between them that fights often broke out between the rival gangs of workers at the excavation sites.

Bernadino Drovetti

Drovetti had served as a colonel during Napoleon's expedition to Egypt. He became Consul General of Egypt in 1810, and for the next 19 years used his position to carve out a career as an antiques dealer. He often directed excavations himself and took an active part in the looting of antiquities, ably assisted by his agent Jean-Jaques Rifaud, a sculptor from Marseilles. When he had amassed a significant collection he offered the finds to Louis XVIII, hoping that they would be bought for the Louvre in Paris. But the king thought the price too high, so Drovetti sold the collection to the King of Sardinia, who presented it to the Turin Museum in 1824. Some of the best pieces of royal sculpture, including the famous seated statue of Ramesses II (c.1279–c.1213 BC), are in this collection today and the Turin Museum was the first to own such an important group.

Drovetti then embarked on another collection, which he again offered to France. This time it was bought by Charles X, on the recommendation of Champollion, on behalf of the Louvre, where it became the nucleus of the Egyptian Antiquities section. Friedrich Wilhelm III of Prussia bought a third collection in 1836 for the Berlin Museum.

Henry Salt

Not to be outdone, the British Consul General, Henry Salt, also collected antiquities on the instructions of Sir Thomas Banks, one of the Trustees of the British Museum. However, he was bitterly disappointed when he was offered a mere £2,000 for what he had assembled. This did not even cover the cost of excavation and transport. Furthermore, the museum refused to buy the best item in the collection, the beautiful alabaster sarcophagus of Seti I (c.1294–c.1279 BC). This was later bought by Sir John Soane, who paid as much for it as Salt had received for the rest of the collection, and it is the centrepiece of Sir John Soane's Museum in Lincoln's Inn Fields, London.

A second collection made by Salt was offered to the British Museum, but was finally sold to the French king Charles X and presented to the Louvre. Among its many important pieces was the Karnak kinglist, which made the Louvre collection as important as that of Turin.

▼ *Belzoni's drawing of the Temple of Karnak. Only the tops of the pillars and pylons stood out from the mounds of accumulated sand and rubble.*

◀ *Bernardino Drovetti, standing centre left, whose collection formed the nucleus of the Turin Museum.*

'The Patagonian Samson'

Belzoni had enjoyed a varied career before entering Salt's service. At one time he had entertained ideas of becoming a monk, but he later appeared as 'The Patagonian Samson' in a music-hall act at Sadler's Wells Theatre in London. He was extremely tall and immensely strong, and the climax of his act was to appear on stage strapped into an iron harness carrying a dozen or so people who formed a 'human pyramid'.

Giovanni Belzoni

Salt's right-hand man in the difficult process of transporting the antiquities to Europe was the adventurer Giovanni Belzoni. He first visited Egypt in 1814 with the idea of interesting the Turkish viceroy, Mohammed Ali Pasha, in a water-raising device he had invented. Unfortunately for Belzoni his machine was rejected, and he was left penniless as he had sunk all his funds into the project. In despair, he left Cairo in 1816. But as luck would have it, he was approached by the scholar and explorer Jean-Louis Burckhardt, who introduced him to Salt. Burckhardt suggested that they should try to remove the colossal fallen bust of Ramesses II from the Ramesseum and transport it to England.

▲ *Giovanni Belzoni, seen here in Turkish dress, was given money by the British Consul General to collect antiquities for the British Museum.*

By means of four great levers the bust was raised sufficiently for a huge raft on rollers to be placed underneath it, and Ramesses began the first stage of his long, slow journey to London. It took ten days to cover less than 2km (1 mile). The local rulers put many difficulties in the way, but eventually the statue reached the River Nile.

While waiting for a ship big enough to carry the bust to Cairo, Belzoni used the time to visit the Valley of the Kings, where he explored the magnificent tomb of Seti I. Belzoni was also a talented artist and faithfully copied all the painted reliefs and texts he found in Seti's tomb. His drawings were later exhibited to great public acclaim in London and Paris. Even Champollion went to have a look at Belzoni's work and copied a number of the texts in support of his theories on decipherment.

During the wait for a ship, Belzoni also excavated at Karnak, where he discovered 18 statues of the lioness-headed goddess Sekhmet, a kneeling statue of Seti II (c.1200–c.1194 BC) and several sphinxes, all of which are today in the British Museum collections. Belzoni also took part in the excavation of Abu Simbel and made accurate records of the temple. ◆

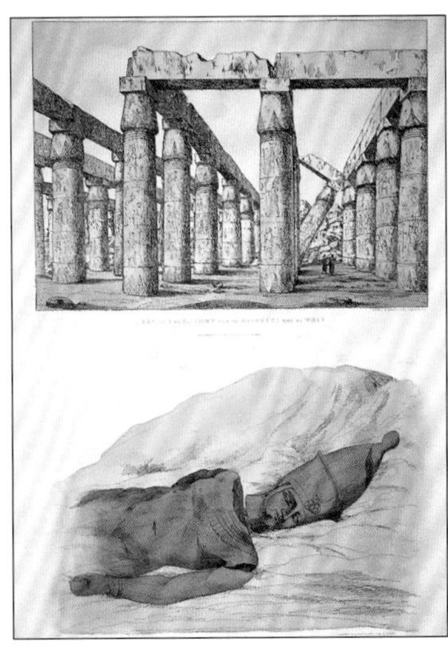

▲ *Illustrations from a book by Belzoni of Karnak and a colossal statue, thought to be of Ramesses II, that he found there.*

The Founders of Egyptology

The nineteenth century saw the development of an ever-increasing body of serious travellers to Egypt. By this time, these travellers' main interest lay in making careful records of the antiquities, rather than in removing them from their original settings to the museums of Europe.

John Gardner Wilkinson

The work of Sir John Gardner Wilkinson (1797–1875) laid the foundations of Egyptology in Britain. Arriving in Egypt in 1821, he spent the next 12 years systematically studying the main archaeological sites of Egypt and Nubia, including Karnak, the tombs of the Valley of the Kings and Gebel Barkal, the sacred mountain near the Fourth Cataract. He made precise copies of the tombs at Beni Hasan, identified the 'Labyrinth' described by the classical authors as the mortuary temple of Amenemhat III (c.1855–c.1808 BC) at Hawara and was the first to draw up a detailed plan of Tell el-Amarna, the city of Akhenaten (c.1352–c.1336 BC). Some of his most valuable work was in the field of epigraphy, which is the study of ancient inscriptions. He made exact copies of the texts he came across during his excavations, and identified the names of many of the ancient Egyptian kings for the first time. The detailed precision of his work far outclassed that of his contemporaries, and it remains a veritable mine of information for modern Egyptologists.

Wilkinson was interested in more than the monuments, however, and on his return to England wrote a massive work entitled *The Manners and Customs of the Ancient Egyptians.* Using his copies of scenes from the tombs, papyri and other inscriptional material, he produced a vivid portrayal of the daily life of the ancient Egyptians. Later, he made a detailed study of the famous kinglist known as the Turin Canon, and helped to establish the correct order of the rulers of ancient Egypt.

▼ *A watercolour painting by Lepsius depicts the city of Thebes, showing the ruins of the temples of Luxor and Karnak.*

▶ *John Gardner Wilkinson was the first British scholar to make a science of Egyptology. He was particularly famous for his copies of tombs and their inscriptions.*

Carl Richard Lepsius

In 1842, Carl Lepsius (1810–84) was commissioned by Friedrich Wilhelm IV of Prussia to lead an expedition to Egypt. Before this he had spent years studying Champollion's grammar in order to learn hieroglyphs, and had visited the major European collections of Egyptian antiquities. As with the earlier expeditions, Lepsius' main task was to record the monuments and to take home antiquities. His team included the artist Joseph Bonomi and the English architect James Wild. On his return he published his findings in a monumental work, *Denkmäler aus Aegypten und Aethiopien* (1849–58), a book comparable in scale to Napoleon's *Description de l'Egypte.*

Lepsius' work is particularly important because it describes many sites where there was considerably more to see at the time of his visit than there is today. Many of them have suffered at the hands of looters as well as from the ravages of time. In fact, some of the most important finds of recent times came about through his work. Professor Geoffrey Martin's rediscovery of the tombs of Maya, Tutankhamun's treasurer, and the king's general, Horemheb, were made possible by surveys and descriptions made by Lepsius of the tombs at Saqqara dating from the New Kingdom (c.1550–c.1069 BC). They lay buried beneath the sand as the joint expedition of the Egypt Exploration Society and the National Museum of Antiquities in Leiden set to work in 1975.

In 1865, Lepsius was rewarded with the post of Keeper of the Egyptian Antiquities Department in the Berlin Museum, and some months later he led another expedition to Egypt, this time to the little-explored area of the Delta. At Tanis, he discovered the Canopus Decree: this document, written in Greek and Demotic, proved useful to scholars engaged in decipherment because it could be compared with the Rosetta Stone. Until his death in 1884, Lepsius produced many more publications, and was also the editor of the leading German Egyptological journal, the *Zeitschrift für ägyptische Sprache und Altertumskunde.* Lepsius did more than anyone else to put Germany, particularly the Berlin Museum, on the map in the field of Egyptology. ◆

▼ *The antiquities and 15,000 casts Lepsius brought home from Egypt formed the nucleus of the Berlin Museum's Egyptian collection.*

Mariette and French Egyptology

Auguste Mariette (1821–81) first became interested in Egyptology in 1842 while he was sorting through some papers left to his family by his cousin Nestor L'Hôte. L'Hôte had accompanied Napoleon's expedition to Egypt and had produced several drawings for Champollion, some as yet unpublished. Mariette spent the next seven years learning hieroglyphs and studying Coptic before finding employment in the Louvre, where he made an inventory of all the museum's ancient Egyptian texts.

The Serapaeum

In 1850, Mariette was sent to Egypt to collect papyri, but because he was given a rather lukewarm reception in the monasteries of the Wadi Natrun he decided to try his luck elsewhere. He eventually arrived at Saqqara, the cemetery site for the ancient capital Memphis. On seeing a sphinx half-buried in the sand he was immediately reminded of the words of Strabo:

▲ *Mariette's discovery in the Serapaeum of an undisturbed Apis burial, with the bull's mummy, jewellery and gold, brought him worldwide fame.*

◀ *Auguste Mariette, the founder of the Egyptian Antiquities Service and the Bulaq (now Cairo) Museum. He discovered the Serapaeum, the burial place of the Apis bulls, and the valley temple of the Old Kingdom king Khafre, at Giza.*

There is also a Serapaeum at Memphis, in a place so sandy that dunes of sand are heaped up by the winds: and by these, some of the sphinxes which I saw were buried even to the head and others were half visible; from which one might guess the danger if a sandstorm should fall upon a man travelling on foot towards the temple.

Mariette felt irresistibly led by these words towards the Serapaeum, which was the burial place of the mummified remains of the Apis bulls. Each of these sacred animals was regarded during its lifetime as the representation on earth of the deity Apis (a manifestation of Ptah, the creator god of Memphis) and was kept in a special stall near his temple. After death the bulls were associated with the Underworld gods Sokar and Osiris, and were laid to rest at Saqqara.

The avenue leading to the temple took two years to clear and it was only in the face of much official opposition that Mariette was allowed to complete his work in the Serapaeum itself. However, he was eventually able to restore some kind of order to the chaos found in the subterranean passages and burial chambers, where the sarcophagus lids had been prised off and many had been smashed. The Serapaeum subsequently became a major tourist attraction and its discovery brought Mariette much acclaim. He often conducted important visitors to the Serapaeum in person and on such occasions the galleries were lit by hundreds of children carrying candles, giving an effect described as dreamlike and magical. Inside the last burial chamber, the guests found a table set with silver goblets and a bottle of champagne, with folding chairs ready to receive them.

▲ *Mariette's excavation methods are criticized today. He often requisitioned the male population of villages to further the work and used dynamite.*

Khafre's valley temple

Mariette's second most important discovery was the valley temple of the pyramid of the Fourth Dynasty king Khafre (c.2558–c.2532 BC) at Giza. At the time of its discovery, it had been virtually reduced to a heap of enormous stones. He began work on it in 1853, when he partly excavated the interior, and completed it in 1858. In the course of the excavation he blew apart some of the collapsed monoliths in order to remove them from the temple. He is often criticized for the fact that here, as elsewhere, he failed to publish his finds adequately. But in this case he did discover one of the masterpieces of the Old Kingdom (c.2686–c.2181 BC), the great diorite statue of Khafre himself (now in the Cairo Museum).

▲ *Found by Mariette in the valley temple, this diorite statue of King Khafre protected by the hawk god Horus is a masterpiece of Egyptian art.*

In 1858, Mariette was appointed Director of the Egyptian Antiquities Service, and the viceroy gave him the authority and means to excavate wherever he wished. He set up the Bulaq Museum near Cairo to exhibit his finds. ◆

Amelia Edwards

It was entirely by chance that Amelia Edwards (1831–92) first became interested in Egypt. She and a friend had gone to France on a sketching holiday and had been plagued by weeks of rain. After discussing whether to return to England or 'push on further still in search of sunshine', they decided to go to Egypt. She later wrote:

> *For in simple truth we had drifted hither by accident with no excuse of health or business or any serious object whatsoever and had just taken refuge in Egypt as one might turn aside into the Burlington Arcade... to get out of the rain.*

In spite of this rather prosaic start to her relationship with Egypt, once she was there it was clearly a case of love at first sight. On looking out of her window on the first morning of her stay she was immediately captivated by the scene:

> *It was dark last night, and I had no idea that my room overlooked an enchanted garden, far-reaching and solitary, peopled with stately giants beneath whose tufted crowns hung rich clusters of maroon and amber dates... Yonder, between the pillared stems, rose the minaret of a very distant mosque; and here where the garden was bounded by a wall and a windowless house, I saw a veiled lady walking on the terraced roof in the midst of a cloud of pigeons. Nothing could be more simple than the scene and its accessories; nothing at the same time more Eastern, strange, and unreal.*

Before going to Egypt, Amelia Edwards had already achieved some success as a writer and journalist. She was to become one of the most prominent writers of her age, and her work included several travel books, the most famous of which is the record of her six-month journey up the River Nile, *A Thousand Miles up the Nile*.

▲ *Amelia Edwards wrote the best-selling book* A Thousand Miles Up the Nile *(1877) and founded what is now the Egypt Exploration Society.*

A Thousand Miles up the Nile

It is typical of Edwards' enterprise and courage that she and her friend decided to make the most of their trip to Egypt by chartering a *dahabeeyah* (a flat-bottomed, wooden boat) and engaging a crew with a view to sailing up the Nile to Aswan and then beyond the borders of Egypt into Nubia. This was in 1873, the year David Livingstone died and before General Gordon had made his first journey to Khartoum, a remarkable feat for two women at that time.

By far the greater part of *A Thousand Miles up the Nile* is devoted to the monuments she visited. The modern tourist sees them in their reconstructed state, but when Miss Edwards went to Egypt over a century ago, many of the tombs and temples were filled with the rubble and driven sand of past centuries. Describing the ruins of Luxor Temple she wrote:

> *These half-buried pylons, this solitary obelisk, those giant heads rising in ghastly resurrection before the gates of the temple were magnificent still. But it was as the magnificence of the*

◄ *A 19th-century painting of the Cairo Bazaar that so fascinated Amelia Edwards on her arrival.*

Preparing for the voyage

The hiring of Miss Edwards' *dahabeeyah* was much more difficult than house-hunting. Added to the problems of weighing up the merits of the available boats was the fact that they frequently changed their position on the river. The prices varied from day to day and the 'certificates of recommendation' by former travellers had 'a mysterious way of turning up again and again on board different boats and in the hands of different claimants'.

Eventually Amelia and her friend found a craft to their liking. After scurrying to the nearest stores to make a few last-minute purchases, they went on board and set about transforming the sparsely furnished saloon of the *dahabeeyah* into a cosy Victorian parlour. As Miss Edwards remarked, 'It is wonderful what a few books and roses, an open piano and a sketch or two will do'.

▲ *Nile cruises became very popular after the publication of Amelia Edwards' book.*

prologue to a poem of which only garbled fragments remain. Beyond that entrance lay a smoky, filthy, intricate labyrinth of lanes and passages. Mud hovels, mud pigeon houses, mud yards, and a mud mosque, clustered like wasps' nests in and about the ruins. Architraves sculptured with royal titles supported the roofs of squalid cabins. Stately capitals peeped out from the midst of sheds in which buffaloes, camels, donkeys, dogs and human beings were huddled together in unsavoury fellowship.

Amelia began work on the book on her return to England in 1874. She read extensively and consulted respected Egyptologists on matters of historical and archaeological detail. She also took up the study of hieroglyphs. By 1878, she was writing reviews and articles on Egyptology for weekly journals such as The Academy, and quickly became an authority in her own right.

The Egypt Exploration Fund

Amelia Edwards' greatest work was the founding of the Egypt Exploration Fund (now Society). She was very concerned about the state of the ancient monuments; many were suffering from neglect; others were being vandalized. The Egyptian government had neither the interest nor the resources necessary to protect them. In 1879, Miss Edwards wrote to Auguste Mariette, the founder of the Cairo (Bulaq) Museum, to ask whether it might be possible to finance excavation in the Delta by public subscription in England. She also enlisted the support of several English Egyptologists and Biblical scholars.

Amelia's most enthusiastic supporter was Sir Erasmus Wilson, an eminent surgeon who was already engaged in writing a popular history of Egypt. He was also very wealthy and had just spent £10,000 transporting the obelisk now known as Cleopatra's Needle to England. When *A Thousand Miles up the Nile* was published, Wilson was so impressed with it that he wrote to Amelia, and thus began a long friendship. She advised him on his book and he was always willing to give financial support to any scientific survey or excavation by the British in Egypt. Others were less easy to persuade. The Oriental Department of the British Museum was totally opposed to Miss Edwards' efforts, although help came from elsewhere in the Museum, notably from the Department of Coins and Medals. The Egypt Exploration Fund was eventually set up in March 1882, with R. S. Poole and Amelia Edwards as Honorary Secretaries and Sir Erasmus Wilson as Treasurer.

The Fund found many supporters in the United States, where Miss Edwards embarked on an extensive and exhausting lecture tour in 1889. During the five months she was there, she lectured 115 times and travelled to 16 different states. Her labours were well rewarded and the subscriptions flowed in.

First chair in Egyptology

The strenuous tour of North America had left Amelia's health seriously impaired, but her devotion to the Fund impelled her to go to Millwall Docks in London in October 1891 to supervise the arrival of antiquities from Egypt and their dispersal to various museums. A lung infection resulted, from which she never recovered. She died the following spring, bequeathing a sum of money to found the first chair in Egyptology at University Collge, London, with the proviso that Flinders Petrie should be the first professor. ◆

The Father of Modern Egyptology

Sir William Matthew Flinders Petrie (1853–1942) was the pioneer of modern archaeological methods in Egypt. In great contrast to his contemporaries, his main anxiety was to halt the destruction of the ancient remains.

Petrie had received little formal education but his father had taught him the principles of surveying and geometry. After practising on Stonehenge, father and son planned to visit Egypt to survey the Great Pyramid. In the end, his father did not go, and Petrie undertook the task alone. Nobody had ever done anything like it before. He spent several weeks setting up the survey points and making accurate plans, which he published in 1883. He also spent much time weighing up the possible methods by which the pyramids might have been constructed.

He was horrified by what he saw going on in the valley temple of Khafre:

> *Mariette most rascally blasted to pieces all the fallen parts of the granite temple by a large gang of soldiers, to clear it out instead of lifting the stones and replacing them by means of tackle... Nothing seems to be done with any uniform and regular plan, work is begun and left unfinished; no regard is paid to future requirements of exploration, and no civilized or labour-saving devices are used. It is sickening to see the rate at which everything is being destroyed, and the little regard paid to preservation.*

In his time, Petrie excavated at most of the important archaeological sites. He worked principally at the Predynastic cemeteries at Naqada, the Delta sites of Tanis and Naucratis, the city of Akhenaten at Tell el-Amarna, the Faiyum pyramids of Senusret II (c.1880–c.1874 BC) and Amenemhat III (c.1855–c.1808 BC), and the remains of the cemetery and ancient city of Abydos.

▲ *Flinders Petrie, the pioneer of modern archaeological methods in Egypt and the first Professor of Egyptology at University College, London.*

Excavations at Abydos

Although frustrated in his ambition for many years, in 1899 Petrie was eventually granted the concession to dig at Abydos. There he found that the site had been dug over many times, both by dealers and by local farmers looking for mudbrick to grind up for use as fertilizer on their land. Mariette had removed statues from the site for the Bulaq Museum. Worst of all, the Frenchman Emile Clément Amélineau had worked over the royal tombs of the Early Dynastic Period (c.3100–c.2686 BC) and had done untold damage in the process. It had been rumoured that he was interested only in large, intact, saleable objects and that he broke those he was not able to carry away: Petrie found that this appeared to be true. Moreover, because Amélineau had treated his workmen badly and offered them no reward for objects they found, there seemed to have been much pilfering from the site.

When Petrie began to rework the site, he found much that Amélineau had missed, including some of the grave stelae that marked the royal tombs and small tablets indicating the graves of officials. Most important of all were the little ivory and ebony labels originally attached to grave goods, which gave the

▼ *The members of Petrie's teams led a spartan life. At the age of 83, Petrie and his wife Hilda (in the helmet) used this old green bus in Palestine.*

▲ *Ivory comb of King Djet from the Early Dynastic cemetery at Abydos.*

names of some of the kings, each one recording an important event in a particular year of the king's reign. From these, Petrie was able to collect the names of all the kings of the First Dynasty (c.3100–c.2890 BC) and to suggest the order in which they had reigned.

During his excavation of the tomb of King Djer (c.3000 BC), Petrie found part of an arm wrapped in bandages, later found to be wearing a set of four exquisite bracelets made of gold, lapis lazuli, amethyst and turquoise. After carefully examining the jewellery, he entrusted the precious burden to James Quibell, the Chief Inspector of Antiquities for Lower Egypt, to deliver to the Cairo Museum. However, the museum's assistant conservator was interested only in the jewellery, and threw away the arm and the linen, thus destroying the earliest evidence for mummification. As Petrie remarked, 'a museum is a dangerous place'.

This discovery also demonstrates the superior way in which Petrie treated his workers. He always believed in paying his men properly for anything that they found so that he could be sure they would bring their finds to him rather than take them to the dealers. In this instance, the workmen could see the jewellery inside the wrappings, but left the arm undisturbed while they went to find one of Petrie's assistants. In the evening, the arm was unwrapped in the presence of the workmen and the gold of the bracelets weighed against sovereigns. The men were paid handsomely 'to ensure their goodwill and honesty for the future'.

Petrie's interest in objects of everyday life also marks him as remarkably astute. In his day, these would usually have been passed over in favour of the more spectacular. From the small finds made at Kahun, the settlement of the workers on Senusret II's pyramid at el-Lahun, it is possible to build up a complete picture of life within the community.

Honeymoon on a coal barge

Petrie was aided in his work by his wife, Hilda Urlin, one of his former students. Their wedding breakfast, a glass of milk and a bun at a café opposite Victoria Station in London, before catching the boat-train to Calais on the first stage of their journey to Egypt, anticipated the austerity of their married life. After nearly two weeks in Cairo they set off for Dendera. The train went no farther than Nag' Hamadi, so they hired a boat for the rest of the journey. Unfortunately, the wind dropped and they were forced to spend the night in cramped conditions under the half deck. They breakfasted on the remains of the previous night's supper of bread, 'little fritters', beans and jam. A colleague, Norman de Garis Davies, was with them, and all three had to share a single knife and tin mug provided by the boatmen. When they were still 16km (10 miles) from their destination at two in the afternoon, they decided to walk the rest of the way. Hilda claimed to have enjoyed this 'most delightful adventure' of her 'honeymoon on a coal barge'. ◆

▲ *This carved ivory label was once attached to a pair of sandals from the royal cemetery at Abydos. King Den is shown smiting his enemies.*

Sequence dating

Petrie devised an ingenious method, called sequence dating, of putting into chronological order the finds from his excavations at Naqada, Hu and Abadlya. He cut 900 strips of cardboard, each 17cm (7in) long, to represent 900 of the 4,000 tombs he had excavated. On each he recorded the number of pots of various types he had found in the grave, as well as other objects such as palettes and beads. By comparing the contents of each grave, he was able to work out a probable chronological order. Assuming that designs would become more complex over time, Petrie assigned the earliest sequence dates to the simplest artefacts, using a numerical sequence from 30–80 (the numbers 1–29 were kept free in case earlier objects were found). He was able to divide the pottery and associated grave goods into two main phases, now usually called Naqada I (c.4000–c.3500 BC; red pottery with white decoration) and Naqada II (c.3500–c.3100 BC; buff-coloured pottery decorated with red motifs such as ships, ostriches and dancing women). Although adjustments have been made in the light of more recent discoveries, the system is still used by archaeologists today.

The Development of the Pyramid Complex

The Predynastic Period in Egypt lasted from around the mid-sixth millennium BC to c.3100 BC. During this long, formative period, the many individual cultures of different parts of Egypt were gradually replaced by those now called Naqada II (c.3500–c.3100 BC) and III (c.3100–c.3000 BC). Naqada was a site in the south of Egypt excavated by Sir Flinders Petrie in 1895, and it gave its name to a particular type of burial that had distinctive grave goods. At the same time, the various settlement centres gradually developed into a politically unified state ruled by a king.

Some of the most impressive archaeological remains of the Early Dynastic Period (c.3100–c.2686 BC) are the mudbrick mastabas, or burial places, of the kings and their officials at Saqqara, Abydos and Naqada. Mastaba, from an Arabic word meaning 'bench', is the name given to a type of tomb that looks rather like the mudbrick benches seen outside Egyptian houses. The burial chamber was below ground, surrounded by storerooms filled with goods for the use of the deceased in the Afterlife. Above ground, a mudbrick superstructure was built with an offering chapel attached. In later examples, the offering chapel was incorporated into the superstructure. It was from these mastaba tombs that the later royal pyramid complexes developed, while the mastaba form continued to be used by high-ranking officials whose burial places were usually clustered around those of the kings they had served.

◄ *Amenemhat III's pyramid at Hawara was the last large pyramid to be built in Egypt.*

Early Dynastic Period Mastabas

The earliest type of mastaba had a pit cut into the desert plateau. This was divided by mudbrick walls into the burial chamber and storerooms. There was no way into the burial chamber from outside, so the tomb was finished only after the burial had taken place. Later in the Early Dynastic Period, access to the burial place was provided by a staircase leading into the tomb, so it could be constructed before the body was buried. Precautions against robbers were apparently necessary, because in several tombs portcullises blocked the stairway.

During the Old Kingdom (c.2686–c.2181 BC) the storerooms were incorporated into the superstructure, from which a shaft led down to the burial chamber below ground. Stones often blocked the shaft. The main offering niche also became part of the internal plan, and eventually developed into a funerary chapel, decorated with scenes depicting the life of the tomb owner.

▲ *These two small dolomite vases with gold lids fastened with gold wire came from the tomb of the 2nd Dynasty king Khasekhemwy at Abydos.*

Abydos

As recently as about a century ago, the history of the earliest dynasties was still unknown. Flinders Petrie described the period before King Sneferu (c.2613–c.2589 BC), first king of the Fourth Dynasty, as 'a blank', but he did more than any other Egyptologist to fill the gap, with his discoveries in the First and Second Dynasty mastaba tombs of Abydos. Emile Amélineau had excavated these between 1894–8, but much had been missed. Petrie re-dug the site much more meticulously and was able to chart the development of the architecture of the tombs, which he was convinced were the burial places of the earliest kings. He also found objects inscribed with the names of previously unknown kings and was able to suggest a tentative chronology. This has recently been confirmed by the find at Abydos, by a team from the German Archaeological Institute led by Gunther Dreyer, of a clay seal, giving the names of the first five kings of the dynasty in order. The members of the team have continued the work on architectural

▼ *Remains of 1st and 2nd Dynasty tombs discovered by Walter B. Emery at Saqqara; thought to be royal tombs when first excavated, they are now known to have belonged to officials.*

▲ *The grave marker of King Djet from his tomb at Abydos. The* serekh *bearing his name is surmounted by Horus, thus associating the king with the god.*

development, and have found evidence for several stages of building in some tombs. They have also studied the links between the Early Dynastic Period tombs and those of the Predynastic Period nearby. They are now postulating a Dynasty Zero preceding the First Dynasty, thus pushing back the boundaries of the known history of Egypt.

Graves of a typical Predynastic type have been found in Cemetery U at Abydos. Here, graves of the Naqada I and II and later periods have been found. Some Predynastic tombs of the latest stage have several chambers, and it is thought that these belonged to the Dynasty Zero kings. One originally had nine rooms, but was later extended to 12. The storerooms were filled with large numbers of pottery vases, some of local origin and others imported from Canaan. In the burial chamber were traces of a wooden shrine and an ivory sceptre very similar to those that later formed part of the royal insignia.

The first tombs of the Early Dynastic Period (c.3100–c.2686 BC) were found in Cemetery B. The most elaborate belonged to King Aha, probably the second king of the First Dynasty. This tomb too, seems to have been extended at various times. Surrounding the tomb were a large number of subsidiary graves for retainers. From a study of the skeletal remains it seems that the bodies were all of young men aged about 25, and that they were killed in order to accompany their royal master to the Afterlife.

The remaining First Dynasty tombs lie a little to the west. They, too, were brick-lined pits but some also had a further lining of wood panelling. They were also surrounded by the graves of servants. The superstructures have long since disappeared, but the grave markers remain, carved with the names of their royal owners.

Lying some distance away from the tombs themselves are the associated funerary enclosures, which were probably used for the funerary cults of the dead kings. Of those belonging to the First Dynasty kings little remains, but some that belonged to the kings of the Second Dynasty are still impressive. The best preserved belonged to King Khasekhemwy (c.2686 BC), and its double walls still stand to a considerable height. The outer surface of the inner wall is built in the 'palace façade' style, with a series of elaborate niches and false doors. Just inside the entrance to the enclosure were some small buildings. The funerary complexes, together with the tombs themselves, may well be the prototype of the Step Pyramid. A further clue may lie in the fact that the entrance to each of the Abydos enclosures is on the south-eastern corner, just like the entrance to the Step Pyramid complex.

The tomb of Djer

According to ancient Egyptian tradition, Abydos was the burial place of Osiris and, in the late Middle Kingdom (c.2055–c.1650 BC), the tomb of the First Dynasty king Djer (c.3000 BC) was remodelled as the god's tomb. Emile Amélineau found a stone statue representing Osiris lying on his side (a reference to the myth in which the god was killed by his jealous brother Seth). However, much of the original burial remained and Petrie, during his re-excavation of the site, found the now famous set of four bracelets still attached to part of a mummified arm.

Saqqara

Between 1936–56, Walter B. Emery found further mastaba tombs at Saqqara, the chief necropolis of Memphis. These had many rooms containing high-quality grave goods arranged around a central burial chamber. The fact that the tombs were much bigger than those at Abydos (excluding the funerary enclosures) led Emery to think that he had found the true royal tombs at Saqqara, and that the tombs at Abydos were cenotaphs only. This theory has now been discounted, and the Saqqara tombs seem to have belonged to high officials. First, the number of tombs at Saqqara was much larger than the number of known kings, and second, seal impressions bearing the names of the same rulers turned up in several tombs. These seals were also inscribed with the names of senior officials. In the case of Mereruka, an official of the First Dynasty king Qa'a (c.2890 BC), a stela bearing his name was found near the main offering niche, making ownership of the tomb clear. This stela was the forerunner of the decoration of the false door of later funerary chapels and of the tomb autobiography, which was intended to justify the life of the deceased and provide his passport to immortality. ◆

The First Architecture in Stone

Until the beginning of the Third Dynasty (c.2686 BC), the main building materials were wood, reeds and mudbrick. The first building in the world to be constructed completely in stone was the Step Pyramid of King Djoser (c.2667–c.2648 BC) at Saqqara. Before this time, only a few details, such as doorways or the paving of a tomb chamber, had been made of stone. According to Manetho (an Egyptian priest who wrote a history of Egypt in the third century BC to impress Ptolemy II with the great splendour and antiquity of the civilization he had inherited), the inventor of the art of building in stone was Imhotep. That he was at any rate in charge of building operations at the Step Pyramid is clear from the discovery there of the pedestal of a statue of King Djoser bearing the words: 'The Chancellor of the King of Lower Egypt, the first after the King of Upper Egypt, Administrator of the Great Palace, Hereditary Lord, the High Priest of Heliopolis, Imhotep, the builder, the sculptor'.

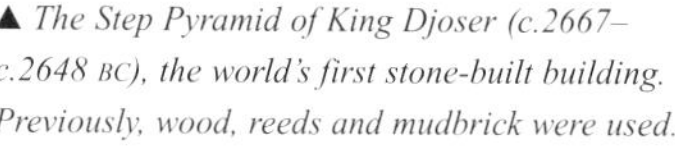

▲ *The Step Pyramid of King Djoser (c.2667–c.2648 BC), the world's first stone-built building. Previously, wood, reeds and mudbrick were used.*

Djoser's Step Pyramid

The Step Pyramid itself developed from the mudbrick royal mastabas of the Early Dynastic Period (c.3100–c.2686 BC) at Abydos. There, a mound of sand covered the burial chamber, perhaps representing the first land that appeared from the primordial ocean and on which creation took place, thus linking the themes of creation and re-creation. The mudbrick mastaba developed into a stone-built tower, and the mound became a ladder, which the king would climb to join the 'imperishable stars', a claim made in the Pyramid Texts, the funerary texts that accompanied royal burials during the Late Old Kingdom and First Intermediate Period (c.2350–c.2055 BC).

In the Step Pyramid complex, architecture that had previously been carried out in mudbrick, wood and reeds has been translated into stone. The wall surrounding the whole complex is built of small blocks of dressed limestone in imitation of the mudbrick 'palace façade' style of Early Dynastic tombs and enclosure walls.

The entrance to the complex is at its south-eastern corner. Roofing in ancient Egypt was usually in the form of palm logs, and the entrance passage was roofed with such 'logs' copied in stone. There are no real doors at the actual entrance, but the vestibule has carvings in stone of huge wooden doors, forever open. Even the hinges have been reproduced, and the right-hand door has a slit to show which panel should be 'closed' first.

Inside the entrance stands a colonnade of 20 pairs of half-engaged columns. These imitate huge bound bundles of reeds. Although no buildings in this medium have survived in Egypt, until very recently the Marsh Arabs of southern Iraq used reeds to build their homes and strengthened the corners with reed bundles. Similar buildings are also known from Sumerian seals of the third millennium BC. It is sometimes

◀ *Papyrus plants made of stone, with triangular stems and open umbels, form half-engaged columns and capitals in the Northern Court.*

▲ *Bundles of reeds are used by the Marsh Arabs of southern Iraq to strengthen buildings. Stone versions were used in the Step Pyramid buildings.*

said that the Step Pyramid columns are half-engaged (joined to the wall) because the architect, uncertain of the new technique, was not sure that they would be strong enough to support the roof if they were free-standing. It is much more likely that they were direct copies of the way reed columns were used in house construction.

Dummy shrines

Plant forms are much in evidence elsewhere in the complex. The dummy buildings of the *heb sed* court and North and South Houses are translations into stone of different types of shrines to local gods, which until this time had been made of wood and reeds. The most common type represents a rectangular wooden-framed tent with an arched roof. The shrine stands on a pedestal. The curved roofs of the larger ones are supported with poles carved in imitation of the trunks of conifers. The poles suggest that the actual shrines were open at the front to reveal the image of the god. They would have been temporary rather than permanent structures in real life, providing a shelter for the god's image at festivals.

The second type of shrine, seen in the North and South Houses of the complex, was larger and stood directly on the ground. These shrines, too, were open-fronted but the image of the god was shielded by a reed screen between the poles over the lower part of the building. The fact that reeds were actually used in this way in the construction of real reed shrines is suggested by the carving of their knotted ends. This stylized knotting became a standard architectural motif known as the *kheker* frieze.

In the third version of the temporary shrine, of which Temple T is an example, all four walls are plain and are strengthened at the corners by bound reed bundles. Another roll lies across the top of the wall, but here the loose ends of the reeds form a plain frieze. Inside, however, is another building, imitating one made of mudbrick.

▲ *Palm-log ceilings are still features of Egyptian village houses. Stone imitations were used in the entrance lobby of the Step Pyramid complex.*

All these designs, including the double shrine, became features of later ancient Egyptian temple architecture, as did the papyrus column and open papyrus capital first seen in engaged form decorating the walls of the Northern Court. ◆

▶ *Stone shrines to house statues of the gods surround the* heb sed *court where the king would be able to celebrate his jubilee in the Afterlife.*

From Step Pyramid to True Pyramid

Two of Djoser's successors, Sekhemkhet (c.2648–c.2640 BC) and Khaba (c.2640–c.2637 BC), attempted to build step pyramid complexes but failed to complete them. There are also some provincial step pyramids, including one at Seila on the fringe of the Faiyum Oasis. It has been suggested that this may have belonged to the first king of the Fourth Dynasty, Sneferu (c.2613–c.2589 BC), which would bring the number of pyramids associated with him to four. Five of the step pyramids are tentatively associated with Huni (c.2637–c.2613 BC), Sneferu's predecessor. However, later kings did not copy this type of royal burial, although some features were incorporated into pyramid complexes belonging to later periods.

▲ *It is possible that the Meidum Pyramid was never finished, explaining its present appearance. This may be why the stelae are uninscribed.*

The Meidum Pyramid

Sneferu's three main pyramids were built at Meidum and Dahshur. Today, the Meidum Pyramid appears across the cultivation as a ghostly three-staged tower surrounded by a great heap of debris. It is often suggested either that the pyramid collapsed in antiquity, leaving the first stages of the building revealed, or that later builders used the pyramid as a quarry. Even the ownership of the pyramid is sometimes disputed. In the past, some scholars preferred to believe it was the work of Huni (largely because, at the time, no other pyramid had been attributed to him). However, all the texts found at the site, albeit from later periods, mention Sneferu rather than his predecessor, and as the ancient name of Meidum is Djed Sneferu ('Sneferu endures'), it seems likely that the pyramid belonged to him. The fact that the two stelae found in the mortuary chapel were uninscribed is rather a puzzle. Not only would a name have definitely established ownership but it was also considered extremely important in ancient Egyptian funerary belief to perpetuate the name of the deceased, otherwise he might cease to exist in the Afterlife.

Sneferu began work on the Meidum Pyramid early in his reign. It was originally conceived as a seven-stepped tower, but a further step was added later. This seems to have been completed by Sneferu's 14th year but then, probably during the latter part of his reign, Sneferu had the steps filled in to form a true pyramid.

The Meidum Pyramid complex set the pattern for the rest of the Old Kingdom (c.2686–c.2181 BC). It consisted of the main pyramid and at least one subsidiary pyramid within an enclosure, together with a mortuary temple, to ensure the king's immortality. This was connected by a causeway to the valley, or lower, temple, situated at the edge of the flood plain. The valley temple was linked to the River Nile by a canal, so that the funeral procession of the king could land here and the body be taken up the covered causeway for burial within the pyramid in relative privacy. The Meidum Pyramid is also remarkable for the first use of corbelling to roof the burial chamber.

The pyramids of Dahshur

For some unknown reason, in mid-reign Sneferu temporarily abandoned Meidum and began to build two further pyramids, the Bent and the Red Pyramids, further north, at the new necropolis of Dahshur.

▲ *The Bent Pyramid is so-called because of the change of angle about halfway up. Much of the high-quality Tura limestone casing remains.*

The Bent Pyramid seems to have been something of an experiment as the angles had not yet been satisfactorily worked out. There is evidence to suggest that the Bent Pyramid began as a small pyramid with a slope of 60 degrees, but that subsidence threatened to cause it to collapse. Thereupon further layers were added round the inner core so that the angle was more gentle. The problems continued, however, and it was eventually decided to proceed at an even less severe angle. Consequently the profile of the pyramid has a distinct bend towards the top.

The Bent Pyramid is noteworthy for the large amount of outer casing of fine Tura limestone that remains in situ. Further, both the burial chamber and the antechamber of the Bent Pyramid are roofed in magnificent corbelling. The mortuary chapel, on the other hand, is a very simple affair. Inside were an offering table and two stelae, both inscribed with the name of Sneferu. However, it was in the valley temple that Sneferu's funerary cult was carried out by later kings.

The Red Pyramid is perfectly constructed. There is no sign of experimentation whatsoever, and it is generally recognized as the first true pyramid. It was built of local limestone containing iron oxide, which gives it the reddish colour from which it gets its name. The outer casing of white Tura limestone has almost entirely disappeared, but the pyramid is otherwise intact. Noteworthy features are the low angle of inclination (43 degrees) and the horizontal line of the core blocks. In earlier pyramids, the blocks were laid at an angle in the belief that this method gave greater stability to the building. As in the Bent Pyramid, the antechamber and burial chamber are roofed with very fine corbelled blocks.

Excavations by Dr Rainer Stadelmann of the German Archaeological Institute have revealed a large number of graffiti scribbled on pieces of limestone casing by the builders of the Red Pyramid. The most interesting thing about these inscriptions is that they are dated. One, from a corner of the pyramid, implies that Sneferu began to build it in the 30th year of his reign. Another, which had originally been placed about 30 courses of stone higher up, was dated four years later. From these marks, it has been possible to deduce the length of time it took to build a pyramid, in this case about twenty years.

The mortuary temple was on the east side of the Red Pyramid and the ground plan has been reconstructed. Enough remained to make possible a reconstruction on paper of the temple's original appearance. It seems to have been much larger than the mortuary temples of the Meidum and Bent Pyramids, and was a worthy forerunner of the even larger Great Pyramid of Khufu at Giza. Lying in the mortuary temple is the reconstructed pyramidion, or solid limestone capstone, that once topped the pyramid. ◆

▼ *The Red Pyramid is second only in base size to the Great Pyramid of Khufu but is about 15m (49ft) lower because of its more gentle angle.*

How the Pyramids were Built

The first step in building a pyramid was to choose a suitable site. This had to be on the west side of the Nile because the west was where the sun set and where the dead were thought to enter the Underworld. The pyramid also needed to be situated on high ground, away from the danger of flooding at the time of the Nile's inundation. However, it could not be too far away from the bank because the river would be used to transport blocks of fine-quality limestone for the outer casing from Tura, on the other side of the Nile. The site chosen would be at a point on the desert plateau that would provide a firm rock base capable of supporting the great weight of the pyramid without any risk of cracking. It would also need to be within easy reach of the capital, so that the king could go to inspect the building work whenever he wished.

Site preparation

No plans for a pyramid exist, although there are extant plans of tombs in the Valley of the Kings. However, the building of a pyramid was not a haphazard affair and the measurements were accurate to a high degree. The workers had first to prepare a firm foundation by removing the loose sand from the rock. Then the rock base had to be made absolutely flat. The workers may have done this by building low mud walls all round the base and cutting channels in a grid pattern over the surface. Then they would have filled the channels with water and marked the level it reached. After the water had drained away, protruding rock would have been cut back to the level indicated, and any depressions filled with stones to make a perfectly level surface.

Each side of the pyramid had to face one of the cardinal points. The builders probably established true north first and worked out the other directions from that. They may have found true north by taking a sighting on a particular star in the northern sky. They would then observe the rising and setting of the star and mark its appearance and disappearance on an artificial horizon. By bisecting the angle thus made, they would obtain a north-south line. They had instruments for drawing right angles, so they would then have been able to find east and west. Next, they had to make the base perfectly square, with all four sides exactly the same length and the corners perfect right angles.

The workforce

Herodotus claimed that the Great Pyramid was built using slave labour, with 100,000 men at a time working in three-monthly shifts, for a period of 20 years. The idea of slave labour is now discounted, and it is thought more likely that the work did not carry on throughout the year, but only during the three months or so of the inundation period, when the workforce could not be employed on the land.

▼ *An artist's impression of the construction of the Giza pyramids, based on a drawing of Heinrich Leutemann. Groups of workers haul the massive blocks into position.*

▲ *Scene from a stela of Ahmose I commemorating the reopening of the quarries at Maasara in his 22nd year, showing oxen hauling a stone block.*

▼ *The production of mudbricks, as depicted in the tomb of Rekhmire at Thebes. Mudbrick remains an important building material in Egypt today.*

Raising the blocks

Sometimes a rocky outcrop was used as the core of the pyramid to save work. The inner chambers and passages would have been constructed independently and the actual pyramid built around them. Some of the royal pyramid builders seem to have changed their minds about their preferred location of the burial chamber. The inner pyramid would then be built of limestone cut from the desert plateau. When the main structure was finished, the pyramid was completed by encasing it in blocks of finely cut and dressed limestone from Tura. Sometimes granite was used for the lower courses.

The precise method of raising the pyramid is not known. Pulleys were apparently not invented until Roman times. However, the Greek historian Herodotus tells of levers being used to raise the blocks from one level to the next. It has also been suggested that workers operating in teams used ramps to haul the blocks into position. As the pyramid grew in size so the ramp would have been raised to enable the workers to reach the next level. The main problem with this is that the ramp would eventually have been as huge as the pyramid itself and would have reached an immense distance into the desert. No trace of such a structure has definitely been identified at any of the various pyramid sites. Another idea is that the ramp wound around the pyramid and was dismantled when the pyramid was completed. Construction methods are still hotly debated. ◆

The Pyramid Texts

The Pyramid Texts are a collection of spells that were meant to ensure the resurrection of the king and his union with the gods in the sky. The texts appear for the first time covering the walls of the burial chamber and adjoining rooms in the pyramid of the last king of the Fifth Dynasty, Unas (c.2375–c.2345 BC), which was erected near the Step Pyramid of Djoser at Saqqara. Similar collections are found in the burial suites of the Sixth Dynasty kings Teti (c.2345–c.2323 BC), Pepi I (c.2321–c.2287 BC), Merenre (c.2287–c.2278 BC) and Pepi II (c.2278–c.2184 BC).

These texts are our best source of information about religious belief in the Old Kingdom. Not only do they shed light on beliefs concerning the king's Afterlife, but they also make many references to ancient Egyptian mythology. One text from the passageway leading to Unas' burial chamber reads:

This Unas comes to you, O Nut,
This Unas comes to you, O Nut,
He has consigned his father to
the earth,
He has left Horus behind him.
Grown are his falcon wings,
Plumes of the holy hawk;
His ba has brought him
His magic has equipped him.

Nut, the sky goddess, welcomes Unas to the Afterlife with the words:

Make your seat in heaven,
Among the stars in heaven.

Another spell, this time from the ante-chamber, calls on the gods for assistance. Shu, the god of air, is asked to lift the king up, while Nut bends down to take his hand. The king is also thought to climb up to the sky on a ladder:

Hail, daughter of Anubis, above the
hatches of heaven,
Comrade of Thoth, above the
ladder's rails,
Open Unas' path, let Unas pass!

Sometimes the king calls on a celestial ferryman, in fact the ferryman of the gods, to take him across the water that was thought to separate earth and sky:

Awake in peace...
Sky's ferryman, in peace,
Nut's ferryman, in peace,
Ferryman of gods, in peace!
Unas has come to you
That you may ferry him in this boat
in which you ferry the gods.

▲ *The first Pyramid Texts were found in the burial chamber of Unas. In these, he climbs a ladder to be united with his father Re-Atum.*

▲ *Texts from the tomb of Teti describe how he takes his seat in the sun god's boat and sails with him across the sky. Another text tells how his father Geb welcomes him into heaven.*

Should the ferryman refuse, a solution to the problem could be found in the form of Thoth, the god of wisdom, who is often represented as an ibis:

If you fail to ferry Unas,
He will leap and sit on the wing of Thoth,
Then he will ferry Unas to that side!

Most of all, the king desires to spend eternity united with his father, Re, the sun god:

Re-Atum, your son comes to you,
Unas comes to you,
Raise him to you, hold him in your arms,
He is your son, of your body, forever!

Although the texts are found in pyramids only towards the end of the Old Kingdom, the material embodied in them may be much older. An indication of this can be seen in a text of King Teti, which seems to make reference to a time when burials were much simpler:

Oho! Oho! Rise up, O Teti!
Take your head,
Collect your bones,
Gather your limbs,
Shake the earth from your flesh!

The same text implies that commoners are excluded from heaven, which is the prerogative of kings:

Stand at the gates which bar the common people!
The gatekeeper comes out to you,
He grasps your hand, takes you into heaven, to your father Geb.
He rejoices at your coming,
Gives you his hands,
Kisses you, caresses you,
Sets you before the spirits, the imperishable stars.

Teti is also seen sailing with the sun god, a theme that first occurs in the Pyramid of Unas:

Teti will take his pure seat in the bow of Re's barque:
The sailors who row Re, they shall row Teti!
The sailors who convey Re about lightland,
They shall convey Teti about lightland!

In the burial chamber of Pepi I there are several references to the myth of Osiris, with whom Pepi is united in the Afterlife. Pepi is said to be:

...the Great One...fallen on his side,
He who...in Nedyt was cast down.

This is an allusion to the murder of Osiris by his jealous brother, Seth. Pepi, like Osiris, hopes to be raised from the dead and to become Orion.

Your hand is grasped by Re,
Your head is raised (by all the gods)
Lo, he has come as Orion,
Lo, Osiris has come as Orion...

You shall live!
You shall rise with Orion in the eastern sky,
You shall set with Orion in the western sky. ◆

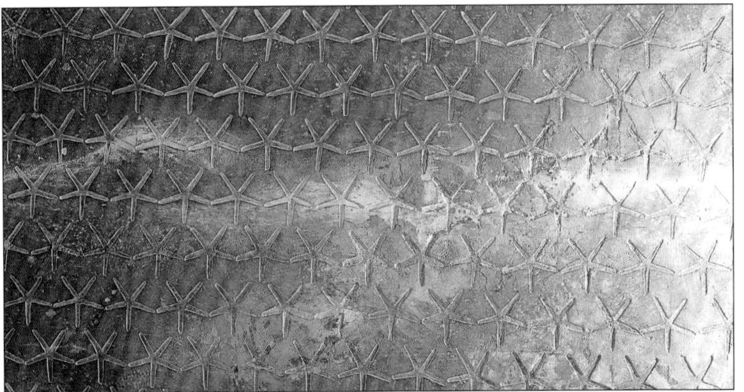

▶ *The ceilings of royal burial chambers were decorated with stars as the king, on death, hoped to take his place in heaven among the 'imperishable stars'.*

The Abusir Necropolis

Several of the kings of the Fifth Dynasty (c.2494–c.2345 BC) built their pyramids at Abusir, a name that is ultimately derived from Per Wsir, which means 'Place of Osiris'. The pyramids here are not as large as those of the Fourth Dynasty kings, and it has been suggested that this smaller size reflects a corresponding decline in royal power. That this might not be so is perhaps borne out by the fact that the quality of the materials used and the standard of much of the workmanship remains high. When in 1902–8 the German Egyptologist Ludwig Borschardt excavated the pyramid complex of Sahure (c.2487–c.2475 BC), the second king of the Fifth Dynasty, he found a great number of painted, delicately carved reliefs.

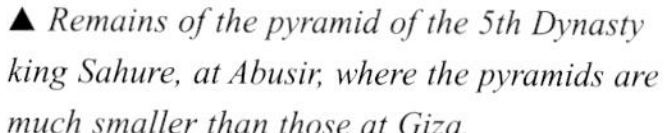

▲ *Remains of the pyramid of the 5th Dynasty king Sahure, at Abusir, where the pyramids are much smaller than those at Giza.*

Pyramid complex of Sahure

Although Sahure's complex is the best preserved of those at Abusir, the pyramid itself is in a dilapidated condition. Once the outer casing had been removed, the inner core deteriorated into a heap of rubble. The core had been formed of five or six steps built with rough blocks of local limestone, held together with mud mortar. Borschardt found evidence for a wide 'construction gap' on the northern side of the pyramid, which gave the builders room to work on the inner chambers while the construction of the pyramid itself went on around them. Granite had been used to line parts of the passageway leading to the burial chamber and for the portcullis that blocked the first section. The burial chamber itself was built entirely of Tura limestone and was roofed with three layers of huge limestone blocks placed at an angle.

Sahure's valley temple was on the edge of the Abusir Lake, from where a ramp led to a portico. The roof of this building was decorated with gold stars on a blue ground and supported by eight granite columns with palmiform capitals. Granite had also been used for the lower part of the walls and black basalt for the floor. The upper walls were of limestone carved with reliefs showing the king as a sphinx trampling his enemies.

The causeway was also decorated in relief and included scenes showing the gods leading prisoners representing Egypt's enemies – Asiatics and Libyans. These set a trend that was followed until the end of the Pharaonic Period.

The mortuary temple is the most interesting part of Sahure's complex, and became a model for those of later kings. It consists of five parts: entrance hall, open court, five niches for statues, storerooms and a sanctuary. The open court was paved with basalt and surrounded by a cloister decorated with scenes of the king receiving booty and smiting his enemies. Granite columns and palm-frond capitals again supported the starry roof. Running around the outside of the court was a wide corridor decorated with an entirely different type of relief. On the northern side the king was shown fishing and fowling in the

◀ *Travertine/calcite altar from Niuserre's sun temple at Abu Gurab. The shape has been interpreted as a huge hieroglyph meaning 'May Re be satisfied'.*

▶ *Following earlier tradition, the great officials of the 5th Dynasty were buried near their royal masters. The tomb of Ptahshepses, shown here, is one of the most splendid.*

marshes, and on the southern side he was depicted hunting with his courtiers and his successor, Neferirkare (c.2475–c.2455 BC). These reliefs are today in the Berlın Museum.

Neferirkare planned a pyramid complex at Abusir. His pyramid was to have been bigger than that of his predecessor, but it was never finished. Although the mortuary temple seems to have been hurriedly completed in mudbrick, only the foundations of the causeway and valley temple had been finished. When his son, Niuserre (c.2445–c.2421 BC), became king, he removed these elements from his father's complex and incorporated them into his own.

Tomb of Ptahshepses

Close to the pyramid of Sahure is the magnificent tomb of his vizier, Ptahshepses. The complex includes a portico, with the earliest-known example of columns with lotus-bud capitals, an offering room with statue niches, a huge courtyard surrounded with square pillars and a burial chamber with the fine granite sarcophagus still in situ.

◀ *Calcite bowls from the court of Niuserre's sun temple, used in the purification of offerings.*

Sun temples

Near to their pyramids, the kings of the Fifth Dynasty built sun temples to honour Re, the Heliopolitan sun god, at Abu Gurab. The Abusir Papyri and other documents mention six, although only two have been found so far, those of Userkaf (c.2494–c.2487 BC) and Niuserre. Userkaf's was the first royal building in this part of the necropolis, his pyramid being at Saqqara, close to the Step Pyramid of King Djoser. The remains, such as they are, were excavated between 1954–7 by a team from the Swiss Institute in Cairo. Niuserre, who also built his own sun temple at the nearby site of Abu Gurab, added extensively to Userkaf's temple.

Niuserre's sun temple is in a much better state of preservation. Although not much remains on the site today, the German expedition of 1898–1902 found enough clues to make possible a reconstruction on paper. It seems that the sun temple was part of a larger complex with the same component parts as a pyramid complex, including a valley temple and connecting causeway. Like the pyramid complex, it may have had a funerary function. The sun god was one of the chief gods of the Afterlife, and was also the main creator god. If the sun temple is considered to be part of the pyramid complex, there is no need to see the monuments of the kings of the Fifth Dynasty as being in any way inferior to those of the Fourth. ◆

The Abusir Papyri

Details of the cult of the dead king can be found in an archive called the Abusir Papyri. They date from the reign of King Djedkare (c.2414–c.2375 BC) and are mostly concerned with the administration of the mortuary cult of King Neferirkare (c.2475–c.2455 BC). They provide an insight into the duties of the priests involved in the daily ritual, as well as important festivals. They laid down which offerings were to be brought on given dates, supplied rotas for guard duty, and indicated the organization of the workforce. There are also inventories of temple furniture and ritual vessels, and sets of accounts of the temple's income and expenditure.

Mudbrick Pyramids

Some of the kings of the Middle Kingdom (c.2055–c.1650 BC) built mudbrick pyramids in the Faiyum Oasis. They do not exactly follow the Old Kingdom model, and display a number of unusual features.

The pyramid of Senusret II

Senusret II (c.1880–c.1874 BC) built his pyramid at el-Lahun, an important agricultural centre near the Middle Kingdom capital, close to where the Bahr Yusef leaves the Nile and enters the Faiyum. The pyramid was built around a core of limestone, over which a limestone framework was erected and filled with mudbrick. The upper part of the pyramid was entirely of mudbrick. The exterior was then cased in limestone, with the blocks of the bottom course set into a trench cut into the rock.

Senusret departed from usual practice by placing the entrance on the southern side of his pyramid instead of on the northern side. This may have been intended to outwit potential robbers but, if so, it failed. All that was left of Senusret's burial was a gold *uraeus*, the royal headdress in the protective form of a rearing cobra, and a few leg bones, presumably of the king.

Very little remains of the mortuary and valley temples or the causeway. Surrounding the pyramid were two walls, one of stone and one of mudbrick. Beyond the outer wall, trees had been planted in pits sunk into the rock and filled with earth. Inside the enclosure wall on the northern side of the pyramid was a row of eight mastaba tombs, at the eastern end of which was a small pyramid. It is not clear whether this was a subsidiary tomb connected with the king's own burial or whether it was intended for a queen. Between the enclosure walls on the southern side of the pyramid were four shaft tombs. One

▲ *A statue of Amenemhet III from his pyramid complex at Hawara. His burial chamber was cut from a single block of quartzite.*

▼ *The first of the mudbrick pyramids belonged to Senusret II who built his final resting place at el-Lahun in the Faiyum.*

▶ *Amenemhet III planned to be buried at Dahshur but seems to have abandoned the idea when the pyramid began to show signs of structural stress. He built a second pyramid at Hawara.*

of these was the burial place of Princess Sithathoriunet, and contained a collection of jewellery, which was part of her funerary equipment.

The Labyrinth

Amenemhat III (c.1855–c.1808 BC), famous for his land reclamation schemes, sited one of his pyramids at Hawara in the Faiyum. Like that of Senusret II, it was built of mudbrick and cased in limestone. It was almost 60m (197ft) tall and was the last large pyramid to be built in Egypt. On the southern side of the pyramid was a vast structure known to Herodotus and other classical authors as the Labyrinth. It covered an area of 6 hectares (15 acres) and had 12 covered courts, six in a row facing north and six facing south, with the gates of the one range exactly fronting the gates of the other, with a continuous wall around the outside of the whole. Inside, the building was of two storeys and contained 3,000 rooms, of which half were underground with the other half directly above them.

Herodotus wrote that he was not allowed to see the underground rooms because they contained the tombs of the kings who built the Labyrinth and also the tombs of crocodiles, which were worshipped in the Faiyum. However, he was allowed to see the rest and could hardly believe his eyes as he wandered through this maze of rooms, galleries and courtyards. None of this remains today, and even when Flinders Petrie excavated the site in 1888–9 he could recognize very few details of this most unusual of mortuary temples. ◆

▼ *Carved limestone crocodiles representing the god Sobek once adorned the 'Labyrinth', in fact the mortuary temple of the Hawara pyramid.*

The workers' town of Kahun

Not far from Senusret's valley temple was the town of Kahun, where the workers on the pyramid lived. This site was exhaustively excavated by Flinders Petrie, who discovered a vast number of domestic objects in the form of pottery, loom weights, mirrors, combs, stone and faience vases for perfumed oils and ointments, pots of kohl used as eye-liner, rush baskets of various shapes and sizes, rush sandals, carpenters' tools, fish hooks, agricultural implements and toys. There was even a rat trap. Different types of houses and their interior decoration also came to light. A large number of documents were found, including wills and some extremely interesting gynaecological and veterinary papyri. From these, it has been possible to build up a full picture of life in this town, which was the first of the pyramid workers' towns to be discovered and excavated.

Royal Jewellery of the Twelfth Dynasty

Several of the daughters of the kings of the Middle Kingdom (c.2055–c.1650 BC) were buried in shaft graves near to their father's pyramid. Some of the shafts contained sumptuous collections of diadems, bracelets, pectorals and collars. Middle Kingdom jewellery is considered to be some of the most exquisite ever made, either in ancient Egypt or elsewhere. Both in terms of inspiration and craftsmanship it is unparalleled.

Jewellery of Princess Sithathoriunet

When Flinders Petrie and Guy Brunton explored the shaft tomb of Princess Sithathoriunet in 1914, they found little apart from her red granite sarcophagus and a set of canopic jars, the vessels which accompanied each burial to house the internal organs. Then they discovered a niche in the wall that had been plastered over. Inside were five boxes containing Sithathoriunet's jewellery, a mirror, razors and pots for cosmetics.

▲ *The stunning gold diadem of Sithathoriunet was found in her tomb in the funerary complex of Senusret II.*

▶ *The silver mirror of Sithathoriunet is a jewellery masterpiece. It is supported by a head of Hathor mounted on an obisidian handle.*

The prize piece in this collection is a diadem in the form of a broad band of gold decorated with the *uraeus* (the royal cobra) and rosettes. It also has two gold plumes and three sets of detachable gold streamers. It would have been worn on top of a wig made up of dozens of long braids held in little gold clasps. The cobra's head is made of lapis lazuli and the eyes of garnets set in gold rims. The rosettes are inlaid with lapis, carnelian and green faience in imitation of feldspar and turquoise. The diadem is now on display in the Cairo Museum.

There are also two pectorals (chest ornaments) in the collection. One has the name of the princess's father, Senusret II (c.1880–c.1874 BC), worked into the design and the other the name of her nephew, Amenemhat III (c.1855–c.1808 BC), during whose reign she died.

The toilet articles are as beautiful as the jewellery. Among them are some elegant black vases for perfumed oils and ointments, but the masterpiece is the mirror. This consists of a thick silver disc surmounting a handle of obsidian in the form of an open papyrus plant. Below the umbel, which is covered in electrum (an alloy of silver and gold) is the head of Hathor, goddess of sexual love, worked in gold with eyes of lapis lazuli. The head has Hathor's characteristic cow's ears, symbolizing her nurturing role: she was worshipped as a universal mother goddess, but was particularly associated with kings. The mirror is double-faced, both sides being identical. Around the neck are four rings inlaid with carnelian, stone and faience, as is the pointed corolla of the base. The triangular shape of the papyrus stem is outlined in granulation work. This mirror would have ensured that the princess, whose name included that of Hathor, putting her under the protection of the goddess, enjoyed her gifts of eternal youth and beauty in the Afterlife.

Jewellery of Princess Neferuptah

A further collection of jewellery and toilet articles was discovered in 1956 at Hawara in the tomb of Princess Neferuptah, possibly a daughter of Amenemhat III. One of the most impressive pieces is a broad collar composed of six bands of tubular beads made of feldspar and carnelian, with little gold beads between them. Below this is a border of golden droplets inlaid with feldspar heads in repoussé work. The collar is balanced by a counterpoise consisting of a miniature falcon head above a series of narrow bands of beads, which match the main part of the collar. Matching pairs of bracelets and anklets complete the set.

▲ *A beautiful pectoral found in Princess Meret's tomb at Dahshur shows her father Senusret III as a griffin trampling his foes.*

Jewellery of Princess Meret

Some of the Middle Kingdom kings built mudbrick tombs at Dahshur. Princess Meret, daughter of Senusret III (c.1874–c.1855 BC), was buried close to his pyramid there. Two finely wrought pectorals were among the funerary equipment found in her tomb. They are made in the form of shrines. Inside at the top, Nekhbet the vulture goddess, protector of kings, hovers with outspread wings above the image of the king trampling his enemies. One pectoral includes the name of her father and the other that of Amenemhat III, her brother.

▲ *Princess Neferuptah's collection included matching sets of bracelets and anklets. They were made of gold, carnelian and feldspar.*

◀ *The intact tomb of Princess Neferuptah, found under a ruined mudbrick pyramid at Hawara, revealed another rich collection of jewellery. The princess was found wearing this collar.*

Jewellery of Princess Sathathor

Princess Sathathor was also buried at Dahshur, close to the pyramid of Senusret III whose sister, and possibly wife, she was. Her jewellery includes a pectoral in the form of a shrine, with the name of her father, Senusret II, inscribed inside it. This is protected on each side by two striped falcons wearing the Double Crown of Upper and Lower Egypt.

Another delightful piece is a belt of gold cowrie shells and tiny beads. The clasp is formed of two half cowrie shells, which slide together along grooves to make a whole as they fasten the belt. ◆

The Pyramids of the Kushite Kings

From the beginning of the New Kingdom (c.1550–c.1069 BC), kings abandoned the practice of burial within a pyramid and opted instead for a tomb in the Valley of the Kings in Western Thebes. The tradition of pyramid burial was, however, revived by the Kushite kings of the Twenty-fifth Dynasty, whose capital was at Napata in Upper Nubia. Egyptian control of Nubia had been lost after the end of the New Kingdom, and Nubia had developed as a separate kingdom. During the same period, several independent rulers, each powerful in his own district, had governed Egypt. The Kushite king, Piy (c.747–c.716 BC), marched north around 728 BC and brought the whole of Egypt under his control. His success was recorded on a great stela originally set up in the temple at Gebel Barkal and now in the Cairo Museum.

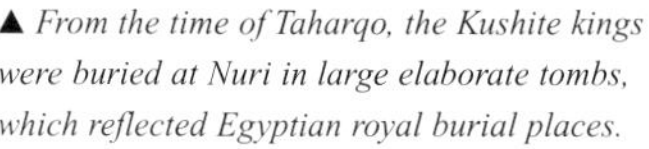

▲ *From the time of Taharqo, the Kushite kings were buried at Nuri in large elaborate tombs, which reflected Egyptian royal burial places.*

Burials at el-Kurru

The Kushite rulers regarded themselves as the true successors of the great Egyptian kings and emulated their activities in many ways, including that of building pyramids. Piy, his father, and several of his successors were buried in pyramids at el-Kurru. The style of these was rather different from the traditional structures, however. They were much more modest in size and had steeply sloping walls. Like the early Egyptian tombs, they seem to have evolved from mastabas. However, they appear to have been modelled on small 'private' pyramids, known from the craftsmen's village at Deir el-Medina, rather than on the vast royal structures from the height of the Pyramid Age. Apart from the kings' tombs, 14 queens were also buried in pyramids at el-Kurru.

Piy and his immediate successors, Shabaqo (c.716–c.702 BC) and Shabitqo (c.702–690 BC) were buried on beds within the tomb chamber. But from the time of Taharqo (690–664 BC), the kings adopted the Egyptian practice of using coffins and sarcophagi. Mummification was practised and the grave goods included traditional *shabti* figures, small statuettes of servants who would do whatever work was necessary in the

◄ *Pyramids of the kings and queens of Meroe in the North Cemetery. They were built on a ridge in imitation of Egyptian pyramids.*

▲ *One of Taharqo's* shabtis. *Kushite kings were buried in Egyptian-style coffins and sarcophagi. Bodies were mummified and provided with* shabtis.

Afterlife. One distinguishing feature was the continuation of the Kushite practice of horse burials. The royal chariot horses were apparently sacrificed, decapitated and buried standing in pits in a special cemetery near the pyramids of el-Kurru.

Nuri

From the time of Taharqo, members of the Kushite royal family were buried at Nuri. Here the pyramids were much larger than those at el-Kurru and the chapels were decorated with reliefs. A stela built into the pyramid showed the king, in Egyptian fashion, before the gods. Taharqo's pyramid was the largest of all and was built in two stages, the inner pyramid having been encased with limestone. The subterranean rooms were also more elaborate than in any other of the Nuri tombs. The entrance was on the eastern side and led eventually to a doorway with a moulded frame and cavetto (concave) cornice. From there a tunnel led to an antechamber with a barrel-vaulted ceiling. In the burial chamber, there were six great pillars cut from the rock. These divided the room into three, each part having a barrel-vaulted ceiling. A shallow pit had been cut into the floor to take the sarcophagus, and four niches were incorporated into the walls. Surrounding the burial chamber was a 'moat' reached by a flight of steps.

The last royal burial at Nuri took place at the end of the fourth century BC. From this time, the city of Meroe in the Sudan became important, and the kings built their pyramids there. Meroe remained the royal cemetery for much of the next 600 years, until the disintegration of the kingdom in around AD 350. ◆

▶ Shabtis *of Taharqo from his pyramid at Nuri. They were exceptionally large and made of serpentine, calcite and black granite. The features of the king indicate that he was Nubian, and the texts reflect the interest of the Kushite kings in earlier periods.*

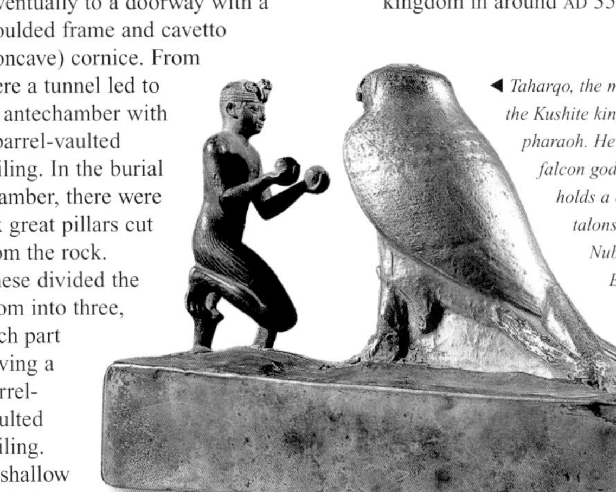

◀ *Taharqo, the most famous of the Kushite kings, dressed as a pharaoh. He kneels before the falcon god, Hemen, who holds a cobra in his talons. The deity is a Nubian version of the Egyptian god Horus.*

The Pyramids of Giza

Giza was the most important royal necropolis of the Fourth Dynasty (c.2613–c.2494 BC), and it is where the most famous of all the pyramids were built. Although today the three main pyramids have been almost engulfed by the sprawling suburb of Giza, they still retain their awe-inspiring majesty. These colossal monuments are not the only sights worth seeing at Giza. They are surrounded by the smaller pyramids of queens and princesses, and the mastaba tombs of high officials, several of which can now be visited. Recent excavation has also revealed a cemetery where dwarfs were buried. In life, these men were highly respected and held important posts, and in death they were considered to be worthy of a tomb close to their royal master.

A further exciting find in recent years has been the discovery of the town inhabited by the workers who built the pyramids. It came to light during work on the construction of a sewage system for the villages near to the Great Pyramid. An extensive settlement site dating from the Old Kingdom (c.2686–c.2181 BC) was discovered near the valley temple of Khufu. Hundreds of objects relating to the daily life of the workers and their families have been found here, and the associated cemetery has also been discovered.

◀ *Visited by Herodotus in the mid-5th century BC, and one of the Wonders of the Ancient World, the Giza pyramids are now closed in rotation as a means of conservation.*

The Great Pyramids

The most famous of all the landmarks of present-day Egypt, and one of the Wonders of the Ancient World, the Giza pyramids were the burial places of the Fourth Dynasty kings, Khufu, Khafre and Menkaure. Each pyramid was part of a larger complex consisting of a mortuary temple, a causeway, a valley temple and subsidiary pyramids, while the pyramid of Khufu is surrounded by five boat pits. The pyramids were robbed in antiquity, but the contents of the concealed tomb of Queen Hetepheres, the mother of Khufu, give some idea of the richness of the burials of the kings. The pyramid complexes are surrounded by 'streets' of mastaba tombs belonging to the officials who served as administrators or were in charge of the funerary cults of the deceased kings. Current excavation is beginning to shed light on the lives and deaths of the workers who toiled to build the memorials to the ancient kings. ◆

▲ *The Great Pyramid of Khufu was the largest of the three pyramids at Giza. It appears smaller than that of Khafre, which was built on higher ground.*

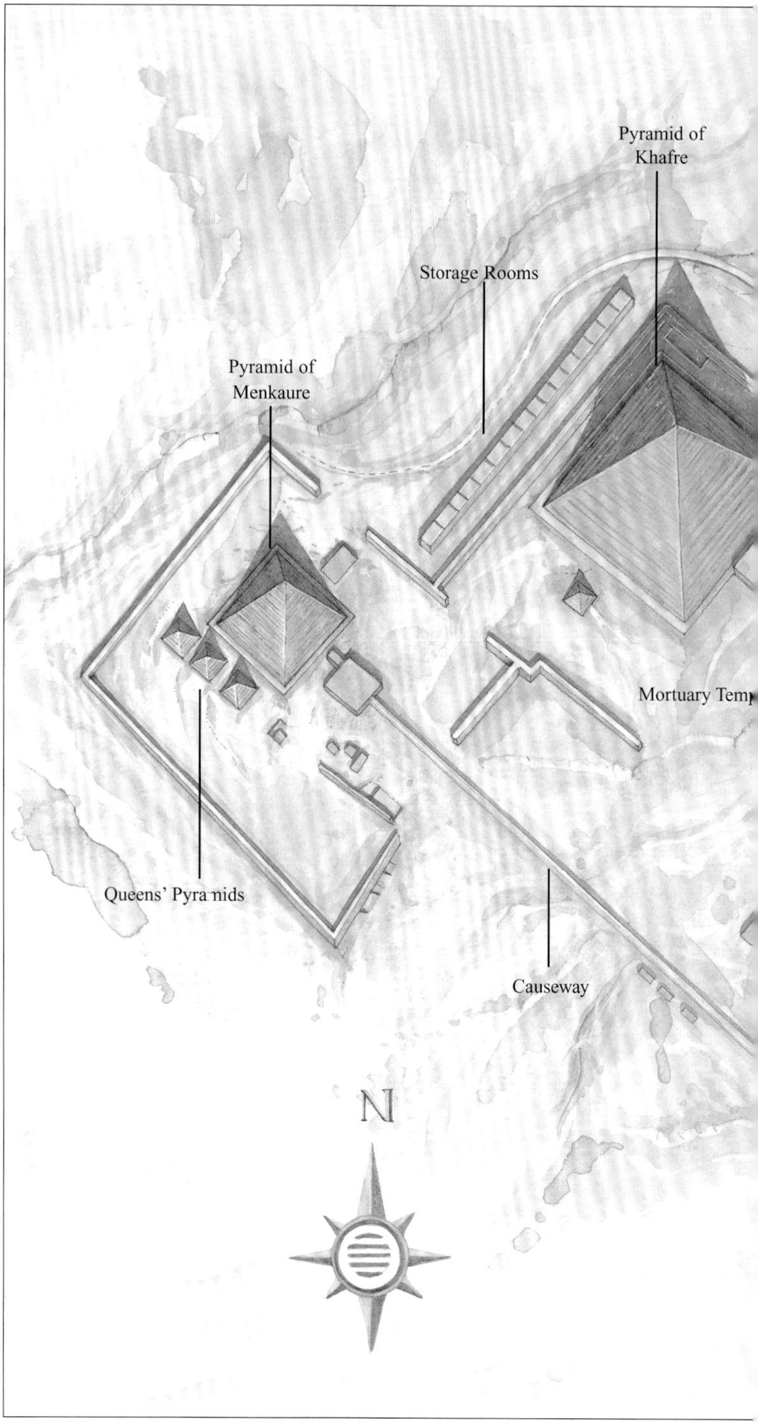

Pyramid of Khafre

Storage Rooms

Pyramid of Menkaure

Mortuary Tem

Queens' Pyramids

Causeway

N

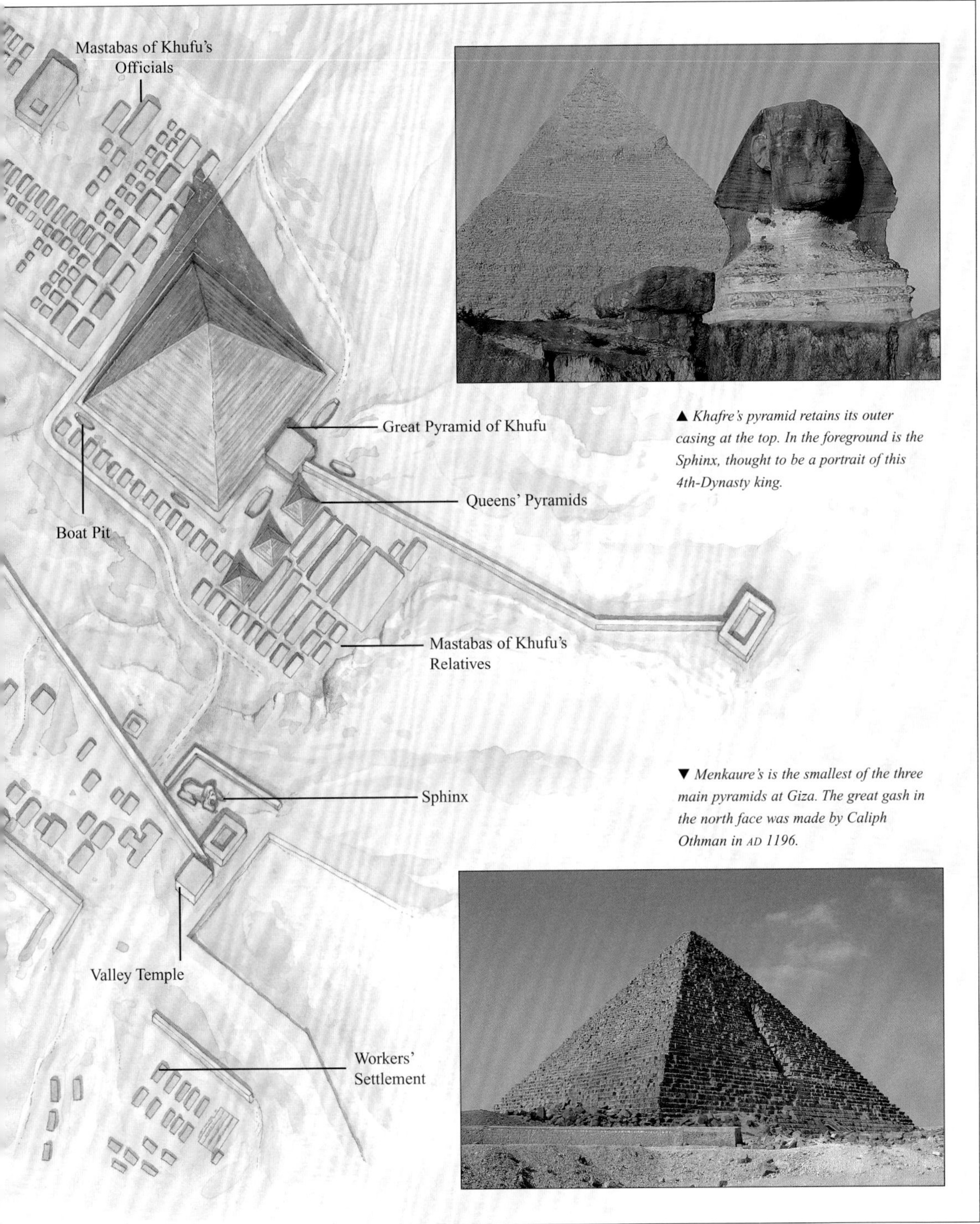

▲ *Khafre's pyramid retains its outer casing at the top. In the foreground is the Sphinx, thought to be a portrait of this 4th-Dynasty king.*

▼ *Menkaure's is the smallest of the three main pyramids at Giza. The great gash in the north face was made by Caliph Othman in* AD *1196.*

The Great Pyramid of Khufu

The Great Pyramid of the Fourth Dynasty king Khufu (c.2589–c.2566 BC) is the largest of all the pyramids. It was originally 140m (460ft) tall but is now 3m (10ft) less. At the base, the sides each measured 140m (460ft), but are now only 127m (417ft) because the pyramid has been stripped of its limestone casing. Some of this was removed in antiquity, but much was also taken in the ninth century AD when the caliphs built the city of Cairo. Amelia Edwards thought this gave the pyramid an unfinished look, as if the workmen 'were coming back tomorrow morning'. It is estimated that about 2,300,000 blocks, each weighing an average of 2.3 tons (although some weigh much more) went into the building of the pyramid.

The original entrance is on the north face and is 15m (49ft) above ground level, surmounted by a double vault. The lower entrance, used by tourists today, was made in the ninth century AD when an entry was forced on the orders of Caliph Mamun.

▲ *The Great Pyramid at Giza, largest of all the pyramids, was stripped of its casing of white limestone in antiquity and during the 9th century.*

Inside the Great Pyramid

There are at least three chambers inside the pyramid. From the entrance, a corridor leads downwards for 18m (60ft) and then divides. One branch leads on down to an underground chamber, which was left unfinished. The other climbs up towards the Grand Gallery, where it again divides. A horizontal tunnel leads to a second chamber, misleadingly known as the Queen's Chamber, while another tunnel winds precipitously to connect with the descending corridor.

The Grand Gallery is corbelled in the manner of Sneferu's pyramids and is a wonderful example of craftsmanship and precision. An antechamber once blocked by three granite slabs leads from it into the King's Chamber, the walls of which are lined with granite. The sarcophagus is plain and uninscribed. It has been suggested that the two chambers lower down the pyramid were intended as burial chambers, but first one and then the other was found to be too small to house the large granite sarcophagus, so it became necessary to alter the plans. This would have been possible, as the internal chambers were constructed while the main work of building the pyramid went on around them. The King's Chamber is roofed with nine granite slabs weighing about 400 tons. Above are five weight-relieving chambers, one above the other, designed to carry the enormous weight of the rest of the pyramid.

Two small shafts, once thought to be for ventilation, lead north and south from the burial chamber to the outside. Recent research by the German Archaeological Institute has shown that they are nothing to do with the circulation of air, but had a purely ritual use. They were to provide a direct route to heaven for the soul of the king. According to the same

▲ *The Grand Gallery leads from the ascending corridor to the burial chamber of Khufu. The walls are 8.5m (28ft) high and 47m (154ft) long and are corbelled, each layer of limestone blocks projecting about 6cm (2½in) beyond the one on which it rests.*

◀ *The only surviving image of Khufu, builder of the Great Pyramid, this tiny limestone statuette is in the Egyptian Museum, Cairo. Although the fugure is tiny, just 7.5cm (3in) tall, the face is full of character.*

study, the three internal chambers also had a ritual purpose and the team would dispute the suggestion that they represent changes in plan.

The Queen's Chamber also has a similar pair of shafts, which were partly explored when the pyramid was closed for conservation in 1992. A tiny robot penetrated 65m (213ft) into the pyramid before it was stopped by a 'door' with two copper handles. It is hoped that exploration will continue in the near future. A new gilded limestone capstone was made to celebrate the turning of the millennium.

The pyramid complex

Although little remains today, the pyramid once possessed a valley temple, causeway and mortuary temple. The mortuary temple was much bigger than those of the Meidum and Dahshur pyramids. It had a colonnade surrounding a large court paved with basalt. The limestone walls had carved reliefs. According to Herodotus, the causeway was also decorated with reliefs, and some pieces have now come to light to support his statement. The valley temple has almost completely disappeared, although some basalt paving blocks found in 1990 by Dr Zahi Hawass, Director-General of the Giza Pyramids and Saqqara, may once have belonged to it.

On the south side of the pyramid, there were three small pyramids belonging to the queens Henutsen, Meritetis and Hetepheres, Khufu's mother. Khufu's own (tiny) secondary pyramid was found in 1991 by Zahi Hawass. The complex is completed by five boat pits, which either represented or contained boats to enable the deceased king, in his identification with the sun god, to make his celestial voyages. To the east of the complex lie the mastabas of his relatives, while those of his officials are to the west. ◆

Images of Khufu

If there were ever any statues of Khufu in the temple complex they have vanished without trace. The only surviving image of this king is a tiny statuette found by Flinders Petrie at Abydos and now in the Cairo Museum. In fact Khufu's only firm link with the pyramid is his cartouche in the topmost of the relieving chambers above the burial chamber.

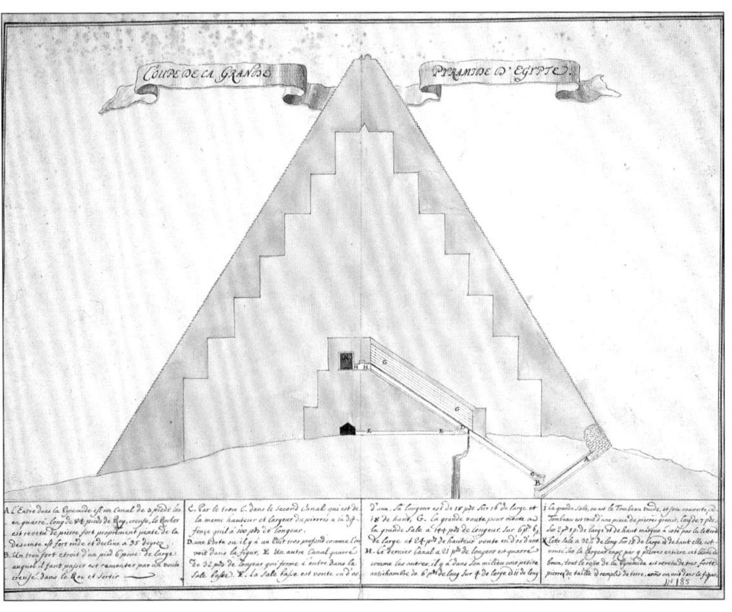

▶ *This plan of the interior of the Great Pyramid by Benoit de Maillet was published in 1735 before the descending corridor had been fully explored.*

The Pyramid of Khafre

The pyramid complex of Khafre is the most complete of all the Giza pyramids. Because it was built on slightly higher ground and rises at a sharper angle, the pyramid itself appears to be larger than Khufu's, although it is actually second in size. Near the top it still retains some of its original casing stones. The other component parts of the complex, especially the valley temple, are also much more in evidence here.

There are two entrances to the pyramid on the north side, of which the lower one is used by tourists today. This leads to a passage that first descends and then rises, before running horizontally to the burial chamber, which is just below ground level. The Italian adventurer Giovanni Belzoni entered the burial chamber on 2 March 1818, as his inscription proclaims. Inside was an empty plain red granite sarcophagus, with no inscriptions.

In its heyday, the pyramid was served by a magnificent mortuary temple, 110m (360ft) long, with two pylons, a transverse vestibule and a rectangular hall, both embellished with columns. Then came a large court surrounded by a columned portico where there would have been statues of the king. Behind this were five small chapels, storehouses and an inner sanctuary. Sadly, the temple has been used as a quarry over the centuries, and little of its ancient splendour can be seen today.

▲ *The pyramid of Khafre, which still retains part of its original high-quality Tura limestone casing. Khafre's funerary complex is the best preserved of the three at Giza.*

Khafre's valley temple

Although it has lost its roof, much remains of the causeway along which the king's body would have been brought from the valley temple. Khafre's magnificent valley temple is the best preserved of any that have come to light so far. It was discovered by Auguste Mariette in 1858, and is sometimes known as the Granite Temple because of

◀ *Khafre spared no expense on the construction of his valley temple. It is lined with huge blocks of polished Aswan granite and the floors are paved with alabaster from Hatnub.*

▲ *The famous Sphinx is carved from an outcrop of rock on the Giza Plateau. The lion's body symbolizes royal power, while the head is a portrait of Khafre. The features strongly resemble the diorite statue of the king.*

the huge blocks of polished red Aswan granite from which it was constructed. These enormous blocks were cut with astounding precision. Some have even been cut so that they turn corners. The floors are of polished alabaster.

In the T-shaped hall are emplacements for 23 statues of Khafre. These would have been illuminated by light entering through slits high up on the walls. Only the bases of most of these statues remain, but Mariette found one splendid complete version lying in a well in the vestibule. It is a little larger than life-size and is made of polished diorite from the quarries at Toshka in Nubia. Khafre is seated on the throne of the Two Lands. Behind him sits Horus, in the form of a falcon, with his wings folded protectively around the king's head.

The king's body would have been transported from the capital, Memphis, by boat. A quay has been discovered in front of the Sphinx temple, and it may have continued in front of the valley temple.

The site of the secondary pyramid has now been located to the east of the pyramid. Only the foundations of the superstructure remain, but when the underground section was explored one of the two passages was found to end in a niche that once contained the remains of a wooden shrine. This may have held a statue of the king; in some tomb scenes such a shrine housing a statue of the deceased is shown being dragged towards the tomb.

◀ *Twenty-three diorite statues of Khafre once graced his valley temple, although only this one, now in the Cairo Museum, survives intact. The king is protected by Horus, the falcon god.*

The Sphinx

Egypt's earliest colossal royal statue, the Sphinx, is also an integral part of Khafre's complex. In spite of some of the more bizarre theories recently put forward, most Egyptologists regard the Sphinx as a portrait statue of the king carved from an outcrop of rock that remained after the quarrying of limestone for the interior of the Great Pyramid. Rather than leaving it as something of a blot on the landscape, it was transformed into this symbol of royal power, a lion's body with the head of the king.

During the New Kingdom (c.1550–c.1069 BC), the Sphinx was regarded as a manifestation of the sun god. Between its paws is the famous Dream Stela, an inscribed tablet that records the promise to the prince Tuthmosis, later Tuthmosis IV (c.1400–c.1390 BC), that the sun god would ensure that he became king of Egypt, though he was not the heir, should he clear away the sand that had drifted around the Sphinx and do any necessary repairs. Much conservation work has been done on the Sphinx in recent years, and the Sphinx Temple has also been restored. ◆

The Pyramid of Menkaure

The pyramid built by the Fourth Dynasty king Menkaure (c.2532– c.2503 BC) at Giza is only about half the size of those of his predecessors, Khufu and Khafre. The reason for this is unclear. Perhaps their building projects had put too great a strain on Egypt's resources. The builders may have been running out of suitable sites on the Giza Plateau. Or perhaps the kings now felt they needed to show more deference to the sun god, as witnessed by the small size of the royal burial places and the contemporary building of sun temples at Abusir during the Fifth Dynasty (c.2494–c.2345 BC).

Architectural innovations

Whatever the reason for its diminished size, the construction still used costly materials and the pyramid was designed with several original features. For instance, although it was partly cased in Tura limestone, 16 courses of red granite blocks were used for the lower section. Further, the entrance on the north side of the pyramid leads down to a horizontal chamber decorated with a false door motif. The lintel above the entrance to the horizontal corridor is carved in imitation of a rolled reed curtain. These are the first signs of decoration inside a pyramid since the time of Djoser (c.2667–c.2648 BC). Another new feature was the complexity of the burial suite. A horizontal passage with three portcullises leads to an antechamber. From here, a second passage leads down to the burial chamber, lined with granite. When the English explorer Howard Vyse entered the pyramid in 1837 he found a sarcophagus carved with the 'palace façade' motif. It was removed for shipment to England, but was unfortunately lost in a storm at sea. A wooden coffin found in an upper

▼ *Despite being only about half the size of those of his predecessors, the pyramid of Menkaure was nonetheless built of costly materials, with granite being used for the casing of the lower part.*

▶ *Remains of the mortuary temple are still visible on the east side of the pyramid. Offerings to the king would have been brought here daily.*

chamber and containing the remains of a mummy was dispatched on a different ship and is now in the British Museum in London. The style of the coffin, however, dates it to the Twenty-sixth Dynasty, or Saite Period (664–525 BC), while the bones are from the Christian era. Attached to the burial chamber was a room divided into six small niches and probably intended as a store for the king's funerary goods.

Mortuary and valley temples

The remains of an unfinished complex mortuary temple can be seen against the eastern face of the pyramid. It consists of a vestibule leading from the causeway, a large open court, a pillared portico leading to the sanctuary and various ancillary rooms, presumably for cultic equipment. Building was started in limestone, although the intention appears to have been to case it in granite. Menkaure seems to have died before it was completed because the temple has been hurriedly finished off in mudbrick. The unfinished nature of the complex made its excavation by George Reisner in 1899 especially interesting, because it provided information about how the work had been done. When Reisner stripped away the mudbrick he could see that the limestone walls were being prepared to take the granite facing when the construction was interrupted. On the core blocks he found levelling lines, measurements and even the names of workers marked in red paint.

Not much remains of the limestone causeway. Like the valley temple, this is often said to have been completed by Menkaure's son, Shepseskaf (c.2503–c.2494 BC), but there is little evidence for this. The valley temple itself, even in Reisner's time, lay beneath the sand. He found it by projecting the axis of the causeway from the entrance of the mortuary temple, and was fortunate enough to make some wonderful discoveries. First he found the pair-statue of Menkaure and his queen, Khamererenebty. He went on to find four more masterpieces of ancient Egyptian art, the famous triads showing Menkaure with the goddess Hathor and a local deity, which are now in the Cairo Museum.

Three small pyramids lie to the south of Menkaure's, one of which might have been intended as the king's subsidiary pyramid, later adapted to accommodate a queen. The body of a young woman was found in the central pyramid. ◆

◀ *The mudbrick valley temple was embellished with beautiful schist triads showing Menkaure protected by Hathor and various local deities.*

Hathor

The king was thought to be the child of the gods. As the living king was regarded as Horus, his mother was often held to be Isis. However, in the triads that decorated Menkaure's valley temple, Hathor, whose name means 'House of Horus', plays that role. As a cow goddess she nurtures the king with her milk. In the Pyramid Texts the king is asked on his arrival in paradise, 'Are you Horus, the son of Osiris? Are you the god, the eldest one, the son of Hathor?'

Stories from Herodotus

In Book Two of *The Histories*, Herodotus related the stories of Cheops (Khufu c.2589–c.2566 BC) and Chephren (Khafre c.2558–c.2532 BC) as told to him by Egyptian priests during his visit to the pyramids in the mid-fifth century BC. He clearly regarded them as tyrants. In contrast, Mycerinus (Menkaure c.2532–c.2503 BC) was seen as a good king.

Oppressive rule

'Cheops…brought the country into all sorts of misery. He closed all the temples, then not content with excluding his subjects from the practice of their religion, compelled them without exception to labour as slaves for his own advantage. Some were forced to bring blocks of stone from the quarries in the Arabian hills to the Nile, where they were ferried across by others who hauled them to the Libyan hills. The work went on in three-monthly shifts, 100,000 men in a shift. It took ten years of this oppressive slave-labour to build the track along which the blocks were hauled, a work, in my opinion, of hardly less magnitude than the pyramid itself, for it is 5 furlongs [1km] in length, 60ft [18m] wide, 48ft [15m] high at its highest point, and constructed of polished stone blocks decorated with carvings of animals. To build it took, as I have said, ten years, including the underground sepulchral chambers on the hill where the pyramids stood: a cut was made from the Nile, so that the water from it turned the site of these into an island. To build the pyramid itself took 20 years: it is square at the base, its height equal to the length of each side; it is of polished stone blocks, beautifully fitted, none of the blocks being less than 30ft [9m] long. The method employed was to build it in steps, or as some say, tiers or terraces. When the base was complete, the blocks for the first tier above it were lifted from the ground by contrivances made of short timbers; on this first tier there was another, which raised the blocks a stage higher, then yet another which raised them higher still. Each tier or storey had its set of levers, or it may be that they used the same one, which being easy to carry, they shifted up from stage to stage as soon as its load was dropped into place. Both methods are mentioned, so I give them both here. The finishing-off of the pyramid was begun at the top and

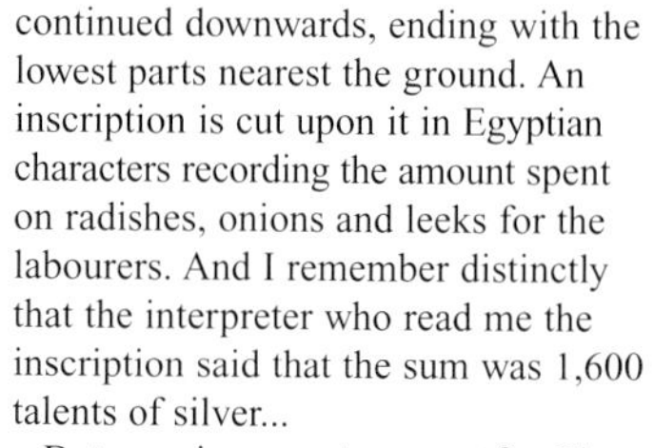

continued downwards, ending with the lowest parts nearest the ground. An inscription is cut upon it in Egyptian characters recording the amount spent on radishes, onions and leeks for the labourers. And I remember distinctly that the interpreter who read me the inscription said that the sum was 1,600 talents of silver...

But no crime was too great for Cheops: when he was short of money, he sent his daughter to a bawdy house with instructions to charge a certain sum, they did not tell me how much. This she actually did, adding to it a further transaction of her own; for with the intention of leaving something to be remembered by after her death, she asked each of her customers to give her a block of stone, and of these stones (the story goes) was built the middle pyramid of the three which stand in front of the great pyramid. It is a 150ft [45m] square.

Cheops reigned for 50 years according to the Egyptian's account, and was succeeded after his death by his brother Chephren. Chephren was no better than his predecessor: his rule was equally oppressive, and, like Cheops, he built a pyramid, but of a smaller size (I measured both of them myself)... The pyramid of Chephren lies close to that of Cheops; it is 40ft [12m] lower than the latter, but otherwise of the same dimensions; its lower course is of the coloured stone of Ethiopia.

Chephren reigned for 56 years, so the Egyptians reckon a period of 106 years, all told, when the temples were never opened for worship and the country reduced to the greatest possible misery...'

◀ *A bust said to be of the Greek historian Herodotus, who was one of the first travellers to Egypt to write of his experiences there.*

▲ *Herodotus visited the pyramids in the mid-5th century BC and was given his information by the priests who looked after the site.*

The reign of Menkaure

'The next king of Egypt to rule after Chephren was Mycerinus, the son of Cheops. Mycerinus, reversing his father's policy of which he did not approve, reopened all the temples and allowed his subjects, who had been brought into such abject slavery, to resume the practice of their religion and their normal work. Of all the kings who ruled in Egypt he had the greatest reputation for justice in the decision of legal causes, and for this the Egyptians give him higher praise than any other… He used to compensate out of his own property any man who was dissatisfied with the results of his suit, and so leave him nothing to complain of… Such were the generosity and mild rule of Mycerinus, when the first of his troubles fell upon him: his daughter, who was his only child, died. Wishing, in the excess of his grief at this calamity, to give his daughter a tomb which should be different from any other, he had a wooden cow made, hollow inside and plated on the outside with gold, to receive her body. The cow was not buried, but was still to be seen in my day at Sais, standing in a richly decorated chamber of the royal palace; incense of all kinds is burnt before it every day, and at night a lamp is always kept lighted in the room. Close by in another chamber, the priests told me, are some statues, which represent the concubines of Mycerinus: there are, indeed, 20 or so naked wooden figures of great size in this chamber, but as to whom they represent I can only pass on such information as was given to me.

There is another, and quite different, story told about the cow and the statues; according to this, Mycerinus conceived a passion for his daughter and violated her, and distress at the outrage drove her to hang herself: she was entombed in the cow, and her mother cut off the hands of the servants who had allowed the king access to her. The statues represent the servants, and like their living originals, have no hands. Personally I think this story is nonsense, especially in its explanation of the servants' missing hands; I could see for myself that they had simply dropped off through age. They are still there, plainly visible, lying on the ground at the statues' feet...

After the death of his daughter, a second calamity fell upon Mycerinus: he received an oracle from Buto to the effect he was destined to live for only six more years and to die within the seventh. He sent back an angry message to the shrine, and reproached the god with the injustice of allowing a man so pious as himself to die so soon, when his father and uncle, who had closed the temples, forgotten the gods, and afflicted their fellow men, had lived to a good old age. In answer to this there was another message from the oracle, which declared that his life was being shortened precisely because he had not done what he ought to have done...Mycerinus, convinced by this that his doom was sealed, had innumerable lamps made, by the light of which he set himself every evening to drink and be merry, and never ceased by day or night from the pursuit of pleasure, travelling about from place to place amongst the pools and woodlands...His object in this was by turning night into day to extend the six remaining years of his life into twelve, and so convict the oracle of falsehood.' ◆

The Tomb of Hetepheres

Queen Hetepheres was the wife of Sneferu (c.2613–c.2589 BC) and the mother of Khufu (c.2589–c.2566 BC). It seems likely that she was originally buried at Dahshur, near her husband, but that her tomb was violated soon after she was laid to rest. Perhaps because of this, her reburial was ordered and a shaft grave assigned to her on the east side of Khufu's Great Pyramid, near the three small pyramids, the northernmost of which is also thought to be hers. The shaft tomb was discovered in 1925 by the staff photographer of the Harvard-Boston expedition led by George Reisner. It was found to contain some beautiful gilded wooden furniture, which is now displayed in a new gallery in the Cairo Museum.

Hetepheres' furniture

The furniture includes a large portable canopy and a box for the curtains that went with it. Both are inscribed with the name of Hetepheres' husband, and the rest of the furniture dates to his reign. One of the best pieces is a beautifully crafted, gilded wooden sedan chair, a mode of transport commonly seen in the tombs of high-ranking officials of the Old Kingdom (c.2686–c.2181 BC). Unfortunately, the wood could not withstand the ravages of time, but the gold work is spectacular. The finials of the carrying poles take the form of elegant palmiform capitals, and the chair is decorated with strips of gold chased in imitation of reed matting. The ebony panels of the backrest are decorated inside and out with exquisite hieroglyphs worked in gold, each one a little masterpiece. The inscription reads:

> *Mother of the King of Upper and Lower Egypt, follower of Horus, controller of the butchers of the acacia house, one for whom everything she says, is done, the god's bodily daughter, Hetepheres.*

There are also two gilded wooden chairs decorated with papyrus clusters and delicate inlay work, as well as a bed and headrest, also of gilded wood. Other objects found in the tomb include a tubular leather case for walking sticks, a large gilded jewellery box containing silver bracelets inlaid with precious stones and a small box containing razors and three elegant golden vessels.

▲ *This gilded wooden chair was placed in Hetepheres' tomb for her use in the Afterlife, but was likely to have seen service in her lifetime.*

▼ *This narrow side panel from one of the boxes found in Hetepheres' tomb shows the name of her husband, Sneferu.*

The body of the queen has not been found. A beautifully carved alabaster sarcophagus was found in the shaft but it was empty. However, an alabaster canopic chest discovered in the tomb was found to contain the queen's internal organs, and it is some of the earliest evidence for the practice of including the organs in the burial in this manner.

However, the American archaeologist Mark Lehner has recently suggested that her original burial place was, in fact, the shaft-grave and it was this that was robbed in antiquity. He thinks her body, but not the canopic chest, was then removed to the satellite pyramid, which was also later violated. This would explain the damage to the funerary equipment found in the shaft grave and the presence there of the canopic chest and the empty sarcophagus. ◆

▲ *Furniture found in the tomb of Hetepheres would have been used by her on royal progresses through Egypt, which took place at regular intervals. It included a portable canopy, a chair, a bed and a headrest.*

Khufu's Boats

Boat pits as part of a funerary complex are known from the First Dynasty (c.3100–c.2890 BC). Boats have always played a significant role in the lives of the Egyptians, and were also important in a funerary context. In the Pyramid Texts, there are many references to the boat of the sun god Re, and to the fact that the king in his Afterlife expected to accompany Re in his daily journeys across the sky.

Five boat pits are associated with Khufu's burial within the Great Pyramid complex. Two lie to the south of the pyramid, and three others were found to the east. Both of the southern pits were sealed by huge blocks of limestone. One of these was opened and was found to contain a large wooden boat that had been taken apart for storage. This was restored over a period of ten years by Ahmed Yussef Mustafa, and was finally reassembled in 1968. It is now housed in a specially constructed museum nearby. The function of the craft is unknown. It may have been a solar boat, in which the deceased king, identified with the sun god Re, would cross the sky each day. It may have been used as a state barge in real life, or it may have been the boat that brought the king's body from the capital at Memphis to his pyramid for burial. That it might have had a practical use before burial is suggested by the fact that it shows signs of having been in water. Nevertheless, it could also have been part of the funerary equipment intended to provide the king with everything he needed in the next world.

The other pit on the southern side has not yet been opened, although there are plans to do so in the future. However, using modern technology it has been

► *One of Khufu's boats reconstructed from timbers found in one of five boat pits surrounding his pyramid is now on display in the Boat Museum at Giza.*

▲ *In this scene from the Valley of the Kings, the sun god Re sails through the Underworld and accompanies the king on his journey to the Afterlife.*

▼ *An aerial view of some of the empty boat pits lying close to the Great Pyramid.*

possible to see inside the pit without opening it. An endoscopic image has been obtained, which proves that there is indeed a boat inside. The other three pits are empty, and it is not known whether they ever contained boats or whether the pits themselves were intended to represent boats.

Khufu's boat was made of cedarwood from Lebanon. Shipments of wood from Byblos are known from the reign of Sneferu (c.2613–c.2589 BC). They are also mentioned on the Fifth Dynasty stela known as the Palermo Stone, which records important events from the beginning of the First Dynasty to the end of the Fifth Dynasty (c.2345). No nails were used in the construction of the boat: the planks were fastened together with ropes and pegs.

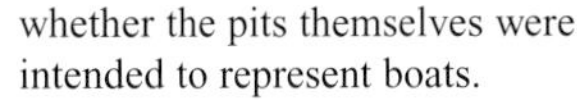

The boat is 43m (141ft) long and 6m (20ft) wide. It has a very shallow draught, making it suitable only for use on the River Nile. There are two cabins, a long central one, presumably for the use of the king, and a smaller one at the prow, probably for the captain. Two large steering oars are located in the stern and the boat was rowed by ten pairs of oars. There is no mast and so no provision for a sail. ◆

The Eastern and Western Cemeteries

The Great Pyramid is the central monument in a large necropolis. Behind the three queens' pyramids to the east of Khufu's pyramid, several members of the royal family were buried, some in mastabas and some in rock-cut tombs. The mastabas of the Sixth Dynasty official Qar and his relative Idu are also situated in the Eastern Cemetery. Officials of Khufu's reign lie in mastaba tombs in a cemetery to the west.

The tomb of Meresankh III

One of the most beautiful and best-preserved tombs in the Eastern Cemetery is that of Queen Meresankh III. She was the granddaughter of Khufu and the daughter of two of his children, Kawab and Hetepheres II. She became the wife of her half-brother King Khafre (c.2558– c.2532 BC), and was about 50 years old when she died.

Her tomb lies below that of her mother and consists of a large, subterranean, rock-cut tomb chapel divided into three main sections. The doorway is inscribed with her name and titles, principally 'Daughter of the King' and 'Royal Wife of Khafre'. It also, unusually, records the time taken to mummify her body. The inscription states that 270 days elapsed between the dates of her death and burial, which is an unusually long time. The embalming process and associated ritual is generally thought to have taken about 70 days, so perhaps her tomb was not finished at the time of her death.

In the first section are scenes common to most tombs of the Old Kingdom (c.2686–c.2181 BC). As well as the usual offering scenes, they show farmworkers engaged in agricultural work, fishermen catching fish by various means, hunters in the marshes and fights between the boatmen. Meresankh and Hetepheres are depicted trapping birds in a net and sailing through the marshes in a papyrus boat, gathering lotus flowers.

▼ *Beyond the square pillars of the first large room is an extension containing statues in high relief of Meresankh III, her mother Hetepheres II and several young female members of the family.*

▲ *Meresankh and Hetepheres are depicted gathering lotus and catching birds with nets in the marshes. Both of these activities have religious significance, the lotus being a symbol of new life and the catching of birds representing the restoration of order over chaos.*

Immediately to the left of the entrance are scenes showing scribes, sculptors, goldsmiths and carpenters at work. The section showing the making of statues is particularly interesting because the names of two of the artists are recorded. Most Egyptian art is anonymous, and it is only very rarely that the names of individual artists come to light. One of the five panels shows Rehay painting a statue of Meresankh, while another shows his colleague, the sculptor Inkaf, at work on another statue of the queen.

The groups of actual statues are another unusual feature of this tomb. Further along from the scenes in the sculptors' workshop there are three niches containing six statues in officials' attire. Unfortunately, these are not inscribed, so their names are not known. Almost opposite, in the extension to this first room, is a huge niche with a group of ten large, female statues, who presumably represent Meresankh, her mother and her daughters, although, again, there are no inscriptions to identify them. The main room also has a false door stela, and offering lists are inscribed on the lintel over the door to the next room. Between the main room and the extension are two pillars decorated in painted, carved relief, with figures of Meresankh wearing a close-fitting dress of white linen. Her two young sons are also shown. One scene shows her father and mother in a papyrus boat.

Beyond the main room is the offerings chapel, decorated with agricultural scenes and others that depict the funerary banquet, where the guests are entertained by singers and musicians. On each side of a false door are two more statue niches. Each houses two statues, presumably of Meresankh and Hetepheres, her mother, placed there to receive offerings.

From the offerings chapel, a shaft leads down to the burial chamber, where George Reisner found a black granite sarcophagus in the course of his excavations in 1927. The mummy of the queen was inside, and this was taken to the Cairo Museum. ▶

▶ *A square pillar in the tomb of Meresankh III shows her dressed in an elegant, close-fitting gown of fine linen. Her two young sons are also depicted. Above her image are her name and titles.*

The mastaba of Qar

Qar lived in the Sixth Dynasty, probably some time during the long reign of Pepi II (c.2278–c.2184 BC). Although he was not an official of Khufu during the king's lifetime, he had responsibilities connected with Khufu's funerary cult and so merited a tomb close to the royal burial place. His titles included 'Overseer of the Pyramid City of Khufu and Menkaure' and 'Supervisor of Priests in the Pyramid of Khafre'. He was also 'Regent of the Pyramid' of Pepi I. His wife, Gefi, was a priestess of Hathor.

Qar's tomb is a stone-built mastaba consisting of a staircase passage, a large main room divided into two sections, and an offering chapel. Like the tomb of Meresankh, it has several interesting sculptures. In a niche in the wall to the left of the entrance is a seated statue of Qar, and on the south wall there is a whole series of statues representing Qar, his young son and other members of his family. The same room has well-preserved scenes showing the presentation of offerings and funeral ritual in painted, carved relief. On the pillar in the centre of this room are Qar's names and titles, together with scenes that show him with his sisters and sitting in a chair with his dog. In the offering chapel, which leads off to the right, is a false door stela.

▼ Qar's tomb is located near to the pyramids of the kings whose cult he served. This view of the interior shows statues of Qar and his relations carved into the face of the rock.

▲ The 6th-Dynasty official Qar and his young son are represented by two statues in his tomb. Qar was in charge of the funerary cult of Khufu, Khafre and Menkaure at Giza.

▲ *A detail of a painted relief of Idu before an offering table shows him wearing an official's wig and a wide collar, which he may have received as a reward for his services to the king.*

The mastaba of Idu

The tomb of Idu, who may be either the father or the son of Qar, is virtually next door. This stone-built mastaba is, in many ways, similar to that of Qar but is much smaller. Idu's tomb has one main room decorated with painted reliefs and rock-cut statues of the deceased and his family. On the jambs of the doorway at the entrance to the tomb are Idu's names and titles, which provide some biographical detail. From these it is clear that he also had duties relating to the funerary cults of the Fourth Dynasty kings. He was inspector of the *wab*-priests of Khufu and Khafre, as well as 'Scribe of the Royal Documents in the Presence of the King'.

The decoration of the tomb is funerary in character. There are few scenes of everyday life, which are otherwise common at this period. The false door stela, where offerings were presented, is in the middle of the east wall and is very unusual in design. A statue of the deceased shows him seated, his hands with upturned palms resting on his knees, as he waits to receive offerings. Above his head is a relief that shows him and his wife seated on each side of an offering table. On the opposite wall are niches containing the statues of Idu and his family. One of the most charming shows Idu wearing his short kilt and official's wig, standing next to his son.

The painted reliefs on the south wall to the left and right of the door are funerary scenes. They show Idu's home, a purification tent and the funeral procession. Facing these, on the back wall, are scenes depicting the preparation of food and drink, dancers and musicians, and the presentation of offerings. Idu oversees these sitting on his palanquin.

The Western Cemetery

Other officials are buried to the west of the Great Pyramid, where there is a whole pyramid 'town' with mastabas laid out in 'streets'. One of the most impressive of these tombs belonged to Iymery, a Fifth Dynasty official who was 'Prophet of Khufu' and 'Overseer of the Great House'. This is a large tomb consisting of an entrance, vestibule, first room, *serdab* (statue room) and offering chapel with a false door stela. Here are the familiar everyday-life scenes that decorate the walls of many of the Old Kingdom tombs. The vestibule has scenes showing carpenters, goldsmiths and sculptors at work. In the first room, there are scenes of cattle-breeding, fishing and fowling in the marshes. The offering chapel has scenes showing offerings being presented to the deceased, who is enjoying the company of his wife and family as musicians and dancers entertain them.

Although many of these tombs have been known for some time, several others have been discovered recently. One of these belongs to a priest called Kai, who remained in royal service from the reign of Sneferu (c.2613–c.2589 BC) to that of Khafre (c.2558–c.2532 BC). His tomb is decorated with elegant reliefs of the tomb owner and offering scenes, in which the colours look as if they were painted yesterday. ◆

False doors

In the offering chapel of a tomb, a stela (stone slab) resembling a door was erected to enable the spirit of the deceased to come out and partake of the daily offerings left in front of it. In some royal tombs, false doors were made of red granite, while in non-royal tombs they were of limestone, which was sometimes painted red in imitation of granite.

▼ *A painted carved relief from the false door of Idu's tomb shows the deceased and his wife at either side of an offering table.*

The Tombs of Pharaoh's Workers

The necropolis containing the tombs of the workers who built the pyramids has only recently come to light. It was found in 1990 when a horse ridden by a tourist stumbled over a low wall, which later turned out to be part of a tomb.

The tombs of this cemetery are very small and inferior in quality to the rather grand stone-built mastabas in the cemeteries of the high officials. They were constructed with odds and ends of different types of building materials left over from the building of pyramids and their associated temples. The first one to be explored was a long vaulted chamber with two false doors. Hieroglyphs in the tomb showed that it belonged to Ptah-shepsesu and his wife. There were three burial shafts at the back of the chamber, so perhaps their son was buried there too. Ptah-shepsesu may have been a supervisor of some sort as his tomb is larger than the others surrounding it. Altogether, about 600 of these small tombs have been found, as well as about 30 larger ones belonging to overseers. The tombs were constructed in all shapes and sizes, many of them appearing to imitate the plans of the tombs of high officials. One has a small ramp, perhaps in imitation of a royal tomb.

Later, an upper part of the necropolis was discovered. Here, the tombs were larger and inscriptions indicated that they were the tombs of the artisans, whereas the lower cemetery seems to have been where the labourers were buried. One of the more imposing tombs was a limestone mastaba with six burial shafts and two false doors carved on its eastern face. Attached to the mastaba was a rock-cut room. The burial was found to be intact, and a sealed niche was found to contain four statues of the deceased, whose name was Intyshedu

▼ *Metalworking processes are common themes in Old Kingdom tombs. Here, the workmen use bellows to increase the heat of the brazier, as depicted in the tomb of Mereruka.*

▶ *The dwarf Seneb and his family, from his tomb at Giza (c.2475 BC). Funerary statues project an ideal view of the deceased so Seneb's deformity has been disguised.*

and who styled himself 'Overseer of the Boat of the Goddess, Neith' and 'King's Acquaintance'. He was a carpenter who made ceremonial boats for the goddess Neith on behalf of the king, and the statues depict him at various stages in life, from youth to old age.

None of the workers' bodies had been mummified, and each had been laid in a small shaft in a foetal position. The skeletal remains, especially in the lower cemetery, showed signs of arthritis and joint injuries incurred during lives of hard physical work, and the lifespan of the workers seems to have been shorter than that of the officials and their wives buried in the officials' cemeteries.

The dwarf cemetery

Another important discovery of recent years is that of the dwarf cemetery. Dwarfs were respected members of society in ancient Egypt and often attained high positions at court. The dwarf Seneb, for example, who has been known for many years from his splendid statue in the Cairo Museum, was chief of all the dwarfs who were responsible for the royal wardrobe. He was also a priest involved in the funerary cults of Khufu and Djedefre. It is known from inscriptions on the false door of his tomb that he was a wealthy man who owned cattle. His statue depicts him sitting cross-legged in the position of a scribe, indicating that he was an educated man. Seneb's wife, Senetites, sits beside him with her arm affectionately around his shoulders, in typical Old Kingdom style. The sculptor has sensitively disguised his deformity, ingeniously compensating for his short stature by placing his two children where his legs would otherwise have been.

Among others, a further dwarf tomb was discovered a few years ago. It is of limestone and has two false doors on the east side, where the name of the dwarf, Prnyankhw, is inscribed. Three shafts were discovered, of which one contained his skeletal remains and the others the remains of two women. Statues of these women were found beside the false doors. Prnyankhw's statue is made of black basalt. He is seated on a chair and is shown as a strong and lively man. The only sign of deformity is that his lower left leg appears to be swollen, and it has been suggested that this might indicate the earliest known case of elephantiasis. Like Seneb, Prnyankhw was highly thought of. An inscription on his right leg describes him as 'One who delights his lord every day'. ◆

Memphis and Saqqara

Memphis, about 24km (15 miles) south of Cairo, was the first capital of the united land of Egypt and remained an important religious and administrative centre throughout the Pharaonic Period. It was the chief cult centre of the god Ptah, and in Egyptian mythology it was the place where he performed the act of creation. It was also where the goddesses Isis and Nephthys took the body of their brother Osiris from the Nile, after he had been murdered by his jealous brother Seth, and where Osiris entered the Underworld to become judge of the dead. The divine court, which finally decided that Horus should inherit the throne of Egypt from his father Osiris, was said to have sat at Memphis.

During the Ptolemaic Period (332–30 BC), the new city of Alexandria overtook Memphis in importance. Memphis never recovered its old status, and the ancient buildings were used as a quarry during the building of the new capital, Cairo, after the Arab invasion in the ninth century AD. Today, there is little to see of the ancient capital city. However, the remains of the tombs of kings and commoners at Saqqara, the cemetery site for Memphis, are spectacular.

◀ *Little remains of the ancient city of Memphis, first capital of Egypt and principal cult centre of the creator god Ptah.*

City and Cemetery

According to Herodotus, the city of Memphis was founded by Min, the legendary first king of Egypt, who would appear to be the Menes of the Egyptian kinglists. First, he prepared the site by building a dam to divert the River Nile. He then built the city and embellished it with the 'large and very remarkable temple of Hephaestus' (actually Ptah, the creator god of Memphis, whom the Greeks equated with their own god).

The name of Memphis may be derived from Men-nefer, the name of the pyramid town of Pepi I at Saqqara. It means 'Established and Beautiful'. Other names included 'White Walls', a reference to the city's fortifications, and 'Balance of the Two Lands', referring to its position at the meeting point of the Nile Valley and the Delta.

▲ *The head of the colossal polished-limestone statue of Ramesses II. Originally erected in front of the Ptah temple, today it is in the museum at Memphis. The statue stood 13m (43ft) high.*

Archaeological remains

In Memphis today, a museum housing a gigantic statue of Ramesses II and various other pieces from the New Kingdom (c.1550–c.1069 BC) and later periods are all the tourist usually gets to see of the ancient city. The remains of a Ramesside temple of Ptah are also visible. Material from earlier structures, including a lintel dating from the Middle Kingdom (c.2055–c.1650 BC), was reused in this building, suggesting the existence of previous temples on the site. However, these have not so far come to light as the high water table makes the site difficult to excavate. It is also possible that the city's location changed during the Pharaonic Period, corresponding to changes in the course of the Nile. Recent attempts to locate the most ancient city have been made by David Jeffreys and the Egypt Exploration Society using drill cores.

Close to the temple of Ptah in Memphis was the stall where the Apis bull, the living image of the god Ptah, was kept. On his death, the bull was mummified in the embalming house. The embalming tables used for this purpose remain on the site and the embalming house built by the Twenty-second Dynasty king Sheshonq I (c.945–c.924 BC) is currently undergoing excavation and reconstruction.

Saqqara

Saqqara was the main cemetery site for ancient Memphis, and was used by kings and/or their officials from the First Dynasty (c.3100–c.2890 BC) to the Christian era. Here are the great mastaba tombs of the First Dynasty élite, once thought to be the tombs of the kings of this period. Here, too, is the Step Pyramid of King Djoser (c.2667–c.2648 BC), the oldest stone building in the world. The officials' tombs of the Old Kingdom (c.2686–c.2181 BC) are grouped around the tombs of the kings they served. Most of the Middle Kingdom kings and their officials were buried further south at Dahshur, in the Faiyum, and at Thebes, but because Memphis continued to be the seat of government in the New Kingdom, many officials of this period were buried at Saqqara, although the kings themselves were usually buried in the Valley of the Kings.

Saqqara continued to be used for private burials from the Saite to the Ptolemaic Periods (664–30 BC). After this time the site was abandoned until the fifth century AD, when the Copts (Egyptian Christians) built a monastery here dedicated to St Jeremiah. The tombs of important Persian officials, dating from the Persian occupation of 525–404 BC, are currently being investigated.

The site is vast and extends for about 6km (4 miles) along the desert edge. ◆

▲ *A block carved in sunken relief from the pyramid complex of King Unas at Saqqara. The name of the king appears in the cartouches.*

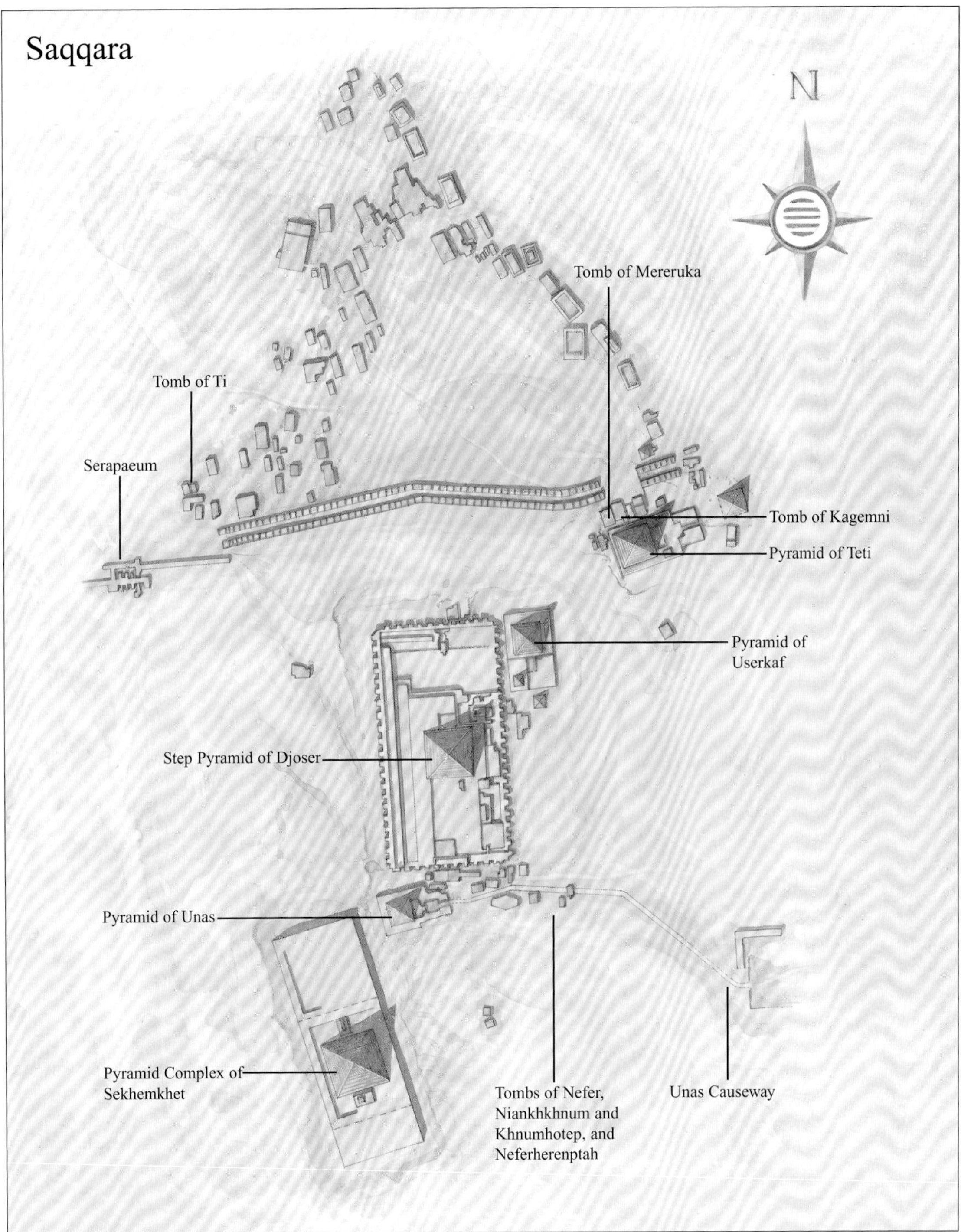
Saqqara
N
Tomb of Mereruka
Tomb of Ti
Serapaeum
Tomb of Kagemni
Pyramid of Teti
Pyramid of Userkaf
Step Pyramid of Djoser
Pyramid of Unas
Pyramid Complex of Sekhemkhet
Tombs of Nefer, Niankhkhnum and Khnumhotep, and Neferherenptah
Unas Causeway

The Step Pyramid of King Djoser

The buildings of the Step Pyramid complex of King Djoser (c.2667–c.2648 BC) are of two different types: some were designed for practical use, while the majority are dummy buildings. According to their excavator, Jean-Philippe Lauer, the latter appear to be primarily symbolic and represent the ancient city of Memphis, so that, just as the subterranean chambers of the pyramid were stocked with food and drink to supply the king's supposed physical needs, he was also provided with a capital city for the Afterlife. The functional buildings may have been used during the king's funeral and for the subsequent daily ritual of his mortuary cult.

▼ *The Step Pyramid of King Djoser, built on the desert plateau, is seen here across the date palm trees of the Nile Valley.*

Entrance to the complex

The complex covers a large area in the form of a rectangle 544 x 277m (1,785 x 909ft), 15 hectares (37 acres) in all, which is thought to be the size of a typical large town of the period. Boundary stelae, inscribed with the name of the king and his two daughters, Hetep-her-nebti and Int-ka-s, mark out the site, and it is entirely surrounded by a wall of fine-quality white Tura limestone. This may well have represented the walls of the city, which gave Memphis one of its epithets, 'White Walls'. Fourteen dummy doorways are set in the walls and the complex is entered on the south-eastern side through a doorway with a door carved in an open position. Inside the door is a small vestibule and a corridor composed of two rows of 20 half-engaged fluted columns, carved in imitation of bundles of reeds. The corridor leads into a small hypostyle hall (a chamber in which the roof is supported by columns) with eight columns arranged in pairs connected by limestone blocks. Beyond is the Great Courtyard in front of the Step Pyramid.

Djoser's pyramid

The Step Pyramid is a tower built in six stages, based on a mastaba 63m (207ft) square and about 8m (26ft) tall. This covers a shaft 28m (92ft) deep, leading to the burial chamber and a whole network of subterranean rooms and tunnels used for funerary goods. A further series of 11 shafts and chambers were constructed to the east, perhaps to accommodate the burial of the royal women. The mastaba seems to have been expanded to cover these extensions, and at some point

further stages were added. This produced a more imposing monument and perhaps represented a stairway to heaven, which, according to the Pyramid Texts found in the pyramid of King Unas (c.2375–c.2345 BC), the king expected to climb.

The Great Courtyard

On the south side of the court is a building called the Southern Tomb, which may have housed the king's internal organs (liver, lungs, stomach and intestines), the chamber being too small to take a body. Another theory is that it was intended for the burial of the king's *ka* statue, a representation of his spirit or vital force as his slightly smaller double. The walls are decorated with reliefs showing the king running his *heb sed* race and naming him as Horus Netjerikhet. The top of the tomb wall has a frieze of cobras, which represent the goddess Wadjet, the protector of kings.

The *heb sed*, or royal jubilee festival, usually took place after the king had been on the throne for 30 years and included a re-coronation ceremony, when the king was reinvested in his position and his royal power was renewed. It would seem that provision was made for this to happen in the Afterlife too, so that the king could be confirmed in his role eternally. In the centre of the Great Courtyard are a couple of semicircular blocks, two of the markers that once indicated the course to be run by the king during his *sed*-festival in the Afterlife. On the eastern side of the court is Temple T, a building that perhaps represents the pavilion where in real life the king would wait at certain points in the *heb sed* ritual. It contains a niche decorated with *djed*-pillars, which were associated with Osiris and symbolized stability, and the king is likely to have been represented here by a statue. ▶

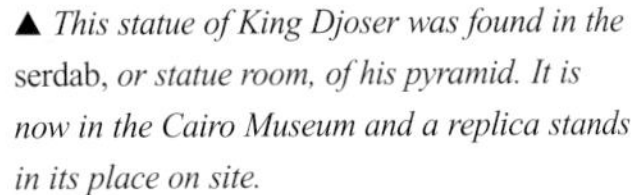

▲ *This statue of King Djoser was found in the* serdab, *or statue room, of his pyramid. It is now in the Cairo Museum and a replica stands in its place on site.*

◀ *Distinctive columns carved to resemble bundles of reeds can be seen when looking east through the colonnaded entrance to Djoser's pyramid complex, which was built by Imhotep.*

◀ *A frieze of royal cobras decorates the top of the so-called Southern Tomb.*

The *heb sed* court

From Temple T the wall curves round, guiding the ceremonial procession into the *heb sed* court where the king would be recrowned, once as King of Lower Egypt and once as King of Upper Egypt. In this court, there is a platform approached by a short flight of steps. Here, there would have been a double canopy, under which the ceremony would have taken place. A tiny ebony label once attached to grave goods in an Early Dynastic tomb at Abydos depicts this ceremony and enabled archaeologists to reconstruct the platform and short flights of steps.The *heb sed* court is surrounded by dummy chapels with beautifully finished façades of dressed limestone, but entirely filled with rubble. They were designed to provide a suitable setting for the ceremonial. Several unfinished statues of the king have also been found in this area, but their precise intended location is not known.

The Southern and Northern Courts

Leading from the *heb sed* court is the Southern Court, the main feature of which is the House of the South. Although it is now restored only to doorway height, Jean-Philippe Lauer, the French architect who has restored the complex, thought that the building would originally have been more than 12m (40ft) high, with a façade embellished with slender, engaged fluted columns. Many of the capitals were found, almost complete, lying in the sand, carved in the form of pendant leaves. Set in a recess in the wall of the court, Lauer found the base of a small round column. He also found the uppermost part of the column, but unfortunately the capital seems to have disappeared. Lauer thought that it would have been in the form of a lotus, the symbol of Southern or Upper Egypt, hence the name given to the court.

Inside the House of the South are some interesting graffiti written by visitors during the New Kingdom (c.1550–c.1069 BC), expressing their admiration for the monument, which was by then about 1,500 years old. One of these is particularly informative because it mentions the name of Djoser, while the other inscriptions in the complex name King Netjerikhet as the owner. It is now recognized that they were one and the same (each king of Egypt having more than one name). This graffito reads:

▶ *The* heb sed *court in Djoser's Step Pyramid complex was meant to provide a setting for the king's celebration of the* heb sed *in the Afterlife.*

▲ *Papyrus-form pillar with a triangular stem and an open-umbel capital in the so-called Northern Court. The papyrus was the symbol of Lower Egypt.*

The scribe Ahmose, son of Iptah, came to see the temple of Djoser. He found it as though heaven were within it, Re rising in it. Then he said, 'Let loaves and oxen and all good and pure things fall to the ka *of the justified Djoser; may heaven drip fresh myrrh, may it drip incense!'*

Next comes the Northern Court, the east wall of which has a recess with three slender triangular columns crowned with open papyrus umbels symbolizing Northern or Lower Egypt and emphasizing the dual nature of the complex. Another building, corresponding to the House of the South in the other court, completes this section.

At the north-eastern corner of the pyramid is the *serdab*, or statue chamber, which housed the *ka* statue of the king to which offerings would have been brought during the daily mortuary ritual. The original statue is now in the Cairo Museum and has been replaced by a replica. The mortuary temple was on the north side of the pyramid. It is largely in ruins now, but must have been imposing in its time and is the earliest example known. Also on the north side is the original entrance to the burial chamber, although this is no longer accessible to tourists. During the Saite Period (664–525 BC) another entrance was made on the southern side. ◆

Imhotep

The architect of the Step Pyramid of King Djoser was Imhotep, the king's vizier. He has been identified by an inscription on the base of a statue of the king. He was later also credited with medical knowledge, and his fame became so great that in the Ptolemaic Period (332–30 BC) he was deified and equated both with Thoth, the ancient Egyptian god of wisdom, and Asklepios, the ancient Greek god of healing.

The Asklepion, his cult centre, was visited by pilgrims who brought offerings of mummified ibises, many bearing the name of Imhotep on the wrappings. Pilgrims also left clay models of afflicted body parts in the hope that Imhotep would heal them. It was in the search for the actual tomb of Imhotep that the sacred animal cemetery at Saqqara was accidentally found.

▶ *The entrance to the Step Pyramid complex of King Djoser.*

The *Sed*-Festival

The *heb sed*, or royal jubilee festival, was a ritual during which the king's right to rule and his royal powers were renewed. In representations of this ceremony, he is usually shown running alongside the Apis bull, proving his fitness to rule, and then being recrowned as 'King of the Two Lands'. Officially, the *sed*-festival was held after the king had been on the throne for 30 years, but reliefs and inscriptions suggest that some kings, including those with relatively short reigns, celebrated earlier. Although this may sometimes have been the case, other kings may simply have been depicted symbolically fulfilling one of the obligations of kingship, just as Queen Nefertiti, for example, perhaps as co-ruler with her husband, Akhenaten (c.1352–c.1336 BC), is depicted smiting enemies.

The origins of the *sed*-festival are not known, although there is evidence that it was held from the very beginning of recorded history. On a small ebony label once attached to a jar of oil from the tomb of King Den (c.2950 BC) at Abydos, a tiny pin-man figure of the king is shown running around a clearly defined course and carrying the *heb sed* insignia. To the left, there is a platform approached by a short flight of steps, on which a double shrine has been erected. Inside the shrine, the king is shown again, sitting on a throne and wearing the Double Crown, having been recrowned twice, once as King of Upper Egypt and once as King of Lower Egypt.

The *heb sed* and the Afterlife

The Step Pyramid complex of King Djoser at Saqqara includes provision for this ceremony to be eternally re-enacted in his Afterlife. The markers in the Great Court that indicated the course the king would have to run perhaps represented the frontiers of Egypt and symbolized the extent of the king's dominion. The figure of the running king can be seen in low relief in the chambers below the Southern Tomb and beneath the pyramid.

▲ *Papyrus-form columns embellish the walls of the House of the North in the Step Pyramid complex, papyrus being the symbol of Lower Egypt.*

Evidence for the view that the king would expect to take part in this important ritual of kingship in the Afterlife is found in a beautiful alabaster

▶ *Queen Hatshepsut in her role as king of Egypt celebrates the* heb sed *by symbolically running around Egypt's boundaries accompanied by the Apis bull.*

vase that was discovered in one of the chambers beneath the pyramid itself. The vase is carved with the figure of a man with arms upraised, holding aloft a square object, perhaps a canopy, although Jean-Philippe Lauer suggests that it is the platform on which the double shrine and the two thrones would have been set up. The handle of the vase is decorated with reliefs of the thrones of the Two Lands. The figure represents the hieroglyph for millions of years and the thrones are those used by the king at his *heb sed*.

The *heb sed* in history

The ritual was practised throughout Pharaonic history. At Karnak, blocks from the reconstructed Red Chapel of Hatshepsut (c.1473–c.1458 BC) show her, as king, running with the Apis bull between the markers. Scenes from the inner walls of the hypostyle hall in the temple at Karnak show Ramesses II (c.1279–c.1213 BC) similarly engaged. Jubilees are also depicted in the mortuary temple of Amenhotep III (c.1390–c.1352 BC) at Thebes, although he seems to have altered the ritual and

▶ *King Djoser, dressed in his* heb sed *costume, runs around the course markers that symbolized the boundaries of Egypt.*

its usual setting somewhat. He celebrated three *heb seds* and descriptions of the ceremonies say that they took place on the great artificial lake he had created at Malkata. Here, the king and statues of the deities sailed along in barges, re-enacting the voyage of the sun god through the Underworld.

Surprisingly, in view of the break with tradition during the reign of the Eighteenth Dynasty king Akhenaten, the *heb sed* was also depicted in the colonnaded court of the Temple of Aten at Karnak, although in this case Akhenaten's queen, Nefertiti, and the royal daughters also took part. The ceremony also took place very early in his reign, before the move to the new capital of Akhetaten. Another remarkable feature is that the Aten, the life-giving disc of the sun, is also seen taking part in a *heb sed* of his own. This is most unusual because the gods are usually seen to give *sed*-festivals to the king; they are never shown taking part in such a ritual themselves. Akhenaten seems to be pointing out that because the god is king, so the king is also a god.

The festival continued to take place in later times. This is confirmed by scenes from the temple of the cat-goddess, Bastet, at Bubastis, where the Twenty-second Dynasty king Osorkon II (c.874–c.850 BC) is shown seated in the *heb sed* kiosk, wearing the typical robe. At Kom Ombo, carved reliefs show Ptolemy VIII (170–116 BC) receiving *heb sed* symbols from the god Horus, showing that even foreign kings liked to depict themselves taking part in the traditional ritual of kingship. ◆

◀ *The* heb sed *court in the Step Pyramid complex makes provision for the king to renew his right to rule in the Afterlife for all eternity.*

The Pyramid of King Unas

The pyramid of King Unas (c.2375–c.2345 BC), the last king of the Fifth Dynasty, is located near the south-western corner of the Step Pyramid complex. Most of the outer casing has disappeared from this pyramid, revealing its inner core of loose blocks and rubble. It is the smallest of all the Old Kingdom pyramids, but also one of the most interesting as it has several unusual features. On the south side of the pyramid, for instance, there is an inscription of Khaemwese, son of the Nineteenth Dynasty king Ramesses II (c.1279–c.1213 BC), saying that he restored the pyramid on his father's instructions and replaced the name of King Unas because by that time it was missing.

The entrance is on the north side of the pyramid at ground level, and was originally closed with a limestone plug. A sloping passage only 1.4m (4ft 6in) high leads to a vestibule and a second corridor, where there are the remains of three granite portcullises. This corridor eventually leads to a small rectangular room with three niches, probably intended for the *ka* statues of the king. A passage leads to the burial chamber, in which Gaston Maspero of the Egyptian Antiquities Service found a basalt sarcophagus containing the remains of a mummy in 1881.

▲ *A roofed causeway ran from the valley temple to the mortuary temple. Next to it were two large boat pits.*

▼ *Although Unas' pyramid was repaired in antiquity, the outer casing has almost disappeared.*

Pyramid Texts

Both the rectangular antechamber and the burial chamber have ceilings made of two large, sloping limestone slabs decorated with gold stars on a blue ground. The walls of both chambers are covered with Pyramid Texts, and this is the earliest known appearance of these collections of spells, which were intended to enable the king to overcome hostile forces and powers in the Underworld, and so to join the sun god Re, his divine father. He would then spend his days in eternity, sailing with Re across the sky in the solar boat:

Re-Atum, this Unas comes to you,
A spirit indestructible...
Your son comes to you, this Unas comes to you,
May you cross the sky united in the dark,
May you rise in lightland, the place in which you shine!
(Utterance 217)

The sky's reed floats are launched for Re,
That he may cross on them to lightland...
The sky's reed floats are launched for Unas,
That he may cross on them to lightland, to Re...
(Utterance 263)

Other spells describe the king climbing a ladder to heaven and joining the gods among the stars, or acting as Re's secretary:

Unas squats before him,
Unas opens his boxes,
Unas unseals his decrees,
Unas seals his dispatches,
Unas sends his messengers who tire not,
Unas does what Unas is told.
(Utterance 309)

The hieroglyphs of the texts are beautifully carved and filled with blue paste, so that they stand out boldly from the white background. Several kings of the Sixth Dynasty, Teti (c.2345–c.2323 BC), Pepi I (c.2321–c.2287 BC), Merenre (c.2287–c.2278 BC) and Pepi II (c.2278– c.2184 BC), also decorated their burial chambers in this way.

The pyramid complex

The mortuary temple of Unas was partly excavated by the Italian archaeologist Alessandro Barsanti in the early twentieth century, and more completely by Sir Charles Firth in 1929. It is almost completely destroyed, although it has been possible to trace the layout. The temple was similar to that of Sahure, although the floor was made of alabaster rather than basalt.

The plan of the temple is not known in its entirety as the remains of the building lie partly under a modern road. However, enough work has been done to show that the temple was embellished with beautifully made granite palmiform columns. There was a lake here, which made a harbour for the temple. The archaeologists also discovered the harbour, including quays and a slipway.

▲ *The causeway was decorated with scenes in carved and painted relief. Here, Unas is depicted smiting his enemies.*

Linking the valley and mortuary temples is an impressive causeway, 750m (2,460ft) long and once decorated with brightly coloured reliefs. The scenes are amazingly varied. Some show agricultural work, others hunters pursuing lions, leopards, hyenas and a giraffe. Ships are depicted transporting granite palmiform columns, and craftsmen work copper and gold. Possibly the most intriguing are the famine scenes. The relief is not complete and it is not possible to identify the starving people with any certainty. Amelia Edwards surmised that they were foreigners to whom Unas probably sent aid, and that the scenes illustrated one of his good deeds that he wished to perpetuate for eternity. Others see them as Egyptian and read into the scenes signs of Egypt's decline towards the end of the Old Kingdom. ◆

◀ *The walls of the long, roofed causeway were also elaborately decorated with beautifully carved hieroglyphs .*

Tombs of Old Kingdom Officials

Alongside the causeway linking the mortuary and valley temples of King Unas (c.2375–c.2345 BC), there are several tombs belonging to officials of the Old Kingdom (c.2686–c.2181 BC). They chose to be buried near to the pyramids of their royal masters so that they could be on hand to continue to serve them in the Afterlife.

The tomb of Nefer

One of the best-preserved is that of Nefer, but it can be visited only with special permission. Nefer was 'Head of the Royal Singers' and 'Inspector of the Court'. He seems to have been close to the king because he calls himself 'keeper of the king's secrets'. Several members of his family were buried here, including his father, Kaha, who also held the position of 'Head of the Royal Singers', and his mother, Khons, who was a priestess of the goddess Hathor. In the tomb, Nefer's father is described as the 'controller of the beautiful voice' and 'unique among the singers of the funerary estate'. Nefer's three sons and his daughter were also musical and had positions as professional singers. The family is depicted in the tomb, which is noteworthy for a unique scene in which Nefer's wife and child are shown watching dancers.

The tomb is very beautifully decorated with lively scenes in painted relief. Some show work going on in a vegetable garden, where onions and lettuce are being planted and grapes are being gathered and pressed. A baboon is lending a hand. Papyrus is being gathered and prepared for transportation, cattle mate and calves are born. An interesting group shows the building of a wooden cargo boat, the construction of a canoe and a papyrus boat. Elsewhere,

▶ *Nefer, dressed in the leopardskin of a priest, sits in front of an offering table laden with loaves of bread. Above are jars of wine, beer and fruit.*

▶ *Papyrus plants are harvested and bound into bundles in preparation for transport. Papyrus was used for paper, making sandals and building boats.*

ships ply up and down the Nile. As usual, much attention is paid to hunting, fishing and the preparation of food.

A pit cut into the floor of the tomb houses one of the oldest mummies extant. It is about 4,500 years old and, even though the mummification process had not been perfected at this stage, it is virtually intact. It had been so carefully wrapped that the bandages bore the impressions of the fingernails and a callus on the sole of the foot. The body was naked apart from a bead collar. A false beard had also been added. When the body was discovered in the 1940s, the deceased was holding his long official's cane in one hand and a short staff in the other. It is not certain whether it is Nefer himself who is lying here, or a family friend called Waty. ▶

The king's officials

The Narmer Palette, which dates from the beginning of the Dynastic Period, and labels attached to grave goods found at Abydos and Saqqara give the names of officials who held positions in the administration of Egypt. These make it clear that an organized central administration existed from the very beginning of the united land, c.3100 BC. Officials carried titles such as 'Sandal Bearer', 'Sole Companion' or 'Royal Seal Bearer'. The 'Chief of Scouts' organized trading expeditions to procure exotic goods for the king.

▶ *Nefer's tomb is one of the most beautifully decorated of the Old Kingdom. Here, a servant brings a deer to sustain Nefer in the Afterlife.*

◀ *Mereruka, vizier and son-in-law of Teti of the 6th Dynasty, receives a procession of offering bearers bringing food to the tomb.*

The tomb of Niankhkhnum and Khnumhotep

Niankhkhnum and Khnumhotep were brothers, probably twins. Like Nefer, they were high-ranking officials. Each held the position of 'Prophet of Re' in the sun temple of Niuserre (c.2445–c.2421 BC) and both were 'Overseers of the Manicurists of the Great House'. They are beautifully depicted, embracing each other, on the wall of the chamber leading to the offering room.

The superstructure of their tomb was almost completely destroyed in antiquity, because King Unas built his causeway over it. It has been reconstructed using the decorated blocks that were found during excavation, and is now open to the public. The part of the tomb that was cut into the rock is well preserved. The quality of the painted reliefs is excellent, especially in the first of the rock-cut chambers. The various scenes on the western side of the tomb include fishing and fowling in the marshes, stock breeding, papyrus gathering and fights among the boatmen. Opposite are agricultural scenes and scenes of sculptors and jewellers at work. There are also the usual offering bearers and banqueting scenes, where the guests are entertained with music and dancing.

The 'bird tomb' of Neferherenptah

Nearer to the boat pit of the pyramid complex of Unas is the mastaba of Neferherenptah, who was 'Head of the Hairdressers'. This tomb is unfinished, and it would appear that building was interrupted by the construction of the causeway of King Unas. However, it is decorated with simple designs of exceptionally high quality. The scenes depict agricultural work and the preparation of food and drink. There is also a fine fowling scene with a large flock of birds, from which the tomb gets its nickname.

The mastaba of Mereruka

Mereruka held office as vizier during the reign of Teti (c.2345–c.2323 BC), the first king of the Sixth Dynasty, and married the king's daughter. His tomb lies close to Teti's pyramid. It was excavated by Jacques de Morgan of the Egyptian Antiquities Service in 1892, and it is the largest of all the non-royal Old Kingdom tombs. There are 32 chambers in all: 17 are in the main suite, which accommodated the funerary arrangements of Mereruka himself, and the rest were used for the burials of his wife, Watetkhethor, and their son, Meryteti. Most of the rooms are decorated, and those that are not were used for stores.

▼ *Kagemni's tomb is decorated with scenes showing many types of fishing. Here, fish are being caught in baskets and nets from a papyrus boat.*

▶ *Lively scenes showing fights between boatmen in the marshes are common in later Old Kingdom tombs. This one comes from the tomb of Kagemni.*

Mereruka appears on the entrance to the tomb together with his name and titles. Just inside the vestibule he is shown hunting in the papyrus marshes, where birds, hippopotamuses and crocodiles are vividly portrayed. In the next room, Mereruka and his wife inspect a jeweller's workshop. All the processes are recorded, from the weighing out of the gold to the making up of the finished pieces. Several of the workers are dwarfs. Other scenes show sculptors, carpenters and makers of stone vases at work.

The main room, the funerary chapel, has a false door in which stands a life-sized painted statue of Mereruka, who appears to be striding forward to receive his offerings of food and drink. The roof is supported by six square pillars, and Mereruka appears on each face carrying his staffs of office. The walls are decorated with a variety of scenes in painted relief. To the right of the statue, another figure of Mereruka watches boys and girls playing boisterous games, while to the left there are some unusual scenes where animals, including hyenas, are being force-fed. Nearer to the entrance agricultural work is being carried out on Mereruka's estates, and on the opposite wall several large ships get ready to sail.

Although in poor condition, this tomb has some charming domestic scenes. The walls of Chamber 7 show Mereruka and his wife sitting together on a large couch, while she plays her harp to soothe him. Just to the left they are shown again, this time standing hand in hand while servants make their bed. On the opposite wall they receive offerings and are entertained by male and female dancers.

▼ *A detail of a beautifully carved relief from the tomb of Kagemni, showing cattle crossing a stream.*

In the area devoted to Mereruka's wife, she is shown being carried on a large sedan chair and receiving offerings in the company of her son and daughter. In another scene, she is portrayed with her three dogs and a pet monkey.

The mastaba of Kagemni

Kagemni was vizier, or chief minister, in the early part of Teti's reign. His large tomb also lies opposite Teti's pyramid, next door to that of Mereruka. Eight of its rooms are beautifully decorated in high relief. There are also five storage areas. The tomb has some unusual features. One is that the *serdab*, or statue chamber, which housed the *ka* statue, is completely sealed off from the rest of the tomb. (There is usually a 'window' from which the statue can see out.) There is also a stairway leading to the roof and two boat-shaped chambers reminiscent of the boat pits of King Unas.

Much of the decoration in Kagemni's tomb is taken up with offering processions, agricultural work and stock breeding. Some of the best scenes are of fishing, and show several different methods of catching fish, including the use of clap nets, trawl nets and a multi-hooked rod. Other scenes show birds trapped in a net and hippopotamuses speared with harpoons. Unusual themes include a piglet being fed and a mother feeding her baby on a boat. Kagemni himself is seen receiving offerings. ◆

New Kingdom Tombs at Saqqara

Saqqara continued to be used as a necropolis in the New Kingdom (c.1550–c.1069 BC). The necropolis was known in the mid-nineteenth century from the work of Carl Lepsius and from loose sculpted and inscribed blocks that had found their way into museums, but some of the most important discoveries of recent times have been made by the joint expedition of the Egypt Exploration Society and Leiden University, headed by Professor Geoffrey Martin.

The tomb of Maya

One of the tombs seen by Lepsius was that of Maya, treasurer of Tutankhamun (c.1336–c.1327 BC) and his two immediate successors in the Eighteenth Dynasty. Maya's tomb was found almost by accident when the EES–Leiden team were led astray by the inaccuracies in Lepsius' map of the necropolis. In 1986, while they were excavating in the tomb of Ramose, a contemporary of Maya and an officer in the Egyptian army, they noticed a shaft leading to the underground chambers of another tomb. Much to their delight it turned out to be the tomb of Maya, which they had been seeking and had so far failed to locate. The following year they began to explore the superstructure and soon found the tops of the mudbrick walls of the inner court and the main cult room with its adjoining chapels. These areas were cleared of sand and the reliefs revealed.

The tomb is decorated with painted, carved reliefs of the highest quality, and with texts that identify the owner and his wife, Meryt. Some that Lepsius had recorded were no longer there. These included some that he had taken to Berlin, but others seem to have been removed by local people and used to make lime. This also seems to have been the fate of several statues known to have been made for the tomb, although three, which were in perfect condition and are masterpieces of Egyptian art, had been acquired by the Leiden Museum in the 1820s and have thus survived. However, the statue group of Maya and Meryt, which Lepsius had noticed, was still there, albeit lying face downwards instead of standing upright against the wall. This revealed the fact that it had been made from a block taken from an Old Kingdom tomb. In fact, much of the material used in the building of this tomb had been 'recycled' in this way.

Some detail concerning the life of Maya was found in an inscription on the south wall of the entrance pylon, or gateway. He wrote about himself thus:

▲ *Prisoners from the city-states of Syria–Palestine are led by Egyptian soldiers into the presence of Tutankhamun.*

...the governance which came into being through me, [was] as something ordained by my god since my youth, the presence of the king having been granted to me since I was a child. I happily reached the end [of my career], enjoying countless favours of the Lord of the Two Lands...In the beginning I was good, in the end I was excellent, one who was revered in peace in the temple of Ptah. I carried out the

plans of the king of my time without neglecting anything he had commanded... [I made splendid] the temples, fashioning the images of the gods for whom I was responsible. I entered face to face to the August Image...

The tomb of Horemheb

Maya's great contemporary was the army commander Horemheb, who later became the last king of the Eighteenth Dynasty (c.1323–c.1295 BC) and was buried in the Valley of the Kings. In the earlier part of his career, he prepared a tomb at Saqqara. This tomb was also found by happy accident in 1975, when the joint EES–Leiden expedition was given permission by the Egyptian Antiquities Department to search for the tomb of Maya. Strangely enough, only a few days after starting work, the team came upon a column that bore the image, name and titles of Horemheb, who was already well known to scholars through inscriptions and reliefs in most of the major museums.

Horemheb's tomb is approached by an undecorated pylon, or gateway, leading to the first court. This is mainly decorated with scenes from his time in office and processions of offering bearers. One is a 'Window of Appearances' scene, which shows Horemheb being rewarded by the king for his services. On the west wall of this court there was originally a stela depicting Horemheb worshipping Re-Horakhty, the sun god, Thoth, the god of wisdom, and Maat, the goddess of truth. It was also inscribed with a long hymn in their honour. The original is in the British Museum in London, but a cast now replaces it on the site.

From inscriptions in his tomb, a great deal is known about Horemheb's career. He had a great many titles conferred on him, many by Tutankhamun, although his military career probably began under Akhenaten (c.1352–c.1336 BC). Among these titles are 'Hereditary Prince and Count', 'Deputy of the King in the Entire Land', 'Overseer of all Offices of the King', 'Generalissimo', 'King's Envoy', 'Overseer of Recruits of the King of the Two Lands', 'Chief of the Entire Land', 'Sealbearer of the King of Upper and Lower Egypt', 'Overseer of all Overseers of Scribes of the King', 'Overseer of all Works of the King in Every Place' and 'Overseer of All Divine Offices'. It was extremely important that all this was recorded so that Horemheb would be able to continue to serve the king in these capacities in the Afterlife. It was his wife Mutnodjmet, possibly the sister of Akhenaten's wife Nefertiti, who was buried here, while Horemheb enjoyed a royal burial at Thebes. ◆

▲ *Nubian prisoners of war are very realistically portrayed awaiting transportation to a work camp.*

▼ *Horemheb receives envoys from Libya and the Near East on behalf of Tutankhamun.*

▼ *Carved in delicate low relief, Maya adores Osiris. The hand of his wife, Meryt, also raised in adoration, is shown behind him.*

The Serapaeum

The Serapaeum was used for the burials and funerary cult of the Apis bulls, which were regarded as the living representation of the Memphite creator god Ptah during their lifetime and were identified with Osiris after death. Herodotus describes the birth and appearance of the Apis bull in Book Three of *The Histories*:

> *This Apis is the calf of a cow which is never afterwards able to have another. The Egyptian belief is that a flash of light descends upon the cow from heaven, and this causes her to receive Apis. The Apis-calf has distinctive marks: it is black, with a white diamond on its forehead, the image of an eagle on its back, the hairs of its tail double and a scarab under its tongue.*

The bulls lived for about 15 years, and when one died its body was taken to be mummified in the special embalming house at Memphis. It then went to the underground galleries of the Serapaeum for burial in a huge granite sarcophagus.

The Serapaeum was first discovered by Richard Pococke in 1738, and then rediscovered and excavated by Auguste Mariette in 1851. Mariette said that he had been led to the Serapaeum and the associated temple by a passage in the work of the Greek geographer and historian, Strabo, who described the avenue of sphinxes leading to it as being virtually buried by drifting sand, 'some having only their heads above the surface'. One day, as Mariette was walking in the desert, he came across the head of a sphinx just visible above the sand, and was immediately reminded of the passage in Strabo. He excavated the site, and found a vast complex of galleries that date from at least the early New Kingdom (c.1550 BC) and which were expanded in the Saite and Ptolemaic Periods.

▲ *The Apis bull, who represented the creator god Ptah while alive and Osiris after death, was kept in a stall outside the Temple of Ptah at Memphis.*

The catacombs

The galleries were extended during the time of Ramesses II (c.1279-c.1213 BC) and his son Khaemwese, who was High Priest of Ptah at Memphis. Another extension took place in the Saite Twenty-sixth Dynasty (664–525 BC) and they continued in use until the Ptolemaic Period (332–30 BC), when a further gallery was added. The galleries were cut into the solid rock and the burial chambers hewn out on both sides. These chambers house the enormous sarcophagi, which weigh up to 80 tons and measure about 4m (13ft) in length by 2m (6ft 6in) in width, with a height of 3.3m (11ft).

Altogether, 24 sarcophagi were discovered by Mariette, and all but one had been robbed. It seems this tomb had defeated the robbers because the lid was so firmly fixed that Mariette had to resort to dynamite to blast it off.

▼ *Large numbers of bronze statuettes of Apis have been found, indicating the popularity of the cult in the Late and Ptolemaic Periods.*

▲ *After death, the Apis bulls were mummified and placed in huge granite sarcophagi weighing up to 80 tons each.*

Inside he found the solid gold statue of a bull, now in the Louvre, Paris, and the mummy of the bull itself, which is now in the Agricultural Museum in Cairo. Elsewhere in the catacombs, Mariette thought that he had found the remains of the mummy of Khaemwese, although some scholars now think that the bones were actually those of a bull.

Mariette was obviously moved by his discoveries:

> *By some inexplicable accident one of the chambers of the Apis tombs, walled up in the thirtieth year of Ramesses II, had escaped the general plunder of the monuments, and I was so fortunate to find it untouched. Three thousand seven hundred years had had no effect in altering its primitive state. The fingermark of the Egyptian who set the last stone in the wall built to cover up the door was still visible in the mortar. Bare feet had left their traces on the sand...*

Votive tablets

What the robbers either overlooked or thought to be worthless were the 500 votive tablets dedicated in antiquity by pilgrims to the site. These, too, are now in the Louvre and, because they are dated, have proved invaluable for establishing the chronology of the Saite and Graeco-Roman Periods. Their use was demonstrated over a century ago. According to Herodotus, Cambyses (525–522 BC), one of the Persian rulers of Egypt, stabbed the Apis bull in a fit of jealous rage, after which 'Apis lay some time pining in the temple, but at last died of his wound and the priests buried him secretly'. Amelia Edwards, however, noted that one of the votive tablets stated that the bull did not die until the fourth year of the reign of Darius I (522–486 BC), the succeeding king. Herodotus may simply have used this tale to confirm his belief that Cambyses was mad, as this would have been considered such a heinous crime. ◆

▼ *Niches in the walls of the Serapaeum originally contained votive tablets set up by pilgrims to the vaults. These were taken by Mariette to the Louvre and are an invaluable source of information on chronology.*

The Valley of the Kings

From the beginning of the New Kingdom (c.1550–c.1069 BC), kings were no longer buried in pyramids in the north of Egypt but in tombs cut into the cliffs of the Valley of the Kings on the west bank of the Nile at Thebes. Throughout the New Kingdom, Thebes was an important religious and administrative centre. The kings were often in residence there, and the Valley of the Kings became the obvious location for their last resting place. During this period, the king was himself regarded as a god. The walls of royal tombs are covered with scenes depicting the pharaoh in the company of the gods on his journey through the Underworld and finally united with them in paradise. It was therefore natural that the Valley of the Kings should have been regarded as one of the most sacred sites of the Two Lands.

For the ancient Egyptians, death was not the end but the entrance to eternal life. Those who could afford to spent the greater part of their adult lives making preparations for it. Soon after his coronation, the king would instigate work on his tomb, where his transfiguration, resurrection and final union with the gods would take place. A suitable spot would be chosen, a plan drawn up, and the decoration of the walls decided.

◀ *From the beginning of the New Kingdom, royalty were buried in the remote Valley of the Kings on the west bank of the Nile.*

The Royal Burial Ground

The Valley of the Kings must have been wild and remote in ancient times. It is still possible to get the feel of the place by approaching the Valley along the mountain path from Deir el-Medina, as the craftsmen did 3,500 years ago on their way to work on the royal tombs. Even today, when motor coaches follow each other nose to tail along the approach roads and disgorge their passengers at the new rest-house, a sense of eternity pervades the site, defying the attempts of the little tourist trains plying their trade along the Valley to bring it into the twenty-first century.

The Valley of the Kings is actually two valleys. Most of the royal tombs are situated in the eastern valley, with the exception of those of Amenhotep III (c.1390–c.1352 BC) and Ay (c.1327–c.1323 BC), which are in the more remote western branch. The area seems to have been chosen because of its situation, remote from the city of Thebes and the village settlements down by the Nile, perhaps in the hope that the royal burials would be safe from the activities of the tomb robbers. If so, this proved to be a rather vain hope. When the tombs were excavated in the nineteenth and twentieth centuries, all were found to have been robbed except for that of Tutankhamun. That, too, had been entered, but was saved by the necropolis priests.

▲ *From the beginning of the New Kingdom, the kings were no longer buried in pyramids but in rock-cut tombs in the remote Valley of the Kings.*

However, there seems to have been another, perhaps more cogent reason for the location of the royal tombs. From a distance, the mountains of the west bank resemble the hieroglyph *akhet* (horizon). Since the sun set in the west, the ancient Egyptians associated it with the entry of the deceased into the Underworld. The *akhet* hieroglyph of the Theban massif, therefore, became the horizon below which the king entered the Underworld, just as the sun god, in the form of the setting sun, did each night. This belief was acted out each time a royal funeral procession wound its way over the mountain from the mortuary temple and down into the Valley of the Kings, sinking like the sun beyond the western horizon. ◆

◀ *Tutankhamun and his wife Ankhesenamun are seen here in an intimate scene from the gilded wooden statue shrine discovered in his tomb.*

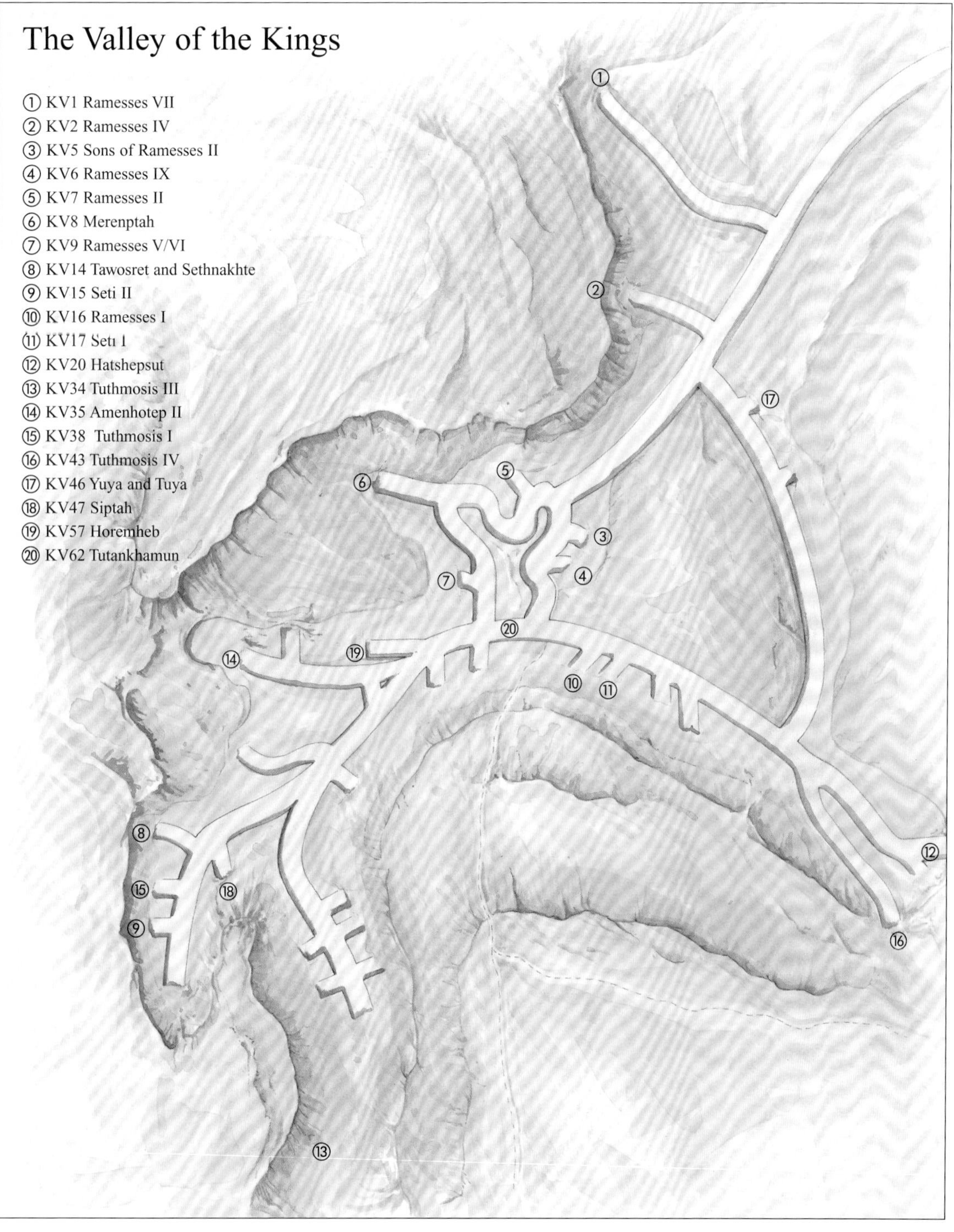
The Valley of the Kings
① KV1 Ramesses VII
② KV2 Ramesses IV
③ KV5 Sons of Ramesses II
④ KV6 Ramesses IX
⑤ KV7 Ramesses II
⑥ KV8 Merenptah
⑦ KV9 Ramesses V/VI
⑧ KV14 Tawosret and Sethnakhte
⑨ KV15 Seti II
⑩ KV16 Ramesses I
⑪ KV17 Seti I
⑫ KV20 Hatshepsut
⑬ KV34 Tuthmosis III
⑭ KV35 Amenhotep II
⑮ KV38 Tuthmosis I
⑯ KV43 Tuthmosis IV
⑰ KV46 Yuya and Tuya
⑱ KV47 Siptah
⑲ KV57 Horemheb
⑳ KV62 Tutankhamun
①
②
⑰
⑤
⑥
③
④
⑦
⑳
⑲
⑭
⑩
⑪
⑧
⑫
⑮
⑱
⑨
⑯
⑬

The Burial of the King

The tombs in the Valley of the Kings are radically different from those of the Pyramid Age. During the New Kingdom (c.1550–c.1069 BC) the royal tombs were not built of stone or mudbrick but were laboriously cut into the mountainside. Whereas the interior chambers of the pyramids had been relatively small and mainly undecorated, the passages and burial chambers of the rock-cut tombs were much larger and were brilliantly decorated with images of the king before the gods and with new texts that would ensure his safe arrival in the Afterlife and his union with both Re and Osiris.

Another distinguishing feature is that the mortuary temple, causeway and valley temple were physically separated from the tomb, although spiritually still connected. The temples now lay on the other side of the mountain, on the desert edge of the Nile Valley. The mortuary temples were grander than the earlier ones, while the valley temples were reduced to little more than landing stages, where the boats of the royal funeral procession would dock. The stone-built causeway was replaced in the later New Kingdom by a canal that led to a small harbour in front of the mortuary temple.

Concealed entrances

The location of the tomb and the basic plan, as well as the images and texts chosen for the decoration, varied from period to period. In the earlier part of the Eighteenth Dynasty (c.1550–c.1295 BC), the royal tombs were usually cut higher up the cliffs of the Valley than those of the later kings, and were often near a cleft in the rock. After the burial had taken place, these tombs were blocked with stones and plastered over. Debris deposited by rainwater pouring down the cleft would then conceal the entrance. Because the tombs of the later Eighteenth and Nineteenth Dynasties (c.1550–c.1186 BC) were built lower

▼ *A scene from the tomb of Ramesses I depicts the king flanked by the falcon-headed 'soul of Pe' and the jackal-headed 'soul of Nekhen' representing Upper and Lower Egypt respectively.*

down the valley, they have been subjected to damage by floodwater.

The latest group of tombs, those of the Twentieth Dynasty (c.1186–c.1069 BC), show no sign of any attempt having been made to seal or hide the entrance. These tombs were simply closed with wooden doors. They were often located at ground level at the ends of rocky spurs, and were protected to some extent by the water channels that ran down each side, although some have suffered from water seeping in through cracks in the rock or from storm damage.

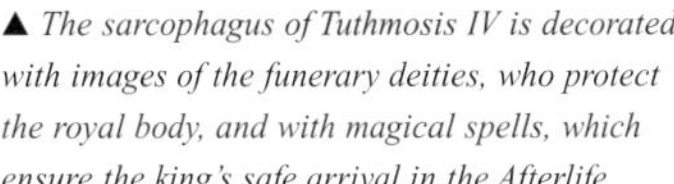

▲ *The sarcophagus of Tuthmosis IV is decorated with images of the funerary deities, who protect the royal body, and with magical spells, which ensure the king's safe arrival in the Afterlife.*

Tomb layouts

The plans of the tombs, although basically consisting in each case of a series of descending corridors, an antechamber and a burial chamber, also varied. The typical tomb plan of the earlier Eighteenth Dynasty was perhaps derived from the general layout used in the pyramids of the Old Kingdom (c.2686–c.2181 BC), and follows a 'bent' axis: a flight of steps leads to three corridors, each known as one of the passages of the sun's nightly journey through the Underworld. This theme is later echoed in the decoration of the walls. Next comes a well or pit, which was perhaps intended to inhibit the activities of tomb robbers, or perhaps simply to drain off water and prevent damage to the tomb. Beyond the well is a small pillared hall. Then the tomb takes a right-angled turn, and a further flight of steps and a sloping ramp lead down into the burial chamber.

Over time, the plans became more complicated. More rooms and passages were added, and it could be that these echo the twists and turns seen in maps of the Underworld, which decorate the floors of the rectangular wooden coffins of officials during the Middle Kingdom (c.2055–c.1650 BC).

From the time of Horemheb (c.1323–c.1295 BC), the last king of the Eighteenth Dynasty, the bent-axis plan was abandoned in favour of the 'jogged-axis' or straight type. Although the passages leading to Horemheb's own burial chamber descend steeply, the general trend was for the inclines to become less acute in the tombs of the Nineteenth Dynasty and, later still, to slope only slightly in those of the Twentieth Dynasty. ◆

◀ *Tuthmosis IV is welcomed into the Afterlife by (from left) Hathor, Anubis and Osiris, in a scene typical of 18th Dynasty decoration of the well shaft and antechamber in royal tombs.*

The Tomb of Amenhotep II

The tomb of Amenhotep II (c.1427–c.1400 BC) is one of the most interesting in the Valley of the Kings. Not only is the decoration of the burial chamber extremely beautiful, but the story of the discovery of the tomb and its contents is also intriguing.

The tomb was discovered in March 1898 by the French archaeologist Victor Loret, then head of the Egyptian Antiquities Service. The previous month he had discovered and cleared the tomb of Tuthmosis III (c.1479–c.1425 BC) high up in the cliffs of the Valley of the Kings, and it was while he was still engaged in this work that he made his next exciting find. He had set his workmen to explore another area in the Valley, where no tomb had yet been discovered. They noticed a large area of loose pieces of cut stone piled at the foot of the cliff. When they cleared this away, they found the top of a tomb entrance. Eventually, Loret was able to enter the steeply descending corridors and cross the well by means of a ladder. He found himself in a small two-pillared hall full of smashed pieces of funerary furniture, including three broken wooden boats. On closer inspection one bore a rather grisly cargo. Loret described his find thus:

> *I went forward with my candle and, horrible sight, a body lay there upon the boat, all black and hideous, its grimacing face turning towards me and looking at me, its long brown hair in sparse bunches around its head.*

Loret had a fertile imagination, and in the heat of the moment he was convinced that he had found a human sacrifice or, at the very least, a tomb robber polished off during a fight over the division of the loot, or by the police interrupting the robbery. In fact, it turned out to be most likely that the body was that of Webensennu, the king's son, who in his lifetime had been in charge of the royal chariot horses. This is suggested by the find in the same room of a *shabti*-figure (or model servant) inscribed with his name.

▲ *The cartouche-shaped red sandstone coffin of Amenhotep II stands in a recess in his burial chamber. Isis and Nepthys guard his feet and head.*

The burial chamber

As Loret entered the burial chamber, he saw six square pillars decorated on each face with images of Amenhotep II, identified by the accompanying cartouches, in the embrace of the deities Anubis, Hathor and Osiris. In the sunken area at the end of the burial chamber there was a sarcophagus. Loret could scarcely contain his excitement as he went to examine it:

> *The sarcophagus was open, but was it empty? I did not dare to hope for the contrary as royal burials had never been found in the necropolis of the Valley, all of them having been moved in antiquity to a safe place. I reached the sarcophagus with difficulty being careful not to break anything underfoot. I could partially read the cartouches of Amenhotep II. I leant over the edge, bringing the light a little nearer. Victory! A dark coffin lay at the bottom, having at its head a bunch of flowers and at its feet a wreath of leaves...*

The journey of the sun god

The walls of Amenhotep II's burial chamber are decorated with a complete version of the Am Duat, or 'Book of What is in the Underworld'. This text describes the king's nocturnal journey with the sun god through the Underworld and his rejuvenation as the sun rises next day.

The work is divided into 12 'chapters', which represent the 12 hours of the night. Vertical borders define these, and each is divided into three horizontal registers. The middle one shows the King and the sun god sailing through the Underworld and overcoming the many hazards of the journey. Finally, the king's mummy is shown propped against the wall as his spirit soars to paradise. The ceiling is painted blue with golden stars.

Later, Loret was able to get a closer look at the coffin. To his relief the body was still inside, and was intact. 'It carried around the neck a garland of leaves and flowers, on the breast a little bouquet of mimosa, which hid the prenomen of Amenhotep II written on the sheet, the name which I later read.'

Apart from the mummy of Tutankhamun, that of Amenhotep II is the only one to have been found lying in his own tomb, albeit in what appears to have been a replacement coffin. Unlike the mummy of Tutankhamun, which still remains in his tomb, Amenhotep's was taken to the Cairo Museum later.

This was not the only surprise. Loret went on to clear the rooms that lay to the side of the burial chamber. The two left-hand ones were filled with storage jars, embalmed provisions, *shabti*-figures and other funerary goods. But on the right he found more mummies. The first chamber on the right contained a woman, a youth and a man. The second contained a further nine mummies, and turned out to be a cache of royal bodies removed from their tombs for safekeeping (see *The Fate of the Royal Mummies*). ◆

▼ *The starry ceiling of Amenhotep II's burial chamber is supported by six square pillars decorated with images of the king welcomed into the Afterlife by Anubis, Osiris and, shown below, Hathor, Mistress of the West. The figures are drawn in outline with only some decorative elements, such as Hathor's headress and the panel surround coloured in.*

The Tomb of Seti I

The tomb of Seti I (c.1294–c.1279 BC) is the longest and deepest royal tomb in the Valley of the Kings. Its decoration is also the most complete, although there are some unfinished scenes. The basic plan is of the 'jogged-axis' type, but here it is complicated by the addition of several extra chambers.

Original features

From the entrance, the three usual corridors lead to a well shaft and a pillared hall. Then a new feature appears in the form of a second chamber, designed perhaps to fool tomb robbers. The burial chamber also has additional pillared rooms and ritual niches. A further innovation is a passage leading down from the burial chamber in the main part of the tomb to another pit deeper down, near the level of the water table. This may have had some symbolic significance, linking the burial chamber to the primordial waters and uniting the concepts of creation and re-creation. In a similar way, the Osireion of Seti's temple at Abydos, built in honour of Osiris, is also sunk deep in the ground so that at times it would be surrounded by water, like the primeval mound.

▲ *Ceilings of the burial chamber are decorated with deities and stars. Below are funerary texts to aid the king on his journey to the Afterlife.*

◀ *Part of the astronomical ceiling in the burial chamber of Seti I showing the constellations.*

Tomb paintings

Another similarity with the Abydos temple is the quality of the decoration in the tomb. Most of it is embellished with beautiful figures of the king and the gods in painted raised relief.

Seti's choice of themes sets a precedent for all the later tombs in the Valley. For the first time, the first two corridors are decorated with texts from the Litany of Re, which praises the sun god under 75 different names. Scenes from the Am Duat are also present in the second corridor, whereas in earlier tombs these appeared only in the burial chamber. The well is decorated with images of the king before the gods, as in some earlier tombs. However, the pillared hall has scenes and texts from the Book of Gates and, again for the first time, an Osiris shrine marking the entrance to the lower part of the tomb. This style was followed in many later tombs. Seti's burial chamber is decorated with the earliest example of an astronomical ceiling, showing some of the constellations and a calendar with the 36 'decans', or groups of stars, into which the night sky was divided by the ancient Egyptians.

▶ *One of the masterpieces of ancient Egyptian art, this shows the goddess Hathor welcoming Seti I into the Afterlife.*

The mummy of Seti I

Giovanni Belzoni discovered the tomb in 1817. His most significant find at the site was the beautiful translucent calcite sarcophagus, also decorated with scenes and texts from the Book of Gates, now in Sir John Soane's Museum in London.

When Belzoni found the sarcophagus, it was empty. However, the mummy was found many years later by Emile Brugsch in the cache at Deir el-Bahri (see *The Fate of the Royal Mummies*). The body was quite well preserved, although the head had been detached from the body during one of several rewrappings by the high priests of Amun during the Twenty-first Dynasty (c.1069–c.945 BC). Inscriptions on the coffin, also restored by the priests, record Seti's removal from his own tomb in Year 10 of the reign of Siamun (c.978–c.959 BC), his reburial three days later in the tomb of Queen Inhapi, and his subsequent transfer to the cache in the reign of Sheshonq I (c.945–c.924 BC). There it remained until 1881 when it was removed with the other royal mummies to Cairo, where it is now on display in the Egyptian Museum. The tomb itself has been closed for restoration since 1991. ◆

The Book of Gates

This collection of magical spells, which decorated the pillared hall of Seti's tomb and his sarcophagus, was intended to enable the king to overcome the demons and powers of the Underworld. The spells provided him with the passwords he needed to get through the gates guarded by snakes and deities as he proceeded on his journey.

The Discovery of Tutankhamun's Tomb

Between 1903 and 1912, an American businessman, Theodore M. Davis, financed a series of excavations in the Valley of the Kings. One of those working for him was the experienced Egyptologist, Howard Carter (1874–1939). Together they made several important discoveries, including the (albeit robbed) tombs of Tuthmosis IV (c.1400–c.1390 BC) and Hatshepsut (c.1473–c.1458 BC), and the intact tomb of Yuya and Tuya, who may have been the great-grandparents of Tutankhamun (c.1336–c.1327 BC).

Davis also found various clues suggesting that the tomb of Tutankhamun might be in the vicinity. One was a robbers' cache containing items of Tutankhamun's funerary furniture. Another was a pit, discovered in 1907, containing seal impressions of Tutankhamun, linen bags filled with natron and other embalming materials, and the remains of his funerary feast. Finally, under a nearby boulder, Davis found a blue faience cup bearing the name of Tutankhamun. However, after several years of fruitless searching, Davis left the Valley convinced there were no more royal tombs to be found.

Howard Carter and his British patron, the fifth Earl of Carnarvon, gained the concession to dig and were ready to start work in 1914, but had to abandon the idea when World War I broke out. They started again in 1917, but had no more luck than Davis. After five unsuccessful seasons Lord Carnarvon was ready to give up, but Carter pleaded for just one more chance. Digging was resumed on 1 November 1921, the first job being to record and remove some ancient workmen's huts apparently used during the preparation of the tomb of Ramesses VI (c.1143–c.1136 BC). As they took down the old building, the top of a flight of steps was revealed.

► *Tutankhamun fulfils his traditional role as Horus harpooning the evil Seth.*

▲ *Discovered in the antechamber of the tomb, this magnificent box shows Tutankhamun charging into battle against his enemies.*

Opening the tomb

By the next afternoon the stairway had been cleared and a doorway, fastened with the seal of the necropolis inspectors, had been found.

The next morning Carter sent a telegram to Lord Carnarvon, announcing his discovery. Lord Carnarvon and his daughter reached Luxor on 23 November. The staircase was again uncovered and the remaining four steps were cleared, revealing the lower part of the doorway. Much to the delight of the excavators, this was stamped with the seals of Tutankhamun, proving that his long-sought tomb was found. The king's seals were on part of the original blocking of the tomb, while those of the necropolis inspectors referred to a resealing, which implied that the tomb might still contain some funerary equipment.

After entering and clearing the sloping tunnel behind the door, they came to another sealed doorway. Carter described the mounting excitement:

Slowly, desperately slowly, it seemed to us as we watched, the remains of the passage debris that encumbered the lower part of the doorway were removed, until at last, the whole door was clear before us. The decisive moment had come. With trembling hands I made a tiny breach in the upper left-hand corner. Darkness and blank space as far as I could reach, showing that whatever lay beyond was empty and not filled like the passage we had just cleared.

▲ *Tutankhamun and his wife, Ankehsenamun, depicted on the back of a gilded wooden throne, which is decorated with glass paste and semi-precious stones.*

Candle tests were then applied as a precaution against foul gasses, and then, widening the hole a little, I inserted a candle and peered in, Lord Carnarvon, Lady Evelyn and Callender standing anxiously nearby to hear the verdict. At first I could see nothing, the hot air escaping from the chamber causing the candle to flicker, but as my eyes grew accustomed to the gloom, details of the room within emerged slowly from the mist, strange statues and animals and gold, everywhere the glint of gold. For the moment, an eternity it must have seemed to those standing by, I was struck dumb with amazement, and when Lord Carnarvon, unable to stand the suspense any longer, inquired anxiously, 'Can you see anything?' it was all I could do to get out the words, 'Yes. Wonderful things!' Then making the hole a little wider we inserted an electric torch.

Finds from the tomb

A painted wooden head of Tutankhamun emerging from a lotus flower was found among the rubble blocking the passage to the tomb. It shows Tutankhamun appearing as the sun god did at the time of creation from a lotus floating on the waters of the primordial ocean. It combines the idea of creation with the king's re-creation.

Three beds were found in the antechamber. One is in the form of a lion, representing the goddess Mehet, associated with Hathor, Sekhmet and Isis. Mehet is the deity responsible for the Nile flood. Another takes the form of a composite deity, part crocodile, part lion and part hippopotamus. She is Ammut, Devourer of the Dead. She stands near the scales in the Judgement Hall and devours anyone who fails to pass the test. The cow goddess depicted on the third bed is Mehet Weret or 'Great Flood'. She represents the primordial cow who rose from Nun, the primordial ocean, and bore the sun god Re, to the sky. She will raise Tutankhamun, too, so that he can join the sun god.

Tutankhamun's mummy was found in a gold coffin. It had been placed inside two more coffins, one inside the other. The innermost was made of gold and the second was of gilded wood covered with precious stones. These are on display in the Cairo Museum, along with the other treasures from the tomb. The body of Tutankhamun, now placed in the outermost coffin, still lies in his tomb in the Valley of the Kings.

◀ *The solid gold mask of Tuthankhamun was placed over the face of the mummy.*

Directly over the mummy's face was a solid gold mask. Tutankhamun is shown wearing the royal headdress, in which the blue stripes are made of glass paste in imitation of lapis lazuli. His eyes are inlaid with quartz and obsidian to make them sparkle and to emphasize that he is a living king. He wears a curved false beard to show that he has become Osiris.

The mummy of Tutankhamun was decorated with 150 pieces of jewellery, all of which are full of symbolism. The winged scarab is the sun god Khepri. He holds the lotus and papyrus, symbols of Upper and Lower Egypt, and *shen*-rings, symbols of eternity. At either side is the *uraeus*, the cobra that spits at Egypt's enemies, wearing a solar disc. Above is the solar boat carrying the *udjat*, or Eye of Horus (the moon). It is flanked by two more *uraei*, wearing moon discs. At the very top is the disc of the moon inside the lunar crescent. On the disc, Tutankhamun is crowned by Thoth and Re-Horakhty. The whole piece symbolizes the king's ascent to heaven and his rule throughout eternity. ◆

Texts from the Tomb of Ramesses VI

The tomb of Ramesses VI (c.1143–c.1136 BC) is a good example of the 'straight-axis' tomb plan. The floors of the first corridors slope only gently before descending to the lower passages and burial chamber. Inscriptions in the tomb state that it was prepared initially for Ramesses V (c.1147–c.1143 BC). There is no sign of Ramesses VI having usurped the tomb, so it is possible that both kings were buried here. Neither of their mummies was discovered in the tomb: both were found in the cache at Deir el-Bahri.

The choice of texts used for the decoration of this tomb is rather different from earlier ones, with a greater emphasis on the sun god Re and on astronomical texts. Unlike most tombs from the time of Seti I (c.1294–1279 BC), however, the Litany of Re does not appear, and is replaced by excerpts from the Book of Gates and the Book of Caverns. Apart from the text inscribed on the sarcophagus of Seti I, the most complete version of the Book of Gates appears in this tomb. The Book of Caverns is particularly concerned with rewards and punishments in the Afterlife, and especially with the annihilation of Re's enemies.

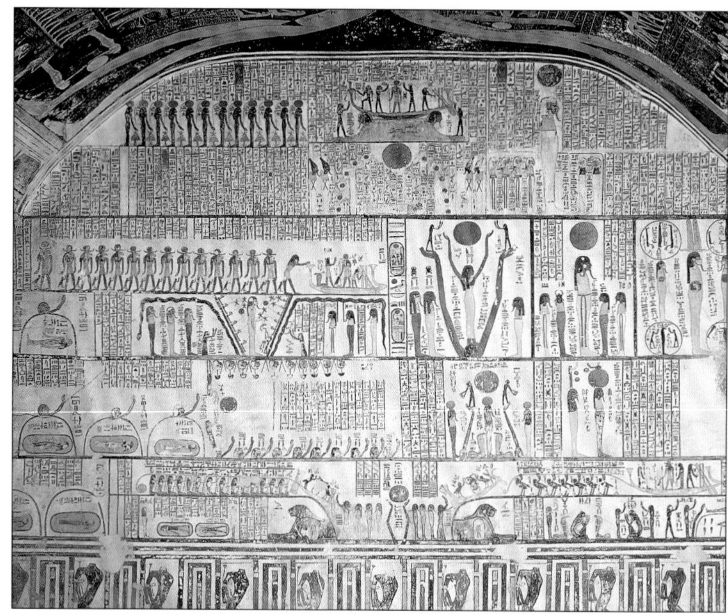

▲ *The magnificent tomb of Ramesses VI is one of the largest and most complete in the Valley of the Kings. The walls are covered with collections of spells to effect the king's resurrection.*

The first three corridors have astronomical ceilings and there are excerpts from the Books of the Heavens in the well room and first pillared hall. These books are a collection of texts that describe the sun's journey across the sky. They include the Book of the Day, the Book of the Night and the Book of the Divine Cow. Further extracts from these books decorate the ceilings of the lower passages and antechamber.

The walls of the corridors are painted with parts of the Am Duat or 'Book of What is in the Underworld', while the antechamber is decorated with images of the gods and sections of the Book of

◀ *The scenes from the Book of the Earth show the rebirth of the sun, which symbolizes the resurrection of the King.*

▶ *Boats in the retinue of the sun god accompany him though the Underworld. Above are avenging deities armed with knives to overcome Re's enemies.*

the Dead. This material is usually found inscribed on papyrus rolls in the tombs of commoners from the beginning of the New Kingdom (c.1550 BC). It is a collection of spells derived from the Middle Kingdom Coffin Texts and ultimately from the Old Kingdom Pyramid Texts, which were used exclusively in royal burials.

The magnificent ceiling of the burial chamber of Ramesses VI combines images of the sun god in the solar barque with the passage of the sun through the body of the sky goddess Nut.

The content of the texts

The funerary texts that decorate the walls of the royal tombs in the Valley of the Kings describe the voyage of the sun god, with whom the king is identified, through the Underworld. They enable the king to enter the Afterlife unmolested by the enemies of Re.

The earliest is the Am Duat. It tells of the sun god's journey through the 12 divisions of the Underworld, which are equated with the 12 hours of the night. Complete copies are found in the tombs of Tuthmosis III (c.1479–c.1425 BC) and Amenhotep II (c.1427–c.1400 BC). Portions decorate the walls of the lower passages of the tomb of Ramesses VI.

Nearer to the entrance are extracts from the Book of Gates, which also describes the sun god's journey through the hours of the night. The name of the book refers to the 12 gates through which the sun god passed and that divide one hour from another. One section of the Book of Gates depicts the Judgement Hall of Osiris where the hearts of the dead are weighed in the balance. The good are justified and wrongdoers condemned.

The Book of Caverns appears in the first three passages, the well room and the first pillared hall along with scenes from the Book of Gates. Osiris figures prominently in these texts where the sun god Re comes for him and punishes his enemies, condemning them to non-existence. In the pillared hall, Osiris wears a solar disc, which identifies him with Re so that they appear to be two aspects of one god. Elsewhere in the tomb, the sky goddess Nut carries the sun god on her hands. He is seen both as the disc of the sun and in human form with a ram's head. Four crocodiles on Nut's left are Re's enemies. On her right is the sun god in different forms.

The Books of the Heavens and a double image of the goddess Nut span the burial chamber. Here, the sun is shown as a disc being swallowed by the sky goddess and passing through her body to be reborn the next morning, and also as a ram-headed god sailing in the solar boat across the sky during the day. The king aspires to accompany the sun god through the Underworld, then to rise and sail with him upon the celestial waters throughout eternity. ◆

▼ *Depicted on the ceiling of the tomb, Nut swallows the sun in the evening whereupon it travels through her body during the night and is reborn at sunrise.*

The Fate of the Royal Mummies

In 1881, in the absence of Gaston Maspero, the then head of the Egyptian Antiquities Service, his assistant Emile Brugsch arrived in Luxor to investigate rumours concerning the discovery of a hitherto unknown tomb. For the previous ten years or so, objects such as funerary papyri, *shabtis* and canopic jars had been mysteriously appearing on the antiquities market from an undisclosed source. Brugsch's arrival in Luxor had, in fact, been prompted by the confession of the head of the Rassul family from Gurna on the west bank, who claimed that members of his family had been responsible for removing these artefacts from a tomb in the cliffs at Deir el-Bahri.

The cache of Deir el-Bahri

How the tomb came to be discovered in the first place is not known, although several romantic stories are told about it. Some members of the Rassul family acted as guides for visiting travellers, and it may be that their intimate knowledge of the area led them to it. The family had certainly been suspected of untoward dealings in antiques, and two of them had been interrogated and tortured by the local mudir, or governor, Daud Pasha. In spite of some brutal treatment they refused to give anything away and it was only in the face of great family opposition that the headman, Muhammad Ahmed Abd el-Rassul, decided to go to the authorities.

Although Brugsch realized that there would be more than one royal mummy in the tomb, he was astounded by the number that met his eyes when he entered the first chamber. In a further chamber, he found even more mummies. In his haste to clear the tomb before local treasure hunters could lay their hands on the contents, however, no proper records were kept.

An Egyptian film made in 1969, *The Night of the Counting of Years*, is based on the story of the discovery of the cache. In one of its most moving scenes, the procession of donkeys and mules bearing their precious burdens reaches the Nile and the royal mummies are put on a boat. Women from the villages come down to the river to wail in mourning for the long-dead kings as they sail downstream to Cairo.

On his return to Egypt, Maspero paid a visit to Luxor to see the tomb for himself, and was soon able to recognize two different groups of mummies. Those from the further chamber were carefully wrapped and placed in distinctive coffins, with their funerary goods around them. These were the mummies of a family of high priests of Amun descended from Herihor, who ruled the Theban area from the end of the Twentieth Dynasty (c.1069 BC). The mummies of the other group proved to be of kings, queens and officials previously buried elsewhere. They included Ahmose, Amenhotep I, Tuthmosis II, Tuthmosis III, Ramesses I, Seti I, Ramesses II and Ramesses III.

On examining the notes written on the mummy wrappings, Maspero discovered that many of the royal mummies had had a somewhat eventful career. The notes revealed that some of the mummies had been restored and rewrapped several times, and moved from one hiding place to another over a period of about 70 years. During this time several mummies had been taken to the tomb of Seti I and restored there before being moved again. The tomb of Queen Inhapi is mentioned many times in these notes, and at one time it was believed that the tomb in which the cache was found was hers. Recent research has shown that her tomb was yet another halfway house, and that the final hiding place was in fact the family tomb of Pinedjem II, High Priest of Amun. The family burials in the end chamber were orderly and intact, whereas the royal mummies seemed to have been pushed into the first chamber rather unceremoniously, Queen Inhapi's among them, suggesting haste.

Royal mummies in the tomb of Amenhotep II

A second cache of nine royal mummies was found in a side chamber in the burial suite of Amenhotep II (c.1427–c.1400 BC) (see *The Tomb of Amenhotep II*). At first, Victor Loret, who discovered the tomb in 1898, thought they must be members of Amenhotep's family. He changed his mind when he examined them more closely:

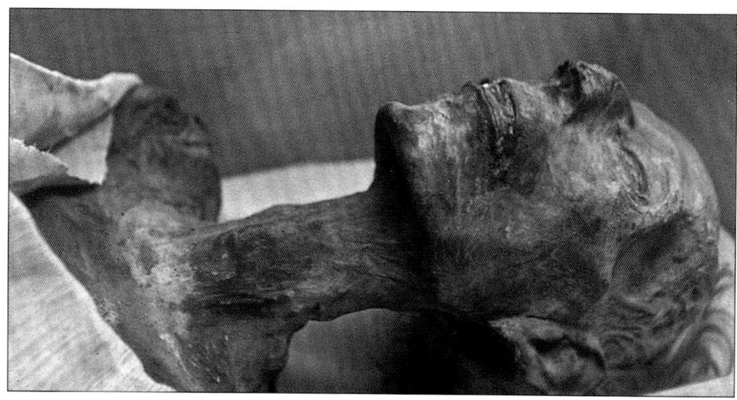

▶ *The mummy of Ramesses II demonstrates the skill of the embalmer and the degree to which the technique of mummification had been perfected.*

▲ *The lid of the coffin of Queen Maatkare, which was found in Deir el-Bahri. The daughter of the High Priest, she was installed as 'God's Wife of Amun', an important religious and political post.*

The coffins and mummies were a uniform grey colour. I leaned over the nearest coffin and blew on it so as to read the name. The grey tint was a layer of dust which flew away and allowed me to read the nomen and prenomen of Ramesses IV. Was I in a cache of royal coffins? I blew away the dust from a second coffin and a cartouche revealed itself, illegible for an instant, painted in matte black on a shiny black ground. I went over to the other coffins – everywhere cartouches.

He realized that he had indeed discovered a cache of royal mummies. The names of the kings proved to be every bit as illustrious as those in the tomb at Deir el-Bahri: Tuthmosis IV, Amenhotep III, Merenptah, Seti II, Siptah, Ramesses IV, Ramesses V, Ramesses VI and an unnamed female, perhaps Tawosret, wife of Seti II.

It is now thought that these mummies, and the various pieces of funerary equipment that were found with them, had been collected from other tombs and caches at the same time as the body of Amenhotep II himself had been rewrapped, since all the bodies bore a similar type of docket. This must have been some time after Year 12 of the Twenty-first Dynasty king Smendes (c.1069–c.1043 BC) because a note on the mummy wrappings of Amenhotep III states that the mummy had been restored that year in his own tomb.

Some of the mummies were in the 'wrong' coffins. Amenhotep III was in a coffin inscribed with the name of Ramesses III, while the lid had originally belonged to Seti II. Merenptah lay in the lower part of a coffin inscribed for Sethnakhte, while the female mummy was lying on the upturned lid.

▲ *This wooden coffin, which housed the mummy of Ramesses II, found in the Deir el-Bahri cache, was possibly originally intended for Ramesses I.*

Is there a third cache?

Not all the bodies of the kings of the New Kingdom have yet been found. The missing mummies include those of Tuthmosis I, Akhenaten, Horemheb, Ay and Hatshepsut. An inscription found by Sir Alan Gardiner at the entrance to the tomb of Horemheb may refer to the restoration of further royal mummies. This is supported by the fact that Theodore Davis found many dismembered skeletons, as well as funeral garlands of a type dating from the Third Intermediate Period (c.1069–c.747 BC), when he was working in the Valley of the Kings in 1908. ◆

The Craftsmen's Village at Deir el-Medina

The craftsmen who lived in the village known to the ancient Egyptians as the Place of Truth, now Deir el-Medina, were highly skilled sculptors and artists who worked on the royal tombs in the Valley of the Kings. Their village is one of the most interesting sites of ancient Egypt for two reasons: not only have very few other occupation sites been discovered but large amounts of written material, often inscribed on limestone chippings called 'ostraca', were found during excavation.

The village was laid out around a main street with side alleys leading from it. It originally consisted of 70 houses, and about 40 more were added during the Nineteenth Dynasty (c.1295–c.1186 BC). The houses were built of rough field stones and mudbrick, and consisted of four or five rooms: an entrance, a main room, two smaller rooms behind that and a kitchen with a cellar. A staircase led to the roof. The windows were high up on the walls, allowing light to enter while excluding the full glare of the sun. A feature of the main room was a mudbrick platform approached by a short flight of steps, which may have functioned either as a shrine or as a birthing bed. The village was about 3km (2 miles) away from the Nile Valley, apparently for security reasons. Bricks stamped with the name of Tuthmosis I (c.1504–c.1492 BC) suggest that the village was founded in his reign.

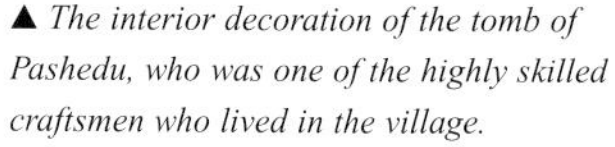

▲ *The interior decoration of the tomb of Pashedu, who was one of the highly skilled craftsmen who lived in the village.*

The craftsmen left the village at the close of the Twentieth Dynasty (c.1069 BC), as from that time the kings were buried in the Delta.

Organization of the workers

The workmen were divided into two gangs, called, like a ship's crew, the gang of the right and the gang of the left. Most lived permanently in the village, although the numbers varied according to the amount of work to be done. New workers were recruited from among the sons of the craftsmen. There were two foremen, one for each gang, who were appointed in the first place by the vizier on behalf of the king. Thereafter the position remained in the family unless something untoward happened, when a new appointment would be made. As well as being in charge of work on the tomb, the two foremen controlled the village and its activities.

Next in importance came the scribe of the tomb. His chief duty was to keep a register of work done and to note absentees. He also recorded the

◀ *The view from the surrounding hills of the village of Deir el-Medina, which housed Egypt's best artisans from the 18th to 20th Dynasties.*

◀ *Anherkhau and his wife depicted in his tomb at Deir el-Medina, where he was foreman.*

distribution of tools, materials and wages. The deputy foremen, usually the sons or near relatives of the foremen, sometimes undertook the supervision and distribution of supplies, while the guardians of the tomb controlled the royal storehouses where the tools and materials were kept. They were aided by doorkeepers, who worked in shifts to guard the entrances to the royal tombs, and the *medjay*, who were stationed outside the village. It was their job to preserve law and order and prevent unauthorized entry to the tombs in the Valley of the Kings.

The villagers were supported by the 'servants of the tomb', who lived outside the village but were sent by the central administration to supply the inhabitants with firewood, water, fish and vegetables. Some were potters and washermen. There were also slaves who ground flour for the villagers. All payment was in kind, and these goods formed part of the wages of the craftsmen. The workers also received monthly rations of emmer wheat and barley, as well as irregular payments of dates, cakes and beer. On special occasions, there were bonus payments of blocks of salt, natron (a salt used in the mummification process) and meat.

Generally, the rations seem to have been more than adequate, and there was usually something over that could be used for barter or even bribes. However, the payment was not always prompt and delays could mean hardship. When their wages did not materialize in Year 29 of Ramesses III (c.1184–c.1153 BC), the workers went on strike and demonstrated in front of the Ramesseum. The 'police' seem to have been sympathetic and arranged for them to be supplied with food to tide them over until they were paid. There were more strikes later in the year and in subsequent reigns.

The working week consisted of eight days, with rest days on the ninth and tenth, so the workers had six days off a month, although they seem to have taken longer 'weekends' quite frequently. They also had holidays on religious festivals. During the week, they may have camped-out near the Valley of the Kings. Otherwise they lived with their wives and children in the village.

Village life

On their days off, the villagers might set to work on their own and each other's tombs. The workmen who excavated and decorated the royal tombs were the best craftsmen of ancient Egypt. They included stonemasons, draughtsmen, sculptors, artists and carpenters. They trained their sons and passed on their skills to them. Consequently, their own tombs are some of the most beautiful on the West Bank. Those who had other skills did a brisk trade in coffins and funeral equipment.

Otherwise, their leisure time seems to have been spent reading, committing adultery or taking each other to court.

Local justice

The village had its own court, composed of the foremen and deputies, the scribe and some of the craftsmen. It is not known when it met, but it was a source of great entertainment. The village court had the authority to deal with all civil action and minor criminal matters. (Major crime was dealt with by the vizier's court at Thebes.) Most of the cases concerned non-payment for goods or services rendered, and were fairly trivial matters. The villagers conducted their own cases, so there were no fees to be paid to lawyers and arguments often dragged on for years. The craftsman Menna, for example, sued the chief of police over non-payment for a pot of fat and certain articles of clothing. The case lasted for 11 years. ◆

The register

The record of attendance kept by the scribe of the tomb shows that many of the craftsmen had days off due to illness. Scorpion stings and eye diseases are often mentioned. Some had time off for family reasons, often to do with funeral arrangements. Other much less reputable reasons were also noted: one man had had a row with his wife and another had been out drinking with his friend Khons and was in no fit state to work the next morning.

Tomb Robbery

The fact that most of the royal mummies were removed from their tombs in the Valley of the Kings and hidden elsewhere suggests that they had been in danger of violation by tomb robbers. There is also clear evidence of a break-in at the tomb of Tutankhamun.

Tomb robbery papyri

A great deal is known about the activities of tomb robbers, and the measures taken to deal with them, from a collection of papyri dating from the end of the Twentieth Dynasty (c.1069 BC). At this time there seems to have been a general breakdown in law and order, and the robbing of tombs was a symptom of these troubled times. The papyri contain the names of the tombs that had been robbed, the confessions of the robbers, and the results of the official inspections of the tombs undertaken in answer to allegations of theft. The discovery of the true extent of the tomb robbing was complicated by the rivalry of the two mayors of Thebes. Puwero, the mayor of West Thebes, was also chief of the necropolis police and particularly resented the implication that he had not been doing his job properly. Eventually, his resistance was broken down and the investigations began. A commission of high officials was set up to look into the reports of robberies in the necropolis and to inspect the tombs for damage.

Apart from the document now known as Papyrus Mayer B, which records the robbery of the tomb of Ramesses VI (c.1143–c.1136 BC), the papyri all refer to the plundering of tombs outside the Valley of the Kings. The royal tombs in question were situated at the nearby necropolis of Dra Abu el-Naga, where the kings of the Seventeenth Dynasty (c.1650–c.1550 BC) were buried. The commission extracted some extraordinary confessions from the accused, such as this one recorded in Papyrus Leopold-Amherst from the stonemason Amenpanufer in Year 16 of the reign of Ramesses IX (c.1126–c.1108 BC):

> *We went in accordance with our regular habit, and we found the pyramid of King Sobekemsef, this being not at all like the pyramids and tombs of the nobles which we habitually went to rob. We took our copper tools and we broke into the pyramid of this king through its innermost part. We found its underground chambers and we took lighted candles in our hands and we went down. Then we broke through the rubble that we found at the mouth of the recess, and found this god lying at the back of his burial place. And we found the burial place of Queen Nubkhaas, his queen, situated beside him, it being*

▼ *The robbery of the tomb of Ramasses VI was documented in antiquity in Papyrus Mayer B. The entrance to his tomb can be seen below centre.*

protected and guarded by plaster and covered with rubble. This we also broke through, and found her there, resting in similar fashion. We opened their sarcophagi and their coffins in which they were, and found the noble mummy of this king equipped with a falchion; a large number of amulets and jewels of gold were upon his neck, and his headpiece of gold was upon him. The noble mummy of this king was completely bedecked with gold, and his coffins were adorned with gold and silver, inside and out and inlaid with all sorts of precious stones. We collected the gold we found on the mummy of this god, together with that on his amulets and the jewels which were upon his neck, and that on the coffin in which he was resting, and we found the queen in exactly the same state. We collected all that we found upon her likewise and set fire to their coffins. We took their furniture which we found with them consisting of articles of gold, silver and bronze, and divided it among ourselves. And we made into eight parts the gold which we found on these two gods coming from their mummies, amulets, jewels and their coffins, and 20 deben of gold fell to each of the eight of us, making 160 deben [14.5kg (32lb)], the fragments of furniture not being included. Then we crossed over to Thebes.

The confessions, from both men and women, were often extracted under torture. A certain Mutemwia, whose husband the measurer, Pawero, had been involved in robbing the tombs, was questioned concerning the whereabouts of the stolen goods, and denied all knowledge of them, but under torture 'with the birch and the screw' confessed that her husband had hidden his loot in the house of his brother-in-law.

The punishments meted out to the robbers are known from the oath that they were required to swear when they gave testimony: 'As Amun lives and as the ruler lives, if I be found to have had anything to do with any one of the thieves may I be mutilated in nose and ears and be placed on the stake.'

▲ *A papyrus records the confession of robbers who entered the tombs of kings and commoners alike and stripped the mummies of their jewellery.*

The tombs of priests and other commoners were not immune from violation by the robbers, who dragged the bodies out of their coffins to strip off their jewellery, and left them out in the desert. The commission also discovered that some of the workmen from Deir el-Medina were involved. Eight of the craftsmen were arrested, including the two deputy foremen. The stolen goods were found in their homes, and various members of other settlements on the west bank were named as receivers of stolen goods. A further investigation led to a complete purge of the village hierarchy, and new foremen and deputies were appointed. ◆

Queens, Princes and Officials

The pharaohs were not the only people to be buried in the Valley of the Kings. Other members of the royal family were buried there too. Tuthmosis III (c.1479–c.1425 BC) prepared a splendid tomb close to his own for his chief wife, Hatshepsut-Merytre, while Isisnofret, the wife of Merenptah (c.1213–c.1203 BC) was buried with him in his tomb in the Valley of the Kings. Royal sons buried in the Valley include the sons of Ramesses II (c.1279–c.1213 BC). Commoners of high rank could also be buried there, the most famous being Yuya and Tuya, the parents of Queen Tiye, and the chancellor Bay, who took charge in the unsettled period at the end of the Nineteenth Dynasty (c.1295–c.1186 BC).

Amenhotep III (c.1390–c.1352 BC) prepared places for two of his wives, Tiye and Sitamun, within his own tomb in the Western Valley. In the Ramesside Period, however, royal wives were usually buried in the nearby necropolis of the Valley of the Queens, although some of the royal children had been buried there since early in the Eighteenth Dynasty (c.1550–c.1295 BC). The most appealing of these tombs is that of Nefertari, Great Royal Wife of Ramesses II, and of the sons of Ramesses III (c.1184–c.1153 BC), Khaemwese and Amun-hir-khopshef. Most of the officials of the Ramesside Period are buried in beautifully decorated tombs in or near the modern village of Gurna.

◄ *This wall painting from the tomb of Nefertari in the Valley of the Queens shows the queen, identified in the cartouche, wearing the vulture headdress, which links her with Isis and Hathor.*

The Tomb of Nefertari

Nefertari was the favourite wife of Ramesses II (c.1279–c.1213 BC), the first of eight that he married during his long reign of 67 years. His other wives included two of his own daughters, his sister and two Hittite princesses. Nefertari seems to have belonged to a high-ranking family, but was not herself royal because she is never given the title of 'King's Daughter'. It is thought that she probably came from Thebes because she is always called 'Beloved of Mut', and Mut was an important goddess in the Theban area. Although she was given the title 'Mother of the King' and had several sons, they all seem to have died before their father. Merenptah (c.1213–c.1203 BC), the next king, was the son of Istnofret, Ramesses II's other chief queen.

Nefertari seems to have played a prominent ceremonial role on state and religious occasions. In the first year of Ramesses' reign she officiated at the investiture ceremony of Nebwenenef as Chief Prophet of Amun at Abydos. She also appears in Year 3 on the New Pylon, a ceremonial gateway, which Ramesses II built at the Luxor Temple, and in diminutive form among the royal statues with which he embellished the forecourt. Ramesses honoured her most of all at Abu Simbel in Nubia. He built two temples there, one for Re-Horakhty and the other state deities, including himself, and the other dedicated to the goddess Hathor and Nefertari.

Tomb paintings

Nefertari's tomb in the Valley of the Queens is the most beautiful of all the royal tombs. It is an absolute feast for the eyes, the bright colours used for the figures being enhanced by the white background and the dark blue of the ceiling. It was discovered in 1904 by Ernesto Schiaparelli, and was closed to the public shortly afterwards because the painted plaster was in such a fragile condition. It has recently been conserved by the Getty Conservation Institute and is now open to the public again for the first time in many years. However, the numbers of visitors to the tomb are strictly controlled, so that this treasure may be preserved for future generations.

▲ *Nefertari, the favourite wife of Ramesses II, is introduced to various deities in scenes from the vestibule of her tomb in the Valley of the Queens.*

Much of the decoration concerns the Heliopolitan creation myth, according to which Atum, the sun god, emerged from the primordial ocean to create Shu,

▶ *Wearing a diaphanous gown of fine linen and the vulture headdress, Nefertari plays* senet, *a board game similar to chess or draughts.*

the god of air, and Tefnut, the goddess of moisture, from his bodily fluid, which contained both male and female elements necessary for creation. Their union produced Geb, the earth god, and Nut, the sky goddess, who also married and produced Isis, Osiris, Seth and Nephthys. Linked to this is the myth of Osiris, in which he, as the highly esteemed king of Egypt, was murdered by his jealous brother Seth. After he had been restored to life he entered the Underworld to become the judge of the dead while his son, Horus, avenged his death to become the next king of Egypt. The upper section of the west wall of Chamber C shows Isis and Nephthys as kites at the foot and head of the dead Osiris. In the myth they beat the air with their wings to enable Osiris to breathe again and so be restored to life. Nefertari hopes to be restored in the same way.

Here, as in several later tombs in the Valley of the Kings, the sun god is assimilated with Osiris. On the west wall of Chamber G, Isis and Nephthys are depicted on each side of a god who takes the form of a mummy, as Osiris did, and is represented with the ram's head of the sun god. The text on the left reads, 'It is Osiris who sets as Re,' and on the right, 'It is Re who sets as Osiris.' Osiris and the sun god Re appear in various forms throughout the tomb, and Nefertari associates herself with both.

Elsewhere in the tomb, deities lead Nefertari into the presence of the gods. In Recess E, Hathor, the cow goddess, who was often depicted as the mother of the king, conducts Nefertari on her way through the Afterlife. She is also shown welcoming her on one of the pillars of Chamber K. ◆

▼ *The elegantly dressed Nefertari offers two* nu-*pots to Hathor; from the southern wall alongside the steps leading to the burial chamber.*

Conservation

The Getty Conservation Institute has cleaned the walls of the salt crystals that had formed over the centuries, and stabilized the plaster. It is adamant that the tomb has not been subjected to 'restoration', by which it means the addition of missing colour. No new paint was added – what can be seen is the original work. Where the original decoration has disappeared, blank patches of plaster, made from local materials, now cover the gaps.

The Tomb of Ay

Ay (c.1327–c.1323 BC) was an army commander who became king of Egypt after the death of Tutankhamun (c.1336–c.1327 BC). He may have been related to the royal family by marriage: there is evidence to suggest that he was the brother of Queen Tiye, wife of Amenhotep III (c.1390–c.1352 BC), while it is also sometimes mooted that he may have been the father of Nefertiti, the wife of Akhenaten (c.1352–c.1336 BC). He is shown on the walls of the burial chamber in the tomb of Tutankhamun, officiating at the young king's funeral, and thus staking his claim to the throne.

Whatever the truth about his relationship to the royal family, it is clear that Ay was a high official at the court of Akhenaten, where he held the title 'Superintendent of the Royal Horses'. Later, he rose to power as vizier and royal chancellor. Not unnaturally, he began work on a large and splendid tomb at Akhenaten's capital Akhetaten (Tell el-Amarna). This was left unfinished but is famous for its inscription of an extended version of the Hymn to the Aten, in praise of the sun disc, which was worshipped exclusively during Akhenaten's reign.

The Western Valley tomb

The tomb that was prepared for Ay as king lies in the wild and rugged Western Valley. Ay had a comparatively short reign of four or five years, and it appears that the tomb may previously have been intended for somebody else. Candidates include Tutankhamun or even Tuthmosis, the elder brother of Akhenaten who died before his father, Amenhotep III, who is also buried in the Western Valley. In any event, the decoration of the tomb is very similar in many ways to that of Tutankhamun's. It was discovered by Giovanni Belzoni in 1816 but was not fully excavated until 1972, when it was cleared by Otto Schaden.

The architecture of Ay's tomb is akin to that of the royal tomb at Tell el-Amarna, having a straight axis but with the burial chamber slightly to one side. A new feature is the slots cut into the walls of the first corridor, to accommodate a beam that was used to lower the sarcophagus into the tomb.

◀ *Ay was considered to be the last king of the Amarna period and consequently his tomb was badly mutilated. All images of Ay have been hacked away.*

▲ *The images of the gods and goddesses were left untouched. Here, the goddess Nut offers Ay the sign for water so he will not die of thirst on his journey to the Afterlife.*

Tomb decoration

The artistic style and the motifs of the tomb decoration so resemble those of Tutankhamun that it would seem that the same artist was responsible for both. In both tombs there are scenes showing the deceased king and his *ka*, or vital essence, being welcomed into the Underworld by Osiris and Hathor. Another scene shows 12 baboons, who represent the 12 hours of the night, while a further scene shows the boat of the sun god in his scarab beetle form, preceded by five deities.

A unique feature for this period is the scene of fishing and fowling in the marshes, in which Ay is shown hunting with his wife. This is a theme more usually found in the tombs of nobles,

although a similar scene appears in the much earlier mortuary temple of the Fifth Dynasty king Sahure (c.2487–c.2475 BC) at Abusir. There may even be another parallel with the tomb of Tutankhamun: although hunting is not part of the painted decoration there, it is perhaps reflected in the hunting scene on the small gilded shrine found among the grave goods. It is also echoed in two statuettes of Tutankhamun on a papyrus skiff, with a harpoon poised to thrust into his prey in the water.

A small room leading from the burial chamber is the canopic chamber, where the internal organs of the king would have been preserved. The entrance has been decorated with two pairs of figures who are sometimes identified with the Four Sons of Horus, the guardian deities of the viscera.

The images of Ay himself, although not those of his *ka*, were destroyed in antiquity, presumably because of his association with the heretical regime of Akhenaten. This probably happened in the early Ramesseside Period, when steps were taken to obliterate the memory of Akhenaten from history. Ay's sarcophagus, also similar to that of Tutankhamun, was found in fragments, although it has now been restored. His mummy has never been found. ◆

▲ *Ay performing the Opening of the Mouth ceremony in the tomb of Tutankhamun. Usually this is done by the son of the deceased. As Tutankhamun had no son, this scene indicates Ay as his successor.*

The Tomb of Yuya and Tuya

Yuya and Tuya were the parents of Queen Tiye, the wife of Amenhotep III (c.1390–c.1352 BC). Because of their close connection with the king, they were allowed the honour of having a tomb in the Valley of the Kings, even though they themselves were not royal. They were very important people in their own right, however. Yuya was in charge of the king's chariotry and Tuya was 'Chief Lady of the Harem'. Yuya was also called 'God's Father', a reference to his relationship to the king.

The tomb of Yuya and Tuya was discovered in 1905 by James Quibell, and was found to contain the most spectacular collection of funerary goods that had yet come to light in the Valley of the Kings. This came as a complete surprise to the excavators, as it was obvious that the tomb had been broken into in antiquity. It had been resealed with a stone wall covered in mud plaster and stamped with the necropolis seal, and there was evidence to suggest that this had happened more than once.

The robbers had gone through the tomb feverishly searching for valuables. The mummy bandages had been ripped apart and the lids of boxes torn off in their haste. However, as was the case with the tomb of Tutankhamun, it appears that the robbers were disturbed just in time. A chariot yoke, a gilded wooden staff and a heart scarab had been abandoned in the corridor as they fled. Nevertheless, the robbers seem to have made away with all the smaller valuables. There was no jewellery in the tomb apart from that found on the mummies themselves. Other costly items such as oils and perfumes were also missing. The many treasures that remained are now in the Cairo Museum.

▲ *Tuya's jewel casket of gilded wood inlaid with elements made of ebony, pink-stained ivory and blue faience. The upper part is decorated with cartouches of Amenhotep III, her son-in-law.*

Quibell was working in the Valley under the auspices of Theodore Davis, who cleared the tomb in great haste while Quibell was away. Unfortunately, as time was at a premium, he did not take the trouble to record the finds properly, particularly their position in the tomb. It is not known whether Yuya or Tuya died first, and such information might have helped to answer that unsolved question.

▼ *The goddess Isis protects the mummy just as she protected Osiris in mythology.*

The mummies

The mummified bodies of Yuya and Tuya were found within the tomb. Although they had been partly unwrapped, they were very well preserved and are two of the finest examples known. Quibell wrote that Yuya's features were perfectly preserved, so that 'The powerful and dignified face of the old man strikes one as something human, as a face one would recognize in a portrait.' Yuya's mummy was placed in a nest of four coffins, one rectangular (but bottomless) and three anthropoid. Of these, the enormous outer one was covered in bitumen and bound with inscribed bands of gilt; the next had similar bands over a background of silver leaf; and the innermost was gilded all over and inlaid with glass hieroglyphs in imitation of jewels.

The faces of both mummies had been covered with masks. Royal mummy masks were usually made of beaten gold, but those of Yuya and Tuya were of gilded cartonnage (linen stiffened with plaster). Yuya's mask had been broken into fragments. That of Tuya was broken in two, but has now been restored. The

▲ *Gilded wooden side panels from a chair with images of the protector deities, Bes and Taweret.*

mask had been covered with a piece of very fine linen. When this was removed it revealed a beautiful portrait of Tuya. She has a charming smile and her eyes have been inlaid with blue glass and quartz, to which red touches have been added in order to give her a lifelike appearance. Her eyebrows have been inlaid and her eyes outlined with glass in imitation of lapis lazuli. She wears a long striated wig that is kept in place with a floral headband. Covering the upper part of her body is a huge collar composed of rows of leaf and petal shapes inlaid into a background of coloured glass, which imitates bands of lapis lazuli, turquoise and carnelian.

The four canopic jars of Tuya are particularly interesting. Each contains one of her internal organs wrapped up in a little mummiform parcel, and each miniature 'mummy' has been given its own small mummy mask.

The grave goods

The tomb was packed with all sorts of funerary goods, including several pieces of furniture, one of which was a beautiful jewel casket that had belonged to Tuya. It is made of gilded wood in the form of a little shrine and is inlaid with ebony, rose-tinted ivory and blue faience. The box is decorated with the cartouches of Amenhotep III, her son-in-law, and her daughter, Queen Tiye. A frieze running around the lower part of the casket is composed of the hieroglyphs for 'life' and 'prosperity', thus wishing the owner a blissful Afterlife.

Three beautiful chairs were also found in the tomb, one of which had belonged to Sitamun, the daughter of Amenhotep III and granddaughter of Tuya and Yuya. It is made of dark red wood and decorated with side panels covered in gold leaf. These show figures of the god Bes, protector of families and helper of women in childbirth, wielding knives and beating on drums to drive away evil spirits. The panel on the chairback shows Sitamun being presented with golden collars by Syrian princesses. There were also three beds whose headboards were decorated with images of Bes.

Yuya took his chariot with him to the tomb. It is made of gilded wood and is in remarkably good condition, being almost complete. It is decorated with spirals and rosettes in gilded plaster. Measures were also taken to ensure that Yuya and Tuya did not go hungry. Some of the boxes found in the tomb contained dried meat, geese and ducks to sustain them throughout eternity. ◆

▼ *The funerary mask of Yuya, father of Queen Tiye. His mummy is one of the best preserved ever found.*

▼ *The gilded plaster mask that once covered the head of the mummy of Tuya, mother of Queen Tiye.*

A royal seat

The Empress Eugénie, wife of Napoleon III of France, visited the tomb while Quibell was finishing its clearance. When he apologized for the fact that all the (modern) chairs had been packed away and there was nowhere to sit, the eye of the empress lit upon the chair of Sitamun and she decided that it would suit her very well. The archaeologists held their breaths as she sat down, but fortunately for both empress and chair it stood up to the strain.

The Tomb of the Sons of Ramesses II

Ramesses II (c.1279–c.1213 BC) had an extremely long reign of 67 years, and must have been over 90 years old when he died. He had several wives and concubines, and fathered a great number of children, many of whom he outlived. His successor, Merenptah (c.1213–c.1203 BC), whose own tomb is in the Valley of the Kings, was his thirteenth son, his older brothers having died before their father. Although they never inherited the throne, these brothers seem to have been given the privilege of burial in the Valley of the Kings (apart from Khaemwese, who may be buried near Memphis, where he was High Priest of Ptah). Other sons of Ramesses II may well have been buried there too.

Only 70m (77yd) from the tomb of Tutankhamun and almost opposite the tomb of Ramesses II, Dr Kent Weeks, an American archaeologist and director of the Theban Mapping Project, discovered an enormous enigmatic structure hailed by many as the most exciting archaeological discovery of modern times. It is thought to be the burial place of the sons of Ramesses II.

▲ *The names of many of Ramesses II's sons are known from inscriptions elsewhere, such as this relief from the Temple of Luxor. They include Meryatum (his sixteenth son) and Seti (shown here), who both died in their twenties as did several of their brothers.*

New discoveries

The existence of this tomb, known as KV5, has long been known, and it was partially explored as long ago as 1825 by the English Egyptologist James Burton. Howard Carter also examined the area around the tomb in 1902, but was not able to penetrate beyond the entrance. Kent Weeks and his team from the American University in Cairo relocated the tomb in 1985–6. As the first two chambers were cleared of debris it became obvious that a great deal of damage had been caused by the tourist coaches using the road above the tomb, and by a broken sewer. After the first season of work on the tomb, Weeks realized that the structure he had found was unique. He went so far as to claim that it was the tomb of at least two, and perhaps as many as eleven of Ramesses' sons. However, since then, many more chambers have been discovered. In May 1995 Kent Weeks made an exciting announcement:

Last February, excavating through the flood-borne debris that fills the tomb, my staff and I found a passageway leading past 20 chambers to a statue of the god Osiris. Two transverse corridors, each with another 20 chambers, extend beyond that. At the end of the corridors there are stairs and sloping corridors apparently leading to even more rooms on a lower level. The tomb could be the largest ever found in Egypt.

There are likely to be about 150 chambers and corridors in the complex, of which fewer than seven per cent have yet been cleared. In fact, Weeks has no intention of trying to complete the excavation himself. He wants to leave parts of the building to be explored by future generations, using new excavation techniques as they are developed. In the meantime, he and his team will concentrate on making the structure safe and recording, conserving and studying the wall decorations, inscriptions and artefacts that have already been discovered.

Tomb layout and decoration

The plan of the complex as a whole is unique, although there are some individual features that are similar to other tombs in the Valley. Some Eighteenth Dynasty tombs have a narrow entrance that leads directly into a chamber, rather than the more usual passage, while some of the chambers have vaulted ceilings like tombs of the Nineteenth Dynasty. In this tomb there are two chambers, which give way to a large pillared hall. Leading from the hall is a huge T-shaped area lined with many alcoves or small chambers. In the centre of the bar of the T is a statue of Osiris and, at each end, a stairway descends to a lower level where two passages slope, in the opposite direction to the upper level, towards the tomb of Ramesses II.

That this unique structure was intended as the burial place of Ramesses II's sons is indicated in the decoration of the first two chambers, where there are painted reliefs showing the king leading his sons into the presence of the funerary deities. These were originally similar to the scenes in the tomb of Amun-hir-khopshef (see *Tombs of the Sons of Ramesses III*), in the Valley of the Queens, but so much damage had been done by floodwater and sewage that the painted plaster had come adrift and lay in fragments among the debris. However, it has been possible, with the help of a skilled conservator, to preserve the south-western corner of the tomb. There, the name, titles and figure of another Amun-hir-khopshef, Ramesses II's eldest son, came to light. He is shown with his father, who introduces him to the goddess Hathor and the funerary deity Sokar.

Another son was 'discovered' on the south wall. He was named Ramesses after his father, who is shown leading him into the presence of Nefertem, the god of the lotus blossom. The name of a further son, Seti, was found on a fragment of a canopic jar in the second chamber, and a fourth, Meryatum, on an ostracon found by Howard Carter. The names of a total of 52 sons of Ramesses II are known from other sources. It will be interesting to see how many eventually come to light in this tomb. The images of several more sons appear in the painted decoration of the tomb, but the inscriptions accompanying them have unfortunately been destroyed. Several skulls and a whole skeleton have been found, but there is, as yet, no clear evidence for their identification.

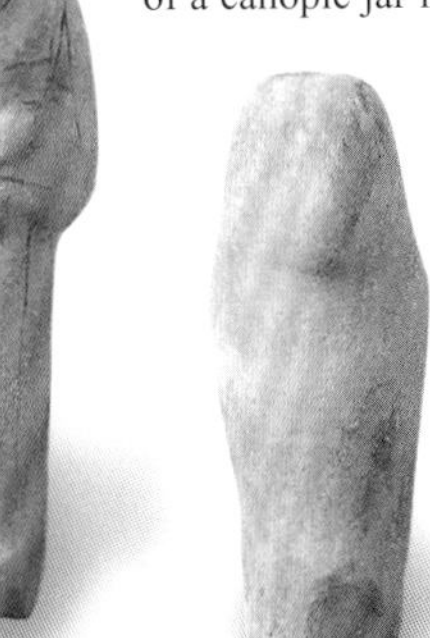

▲ *This rock-cut figure of Osiris, King and Judge of the Dead, was found in his shrine in the T-shaped tomb of the sons of Ramesses II.*

Another puzzle is that the entrances to the side chambers of the T-shaped section are too small to accommodate sarcophagi, so what was the purpose of these chambers? It is known that the main doorways of the tomb were widened at some time, as the alterations have cut into figures and texts already carved on the walls. This would have made it possible to bring sarcophagi inside the tomb itself. Perhaps they were then placed in parts as yet unexplored. ◆

◀ *Inscribed* shabtis *were found among the funerary equipment.*

The Tombs of the Sons of Ramesses III

Of the five tombs prepared by Ramesses III (c.1184–c.1153 BC) for his sons, three were found by Ernesto Schiaparelli in the early 1900s. The most beautiful are those of Amun-hir-khopshef and Khaemwese, both of which were commissioned in Year 28, towards the end of the reign of Ramesses III. The tombs are decorated in painted carved relief.

Little is known of these two princes and nothing at all about the circumstances of their deaths, although the sequence in which the tombs were prepared can be worked out from developments in their decoration. Even the names of the princes are something of a mystery as they do not match up with a list of 13 sons in Ramesses III's mortuary temple at Medinet Habu. It is sometimes suggested that the princes suffered from some kind of congenital disease that led to an early death, and for this reason Ramesses made provision for them during his later years. Or were they perhaps carried off by some kind of epidemic? The ages of the princes are also uncertain. They are represented with the distinctive hairstyle known as the 'sidelock of youth', which suggests that they were very young, although it may simply indicate that they were sons. However, the fact that their father accompanies them into the Underworld and introduces them to the funerary deities seems to confirm their youth.

An unusual feature of these tombs is that it is the king, and not a god or goddess, who introduces his sons to the various deities. The main theme of the decoration in each tomb is that of the prince undertaking a ritual journey. Eventually, he finds himself alone in the Afterlife, which is symbolized by the tomb. By using the correct 'passwords' from the Book of the Dead he is able to proceed through the gates of the Underworld and join Osiris in paradise. Finally, he is reborn and becomes one of the 'imperishable stars'. ◆

◀ *Amun-hir-khopshef is depicted wearing the 'side-lock of youth' to show he is the son of Ramesses III; from his tomb in the Valley of the Queens.*

▲ *Ramesses III is received by Hathor, in her roles as Mistress of the West and as one of the main funerary goddesses.*

▼ *Ramesses III introduces his son Amun-hir-khopshef to the deities of the Underworld. The age at which he died is uncertain.*

The Tomb of Rekhmire

The vizier was the king's chief minister and the most important official in the land, and Rekhmire held this position under Tuthmosis III (c.1479–c.1425 BC) and Amenhotep II (c.1427–c.1400 BC). His tomb is one of the most attractive and informative of all the tombs of the New Kingdom (c.1550–c.1069 BC). It is located in the modern village of Gurna near the Valley of the Kings, the burial place of the rulers Rekhmire served during his lifetime.

Plan of the tomb

The tomb is cut into the rock and follows the usual plan of officials' tombs of this period. The doorway leads into an oblong chamber, with a long corridor leading from the centre of the back wall, opposite the entrance. The texts that form part of the wall decoration in this tomb are particularly interesting. They describe Rekhmire's installation as vizier and the wide-ranging nature of his work. As well as holding a number of priestly offices, he was also in charge of every government department and was also chief judge. His installation as vizier would have been the climax of an illustrious career.

One intriguing fact about this tomb is that there is no burial shaft, so it would seem that Rekhmire was eventually buried elsewhere. It is possible, as he was such an important person, that he was buried in the Valley of the Kings, although this is not known for certain.

The role of the vizier

The procedure followed in the court of the vizier is described in some of the texts inscribed on the tomb walls. The vizier sat on a chair wearing a cape and his chain of office, with an animal skin behind his back and another at his feet. He had his staff close by and 40 leather rods set out in front of him.

▼ As vizier, part of Rekhmire's duties was to supervise activities in the state workshops. These carpenters are working on a fine chest.

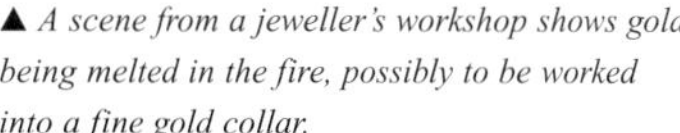

▲ *A scene from a jeweller's workshop shows gold being melted in the fire, possibly to be worked into a fine gold collar.*

Other senior officials and his scribes also sat with him in the court.

The vizier's other duties included reporting daily to the king about all the comings and goings in and out of the palace. He had to inform the king about the income and expenditure of the royal estates, the government finances and the border fortifications. He appointed officials and saw that the local governors were aware of the king's commands, and that they sent in their reports as required. The army was mobilized and the system of compulsory state labour (the corvée) was organized by the vizier, who also conducted land surveys, fixed local boundaries and fitted out ships. He was responsible for law and order, as well as reporting on the height of the Nile and the rise of Sirius, the dog star, the appearance of which heralded the Egyptian New Year.

The tomb's painted decoration includes many scenes depicting all sorts of agricultural operations and craft work. Farmworkers, sculptors, brickmakers and jewellers mingle on the tomb walls. The oblong hall has registers of gifts and shows tribute bearers from Nubia, Syria and Crete. They are all recognizable from the faithful depiction of the physical characteristics of the various ethnic groups and by the objects and animals they bring to the vizier. Other scenes show emissaries from the different regions of Egypt coming to present their taxes, while elsewhere in the tomb there are depictions of funerary and ritual scenes. ◆

▼ *Dancers and musicians entertaining guests at a funerary feast is a common theme depicted on the tomb walls of this period.*

The ship of state

During his long career, Rekhmire was close to the king. He served him well and helped him steer the ship of state, while as a judge he felt his conduct was impeccable:

I was the heart of the Lord, the ears and eyes of my Sovereign. I was his skipper, and knew not slumber by night or by day. Whether I stood or sat, my heart was set upon prow rope and stern rope, and the sounding pole was never idle in my hands... I judged rich and poor alike. I rescued the weak from the strong... I defended the widow. I established the son and heir on the seat of his father... I judged great matters... I caused both parties to go away satisfied. I did not pervert the course of justice for reward. I was not deaf to the empty-handed. I did not accept anyone's bribe...

The Tombs of Eighteenth Dynasty Officials

The ancient Egyptians believed that the Afterlife would be very much like life on earth. They painted scenes on the walls of their tomb chapels recreating their current life to perpetuate it for eternity, and these scenes tell us a great deal about everyday life in ancient Egypt.

The tomb of Nakht

Although it is very tiny, the tomb of Nakht is one of the most charming in the Theban necropolis. Nakht was 'Chief of the Granaries', 'Keeper of the King's Vineyards' and 'Royal Astronomer' under Tuthmosis IV (c.1400–c.1390 BC). Both Nakht and his wife, Tawi, who was a chantress of Amun, were buried here.

On the left of the entrance to Nakht's tomb there are several scenes depicting life on an estate. Two farmworkers are planting seeds, while others plough with wooden ox-drawn ploughs. Farther along are scenes of harvesting, where the corn is cut with sickles and flax is pulled out by the roots. In the next section, the workers use wooden blades to scoop up the threshed grain to separate the grain from the chaff. Meanwhile, Nakht sits in his booth and oversees the work.

Opposite the agricultural scenes is a depiction of a funerary banquet. This is one of the most famous scenes in ancient Egyptian art. The guests are seated on elegant chairs and have cones of scented ointment on their heads. Young girls present bead collars to the ladies, who are dressed in glamorous diaphanous dresses and wear complicated wigs and enormous gold earrings. Musicians playing the harp, lute and some kind of flute entertain the guests. Under a chair, a cat is hastily devouring a stolen piece of fish.

To the right of the door, Nakht and his wife sit in front of an offering table. A similar scene is almost opposite. On the left side of the chapel is a false door, which supplies details of Nakht's life and implies that he hopes to enjoy this same rank and status in the next life. At the bottom, Hathor, goddess of the west, welcomes him into the Afterlife.

Just beyond there is a scene in which Nakht is fishing and fowling in the marshes with his wife and son. Nakht is shown twice, almost as a mirror image of himself, on a skiff in the papyrus marshes. To the left he is aiming a throwing-stick at a flock of birds, while to the right he is about to harpoon a fish.

Further along are two scenes showing the preparation of food and drink. In the top register, the workers are picking large bunches of grapes in the vineyard. Others are trampling the grapes, while another man catches the grape juice in jars and sets them up on a shelf to let the wine ferment. Below, a net is spread to catch birds. When the net is full, a cord is pulled tight and the birds are trapped. The sequel shows the birds being plucked and hung in preparation for cooking.

▲ *Part of a scene from the tomb of Nakht shows him catching wildfowl in the marshes. The other 'half' is a mirror image, which shows him fishing.*

▼ *These musicians, playing a harp, a lute and a double flute, entertain guests at a funeral banquet; from the tomb of Nakht.*

▲ *Sennefer, overseer of the gardens of the god Amun, and his wife in his Theban tomb, which is decorated with a trailing vine.*

The tomb of Menna

Menna was 'Scribe of the Fields of the Lords of the Two Lands of Upper and Lower Egypt' during the reign of Tuthmosis IV. Not surprisingly, a whole wall of his tomb chapel is devoted to agricultural scenes. The top register shows officials measuring the land and assessing the crop. Other sections depict the harvesters reaping in the fields. The grain is carried off to the granary in huge baskets. Scribes, perched on great heaps of grain, record the amounts harvested under the eagle eye of Menna himself, whose status is emphasized by the rather smart horse and chariot waiting to convey him to Thebes. Although such scenes were common to many tomb chapels of this period, the artist has included many details that make it an individual work. A mother is nursing her baby under a tree and two girls are quarrelling. Another vignette shows a girl taking a thorn out of her friend's foot.

The usual scene of hunting in the marshes is also included in this tomb. Like Nakht, Menna is shown in a papyrus boat with his wife and children. He is catching two fish and is about to hurl his throwing-stick in the direction of a papyrus thicket, which is full of nesting birds and small animals.

A different scene shows Menna on a voyage to Abydos, possibly recording a pilgrimage he made to the tomb of Osiris. However, below this are scenes showing the rites performed on the mummy before burial, so it is equally likely that the upper scene is connected with Menna's funeral. In the opposite corner at the far end of the chapel is a painting showing the ritual of the Weighing of the Heart.

The tomb of Sennefer

Sennefer was Mayor of Thebes and 'Overseer of the Granaries and Gardens of Amun' during the reign of Amenhotep II (c.1427–c.1400 BC). Judging from the decoration of his tomb chapel, he may also have been the king's chief vintner. One of the most delightful aspects of the tomb is the vine that is painted growing up the chapel wall and trailing across the ceiling. The surface of the ceiling is rough and the artist has made ingenious use of any raised areas by transforming them into bunches of grapes.

The wall paintings are equally charming. In the antechamber, Sennefer is brought offerings by his daughter and priests. Other scenes show Sennefer and his wife, Meryt, worshipping Osiris. In the main chamber, they are depicted entering the Underworld, sitting side by side on elegantly carved chairs, and accepting offerings. In one of the most attractive scenes, Sennefer is seated in front of an offering table holding to his nose a lotus flower (the symbol of re-creation). His wife sits at his feet, affectionately clasping his leg. ◆

▶ *Sennefer sails upstream from Abydos having completed his pilgrimage to the shrine of Osiris.*

The Tomb of Ramose

Ramose was governor of Thebes and vizier under Amenhotep III (c.1390–c.1352 BC) and Akhenaten (c.1352–c.1336 BC). His tomb is very grand and consists of a spacious hypostyle hall, internal hall and chapel. It is an extremely interesting tomb because both the traditional and the Amarna styles of carved relief are present. The tomb is unfinished, perhaps because the owner moved with Akhenaten's court to the new capital called Akhetaten (Tell el-Amarna), where he may have contemplated preparing another tomb.

The ceiling is supported by 32 rather squat papyrus-bud columns, which have been heavily restored. In the inner hall there are eight more. The inner hall is undecorated and the shrine in the chapel is empty. Two shafts lead down to burial chambers on a lower level, but no bodies were found there.

▲ *Women mourners raise their arms in grief at the passing of Ramose, vizier during the reigns of Amenhotep III and Akhenaten.*

▼ *Servants carry furniture into the tomb. A bed and headrest, four chests and a chair ensure Ramose's comfort in the Afterlife.*

Wall decorations

The carved relief in the traditional style is of the highest quality. Ramose apparently had no children, and his brother Amenhotep built the tomb for him. Amenhotep was an official in charge of the royal building works at Memphis, which may explain the high standard of the decoration. Just inside the hypostyle hall, on each side of the entrance, are funerary scenes. To the left of the door Ramose appears as vizier with his wife and relatives; priests make offerings, Ramose is purified, incense is burnt and three girls shake their *sistra*, the sacred instruments of Hathor, goddess of the west, who was believed to welcome the deceased into the Underworld. On the right is the funerary banquet. In this scene, the wigs, clothing and jewellery worn by the guests are the height of elegance. Ramose, his family and other guests are dressed in high-quality fine linen, which is very delicately portrayed, but the wigs

are particularly fascinating. A great variety are shown, composed of many different combinations of tiny plaits (braids) and curls, all obviously very expensive and the latest thing in fashionable Thebes.

On the opposite wall, to the right of the doorway to the internal hall, there is a typical Amarna-style scene known as the 'Window of Appearances'. Akhenaten and Nefertiti, the king and queen, stand at the palace window and reward Ramose for his services by decorating him with gold collars. Courtiers and fan bearers, who bow low in adoration of the king, accompany him. The royal pair stand below the Aten, the sun disc worshipped to the exclusion of all other deities by Akhenaten, and the rays of the Aten shine down on them. Several end in tiny hands that hold the ankh, the symbol of life, before the noses of the king and queen.

The next scene, further to the right on the west wall, is unfinished. The figures are merely sketched in, ready for carving, and vestiges of a grid remain on the wall. Ramose is shown wearing his gold collars and receiving representatives of foreign countries. Nubians, Libyans and 'Asiatics' are easily recognizable.

The funeral procession

This tomb also has scenes that were not carved but painted straight on to the walls of the tomb. These show Ramose's funeral procession progressing towards his tomb. On the lower register, food and drink, a bed and headrest, a chair, four chests with curved lids and personal possessions such as his sandals and scribal equipment, are carried to the tomb to ensure that his needs in the Afterlife will be catered for. The upper register shows three sleds, one carrying the coffin in a gilded wooden shrine, another carrying a canopic chest containing the internal organs of the deceased, and a third transporting a huge black object called the *tekenu*, the symbol of the 'sun in the form of a bull'. The procession is greeted by wailing women mourning the passing of Ramose. ◆

▲ ▼ *One wall of the hypostyle hall is decorated with finely carved reliefs depicting the funerary feast. Ramose, his family and guests are shown wearing fine linen clothing, which is beautifully portrayed. Their intricate wigs, their jewellery and facial features are also realized in exquisite detail. The reliefs are a fascinating insight into high Theban fashion of the 14th century BC.*

The Tomb of Sennedjem

The tomb of Sennedjem at Deir el-Medina is a small masterpiece. Every surface is brightly painted and the tomb is in perfect condition. The high quality of the tomb decoration is, perhaps, not surprising, as Deir el-Medina is the site of the 'Place of Truth', the village of the master craftsmen who worked on the royal tombs in the Valley of the Kings. Sennedjem was called 'Servant in the Place of Truth', a title that does not have any particular significance, so it is not known whether he had the special status in the village that the high quality of the work might suggest. It is not even known whether he was a draughtsman, sculptor or artist, so it is impossible to know if he did the work himself. As with most ancient Egyptian art, the work is anonymous.

Dispersal of the finds

Most unusually, Sennedjem's tomb was found intact. It was discovered in 1886 by a local man who reported his find to the Director of the Egyptian Antiquities Service, Gaston Maspero, who was luckily in Luxor at the time. The tomb was found to contain the burials not only of Sennedjem, but also of his wife, Iineferti, their son, Khons, their daughter-in-law, Tameket, and a woman named Isis whose precise relationship to the others is not known. Coffins and funerary goods belonging to other members of the family were also found in the tomb, which had been used for at least two generations as a family vault.

Although the contents of the tomb were first taken to Cairo, they are now tragically dispersed. The mummy of Sennedjem remains in Cairo but the other members of the family were scattered, even their mummies and coffins ending up in different American and European museums. The mummies of Sennedjem's wife and son are in Cambridge, Massachusetts, while their

▲ *Sennedjem and his wife plough the Field of Iaru where, according to the Book of the Dead, the deceased harvests crops of grain and dates.*

▼ *Their eldest son, wearing his priest's leopard skin, pours libations before his parents. Below the chair are younger members of the family.*

coffins are in the Metropolitan Museum of Art in New York. His daughter-in-law is in Berlin, and the funerary goods are divided between the museums of Cairo, Moscow, Copenhagen and Paris. These include the sled that transported the coffins to the tomb, a bed, a table and two stools, loaves of bread, eggs, fruit, floral garlands and two pairs of papyrus sandals.

The tomb decoration

Virtually the entire end wall of the burial chamber is given over to a delightful scene showing Sennedjem and his wife working in the Field of Iaru, the ancient Egyptian version of the Elysian Fields. During their lifetime they would never have done agricultural work themselves; the purpose of the scene is to show them in paradise, a land of plenty, where they are enjoying the reaping of a bumper harvest.

At the opposite end of the tomb, Sennedjem and Iineferti worship Osiris, Re-Horakhty and other funerary deities. The upper registers of the side walls show Anubis, the god of mummification and the necropolis, preparing the mummy. This is matched on the opposite side by a scene showing Sennedjem as a mummy, having become Osiris. Isis, the wife of Osiris, and their sister, Nephthys, are depicted as kites. As in the Osiris myth, they beat the air with their wings to create the breath that would restore Osiris to life; here, they are doing the same for Sennedjem. Below this scene Sennedjem's family are shown at the funerary feast. Their eldest son performs the funeral rites in front of them, and the other children are shown as tiny figures below the chairs of their parents and the guests.

The vaulted ceiling has scenes from the Book of Gates, a collection of spells containing the passwords that enable the deceased to get through the gates of the Underworld. One charming vignette shows the goddess of the sycamore tree offering the couple refreshing drinks so they will not die of thirst in the Afterlife. Presiding over the entire event is Osiris, who is shown in a large scene immediately opposite the entrance. This ensures that Sennedjem will come back to life again, just as Osiris did in mythology. ◆

▲ *Osiris, god of the Underworld and King and Judge of the Dead, presides over the tomb of Sennedjem. The Eye of Horus and fetishes of Anubis ensure his resurrection.*

▶ *The elegantly dressed Sennedjem and his wife worship the gods of the Underworld who will protect them on their journey to paradise.*

Part Two: Religious Centres

From earliest times, Egypt has been the home of religious thought. There is evidence for belief in an Afterlife in the contents of graves from the Predynastic Period, when the gods seem to have been worshipped in portable shrines. The first permanent structures are those at the late Predynastic centre of Hierakonopolis and the Early Dynastic shrine at Elephantine by the First Cataract. Many ancient sites were built over by succeeding generations, so that a whole series of temples may occupy the same site. Very occasionally, as at Elephantine, excavations have revealed a succession of temples dating from the Early Dynastic to the Ptolemaic Periods (c.3100–30 BC).

In the Christian era, the ancient temples became churches. The Temple of Isis at Philae was converted to use as a church dedicated to the Virgin Mary. Many Jews settled at Aswan, where there is evidence of a Jewish temple. Egypt was largely converted to Islam in the seventh century AD, although the Christian Church continued to flourish in some areas.

Temples to the Gods

The ancient Egyptians built two main types of temple: mortuary temples, where rituals connected with the deceased kings were performed, and cult temples erected in honour of particular gods. Some, like the temple of the Nineteenth Dynasty king Seti I (c.1294–c.1279 BC) at Abydos, served both purposes.

The temples dedicated to the gods were not places of worship in the modern sense, since the Egyptian people did not congregate inside them to take part in religious ritual. Usually, only the priests seem to have been allowed into the temple to carry out the rites, which were centred on the statue of the deity housed in a shrine in the innermost part of the sanctuary. Only the outermost parts of the temple were accessible by other people, and only then at the time of the great festivals.

Most of the temples seen by visitors to Egypt today were built during the New Kingdom (c.1550–c.1069 BC) and later. This is generally because one of the most important duties of a king was the erection of temples to the gods, so earlier structures were frequently replaced by the buildings of later rulers. In addition, in the Delta, the earlier temples have disappeared because they were pillaged for building materials.

◄ *The First Pylon of the Luxor Temple, erected by Ramesses II, was originally embellished with six statues and two obelisks.*

Temple Architecture

Each temple built by the ancient Egyptians represented the Mound of Creation, which had risen from the primordial ocean at the beginning of time. In temple architecture, the mound was marked by a gradual rise in ground level between the entrance and the innermost shrine, while the columns of the hypostyle hall represented the first plant life to appear on the mound. Every temple had a sacred lake and was surrounded by an undulating mudbrick wall: it is thought that both these feaures were intended to represent the primordial ocean from which the mound arose.

The home of the god

A temple built for the worship of a god was regarded as 'the god's house', quite literally the place where he or she resided. The deity would be represented by a cult statue placed in the innermost part of the temple, in the sanctuary, which was the most secret and sacred area. Although the deities were often thought to possess creative powers, to represent parts of the universe and to embody natural forces, they were also seen in human terms, hence the god's need for a house, food and family.

In general terms, temple architecture provided for the physical needs of the god, and parallels can be drawn with the homes of private individuals. The pylon, or monumental gateway, formed the entrance, with the open courts representing the place where, in an ordinary house, visitors would have been entertained. The hypostyle hall, with its roof supported by tall columns, and the sanctuary were comparable with more private areas in the home such as bedrooms. Only the king, in his capacity as high priest, and other important functionaries would have been allowed to penetrate these inner chambers.

Temples did, however, provide dramatic settings for occasions in which the public could take part. These were the festivals of the gods, when sacred boats bearing the shrines containing the images of the deities were carried in procession along the banks of the Nile and from temple to temple amid scenes of great rejoicing, and even depravity, if we are to believe Herodotus.

▲ *Every temple had a sacred lake that represented the waters of chaos from which creation arose. This is the Sacred Lake at Karnak.*

Many of the places where temples stand today have been sacred sites since the dawn of history. Most of the remains

▲ *The Temple of Philae was said to be sited on the mound that appeared from the waters of chaos at the time of creation.*

▶ *The columns in the Hypostyle Hall at Karnak represent the plants that came into being on the Mound of Creation.*

that can now be seen, however, date to the New Kingdom (c.1550–c.1069 BC) or the Graeco-Roman Period (332 BC–AD 395), so are relatively modern in the context of the history of ancient Egypt. These buildings represent only the latest stage of a series of temples built over a long period of time. At Karnak, however, the development of the complex from the simple Middle Kingdom shrine of Senusret I to the prosperous New Kingdom and Graeco-Roman Periods can be clearly seen. ◆

The Temple of Satet at Elephantine

Elephantine is an island in the Nile, which lies opposite the modern town of Aswan near the First Cataract, where the river becomes unnavigable as it flows over a series of granite outcrops. The southern tip of the island is the site of an ancient settlement, also called Elephantine.

As it lay on the border with Nubia, the town was of great strategic importance and was fortified from the Early Dynastic Period (c.3100–c.2686 BC). Elephantine was also important commercially, and it was from here that expeditions set off into Nubia to procure gold, incense, precious oils, animal skins, ivory and other exotic goods for the Egyptian kings. The tombs of the governors of the South, who organized such expeditions, are carved out of the rocky hillsides on the west bank. Their autobiographies tell of the arduous nature of the trips they made to the south.

Successive buildings

During its long history, Elephantine was served by several temples dating back from the Ptolemaic Period (332–30 BC) to the Early Dynastic Period. A team from the German Archaeological Institute under Dr Günter Dreyer has recently brought the whole series of temples to light. In other places, later kings destroyed earlier buildings while erecting their own, but this was not the case at Elephantine. The earliest shrine was set up among the rocks of the cataract. Space was limited, so when later builders wanted to enlarge the shrine they filled it in, paved over it and built above it, thus creating a time capsule and providing a record of the earlier shrines, complete with votive offerings.

The shrine in the rocks

The earliest shrine was set in a niche formed by the granite rocks of the cataract. It is thought that the cult image would have stood here, but unfortunately it is no longer extant. In the later temples the goddess Satet, guardian of the cataract, was worshipped here, but it is not known if that was the case at this early stage. Many of the votive offerings found within the shrine are figures of children and it has been suggested that the shrine may have been frequented by mothers either hoping to give birth or bringing a thanksgiving offering for a newly born child. No texts have been found that throw light on the subject.

▼ *On the island of Elephantine is a series of temples dating back from the Ptolemaic to the Early Dynastic Period, when a simple shrine was set up among the rocks of the First Cataract.*

▲ *The New Kingdom temple of Tuthmosis III was built over the ancient shrine of earlier temples and dedicated to Satet.*

▲ *Alexander II worships Khnum, one of the deities of the cataract who protected royal expeditions.*

Whatever form it took, the cult image of the earliest shrine was protected by two small mudbrick rooms. In front of these was either a courtyard enclosed by more walls or possibly even a roofed hall. By the later Old Kingdom (c.2686–c.2181 BC) the small shrine had been replaced by a larger court or hall, in the centre of which was a pedestal made of layers of mudbrick and matting, with a wooden pole at each corner. This may well have been a stand on which to rest a portable tent shrine housing the image of the cult deity.

Among the votive offerings found at the shrine were objects inscribed with the names of some of the kings of the Sixth Dynasty (c.2345–c.2181 BC), perhaps produced in honour of their *sed*-festivals. Most were plaques bearing the names of Pepi I (c.2321–c.2287 BC) and Pepi II (c.2278–c.2184 BC) while one was inscribed with a squatting ape holding its young. Rock inscriptions of the kings Merenre (c.2287–c.2278 BC) and Pepi II were found on the walls of the niche.

Stone temples

In the early Middle Kingdom (c.2055–c.1650 BC), a completely new shrine was built, partly of mudbrick, but also using carved and painted stonework. This was in turn replaced in the Twelfth Dynasty (c.1985–c.1795 BC) by a temple built completely of stone. Both these structures were basically extensions of the Old Kingdom temple.

There was a dramatic change in the New Kingdom (c.1550–c.1069 BC), when the Twelfth Dynasty stone temple was dismantled and the ancient shrine filled in with blocks of stone to the level of the top of the boulders. The area was paved over and the Eighteenth Dynasty king Tuthmosis III (c.1479–c.1425 BC) built a new stone temple on top, although a shaft was constructed in the floor to connect it with the original shrine below. Further extensions or embellishment of the temple took place in later reigns until the Ptolemaic Period.

◀ *Reliefs recently restored by the German Archaeological Institute show Tuthmosis III and Satet wearing her distinctive headdress.*

▶ *Tuthmosis III adores the creator god Khnum, who was also worshipped at Elephantine.*

Satet, Khnum and Anuket

It is only with the building of the Middle Kingdom temples that the deity worshipped here is known with any certainty. The carved and painted stone blocks show the goddess Satet embracing the king. In mythology she was the wife of the ram-headed creator deity Khnum, who also had his cult temple at Elephantine from the Middle Kingdom, and the mother of Anuket, goddess of the First Cataract. All three deities were worshipped as guardians of the cataract area and protected the royal expeditions that had to pass Elephantine on their way to Nubia. The rocky island of Sehel, to the south of Elephantine, is covered with the inscriptions of the expedition leaders, who are shown making offerings to the deities of the cataract in the hope of gaining their protection. ◆

The Temple of Luxor

Luxor Temple lies in the centre of the modern town on the east bank of the Nile. It is connected by an avenue of sphinxes to the temple complex of Karnak, about 3km (2 miles) to the north. The ancient Egyptian name of the temple was *ipet-resyt*, which means 'southern harem'. It was dedicated to the cult of Amun in his fertility aspect, his wife, Mut, and son, Khonsu. The temple's main purpose was to provide a setting for the annual *opet*-festival, when the cult images of the gods were taken in procession by land and by boat from Karnak to Luxor.

Although blocks have been found that show that the temple was begun in the Middle Kingdom (c.2055–c.1650 BC), the buildings visible today date from the reign of Amenhotep III (c.1390–c.1352 BC), the great temple builder of the Eighteenth Dynasty (c.1550–c.1295 BC), a time when Egypt was very prosperous and powerful. On a black granite stela some 3m (10ft) tall, now in the Cairo Museum, his inscription records that he built the temple of:

> *...fine limestone, wide, very great, and exceedingly beautiful. Its walls are of fine gold, its pavements of silver. All its gates are worked with the pride of lands. Its pylons reach to the sky, its flagpoles to the stars.*

An ancient view of the temple façade, carved in miniature on the west side of the south wall of the Peristyle Court, gives some idea of what it was like. Ramesses II (c.1279–c.1213 BC), Alexander the Great (332–323 BC) and other later kings extended and embellished it, and the remains of the Roman town can still be seen.

The temple entrance

The complex is entered by the First Pylon, the great monumental gateway added by Ramesses II. On it is emblazoned the story of Ramesses' self-styled great victory over the Hittites at the Battle of Qadesh in 1274 BC. Ramesses is shown heroically taking on the Hittite army in the top registers, while scenes of life in the camp and preparation for battle are depicted below. Written accounts of the battle in both prose and poetry accompany the carved reliefs, which would once have been painted in bright colours.

Originally, there were two seated and four standing figures of Ramesses II, as well as two obelisks in front of the pylon. Only the seated statues, one standing statue and one of the obelisks are still in position. The rest are now in Paris, where the obelisk adorns the Place de la Concorde.

The First Pylon leads to the Peristyle Court, a large open area surrounded by a colonnade added by Ramesses II. Its squat papyrus-bud columns are in sharp contrast to the much more delicate versions seen in the sacred boat shrines of Amun, Mut and Khonsu in the north-west corner, built by the earlier rulers Tuthmosis III (c.1479–c.1425 BC) and Hatshepsut (c.1473–c.1458 BC). The court also sports numerous statues of Ramesses II, accompanied mainly by diminutive representations of Nefertari, his chief queen, between the columns.

▲ *Two seated statues of Ramesses II in front of the First Pylon of the Luxor Temple show him seated on the throne of the Two Lands.*

Above the eastern colonnade of the court is the Mosque of Abu el-Hagag, built in the nineteenth century on top of the accumulated debris. Until 1855, when the clearing of the temple was begun, there was also a village here.

The processional way

The entrance to the Great Colonnade of Amenhotep III is guarded by two further colossal statues of Ramesses II, with Nefertari tenderly embracing his lower

▶ *An avenue of sphinxes once connected the temples of Luxor and Karnak. It is currently being restored.*

leg. Each is seated on a throne decorated with the heraldic motif symbolizing the union of the Two Lands: lotus and papyrus plants tied to a windpipe and lungs. The defeated enemies are depicted underneath the feet of Ramesses.

The Great Colonnade is a processional way composed of 14 huge columns with open papyrus capitals. The sacred boats bearing the images of the gods would have been carried along this way at the time of the *opet*-festival. The inner walls of the court are decorated with scenes of the festival. The procession is shown leaving Karnak Temple, with the sacred boats carried by priests accompanied by musicians and soldiers carrying standards. Other boats are shown in the water, either rowed by energetic crews or towed by men on the banks. Nubian musicians and female acrobats entertain the crowd, and two royal chariots and horses are led by grooms. Finally, King Tutankhamun (c.1336–c.1327 BC) is shown making offerings to the gods. On the east wall, the gods are seen returning to Karnak.

At the southern end of the processional way there would originally have been a pylon, but today the Great Colonnade leads directly out into the Court of Amenhotep III. This too is surrounded on three sides with a double row of columns with papyrus-bud capitals, but the proportions here are much more harmonious. Originally, the colonnade would have been roofed over.

The inner sanctum

Behind the court is the Hypostyle Hall, with its 32 papyrus-bud columns. On the east wall, Amenhotep III is making offerings to Amun, Mut and Khonsu. Near the doors of the small chapels to the south are inscriptions of Ramesses II, indicating that he made some repairs to the temple.

The main Sanctuary, which lies behind the Hypostyle Hall, may have fallen into disrepair and was redesigned by Alexander the Great. The columns of one of the smaller rooms were removed to make room for a sacred boat shrine. Alexander is shown making offerings in the traditional manner of the pharaohs. However, in the Roman Period (30 BC–AD 395) the temple became a shrine to the imperial cult. An altar has been found dedicated to Emperor Constantine (AD 312–337), while the carved reliefs of Amenhotep III in the small court behind the Hypostyle Hall were plastered over and repainted with figures. These were once assumed to represent Jesus and his disciples but are now thought to show the emperor and his court.

A suite of rooms behind the sacred boat shrine represents the 'bedroom' of the god, where the secret rituals of the *opet*-festival took place. Reliefs in the birth room of Amenhotep III show the impregnation of Amenhotep's mother, Queen Mutemwiya, by the god Amun, while the ram-headed creator god Khnum forms the royal child on his potter's wheel. The queen is taken to the birth room by Khnum and Hathor. The child is born and presented to Amun. The last scene shows Amenhotep as an adult blessed by the gods and confirmed in his role as son of the sun god. ◆

◀ *The Court of King Amenhotep III is possibly the precursor of the open Aten temples at Amarna.*

The Temples of Karnak

The vast complex of temples at Karnak demonstrates the religious significance of the area in ancient times. The main Sanctuary is devoted to the worship of Amun, who rose from humble beginnings as a local god of Thebes to become a deity of national importance in the New Kingdom (c.1550–c.1069 BC), when his cult was linked to that of Re, the sun god of Heliopolis. However, the site is extremely complicated as it includes several temples dedicated to other gods. The Temple of Mut, the wife of Amun, lies to the south while the Temple of Khonsu, his son, is within it. Montu, a local war god, Ptah, the creator god of Memphis, and Osiris, the King and Judge of the Underworld, were also worshipped in their own temples inside the sacred area.

Unusually, the temple was built on two axes and spread outwards from the small shrine of King Senusret I (c.1965–c.1920 BC) as successive kings made their own contributions to the complex in the form of pylons, chapels and obelisks. Some buildings were dismantled by later kings and the blocks reused inside pylons. Some of these have now been removed and reconstructed in the Open Air Museum to the north of the main Temple of Amun. One such is the exquisite little shrine of Senusret I,

▲ *This statue of Ramesses II was usurped by Pinedjem, High Priest of Amun, and ruler of Thebes after the end of the 21st Dynasty.*

which was found in pieces in the foundations of the Third Pylon, having been removed from its original position at the heart of the Sanctuary.

Entering the complex

In antiquity, the temple was connected to the Nile by canal, and the remains of the landing stage and a small boat shrine of Amun can still be seen at the entrance to the complex. Leading to the First Pylon, which is thought to be the work of the Thirtieth Dynasty king Nectanebo I (380–362 BC), is an avenue of ram-headed sphinxes protecting the figure of a king. Some are inscribed for Ramesses II (c.1279–c.1213 BC) and Pinedjem, one of the high priests of Amun who ruled the South after the division of Egypt at the end of the Twenty-first Dynasty (c.1069–c.945 BC). However, it is likely that they were usurped from Amenhotep III (c.1390–c.1352 BC) or Horemheb (c.1323–c.1295 BC).

The First Pylon leads into the Great Court of the kings of the Twenty-second Dynasty (c.945–c.715 BC), whose achievements are recorded on its south side, next to the Temple of Ramesses III (c.1184–c.1153 BC). Both this temple and the sacred boat shrines opposite of Seti II (c.1200–c.1194 BC) once stood outside the main temple but were later incorporated into it, while the sphinxes of the avenue that linked the earlier temple to the Nile have been pushed unceremoniously to the side. In the centre of the court is an impressive open papyrus column of an even later king, Taharqo (690–664 BC), which was once part of a kiosk.

▼ *This view of the Karnak temples built by successive rulers from the Middle Kingdom to the Roman Period shows the scale of the complex.*

▲ *The Hypostyle Hall was originally roofed in by huge stone blocks. Clerestory windows let light into the building.*

A mudbrick ramp behind the First Pylon gives some insight into the way these huge structures were built. Another point of interest is the royal statue in front of the pylon. An inscription found under the base shows that it belonged to Ramesses II, while that on the statue itself shows that it was usurped by Pinedjem. The pylon was probably erected by Horemheb, who filled it with small blocks taken from the Temple to the Aten which the heretical Eighteenth Dynasty king Akhenaten (c.1352–c.1336 BC) built at Karnak before his move to Tell el-Amarna. Pylons Nine and Ten were also found to contain such blocks, known by the Arabic word *talatat*. It has been possible to use many of them to reconstruct one of the walls of the Aten Temple and this is now on display in the Luxor Museum.

The Hypostyle Hall

Between the Second and Third Pylons is the Hypostyle Hall, the most famous of the remains at Karnak. This was built in the early Nineteenth Dynasty (c.1295–c.1186 BC). The roof of massive sandstone blocks is supported by a forest of 134 columns, 122 in the closed papyrus-bud style and 12 open papyrus columns in the central aisle. This part of the building would have been completely dark but for the clerestory windows, which allowed shafts of light to penetrate and illuminate parts of the hall. The scenes carved by Ramesses II and his father, Seti I (c.1294–c.1279 BC), show the king worshipping the gods or being blessed and invested with royal authority by them. Those of Seti I are in delicate low relief and are highly superior to the deeply gouged work of Ramesses II. Traces of the original colour remain.

Eighteenth Dynasty monuments

Beyond the Third Pylon of Amenhotep III lies the area built by the kings of the earlier Eighteenth Dynasty. Here stood the alabaster shrine of Amenhotep I (c.1525–c.1504 BC), now in the Open Air Museum. Here, too, is the suite of Hatshepsut (c.1473–c.1458 BC), where the hacked image of the female pharaoh is seen running her *heb sed* race and, again virtually obliterated, being recrowned by Horus and Thoth. In the same area were her obelisks and those of her father. One of her obelisks still stands, while the upper part of the second is now by the Sacred Lake.

Just beyond the Sixth Pylon (also his work) Tuthmosis III (c.1479–c.1425 BC) built his Hall of Records, where the hieroglyphic accounts of his military campaigns are preserved. Somewhat incongruously, the sacred boat shrine lying slightly ahead was the work of Philip Arridaeus (323–317 BC), the half-brother and successor of Alexander the Great. This, however, replaced an earlier shrine, the Red Chapel of Hatshepsut, now also reconstructed in the Open Air Museum.

Royal records

One of the main duties of a king was to quell Egypt's enemies. His campaigns were undertaken at the behest of the gods, who granted him victory in battle. The king, in turn, dedicated the booty and prisoners to the gods, principally to Amun at Karnak. As a result, the temple became a vast storehouse of historical knowledge.

The outer walls of the Hypostyle Hall are inscribed with accounts of the campaigns of Seti I in Syria–Palestine and Ramesses II's triumph over the Hittites at the Battle of Qadesh. The terms of the consequent peace treaty are also inscribed. One of the small rooms adjoining the Festival Hall once contained an important list, now in the Louvre in Paris, of Ramesses' 57 ancestors. Other important documents include the Kamose Stela, an account of the attempt by King Kamose (c.1555–c.1550 BC) to free Egypt of Hyksos rule in the north, and the stela of Psamtek II (595–589 BC), which records his 591 BC Nubian campaign.

The original temple

The site of the original Middle Kingdom temple was in the open space between the Eighteenth Dynasty buildings and the Festival Hall of Tuthmosis III. Only a few vestiges of the early temple remain, but the Festival Hall is most interesting. The columns that support the ceiling are unique in temple architecture and are said to represent tent pegs, reflecting the fact that Tuthmosis III was the great empire builder of the New Kingdom and spent much of his reign on campaign. The columns are decorated with paintings of the heads of saints dating from the Christian era, when the hall was converted into a church. Behind the hall is a series of small rooms decorated in relief with exotic plants and birds, said to have been brought back by Tuthmosis III from his travels. ◆

Temples to the Aten

During the reign of the Eighteenth Dynasty king Akhenaten (c.1352–c.1336 BC), the emphasis of religion changed radically. Akhenaten, who began his reign as Amenhotep IV, attempted to elevate a single deity, the Aten, from the vast Egyptian pantheon to the status of sole god. Old traditions of worship, ritual and art were swept away, and a new capital was built. But neither Akhenaten's new religion, nor his city, survived him.

▲ *Akhenaten and Nefertiti worship the Aten whose rays shine down on them in blessing. The king links himself with Aten as a creator god.*

Sun deities

The sun, with its life-giving properties, had always been worshipped as a god who appeared in many different forms. Khepri, represented as a scarab beetle, was the rising sun; Re, in the guise of a hawk, was the noonday sun; and Atum, depicted as an old man leaning on a stick, the setting sun. Horus, the falcon god, was also sometimes seen as a sun god, as was another falcon god, Re-Horakhty. The Aten, another manifestation of the sun god, was always represented as the sun's disc, without any human, bird or animal form.

The most important of these deities was Re, the sun in the sky and the creator of life. During the day he was thought to sail across the sky in his boat and at night, in his ram-headed form, to sail through the Underworld shedding his recreating light as he went. Suti and Hor, two important officials in charge of the building works of King Amenhotep III (c.1390–c.1352 BC), wrote two hymns in praise of the sun god in all of these different forms, which are inscribed on a black granite stela now in the British Museum, London.

Akhenaten's new religion

Amenhotep III's son and successor, however, preferred the Aten to all the other forms of the sun god. All the other manifestations of the deity were abandoned and only worship of the Aten was allowed. Changing his name to Akhenaten ('Beneficence of the Aten'), in the fifth year of his reign, the king founded a whole new city dedicated to the deity and called Akhetaten ('Horizon of the Aten'). The new capital was built on a virgin site in Middle Egypt now known as Tell el-Amarna, and Akhenaten set up 14 boundary stelae in the cliffs around it, three on the west bank of the Nile and eleven on the east.

The earliest of these stones records that the king had been led to the site by the Aten himself, who had chosen it as his special city, and points out that no other deity had been worshipped there previously. It mentions the temples and palaces, which were to be built on the east bank, and also the agricultural land and the villages on the opposite bank, which were all to be included in the new city. The city was also to include harbours and several suburbs. A year or so later the king revisited the city and drove round it in his 'great chariot of fine gold, like Aten when he dawns in

▲ *A typical scene from the officials' tombs at Amarna shows the royal couple at worship.*

lightland and fills the Two Lands with his love'. He promised never to alter the boundaries and celebrated the occasion with 'a great offering of bread and beer, large and small cattle, fowl, wine, fruit, incense and all good herbs'. At the top of each stela, Akhenaten, his wife Nefertiti and two of their small daughters are shown before a great offering table. As they worship, the disk of the Aten shines down on them in blessing. The rays of the sun end in little hands and each of those nearest to the noses of the king and queen holds a tiny *ankh*, thus infusing them with life.

The Great Temple

The design of the temples of the new city was completely different from traditional ancient Egyptian temples, the inner parts of which were roofed over. The Amarna temples lay open to the sun. Although Akhenaten's city was destroyed after his death and the building blocks removed and reused elsewhere, it is still possible to gain some idea of what these temples looked like. Fortunately, officials like Panhesy, who moved with the royal court to Akhetaten, prepared tombs in the cliffs surrounding the city, and in these they showed the royal family worshipping in the temple.

▼ *These scenes show the king and queen playing with their little daughters, and are unique to the Amarna period. Such displays of affection are otherwise never depicted in royal art.*

The Great Temple was enormous. The temple enclosure measured 229 x 730m (750 x 2,400ft). As so much of the interior seems to have been an empty space, it is assumed that the temple was unfinished. To provide a setting for worship, the buildings were initially put up rapidly using mudbrick, which was then gradually replaced in stone. Even so, only two main parts seem to have been completed, the House of Rejoicing and the Gem Aten ('Aten is Found'). Entrance to the temple was by way of two pylons, leading to a series of offering tables in open courts. The Gem Aten was at the back of the building and was similar in layout to the rest. In these sections of the temple, ceremonies celebrating the daily rising of the sun took place at dawn. Beyond this was the main Sanctuary, with a raised platform on which Akhenaten and Nefertiti made offerings to the Aten, as shown in the scene from the tomb of Panhesy. There were 772 offering tables in the temple itself and about 900 in the sacred area around it.

Royal temples and shrines

There was also a smaller temple in the city centre called the Mansion of the Aten. This was a scaled-down version of the Great Temple and resembled a chapel royal. As it is in line with the Royal Wadi, the site of the royal tomb, it has been suggested by the excavator, Barry Kemp, that it may also have doubled up as a mortuary temple where the cult of the king would have been perpetuated. Within this temple is a small building, which Kemp feels might have contained a robing room and a 'Window of Appearances', both features of the royal funerary temples at Thebes.

Elsewhere in the city were shrines that housed the king's statue as an object of veneration, and some of these have been found in the gardens of private houses. A further group of buildings beyond the main city was called the Maru Aten and was composed of two walled enclosures containing lakes and gardens, pavilions, shrines and 'sunshades' (platforms reached by steps). Recently, another complex to the south of the city has been excavated, although its ancient name is not yet known. Here, the main temple building was surrounded by a garden and was served by a bakery and other workshops within the temple enclosure. ◆

Abydos

Abydos was one of the most sacred sites in ancient Egypt. According to one tradition, it was where Osiris himself was interred; in another myth his head, after his murder and dismemberment by his brother Seth, was buried here. Temples were built on the site from the Predynastic Period to Christian times – from about 4000 BC to AD 641.

Because of its association with Osiris, the Judge of the Dead and King of the Underworld, Abydos was also an important cemetery site. The kings of the earliest dynasties were buried here: Flinders Petrie found and identified the tombs of the kings of the First Dynasty (c.3100–c.2890 BC), and some of those of the Second Dynasty (c.2890–c.2686 BC). More recently some even earlier royal tombs have been found, belonging to the period now known as Dynasty Zero. Later, when the kings were buried elsewhere, they often built cenotaphs at Abydos to identify themselves with Osiris. Private individuals also set up chapels and commemorative stelae in the hope that they would receive divine blessing and be restored to life again, as Osiris was.

Khentamentiu

Osiris was not the first god to be worshipped at Abydos. He was preceded by Khentamentiu, whose name means 'Foremost of the Westerners', signifying that he was a god of the dead. His cult was identified with that of Osiris when the latter came to prominence, and Osiris used the name Khentamentiu as one of his epithets.

There was a city on the site from the Predynastic Period, the most important feature of which was the temple. It stood on the mound today called Kom es-Sultan, which is surrounded by a huge mudbrick wall dating from the Thirtieth Dynasty (380–343 BC). Very little remains of the early temple itself as it was built mainly of mudbrick, but the finds from the site cover a long period of time and suggest that it remained in use until the Graeco-Roman Period (332 BC–AD 395).

▲ *The temple of Seti I at Abydos has the best account of daily ritual in ancient Egypt. Seti I as High Priest is seen here offering incense to Horus.*

▼ *The Abydos temple built by Seti I is dedicated not only to Osiris, his wife Isis and son Horus, but also to the national gods, Amun-Re, Ptah and Re-Horakhty, and to the dead king himself.*

◀ *Horus is shown pouring a libation for Seti I and offering him the hieroglyphs* djed, ankh *and* was, *symbolizing the king's resurrection and confirmed wellbeing in the Afterlife.*

Temples of Seti I and Ramesses II

Today, visitors to Abydos can explore the New Kingdom temples of Seti I (c.1294–c.1279 BC) and his son, Ramesses II (c.1279–c.1213 BC), which lie to the east of the site. That of Seti I is the better preserved. The temple has a deceptively conventional appearance from the outside, although the interior is highly unusual, reflecting the fact that it was dedicated to several gods rather than a single deity. It also combines the functions of a temple built in honour of the gods and a mortuary temple (in this case a duplicate mortuary temple).

The plan is L-shaped. Two pylons, now virtually destroyed, lead into open courts with pillared porticoes. Then come two hypostyle halls and seven chapels, standing side by side and dedicated to the main deities of New Kingdom Egypt. Seti I is also honoured as a god, probably in order to underpin his right to rule, as his dynasty was newly established. His chapel is at the opposite end of the row to that of Horus, perhaps a reminder that as king he embodies Horus. The seven chapels are each reached by their own individual processional way from the First Hypostyle Hall. Originally there were seven entrances from the portico but, except for the central one, they were all blocked by Ramesses II, who completed the building of the temple after his father's death.

Reliefs and inscriptions

It is easy to tell the parts of the temple decorated by Seti I and those by Ramesses II. As at Karnak, Ramesses' reliefs are cut deeply into the stone, whereas Seti's are in delicate raised relief. These are considered by many to be the best work of the sculptors of ancient Egypt.

In the Second Hypostyle Hall, Seti is famously seen offering a figure of the goddess Maat to Osiris, Isis and Horus. Maat represented the perfect world order, based on truth, righteousness and justice, and Seti was thus depicted as the ideal king whose reign was the epitome of these concepts. As the temple doubled as a cenotaph to the deceased king it was important that his reign was seen in this light, so that he would not only spend eternity in the presence of Osiris but become Osiris himself. The funerary aspect of the temple is emphasized by the false doors that occupy the end wall of the shrines and by further suites of rooms dedicated to Osiris and to Ptah-Sokar and Nefertem, the funerary gods of Memphis.

Leading from the Second Hypostyle Hall is the Gallery of Kings, where a list of the predecessors of Ramesses II is carved on the walls.

The Osireion

Behind the temple is the Osireion, which at one time was held to be the burial place of Osiris, but is now thought to be a duplicate tomb of Seti I. The granite structure representing the burial chamber is approached from the desert by a long sloping decorated corridor, which imitates the royal tombs in the Valley of the Kings. It is the most elaborate of all the cenotaphs that kings of different periods built at Abydos to stress their devotion to Osiris and their hope of resurrection. ◆

▲ *Seti I offers to Amun. In Seti's cartouches, the Isis knot hieroglyph replaces the usual Seth animal to avoid any association with the murder of Osiris.*

The Myth of Kingship

Abydos was very important to the kings of ancient Egypt. It was here that their divinity, through their identification with the gods Horus and Osiris, was most clearly expressed. Basic to these concepts is the myth of Osiris. There are allusions to the myth in the Pyramid Texts inscribed in tombs of the Old Kingdom (c.2686–c.2181 BC) and odd episodes are mentioned in works such as the Great Hymn to Osiris, the Memphite Theology and, at greater length, in the complicated story of The Contendings of Horus and Seth. However, for a full version of the story we must look to the work of the second-century Greek writer, Plutarch.

The death of Osiris

In his essay Peri Isidos kai Osiridos, Plutarch states that Osiris was once a real king of Egypt. He was a great king who taught his people all the skills of civilization and was so popular that his wicked brother Seth became jealous of him and planned to get rid of him and take the throne for himself. Seth invited Osiris to a banquet, where he produced a beautifully carved and painted box, which he said he would give to anyone who could fit inside exactly. Everyone tried, but they were either too tall or too short. Then Osiris tried his luck. As soon as he was inside Seth slammed down the lid and threw the box into the Nile. According to the Memphite Theology, Osiris was drowned and his body was taken from the river by Isis and Nephthys (his wife and sister) at Memphis, the place where he entered the Underworld. Plutarch, however, claims that the body was washed right down the Nile and out into the Mediterranean Sea, where the current swept it up the coast until it came to rest at Byblos, in modern Lebanon. There it caught against a sapling, which proceeded to grow at a rapid rate until it completely enveloped the box containing the body. The king of Byblos had the tree cut down and used it to support the ceiling in a room in his palace.

Isis's quest

According to Plutarch, Isis, mourning the loss of her husband, travelled the world searching for him. Eventually, she heard the story of the tree. She arrived at Byblos and begged the king for the body of Osiris. Returning to Egypt she lay down to sleep in the Delta marshes. Unfortunately, Seth came upon the sleeping goddess, snatched the body, cut it up into 14 pieces and scattered them throughout the land.

When Isis discovered what had happened she and her sister set off to recover the various parts of the body. They found all except the penis, which had been eaten by an oxyrhynchus fish. Anubis and Thoth, the funerary deities, helped them to embalm and restore the body, and Isis replaced the lost penis with a clay model by which Osiris was able to impregnate her. She then gave birth to Horus. Isis and Nephthys turned into kites and beat the air with their wings to create breath that Osiris could inhale and so be restored to life. Osiris became King of the Underworld and Judge of the Dead. Isis and Nephthys are often shown at the foot and the head of royal coffins, beating the air with their wings to help restore the dead king to life.

This was not the end of the story, however. The throne of Egypt was now vacant: who would be king next? The wily Seth claimed the kingship but was challenged by Osiris's son, Horus. The matter was angrily debated in the divine court for over 80 years. At one point it was decided to divide the kingship between them. Seth was to be king of the South and Horus, king of the North. Eventually, this decision was overruled and Horus became king of the Two Lands.

▲ *Seti I is suckled by Isis, mother of Horus, thus demonstrating that he is the living Horus.*

Royal identification with Horus

The story explains much about ancient Egyptian ideas concerning kingship. From earliest times, the records show that the kings regarded themselves as Horus, the rightful heir of Osiris. Grave markers found by Petrie outside the tombs of the First Dynasty (c.3100– c.2890 BC) show Horus as a falcon perched above the *serekh* (a device carved in imitation of a niched palace façade) containing the name of the king. The 'Horus name' of the king was always the first of the five by which the king was known in the fully developed titulary. The title *nesw bity*, King of Upper and Lower Egypt, is a further reference to this myth. It literally means 'He of the Sedge and the Bee', the sedge being an emblem of the Nile Valley and the bee of the Delta.

On the walls of the Sokar Chapel at Abydos is a scene of special significance. It shows the posthumous conception of Horus as the deceased Osiris impregnates Isis, who hovers above him as a kite. As the temple is dedicated to Seti I (c. 1294–c.1279 BC) as well as the Abydos triad (Osiris, Isis and Horus), it neatly identifies the king with Horus and substantiates his claim to be the son and heir of Osiris. When the king died he was said to fly off on his falcon wings to join the sun god or to take his place among the stars. In other texts the king became Osiris while his son became the next living Horus.

Horus played an important part in his father's resurrection. Many of the Pyramid Texts refer to the fact that Horus restored Osiris to life by giving him his Eye. In one episode in the dispute between Horus and Seth, Seth was turned into a hippopotamus and was harpooned by Horus. An inscription of Ramesses II (c.1279–c.1213 BC) details all the many good deeds he has done on his father's behalf, claiming to have done as much for his father as Horus did for Osiris. ◆

▲ *This selective list of the kings of Egypt is carved on the walls of the Gallery of Kings at Abydos. Ramesses reads the same names from his scroll.*

▼ *Ramesses II makes an offering of two* nu-*pots to the gods.*

The kinglist

In the temple at Abydos, an important description shows Seti I (c.1294–c.1279 BC), with a youthful Ramesses, reading from a scroll bearing the names of all his royal ancestors. It thus purports to be a complete list of all the kings of Egypt down to Seti I. It is, however, selective, and includes only 'approved' kings, or those who adhered to the concept of *maat* (justice and order). There are therefore no kings of the Intermediate Periods, when Egypt sometimes had several rulers. This contravened the ideal of a single king who ruled a united country. Female rulers were also excluded, as were the kings of the 'heretical' Amarna period – Akhenaten, Smenkhkare, Ay and Tutankhamun. The Nineteenth Dynasty kings seem not to have been related to those of the previous dynasty and were anxious to prove that they were 'proper' kings of Egypt and the true heirs of Osiris. They therefore had their claim to legitimacy carved on the walls of Osiris' main sanctuary.

Pilgrimage and Pageant

From at least the Middle Kingdom (c.2055–c.1650 BC) the tomb of the First Dynasty king Djer (c.3000 BC) in the royal cemetery at Abydos was held to be the actual burial place of Osiris. When it was first excavated by Emile Amélineau at the end of the nineteenth century it contained a statue of Osiris lying on a funerary couch. This has parallels with the Pyramid Texts, which refer to him 'lying on his side', a subtle allusion to his murder by Seth. The tomb became a place of pilgrimage and many people aspired to visit the site, either in this life or the next. In the New Kingdom (c.1550–c.1069 BC), a common scene in the tombs of officials at Thebes shows two boats, one with sails down sailing downstream and the other coming upstream against the current with the sails raised. This is often interpreted as the 'pilgrimage to Abydos', which the tomb owner had either made during his lifetime and hoped to continue in the Afterlife, or planned to do then if he had failed to do it before his death.

From the end of the Old Kingdom (c.2181 BC), people who came from different parts of Egypt were either buried at Abydos near Osiris himself or, if this was not possible, they erected a chapel or commemorative stela to themselves in his presence, hoping in this way to share in his resurrection. Hundreds of *ka* statues (representing the spirit of the deceased), offering tables and stelae have been recovered from the site and are now in museums all over the world. Some of the stelae shed light on the nature of the festivals that were held at Abydos and make it possible to imagine what the shrine of Osiris and the cult statue, gilded and decked out in jewellery, looked like.

▼ *This painted carved relief from the Osiris temple at Abydos shows the god's sacred barque with its statue shrine, which was carried in procession during the annual pageant to commemorate his death and resurrection.*

◀ *After Isis retrieved the scattered remains of her husband's body, she turned herself into a kite and uttered spells so that Osiris was able to impregnate her.*

Ikhernofret's pilgrimage

One of the most important stelae belonged to Ikhernofret, a high-ranking official of the Twelfth Dynasty king Senusret III (c.1874–c.1855 BC). Ikhernofret was commanded by Senusret to go to Abydos to make a portable shrine and to gild the cult statue of Osiris with Nubian gold. On his stela (now in Berlin) he describes what he did:

> *I did all that His Majesty commanded [regarding] his father Osiris, Foremost of the Westerners, Lord of Abydos...I acted as 'his beloved son' [a priestly title for those concerned with this work] for Osiris, Foremost of the Westerners. I furnished his great barque, the eternal everlasting one. I made for him the portable shrine that carries the beauty [statue] of the Foremost of the Westerners, of gold, silver, lapis lazuli, bronze, sandalwood and cedarwood. The gods who attend him were fashioned, their shrines made anew. I set the hour-priests to their tasks. I made them know the ritual of every day and of the feasts of the beginnings of the seasons.*
> *I directed the work of the neshmet-barque, I fashioned the cabin. I decked the breast of the Lord of Abydos with lapis lazuli and turquoise, fine gold and all costly stones which are the ornaments of a god's body. I clothed the god with his regalia in my rank of master of secrets...I was pure of hand in decking the god, a priest whose fingers are clean.*

Ikhernofret was also in charge of the great festival of Osiris. This seems to have been an annual pageant when Osiris's murder by Seth and his subsequent revival were acted out:

> *I conducted the Great procession, following the god in his steps. I made the god's barque sail, Thoth steering the boat. I equipped with a cabin the barque 'Truly is Risen the Lord of Abydos'. Decked in his beautiful regalia he proceeded to the domain of Peqer. I cleared the god's path to his tomb in Peqer. I protected Wen-nofer on that day of great combat. I felled his foes on the shore of Nedyt.*

In this part of the proceedings the shrine of Osiris was carried on another boat in a procession that wended its way from the temple of Osiris at Abydos to his symbolic tomb in the desert. The focal point of the drama was the fight against the enemies of Osiris and their defeat at a place called Nedyt. This was the place where, in mythology, Osiris was killed by Seth. Finally, the procession came back in triumph to Abydos by boat, and the god returned to his temple.

> *I made him enter the great barque. It bore his beauty. I gave joy to the eastern deserts; I caused rejoicing in the western deserts. They saw the beauty of the neshmet-barque as it landed at Abydos. It brought Osiris, Foremost of the Westerners, Lord of Abydos to his palace. I followed the god to his house. His purification was done: his seat made spacious...* ◆

◀ *This gilded wooden statue of Tutankhamun may be similar to that of Osiris that Ikhernofret restored at Abydos.*

Temple Ritual

One of the duties of the king was to see that the temple ritual was carried out and the festivals celebrated properly. By doing this he was trying to ensure that *maat*, the perfect world order, was maintained. The king of Egypt was officially high priest in every temple in the land, though of course it was not physically possible for him to carry out the ritual everywhere on a daily basis. Other priests must have substituted for him most of the time, although he probably took part personally on special occasions. However, only the king is ever shown on temple walls officiating in the cult. Of all the temples of the New Kingdom (c.1550–c.1069 BC), that of Seti I (c.1294–c.1279 BC) at Abydos has the most complete record of the daily ritual. All the stages are depicted in beautiful painted relief.

The morning ritual

Each morning, before the king took part in the cult, he was purified by two priests acting the parts of the gods Horus and Thoth. Dressed in a very simple manner to show his humility before the god, the king approached the sanctuary bearing a censer. The sanctuary contained the sacred boat and a shrine housing the god's statue. As it was dark in the sanctuary, the king would light a lamp. He sprinkled incense on the censer to perfume the air. Reaching the shrine he broke the seal and removed the bolt, called the 'Finger of Seth'. Echoing the myth of Osiris, the king told the god he had brought him the 'Eye of Horus' to restore him to life. He then opened the doors of the shrine, which are described as the 'Doors of Heaven', and gazed on the face of the god. He bowed twice before the god, rose again and sang hymns of praise. The king then anointed the god and burnt incense before him.

Entering the shrine the king embraced the statue and restored him to life by offering him the Eye, just as Horus did for Osiris in the myth. He repeated this part of the ritual in his capacity as king of

▲ *Seti I assists Isis in the ceremony of 'Raising the* Djed-*pillar', which symbolically re-enacts the resurrection of Osiris.*

▲ *Detail of a raised relief in the Hypostyle Hall at Karnak. Seti I offers flowers to the Theban triad, Amun, Mut and Khonsu.*

▲ *A painted carved relief of Seti I in the Osiris temple of Abydos. He stands before an offering table and sprinkles incense.*

the Two Lands. At the end of the repeat ceremony, the king offered a tiny figure of Maat, the goddess of truth and justice.

In the next part of the ceremony, the king took the god's statue from its niche and set it up on a mound of sand. Next, he presented four baskets containing linen, precious ointments and incense. After this, he walked four times round the statue and purified it with water and incense. He then dressed the statue, decked it in jewellery and anointed it with perfumed oils and ointments. Wine and bread were offered. Finally, the statue was put back in its shrine and the doors were bolted and sealed. The king then withdrew, sweeping away his footprints with a broom.

Raising the *Djed*-pillar

One special festival depicted on the walls of the Abydos temple is that of 'Raising the *Djed*-pillar'. The origins of the *djed*-pillar are uncertain, although it is thought by some to represent a pole with grain tied around it. At first it was associated with Ptah-Sokar, a funerary god of Memphis, but by the New Kingdom it represented the backbone of Osiris. The ceremony referred to the resurrection of Osiris and the *djed* motif is often found painted on the bottom of coffins so that the backbone of the deceased would rest on the image of the backbone of Osiris. Its restorative power would then ensure that the dead would return to life, just as Osiris had in mythology. The ceremony of 'Raising the *Djed*-pillar' was also part of the king's *heb sed* or jubilee festival, when he was rejuvenated and reinvested with his royal power. The *djed* symbolized stability and continuity so the ceremony linked the reign of the king with the rule of Osiris in the Underworld. ◆

▶ *The inner walls of the Hypostyle Hall at Karnak are decorated in raised relief scenes showing Seti I offering to Amun and his wife Mut.*

Temples of Hathor

Hathor was one of the most commonly worshipped goddesses in ancient Egypt, beloved of royalty and commoners alike. She was principally a mother goddess and was often regarded as the mother of the king. Her name means 'House of Horus', signifying the womb that sheltered Horus. Hathor was believed to enable women to conceive, and she also helped them in childbirth. In another capacity, as Mistress of the West, Hathor figured in both royal and private tombs as the deity who welcomed the deceased into the Afterlife. She was also Mistress of Foreign Lands, Mistress of Turquoise, and a goddess of music, dance and sexual love.

As early as the Fourth Dynasty (c.2613–c.2494 BC) there is written and archaeological evidence for temples dedicated to Hathor, and the wives of high-ranking officials are known to have been her priestesses. She was also revered by the kings of the New Kingdom (c.1550–c.1069 BC). The Eighteenth Dynasty female ruler, Hatshepsut (c.1473–c.1458 BC), added a small shrine dedicated to Hathor to her mortuary temple at Deir el-Bahri and Ramesses II (c.1279–c.1213 BC) built the lesser of his two temples at Abu Simbel for Hathor and his principal wife, Nefertari. Hathor retained her popularity until the Ptolemaic Period (332–30 BC), when the great temple at Dendera was built in her honour.

◄ *The Roman* mammisi *(birth house) is part of the temple complex at Dendera, where Hathor was worshipped as the mother of kings.*

Hathor in Art and Architecture

Hathor, the cow goddess, seems to have been popular at all periods of ancient Egyptian history. A cow goddess appears on the Narmer Palette, which dates from about 3100 BC. She is not named but may well be Hathor. Even earlier, in the Predynastic Period, vases were painted with pictures of cows and dancing women holding up their arms in imitation of cows' horns. They are thought to be performing 'cow dances', as the women of the southern Sudan do today. These ancient dances were possibly in honour of Hathor.

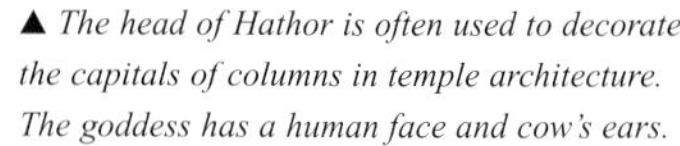

▲ *The head of Hathor is often used to decorate the capitals of columns in temple architecture. The goddess has a human face and cow's ears.*

The nurturing mother goddess

Hathor was often represented entirely as a cow. In the Egyptian Museum in Cairo there is a famous statue of her in this form. King Amenhotep II (c.1427–c.1400 BC), portrayed as an adult, stands in front of Hathor under her protection. He is also shown as a child kneeling down to drink from her udders. Hathor was otherwise depicted as a beautiful, slender woman wearing a headdress of a pair of cow's horns with a sun disc between them, or in human form with cow's ears. Very occasionally, she was represented as a woman with the entire head of a cow. She thus represents divine motherhood.

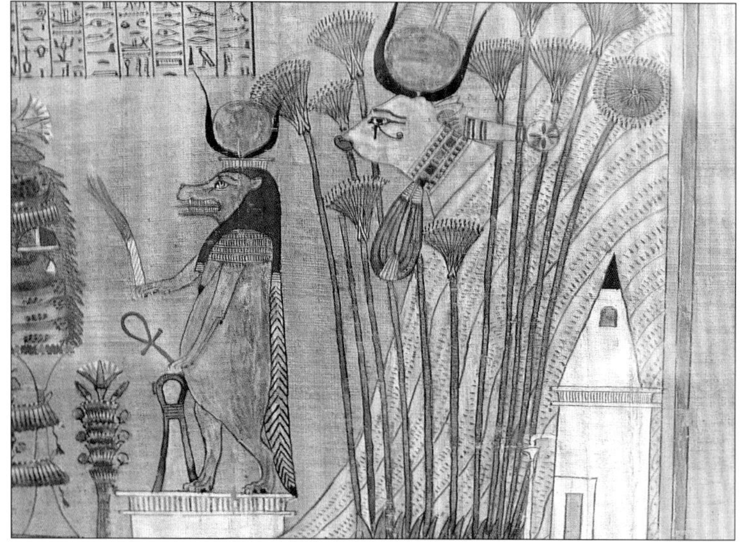

One of the most beautiful depictions of Hathor comes from the tomb of Seti I (c.1294–c.1279 BC) in the Valley of the Kings. This was removed at the beginning of the nineteenth century by Giovanni Belzoni, and is now in the Louvre, Paris. It shows Hathor lovingly holding Seti by the hand and welcoming him into the Afterlife. The delicacy and tenderness of the carving are unique, and the way in which the king's diaphanous linen clothing reveals the fine modelling of his limbs is unsurpassed in the art of ancient Egypt. Hathor wears a dress embroidered with a design based on the king's name and titles. She holds out her *menat*-necklace to him. This is made of dozens of strings of tiny metal beads,

◀ *Hathor as depicted in the Book of the Dead, where she appears as a cow emerging from the Mountain of the West to welcome the deceased into the Afterlife. The papyrus plant is sacred to her.*

▶ *A delicately carved and painted raised relief, originally from Seti I's tomb in the Valley of the Kings, shows Hathor embracing Seti.*

which jingle when shaken; it is a sign of rebirth, so the scene reflects the re-creation of the deceased king.

Mistress of the West

Another scene from the royal tombs in the Valley of the Kings shows Horemheb (c.1323–c.1295 BC) making an offering of wine to Hathor. Here she wears a different headdress which is the hieroglyph for 'west'. It identifies her as the Mistress of the West, and signifies that she was goddess of the necropolis on the west bank of the Nile, the place of the setting sun where the dead entered the Underworld. In this form, Hathor offered the deceased protection on their hazardous journey to the next world. In the text accompanying the relief, she assures Horemheb that she will give him protection and guarantees him 'the throne of Osiris forever'.

Sekhmet the lioness

Usually Hathor was a benign goddess. However, in the myth The Destruction of Humankind she was sent by her father, the sun god Re, to punish the Egyptians for their disloyal murmurings against him. She changed from her maternal cowlike self and became a raging lioness, Sekhmet. She was diverted from devouring all in her path by a trick. The people brewed hundreds of jars of beer dyed with red ochre, which Sekhmet took to be blood and greedily drank. She fell into a drunken stupor, forgetting when she awoke what she had been sent to do. Her motherly aspect returned and the Egyptians were saved.

The symbols of Hathor

In the Book of the Dead of Ani, Hathor is depicted as a cow emerging from the western mountains wearing her *menat*-necklace, welcoming the dead to the Afterlife. In the text she is also associated with the papyrus plant, since thickets of papyrus were the habitat of the wild cow. Another of her symbols was the *sistrum*, a musical instrument which, when shaken, made a noise like a tambourine. The instrument was decorated with the head of Hathor and priestesses played it in temple rituals. As Hathor was a goddess of love and beauty, the shape of the *sistrum* was also used as a handle for mirrors. The *sistrum* was also used as a decorative motif in architecture. It was carved on the sides of square columns, while round columns represented the handle of the *sistrum*, with Hathor's head as the capital, surmounted by the instrument itself. ◆

The Temple at Dendera

Dendera, which lies about 60km (37 miles) north of Luxor, was the capital of the Sixth Nome of Upper Egypt and Hathor's chief cult centre. The ancient Egyptian name of the town was Iunet, which the Greeks translated as Tentyra. The antiquity of Hathor's link with the city is suggested by the discovery of an ancient cemetery there that included some cow burials. Her husband, Horus of Edfu, or Horus the Elder, and their son, Ihy, were also worshipped at Dendera. Their son is also identified as Hor-sema-tawy, the Younger Horus, whose name means 'He Who Unites the Two Lands'.

Early temples

A shrine to Hathor existed at Dendera from the Predynastic Period (c.5500–c.3100 BC) when she was worshipped as She of the Pillar, a reference to the fetish associated with her. This shrine was rebuilt in the Pyramid Age by the Fourth Dynasty king Khufu (c.2589–c.2566 BC) and was dedicated to Hathor, Lady of the Pillar, and her son Ihy, the *Sistrum* Player. Ihy was depicted as a child, that is naked, wearing the sidelock of youth and pointing to his mouth with his index finger, playing the *sistrum*, the musical instrument sacred to his mother. The Sixth Dynasty king Pepi I (c.2321–c.2287 BC) presented a gold statue of Ihy to the temple, and the interest of the Old Kingdom kings is further attested by a fragmentary inscription of Pepi II (c.2278–c.2184 BC).

The Middle Kingdom kings also paid their respects to the goddess. Mentuhotep III (c.2004–c.1992 BC) added a limestone *naos*, or raised shrine, to the temple, while the name of Amenemhat I (c.1985–c.1955 BC) has been found on a granite lintel. An incense altar was presented by one of the Thirteenth Dynasty kings.

The temple was extended and embellished by several of the New Kingdom kings. Inscriptions on some of the columns indicate that Tuthmosis III (c.1479–c.1425 BC) rebuilt the temple at Dendera and revived the ritual. Amenhotep III (c.1390–c.1352 BC) presented a gold statue of Hapi, the god of the Nile inundation, offering stalks of papyrus. Ramesses II (c.1279–c.1213 BC) is shown in relief on a block recovered at the site, presenting two *sistra* to Hathor.

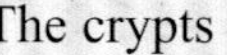

The crypts

An interesting feature of the temple is the existence of crypts below the floor and built into the thickness of the walls. Some of these can be visited and, uniquely, they are very beautifully decorated with carved relief. Strangely, in view of this artistry, they seem to have been used as storage spaces rather than for secret ritual. The lavish decoration is, perhaps, a comment on the valuable nature of the ritual vessels and cult statues that would have been stored there. The carved reliefs include Horus in falcon form, wearing a gold collar with counter-poises decorated with heads of Hathor.

The temple site

The building that the visitor can see today was built during the Graeco-Roman Period (332 BC–AD 395). It is difficult to be precise about its dates as many of the cartouches of the kings have been left blank or simply say 'pharaoh'. However, it is likely that building began during the reign of Ptolemy XII (80–51 BC) and was abandoned during the first century AD.

The temple is vast and largely intact. The site is entered by a Roman gateway, the work of Domitian (AD 81–96) and Trajan (AD 98–117). The former is shown on the outer face making offerings to Hathor, Horus the Elder and Ihy. The temple is unfinished so there is no pylon or open court in front of the main part of the building, the Hypostyle Hall.

◄ *Hathor's chief cult centre was at Dendera, where a shrine or temple stood on the site from the Predynastic to the Roman Periods.*

▲ *A figure of Bes, a dwarf-like god, who was believed to aid mothers in childbirth. Images of the god are used on the pillar capitals of the* mammisi *(birth houses) of the king at Dendera.*

▲ *A carved relief of Hathor and her son Ihy on the rear wall of the Dendera temple (shown here) is balanced by the figures of Cleopatra and her son Caesarion at the opposite end.*

The temple halls

The façade of the Hypostyle Hall dates from the reign of the Emperor Tiberius (AD 14–37). The screen wall is decorated with relief panels and the design incorporates six columns decorated with heads of Hathor. Much of the original colour remains. Inside the temple, the roof of the main hall is supported by massive columns, 15m (49ft) high, representing *sistra* and carved with offering scenes and mythological texts. They are topped with square capitals, on each side of which is a head of Hathor, in human form but with cow's ears.

The ceiling is divided into seven bands. The central one shows the vulture goddess Nekhbet, wearing the crown of Upper Egypt, and winged sun discs with the crown of Lower Egypt. These symbolize the union of Hathor and Horus. The other bands are decorated with astronomical scenes. At each end is an elongated figure of Nut, the sky goddess, along which sail the boats of the gods who represent the stars. On the bands inside these, the gods represent the hours of the night, the signs of the zodiac and the planets. The bands on either side of the centre show the daily course of the sun and the moon.

Beyond is a second hall, a Hall of Appearances, where the walls are decorated with scenes depicting the temple foundation ritual. The approach to the Sanctuary is through the Hall of Offerings and the Hall of the Gods, where the statues of the gods were brought on festival days when they were carried in procession to the roof. The Sanctuary itself originally contained a shrine that housed the statue of the goddess. Unfortunately, this is now missing but it appears in the carved reliefs on the Sanctuary walls, as does the sacred boat, which once a year took Hathor to visit her husband, Horus, whose temple was at Edfu, where a sacred marriage took place before the boat returned to Dendera.

The public shrine

Generally, the public were not allowed into the temple proper: this was the prerogative of the king and the priests. At Dendera, some provision was made for those otherwise excluded. In the centre of the outside wall at the back of the main temple was a small shrine to Hathor. It took the form of a carved relief of the goddess, which was originally protected by a gilded wooden canopy. Here, the public could approach the goddess and offer their prayers and petitions.

This wall is also decorated with a rare, clearly identifiable representation of the famous Queen Cleopatra (51–30 BC). She is shown here with Caesarion, her son by Julius Caesar. Together they are making their own offerings to the gods.

Behind the main temple is the smaller, ruined temple of Isis, probably destroyed by the early Christians. From the New Kingdom (c.1550–c.1069 BC), the mother goddesses, Isis and Hathor, were closely associated, Isis frequently adopting the iconography and attributes of Hathor. ▶

◀ *The statue of Hathor was carried each year to the Chapel of the Union with the Sun's Disc, to be exposed to the re-creative powers of the sun.*

Union of Hathor with the sun

The walls of the temple contain stairways leading to and from the roof, which are decorated with carved reliefs depicting the processions that took place here annually. The figures of priests, some of whom wear masks, are shown carrying shrines of Hathor and other offerings to the little chapels on the flat roof of the temple. The most important festival took place at the New Year, when the statue of Hathor was taken to the roofless Chapel of the Union with the Sun's Disc, so that the sun could shine in on her to reinvigorate her.

A scene showing this ceremony is used to great effect on the ceiling of the Nut Chapel near the foot of the stairway that leads up to the roof from the Hall of Offerings. Here, the sun, swallowed by the sky goddess, Nut, passes through her body during the hours of the night and re-emerges at dawn. As Nut gives birth to the sun it shines down on to an image of Hathor in her shrine. She is then rejuvenated for another year.

The temple roof

Other chapels were used to celebrate the resurrection of Osiris, and they show scenes of the posthumous impregnation of Isis. One is decorated with a copy of the Zodiac of Dendera (the original is in the Louvre, Paris). This is a map of the sky with the constellations divided into 36 decans, or sections, which were used by the Egyptians to tell the time at night. Each decan was visible for ten days at a time (hence the name). The point at which it appeared above the horizon indicated the hour.

From the flat roof it is possible to climb up to an even higher level. A procession of gods and goddesses is carved into the temple wall alongside the ancient flight of steps leading upwards. (Visitors now climb an iron staircase.) From the topmost level there are superb views over the surrounding countryside and the rest of the temple buildings.

The birth houses

From the roof of the main temple many other buildings associated with the cult of Hathor can be seen. To the west are two birth houses or *mammisi*. One of these was built in the reign of Nectanebo II (360–343 BC), the last of the Egyptian pharaohs, and is decorated with carved reliefs, which depict his divine birth. Hathor is shown as his mother and Amun (not Horus) as his father. As they sit together on a bed, Amun gives Hathor the *ankh*, or sign of life, and so impregnates her. Thoth announces the

▶ *This detail of the ceiling of the Hypostyle Hall at Dendera shows the nocturnal passage of the sun, which shines down on Hathor as it is reborn.*

▲ *A large Coptic church lies between the two* mammisi *(birth houses) and is one of the earliest Christian churches in Egypt.*

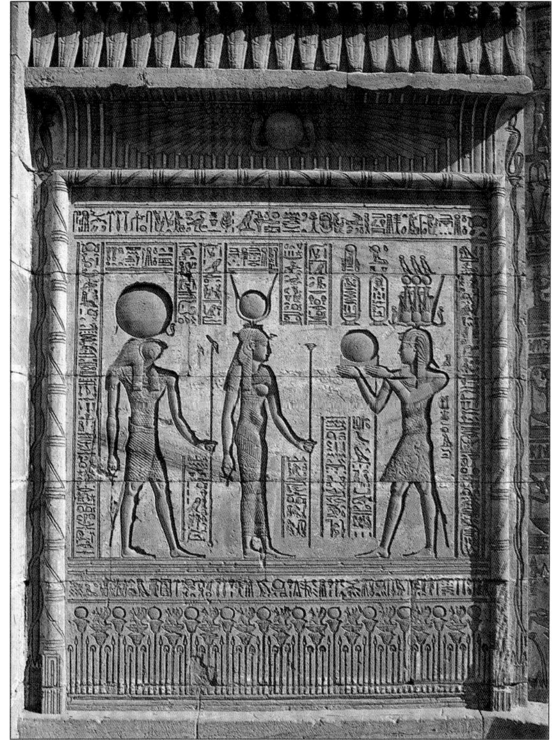

▲ *A detail from the Roman* mammisi *(bath house) shows the emperor offering to the mother goddess. The building was dedicated to Hathor and her son Ihy.*

birth to the assembled gods and goddesses, and the ram-headed god Khnum creates the divine child on his potter's wheel, while the frog goddess Heket holds out the *ankh*. In a double scene on the rear wall the goddess is shown suckling the child while Thoth and Seshat, deities of writing, record the years of his life. These scenes are very similar to the ones at Luxor and Deir el-Bahri, which depict the pharaohs Amenhotep III (c.1390–c.1352 BC) and Hatshepsut (c.1473–c.1458 BC) as children of the god Amun.

Nearer to the temple gateway is the Roman Birth House, begun in the reign of Augustus (27 BC–AD 14) with decoration completed by Trajan (AD 98–117) and Hadrian (AD 117–38). Here, the scenes relate to the birth of Hathor's divine son rather than the king, who is shown presenting offerings. The outer screen walls also show the king adoring the goddess and her son. Above the capitals are *abaci* (slabs supporting the stone beam, which in turn supports the roof) carved with images of Bes, the god who helped mothers in childbirth.

Between the two *mammisi* is a large Coptic church. It dates to the late fifth century AD and was largely built of reused material removed from the Roman Birth House. It is a very good example of the layout of an early Egyptian church, consisting of three main parts: narthex, nave and apse.

Surrounding buildings

Between the temple proper and the Birth House of Nectanebo is a collection of mudbrick rooms and a bath. This complex has now been recognized as a sanatorium. Pilgrims came from near and far to be cured by spending some time in this famous centre of healing. The patients either drank or bathed in water that had been poured over a divine statue inscribed with magical texts, which was considered to have healing properties. Others slept in the cubicles and hoped to receive a dream that would restore them to health.

To the south-west is the Sacred Lake, which represents the primordial ocean. The complex is surrounded by a massive mudbrick wall built in a wavy design, which reflects this symbolism. ◆

Hathor as healer

In mythology, Hathor had healing powers. At one point in The Contendings of Horus and Seth, Seth gouged out the eyes of Horus. Hathor found him weeping in the desert. She caught a gazelle and milked it, and by pouring the milk into Horus's eye sockets she restored his sight.

The Temple of Philae

Hathor was honoured with a shrine at Philae, the main sanctuary of Isis, just as Isis was worshipped at Hathor's cult centre, Dendera. In later ancient Egyptian history, the two deities were often regarded as one because they were both principally mother goddesses. From the New Kingdom (c.1550–c.1069 BC), both were depicted wearing the same headdress – a pair of cow's horns with a sun disc between them. The two goddesses often look so much alike that it is difficult to tell them apart if there are no hieroglyphs to distinguish them. Where there are, Isis is identified by a small throne and Hathor by a square containing Horus as a falcon.

Both Isis and Hathor were important in relation to the king, although in different ways. As far as the succession was concerned, the legitimate king regarded himself as Horus, the heir of Osiris, while his other identity as Horus,

▲ *A view of the approach to the Temple of Philae from Lake Nasser shows the outer walls and two pylons.*

▼ *Images of Hathor decorate the pillars of the First Court at Philae, principally a temple of Isis. Both goddesses were mothers of the kings of Egypt.*

▲ *Bes, a dwarf-like god who helps mothers in childbirth and is often associated with Hathor in this capacity, plays the harp in her honour.*

▲ *An ape plays the lyre, an instrument often shown in 18th-Dynasty tomb paintings being played by female musicians at a banquet.*

son of Hathor, emphasized his divinity. Both aspects of divine motherhood are represented at Philae. On the First Pylon of the Temple of Isis, Ptolemy XII (80–51 BC) is shown smiting his enemies while Isis, Horus of Edfu and Hathor look on. Beyond the First Pylon is the *mammisi* (birth house), where the walls are decorated with scenes depicting the birth of Horus in the Delta marshes. In this myth, his mother was Isis. Nonetheless, the screen walls of the surrounding ambulatory are linked with columns, whose capitals are heads of Hathor.

Musicians and dancers

Outside the Temple of Isis, Hathor has a charming little chapel all to herself. This, like the main temple, was built by the Ptolemies, with later additions by Augustus (27 BC–AD 14). Here, Hathor is commemorated as a goddess of music and dance. The columns of the vestibule are decorated with lively and humorous carved reliefs of musicians of various kinds, including flute players and harpists. There are even some monkeys playing the lyre. The protective god Bes, who often aided Hathor in her capacity as goddess of childbirth, is seen here playing a tambourine. Elsewhere, he is dancing and playing a harp. On the screen walls separating the columns, the emperor Augustus is shown making offerings to various personifications of Hathor. Kings sometimes worshipped Hathor with music and dancing as well as with offerings of food and wine.

The worship of Isis at Philae continued long after the introduction of Christianity. It was not until the reign of the emperor Justinian (AD 527–565) that the temple was closed and a Christian church, dedicated to the Virgin Mary, established on the site. ◆

▲ *Another pillar is decorated with an image of Bes playing a tambourine resembling those often depicted in ceremonial scenes.*

▲ *A priest plays a double flute before a clump of papyrus, a plant sacred to Hathor in her form as a wild cow.*

The king dances

The King, Pharaoh, comes to dance,
He comes to sing;
Mistress see the dancing,
Wife of Horus, see the skipping!

He offers it to you,
This jug:
Mistress see the dancing,
Wife of Horus, see the skipping!

His heart is straight, his inmost
being open
No darkness is in his breast:
Mistress see the dancing,
Wife of Horus, see the skipping!

O Golden One, how good is
this song!
Like the song of Horus himself;
Re's son sings as master singer,
He is Ihy, the musician!

O beauteous one, O cow,
O great one,
O great magician, O splendid
lady, O queen of gods!
The King, Pharaoh, reveres you,
grant that he live!
O queen of gods, he reveres you,
give that he live!

(Extracts from Ptolemaic hymns at Dendera)

Hathor at Deir el-Medina

In the New Kingdom Period (c.1550–c.1069 BC) Hathor was very popular among the inhabitants of Deir el-Medina, the village occupied by the craftsmen who built the tombs in the Valley of the Kings. Some of the village women had the title 'Songstress of Hathor'.

There were several chapels dedicated to Hathor in the village. The Nineteenth Dynasty king Seti I (c.1294–c.1279 BC) built a chapel dedicated to her, as did his son, Ramesses II (c.1279–c.1213 BC), who endowed it with offerings from his own mortuary temple nearby. This was replaced in the Ptolemaic Period (332–30 BC), long after the village had been abandoned, by the rather grand temple surrounded by a massive mudbrick wall that still dominates the site today.

Excavation of the temple revealed the statue of a snake goddess, Mertseger, who was regarded as another form of Hathor. She was often depicted as a cobra and was associated with the peak, covered with shrines, that dominated the west bank. A beautiful head from a statue of Hathor in the form of a cow also came to light. It was made of calcite and the eyes had been inlaid with rock crystal and lapis lazuli.

The craftsmen's stelae

Several of the craftsmen set up stelae in honour of the goddess. The stela of Nefersenut shows him kneeling in front of Hathor, holding a brazier containing an offering. Below, his sons join him in adoration of the goddess. Nefersenut's stela shows Hathor in the form of a woman, while on the stela of Khabekhenet she is shown as a cow emerging from the mountains of the west.

The heartache of a childless couple can be seen in the prayers of another

► *A Hathor column from the interior of her temple at Deir el-Medina is decorated with snakes, representing the goddess Mertseger, with whom Hathor is associated.*

▶ *The Ptolemaic temple to Hathor at Deir el-Medina was built long after the craftsmen's village had ceased to exist.*

craftsman, Ramose. He set up two stelae to the deities of fertility and childbirth, probably in a shrine to Hathor, and also dedicated a stone phallus to her. Inscribed on it was his plea to the goddess to send him a son, expressed in these words:

O Hathor, remember the man at his burial. Grant a duration in thy House as a rewarded one to the scribe Ramose...cause me to receive a compensation of thy house as a rewarded one.

Unfortunately his cries fell on deaf ears and he had to be content with an adopted son.

▼ *A rare representation of Hathor, from the Ptolemaic temple at Deir el-Medina, shows her with a complete cow's head rather than the more usual human head with cow's ears.*

Hathor in literature

The craftsmen of Deir el-Medina appear to have been avid readers, if the amount of ancient Egyptian literature found in the village is anything to go by. Hathor appeared in The Contendings of Horus and Seth when her father, the sun god Re-Horakhty, was angry because the other gods wanted to give the throne of Egypt to Horus while he favoured Seth. He was lying sulking in his tent when Hathor restored his good humour by hitching up her skirts and 'revealing her nakedness'. In a later episode in the same story, she restored the sight of Horus after he had been blinded by Seth.

Hathor also appeared in love poetry, where she was called the 'Golden One' and was regarded as instrumental in bringing lovers together:

O Golden One,
I worship her majesty,
I extol the Lady
of Heaven;
I give adoration
to Hathor,
Praise to my Mistress!
I called to her, she
heard my plea
She sent my mistress
to me:
She came by herself to see me,
O great wonder that happened
to me!
I was joyful, exulting, elated,
When they said, 'See, she is here!'
As she came the young men bowed,
Out of great love for her.
I make devotions to my goddess,
That she grant me my sister
[the girl he loves] as a gift
Three days now that I pray to
her name
Five days since she went from me. ◆

▼ *This limestone chipping shows the snake goddess Mertseger adored by one of the craftsmen at Deir el-Medina. Mertseger was one of the aspects of Hathor.*

Serabit el-Khadim

Hathor was the goddess most often associated with foreign countries and desert areas. She was particularly closely linked with the Sinai region, where she was known as *nebet mefkat* ('Mistress of Turquoise'). Turquoise was highly prized in ancient Egypt and was used in jewellery from the Predynastic Period. One of the most beautiful early examples of royal jewellery was found by Flinders Petrie in the Abydos tomb of the First Dynasty king Djer (c.3000 BC). It was a bracelet formed of tiny *serekhs* (plaques bearing the king's Horus name) surmounted by a Horus falcon. The 13 gold plaques and 14 of turquoise were used alternately to make a stunning piece of jewellery. It is now in the Cairo Museum.

Expeditions to Sinai

Sinai was the most important source of turquoise for the Egyptians throughout the Pharaonic Period. Inscriptions from Wadi Magara and Serabit el-Khadim show that from as early as the beginning of the Old Kingdom (c.2686 BC) the kings mounted expeditions to obtain turquoise from those areas. At Serabit el-Khadim a temple was built in honour of Hathor, whose blessing was sought by the leaders of the expeditions.

A wealth of information on the expeditions to Sinai comes from the stelae set up by the leaders along the approach to the Temple of Hathor. Most of these date from the Middle Kingdom (c.2055–c.1650 BC). Many are badly eroded but it has been possible to use all the available information to build up a more or less complete picture. They describe the numbers of men involved in such an expedition, what part they took in the proceedings, what the transport arrangements were and even when was the best time to go.

The expedition leaders were usually called 'Seal-bearer of the God (meaning the king) and Director of Gangs'. There was also an official in charge of transport. He arranged for boats to bring men and supplies to the nearest accessible point on the coast and organized the donkeys for the rest of the journey. An expedition would need about 500 donkeys, each of which had to carry the food for one man for five days, as well as its own fodder and water. Most of the workforce were quarrymen and stonecutters but the party also included quartermasters, donkey-men and a scorpion-magician.

The best time for the expeditions was in the cooler weather, after the inundation had receded and the sowing had been done. One inscription reads:

By the time the hot weather came on, all this body of men were on their way back to Egypt accompanying the bags full of the precious gifts of the Mistress of Turquoise.

Not all expeditions were so fortunate, however. The expedition leader, Horrure, at first had difficulty locating the turquoise, and had to toil in the scorching sun, having been forced to travel 'when it was not the proper season for coming to this mining region'.

The Temple of Hathor

The original shrine of Hathor was a sacred cave, and seems to have been founded by the Fourth Dynasty king Sneferu (c.2613–c.2589 BC). Although there is no direct link between Sneferu and the Sanctuary, the form of hieroglyphs on an inscribed hawk found in it was thought by Petrie to be contemporary with him, and later kings mention him in terms that suggest that they considered him to have been the founder. The throne of a statuette of the Twelfth Dynasty king Senusret I (c.1965–c.1920 BC) bears a dedication to Sneferu and a stela of Amenemhat III

▼ *Hathor's temple at Serabit el-Khadim contains many inscribed stelae recording successful royal expeditions to Sinai to procure turquoise for the Egyptian kings.*

▲ *This stela was dedicated to Hathor by an expedition leader and names her* nebet mefkat *('Mistress of Turquoise'). Her blessing was thought to bring success to the mission.*

(c.1855–c.1808 BC) refers to himself as 'Beloved of Sneferu'. Sneferu is also the only king from before the Twelfth Dynasty to be named in the Hall of Kings by Hatshepsut (c.1473–c.1458 BC), when she extended the Sanctuary in the New Kingdom. A stela belonging to a Middle Kingdom expedition leader mentions that he had mined more turquoise than anyone else since the time of Sneferu.

The Sanctuary was extended in the Middle Kingdom by the Twelfth Dynasty king Amenemhat III. He enlarged the sacred cave, set up altars and began the building of a portico. The New Kingdom kings were also very active here. Several vases and *menat*-necklaces were dedicated to Hathor by Ahmose-Nefertari, wife of Ahmose (c.1550–c.1525 BC), the first king of the

▶ *A fallen capital from a column in the Hathor temple shows her, in typical style, with a human face, a bouffant hairstyle and cow's ears.*

Eighteenth Dynasty, and by their daughter, Merytamun. However, the most enthusiastic builders were Hatshepsut and Tuthmosis III (c.1479–c.1425 BC). Their most important addition to the Sanctuary was a court surrounded by four great columns with Hathor heads on the capitals. There was a basin for ablutions in the centre. At least a partial remodelling of the cave was carried out at this time, and the main hall of the temple was built.

Hatshepsut also built the Hall of Kings, which contains a relief showing the queen making offerings to Sneferu and depictions of King Amenemhet III and the deities Hathor and Sopdu. The work of Hatshepsut and Tuthmosis III was completed by a Great Pylon. Other rooms were added by later Eighteenth Dynasty kings and some major reconstruction work was done in the Ramesside Period (c.1295–c.1069 BC). However, the kings of later dynasties do not seem to have had much interest in the shrine and it was eventually abandoned.

The temple remains

Today, the temple can only be reached on foot after an exhilarating climb. The views across the mountains are stupendous and well worth the effort. On your return you may well be rewarded by a cup of tea provided by local people, but only after you have bought one of the fragments of turquoise, which is all the mines produce today.

It is also a humbling experience to clamber up the hillsides as the donkey caravans of the expeditions did so long ago. As you survey the bleak ridges of mountains that roll away to the Red Sea, it is easy to imagine their heartfelt need of the goddess's blessing, especially when they were forced to come at the 'wrong' time of year, and their great joy when she led them to stones of 'a good colour', as she eventually did for Horrure, who returned with more turquoise 'than any who had come before':

Offer, offer, to the Lady of Heaven!
May you propitiate Hathor!
May you do this, it is good for you!
Increase this, it will be well for you! ◆

A prized turquoise

A story about King Sneferu tells that he was feeling bored one day and was advised to take some young court ladies out on the palace lake to cheer himself up. He ordered them to change their usual dresses for bead-net versions and apparently 'his majesty's heart was happy seeing them row'. After a while the boat started drifting around in circles, because the women on one side of the boat had stopped rowing. Their leader had dropped her turquoise hair ornament into the water and was so distressed that she refused to go on. The king offered to get her another but she refused. Eventually the king had to send for a magician to roll the water back and retrieve her precious jewel for her.

Hathor, Mistress of Foreign Lands

Foreign lands were regarded as the personal property of Hathor, and the goods that the Egyptians obtained from these countries were said to be her 'gifts'. Temples were erected in her honour in such countries. In the Middle Kingdom (c.2055–1650 BC) she was worshipped at Byblos in Lebanon. Egypt had trading connections with this city that went back at least to the Pyramid Age. The Palermo Stone, on which the annals of the first five dynasties are recorded, notes the arrival from Byblos of 40 shiploads of timber in the reign of King Sneferu (c.2613–c.2589 BC). Excavations have revealed evidence of a cult to Hathor in this ancient commercial centre, where she was called Lady of Byblos.

Imports from Nubia

Egypt had longstanding trading relations with Nubia. In his famous autobiography engraved on the façade of his tomb at Aswan, Harkhuf, a governor of the South, described the expeditions that he undertook on behalf of the king to fetch exotic goods such as incense, ebony, ivory and panther skins. The king was especially pleased about the pygmy that Harkhuf had brought to dance for him, and wrote to congratulate him. Harkhuf was very proud of this letter and had it carved on the front of the tomb next to his autobiography:

> *The King's own seal: Year 2, third month of the first season, day 15. The king's decree to the Sole Companion, Lector-priest, Chief of Scouts, Harkhuf. You have said in this despatch of yours that you have brought a pygmy of the god's dances from the land of the horizon-dwellers, like the pygmy whom the god's seal-bearer Bawerded brought from Punt in the time of King Isesi. You have said to my majesty that his like has never been brought by anyone who did Yam previously.*

The writer of the letter was Pepi II (c.2278–c.2184 BC) who would have been a child of about eight at the time.

▼ *The smaller of the two temples built by Ramesses II at Abu Simbel was dedicated to Hathor of Abshek, a local form of the goddess.*

◀ *The Kiosk of Qertassi, now reconstructed at New Kalabsha, originally stood at the entrance to the sandstone quarries further south.*

Nubian sanctuaries

Temples were built in honour of Hathor in Nubia. One of the most charming is the little Kiosk of Qertassi, which today stands close to the Temple of Kalabsha. It was one of several temples moved to higher ground to save it from the rising waters of Lake Nasser after the building of the Aswan High Dam. Originally, the kiosk stood at the entrance to the old sandstone quarries about 40km (25 miles) further south. As at Serabit el-Khadim in Sinai, Hathor was regarded here as a patron goddess of miners and quarrymen, so it is not surprising that the capitals of the two columns on either side of the entrance are in the form of Hathor heads.

Hathor was also worshipped at Faras, where Queen Hatshepsut (c.1473–1458 BC) founded a sanctuary to her at the time when Egypt was bringing Nubia under direct control. The British Museum's collection includes several figurines of Hathor that were brought to the shrine as votive offerings by the workers of this desert region. She is represented in the Temple of Ramesses II at Wadi es-Sebua, where she appears, unusually, in human form but with the head of a cow. Hathor is one of the most frequently depicted deities in the Ptolemaic Temple of Dakka and was also honoured in the New Kingdom shrines at Qasr Ibrim.

Abu Simbel

Hathor's most important Nubian shrine is at Abu Simbel, where Ramesses II (c.1279–1213 BC) built two temples. In the larger of the two, Ramesses is shown worshipping himself as one of the gods honoured in the temple. The smaller temple he dedicated to Hathor of Abshek, a local goddess of beauty, love and motherhood, and also to Nefertari, Ramesses' principal wife, who was identified with Hathor. It should be remembered that the New Kingdom rulers built temples in Nubia to demonstrate their power and control over the area, and the monuments also served as storehouses for the precious commodities the ancient Egyptians extracted from the area. So Hathor's role as Mistress of Foreign Lands is in evidence here, as she protects the king's dominions on his behalf. However, it is her gentler aspects that are emphasized at Abu Simbel, where the square columns of the rock-cut temple are decorated with the *sistrum*, the sacred instrument that identifies her as a goddess of music and sexuality. ◆

▶ *The Temple of Dakka is dedicated to 'Thoth of Pnubs', Pnubs referring to the sycamore tree where Thoth waited for his wife Tefnut, associated with Hathor, to persuade her to return to Egypt.*

Hathor, Mistress of the West

In her capacity as Mistress of the West, Hathor welcomed the dead into the Afterlife. She is shown in many of the royal tombs, especially on the pillars around the burial chamber, where she is depicted embracing the king and holding out to him the *ankh,* or sign of life, used here as a symbol of the new life that awaits him. On the walls of private tombs and on stelae and funerary papyri of the Ramesside Period (c.1295–c.1069 BC), Hathor appears most commonly as a cow emerging from the western mountain. She comes to protect the deceased in the Underworld and grant them safe passage to the Afterlife.

Beautiful Feast of the Valley

Every year, in the second month of Shomu, there was a special festival connected with this aspect of the goddess. It was called the Beautiful Feast of the Valley. The images of the gods Amun, Mut and Khonsu were carried in their sacred boats from Thebes and were taken to the various Hathor sanctuaries at Deir el-Bahri and the royal mortuary temples on the west bank. Inscriptions in the temples make reference to this festival. The best source of information on the subject comes from the mortuary temple of Hatshepsut (c.1473–c.1458 BC) at Deir el-Bahri, where the reliefs show soldiers and standard bearers taking part in the procession.

The festival was extremely important to private individuals as well as to royalty. Local people would use the opportunity to visit the tombs of their ancestors, where there would be a reunion of past and present members of the family and the sharing of a meal. This idea lingers on in a Muslim context today.

Deir el-Bahri

The association of Hathor with Deir el-Bahri is evident in the number of shrines and chapels dedicated to her in the area. The most important is the chapel to Hathor attached to the mortuary temple of Hatshepsut. It lies on the second level and consists of a vestibule and hypostyle hall and a rock-cut sanctuary. The columns are topped by Hathor-head capitals and the walls are decorated with offering scenes and episodes from the festivals held in her honour. Hathor is represented as a cow standing on her sacred boat. The most secret parts of the ceremonies took place in the rock-cut

◀ *This statue shows Hathor in cow form protecting King Amenhotep II. He is also seen as a child being suckled by the goddess in the Chapel of the Sacred Cow of Tuthmosis III at Deir el-Bahri.*

Sanctuary. Here, Hathor is depicted as a cow who both suckles and protects Hatshepsut. At the very back of the Sanctuary, Hathor and Amun are shown consecrating Hatshepsut as king.

The association of Hathor with this area was probably one of the reasons that the first king of the Middle Kingdom, Mentuhotep II (c.2055–c.2004 BC), built his mortuary temple at Deir el-Bahri, on what was then a virgin site. The princesses who were buried near the temple were priestesses of Hathor.

Between this temple and that of Hatshepsut was the Temple of Tuthmosis III (c.1479–c.1425 BC). A small chapel, a subsidiary shrine of this temple, was found quite by chance after a fall of rock by the Swiss Egyptologist Edouard Naville in 1906. Both the chapel and the statue it contained of Hathor as a cow, suckling and protecting a king, were in an excellent state of preservation and are now in the Cairo Museum. Although the chapel was built by Tuthmosis III, the name of the king depicted turned out to be his son Amenhotep II (c.1427–c.1400 BC). The walls of the chapel are decorated with scenes showing Tuthmosis III making offerings to Hathor in the form of a woman.

Until the death of Hatshepsut her temple was the final destination of the procession of the sacred boats during the Beautiful Feast of the Valley. Later, the Temple of Tuthmosis III took over this function. According to inscriptions found in the area, the cult of Hathor was maintained here until the Ramesside Period, when earthquakes caused the destruction of the main temple and the entrance of the little Chapel of the Sacred Cow was blocked. ◆

▲ *A painted relief from the chapel dedicated to Hathor at Deir el-Bahri shows festivities held in her honour, including a running race and a falconry competition.*

▼ *A vignette from the Book of the Dead shows Hathor, in the form of a cow, emerging from the western mountain to welcome the deceased into the Afterlife.*

Mortuary Temples

Mortuary temples were often called 'House of Millions of Years', and this helps to explain their function. The ancient Egyptians believed that the spirit of an individual, called the *ka*, came into existence at birth and was intimately linked to the physical body during life and after death, when it continued to need sustenance in the form of offerings of food and drink. In a royal mortuary temple, offerings were presented daily for the king's *ka*, and in theory this was to continue in perpetuity.

In the Old Kingdom c.2686–c.2181 BC), mortuary temples were usually built against the east side of the pyramid itself. In the New Kingdom (c.1550–c.1069 BC), when the kings were buried in the Valley of the Kings, mortuary temples were physically quite separate from the tombs, although they were still part of the concept of a funerary complex. They were built on the edge of the desert, just beyond the cultivation, and were separated from the royal tombs by a steep range of cliffs. The layout of the interior was usually the same as that of a cult temple.

The mortuary temples were served by priests who officiated in various capacities. While some presented the *ka* statue of the deceased king with offerings to satisfy his physical needs, others were involved in the running of the temple estates or engaging in trade to finance the mortuary cult.

◀ *The mortuary temple of Hatshepsut at Deir el-Bahri was built in the great bay of the cliffs next to the funerary complex of Mentuhotep II, in an area sacred to Hathor, as Mistress of the West.*

Western Thebes

In ancient times, Thebes was a significant religious centre, with the city of the living and the temples to the gods situated on the east bank of the Nile while the west side was devoted to the dead. Although kings had been buried there since the Eleventh Dynasty (c.2055–c.1985 BC), western Thebes was especially important in the New Kingdom (c.1550–c.1069 BC) when the royal tombs were in the Valley of the Kings. Even in the Ramesside Period (c.1295–c.1069 BC), when the kings ruled from their northern capital of Per-Ramesses, they continued to be buried in western Thebes. The royal mortuary temples, such as Medinet Habu and the Ramesseum, which served the *ka* of the kings buried in the valley, are strung out along the desert fringe. ◆

▲ *This Hathor column, with the capital in the form of a* sistrum, *is from the mortuary temple of Queen Hatshepsut at Deir el-Bahri.*

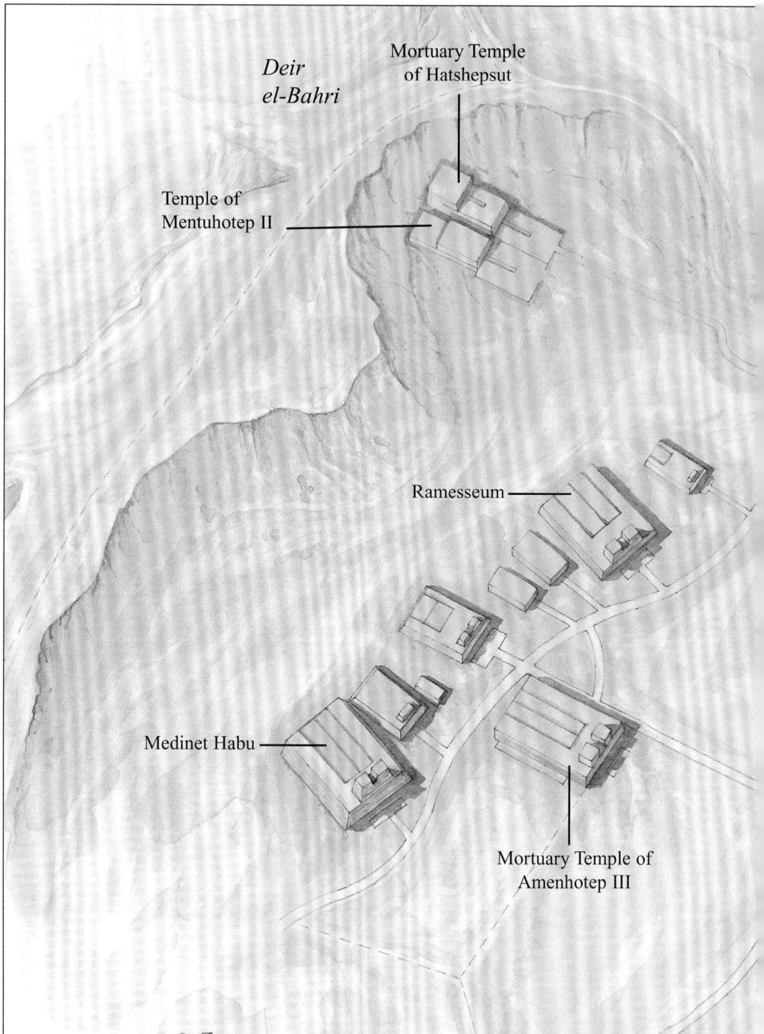

Deir el-Bahri

Mortuary Temple of Hatshepsut

Temple of Mentuhotep II

Ramesseum

Medinet Habu

Mortuary Temple of Amenhotep III

N

▲ *The statues of Ramesses II as Osiris as seen in the Second Court of the Ramesseum.*

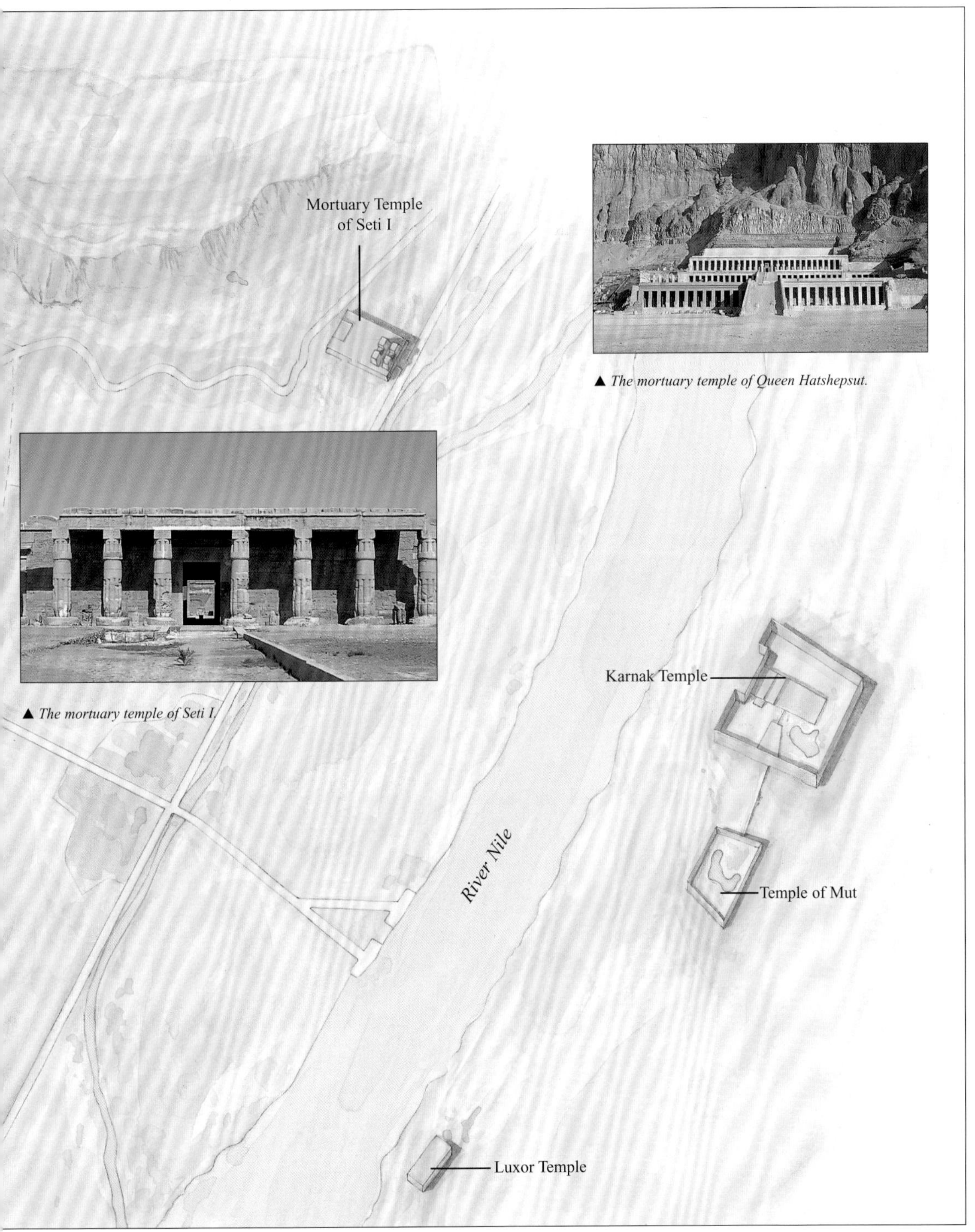

▲ *The mortuary temple of Queen Hatshepsut.*

▲ *The mortuary temple of Seti I.*

Deir el-Bahri: The Funerary Complex of Mentuhotep II

Mentuhotep II (c.2055–c.2004 BC), the Eleventh Dynasty king who reunited Egypt at the beginning of the Middle Kingdom, built a very unusual funerary complex. His mortuary temple was built on different levels in the great bay of cliffs at Deir el-Bahri. It was approached by a 46m (150ft) wide causeway leading from a valley temple, which no longer exists.

The mortuary temple itself consists of a forecourt, enclosed by walls on three sides, and a terrace on which stands a large square structure that may represent the primeval mound that arose from the waters of chaos. As the temple faces east, the structure is likely to be connected with the sun cult and the resurrection of the king. From the eastern part of the forecourt, an opening called the Bab el-Hosan ('Gate of the Horseman') leads to an underground passage and an unfinished tomb or cenotaph containing a seated statue of the king. On the western side, tamarisk and sycamore trees were

▲ *The remains of Mentuhotep's funerary complex can be seen cut into the cliffs at Deir el-Bahri. Facing east, it celebrates the sun cult and the resurrection of the king.*

▼ *A painted carved relief of Mentuhotep II from his mortuary temple at Deir el-Bahri reveals the hieroglyphs for 'one thousand' and 'duration', wishing him eternal life.*

planted beside the ramp leading up to the terrace. At the back of the forecourt and terrace are colonnades decorated in relief with boat processions, hunts and scenes showing the king's military achievements. Statues of the Twelfth Dynasty king Senusret III (c.1874–c.1855 BC) were found here too.

The inner part of the temple was actually cut into the cliff and consists of a peristyle court, a hypostyle hall and an underground passage 150m (492ft) long leading to the tomb itself. The cult of the dead king centred on the small shrine cut into the rear of the Hypostyle Hall.

Mentuhotep's statue

The seated statue of Mentuhotep II was discovered accidentally when the horse on which Howard Carter was riding trod on the paving stone over the entrance to the cenotaph. This caused the covering to collapse, and horse and rider fell into the tomb. The statue had been ritually interred. It was wrapped in a linen cloth and it is thought that the flesh was painted black just before it was buried. The king is wearing the red crown of Lower Egypt and the jubilee robe. His arms are crossed and he would once have carried the crook and the flail, the symbols of kingship. This stance, his curved beard and black flesh identify him with Osiris, with whom he hoped to become assimilated after death.

The royal princesses

The mastaba-like structure on the terrace is surrounded by a pillared ambulatory along the west wall, where the statue shrines and tombs of several royal wives and daughters were found. The princesses were priestesses of Hathor, one of the main ancient Egyptian funerary deities. Although little remained of the king's own burial, six sarcophagi were retrieved from the tombs of the royal ladies. Each was formed of six slabs held together at the corners by metal braces and carved in sunk relief.

The sarcophagus of Queen Kawit, now in the Cairo Museum, is particularly fine. She is shown as the picture of elegance, her slender form set off by a close-fitting dress and simple jewellery. One of her attendants arranges her hair, while others present offerings of perfumed oils and milk. Another sarcophagus belonged to Ashait. When found, her mummy was still lying in a wooden inner coffin, brightly painted with scenes of palace life. Similar scenes were carved on the limestone sarcophagus.

Ashait is shown as a young woman sniffing a lotus flower and seated before an offering table. To the right of her, workers hurry to the granary with sacks of grain, thus ensuring a plentiful supply of food for her in the next life. ◆

▶ *This painted sandstone figure of Mentuhotep II was found in what was probably the original tomb below the terrace of the mortuary temple. His black skin, curved beard and crossed arms identify him with Osiris.*

Deir el-Bahri: The Temple of Hatshepsut

Next to the mortuary temple of Mentuhotep II (c.2055–c.2004 BC) at Deir el-Bahri is that of Hatshepsut (c.1473–c.1458 BC), the female pharaoh of the Eighteenth Dynasty. For a woman to rule Egypt for over 20 years was extremely unusual. Other royal women had ruled as king previously, but only when there were apparently no male heirs to the throne. Their reigns were short and generally came at the end of a dynasty. Women were usually omitted from the kinglists, as the idea of a woman on the throne did not fit in with the Egyptian concept of *maat*, the correct order of things as laid down by the gods at the time of creation.

Hatshepsut's succession

Hatshepsut's father was Tuthmosis I (c.1504–c.1492 BC) and she was married to her half-brother, Tuthmosis II (c.1492–c.1479 BC). On his untimely death, his heir was his son by a secondary wife, but as the young Tuthmosis III (c.1479–c.1425 BC) was still a child, Hatshepsut became regent and ruled on his behalf for about seven years, before proclaiming herself king and ruling jointly with him for a further 14 years.

In the past, Hatshepsut has often been portrayed as a ruthless, scheming woman, hated by her stepson, who had her done away with as soon as possible and subsequently had her name and image removed from her monuments. In the light of modern scholarship, however, this does not seem to have been the case. Rather, Hatshepsut and Tuthmosis III seem to have enjoyed a highly successful and prosperous joint reign, with Tuthmosis undertaking military campaigns while Hatshepsut maintained the royal authority at home. The later obliteration of her name and image from monuments was in any case partial and seems to have had more to do with the concept of *maat* than with the jealousy and hatred of Tuthmosis III.

▲ *The head from a painted statue of Hatshepsut. Although she was a woman, she projected her official image as that of a king, and even wore the royal false beard.*

Hatshepsut's mortuary temple

Like the temple of Mentuhotep II, that of Hatshepsut is partly free-standing and partly rock-cut, and imitates the terraced layout of its predecessor. In antiquity the building must have been a very impressive sight, embellished with sphinxes and statues, as well as trees and flowerbeds.

A monumental causeway led from the valley temple, which has now vanished, although its location is known from foundation deposits. An avenue of sphinxes

▲ *The mortuary temple of Hatshepsut, the female pharaoh, at Deir el-Bahri was built next to the funerary complex of the first Middle Kingdom king, Mentuhotep II.*

lined the causeway and there was a sacred boat shrine in the temple forecourt.

The temple itself is laid out on three terraces, each approached by a ramp. At the rear of each terrace is a portico protecting the lively reliefs carved on the rear wall. On the lowest level, these show barges bringing Hatshepsut's famous obelisks from Aswan to Karnak, while in the middle section there are scenes depicting her divine birth to the right of the ramp, and scenes of the expedition to the land of Punt on the left. At the entrance to the topmost level were Osiris pillars and colossal statues of Hatshepsut. At this level, vaulted rooms on both sides of the court were dedicated to Hatshepsut and her father, Tuthmosis I, and to the gods Re-Horakhty and Amun. There were further statues of the queen on the back wall of the hall around the original entrance to the Sanctuary, although the sanctuary seen by modern visitors to the temple was cut by Ptolemy VIII (170–116 BC) over 1,000 years later.

As well as maintaining the king's cult, mortuary temples were usually also dedicated to the cults of various gods. On the south side of the main complex is a small chapel dedicated to the goddess Hathor, where the columns are topped with Hathor-head capitals. Hathor was paramount on the west bank and is particularly significant here. Another chapel is devoted to Anubis, the god of embalming and funerary rites.

Hatshepsut's mortuary temple was intended to be closely connected with her second tomb in the Valley of the Kings (the first having been located in a remote valley to the west). The original idea seems to have been to excavate a passage from the tomb entrance in the Valley of the Kings to a burial place under her sanctuary in the temple of Deir el-Bahri. However, the tomb builders struck bad rock and had to make a great loop backwards in the direction of the entrance. ◆

▼ *This column is in the form of a* sistrum, *the musical instrument sacred to Hathor. The column is the 'handle' and is decorated with a Hathor head. Above the head, the metal loop of the instrument itself is depicted.*

The Colonnades of the Queen's Temple

In the Southern Colonnade to the left of the ramp are scenes depicting Hatshepsut's celebrated expedition to the land of Punt, the prime object of which was to obtain incense for the cult of her 'father', the god Amun. The accompanying text reveals that a wide variety of exotic goods was obtained, including fragrant woods, ebony, ivory, gold, spices, eye paint, panther skins, apes, monkeys, dogs and native people. Punt is thought to be either modern Somalia or Eritrea.

Some of these reliefs remain clear, colourful and lively, while others, such as the birth scenes, are extensively damaged. Among those that are less easy to see are the scenes showing Hatshepsut (c.1473–c.1458 BC) dedicating the fruits of the expedition to Amun, where the image of Hatshepsut has been obliterated. Another scene shows gold being weighed, with Horus in charge of the scales. Seshat, the goddess of writing, keeps account of the weight, while Thoth, the god of wisdom and patron of scribes, records the amounts of incense obtained. Hatshepsut is shown in the presence of Amun, while Tuthmosis III (c.1479–c.1425 BC) offers incense to the sacred boat.

▲ *As well as incense resin, incense trees in baskets were carried on board ship for transport to Egypt, where they were planted on the terraces of Hatshepsut's temple at Deir el-Bahri.*

▼ *This relief from the South Colonnade shows the King and Queen of Punt receiving Hatshepsut's expedition. The queen appears to suffer from elephantiasis.*

The birth scenes of Hatshepsut

In spite of her female form, Hatshepsut was in every respect a king. She had herself depicted on her monuments as pharaoh, wearing male dress and with the royal regalia. She undertook the customary activities of a king: building temples, sending expeditions to foreign countries and taking part in the *heb sed*, or jubilee

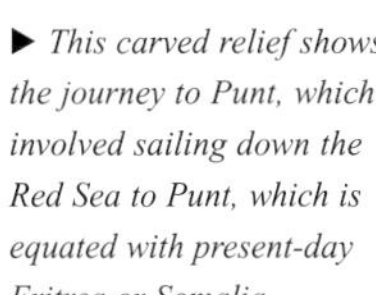

▶ *This carved relief shows the journey to Punt, which involved sailing down the Red Sea to Punt, which is equated with present-day Eritrea or Somalia.*

festival. As other kings before her, she regarded herself as divinely appointed and took the title 'Son of Re'. Going further than this, she had her divine birth recorded on the walls of her funerary temple at Deir el-Bahri. These painted reliefs should not be interpreted as a political ploy to uphold a doubtful claim to the throne, but as Hatshepsut following in the royal religious tradition. They are now very difficult to see and interpret. The god Amun, disguised as Tuthmosis I (c.1504–c.1492 BC), impregnates her mother, Queen Ahmose. The accompanying text describes the scene:

> *Amun made his form like the majesty of her husband, Aakheperkare [Tuthmosis I]. He found her as she slept in the palace. She was woken by the god's fragrance. She smiled at his majesty. He went to her immediately, his penis erect before her. He gave his heart to her...his love passed into her limbs. The palace was flooded with the god's fragrance and all his perfumers were from Punt...Khenmet-Amun-Hatshepsut shall be the name of this daughter I have placed in your body. She shall exercise kingship over the whole land.* ◆

▶ *The pregnant queen is led to the birth chamber by gods concerned with childbirth. After the birth, the child is presented to Amun.*

The Ramesseum

The mortuary temple of the Nineteenth Dynasty king Ramesses II (c.1279–c.1213 BC), known as the Ramesseum, is one of a string of such temples that lay along the desert edge a short distance from the tomb of the king to whom the temple was dedicated. The Ramesseum was also dedicated to Amun, the chief god of the state pantheon. Much of the temple has been destroyed, but the remains are nonetheless impressive.

The victorious king

The decoration of the temple records the military successes of Ramesses and otherwise depicts him as a pious ruler, worshipping the gods and taking part in religious festivals. The reliefs and related texts are thus a sort of justification of the king's reign. Although the kings held that they were appointed by the gods, they also believed that they were responsible to them for the wellbeing of the people. From the kings' accounts of their campaigns it can be seen that they considered military action to be one of their chief duties. The gods, especially Amun in the New Kingdom (c.1550–c.1069 BC), instigated the campaigns and frequently proposed the strategy. They came to the king's aid in battle and rewarded him with victory.

Ramesses recorded his Syrian campaigns on the Great Pylon at the entrance to the temple. The Syrian fortresses he destroyed in the eighth year of his reign are depicted on the North Tower. There are also scenes from his much vaunted war against the Hittites, including depictions of the Egyptian army on the march, and the Egyptian camp surrounded by a 'fence' of shields, within which the soldiers prepare to do battle. To the right at the end is a scene depicting the king holding a council of war and another showing captured spies being beaten.

▲ *Painted carved reliefs on the papyrus columns of the Ramesseum's Hypostyle Hall depict Ramesses II offering to the gods.*

The whole of the South Tower is taken up with the great victory Ramesses claimed to have won against the Hittites at the Battle of Qadesh. Ramesses is seen larger than life, charging into battle in his chariot, while the Hittites, pierced by his arrows, fall into the River Orontes and are drowned, or else flee before him.

Temple courts and halls

Apart from fragments of the west wall, the First Court is totally ruined. Part of a colossal statue of Ramesses lies on the floor. From the measurements of the remains it has been estimated that the statue must have been 17.5m (57ft) high and weighed over 1,000 tons. The head of another colossal head of Ramesses from this temple is now in the British Museum, London. The Second Court has also largely been destroyed, although some of the Osiris pillars representing the

▶ *The statues of Ramesses II as Osiris in the Second Court of the Ramesseum are now largely in ruins.*

deceased Ramesses are still standing. The surviving part of the front wall is decorated with interesting scenes concerning the king's accession. On the left is the festival of Min, the fertility god, which was celebrated at this time. Ramesses is shown watching the procession, in which statues of his ancestors are carried by priests. In front of him are two poles decorated with the headdress of Min. Priests then send off carrier pigeons to the four corners of the earth, bearing the news of the king's accession.

On the right, Ramesses is seen cutting a ceremonial sheaf of corn in honour of Min as a harvest god. Several fragments of colossal statues are scattered in this court, including a piece from a throne inscribed with the name of Ramesses II. From here, three steps lead up into the portico where Ramesses is seen honouring the gods. Beyond this is the Hypostyle Hall, which is similar to that of the Karnak Temple. The roof was supported by a colonnade with three rows of lower columns at each side. The central columns have capitals of open papyrus flowers while the lower ones have buds, the whole representing the Mound of Creation. The columns are carved with images of Ramesses making offerings to the gods. As at Karnak, the temple was lit by clerestory windows set high up in the walls.

In the next hall, the First Small Hypostyle Hall, the reliefs show priests carrying the sacred boats of Amun, his wife Mut and their son Khonsu. At the end, Ramesses is seated under the sacred tree, while Thoth and Seshat inscribe his name on the leaves, thus acknowledging him as the worthy successor of his illustrious forebears. ◆

▲ *Ramesses II is blessed by the seated king of the gods, Amun, his wife Mut and son Khonsu.*

▲ *The fallen head of Ramesses II shows him wearing the double crown of the kings of Egypt.*

The granary

Around the temple itself lie an enormous number of vaulted mudbrick storage chambers which formed one of the state granaries. It has been estimated that, when full, this granary could have provided for the needs of 3,400 families for one year. The craftsmen of Deir el-Medina staged a strike outside the Ramesseum when their rations failed to turn up and were given food from these stores to tide them over until their 'pay' arrived.

Medinet Habu

The mortuary temple of Ramesses III (c.1184–c.1153 BC), the last great king of the New Kingdom Period (c.1550–c.1069 BC), was built at Medinet Habu and was closely modelled on the Ramesseum, both in layout and decoration. The temple takes its name from the associated village that grew up within its precincts. This was named after Amenhotep, son of Hapu, a very influential official of the reign of Amenhotep III (c.1390–c.1352 BC), who was so highly regarded that he was allowed to build himself a mortuary temple on the west bank among those of the kings (see *The Colossi of Memnon*).

Like the Ramesseum, the temple at Medinet Habu was dedicated to Amun. The king is depicted performing his cultic duties, and his military successes are prominently displayed. However, an unusual feature is the entrance to the temple. This was constructed in the form of a *migdol* or Syrian fortress. A massive mudbrick wall surrounded the whole complex and the temple became a place of security in unsettled times. The craftsmen of Deir el-Medina moved there at the end of the Twentieth Dynasty (c.1069 BC), when there was a constant threat of Libyan invasion.

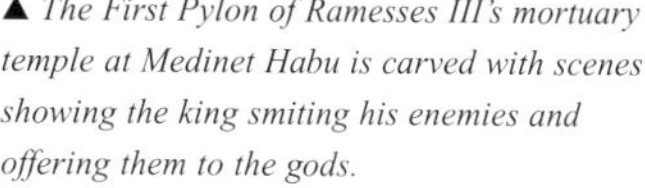

▲ *The First Pylon of Ramesses III's mortuary temple at Medinet Habu is carved with scenes showing the king smiting his enemies and offering them to the gods.*

Temple reliefs

Ramesses III's victories are a constant theme. Inside the *migdol*, the heads of defeated enemies are used as a sill on which the king would tread when he appeared at the window. The outer walls of both the *migdol* and the Pylon at the entrance to the temple proper show the king in his traditional pose of smiting enemies and offering them, on the left to Amun and on the right to Re-Horakhty.

Between the grooves intended for flagstaffs is a long, bombastic account of Ramesses III's victory over the Libyans in the second year of his reign. This theme is repeated on the inner walls of the Entrance Pylon, where some rather grisly war trophies in the form of piles of hands and penises are also displayed, while on the face of the Second Pylon Ramesses' victories over the enigmatic Sea Peoples are recorded. This theme is expanded along the

◀ *Ramesses III ritually cuts a sheaf of corn and offers it to Hapy, the Nile god. A companion scene shows him ploughing the Field of Iaru.*

▲ *A lintel shows Ramesses III, accompanied by baboons, greeting the rising sun. This symbolized the king's resurrection.*

greater part of the northern exterior wall of the temple, where Ramesses is seen charging into battle against his Libyan enemies and their Sea People allies. Further scenes show a vast sea battle taking place.

Otherwise, the painted carved reliefs depict the king honouring the gods. Those of the Second Court, where an amazing amount of colour remains, are particularly beautiful. As in the Ramesseum, the festival of Min is being celebrated. On the rear wall of the North Colonnade, the king is seen carried in procession from the palace on a canopied litter. He is preceded by priests carrying censers, a lector-priest and soldiers, with a retinue of courtiers bringing up the rear. The procession is accompanied by trumpeters, drummers and castanet players. In the next scene, the king makes an offering to Min and a further section shows the god carried in a procession led by the king and queen. They are followed by priests carrying standards, ritual vessels and images of the king and his ancestors. The ritual is again connected with the king's coronation, and the event is announced by the release of pigeons who carry the message in all directions. The ritual closes with the ceremonial cutting of a sheaf of corn, which is offered to Min, and the burning of incense.

The Hypostyle Hall

The roof is missing, and only the lower parts of the columns that once supported it are extant, although the roof slabs of the colonnade of the Second Court have been restored and are most impressive from above. In the Hypostyle Hall beyond there are two pairs of statues, one of Amun and Maat, the goddess of truth and justice, and another of Thoth, the god of wisdom, and the king. These gods were very important in the ideology of kingship. Amun appointed the king and was regarded as his father, while the king had to reign in accordance with the concept of *maat* personified by the goddess. Thoth, the scribe of the gods, recorded the deeds of the king and so justified his reign. Some of the pillars in the preceding courts are in the form of Osiris, and associate the king with the god, with whom he hoped to become one in the Afterlife.

Ancillary buildings

The temple treasuries were built to the left of the Hypostyle Hall and are decorated with scenes showing the king offering to Amun costly ritual vessels, heaps of gold and bags of precious stones. Another chamber off this hall has an unusual scene showing the king ploughing and harvesting in the Field of Iaru (the 'Field of Reeds'), the name given to the domain of Osiris. This scene is more usually seen in the tombs of commoners of this period.

Adjoining the temple are the remains of a palace used by the king for occasional visits during his lifetime as well as being intended as a spiritual royal residence for use in the Afterlife. Although small, it was sumptuously decorated with glazed tiles and had bathrooms lined with slabs of limestone to protect the mudbrick. A church was built in the Second Court in the early Christian era. This has now been dismantled by the excavators. ◆

A plot against the king

In rooms at the top of the *migdol* are scenes showing the king enjoying himself among the ladies of his harem. It has been suggested that the plot to assassinate Ramesses III was possibly hatched here. This concerned one of the lesser queens, who wanted to install her son on the throne. The conspiracy involved several of the harem ladies, one of whom had a brother, a captain in the army, who was instructed to stir up revolt in Nubia in order to create a diversion. Some of the male officials procured wax images, which could be melted, with the intention of magically weakening the limbs of the guards. The plot was discovered and many of those implicated were put to death. Ramesses seems to have survived the conspiracy but the shock of its discovery may well have hastened the old king's end.

▲ *These ritual scenes from the Sacred Court show the king in his capacity as high priest taking part in the annual festival held in honour of the fertility god Min.*

The Temple of Seti I

Many of the mortuary temples on the west bank are barely recognizable today, but one that remains in relatively good condition is that of the Nineteenth Dynasty king Seti I (c.1294–c.1279 BC), the father of Ramesses II (c.1279–c.1213 BC). As well as being built for the *ka* of the deceased king, it was also dedicated to Seti's predecessor Ramesses I (c.1295–c.1294 BC), who reigned for only a few months so was not able to build a mortuary temple for himself, and to Ramesses II, who completed it after his father's death. Amun, the chief god, was also revered here.

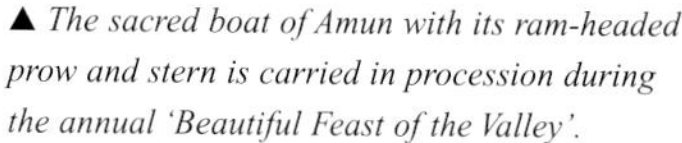

▲ *The sacred boat of Amun with its ram-headed prow and stern is carried in procession during the annual 'Beautiful Feast of the Valley'.*

Seti I was interred in one of the most spectacular tombs in the Valley of the Kings. However, he also had a cenotaph at Abydos, where Osiris himself was thought to be buried. Conversely, the Abydos temple, which was the main sanctuary of Osiris, also doubled as a secondary mortuary temple for the king. The Abydos temple was decorated in a similar way to the actual mortuary temple. In both cases, Seti is seen officiating in the cult and as a child being suckled by a mother goddess; at Abydos, Isis, the wife of Osiris, fulfilled this role.

▼ *The mortuary temple of Seti I in western Thebes includes a chapel dedicated to Ramesses I, who reigned for too brief a time to build a mortuary temple of his own. The Theban triad were also worshipped here.*

The temple layout

Seti's mortuary temple was built of white sandstone on the usual plan of two courtyards, each with their own pylon, a six-columned hypostyle hall and a sanctuary where the sacred boat of Amun originally stood. Until the middle of the nineteenth century the temple was approached by an avenue of sphinxes. Only one now remains and even that has been damaged by recent floods. However, it is still possible to see that the base is inscribed with the motif of the 'Nine Bows', representing Seti's conquered enemies.

The central part of the temple is dedicated to Seti, while the southern part is dedicated to Ramesses I. The

▶ *Papyrus bundle columns support the portico of Seti's mortuary temple, plant forms being powerfully suggestive of creation and the re-creation of the king as he enters the Afterlife.*

cartouches of both Seti I and Ramesses II appear on the First Pylon. Most of the decoration of this temple refers to the cultic activities of Seti, but Ramesses II is also seen offering to the gods in the Hypostyle Hall and the side chapels. Seti makes offerings to the gods of the Ennead (the nine deities of the creation myth of Heliopolis). Ramesses, followed by Mut, the wife of Amun, and their son Khonsu, performs the rites of the *heb sed*, or royal jubilee festival, before Amun. In the main hall both kings are represented as children being suckled by goddesses, Seti by Hathor, the cow goddess, and Ramesses by Mut.

In the Sanctuary, which originally housed the sacred boat, there are scenes showing the boat of Amun with its ram-headed prow and stern, and Seti offering to the boat in procession. In the southern section there are dedication texts of Seti I and the figure of the deified Ramesses I.

Behind the temple is a pool, possibly the remains of a sacred lake, an essential element of any temple, representing as it did the primeval ocean from which creation arose. This would also have been appropriate in a mortuary temple as it was linked with the concept of re-creation and the king's passage to eternity. There are also the remnants of mudbrick houses, where the priests would once have lived, and storerooms where the ritual vessels and other treasures would have been kept.

The complex included mudbrick storerooms on its northern side and a royal palace, probably used for ritual purposes, on the south side. This feature was copied by later kings, such as Ramesses II at the Ramesseum and Ramesses III (c.1184–c.1153 BC) at Medinet Habu. A Coptic church was built in the Northern Courtyard with the coming of Christianity and the temple was used as a quarry to provide stone to build houses within the complex, as was the case in several of the temples on the west bank of the Nile at Thebes. ◆

◀ *A scene from the tomb of Seti I in the Valley of the Kings, which his mortuary temple served, shows Ptah, god of creation, offering him life, wellbeing and stability in the next world.*

The foundation of a dynasty

Seti I was the second king of the Nineteenth Dynasty. His father, Ramesses I, had been an officer in the army and was appointed as king by Horemheb (c.1323–c.1295 BC), who had himself served previous kings as a general. Ramesses I seems to have had no family connections with the previous dynasty, but he was elderly when he came to the throne and already a grandfather, so brought with him a ready-made dynasty. This may be why he was appointed – in order to prevent future disputes over the succession.

Although Ramesses I's own reign was brief, Seti I reigned very successfully for 17 years, during which he fought campaigns in the Levant and against the Libyans and Hittites, thus securing Egypt's prestige in North Africa and the Near East. Seti's success is reflected in the splendour of his tomb in the Valley of the Kings.

The Colossi of Memnon

Although the mortuary temple of the Eighteenth Dynasty king Amenhotep III (c.1390–c.1352 BC), one of the most illustrious of the New Kingdom rulers, was the largest on the west bank, very little of it remains today. It was used by later kings as a quarry when they built their own mortuary temples and had already been destroyed by the reign of the Nineteenth Dynasty king Merenptah (c.1213–c.1203 BC), who incorporated various architectural elements from Amenhotep's temple into his own. However, the site is currently under excavation and the pillar bases of the Hypostyle Hall and several pieces of colossal statues have now come to light.

The temple remains

The remaining features include a strange type of sphinx with the body of a crocodile lying near the road, a huge stela with a dedication text excavated in the nineteenth century, some recently unearthed statues of the lioness-headed goddess, Sekhmet, and the two colossal statues of the king, which once stood at the entrance. Many other statues that once adorned the temple have long since been removed and taken to museums around the world. Of these, some are conventional statues of the king and some are in a budding Amarna style.

The statues of the king

The two huge seated figures known as the Colossi of Memnon both represent King Amenhotep III and once must have stood more than 20m (65ft) high. In each case, the king sits on a huge throne decorated on the sides with the symbol of the united land of Egypt: two images of Hapy, the god of the Nile inundation, tie the heraldic plants of Upper Egypt (the lotus) and Lower Egypt (the papyrus) to the hieroglyph meaning 'to unite'. The South Colossus is better preserved and has the figures of the

▼ *Colossal statues, nearly 18m (59 ft) high, depicting King Amenhotep III, mark the entrance to his mortuary temple. Diminutive figures of his mother, Mutemwiya, and Queen Tiye, his wife, surround the legs of the southernmost statue.*

▲ *A black granite statue of the goddess Sekhmet found at the site. Hundreds more were discovered at Karnak in the temple of Mut, with whom Sekhmet is associated.*

king's mother, Mutemwiya, on the left, and of his wife, Queen Tiye, on the right. Both female figures are minuscule in comparison to the image of the king. There is another small figure between the king's knees but it is not clear who this represents.

▲ *This unusual sphinx with the body of a lion and tail of a crocodile may once have formed part of a processional way.*

The singing statue

The North Colossus was famous for its 'singing' in the Graeco-Roman Period (c.332 BC–AD 395). It was said that an earthquake in 27 BC had damaged the statue, which thereafter emitted a whistling sound early every morning. This was interpreted by visitors as the Homeric hero, Memnon, singing to his mother, Eos, the goddess of the dawn. The phenomenon is described by the first-century Greek geographer, Strabo, who wondered whether the whole thing was a trick, but later claimed to have been convinced that the noise was of divine origin. The life of the singing statue as a tourist attraction was short-lived, however, since the Roman emperor Severus (AD 193–211) repaired the damage, after which the statue no longer 'sang'. ◆

▼ *An aerial view shows the vast area originally covered by the mortuary temple of Amenhotep III.*

The royal architect

Amenhotep, son of Hapu, had an illustrious career during the reign of Amenhotep III. One of his titles was 'Director of all the King's Works' which roughly translates as 'Chief Royal Architect'. This means he would have been in charge of all the processes involved in the building of temples, from the quarrying of the building material and the construction and embellishment of the monuments with painted reliefs to the provision of statues. He may well have been responsible for the Colossi of Memnon.

Amenhotep's career is known from texts on the statues of himself that he was allowed to set up in the Temple of Amun at Karnak. That he was allowed both to do this and to build his own funerary temple among those of the kings indicates his importance. Several of his statues show him as a seated scribe, the epitome of the educated man.

Temples of Nubia

Nubia, Egypt's neighbour to the south, lay along the Nile between Aswan and Khartoum (in present-day Sudan). Ancient Egyptian interest in the area went back at least to the Predynastic Period (c.3500–c.3100 BC) and by the Early Dynastic Period (c.3100–c.2686 BC) the kings were mounting expeditions into Nubia, attracted by its rich resources. They returned bearing ivory, ebony, incense, animal skins and other exotic goods. From the Middle Kingdom (c.2055–c.1650 BC), the Egyptians began to exploit Nubian mineral deposits, especially gold.

The tomb autobiography of the late Old Kingdom official, Harkhuf, gives a wealth of information about Egyptian relations with the Nubian chiefs and the exotic goods he procured on behalf of the Sixth Dynasty king Pepi II (c.2278–c.2184 BC). Rock inscriptions of kings and officials on the island of Sehel provide further details, both about the expeditions and the royal attempts made to dig canals around the First Cataract, just to the south of Aswan. The kings of the Middle Kingdom also built fortresses at the Second Cataract to protect the trade routes. In the New Kingdom (c.1550–c.1069 BC) Egypt ruled Nubia directly, and several kings built temples to help maintain tight control over the territory.

◀ *The First Cataract is immediately to the south of the island of Elephantine and the town of Aswan. This was a major obstacle to trade in ancient Egypt.*

Aswan Dam Rescue Operations

Before the building of the dams at Aswan, the Nile flooded the cultivated areas in the Nile Valley every year between June and October. It then receded, leaving behind a rich deposit of alluvial silt, which replenished the fertility of the soil. In addition, by digging a system of dikes and ditches at the start of the inundation it was possible to bring additional land, some distance from the river and beyond the natural flood plain, under cultivation.

The inundation was so important to the ancient Egyptians that the time when the Nile began to rise – in conjunction with the dawn appearance of Sirius, the dog star, above the horizon after a long absence – was regarded as the start of the New Year. The population faced serious hardships and even death if the inundation was either too high or too low, which could result in disastrous floods or starvation.

Controlling the inundation

As the Egyptian population began to rise sharply at the end of the nineteenth century, the government began to make plans to control the waters of the Nile. The first dam at Aswan was designed by a British engineer, Sir William Wilcox, and was completed in 1902. The Nile Valley was flooded as far south as Wadi es-Sebua. However, this proved to be inadequate and the dam was raised twice, in 1912 and 1934 when the flooding extended to Wadi Halfa and the water level to between 87–121m (285–397ft). This caused many of the ancient temples above the dam to be submerged for much of the year.

▼ *Known as Elephantine in antiquity, this island on the Nile near Aswan was the point from which royal expeditions set out for Nubia to obtain ivory and gold. With the building of the High Dam, Aswan is again an important ecomomic centre.*

Nilometers

The kings of ancient Egypt had been interested in the height of the inundation from earliest times. The Palermo Stone, of which only fragments now remain, was once a record of the important events of every year of the reign of each king of the first five dynasties. It also gives the height of the Nile for each year. The king in his capacity as shepherd of his people needed to be warned of poor harvests: a concept that may be reflected in the biblical stories of Joseph interpreting Pharaoh's dreams. It is also seen in numerous Nilometers, such as the one at Aswan, constructed to gauge the river's rising level.

▲ *To the north of Aswan lie the tombs of the Old and Middle Kingdom Governors of the South, who led the expeditions to Nubia. Among them is the tomb of Harkhuf with its famous autobiography.*

The High Dam

The population continued to grow apace, and after the revolution of 1952 the new regime, under President Gamal Abdul Nasser, decided a new dam was needed. When completed in 1971, the new reservoir, now known as Lake Nasser, stretched 510km (317 miles) to the south. It has a capacity of 150 billion cubic m (5,300 billion cubic ft).

When the decision was made to build the High Dam it was realized that unless drastic measures were taken, many of the Nubian temples would be lost forever. Eventually, UNESCO responded to the appeals of Egypt and Sudan and mounted the Nubia Rescue Campaign. Fifty countries took part and between 1960–80 provided money and expertise in various fields. Wherever possible, the monuments were taken down or cut free from the rock into which they were built and reassembled in areas safe from the rising waters. It was not feasible to move the mudbrick fortresses, such as Buhen, but they were carefully excavated and recorded in detail. Surprisingly, these are at present still in remarkably good condition below the water. Unfortunately, the Nubian people did not fare so well. Their villages were drowned in the flood of water and the population moved elsewhere, some north to Kom Ombo and others to Khasm al-Girba, far to the south of Wadi Halfa. ◆

▶ *This memorial was set up to celebrate the completion of the High Dam in 1971. The dam provides most of Egypt's electricity and makes a major contribution to industrial development.*

Abu Simbel

The most famous of the Nubian temples that were moved to safety by UNESCO are those of Abu Simbel, some 250km (155 miles) south-east of Aswan. They were rock-cut in the reign of Ramesses II (c.1279–c.1213 BC), when Egyptian control of Nubia was possibly at its height. The larger one was dedicated to Re-Horakhty, Amun-Re, Ptah and the deified Ramesses II, and the smaller one to the goddess Hathor and Ramesses' favourite wife, Nefertari.

The two temples were rediscovered in 1813 by the explorer Jean-Louis Burckhardt, who found the heads of the statues of Ramesses protruding from the sand but was neither able to ascertain what they were nor to get inside. The temples were cleared four years later by Giovanni Belzoni, who was rather disappointed that there was little inside that he could take back with him to display in the museums of Europe. In the 1960s they were raised to a new position 65m (213ft) higher up the cliffs and 210m (690ft) to the north-west.

Moving the temples

Various schemes were proposed when the suggestion to move the temples was first put forward. The proposal from the USA was to float both temples on pontoons, which would carry them to the new site as the water rose, while the Polish suggestion was to enclose the site in a spherical shell: tourists would then have been able to visit the temples by going down in lifts within the sphere. Yet other proposals included encasing the site in a transparent tank, through which visitors could view the temples from glass cabins, and cutting the monuments free, setting them up on concrete bases and then using hydraulic jacks to raise the whole lot to safety. In the end it was decided to dismantle the temples by cutting them into carefully numbered blocks and to re-erect them on higher ground close to the original site.

▼ *The larger temple at Abu Simbel was dedicated to the sun gods Re-Horakhty and Amun-Re, the creator god Ptah and the deified Ramesses II.*

▲ *The head of one of the four statues from the façade of the main temple is 19.5m (31ft) high.*

▲ *Ramesses II destroys his enemies in this scene from the main Abu Simbel temple.*

Before the work began, a coffer dam had to be built to protect the temples from the rapidly rising water. Then the temples were sawn into blocks, taking care that the cuts were made where they would be least conspicuous when reassembled. The interior walls and ceilings were suspended from a supporting framework of reinforced concrete. When the temples were reassembled, the joins were made good by a mortar of cement and desert sand. This was done so discreetly that today it is impossible to see where the joins were made. Both temples now stand within an artificial mountain made of rubble and rock, supported by two vast domes of reinforced concrete.

The statues

The visitor is first confronted by the four colossal statues, each 20m (65ft) high, of the deified Ramesses II, which adorn the façade of his temple. Above and between the central statues, his throne name appears in the form of a rebus. In the centre is the figure of the sun god Re, flanked by the *user*-staff and the goddess of peace and justice, Maat. This spells out the king's throne name 'User-maat-re'.

Below the feet of the enthroned king are his traditional enemies: Nubians on the left and Libyans and Hittites on the right. Each throne is decorated with the heraldic plants, the lotus and papyrus, entwined around the hieroglyph for 'unite', to emphasize the fact that Ramesses is in firm control of both Upper and Lower Egypt. Statues of members of the royal family, diminutive in comparison with those of Ramesses but actually more than life-size, are arranged around the king's legs. A row of statues of the hawk-headed sun god Re-Horakhty stand on the platform in front of the statue of the king. ▶

The fallen statue

An earthquake in the 31st year of Ramesses' reign caused a great deal of damage to the temple. The pillars of the Hypostyle Hall cracked and one collapsed. The right arm of the colossus to the right of the doorway fell off, while the upper part of the statue on the left crashed to the ground. Paser, then viceroy of Kush, ordered the restoration of the temple and all but the upper part of the statue was restored. This was still lying where it had fallen when the temple was rediscovered. When it was moved to its new position, the engineers decided to leave the statue as it was found.

▲ *Nefertari is depicted in the temple dedicated to herself and Hathor presenting offerings to Anukis, the guardian goddess of the cataract at Aswan.*

▲ *Seth and Horus are shown crowning Ramesses as king of the Two Lands in this painted relief from the Nefertari temple.*

The temple of Ramesses II

Inside the temple, the ceiling is supported by square pillars embellished with half-engaged figures of the king holding the royal crook and flail. The ceiling itself is painted in the centre with flying vultures and at the sides with stars. The painted reliefs of the walls are very impressive and contain much of historical interest. The two usual themes are present: the king worshipping the gods and celebrating his military triumphs.

Ramesses' most famous victory was at the Battle of Qadesh in 1274 BC. The north wall of the Hypostyle Hall presents a lively account in both reliefs and text. Preparations for battle are being made in the Egyptian camp. Horses are harnessed or given their fodder while one soldier has his wounds dressed. The king's tent is also depicted while another scene shows a council of war between Ramesses and his officers. Two Hittite spies are captured and beaten until they reveal the true whereabouts of Muwatallis, the Hittite king. Finally, the two sides engage in battle, the Egyptians charging in neat formation while the Hittites are in confusion, chariots crashing, horses bolting and soldiers falling into the River Orontes. In the text, Ramesses takes on the whole of the Hittite army single-handed, apart from support rendered by Amun who defends him in battle and finally hands him the victory.

In the Sanctuary, the deified Ramesses sits with Amun-Re, Re-Horakhty and Ptah. Twice a year, on 21 February and 21 October, the rising sun shines directly into the Sanctuary and illuminates the figures of Ramesses and Amun-Re.

Temple of Hathor and Nefertari

The smaller of the two temples at Abu Simbel was dedicated to the local goddess Hathor of Abshek, goddess of love, beauty and motherhood, and to the deified Nefertari, the favourite wife of Ramesses II. The façade is hewn from the rock in imitation of a pylon and is embellished with colossal statues over 10m (32ft) high – four of Ramesses II and two of Nefertari. Here, the statues of Nefertari are the same size as those of her husband, but the royal children placed around their legs are much smaller, although the princesses are bigger than the royal sons.

The central doorway leads to the Hypostyle Hall, which is divided into three aisles by six pillars decorated on the inner side with Hathor-headed *sistra*, the goddess's sacred musical instrument. The other three sides show Ramesses and Nefertari making offerings to deities.

▲ *Nefertari, 'Beloved of Mut', styled here as 'Great Royal Wife and Mistress of the Two Lands', offers a lotus and a* sistrum *to Hathor.*

Although it is dedicated to Nefertari, Ramesses figures largely in the interior of the temple as well as outside. On the south wall is a painted carved relief of the gods Horus and Seth crowning the king. It was usually Horus and Thoth who performed this rite, Seth often being cast in the villain's role because of his murder of Osiris. However, in the Underworld, Seth was seen in a better light as he destroyed the great snake, Apophis, the archenemy of the sun god. Moreover, the family of Ramesses II came from the Delta, where Seth was an important deity, and Ramesses II's father was called Seti after him. On the east wall, Ramesses is shown smiting enemies while Nefertari looks on approvingly. He is also shown offering a tiny image of Maat, goddess of truth and justice, to Amun as a justification of his reign.

Nefertari comes into her own in the Vestibule. She appears on the right of the doorway as a slender figure wearing a close-fitting dress between the mother goddesses Hathor and Isis, who crown her. To balance this, on the left of the doorway, Ramesses, accompanied by Nefertari, offers flowers to Taweret, the goddess of pregnancy and childbirth. She is usually depicted as a pregnant hippopotamus, but here she takes the form of a woman. (Nefertari herself had seven or eight children, although none of her sons lived to become king.) At either end of the Vestibule is a painted relief showing Hathor as a cow emerging from a papyrus thicket. She is worshipped by Nefertari on the south wall and by Ramesses on the north wall.

Leading from the Vestibule is the Sanctuary, on the back wall of which Hathor is seen as a cow coming from the mountain. She is protecting the figure of Ramesses II, who stands under her chin. Otherwise the king and queen are shown making offerings to various deities. One of the most interesting scenes shows Ramesses II burning incense and pouring a libation in front of an image of himself and Nefertari, thus making the statement that they are also gods. Nefertari may not have been well enough to take part in the inauguration ceremony for the temple, and her place was possibly taken by the Princess Merytamun. In any case, she seems to have died shortly afterwards and to have been replaced by Queen Istnofret.

The Abu Simbel stelae

Several stelae were also rescued from the rising water and have been restored as near as possible to their original positions in relation to the two temples. One of the most interesting is on the left of the forecourt of the main temple. This records the marriage of Ramesses II to Naptera, daughter of a later Hittite king, Hattusilis III, which ratified the peace treaty drawn up 15 years after the Battle of Qadesh. Ramesses sits on a throne as the princess is led into his presence by her father. The text says that Ramesses asked Seth, the weather god, to withhold the winter storms until she had safely arrived in Egypt. When he saw her he was bowled over by her beauty and loved her more than anything.

Nearby is the stela of Heqanakht, viceroy of Kush at the time of the temple's dedication in the twenty-fourth year of Ramesses' reign. On the upper part of the stela, the king is shown with his daughter, Merytamun, making offerings to the gods, including the deified Ramesses. On the lower section, Heqanakht is depicted offering to Nefertari.

Further to the south is a double stela showing Ramesses smiting enemies before Amun and Horus, and Setau, another viceroy of Kush, who built the temples of Wadi es-Sebua and Gerf Hussein. The latter is now submerged, although a colossal statue of Ramesses from the site can now be seen in the Nubian Museum in Aswan.

Immediately to the north of the Temple of Hathor is the stela of Iuny, who was viceroy of Kush when the work on the temples was initiated. To the right of this stela is that of Asha-hebsed, who was in charge of the work force. The text tells of Ramesses' decision to build and to give Asha-hebsed the job of organizing the workmen. ◆

Beit el-Wali

The first of a series of temples built in Nubia by Ramesses II (c.1279–c.1213 BC), the Temple of Beit el-Wali lies near to the Ptolemaic Temple of Kalabsha. Both buildings were moved by the UNESCO project to their present location on the western side of Lake Nasser, near the High Dam at Aswan.

The name Beit el-Wali means 'House of the Holy Man' and may indicate its use by a Christian hermit at some point. Although it is relatively tiny, the temple is well worth a visit.

Political control

The Nubian temples of Ramesses II were part of a policy designed to maintain Egyptian control over the region. In the New Kingdom (c.1550–c.1069 BC) Nubia was not only administered by Egyptian officials, there was also a deliberate policy of acculturation, the intention of which was to break down Nubian identity. Many leading Nubians were educated in Egypt and adopted Egyptian dress, burial customs and religion. They spoke the Egyptian language and even changed their names to Egyptian ones. The decoration of the temples was to some extent royal propaganda intended to intimidate the population.

The temple Forecourt

There is a surprising amount of colour left in the inner part of this rock-cut temple, though unfortunately the colour has vanished from the interesting historical scenes in the Forecourt. In the early nineteenth century, the artist Joseph Bonomi removed much of it by taking casts of the painted reliefs. However, he also made careful notes about the colours used so that they could be reproduced later. His casts are now displayed in the British Museum in London. They are of great historical interest as they relate to the earlier part of Ramesses II's reign, when he ruled jointly with his father, Seti I (c.1294–c.1279 BC), and undertook campaigns against the Libyans, Syrians and Nubians.

▼ *A cast of a scene originally in the Forecourt of the Temple of Beit el-Wali shows Nubians presenting their annual tribute of exotic goods to Ramesses II.*

▶ *Ramesses II presides over the annual ceremony when Nubian chieftains and officials presented leopard skins, live animals, gold, precious woods and other exotic items to the king.*

Near the middle of the south wall, Ramesses charges into battle against the Nubians. The reins are tied loosely around his waist so that his hands are free to shoot with his bow and arrow. His young sons, Amenhirwenemhef and Khaemwese, who were then only six and four respectively, are also present. The Nubians flee before the Egyptian onslaught, taking a wounded comrade with them back to their camp among the palms, where all is confusion. The next section shows Ramesses enthroned, receiving the tribute of Nubia. The ceremony is recorded in two registers. In the upper register, Ramesses' eldest son and the viceroy Amenemope present the tribute procession. The viceroy is rewarded for his efforts with gold collars. Among the goods presented are logs of ebony, elephant tusks, ostrich eggs and ostrich-feather fans, rings of gold, elegant chairs and weapons. Below, animal skins, cattle and an exotic collection of monkeys, leopards, a giraffe and a gazelle are brought by the Nubians, some of whom are part of the tribute and would be destined to be taken to Egypt to work on the king's building projects, act as policemen or be recruited into the army for service in Syria.

The theme of Egyptian military success is hammered home on the opposite wall, where Ramesses II's campaigns in Libya and Syria are recorded. Here, Ramesses tramples enemies and holds others by their hair in his left hand while smiting them with his right. The king's personal heroism and military prowess is further displayed in the scene where, charging Bedouin in his chariot, he is shown with his left leg over the front, his foot on the shaft and the reins around his waist, allowing him to seize yet more enemies by the hair and brandish his scimitar at the same time.

The interior of the temple

The theme of the king's military might is carried inside the temple. On the walls of the Vestibule are further smiting scenes to the right and left of the doorway. Otherwise the theme of Ramesses as a pious ruler is taken up, and he is shown worshipping various deities. Beside the doorway leading to the Sanctuary are niches containing statues of the king with (on the left) Isis and Horus and (on the right) Khnum and Anuket, the gods of Elephantine and the First Cataract.

The Sanctuary is also decorated with fine painted reliefs of Ramesses offering to the gods. The most charming scenes are on either side of the doorway and show Ramesses as a child being suckled by the goddesses Isis and Anuket. The statue niche, however, has been destroyed, presumably in the Christian era when the temple was converted into a church. It probably contained a statue of the deified Ramesses sitting between two gods. ◆

◀ *Ramesses II built temples not only to honour the gods but to maintain his authority over a region vital to the Egyptian economy.*

Wadi es-Sebua

The temple at Wadi es-Sebua, which was rescued from the rising waters of Lake Nasser by the Egyptian Antiquities Department in the early 1960s, is perhaps the most attractive of all the Nubian temples. Like those at Abu Simbel, it was built by the Nineteenth Dynasty king Ramesses II (c.1279–c.1213 BC), and was dedicated to the gods Amun-Re, Re-Horakhty and the deified Ramesses II himself. An avenue of sphinxes leads to the temple and affords a most romantic view as it is approached across the desert. The scene from the temple down towards Lake Nasser is equally appealing.

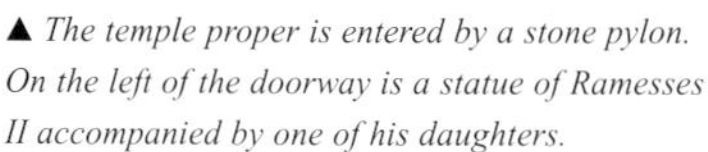

▲ *The temple proper is entered by a stone pylon. On the left of the doorway is a statue of Ramesses II accompanied by one of his daughters.*

The temple precinct

The temple is partly free-standing and partly rock-cut. The gateway to the First Court is embellished with a large standing statue and sphinx of Ramesses II at either side, standing on bases carved with captured enemies. Inside the court there is a short avenue of sphinxes with portrait heads of the king. The avenue continues into the next court but here the four sphinxes represent various local forms of the god Horus. A small figure of Ramesses stands between the paws of each.

The main part of the temple is entered by a stone pylon with a central doorway, which originally had a statue of Ramesses on either side. Only the left-hand one remains in situ, while the other lies a short distance away, out in the desert. The remaining monument is a large standing statue of the king carrying the ram-headed staff of Amun. Ramesses' daughter, Bint-Anath, stands behind his left leg. The pylon itself is decorated in a conventional way, with the king smiting enemies and making offerings to the gods, including himself.

Next comes an open colonnaded court, with columns adorned by Osiris statues of the king. In mythology, before Osiris was murdered by his brother, Seth, he was a real king of Egypt who civilized his people, giving them laws and teaching them agriculture and to worship the gods. The Osiris statues are therefore an appropriate motif in this context, as well as in a mortuary temple, emphasizing Ramesses' role as both king and god, with the wellbeing of his people at heart.

▼ *Looking towards Lake Nasser, the First and Second Courts can be seen. An avenue of sphinxes leads to the main temple.*

Rock-cut halls

The rest of the temple is cut out of the rock and is possibly the most interesting part. It was later used as a Christian church and the original entrance was bricked up to form a double doorway with arches. (This has now been restored to its original state.) The Pillared Hall itself has 12 square pillars, of which

◀ *Ramesses II offers to Re-Horakhty, one of the gods to whom the temple was dedicated.*

the central six were once adorned with Osiris statues of the king: these were chiselled off by the Christians. However, the offering scenes on the walls survive, and some retain their colour. Better still are those of the Vestibule.

The subject of the scenes is traditional, Ramesses is again offering to the gods, but the representation of the goddess Hathor is very unusual. She is usually shown as a woman wearing a sun disc and cow's horns on her head; her face is human and only her ears identify her as a cow goddess. Here, however, she has the head of a cow.

The painted reliefs are in better condition where they were covered over with plaster during the Christian period and so preserved for posterity. The best examples of all are in the Sanctuary and its associated chapels, where there are colourful scenes showing Ramesses adoring the sacred boats of Amun-Re and Re-Horakhty. The central niche once held statues of these gods on either side of Ramesses II. These were hacked away by the Christians and replaced by an image of St Peter, complete with halo and large key. With the plaster removed from the offending carved reliefs the effect is somewhat bizarre, as Ramesses now appears to be offering flowers to St Peter, who has usurped him.

Viceroy Setau

The temple at Wadi es-Sebua was built on behalf of Ramesses II by Setau, who was viceroy of Nubia around 1236 BC. Eleven of his stelae were found in the courtyard of this temple and are now in the Cairo Museum. From these it is possible to trace his own career and to appreciate what the duties of a viceroy were:

I was one whom his Lord caused to be instructed...as a ward of the palace. I grew up in the royal abode when I was a youth...I was provided for, with bread and beer from all the royal meals. I came forth as a scribe from the school, I was appointed to be Chief Scribe of the Vizier; I assessed the whole land with a scroll, I being equal to the task.

Setau attracted the king's attention and was promoted to the posts of 'High Steward of Amun', 'Superintendent of the Treasury of Amun' and 'Festival Leader of Amun' and finally to 'Viceroy of Nubia':

My Lord again found my worth...So I was appointed Viceroy of Nubia... I directed serfs in their thousands and ten-thousands, and Nubians in hundred-thousands, without limit. I brought all the dues of the land of Kush in double measure. I caused the people to come in submission. Then I was commissioned to build the Temple of Ramesses II in the Domain of Amun [Wadi es-Sebua].

He goes on to say that the labour was provided by captives and funded by the booty captured by Ramesses on his campaigns. This statement is backed up by the inscription of an army officer, Ramose, who says:

Year 44: His Majesty commanded... the Viceroy of Nubia, Setau, together with the army personnel of the company of Ramesses II, Amun protects his son, that he should take captives from the land of the Libyans, in order to build the Temple of Ramesses II in the Domain of Amun... ◆

▼ *Ramesses II offers to Horus a figure of the goddess Maat, who represents the ideal world order, to demonstrate his fitness to rule.*

New Amada

The oldest of the temples rescued from Lake Nasser is that of the Eighteenth Dynasty king Tuthmosis III (c.1479–c.1425 BC) at Amada. Like many of the Nubian temples, it was dedicated to Amun and Re-Horakhty. The temple was moved by a team of French engineers, who dismantled the front section and then jacked up the rear on to flat-cars and painstakingly moved it backwards 2.6km (1.6 miles) to its present position.

Although the temple looks rather dull from the outside, it is well worth a visit. Inside, the painted carved reliefs are some of the most attractive in Nubia: they are finely cut and the colours are astonishingly bright and fresh. Like those of Wadi es-Sebua they have been protected by a layer of plaster placed over them by the Christians when the temple was used as a church.

▲ *Built by the Eighteenth Dynasty kings, this is the oldest of the temples dedicated to Re-Horakhty and Amun.*

The temple interior

The original plan of the temple had a pylon, forecourt and portico leading to a vestibule and sanctuary. However, Tuthmosis IV (c.1400–c.1390 BC) roofed over the forecourt and turned it into a pillared hall. The pillars and walls are decorated with offering scenes, with those involving Tuthmosis IV on the left and, on the right, Tuthmosis III and Amenhotep II (c.1427–c.1400 BC), his grandfather and father respectively. The strategic aspect of this Nubian temple can be seen in the title used here by Tuthmosis IV, 'Beloved of Senusret III'. This famous Middle Kingdom king was regarded as a god by the kings of the Eighteenth Dynasty because of his earlier conquest of Nubia.

The best painted reliefs are in the innermost part of the temple, where Tuthmosis III and Amenhotep II are shown being embraced by various deities or making offerings to them. On the left-hand side of the Vestibule, coronation rituals are illustrated: Amenhotep II is crowned by the gods Horus and Thoth and is shown running with oar and *hap* (a navigational instrument). The small cult room at the side of the Sanctuary contains some interesting scenes depicting the foundation ceremony and the consecration of the temple. They include the ritual of the 'stretching of the cord', the ceremonial making and laying of bricks, and the offering of the temple to its gods. Animal sacrifice and the consecration of ritual vessels and temple vestments are also shown.

Temple stelae

The temple contains several interesting inscriptions, which reveal something of the history of Egypt and Nubia, as well as of the temple itself, during the reigns of some of the New Kingdom rulers. From these it can be seen that the work was begun by Tuthmosis III and later completed by Amenhotep II and Tuthmosis IV, with restoration work and further decoration by kings of the Ramesside Period (c.1295–c.1069 BC).

▶ *Tuthmosis IV converted an open court to a roofed, pillared hall in the temple of Amada. His cartouche can be seen on the pillar.*

During the Amarna Period, the 'heretic' king Akhenaten (c.1352–c.1336 BC) obliterated the name of the god Amun throughout the temple, although this was later restored by Seti I (c.1294–c.1279 BC). The stelae of the viceroys Setau, Heqanakht and Messuy tell of their building activities on behalf of the Nineteenth Dynasty kings Ramesses II (c.1279–c.1213 BC) and Merenptah (c.1213–c.1203 BC), and of the chancellor Bay under Saptah (c.1194–c.1188 BC).

The two most important historical inscriptions deal with the military exploits of Amenhotep II and Merenptah. A large stela describes the success of Amenhotep's campaign against the rulers of Retenu, the city-states of

▶ *Part of a coronation scene from the vestibule of the Sanctuary shows Thoth, god of wisdom, purifying Amenhotep II.*

Syria–Palestine, and show that he dealt with them ruthlessly:

> *...His Majesty returned with joy of heart to his father, Amun, when he slew with his own mace the seven princes who had been in the district of Tikhsi. They had been put upside-down at the prow of His Majesty's barge...He put six of those fallen ones on the wall of Thebes, and the hands as well. Then the other fallen one was taken up-river and hanged on the wall of Napata [a frontier city near the Fourth Cataract] to show His Majesty's victories forever and ever in all lands...to the ends of the earth, so that he may set his boundary wherever he wishes without opposition according to the command of his father, Amun-Re, Lord of the Thrones of the Two Lands...*

The message is clear. Although the campaign had been conducted far away from Nubia, the hanging of the body of one of the princes of Retenu on the walls of Napata acted as a dreadful warning of the consequences of rebellion – and all in the name of Amun. Merenptah's inscription records the suppression of an insurrection in Nubia itself, which had Libyan backing. These inscriptions clearly show the way temples were used by the New Kingdom kings to maintain their hold on Nubia. ◆

The tomb of Penmut

Nearby is the tomb of Penmut, 'Deputy of Wawat' (Lower Nubia), 'Chief of the Quarry Service' and 'Steward of Horus, Lord of Miam', during the reign of Ramesses VI (c.1143–c.1136 BC). He was the chief administrator in Lower Nubia, second only in importance to the viceroy of Kush. So thoroughly did the Egyptians replace the native culture with their own that it is not possible to tell whether Penmut was Egyptian or Nubian. He was probably an Egyptianized Nubian, as members of his family also had tombs in the area, while there is a great deal of evidence to show that the Egyptians chose to be buried at home even when they died abroad. Penmut's tomb is rock-cut and has a small offering chapel decorated with scenes of his life: several concern his dedication of a statue of Ramesses VI and his reward of a gold collar.

▶ *Pillars in the Hypostyle Hall are decorated with cartouches of Tuthmosis IV and carved reliefs of the king.*

Expeditions to Nubia

From the beginning of ancient Egyptian history, the kings had been anxious to exploit Nubia in order to obtain the exotic luxuries it could supply. The expeditions they ordered for this purpose are described in the tomb inscriptions of Upper Egyptian officials and others who were responsible for organizing such missions.

Some tell of the hazards of their trips. Sabni, a governor of the South, writes that his father Mekhu was killed undertaking an expedition. Sabni set off in hot pursuit and managed to recover his father's body and bring it home for burial in Egypt. When the king heard about it he congratulated Sabni on his prompt action and provided the embalming materials for the burial of Mekhu.

Harkhuf's expeditions

Many of the expeditions used donkey caravans, as the autobiography of Harkhuf attests. It is inscribed on the façade of his tomb opposite modern Aswan. Harkhuf was a very important official during the reigns of the later Old Kingdom kings, Merenre (c.2287–c.2278 BC) and Pepi II (c.2278–c.2184 BC). His titles included 'Governor of Upper Egypt', 'Royal Seal Bearer' and 'Chief of Scouts', the two latter making clear that one of his main tasks as governor was to mount expeditions on behalf of the king.

Harkhuf's autobiography records three such missions, the first being undertaken with his father, another senior official, which was apparently very successful: 'I did it in seven months, I brought from it all kinds of beautiful and rare gifts and was praised for it very greatly.' A second expedition was equally successful, but Harkhuf experienced some difficulty on his third mission. The local chiefs put up some resistance until he won the support of the Chief of Yam. Then he was able to come home triumphant with 'three hundred donkey loads of incense, ebony, [precious] oils, panther skins, elephant tusks, throw sticks and all good products'.

However, the autobiography reveals that the thing that most delighted the child king Pepi II was a dancing pygmy (perhaps a dwarf) whom Harkhuf had obtained for him, and he anxiously insisted that great care was taken to look after him. The young king wrote a letter of thanks to Harkhuf, who proudly had a copy of it displayed on his tomb:

▲ *This typical fishing and fowling scene comes from the tomb of Mekhu and Sabni at Aswan. Sabni retrieved his father's body from Nubia after he was killed while on an expedition.*

Come north to the residence at once! Hurry and bring with you this pygmy whom you have brought from the land of the horizon-dwellers live, hale, and hearty, for the dances of the god, to gladden the heart, to delight the heart of King Neferkare [Pepi II] who lives forever! When he goes with you down into the ship, get worthy men to be around him on deck, lest he fall into the water! When he lies down at night, get worthy men to lie around him in his tent. Inspect ten times at night! My Majesty desires to see this pygmy more than the gifts of the mainland [Sinai] and of Punt.

Bypassing the cataract

The First Cataract, with its rocks and rapids, was a serious obstacle to river traffic south of Aswan. Attempts were made at an early stage to get around it by digging canals. The Autobiography of Weni, a governor of the south during the Sixth Dynasty (c.2345–c.2181 BC), mentions that he was instructed by the king to dig five canals in Upper Egypt. This may be a reference to such a venture.

The island of Sehel, which lies about 4km (2.5 miles) south of Aswan, is covered with over 200 rock inscriptions. They are dedications to the deities of the cataract, Khnum, Satet and Anuket, placed there to seek a blessing for the hazardous journey ahead into Nubia, or in thanksgiving for a safe and successful return home. Most date from the Eighteenth and Nineteenth Dynasties (c.1550–c.1186 BC) and several refer to the canals.

▲ *This inscription of Amenhotep II on the island of Sehel at the First Cataract commemorates an expedition to Nubia to procure luxury goods.*

▲ *Part of the letter from the child king, Pepi II, expressing his gratitude to Harkhuf for the dancing pygmy the official brought for him.*

Two of the inscriptions are of the Twelfth Dynasty king Senusret III (c.1874–c.1855 BC), and record his instructions for the digging of a canal as well as his conquest of Nubia. Later kings found the canal blocked and had to redo the work.

Two inscriptions from the reign of Tuthmosis I (c.1504–1492 BC), an early Eighteenth Dynasty king, have also come to light. One, in the name of Thure, the king's son, is incomplete but it has been possible to restore the text by comparison with an inscription of Tuthmosis III (c.1479–c.1425 BC), which repeats part of it:

Year 3, first month of the third season, day 22, under the majesty of the King of Upper and Lower Egypt, Aakheperkare [Tuthmosis I] who is given life. His Majesty commanded to dig this canal after he found it stopped up with stones [so that] no [ship sailed upon it]. He [sailed downstream] upon it, his heart [glad having slain his enemies].

Another inscription, also dedicated by Thure states:

'Year 3, first month of the third season, day 22, His Majesty sailed this canal in victory and in the power of his return from overthrowing the wretched Kush'.

In the inscription of Tuthmosis III, he adds:

The name of this canal is: Opener of the Way in the Beauty of Menkheperre [Tuthmosis III] Living Forever. The fishermen of Elephantine shall clear this canal every year. ◆

◀ *This agricultural scene is from one of the tombs of the high officials at Aswan.*

Nubian Temples of the Graeco-Roman Period

From the end of the Twentieth Dynasty (c.1069 BC), Egyptian power declined and Nubia became an independent state ruled from Napata. Three centuries later, the Nubians came into their own when the Kushite kings of Napata took over Egypt and ruled as the Twenty-fifth Dynasty. Unfortunately, in 701 BC one of their most illustrious kings, Taharqo (690–664 BC), antagonized the Assyrian king, Sennacherib, by going to the aid of his rebellious vassal, King Hezekiah of Jerusalem. This resulted in the Assyrian invasion of Egypt, culminating in the devastation of Thebes by Ashurbanipal in 664 BC, after which the Kushites were forced to retreat.

Not long afterwards the Nubians moved their capital further south to Meroe, between the Fifth and Sixth Cataracts. This Meroitic kingdom was contemporary with the Twenty-seventh to the Thirtieth Dynasties and the Ptolemaic and Roman Periods (525 BC–AD 395) in Egypt. During the Ptolemaic Period (332–30 BC), the two powers seem to have been on good terms and collaborated in the building of some of the temples in Nubia. All these have been rescued from the rising waters of Lake Nasser and removed to higher ground, except for Dabod, which was taken to Madrid, and Dendur, which is now in the Metropolitan Museum of Art, New York.

▲ *Originally located 50km (31 miles) south of the High Dam, the Temple of Kalabsha has been moved to higher ground much closer to Aswan. Built largely in the late Ptolemaic and Roman Periods, it was never completed, but is regarded as one of the best examples of Egyptian architecture in Nubia.*

Dakka

The Temple of Dakka was begun by the Kushite king, Arkamani, and was extended by his contemporary Ptolemy IV (221–205 BC). A pylon and sanctuary were added in the Roman Period (30 BC–AD 395).

The temple was dedicated to Thoth of Pnubs. The god's title is a reference to the sycamore-fig tree under which he waited for Tefnut, his wife, to return to Egypt. Tefnut was the goddess of moisture, born from the expectoration of her father, Atum, and in Ptolemaic temples her name was sometimes written with the hieroglyph of two lips spitting. In a demotic papyrus she appears as the eye of Re, who quarrelled with her father and rampaged through Nubia. Thoth, the god of wisdom, and Shu, the god of air, were sent to try to persuade her to come back. This story was used as the starting point for a series of further tales told by Thoth to entertain his wife on the return journey. A carved relief in the Sanctuary shows Thoth in his baboon form sitting under the sycamore-fig tree. In the Roman side chapel, Thoth, again in the form of a baboon, is depicted worshipping Tefnut in the form of a lioness. The son of Thoth and Tefnut was Arsenuphis, a Meroitic god. In this temple both Thoth and Arsenuphis wear short Nubian wigs and headdresses of four feathers. Throughout the temple the Ptolemies are shown as traditional Egyptian kings worshipping many of the Egyptian gods.

▲ *The Kiosk of Qertassi was possibly a way station on the processional route around Lower Nubia, which was regarded as the estate of Isis.*

Kalabsha

The extant Temple of Kalabsha appears to be Roman in date, although representations of Amenhotep II (c.1427–c.1400 BC) and one of the Ptolemies in the Hypostyle Hall suggest that it was built on the site of an earlier construction. The temple was dedicated to Mandulis, a Nubian form of Horus, and was also associated with Osiris and Isis. Mandulis was usually depicted wearing an elaborate headdress of ram's horns, cobras, and plumes surmounted by sun discs. Sometimes he is seen in the form of a hawk, but with a human head. His wife was Wadjet, the cobra goddess, and their child was a young form of Mandulis, so they appear in the temple decoration as counterparts of Osiris, Isis and Horus.

Traditional scenes occur throughout, of Horus and Thoth purifying the king and the king or emperor making offerings to various deities. There are also some interesting inscriptions on the forecourt wall opposite the pylon. One, in Greek, is by a governor of Elephantine, ordering the pigs to be driven from the temple. Another is in the cursive Meroitic script and was written by one of the kings of the Blemmyes (c. AD 4), while the most interesting is an account by Silko, the Christian king of the Nubian kingdom of Nobatia, celebrating his victory over the Blemmyes.

▲ *Hathor, identified by her diadem and erect* uraeus, *is often associated with Isis as the mother of Horus and, by analogy, of the king, to whom she offers her breast.*

Philae

The great cult centre of Isis, wife of Osiris and mother of Horus, was at Philae. The temple was built by the Ptolemies and Roman emperors between about 200 BC and AD 300. Isis was the epitome of motherhood and had a reputation for healing. Inscriptions show that Philae was an important centre of pilgrimage, dear to both Egyptians and Nubians, who remained faithful to Isis long after the introduction of Christianity. The temple was essential to the Ptolemies and Roman emperors who, although foreigners, continued to regard themselves, as the pharaohs had done, as reincarnations of Horus, and were depicted as such in the temple decoration.

The Kiosk of Qertassi

This charming little kiosk has been re-erected near to the Temple of Kalabsha, but once stood at the entrance to the sandstone quarries. The capitals are decorated with Hathor heads, in honour of the goddess who was patron of quarry-men and miners. As Hathor was often associated with Isis, as she is at Philae, it has been suggested that this kiosk and the small temples of Dabod and Dendur were way stations on the processional route taken by priests bearing the image of Isis around Lower Nubia, which was held to be her estate. ◆

Qasr Ibrim

Viewed from the deck of a Lake Nasser cruise ship, Qasr Ibrim appears to be an island. The site, however, once stood on the highest of three headlands on the east bank of the Nile, 70m (230ft) above the river. The waters of the lake have recently reached unexpected levels and each year encroach further on the site. Visitors are no longer allowed to wander around the ruins as they once did and can only view them from the ships, which moor close to the site while the guides point out the salient features. The Egypt Exploration Society continues its work at the site.

History of the site

The name means Fort of Ibrim and is ultimately derived from its ancient Meroitic name, Pedeme. In classical texts it was called Primis and in Coptic, Phrim, which was corrupted to Ibrim in Arabic. The fort may well have originated in the Middle Kingdom (c.2055–c.1650 BC) when the Twelfth Dynasty kings were establishing control of the trade route along the Nile, although the earliest archaeological evidence for fortification dates to c.1000 BC. The strategic importance of Qasr Ibrim was widely recognized, and fighting for the possession of the site took place for centuries until modern times. It was not finally abandoned until 1811.

The earliest inscriptional evidence at Qasr Ibrim is from the reign of Amenhotep I (c.1525–c.1504 BC) of the early New Kingdom. It is a stela dated to the eighth year of his reign and is now in the British Museum in London. The stela was not found in situ but in the cathedral, where it had been reused in one of the crypts.

That the site was of religious as well as strategic importance is clear from four New Kingdom shrines cut low down into the cliffs facing the ancient district capital of Miam (modern Aniba). These shrines were dedicated by high officials of the Eighteenth Dynasty (c.1550–c.1295 BC) and were dedicated to local forms of Horus as well as to the deities of the First Cataract and to Hathor, protectress of expeditions. Although the site in general was thought to be in no danger from the lake, these shrines, lying as they did close to the water's edge, were removed. The shrine of Usersatet, viceroy of Kush in the reign of Amenhotep II (c.1427–c.1400 BC) has been re-erected in the new Nubian Museum in Aswan, and there are plans to relocate the others at New Sabua. A stela of Seti I (c.1294–c.1279 BC) has already been moved to New Kalabsha where it has been re-erected just to the south of the main Ptolemaic temple.

After the defeat of Antony and Cleopatra at the Battle of Actium in 31 BC, Egypt became part of the Roman Empire and a Roman garrison was established at Aswan. This was

▼ *An important fortress in Pharaonic and Roman times, Qasr Ibrim is also the site of several temples, dating from the reign of Taharqo to the late Meroitic period.*

▲ *After Christianity had been introduced to Nubia, the Temple of Taharqo became a church. In the 7th century, a cathedral was built on the site and dedicated to the Virgin Mary.*

attacked by a Nubian queen, probably Amanirenas, and Aswan, Elephantine and Philae were briefly occupied by the Nubians. The bronze statue head of Emperor Augustus (27 BC–AD 14), now in the British Museum in London, was probably taken by the Nubians during this raid. It was found at Meroe, buried in front of the small temple there. The Nubians were driven south and the Romans occupied Qasr Ibrim where they hoped to fix their southern boundary. However, the Nubians again attacked, after which a peace treaty was drawn up and the Romans withdrew.

Temples and churches

The earliest religious building on the site was the mudbrick Temple of King Taharqo (690–664 BC). This was later converted into a Christian church. In the Roman Period (30 BC–AD 395), the traditional Egyptian gods continued to be worshipped here long after Christianity had taken root and become the official religion of the Empire. Christianity also had a long history at Qasr Ibrim and for several centuries held out against the growing influence of Islam.

Qasr Ibrim prospered in the years following the Nubian raids. Several new temples were built and the old Temple of Taharqo was repaired. These establishments gained reputations as healing centres and were much visited by those seeking cures. Although most of the temples dedicated to the old gods were formally closed by Theodosius I in AD 390, those of Qasr Ibrim continued to flourish.

At some point that has not yet been determined, Christianity was introduced at Qasr Ibrim. The Temple of Taharqo became a church and the Temple of Isis was destroyed. In the seventh century a cathedral church dedicated to the Virgin Mary was built on the headland, using some of the blocks from the old temples. Qasr Ibrim then became a great centre of pilgrimage and later, a bishopric. It was not until the sixteenth century that Christianity was replaced by Islam, when Egypt was conquered by the Ottoman Turks and a garrison of Bosnian mercenaries was installed. ◆

The grave of Bishop Timotheos

The intact grave of Bishop Timotheos was found in the north crypt of the cathedral. He had been buried in the late fourteenth century together with his letters of appointment from the Patriarch of Alexandria, which are dated 1372. At this time Christian burials were usually very simple, the body being wrapped in a shroud and laid in a pit covered with stones or a brick canopy. Grave goods were no longer provided in the burials of ordinary people. However, those of clerics were rather more splendid. Bishop Timotheos was buried in his bishop's robes with his benedictional iron cross and other belongings. These are now in the British Museum in London, which also has a page from the Book of Revelation written in the Old Nubian language using the Coptic alphabet. This, too, was found at Qasr Ibrim.

The Delta and Oases

The Delta is the triangular area to the north of modern Cairo, named by the Greeks after the fourth letter of their alphabet because it resembled its shape. In antiquity, the ancient capital of Memphis stood at the point where the River Nile, on leaving the Valley, divided into several branches as it wended its way to the sea. At least five channels existed in the Pharaonic Period, but most dried up between the tenth and twelfth centuries AD, leaving only two in evidence today. Low-lying and fringed by lagoons, wetlands and lakes, the Delta was a very fertile area famous for its rich pastures where goats, sheep and especially cattle were raised. Milk, honey and wine were also produced. Ancient cities grew up across the region, including Tanis, Bubastis and Alexandria.

In the Libyan Desert to the west of the Nile Valley, a string of oases lies virtually parallel to the Nile, the most important of which are Kharga, Dakhla, Farafra and Bahariya. They have been settled since the Stone Age and at Kharga there are traces of early agriculture. From the beginnings of Egyptian history, the inhabitants traded with Egypt, supplying aromatic woods, leather goods, agricultural produce, salt, natron and minerals.

◀ *The Siwa Oasis is a natural depression in the Libyan desert and the site of the famous oracle visited by Alexander the Great in 332 BC.*

Tanis

One of the most important Delta sites was Tanis. At the end of the Twentieth Dynasty (c.1069 BC), the rule of Egypt was divided: the kings ruled from new capital cities in the Delta while the high priests of Amun at Karnak governed the South from Thebes. Tanis was the capital city of King Smendes (c.1069–c.1043 BC), the first king of the Twenty-first Dynasty, and it retained its importance throughout the Late Period (c.747–332 BC). So many statues, carved reliefs and inscriptions of the Nineteenth Dynasty king Ramesses II (c.1279–c.1213 BC) were found there, however, that when the site was first excavated, it was assumed that Tanis was the site of Per-Ramesses, the brand new capital established by Ramesses and his father Seti I (c.1294–c.1279 BC). This caused great excitement because it was thought that the excavators had found the city where, according to the Bible, the Hebrews had worked as slaves. Modern excavation, however, has proved that it was not the city of Ramesses II, which lies a short distance away near the modern village of Qantir. Later kings used Per-Ramesses as a quarry when they were building the temples of Tanis, and this explains why there is so much Ramesses II material there.

The site of Tanis was first excavated by Auguste Mariette and Flinders Petrie towards the end of the nineteenth century. Since then, French archaeologists have been working at Tanis, in particular Pierre Montet, who made spectacular discoveries between 1921 and 1951.

▲ *A sphinx of Amenemhat III found at Tanis was originally from the Temple of Bastet at Bubastis. It was taken to Per-Ramesses in the eastern Delta and subsequently to Tanis by Psusennes I.*

The Temple of Amun

Excavation has revealed an enormous mudbrick enclosure wall surrounding the great Temple of Amun. The monumental gateway, or Propylon, was decorated in the reign of the Twenty-second Dynasty king Sheshonq III (c.825–c.773 BC), who is depicted on some of the blocks. Statues of Ramesses II, brought from Per-Ramesses, were also used to embellish the entrance to the temple precinct, including a fine quartzite colossus. On the right is a triad carved in high relief showing Ramesses II between the gods Re and Ptah-Tatenen. Another colossal figure, itself from an earlier period and usurped by Ramesses II, was also used to adorn the entrance.

Beyond the monumental gateway, fragments of yet more colossal statues and carved blocks, obelisks and columns can be seen. These had been used as fill

▶ *Strewn all over the site at Tanis are blocks bearing the names and image of Ramesses II, which led archaeologists to believe that Tanis was the Ramesside capital.*

for the Propylon. One block shows Ramesses II running his *heb sed* race before the god Horus. Sections of four columns with palm-leaf capitals, originally part of an Old Kingdom structure and also usurped by Ramesses II, had been reused in the building of a kiosk in the outer court of the temple. The entrance to the temple proper was once marked by two obelisks, as were the Second and Third Pylons. Beyond the wall is the smaller Sanctuary of Mut and Khonsu, the wife and son of Amun. Astarte, a goddess of Syrian origin regarded as the daughter of either Re or Ptah, was also worshipped here.

▶ *It is now known that statues and other architectural remains of Ramesses II were brought to Tanis from the Ramesside capital by the kings of the 21st Dynasty.*

Statues from the temple

From the Second Court of the temple came some of the statues now in the Cairo Museum. One of the most remarkable shows Ramesses II as a child, naked and with his index finger in his mouth, squatting in front of the Canaanite god, Horon. He wears a sun disc on his head and holds a plant in his hand. The whole thing is a rebus that spells out his name. The sun disc stands for Ra (Re), the child is *mes* and the plant *sw*. Ramesses is protected by the huge falcon representing Horon, who was worshipped mainly in the Giza area where workers from Canaan were installed during the New Kingdom Period (c.1550–c.1069 BC). They seem to have associated Horon with Horemakhet or 'Horus-in-the-Horizon', the Great Sphinx at Giza, which was regarded as the sun god at this time. According to the Egyptian tradition revealed in the Dream Stela of Tuthmosis IV (c.1400–c.1390 BC) erected between its paws, the Sphinx was the god who chose the next king. Thus, in the Tanis statue, Ramesses is shown as crown prince, chosen and protected by the sun god.

Another interesting statue from the Second Court takes the form of a sphinx. The unusual features of the king, and the fact that the statue was inscribed with the cartouches of one of the Hyksos kings of the Second Intermediate Period (c.1650–c.1550 BC), led the excavators to think that it was a Hyksos work. However, comparison with other statues has revealed that this was actually a portrait statue of the Twelfth Dynasty king Amenemhat III (c.1855–c.1808 BC), probably originating from the Temple of Bastet. It had been usurped first by the Hyksos king, Nehesy, then by Ramesses II who transferred it to his new capital at Per-Ramesses, and by his son Merenptah (c.1213–c.1203 BC). Finally, it was brought to Tanis by the Twenty-first Dynasty king Psusennes I (c.1039–c.991 BC), who added his own name to it and used it to embellish the Temple of Amun. ◆

The Royal Tombs of Tanis

The kings of the Twenty-first and Twenty-second Dynasties (c.1069–c715 BC) were buried at Tanis, rather than in the Valley of the Kings. The tombs were originally underground and were built of mudbrick and reused inscribed stone blocks. Those belonging to Psusennes I (c.1039–c.991 BC), Amenemope (c.993–c.984 BC), Osorkon II (c.874–c.850 BC), and Sheshonq III (c.825–c.773 BC) have been discovered. The tomb of Psusennes I, however, contained the silver hawk-headed coffin of Sheshonq II (c.890 BC) and the coffin and sarcophagus of Amenemope, while that of Takelot II (c.850–c.825 BC) turned up in the tomb of Osorkon II. Two other tombs have been found but the identities of their owners are not known.

▶ *Found in the intact tomb of Psusennes I, this elegant vase was used to pour libations to the gods. It is decorated with the name of Amenemope, Psusennes' son and successor.*

▼ *The funerary mask of Psusennes I depicts the idealized features of the king. It is made of gold and lapis lazuli with inlays of black and white glass for the eyes and eyebrows.*

The royal jewellery

During his excavations in Tanis, Pierre Montet found some wonderful jewellery in the tombs. It is considered to be even more splendid than the jewellery of Tutankhamun. Little attention was given to the discovery at the time, however, because Montet found it in 1939, just at the outbreak of World War II, when there were more urgent concerns. The royal jewellery is today on display in the Cairo Museum and is well worth a visit.

Ancient Egyptians of all walks of life loved jewellery. From the earliest days of Egyptian history there is evidence of gold-working and the use of semi-precious stones such as amethyst, carnelian and turquoise in jewellery-making. Much has been found in tombs, as the Egyptians took the jewellery they had worn during their earthly life with them to the Afterlife. They also had some jewellery made specially for the tomb.

The jewellery found at Tanis is full of religious imagery and significance. Worked into the designs are many amuletic devices to enable the king and his high officials to journey safely through the Underworld and become united to Osiris and the sun god in the Afterlife. The jewellery and other artefacts from the Tanis tombs are the most important evidence found so far concerning royal funerary equipment in the Third Intermediate Period.

▲ *This small vase with 24 gadroons is a type known since the Middle Kingdom. Found in the tomb of Psusennes I, it is decorated on the right with the king's cartouches and on the left with those of his mother, Queen Henuttawy. Part of the king's funerary equipment, it is a fine example of the craftsmen's work at Tanis.*

The pectoral of Psusennes I

An openwork gold cloisonné pectoral, or chest ornament, was found on the mummy of King Psusennes I. The decoration includes images of Isis on the right, and Nephthys on the left, on either side of a winged scarab. In mythology, Isis, the wife of Osiris, and Nephthys, his sister, searched for the body of Osiris after he had been murdered by Seth. When they had found it, they restored Osiris to life. The hope expressed here is that they will do the same for King Psusennes.

The winged scarab, of lapis lazuli, represents Khepri, the sun god of the morning. He is pushing the ball of the sun along in front of him, showing that he is responsible for its rising. The sun is placed over the cartouche of King Psusennes, and the imagery suggests that the king will enter his new life after his hazardous journey through the Underworld, just as the sun, having overcome his enemies during the hours of darkness, rises again as the new day dawns.

Below the main section is a row of alternating *djed*-pillars. These represent the backbone of Osiris, and in this context his resurrection, and the girdle of Isis, which she tied around her little son, Horus, to give him magical protection.

The pectoral of Sheshonq I

Some of the jewellery found at Tanis had been reused. Another pectoral, also made in gold-inlaid openwork, had been made for Sheshonq I (c.945–c.924 BC) but was found on the mummy of Sheshonq II. The inscribed lapis lazuli sun disc, sailing in the sun god's boat through the Underworld, is protected by images of Maat, goddess of justice and truth. The Eye of Horus between the wings of the goddess is a symbol of new life, as in mythology Horus restored Osiris to life by giving him his Eye. Lotus flowers are suspended below: they represent creation, as the sun god was born from a lotus. In this instance, however, they symbolize re-creation and the beginning of the Afterlife.

The bracelet of Sheshonq II

A particularly fine piece is the gold bracelet of Sheshonq II. It is made in imitation of a finger ring, with the bezel in the form of a lapis lazuli scarab beetle standing on a gold base decorated with braiding. The main part of the bracelet is beautiful in its simplicity, completely unadorned apart from the two stylized papyrus heads at either side of the bezel.

The bangles of Psusennes I

A pair of solid gold bangles was found on the mummy of Psusennes. Each is extremely heavy, weighing almost 1.8kg (4lb). The outside is plain, but the king's name is inscribed on the inside, together with a blessing to guarantee his safe arrival in the Afterlife. ◆

▼ *This gold and lapis lazuli bangle was found on the right arm of Psusennes I. Another lay in the sarcophagus beside him. Made of two unequal parts slotted into each other and fastened with a pin, the joins are hidden by the lapis lazuli set in the hollow ring of sheet gold.*

Bubastis

The ancient name of Bubastis was Per-Bastet, and the city was the cult centre of Bastet, the cat goddess. The town and the temple lie 80km (50 miles) north-east of Cairo.

Bubastis was an important town from the Old Kingdom (c.2686–c.2181 BC) to the Roman Period (30 BC–AD 395). The chief attraction was the Temple of Bastet, built of red granite and embellished with images of the goddess and the various kings who paid their respects to her here. Apart from the main temple, Bubastis is the site of the *ka*-temples of the Sixth Dynasty kings Teti (c.2345–c.2323 BC) and Pepi I (c.2321–c.2287 BC), and the jubilee chapels of the Twelfth Dynasty king Amenemhat III (c.1855–c.1808 BC) and the Eighteenth Dynasty king Amenhotep III (c.1390–c.1352 BC), as well as temples to Atum, the creator god, and Mihos, a lion god and son of Bastet.

The Temple of Bastet

Herodotus, the ancient Greek traveller and historian, visited the town in the fifth century BC and much of his description of the site tallies with what Edouard Naville found during his excavations at the end of the nineteenth century. Bubastis is in a rather ruinous condition today, having been used as a quarry at various times, although strenuous attempts are now being made to restore the temple to its former glory. The work was begun by the Fourth Dynasty kings Khufu (c.2589–c.2566 BC) and Khafre (c.2558–c.2532 BC), builders of the largest of the Giza pyramids, and continued by Amenemhat I (c.1985–c.1955 BC) and Ramesses II (c.1279–c.1213 BC).

Bubastis was also the home of the kings of the Twenty-second Dynasty (c.945–c.715 BC) and so grew in importance at this time, although the capital remained at Tanis. Osorkon II (c.874–c.850 BC) built a new hypostyle hall in the temple, and added a further

▼ *Bubastis, the cult centre of the cat goddess Bastet, is now in ruins. Little remains of the red granite Temple of Bastet.*

◀ *This bronze cat depicts Bastet. Her nose ring and earrings are ancient but may not have belonged to the statue originally.*

hall to celebrate his *heb sed*, or jubilee festival. He also decorated the walls and monumental gateway in relief. Many of these carved reliefs are now scattered in museums throughout the world. There is a fine example in the British Museum in London showing Osorkon and his wife, Karoma, making offerings to Bastet and recording his jubilee.

Further work was done by Nectanebo II (360–343 BC), the last king of the Thirtieth Dynasty. Present work on the site includes the restoration of the hypostyle hall of Osorkon II, with its closed papyriform columns. Numerous statues of Ramesses II and Bastet have also come to light.

Bastet, the goddess

Although Bastet was a local deity, she was of great importance to the kings of Egypt. Like Hathor and Sekhmet, the lioness goddess, with whom she could be associated, she was regarded as the daughter of the sun god. Cat-like, she had both gentle and fierce aspects to her nature. To the ancient Egyptians of the Late Period (c.747–332 BC) the cat epitomized the protective aspects of motherhood, so Bastet was honoured as one of the mothers of kings. She was mentioned on the façade of the valley temple of Khafre at Giza together with Hathor, another of the king's mothers, and in one of the spells in the Pyramid Texts she is specifically named as 'My mother Bastet [who] has nursed me'.

Although the earliest representations of Bastet, from the Second Dynasty (c.2890–c.2686 BC), depicted her with the head of a lioness, by the Late Period she was usually shown with the head of a domestic cat, often accompanied by her kittens. She was often shown carrying a *sistrum*, linking her with Hathor.

Bastet's festival

The fifth-century BC Greek writer Herodotus described the annual festival of Bastet at Bubastis, although he actually called the goddess Artemis. Artemis was the Greek goddess of hunting and so was appropriately equated with Bastet, the cat goddess:

The men and women come together in barges, each boat packed with large numbers of people. On the way the women shake their castanets and some of the men play flutes. Everyone else sings and claps their hands. Whenever they pass by a town on the river bank, they bring the barge close to the shore...Some of the women hurl abuse at the women of the town or start dancing and hitch up their skirts (in an unseemly manner). When they get to Bubastis they offer sacrifices and consume huge amounts of wine, more than that drunk during the whole of the rest of the year.

Cat cemeteries

Associated with the cult of Bastet were the cat cemeteries, which lay to the north of the city. These were underground vaulted galleries where mummified cats and hundreds of bronzes of Bastet were buried. The cemeteries were excavated by the Egyptian Antiquities Service in the early 1960s but most of the galleries had been robbed, the attractive figures of Bastet and her kittens being a favourite with antique collectors. In fact they were so popular that many fakes were produced and found their way on to the antiquities market. ◆

▶ *In the Late Period, Bastet was often shown as a mother cat with her kittens. The* sistrum *links her with Hathor, one of the traditional mothers of kings.*

Alexandria Lost and Found

According to the Greek historians, Plutarch (c. AD 46–c.126) and Arrian (c. AD 95–180), the city of Alexandria was not only named after, but also founded by Alexander the Great, who ruled Egypt from 332 to 323 BC. In his history of Alexander's campaigns, Arrian wrote, 'He designed the general layout of the new town, indicating the position of the market square, the number of temples to be built, and what gods they should serve...and the precise limits of its outer defences.'

Alexander, however, did not live to see the city take shape, and it fell to the early Ptolemies to carry out his plans. Strabo (c.63 BC–c.AD 21), the Greek geographer, described the city in such detail that it has been possible to draw a plan of it, including the island of Pharos with its famous lighthouse, the Heptastadium, which joined the island to the mainland, thus forming its two harbours, the royal palace, the Museum and Library, the Serapaeum and the necropolis.

▼ *Since 1994, major discoveries have been made during underwater excavations made by Jean-Yves Empereur and his team in Alexandria.*

▲ *A 13th-century mosaic in St Mark's, Venice, shows St Mark passing the famous lighthouse on his way to bring Christianity into Europe.*

The new city on the Mediterranean coast, designed by Deinocrates of Rhodes, was built on a strip of land between Lake Maroitis and the sea. It consisted of a network of streets lying at right angles to one another, embellished with the many impressive buildings mentioned by Strabo.

The Library

Alexandria's famous Library seems to have been initiated by Ptolemy I (305–285 BC) and developed by Ptolemy II (285–246 BC), who is credited with the idea of writing to the rulers of every other state asking them to contribute books. The Library eventually included most Greek literature, a complete collection of Egyptian literature and works on the religions of the ancient Near East. There was room for up to 70,000 papyrus rolls. Most of the items were bought, but other means were sometimes used. In order to procure coveted works, all ships entering the harbour were searched. Every book found was taken to the Library, where it was decided whether to give it back or confiscate it and replace it with a copy.

The Pharos

The lighthouse was one of the earliest buildings to be erected. The island of Pharos was chosen as the site and gave its name to the lighthouse itself. The construction began under Ptolemy I, and was completed by his successor.

The Pharos was an enormous building, said to be over 100m (330ft) high, built in three tiers, and was described in ancient and later Islamic sources. The lowest level was a square tower, 60m (200ft) in height. This was surmounted by a second tier, 30m (100ft) high and octagonal in shape. The top level was cylindrical, about 15m (50ft) high, and was crowned by a statue of Zeus the Saviour. (In the Islamic period this third tier was replaced by a mosque.) It seems, from the reports of travellers in the Middle Ages, to have been in ruins in the mid-fourteenth century, although it was apparently still in good condition around 1200, when it was depicted in a mosaic in the Chapel of St Zeno in St Mark's, Venice.

According to the descriptions of classical authors and the first-century Jewish historian, Josephus, a great fire was kept burning all night at the base of the lighthouse. This was reflected by mirrors from the top and could be seen from an enormous distance out at sea.

The Museum

In order to legitimize their rule, the Ptolemies had to project their city as the home of Greek culture and the main centre of scientific research. They invited all the great scholars of the age to come to work in Alexandria and offered them favourable conditions to do their work. It was a true intellectual centre, where all the disciplines were found.

Almost all of the great minds of the third century BC lived in Alexandria, at least for a while. Among them were Eratosthenes (c.276–c.194 BC), who calculated the circumference of the earth to within 80km (50 miles), and Aristarchus of Samos, who first put forward the idea that the earth turned on its own axis and at the same time moved around the sun. The mathematician Euclid also lived and taught at Alexandria around 300 BC, and Archimedes (c.287–212 BC) corresponded with the scholars and may have visited the city. It was also here that the Old Testament was translated from Hebrew into Greek, for the benefit of the Jews of Alexandria.

The Serapaeum

Under Ptolemy I the Egyptian cult of Osiris-Apis at Memphis was transferred to Alexandria, where the god was called Serapis. He was given the form of a Greek god but embodied both Greek and Egyptian deities: he was not only Osiris-Apis, but also Zeus, Dionysus, Hades and Asklepios. Serapis was thus a god of the Underworld, a healing god, a god of fertility and also the protector of sailors. He was depicted as a mature man with a beard and curly hair. On his head he carried a basket overflowing with good things. A temple, the Serapaeum, was built in his honour.

Rediscovery

Until recently, apart from the Serapaeum, very little of Ptolemaic Alexandria could be seen. However, since 1994, Professor Jean-Yves Empereur and his team have been uncovering the remains of the ancient city. A team of underwater archaeologists has been exploring the sea bed off Qaitbay Fort and has discovered thousands of columns, bases and capitals, many of red granite, removed from buildings of the Ramesside Period (c.1295–c.1069 BC) and reused by the Ptolemies. Parts of six colossal statues have been recovered, including a head of one of the Ptolemies. Other discoveries include obelisks, sphinxes and an enormous statue of a queen as the goddess Isis.

Work is also going ahead on land. One of the most exciting discoveries has been that of a Roman house with mosaic floors, one of which is decorated with a huge head of Medusa. Another is that of the Ptolemaic necropolis, already known from maps made during Napoleon's expedition of 1798. It was recently rediscovered during the construction of a bridge and new road to Cairo. The necropolis contained tiers of collective burials, with tombs that had been used and reused over several generations. They are dated to the Ptolemaic Period by their Greek inscriptions with Egyptian connotations, and decorative elements such as the classical hand-shake farewell. The deceased is often depicted as a cavalry man, or, if a woman, as a young mother with her new baby. ◆

▼ *A painted scene in the Tigrane tomb shows Isis and Nephthys guarding the mummy of Osiris.*

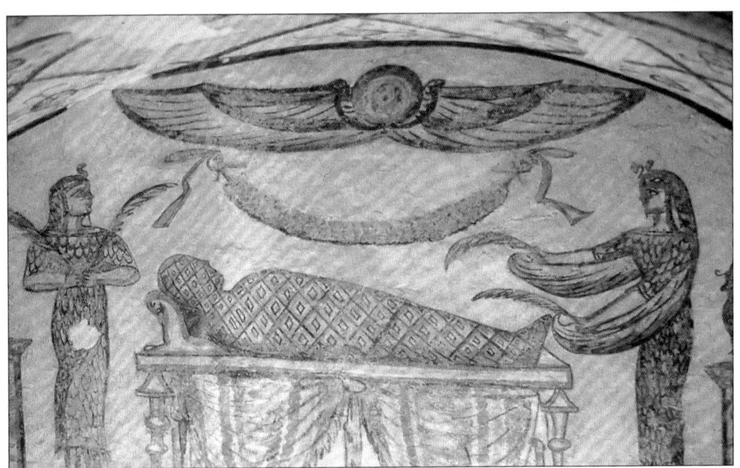

The Siwa Oasis

The Siwa Oasis lies in the Western Desert, not far from the border with Libya and about 300km (186 miles) inland from Mersa Matruh. It lies in a great depression, which is up to 60m (200ft) deep in parts. The oasis is enormous, about 80km (50 miles) long and 28km (17 miles) across at its widest point, with a population of about 10,000.

Water and salt are big problems in Siwa. Although there are more than 1,000 springs in use, the water is very saline and is of little use for agriculture. The crops produced are limited to dates, olives and a few vegetables. The lake is too salty for fish to survive.

The soil, which is used to make the traditional mudbrick houses of Siwa, is also full of salt. The salt appears in great chunks, which help to strengthen the walls. Unfortunately, on the rare occasions when it rains, the lumps of salt dissolve, causing the houses to collapse.

As the depression is well below sea level, drainage is another problem. In order to make any sort of agriculture possible the soil must be washed, but there is nowhere for the water to go. This also creates problems when there is a storm. There was major flooding in 1982, when it rained continuously for two days. The resulting floods devastated crops, killed livestock and destroyed houses throughout the oasis.

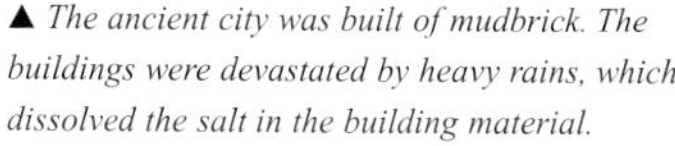

▲ *The ancient city was built of mudbrick. The buildings were devastated by heavy rains, which dissolved the salt in the building material.*

The history of Siwa

The ancient city was at Aghurmi, where the Temple of the Oracle and the Temple of Umm'Ubaydah still stand. It was probably founded during the Saite Dynasty (664–525 BC). Esarhaddon of Assyria had invaded Egypt in 671 BC, as did his son, Ashurbanipal, shortly afterwards. The Kushite king, Taharqo (690–664 BC), at first resisted but was forced to flee. Eventually, the Saite kings restored stability but in the intervening period unsettled conditions caused a diversion of trade from the Nile Valley to the oases and thence to the Mediterranean. Siwa thus lies at the hub of a network of desert routes.

Aghurmi was attacked by Bedouin in the Middle Ages and a new settlement, the Shali, was founded in 1203. The people were not allowed to build outside the walls so, as the population grew, the town extended upwards. Some of the salt-impregnated mudbrick houses reached seven or eight storeys high. After a rainstorm in 1928

◀ *The Temple of the Oracle at Siwa was famous throughout the ancient world. It was consulted by Croesus of Lydia before his disastrous attack on Cyrus of Persia in 546 BC.*

▶ *The tombs in the necropolis of Jabel al-Mawta (Hill of the Dead) were founded in the Saite Period during the 7th century BC and used by both Egyptians and Greeks.*

the ancient town had to be abandoned when the houses collapsed. No one lives there now but it is still possible to visit it. The modern town, with the mosque of Sidi Soliman, lies at its foot.

The Temple of the Oracle

During the reign of the Twenty-sixth Dynasty king Ahmose (570–526 BC), the Temple of the Oracle was built on the rock of Aghurmi, probably on the site of an earlier shrine to Amun and various local deities. In antiquity, the temple was famous all over the Mediterranean world.

Alexander the Great's visit to the oracle was recorded by the second-century AD Greek writer Arrian:

> *...[Alexander] suddenly found himself passionately eager to visit the shrine of Ammon [Amun] in Libya. One reason was his wish to consult the oracle there, as it had a reputation for infallibility and also because Perseus and Herakles were supposed to have consulted it...[and] Alexander longed to equal their fame [as] the blood of both flowed in his veins, and just as they traced their descent from Zeus so he, too, had a feeling he was descended from Ammon. His main concern was to have this confirmed.*

He seems to have had his wish granted; the priest meant to greet him in Greek with the words 'O, paidion' ('O, my son') but because he was Egyptian and speaking a foreign language he made a mistake and actually said 'O, pai Dios' ('O, son of god'). Alexander was delighted to have his divine origins confirmed.

The temple itself is relatively well preserved, although much remains to be excavated. The First Court has almost disappeared. Still standing are two halls and the Sanctuary, which Alexander the Great entered to hear the oracle. The Sanctuary is decorated with images of King Ahmose offering to Amun, Mut, Khonsu and other deities whose identity is not clear. To the right of the Sanctuary is a narrow corridor that leads around to the back. This could have been used to store ritual vessels or may have been involved in the delivery of the oracle's messages.

▶ *Alexander the Great was the ruler of Egypt from 332 to 323 BC, and visited the Temple of the Oracle so that it could confirm his divinity.*

The tombs at Jabal al-Mawta

Greek influence can be seen in the decoration of the tombs at Jabal al-Mawta, a short distance from the centre of Siwa. Of these, the tomb of Si-Amun is the most beautiful. The decoration is a mixture of Greek and Egyptian styles, explained by the number of Greeks encouraged to settle in Egypt during the Saite Period (664–525 BC). The owner, Si-Amun, is shown with a fair complexion but dark curly hair and beard, which suggest his Greek origins. Unusually, no titles appear in the tomb, which suggests he might not have had an administrative or religious post.

The tomb is decorated with Egyptian themes. Osiris is seated in his shrine beside a depiction of the ceremony known as the 'Weighing of the Heart'. The goddess of the sycamore tree pours cooling drinks in the time-honoured way. The sky goddess Nut appears on the ceiling near the entrance, with the morning sun emerging from her body. Further into the tomb Nekhbet the vulture goddess stretches her arms protectively. ◆

The Faiyum

About 60km (37 miles) south-west of Cairo, the Faiyum is another large depression in the Libyan Desert. It is a very fertile area surrounding a large lake, the Birket Qarun, called Lake Moeris by the classical writers. Originally, this was a vast salt-water lake but since the Palaeolithic period it has become smaller and the water has become fresh. Water is brought to the region by the Bahr Yusef, a branch of the Nile, which leaves the main river north of Asyut.

Farming is the main industry and yields are abundant. A wide variety of crops are grown and the orchards of the western Faiyum are among the best in Egypt and are famous for their oranges, lemons, apricots, guavas and mangoes. The Faiyum is also noted for its poultry farms, honey and flowers, which are exported to the perfume producers of Europe and America. Fishing on the lake and canals is important and fishermen can often be seen casting their nets and beating the water to attract the fish.

In Pharaonic times, the kings would visit the Faiyum to indulge in the sports of fishing and fowling. In the reign of Ramesses II (c.1279–c.1213 BC) some of the ladies of the harem were employed in the production of textiles in the Faiyum. One such was Maathorneferura, the daughter of the Hittite king, Hattusilis. She is known to have lived in a palace at Miwer (modern Medinet el-Ghurab), which seems to have been a textile production centre. Today, there is a cotton mill there, as well as a canning factory and hydro-electric station.

The history of the Faiyum

The area has been inhabited since the Stone Age, but really came into its own during the Middle Kingdom (c.2055–c.1650 BC), when a new capital city was established at Itjtawy. This has not yet been located but is thought to be near el-Lisht. Several of the Middle Kingdom kings built pyramids in the Faiyum and King Amenemhat III (c.1855–c.1808 BC) is known to have had a special interest in the area and was responsible for land reclamation work. He constructed a barrage to control the amount of water coming into the Birket Qarun and so was able to bring a large area of fertile land under cultivation.

Important work on the earliest settlers was done early in the twentieth century by Gertrude Caton-Thompson and Elinor Gardner in the northern Faiyum. In 1894, Flinders Petrie excavated the site of Kahun, the town that housed the workers on the pyramid of King Senusret II (c.1880–c.1874 BC) at nearby el-Lahun. From the wide variety of household objects and documents found, it was possible to build up a complete picture of life in the town.

▲ *Waterwheels are used in the Faiyum today to irrigate the exceptionally fertile land.*

Apart from the pyramids of the Middle Kingdom kings, most of the other archaeological remains belong to the Graeco-Roman Period (332 BC–AD 395), when the towns of Karanis, Tebtunis and Bacchias were flourishing. Many new settlers came into the Faiyum at this time, as the Ptolemies rewarded their veterans with plots of land. Thus it was necessary for the Ptolemies to continue the work of the Middle Kingdom kings by expanding the area of cultivable land. They too embarked on the work of draining the lake and building networks of canals.

Karanis was one of the largest of the Graeco-Roman cities. It was founded in the third century BC and inhabited by veteran settlers. Judging by the

▲ *The ruins of the city of Karanis, which was a flourishing agricultural and administrative centre in the Graeco-Roman Period.*

The Labyrinth

Attached to the pyramid of Amenemhat III at Hawara was his mortuary temple, known to the classical authors as the Labyrinth. It was said to be bigger than all the other Egyptian temples put together. Herodotus paid it a visit during his travels in the mid-fifth century BC and described it as having 3,000 rooms connected by winding passages, hence its name. Pliny claimed that the Knossos labyrinth was actually copied from this building, and mentioned crocodile vaults in his description of the site.

When the area was explored by Flinders Petrie at the end of the nineteenth century he found only scanty remains. However, a bed of limestone chippings showed that it had been about 300m (1,000ft) long and 250m (820ft) wide. He also found crocodile burials, indicating that the temple had been dedicated to Sobek, the crocodile god.

numerous granaries and tax returns found here, Karanis was an important agricultural centre. The main crop was wheat, which was exported to Rome by way of Alexandria. Hundreds of houses, several temples and some splendid baths have been found. An important find was the discovery of a temple to the crocodile gods Pnephorus and Petesouchos, local variants of the Egyptian crocodile god, Sobek. Other temples to the crocodile god have been found at Narmouthis, where the Ptolemies extended a Middle Kingdom temple of Amenemhat III, and at Tebtunis where there was also a crocodile cemetery. One city, Crocodilopolis, was named in honour of the god. ◆

▼ *This granite statue depicts Amenemhat III, who was famous for his land reclamation schemes and who built a mudbrick pyramid in the Faiyum.*

The Faiyum Portraits

In 1887, while searching for the entrance to the pyramid of Amenemhat III (c.1855–c.1808 BC), Petrie found a huge Roman cemetery. The mummified bodies were lying in brick tomb chambers, their faces covered with wooden panels on which portraits of the deceased had been painted: 'One was a beautifully drawn head of a girl, in soft grey tints, entirely classical in its style and mode. Another was of a young married woman of about 25; of a sweet but dignified expression, with beautiful features and a fine complexion. She wears pearl earrings and a gold necklace.'

From then on they came thick and fast and Petrie, somewhat overwhelmed by the great numbers that were coming to light, had to build a special store in which to house them. The mummies certainly seem to have kept him very busy. Giving an account of his activities he explained that he had to make containers for all the mummies himself, wash their garments and make accurate drawings of the sarcophagi. Always far ahead of his time, he realized the significance of his finds. When he found the burial of the young married woman, the mummy was in a fragile condition. However, aware of the importance to anthropologists of being able to match the portrait with a body, Petrie retained the skull.

▲ *For this portrait of a young woman, lead white was used as the background, haematite for the robe, a copper-based paint for the necklace and iron sulphate for the flesh tones.*

▲ *This portrait in encaustic on limewood was found by Petrie at Hawara in 1888. The clothes and jewellery indicate a 3rd–4th century date.*

The question of identity

The matching of the physical remains with portrait likenesses in modern times has had some interesting results, especially in answering the question of who these people were. This has proved quite tricky, and the answers are complicated by fashions in costume and burial customs. The portraits obviously belonged to members of the upper classes, as no one else would have been able to afford them. The question is, however, were the people of the Faiyum just like the upper-class inhabitants of the rest of Egypt at this time? As Petrie noted, the portraits have a distinctly Greek look. Does this mean that their owners were Greek? For instance, it is known that the Faiyum population was swollen in the Ptolemaic Period (332–30 BC) by numbers of Greek veteran soldiers who were settled here. However, they did not work their plots of land themselves but hired the services of Egyptian agricultural workers, who must also have been immigrants to the area. Evidence for this is seen in Egyptian personal names and the names of gods and villages. Moreover, they seem to have come from all over Egypt, resulting in a very diverse population.

The Romans seem to have categorized people either as 'Greek' or 'Egyptian', but instead of simplifying things this makes the issue more complicated as the term 'Greek' really meant 'non-Egyptian' and could include people who were not Greek in the modern sense. The diversity of population is reflected in the adoption of Graeco-Roman hairstyles and Egyptian funerary practices, by people of whatever ethnic origin.

Historic survivals

The portraits are very important in the history of art, as all other examples of Greek painting elsewhere in the Mediterranean world have been lost. Only in Egypt has the climate been kind enough for them to have been preserved. Most of the Faiyum portraits were painted on wood, either in tempera (for which the pigments were mixed with a water-based binding agent, such as animal glue) or encaustic (using pigments mixed with beeswax). The actual 'recipes' used remain a mystery.

▲ *The large size and high quality of this portrait suggest that the man came from an important family. It was excavated in 1911 by Petrie who dubbed it 'the Red Youth'.*

It is now thought that the paintings were made specifically for funerary purposes. As some of the portraits show signs of having been cut down to 'fit' the mummy, it has sometimes been suggested that they may have been painted during the lifetime of the deceased and hung for years on the walls of the family home; in support of this argument the point was made that many of the portraits were of young people. However, this is not now considered the case, and the youth of those portrayed is thought to show that many people died at a very early age.

◀ *This painting in tempera of a young man holding a glass of red wine and a garland probably came from er-Rubayat, as it is similar in style to others known to be from that site. It has been dated by the hairstyle, with receding hairline, to the reign of Severus (AD 193–211).*

Throughout their long history, life after death was a belief firmly held by the ancient Egyptians. They aspired to become an *akh* or transfigured spirit. In order to do this, the deceased had to overcome death by ensuring that his body did not decay and by providing for the needs of his *ka*, either by actual offerings of food and drink or by magical spells. These funerary beliefs and practices continued until the introduction of Christianity. The Faiyum portraits are more moving than the likenesses on earlier mummy cases as they are clearly pictures of real people. They are touching reminders of the eternal quest for immortality. ◆

The Islands of the Blest

The oases of the Western Desert are depressions in the desert floor where life is sustainable thanks to the easily accessible water supplies. Much of the water comes from springs or, where the water is trapped underground, from wells. Wherever water is available, settlements have grown up within each oasis. How these depressions developed is still a matter of conjecture, but most geologists believe that they are the result of tectonics and water and wind erosion during the Pliocene period, while Europe was undergoing the ice age.

Herodotus called the oases 'the Islands of the Blest'. Their history reflects that of the Nile Valley, although most is known about the settlements from the Saite (664–525 BC) and Graeco-Roman (332 BC–AD 395) Periods. The people who live there now are largely farmers, and Bedouin who no longer roam the desert but have settled on the fringes of the agricultural land.

▲ *Qasr el-Ghueida, the Fortress of the Beautiful Garden, within which is a well-preserved sandstone temple, dedicated to Amun, Mut and Khonsu.*

Kharga

The Kharga oasis lies about 175km (109 miles) east of Luxor. Although there is evidence for agriculture here in the Neolithic period, there is little history of the area in Pharaonic times until the New Kingdom (c.1550–c.1069 BC), when records in Theban tombs state that the inhabitants of Kharga paid tax in the form of dates, grapes, wine and minerals such as ochre. Rebellions, and the expeditions mounted to quell them, are also mentioned. It seems, too, that the oasis was used as a place of exile then as it was for centuries later.

◀ *The el-Qasr mosque in Dakhla was built during the reign of Saladin (AD 1171–93). Its 21m (69ft) high minaret is typical of this brilliant period of Islamic architecture.*

By the Twenty-second Dynasty (c.945–c.715 BC), when the kings were of Libyan stock, there was much more royal interest in the area. Sheshonq I (c.945–c.924 BC) ordered the improvement of the desert tracks and also had to deal with a rebellion. During the Persian occupation, Darius I (522–486 BC) built temples to Amun-Re at Hibis and Qasr el-Ghueida.

The time of greatest prosperity was in the Roman Period (30 BC–AD 395), when the caravan routes were protected by a chain of fortresses, and new roads and wells were constructed. The period is marked by the building of temples, many as part of fortress complexes. By AD 390 Kharga was Christianized and many of the old fortresses and temples were converted to use as churches and monasteries. At Gebel el-Teir, in the mountains, several churches and hermitages came into being, and these are among the earliest Christian buildings in Egypt. Two famous exiles to the oasis were Athanasius (c.AD 296–373), Patriarch of Alexandria and Primate of the Church in Egypt, and Nestorius, Patriarch of Constantinople (AD 428–431), who were both banished here when their beliefs conflicted with the prevailing dogma.

Dakhla

Several settlement sites and cemeteries have been found dating from the Old Kingdom (c.2686–c.2181 BC) in this

◀ *The view over the Dakhla Oasis, with its high fields and overlands and the distant escarpment. Dakhla is regarded as the bread basket of the area.*

region, the most important being the town and associated mastaba tombs of Sixth Dynasty officials near the modern village of Balat. As Dakhla lies about 300km (186 miles) west of Luxor, these clearly demonstrate the extent of Egyptian control at this very early period.

Near modern Arnhada there is a cemetery belonging to the First Intermediate Period (c.2181–c.2055 BC) and a late Ramesside temple (c.1130 BC) to the goddess Mut near Ezbet Bashindi. Otherwise, the most important remains again belong to the Graeco-Roman Period. These include a temple of Thoth at el-Qasr and a further temple dedicated to Amun, Mut and Khonsu at Deir el-Hagar. There are decorated tombs of the Roman Period at Qaret el-Muzawwaqa, while the most exciting finds so far come from Arnhada, where a Canadian team have excavated a two-storey building of 15 rooms, each decorated with scenes from Greek and Roman mythology.

Bahariya

The Bahariya Oasis lies in the Western Desert, about 200km (125 miles) west of the Nile. The earliest archaeological remains date to the New Kingdom (c.1550–c.1069 BC), represented by the tomb of the Nineteenth Dynasty provincial governor, Amenhotep Huy, near Bawit. The necropolis contains the tombs of several officials from the Saite Period. Nearby is a sacred bird cemetery associated with the worship of Horus and Thoth. This is partly of Saite and partly of Roman date. There are also two temples at Bawit, one built by the Twenty-sixth Dynasty king Apries (589–570 BC) and the other by Alexander the Great (332–323 BC). From the Roman Period there is a triumphal arch, also at Bawit, and a garrison, basilica and small settlement at el-Hayz.

Farafra

The Farafra oasis is about 300km (186 miles) west of Assiut. Texts mention occupation of the area from the Old Kingdom but as yet there is no archaeological evidence for settlement before the Roman Period. There are the remains of a town of the early Christian Period (c.AD 450) at Ain Dallaf. ◆

New discoveries

By far the most exciting find in the region in the last few years has been the discovery of hundreds of the most beautiful and well-preserved mummies ever found in Egypt. The cemetery lies near the Temple of Alexander the Great at Bawit and is vast. Eventually, thousands of mummies may be recovered.

There are four different styles of mummy in the necropolis. The first has a gilded mask placed over the face of the mummy, while the second is covered with cartonnage (plaster-stiffened linen) painted with the funerary gods, Anubis, the four sons of Horus, Osiris, Isis and Thoth. The third style is a burial of an undecorated mummy within a pottery coffin, while a fourth group was simply wrapped in plain linen and not placed in any kind of coffin.

The Antiquities Service is preparing to open the Temple of Alexander to tourists, but the mummies will not be on view.

▶ *Wind-eroded chalk sculptures create the surrealist landscape of the White Desert in the Farafra Oasis. The powdered chalk makes much of the spring water undrinkable.*

Monasteries, Mosques and Synagogues

The temples of the old gods are not the only sacred sites in Egypt. From the time of the Hebrew Exile there had been a Jewish settlement on the island of Elephantine, and in the Graeco-Roman Period (332 BC–AD 395) a substantial Jewish population existed in Alexandria.

According to tradition, Egypt was one of the earliest places to accept Christianity, which was said to have been introduced in the middle of the first century AD by St Mark. It was first adopted by the Greek-speaking upper classes of Alexandria, and spread only gradually to ordinary Egyptians during the third century AD. Egyptian Christians, known as Copts, denounced the ancient religion, although some elements of the old beliefs survived. Egypt was also the home of monasticism; the desire for a life of seclusion was perhaps stimulated by the Roman persecutions of the third century.

The conversion of the country to Islam effectively began with the capture of Alexandria by the Arab general, 'Amr Ibn el-'Asi in AD 641. The Fatimid caliphs who ruled Egypt in the tenth century were great builders. They founded the new capital, Cairo, with the intention of making it as splendid as Baghdad, and some of the mosques they constructed can still be seen today, together with the medieval mausoleums of the Mamelukes.

◀ *The skyline of Cairo reveals the domes of the many Muslim mosques that have been erected in the city since the 10th century AD.*

Early Christianity in Alexandria

The Egyptian Church claims to be the oldest in Christendom, but its origins are actually obscure. In his *Ecclesiastical History* written in the fourth century, Eusebius of Caesarea (c.AD 264–340) stated that Christianity was brought to Egypt by the gospel writer St Mark and that he established the first churches in Alexandria itself. This was early in the reign of Claudius, about AD 41–3, and only a few years after the death of Christ. Eusebius further wrote that Mark stayed in the Jewish quarter of Alexandria and that his first convert was a shoemaker. However, there is no reliable contemporary literary evidence for this. Neither has the early Church left any trace in the archaeological record.

Whatever the truth concerning its beginnings, the Church in Egypt was certainly established by the reign of Commodus (AD 180–92), as it is known that one of his concubines was a Christian. By this time, too, the Egyptian Church was presided over by a Patriarch.

Eusebius also credited Mark with the foundation of the See of Alexandria. He claimed that Mark was the first Patriarch and gave a list of those who followed. The list is, however, considered to be suspect, as the reigns of the first 11 are all of 12 years, which seems rather too much of a coincidence. There is evidence, though, for the twelfth, Demetrius, who held office from AD 190–223. In spite of all the doubts, the head of the Coptic Church in Egypt is still called the Patriarch of the See of St Mark and Pope of Alexandria.

The scholars of Alexandria

The Church in Alexandria was very well organized and converts were given training in the Christian faith in the Catechetical School. The catechetes, or teachers, could be either clergy or lay people. They taught the converts and prepared them for baptism. Two of the most famous scholars to be head of the Catechetical School in the late second and early third centuries were Clement (c.AD 150–215) and his pupil Origen (c.AD 185–254).

Clement may have been born in Athens. He was very interested in philosophy and seems to have spent much of his life visiting the great centres of learning in the Mediterranean world. He converted to Christianity in Alexandria and went on to become a presbyter and then head

▼ *St Sebastian is depicted before the Emperor Diocletian, under whom the Egyptian Church suffered its most severe persecution when church buildings and the scriptures were burnt.*

of the Catechetical School. In his teachings, he emphasized the intellectual approach to Christianity. He appealed to the Greek population through discussions on the philosophers and tried to demonstrate the superiority of Christianity by attacking paganism.

Origen was born in Alexandria. When he was about 17 years old, the Roman emperor Severus (AD 193–211) visited Egypt and issued an edict forbidding conversion to Judaism or Christianity. Origen's father was arrested and imprisoned and Origen encouraged him to suffer martyrdom rather than give up his faith. In fact, Origen was eager to seek martyrdom himself but it is said that his mother hid his clothes so that he was unable to go out. When he became a catechete he castrated himself in order to avoid a scandal concerning himself and a female student, although he is said to have regretted this later.

Origen became head of the Catechetical School after Clement's death. By this time he was very famous and was invited all over the Near East to discuss knotty theological problems, much to the annoyance of the Patriarch Demetrius, who exiled him from Alexandria. Altogether, Origen wrote about 6,000 learned works, including the *Exhortation to Martyrdom*. His most important work was the *Hexapla*, in which the Old Testament is presented in six different versions, in Hebrew and Greek, arranged in columns for comparison. Origen died at Tyre as a result of the torture he had suffered during the persecution ordered by Diocletian (AD 284–305).

▲ *A mosaic in St Mark's, Venice, shows St Mark passing the Alexandria lighthouse as he brings the gospel to Egypt.*

The spread of Christianity

Christianity encountered opposition from Gnosticism and the cult of Serapis and it spread only slowly to other parts of Egypt, and then only to the Greek-speaking areas. By the third century, churches were established in Oxyrhyncus, Antinoopolis and Panopolis. As Christianity spread, the need arose to provide the converts with scriptures. This led to the emergence of Coptic, the ancient Egyptian language written using Greek letters, as a standardized literary form in the third century. The earliest surviving books in Coptic, which are versions of the Old and New Testaments, date from the early fourth century.

With the acceptance of Christianity, Coptic styles of architecture and sculpture were also introduced. These were based on Greek classical style rather than Christian motifs, and were imitated in the images used to decorate textiles. Biblical themes did not appear until the eighth century. However, in mural painting, Old Testament themes such as Adam and Eve, Noah's Ark, Daniel and the three Hebrews in the fiery furnace, and local saints, such as Damien and Cosmos, were popular. New Testament scenes commonly used were the Massacre of the Innocents, the Flight into Egypt, the Wedding at Cana, the Baptism of Christ and the Last Supper, though otherwise there were few scenes relating directly to the life of Christ. After the fifth century, when Egypt became mainly monophysite (believing that Christ is divine only), the Nativity and the Crucifixion disappeared entirely from the repertoire. Burial customs also changed: bodies were wrapped in a shroud and buried without grave goods, a complete break with the long tradition of ancient Egypt. ◆

▶ *The Serapaeum, the cult centre of Serapis, is marked by 'Pompey's Pillar', in reality set up in AD 297 in honour of Diocletian.*

The Monasteries of Wadi Natrun

The Wadi Natrun is a depression in the Western Desert, 32km (20 miles) long, which lies midway between Cairo and Alexandria. A series of salt lakes, joined to the Nile by subterranean channels, lies along the valley floor. These evaporate in the summer, leaving behind deposits of salt and the natron that gave the valley its name. Natron was extremely important to the ancient Egyptians for mummification. Today it is used for bleaching cloth and in the manufacture of soap and glass.

Persecution

Wadi Natrun is also famous for its monasteries and hermitages, founded following the persecutions of early Christian communities by the Romans. The worst was under Diocletian (AD 284–305), when churches were razed, scriptures burnt and clergy and laymen imprisoned and tortured. Those who persisted in declaring their faith were often put to death. In an attempt to stamp out Christianity, an earlier emperor, Decius (AD 249–251), had issued an edict requiring all inhabitants of the empire to take a loyalty test, which involved making an offering to the emperor as a god. Those who did so were given a certificate to say they had. About 50 of these certificates are extant. Some Christians, fearing for their lives, performed the sacrifice and received certificates. This was the cause of much bitterness later when Christianity became acceptable and those who had thus denied their faith sought readmission to the Church.

The desert fathers

The traditional founder of monasticism in Egypt was St Anthony (AD 251–356), who lived at a time when the empire-wide persecutions were at their height. Coming from an affluent family, Anthony was moved by the gospel story of the rich young man who came to Jesus seeking the Kingdom of God and was advised to sell everything he had and give to the poor. He went off to the Eastern Desert and lived as a hermit. Others followed his example, including Abu Maqar, the founder of monasticism in the Wadi Natrun. Formerly a camel driver, Abu Maqar felt called by a vision to seek a solitary life and thereafter lived in the Wadi Natrun as a hermit. He seems to have attracted others and a small community grew up. Each monk had his own cell, well removed from

▲ *Five churches lie inside the walls of the monastery of St Bishoi. The monastery is named after a disciple of Abu Maqar.*

those of his neighbours, although they met weekly to celebrate the Eucharist.

This remains the basis of the monastic system in the Wadi Natrun today. Some of the monks still seek the solitude of their predecessors, but they first have to spend ten years in a monastery before they are allowed to apply for permission to become hermits. If this is granted, the monk has to go into the desert to look for a suitable cave. A truck from the monastery delivers food once a week, and once a month the hermit has to go back to the monastery to take part in the liturgy with the other monks.

There are four monasteries in Wadi Natrun today. Each is surrounded by a high protective wall (which originally had no entrance) and a keep where the monks of the Middle Ages could hide

▼ *Deir Abu Maqar was founded by Abu Maqar, the first of the thousands of monks and hermits to seek the solitary life in Wadi Natrun.*

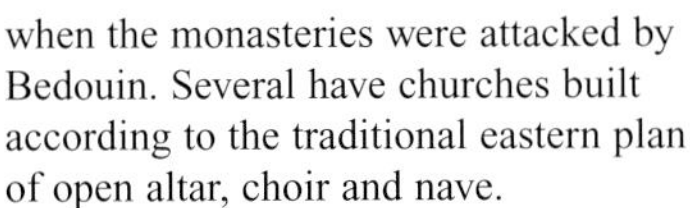

when the monasteries were attacked by Bedouin. Several have churches built according to the traditional eastern plan of open altar, choir and nave.

Deir el-Baramus

Called the Monastery of the Romans, Deir el-Baramus is the oldest of the surviving monasteries. It was founded in AD 340, and is said to have been named after two sons of the emperor Valentinian (AD 364–75), St Maximus and St Domidus, who came to stay in the area, having been ordained as monks in Syria. They lived in a cave 3km (2 miles) away from the monastery. After they died, three days apart, they were buried under the middle altar of the Church of the Virgin Mary, to whom the monastery was originally dedicated, and it was then renamed in their honour.

The monastery church contains the relics of another fourth-century saint, Moses the Black, who before his conversion had been a thief and a murderer. Afterwards he became the founder of a now ruined monastery near Deir el-Baramus. The church also contains the pillar of St Arsenius (AD 354–450), who was tutor to the sons of Theodosius I (AD 379–95) before he came to Wadi Natrun. The most important antiquities in the church are the frescoes. They were discovered recently behind four layers of plaster and are thought by the French team engaged on restoration work to date from the fourth century. They include scenes from the life of Christ, images of Jesus, six of the Apostles, the Virgin Mary and the monastic fathers.

▲ *Deir el-Baramus, also founded by Abu Maqar, is the oldest of the four monasteries remaining in the Wadi, dating from AD 340.*

The Monastery of the Syrians

Founded in the sixth century, the Monastery of the Syrians was given its present name in the ninth century, when it was bought by a merchant from Syria for Syrian monks. The monastery once housed a vast library but the manuscripts have now been dispersed. The Church of the Holy Virgin within the walls is the most interesting in Wadi Natrun and is decorated with tenth-century frescoes.

The Monastery of St Bishoi

Opposite the Monastery of the Syrians is the Monastery of St Bishoi, named after one of the first hermits who lived in Wadi Natrun. His relics are housed in the Church of St Bishoi within the walls, and are often visited by pilgrims.

The Monastery of Abu Maqar

This monastery was named after Abu Maqar, also known as Father Macarius, the first of the hermits and monks to live in Wadi Natrun. Although he founded this monastery as well as the Monastery of the Romans, he remained a hermit to the end of his life. In the eleventh century, this monastery became the seat of the Coptic Church. ◆

Abu Mena

According to Coptic tradition, St Mena was an Egyptian who was martyred in Phrygia during the persecution of the Christians under Diocletian (AD 284–305). Originally a soldier, he had left the army when the persecution began. He went out into the desert where he had a vision in which he was told that he would be martyred and his martyrdom would be of great importance. A sanctuary would be built in Egypt in his honour and would draw pilgrims to it from all over the world. It was also foretold that miraculous cures would be effected there.

Mena himself subsequently entered the arena at Kotyaion during a festival and declared himself a Christian, whereupon he was arrested and tortured before being beheaded. Before he died, he begged that his body should be taken to Egypt for burial. The body was retrieved by fellow Christians and given to an officer in the Phrygian army, Athanasius, who had been ordered to Egypt. He was reluctant to bury the corpse because, apparently, he thought it brought him good luck. Eventually, however, he had no option, as the camel carrying the body refused to go any further. At the spot where St Mena was buried, between Alexandria and the Wadi Natrun, springs of healing water gushed from the desert floor, and pilgrims began to flock to be cured.

St Mena, whose image is often seen standing between two camels on the famous pilgrim flasks associated with the site, may once have been a camel driver himself. Whether this is the case or not, his association with the animals led to his becoming the patron saint of merchants and camel drivers. Between the fifth and seventh centuries a great

▶ *The remains of the city of Abu Mena have been excavated since 1905 by German and Egyptian archaeologists. Attacked by Bedouin and Arabs in the early Middle Ages, it was deserted by AD 1000.*

◀ *The monastery of St Mena is now in ruins but it was an important focus for pilgrims from the 4th to the 10th centuries. A new monastery was built near the original site in the 1980s.*

▶ *St Mena is here depicted between two camels, which were said to have knelt beside his body after its miraculous transportation from Asia Minor.*

city, Abu Mena, arose near the springs. Within the city, the Byzantine emperor Arcadius (AD 395–408) built a splendid basilica over the saint's burial place, while the emperor Zeno (AD 474–91) built a palace near the basilica and garrisoned the city to protect the pilgrims.

The pilgrim flasks

When pilgrims came to the site to honour the saint and be cured of their ailments they took home with them little pottery flasks of the healing waters. These were made locally and are often decorated in high relief with the characteristic scene of St Mena standing between two camels. These flasks have been found all around the Mediterranean and in other parts of the Christian world, indicating how far pilgrims would come to visit the site. So many flasks were found at the site by the German archaeologist Kaufmann in 1905 that he was able to identify it as Abu Mena, even though the city itself was completely ruined.

The end of Abu Mena

The city flourished after its foundation, but in the seventh century it was attacked by Bedouin tribes and again later by the forces of Islam during the Abbasid era. Its buildings were dismantled and architectural elements were taken to Cairo and Alexandria and incorporated into new buildings there.

The city of Abu Mena was seen and described by an Arab traveller around AD 1000. He mentions the palaces, marble sculptures and holy icons that he saw, as well as the famous vineyards and gardens with their almond and carob trees. But by that time the city was already a ghost town, solely inhabited by marauders and thieves.

The rediscovery of the city

The site seems then to have been largely avoided by travellers until the nineteenth century, when J. R. Pacho went there in 1825. So little was left by this time, he assumed it was a Roman ruin. It remained unrecognized as the great pilgrim centre it had once been until the arrival of the German cleric and archaeologist, Kaufmann, in 1905. Since then it has been extensively excavated by a team from the Coptic Museum in Cairo and by German archaeologists. They have discovered the ruins of several churches, a monastery, a pilgrim hostel, baths where the pilgrims could immerse themselves in the healing waters, potters' workshops and kilns where the pilgrim flasks were produced, cisterns, private houses, shops and two cemeteries. Many of the finds from the site can now be seen in the Coptic Museum in Cairo. ◆

The Monasteries of the Eastern Desert

The life of St Anthony (AD 251–356), traditionally the founder of Egyptian monasticism, was recorded in a mixture of fact and legend by the fourth-century theologian and Patriarch of Alexandria, St Athanasius (c.AD 296–373). According to his account, Anthony was born into a wealthy Christian family at Coma, near Beni Suef. He seems to have been a serious youth, and after his parents died he decided to leave home and lead an ascetic life. At first he lived just outside his village supporting himself by his handiwork and giving part of what he earned to the poor. Then, under the influence of an old man who had practised asceticism since his youth, Anthony travelled about meeting like-minded men from whom he learned much about this way of life. He went without food for several days at a time and when he did eat he only ever had bread, salt and water. He also deprived himself of sleep.

Eventually he went to live in an ancient tomb and blocked up the entrance. While he was there he was attacked one night by the Devil. He was discovered by a friend coming to bring him food, who carried his apparently lifeless body back to the village and laid him in the church, where the people came to pay their respects to the dead man. In the middle of the night, Anthony came round and asked to be taken back to his cave. Once more, the Devil attacked him, aided this time by an army of demons and monsters. However, Anthony was able to withstand the onslaught and his ordeal was eventually brought to an end by a beam of light shining down from the roof. Anthony heard a voice telling him that because he had stood firm he would always receive divine help and would become famous everywhere.

▲ *The Monastery of St Anthony today. Although the foundations date to the third century AD, most of the building dates to 1560.*

Anthony's troubles were not yet over, however, as the Devil put several temptations in his way. He always resisted, and at last took refuge in an abandoned fortress at Pispir, on the east bank of the Nile. Anthony lived here for the next 20 years, never going out and seeing no one. He became famous for his asceticism. One day a crowd came to Pispir and broke down the door of his cell, expecting to find him pale and emaciated. To their amazement he was fit and well and of a sound mind. Many of their number were sick and Anthony cured them. He also managed to persuade many to take up the hermit's life, and so began the monastic movement.

▶ *This is an icon of St Paul, said by Jerome to be the first of the hermits.*

At first there was no organized community. The hermits lived alone in caves near to the fortress of Pispir. Gradually two different types of community developed: one where the hermits lived entirely alone, and the other where they lived alone but met at times for prayer.

The Monastery of St Anthony

After a time Anthony withdrew from Pispir to seek solitude in the Eastern Desert. Even here his fame attracted visitors, so leaving behind a second community of anchorites he moved into a cave in the mountains. Anthony is said to have died at the ripe old age of 105, having sworn two trusted monks to secrecy concerning the whereabouts of

▶ *Frescoes from the church of St Paul in his monastery in the Eastern Desert.*

his body. He did not want his tomb to be venerated. Some say he was buried under the floor of the cave. Another tradition maintains that the body was moved in AD 561 to the Church of St John the Baptist in Alexandria and thence to St Sophia in Constantinople. Otherwise, the body is said to rest in various locations in France. Whatever the truth, a monastery was eventually set up in the fourth century in the Wadi Araba in the Eastern Desert, near the cave where Anthony lived for the last years of his life.

St Anthony's Monastery is the oldest and largest Coptic monastery in Egypt. There is little to see of the original monastery today, as it was rebuilt in later centuries. It remained a great centre of scholarship where Coptic works were translated into Arabic until 1483, when it was attacked by the Bedouin and the monks killed or expelled. It has now been reoccupied, and a self-supporting community carries on its tradition.

▼ *The monastery of St Paul is the second oldest Coptic monastery in Egypt. It is situated in the Wadi el-Deir.*

The Monastery of St Paul

St Paul's Monastery in the Wadi el-Deir is the second oldest Coptic monastery in Egypt. The life of St Paul the Hermit (AD 228–341) was recorded by St Jerome (c.AD 342–420) but it contains much that is tradition and legend. Born to a wealthy family in Thebes, he fled into the desert during the persecution instigated by Decius (AD 249–251) to become a hermit. He is said to have lived on dates and the bread brought to him by a raven that visited him daily. As he lay dying, he was visited by St Anthony, who buried him with the help of two lions.

By AD 460, a church had been built over his grave and by the sixth century this had become a place of pilgrimage. The monastery was built in the Middle Ages. It is surrounded by defensive walls, from the top of which there are magnificent views of Mount Sinai. There is a Chapel of the Virgin in the watch tower and next door is the Church of St Michael, which contains an icon said to have been painted by St Luke. ◆

Pachomius

St Pachomius also lived in the fourth century and developed a different sort of monasticism. He started a community of ascetics near the Nile at Tabennisi around AD 323. Here, the monks lived an organized, communal life that involved strenuous manual labour and strict discipline. Prayer was an important part of life in the monastery. The monks were divided into houses according to their trade or nationality. Each house had a head and the whole monastery was presided over by the superior-general and his deputy. Pachomius died of plague in AD 346, by which time he had established 11 such communities, including two for women.

St Catherine's Monastery

At the foot of Mount Sinai, according to tradition, lies the place where Moses tended the flocks of Jethro, his father-in-law, and where he saw the Burning Bush. From the end of the third century the area was settled by small communities of monks escaping persecution by the Romans and seeking the spiritual life in the isolation of the mountains. Some time after AD 313, when Constantine (AD 312–337) had granted freedom of worship throughout the Roman Empire, the monks of Sinai petitioned his mother, Helena, for patronage. Helena answered this request in AD 330 by erecting a small church dedicated to the Virgin Mary, and also a tower on the traditional site of the Burning Bush to provide refuge for the monks.

In about AD 530 Emperor Justinian (AD 527– 65) ordered the building of the great walled monastery, with its magnificent church, which remains to this day. The church incorporated Helena's earlier building and was also dedicated to the Virgin Mary, since the church fathers saw the Burning Bush as a symbol of the Annunciation. The monastery was originally called the Monastery of the Transfiguration but since the eleventh century it has also been known as St Catherine's.

▲ *To protect the monks who settled around the site of the Burning Bush from marauding Bedouin, the Byzantine emperor Justinian ordered the building of a fortified monastery.*

The life of St Catherine

St Catherine was born into an aristocratic family of Alexandria in AD 294. She was clever, highly educated and, according to tradition, beautiful. However, she was converted to Christianity by the teaching of a Syrian monk and rejected all her many suitors. During the last years of the persecutions she publicly confessed her faith. The story goes that 50 wise men from all over the Roman world were brought to reason with her, but to no avail: instead, she converted them to Christianity by her persuasive arguments. When she was later tortured, she even managed to convert members of the imperial family and the Roman aristocracy.

Catherine was executed. Her body vanished and tradition has it that it was carried by angels to the peak of Mount Sinai. Some three centuries later, the monks brought it down and buried it in the church.

The sanctity of the monastery

A tradition claims that in AD 625 the monks of St Catherine's sent a delegation to Medina to ask for Muhammad's patronage and protection. The request appears to have been granted, as in the Icon Gallery there is a copy of a document stating that the Muslims would defend the monks and that they were exempted from taxation. According to another legend, Muhammad actually visited the monastery while he was a merchant.

When the Arabs invaded Egypt in AD 641 the monastery itself was not harmed. However, the number of monks began to decline until, by the early ninth century, only 50 were left. Many of the Christians of Sinai converted to Islam, and in the eleventh century a mosque was built within the complex. During the Crusades, pilgrims from Europe came to St Catherine's in ever-increasing numbers and a special order of Crusaders was formed to protect them. The story of St Catherine's martyrdom was brought to Europe by the Crusaders, and she became a major saint.

Conditions were more difficult under the rule of the Mamelukes but the monastery's fortunes revived in the early sixteenth century under the rule of the Ottoman sultan Selim I (1512–20), when the rights of the monks were respected and the archbishop was granted special status.

By the seventeenth century the monastery owned property in several other countries, as branches had been established in other parts of Egypt, Palestine, Turkey, Romania, Russia, India and Greece. Especially important was the school at Heraklion in Crete, where the greatest Greek scholars of the time were educated. At the end of the eighteenth century the monastery came under the protection of Napoleon, who also paid for the reconstruction of the north wing. During the later nineteenth and earlier twentieth centuries, however, the monastery lost much of its property abroad. In spite of this it continues to function and in 1951 a new wing was added to house the library, Icon Gallery, a new refectory and the archbishop's apartments. The monastery celebrated its 1,400th anniversary in 1966.

▼ *The interior of the church of St Catherine, from a painting by David Roberts. The decoration and iconostasis date from the 17th and 18th centuries.*

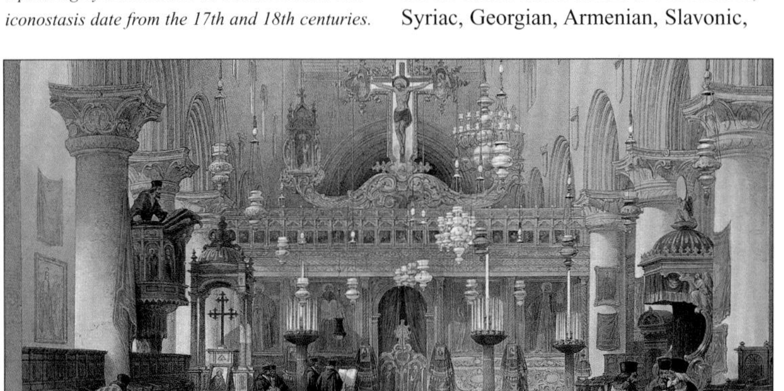

The Icon Gallery

The monastery owns a large collection of 2,000 icons, of which 150 are on display. They are of great artistic and historical importance. Twelve of the oldest and rarest icons date from the sixth century and were painted using the encaustic method (mixing pigment with beeswax). Part of the collection is Byzantine, dating from the sixth to the tenth centuries, while most of the icons date from the eleventh to the fifteenth centuries.

The library

The monastery's library is second only to that of the Vatican in importance and contains about 3,000 manuscripts. Most are in Greek while others are in Arabic, Syriac, Georgian, Armenian, Slavonic, Coptic and Ethiopian. Most of them are Christian works but there are also historical documents in the collection granting rights and privileges to the monastery and authorized by the seals of emperors, patriarchs, bishops and even Turkish sultans. At present the oldest document is the Codex Syriacus, dating to the fifth century, which is the oldest translation of the gospels. Until the mid-nineteenth century the Library also owned the even more important fourth-century Codex Sinaiticus, which is now in the British Library in London. ◆

Codex Sinaiticus

The Codex Sinaiticus was found in 1844 in the library of St Catherine's by the German scholar Konstantin von Tischendorf (1815–74). His interest was aroused when he saw some manuscripts in a basket waiting to be burned. Concealing his excitement, he asked for the pages, which he recognized as part of a very early Bible, and presented them to Frederick Augustus of Saxony. He managed to obtain the remaining pages on a later visit in 1859, as the result of a rather dubious deal, which the monks still resent. This document was presented to Tsar Alexander II of Russia as head of the Orthodox Church, and was purchased from the Russians in 1933 by the British Library.

Until the nineteenth century the Codex was complete. It once contained both Old and New Testaments, as well as several books of the Apocrypha. Unfortunately, about 300 pages are now missing. It is still the oldest complete New Testament in the world and has proved invaluable to Biblical scholars. Notes in the margins of the Codex show that it had been checked in antiquity against the *Hexapla* of Origen, the second-century scholar, and corrected by Antoninus and Pamphilius in the fourth century.

The Islamic City of Cairo

The city of Cairo is the largest in Africa and in the Islamic world. It came into being after the Arab conquest of Egypt in AD 641. The main part of the city lies on the east bank of the Nile, where there had been a settlement from the beginning of ancient Egyptian history. The settlement was called Kher-aha, meaning 'Place of Combat', because it was said to be the spot where Horus and Seth had fought over the succession to the throne of Egypt after Osiris had gone to be the ruler of the Underworld.

Cairo is an exciting place to visit. As well as the mosques and mausoleums there are the medieval bazaars of the Khan el-Khalili, the Museum of Islamic Art and the Wakal of Kait Bey, a caravanserai built in 1480.There is also the seventeenth-century House of Sheik es-Sihaimi, the Bab el-Futah ('Gate of Conquests'), which marks the northern limits of the Fatimid city, and the Nilometer on the southern end of Roda Island, constructed by the Omayyads in AD 716.

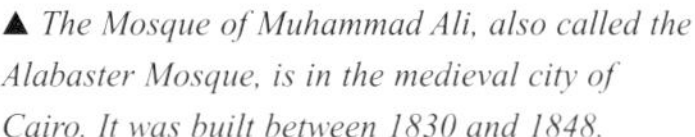

▲ *The Mosque of Muhammad Ali, also called the Alabaster Mosque, is in the medieval city of Cairo. It was built between 1830 and 1848.*

Babylon and Fustat

The Ptolemies called the area Babylon, perhaps a corruption of Per-Hapi en Yun, the Egyptian name of the island of Roda nearby. Later the Romans built a fortress here, the remains of which can still be seen today. This stronghold was besieged and conquered by the armies of Caliph Omar in AD 641, after which a new city, Fustat, was founded just to the north of Babylon. The first mosque was built here but this was destroyed in 1158, along with the rest of Fustat, to prevent it falling into the hands of the Crusaders. Until AD 868 Egypt was ruled by governors representing Arab dynasties based in Damascus (the Omayyads) and Baghdad (Abbasids). Then, for a brief spell of about 40 years, Egypt became independent under Ahmed ibn-Tulin, who built the mosque named after him that still stands today.

El-Kahira

Egypt was finally conquered in AD 969 by Gawhar of the Fatimid dynasty, who traced their descent back to Fatima, the

◀ *The mosque of ibn-Tulin, built in AD 876–9, is the second oldest in Cairo. The fountain in the central courtyard was added in the 13th century.*

▲ *Originally built by Saladin in 1176, the Citadel was the stronghold of the city until the time of Muhammad Ali, and home to Egypt's rulers for nearly 700 years.*

daughter of Muhammad. Gawhar then founded a new capital city called el-Kahira, meaning 'the Victorious One'. It was named after the planet Mars (el-Kahir in Arabic), which was apparently passing over the city at the time when the foundations of the ramparts were being laid. The Fatimids were followed by the Ayyubids, a new dynasty founded by Saladin, and the Ayyubid period is the most brilliant in the medieval history of Cairo. One of Saladin's claims to fame is that he began the building of the citadel and the city walls, although he himself spent only eight years in the city. For the rest of his reign he was on campaign in Syria, Palestine and Mesopotamia.

The Mamelukes

The Ayyubids were followed by the Mamelukes, originally slaves bought by the sultans and trained to become both their bodyguards and an élite force of troops. During the thirteenth and fourteenth centuries they further embellished the city with mosques, the most important being the Mosque of Sultan Hasan. They also began the practice of building elaborate mausoleums. Those of the later (Circassian) Mamelukes are in the eastern part of the city, that of Kait Bey, one of the last independent Mameluke rulers, being particularly noteworthy. It was built in 1474 and restored at the end of the nineteenth century. With its intricately carved arabesques and interlaced patterns it is considered to be one of the jewels of Islamic art.

Egypt was conquered by the Turks in 1517 and remained under their rule for the next 300 years. The power of the Turkish sultans and their governors, the pashas, soon declined however, the pashas being required to obtain the consent of the Mameluke beys (the district governors) before bringing in any new measures. The beys collected the taxes and commanded the army but paid tribute to the pasha.

European influence

In 1798, Napoleon's fleet appeared off Alexandria. Although the French were defeated by Nelson at the Battle of Abukir Bay, Napoleon went on to conquer Middle and Upper Egypt the following year. However, his triumph was short-lived as in 1801 he surrendered to the British in Cairo and Alexandria and was forced to leave Egypt.

The French withdrawal saw the rise to prominence of Muhammad Ali, who threw out the Turkish governor, proclaimed himself pasha and took possession of the Citadel in Cairo. He and his successors enjoyed some military successes and introduced railways, bridges, canals, a postal and telegraph service and factories, as Egypt came under increasing European influence. The Suez Canal was one of the major enterprises undertaken during this time, though these public works resulted in a huge rise in the national debt. ◆

▼ *Khan el-Khalili, the main Cairo bazaar, where brassware, perfume, jewellery and leather goods are on offer. Having always drawn in foreign merchants, it is now a major tourist attraction.*

The Coptic Churches of Old Cairo

The oldest Coptic churches in Cairo are within the Roman fortress of Babylon. Their plan seems to have been based on the Roman basilica used for administrative purposes, which was oblong in shape with a double colonnade and a semicircular apse at one end. The churches are aligned east–west, with the main entrance at the west end and the sanctuary at the east. In some cases there are three sanctuaries, said to represent the Trinity. There is a dome over the main sanctuary and if there are more sanctuaries these will have a dome too, each topped by a cross. The windows are high up on the wall to cut down on the amount of light, heat and sand entering the building.

In order to protect the congregation from Muslim attacks, the outside of the church was made to look little different from an ordinary house. The main door was often blocked up and the church entered through an unobtrusive side entrance. Bells were forbidden under Muslim law, so there are no bell towers in Coptic churches.

Inside, the churches are divided into narthex, nave, chancel and sanctuaries. In the narthex or entrance hall of the oldest churches a large basin, about 3m (10ft) long and 2m (6ft 6in) wide, is set into the floor. This was used for the blessing of the water on the night of Epiphany, when the congregation bathed in it, and for baptism. The nave is usually divided into three aisles by two rows of superimposed columns. A gallery often runs around the top, which was originally used by the women in the congregation. Another basin is usually found at the west end of the nave, for use during the ceremony of Washing the Feet on Maundy Thursday.

The chancel, which goes across the whole width of the building, is a very important part of the Coptic church as it is the place from which the choir leads the worship. Apart from occasional use of triangles or cymbals, Coptic church music is purely vocal. At the back of the chancel an iconostasis, or screen, separates the sanctuary from the rest of the church. This is made of intricately carved wood, inlaid with ivory. The upper part is decorated with icons and lamps, and ostrich eggs are suspended in front.

A central door with a window to either side leads into the sanctuary. Nearly all Coptic churches have three sanctuaries, each with its own altar. The central altar is covered by a wooden dome, the underside of which is painted with images of Christ in glory surrounded by cherubim and seraphim. Behind the altar is the bishop's throne, with a perpetually burning lamp in front of it. Every church also has a baptistry, with a font deep enough to allow the priest to immerse the baby completely.

▲ *Dedicated to the Virgin Mary, this church is known as the 'Hanging Church' as it rests on the bastion of the old Roman fortress of Babylon.*

▶ *The Coptic cross on the gate of the Hanging Church in Babylon. Crosses are not used in the altars of Coptic churches.*

The Church of St Sergius

Built in the fourth or fifth century, St Sergius is one of the oldest churches in Cairo and traditionally stands on the place where the Holy Family rested during the Flight into Egypt. A round stone font in the south aisle of the crypt chapel marks the exact spot, and the event is commemorated annually on 1 June. The church is dedicated to Sergius and Bacchus, two soldiers in the Roman army said to have been put to death in the third century for refusing to take part in sacrifices to Jupiter. The wood and ivory iconostasis is also decorated with panels of ebony inlaid with ivory crosses, above which is a row of icons depicting the 12 Apostles and the Virgin Mary. The Nativity and the Last Supper, together with three warrior saints, are portrayed either side of the sanctuary door.

The Church of St Barbara

There are two churches on this site. The first was built by a rich scribe, Athanasius, in AD 684 and was dedicated to St Cyrus and St John. The second was built later when the body of St Barbara, a young woman put to death by her father when she converted to Christianity, was brought here. It is one of the largest and most beautiful old churches in Egypt. The icon of the Virgin and Child, in a frame of carved wood inlaid with ivory, is particularly fine.

The Church of St George

This church is also said to have been built by the wealthy scribe Athanasius, in AD 684. Unfortunately, it was burnt down in the nineteenth century and only the fourteenth-century Wedding Hall remains.

The Church of the Virgin

The Church of the Virgin was built in the ninth century and is also known as the Church of the Pot of Basil, which may be a reference to the use of basil in the Greek Orthodox ceremonies of Blessing the Water, which take place every month and on the feasts of the Holy Cross. It is thought that the church may have acquired this name when it was taken over temporarily by the Greek Orthodox Church during the caliphate of el-Hakim, whose mother belonged to that faith. The original church was destroyed and then rebuilt in the eighteenth century.

◀ *An icon of the Virgin and Child from the church of St Sergius, associated with the Flight into Egypt.*

▶ *The interior of the church of St Barbara with its beautiful 13th-century screen of wood inlaid with carved ivory.*

The Hanging Church

One of the most beautiful in Old Cairo, the Hanging Church was built in the late seventh century. Its name is derived from the fact that it rests on the remains of the bastions of the Roman fortress of Babylon. The original church was replaced by a larger one as it increased in importance. It became the seat of the Coptic Patriarchs in the eleventh century, when the Patriarchate was moved from Alexandria to Cairo, and remained so until the fourteenth century. ◆

Jewish Synagogues and Temples

Jews probably settled in Egypt at the time of the Exile at the beginning of the sixth century BC, when they were not only taken to Babylon by King Nebuchadnezzar, but were dispersed throughout the known world.

The Synagogue of Ben Ezra

One of the most interesting sacred sites of Old Cairo is the Synagogue of Ben Ezra, which stands in a pleasant, shady garden near the churches of St Sergius and St Barbara (see *Coptic Churches of Old Cairo*). According to tradition, there has been a Jewish community in Old Cairo since the time of Moses. The earliest written records, however, are those of medieval travellers, such as Benjamin of Tudela (died 1173), who visited the synagogue and claimed to have seen the Torah of Ezra the Scribe.

The first synagogue was destroyed when the Romans took Egypt. Later, at the time of the Arab conquest in AD 641, the site was given to the Copts by the Muslim general, Amr. The Copts built a church there and dedicated it to St Michael. This church, in turn, was destroyed by Caliph el-Hakim and in the twelfth century the site was given back to the Jews and a new synagogue built by Abraham Ben Ezra, the great Rabbi of Jerusalem.

At the end of the nineteenth century, a hoard of ancient manuscripts was found here, including the ancient Torah. Sadly, this was split up and portions are now owned by various institutions in Europe and America. However, some interesting documents remain, including a copy of the Torah dating to the fifth century BC written on gazelle skin, a drawing of a seven-branched candlestick on deer skin, and the manuscript known as the Atlas of Moses.

Elephantine

A small community of Jews also existed at Elephantine: they and their temple are known from Aramaic papyri of the fifth

▼ *The Roman city on the island of Elephantine is now in ruins. In the sixth century BC, the island was inhabited by a small community of Jews.*

▲ *Rams sacred to Khnum were buried next to his temple at Elephantine. Antagonism between the Jews and the priest of Khnum can be seen in the Aramaic papyri.*

century BC. The Temple of Yahweh was in existence before the invasion of Egypt in 525 BC by the Persian king, Cambyses, but its precise location is not known. The papyri reveal that in 410 BC the priest of the nearby Temple of Khnum persuaded the local governor, in the absence of the Persian satrap (the provincial governor), to attack and destroy the Temple of Yahweh.

The Jews wrote to Bagoas, Governor of Judea, and Yohanan, High Priest in Jerusalem, in protest. At first their communication was ignored, but two years later they wrote again to Bagoas and to the two sons of Sanballat, an earlier governor of Samaria. This time they had the answer they were hoping for. A messenger was sent to request the permission of the Persian satrap to rebuild the temple. The temple was restored and in 401 BC is mentioned in a document, but shortly after the end of Persian rule in Egypt in 332 BC, the Jewish colony was dispersed and its temple disappeared.

Leontopolis

A later Temple of Yahweh, at Leontopolis in the Delta, is known from the work of the first-century Jewish historian, Josephus. He wrote that, after the murder of the High Priest Onias III, his son Onias fled to Egypt where he became commander of the Jewish military colony at Leontopolis (Tell el-Yahudiyeh). While in this post he obtained permission from Ptolemy VI (180–145 BC) to build a temple to Yahweh. According to Josephus, this was built on the site of an old Egyptian temple and was modelled on the Temple in Jerusalem, although it was smaller and not so splendid. The temple was founded in 160 BC but was destroyed by the Romans in AD 74 after the Jewish Revolt. ◆

The 70 scholars

Under the Ptolemies, there was also a large Jewish community in Alexandria. They were mostly Greek-speaking and the Old Testament was translated from Hebrew into Greek mainly for their benefit. The tradition of the 70 scholars who gave their name to the translation comes from a fictional work, The Letter of Aristeas to his friend Philocrates. This says that Ptolemy II (285–246 BC), at the suggestion of Demetrios of Phaleron, decided to make a collection of all the books in the world. When it was realized that the Library of Alexandria did not contain a copy of the Jewish Law, Ptolemy sent a letter to Eliezer, High Priest of Jerusalem, asking him to send to Egypt six elders from each of the 12 tribes, all of whom must be experts in Hebrew and Greek, in order that a translation might be made. On arrival in Alexandria, they were taken to the island of Pharos and set to work.

According to Philo of Alexandria (c.20 BC–c.AD 40), the scholars were inspired as if by an invisible authority, while an anonymous third-century source claims that the scholars were isolated from one another in separate rooms while they translated. St Epiphanius (c.AD 315–403) claimed they were given 36 little houses in which they were installed two by two and locked in from dawn to dusk. Whatever the story, the result was the same: when the translations were compared they all turned out to be identical.

The Mosques and Mausoleums of Cairo

There were no mosques at the time of Muhammad. He and his followers prayed in his home, which consisted of a collection of huts around an open courtyard, surrounded by a high wall. This court was later roofed over and became a place of prayer. After Muhammad's death, when the new faith was spread by military conquest, the Arab armies came into contact with Byzantine and Sassanian culture and this eventually had a great influence on Islamic architecture. In the later seventh and eighth centuries, the semicircular Islamic prayer niche, the pulpit and the screened-off area where the caliph sat were all inspired by the art and architecture previously encountered abroad.

In Syria, the first mosques had originally been churches. The old entrances on the west side were blocked and new ones opened up in the north side. A niche would be made in the south side to indicate the direction of Mecca. A different type of mosque developed in Mesopotamia when the seat of government of the Arab world moved eastwards. The first large mosque to be built in Baghdad occupied an area 120m (1,292ft) square. It consisted of a central court surrounded by a large prayer hall on the south side and on the three other sides by roofed and columned halls or liwans.

▲ *The Sultan Hasan Mosque is possibly the finest example of Islamic architecture in the world.*

The Mosque of Ahmed ibn-Tulin

For about 50 years in the mid-ninth century, the Caliphate was at Samarra, about 100km (60 miles) north of Baghdad, where excavation of the palace has revealed pointed arches and carved stucco. When Ahmed ibn-Tulin, a native of Samarra, became ruler of Egypt, he brought with him the architectural ideas from his own part of the world.

The mosque of Ahmed ibn-Tulin has a ground plan similar to that of the mosque in Baghdad and the decoration is like that found in the caliph's palace at Samarra. All the main types of ornamentation in carved wood and stucco are repeated here. Pointed arches are integrated into the structure. The lower parts of the arches on the south-west side of the court are decorated with the earliest-known examples of geometric patterns in Islamic art.

The el-Azhar Mosque

Of all the Fatimid examples, the el-Azhar Mosque is considered to be the finest. It was finished in AD 972 by Gawhar. In AD 988, it was given university status by Caliph el-Aziz. It was rebuilt after an earthquake in 1303 and since then several rulers and governors have made it their religious duty to restore and maintain the buildings. It remains the leading university of Islam.

The principal lecture hall is the vast liwan on the south-east side of the central court, while the smaller ones on the

▲ *The Sultan Hasan Mosque was built between 1356 and 1363 and was once used as a fortress.*

▲ *An interior view of the richly decorated dome of the Muhammad Ali Mosque, also known as the Alabaster Mosque, which stands on the site of a former Mameluke palace.*

south-west and north-east are used as student workrooms and sleeping quarters. Around the central court there is an arcade with Persian-type arches, decorated with niches and medallions and crowned by crenellations. The mosque owns a magnificent fourteenth-century library, which houses 60,000 volumes.

◀ *The minaret of the el-Azhar Mosque was added to the building in the 15th century. The original mosque dates from the founding of the new city of Cairo in* AD *970–971.*

The Sultan Hasan Mosque

The Sultan Hasan Mosque was built in 1356–63 and is often said to be the finest example of Islamic architecture in Egypt. It is also one of the largest and it has been suggested that it may have been designed by a Syrian architect.

The ground plan is in the shape of an irregular polygon with the liwans arranged around the central court in the form of a cross. The outer walls are plain except for blind niches and twin round-arched windows. The impressive main doorway is 26m (85ft) high, while the minaret, which is well over 81m (265ft), is the tallest in Cairo. The central courtyard contains an elegant fountain and the decoration of the inner walls is in coloured marble cut into attractive geometric shapes. All the liwans are used as prayer halls while the medrese, or teaching rooms, occupy the areas between them.

The main liwan has a carved stucco frieze of kufic lettering. A doorway on the left of the pulpit leads to the Mausoleum of Sultan Hasan, containing a very simple sarcophagus under a dome decorated with carved stalactites.

The Citadel

The Cairo skyline is dominated by the Citadel. It was begun in 1176 by Saladin, who is said to have used the Pyramids at Giza as quarries to provide the stone. Very little remains today of the original structure, except for the walls on the eastern side and some of the internal towers. The two Ayyubid palaces that stood on the site at the time of Saladin's conquest have vanished completely.

One of the most striking sights on entering the Citadel is the Mosque of Muhammad Ali, otherwise known as the Alabaster Mosque. Begun by Muhammad Ali in 1824, it was finished some 30 years later by his successor. The architect was a Greek from Istanbul, whose design was ultimately derived from the Byzantine Church of St Sophia. As in other mosques, there is a fountain for ablutions in the central courtyard, which is surrounded by various halls. The huge main prayer hall has Byzantine-style domes resting on square piers and is impressively lit. The mosque also houses the Mausoleum of Muhammad Ali. ◆

Index

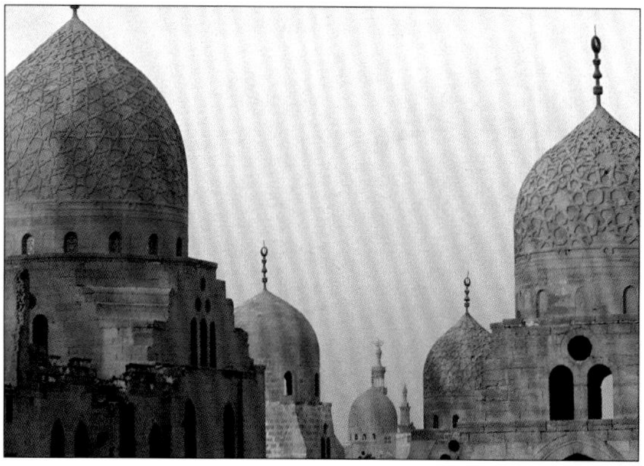

Acknowledgements

Picture Credits

AKG Photographic: pages 4, 8 (inset), 12/13, 14, 15 t, 18 (Musee des Beaux Arts, Liege), 19 tr, 19 b, 20, 23 t b, 25 b, 26 br (private collection), 39 t, 40, 41 b, 51 b (Louvre, Paris), 61 b (Egyptian Museum, Cairo), 90 (Rijksmuseum van Oudheden, Leiden), 105 b (National Museum, Cairo), 112, 117 b, 126, 127 t b, 129 b, 130 t, 151 b, 152, 153 b, 154, 163 t, 179 (Egyptian Museum, Cairo), 180 (Egyptian Museum, Cairo), 182 b (Egyptian Museum, Cairo), 183 t, 189 b, 197 l, 207 b, 209 b, 218, 220 t, 226 l r (British Museum, London), 227 r (Petrie Museum of Egyptian Archaeology).
Alan Fildes: pages 43 t, 91 br.
Ancient Art and Architecture Collection: pages 51 tl, 83 b, 85 b, 91 t bl, 113, 178 t.
Ancient Egypt Picture Library: pages 3, 6, 8, 26 bl, 34 b, 39 b, 44 t, 48 b, 49 all, 55 b, 56 t, 58 t, 59 t, 60, 64 t, 66, 82 b, 84 b, 86, 87 t b, 88 b, 89 b, 102 b, 104 t, 109 l r, 110 b, 111, 118 t, 120 t, 121 all, 128 t b, 129 t, 130 b, 131 b, 140, 142, 143 t b, 148 b, 149 t, 166, 170, 171 t b, 181 t, 191 tr, 197 r, 199, 200, 201 b, 206, 210, 215 t b, 251, 254.
The Art Archive: pages 5 l, 22, 24 (Louvre, Paris/Dagli Orti), 27 (Egyptian Museum, Cairo), 37 b, 38, 120 b (Egyptian Museum, Cairo), 173 t (Dagli Orti), 216 l (Archaeological Museum, Cairo) r.
Axiom: pages 52/53, 63 (Luke White); 54, 55 t, 80 t b, 81 b, 136/7, 138, 144 b, 147 t b, 148 t, 149 b, 15 1 t, 176 l, 177 t b, 188 t b, 189 t, 198 l r 202 t, 212/213, 222 b, 224, 228 t b, 229 t b, 230/231, 239 t b, 242 b, 252 (James Morris); 158 t, 255 (Chris Caldicott).
The Bridgeman Art Library: pages 15 b (National Archaeological Museum, Naples), 28 b, 56 b (private collection), 57 b (private collection), 59 b (Egyptian Museum, Cairo), 107 t, 132 t, 150, 161 tr, 184, 185 c, 187 t, 219 t (Ashmolean Museum, London), 233 b (private collection), 241 (Stapleton Collection), 256.
The British Museum: pages 34 t, 51 tr, 92 b.
J L Charmet: pages 16 (Biblioteque de Mazarine, Paris), 21 t, 26 t.
Christine Osborne Pictures: pages 234, 235 t b, 238 t b, 243 t, 244, 245 all.
Corbis: 46 t (Gianni Dagli Orti), 65 (Roger Wood), 73 (Roger Wood), 81 t (Roger Wood), 83 t (Roger Wood), 93 t b (Roger Wood), 100 (Gianni Dagli Orti), 101 (Gianni Dagli Orti), 114/115 (Roger Wood), 117 t (Roger Wood).
A M Dodson: pages 67 t, 221.
Dyan Hilton: page 167 bl.
Egyptian Museum, Cairo: page 108.
Eye Ubiquitous: page 222 t.
The Hulton Archive: pages 25 t, 28 t, 29, 30 t b.
Jacke Phillips: pages 50.
Dr Joann Fletcher: page 69 t, 158 b.
Jurgen Liepe: pages 32/33, 57 t, 134/135, 139 t, 162 t, 164 t b.
Liason International/© Kurgan-Lisnet: pages 10/11.
The London Library: page 17.
Lorna Oakes: pages 36 b, 37 tr, 44 b, 47 b, 61 t, 76 l, 85 t, 92 t, 110 t, 124, 125 t b, 141 all, 146, 153 t, 155 all, 165 all, 167 br, 168, 169 tl tr, 182 t, 183 b, 186 b, 187 b, 191 tl b, 194, 195 t b, 202 b, 204 t b, 207 tl tr, 225 t b, 236 t b, 237, 246, 247, 249 tl.
Mary Evans Picture Library: pages 19 tl.
Michael Holford: pages 21 b (British Museum, London), 31 r (British Museum, London), 219 b (British Museum, London).
Nowitz Photography: page 243 b.
Panos Pictures: page 249 tr.
Paul Hardy: page 242 t.
Peter Clayton: pages 67 b, 167 t, 181 b, 201 t, 203 t b, 205 t b, 211.
Peter Sanders: page 249 bl.
Rick Strange: page 196.
Robert Harding Picture Library: pages 1, 7, 74/75, 76 r, 94/95, 96 b, 104 b (F L Kenett),105 t, 106 b (R Ashworth), 107 b (R Ashworth), 116 (Tetrel), 131 t, 132 b, 139 b, 144 t, 145, 156/157 (Julia Bayne), 160, 174/175 (Gavin Hellier), 176 r, 185 t (Etan Simanor) b (Gavin Hellier), 186 t (Philip Craven), 208 (Philip Craven), 209 t (Philip Craven), 248 (Nigel Francis), 253.
Scala: pages 41 t (Egyptian Museum, Cairo), 62 (National Archaeological Museum, Naples), 98, 99 t b, 106 t, 159 (Louvre, Paris), 162 b, 172 (Egyptian Museum, Cairo), 223 b (Acropolis Museum, Athens), 232, 233 t.
A Siliotti: pages 46 b, 47 t, 68, 69 b, 70 t, 71 t b.
Silvia Cordaiy Photo Library: pages 192/193.

Sonia Halliday Photographs: pages 37 tl, 78, 79 b, 133 t, 190, 240.
Spectrum Colour Library: pages 161 tl, 163 b.
Sygma/Stephane Compoint: page 220 b.
Theban Mapping Project: pages 122, 123 t b.
Travel Ink/Stephen Psallidas: page 96 t.
Trip: page 118 b.
Veneta Bullen: page 36 t.
Werner Forman Archive: pages 2, 5 c r (Egyptian Museum, Cairo), 31 l (Egyptian Museum, Cairo), 35 (Louvre, Paris), 42, 43 b, 45 t b, 48 t (Metropolitan Museum of Art, New York), 50 t, 58 b, 64 b (Egyptian Museum, Cairo), 70 b, 72, 79 t (Egyptian Museum, Cairo), 82 t, 88 t, 89 t, 102 t, 119 (Dr E Strouhal), 133 b (Dr E Strouhal), 173 b (Egyptian Museum, Cairo), 214 (Egyptian Museum, Cairo), 217 t b (Egyptian Museum, Cairo), 227 l (J Paul Getty Museum, Malibu), 250.

Acknowledgements

The author would like to thank Hany Zarif for his information on the temples of Nubia and Elephantine.

Sources of Quotes

The author and publishers would like to thank publishers for permission to quote from the following titles. Every effort has been made to identify sources and we apologize for any omissions:

Page 14: Austin, M M, *The Hellenistic World from Alexander to the Roman Conquest*, Cambridge, 1981
Page 19: Denon, V, *Travels in Upper and Lower Egypt*, London, 1802
Pages 26, 93: Vercoutter, J, *Search for Ancient Egypt*, London, 1992
Pages 28–29: Edwards, A, *A Thousand Miles Up the Nile*, London, 1877
Page 30: Petrie, W M F, *Seventy Years in Archaeology*, London, 1939
Pages 42–43, 84–85, 142, 165, 170, 206–207: Lichtheim, M, *Ancient Egyptian Literature*, Vols 1–111, Berkeley, 1973, 1976, 1980
Pages 62–3, 92, 219: Herodotus, *The Histories*, (trans. Aubrey de Selincourt), London, 1954
Page 81: Lauer, J-P, *The Pyramids of Sakkara*, Paris, 1991
Page 90–91: Martin, G T, *Hidden Tombs of Memphis*, London, 1991
Page 100: Romer, J, *Valley of the Kings*, London, 1881
Pages 104–105: Carter, H, *The Tomb of Tukankhamun*, London, 1923
Pages 112–113: Spencer, A J, *Death in Ancient Egypt*, London, 1982
Page 123: Weeks, K, *The Lost Tomb*, London, 1998
Pages 153, 168–169: Gardiner, A H, Peet, T E, and Czerny, J, *Inscriptions in Sinai*, London 1952–55
Page 167: Bierbrier, M L, *Tomb Builders of the Pharaohs*, London, 1982
Page 183: Naville, E, *The Temple at Deir el-Bahri*, London, 1894-1908
Page 203: Kitchen, K A, *Pharaoh Triumphant*, Warminster, 1982
Page 205: Breasted, J, *Records of Ancient Egypt*, London, 1906
Page 207: de Morgan, J, *Sehel Inscriptions*, Paris
Page 223: Arrian, *Life of Alexander*, (trans. Aubrey de Selincourt), London, 1958

GODS & MYTHS OF

ANCIENT EGYPT

GODS & MYTHS OF ANCIENT EGYPT

AN ILLUSTRATED GUIDE TO THE MYTHOLOGY, RELIGION AND CULTURE

LUCIA GAHLIN

LORENZ BOOKS

For Richard and Dexter

This edition is published by Lorenz Books, an imprint of Anness Publishing Ltd, Blaby Road, Wigston, Leicestershire LE18 4SE; info@anness.com

www.lorenzbooks.com; www.annesspublishing.com

Anness Publishing has a new picture agency outlet for images for publishing, promotions or advertising. Visit www.practicalpictures.com for more information

A CIP catalogue record for this book is available from the British Library.

Publisher: Joanna Lorenz
Project Editor: Debra Mayhew
Designer: Jez MacBean
Illustrator: Stuart Carter
Production Manager: Steve Lang
Picture Researcher: Veneta Bullen
Illustrator: Stuart Carter

CONTENTS

Introduction

▲ *In this intimate scene decorating the side of Tutankhamun's small gold-plated shrine, the queen ties her husband's floral collar behind his neck. 18th Dynasty.*

Though the civilization of the ancient Egyptians was arguably not the earliest to flourish, it endured longer than any other, and in its heyday it was the most spectacular on earth. It emerged about 5,000 years ago and continued to flourish for three millennia. Much of the information about this remarkable country, and the people who lived there so long ago, has lain hidden in the sands for thousands of years. Their secrets are being gradually unearthed.

It was in the fertile areas around the great rivers of the Near East and North Africa that agriculture began, and with it came the beginnings of a settled, civilized way of life which proceeded to bear rich cultural fruits. The earliest evidence of settled farming communities beside the Nile dates from c.5500 BC. These grew into a number of chiefdoms, with distinctive regional cultures, in Upper and Lower Egypt. In Upper Egypt, social stratification and craftsmanship began to evolve and the cultural developments of the south gradually penetrated Lower Egypt to the north during the Predynastic and Protodynastic Periods, leading up to the country's political consolidation as a single state in c.3100.

▼ *The king was the only mortal who could be depicted face-to-face with a deity. Here Ramesses II encounters Amun. 19th Dynasty.*

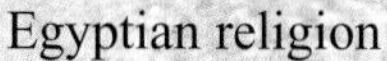

Egyptian religion

When Egypt was unified under a succession of pharaohs, many local gods were admitted into the national pantheon, giving rise to a vast number of deities and a complex system of beliefs and ritual. Religion was a fundamental part of the life of every Egyptian, from the mighty pharaoh down to the most humble agricultural worker, and the annual flooding of the Nile inspired many of the myths and beliefs of ancient Egypt. The people recognized their utter dependence on the revival of their agricultural land. The arid desert in which the people of Egypt were buried also shaped their identity and inspired their religious beliefs. For us, their religion is one of the most intriguing aspects of the ancient Egyptians' culture – a wealth of gods and temples, mummies, ornate tombs and fabulous treasure. Centuries of plunder by grave robbers, followed by more systematic excavations by archaeologists, have revealed an incredible quantity of artefacts, buildings, imagery and writing that provide a fascinating account of the beliefs and practices of these ancient people. The wealth of documentary information left in the form of carved inscriptions and inscribed papyrus rolls provides us with an insight into all aspects of their religion and ritual.

A vast number of graves and tombs have been excavated. They reveal that the ancient Egyptians aspired to an Afterlife that was pretty much a continuation of their existence on earth (only more fruitful and prosperous), preserving their social status, family connections and even their physical possessions. They thought of their deities, too, as leading lives very much like their own. Their tombs and temples are therefore rich in decoration, inscriptions and artefacts that offer a detailed and vibrant account of every aspect of life in ancient Egypt. ◆

Timeline of Ancient Egypt

Before c.5500 BC

Early settlers in the Nile Valley; beginning of crop farming, growing wheat and barley.

c.5500–c.3100 BC
Predynastic and Protodynastic Period

Development of craftsmanship and animal husbandry.

Beginnings of social stratification.

Boats used on the Nile.

Construction using wattle and daub and beginning of mud brick.

Early wall painting and stone carving.

c.3100–c.2686 BC
Early Dynastic Period

Unification of Egypt.

Memphis established as capital.

Development of hieroglyphs.

c.2686–2181 BC
Old Kingdom

c.2650 BC

Step pyramid built at Saqqara during reign of Djoser.

c.2615 BC

Pyramid built at Meidum.

c.2580 BC

Great Pyramid at Giza built during reign of Khufu.

c.2530 BC

Great Sphinx built at Giza.

▶ *The Great Sphinx guards the Valley Temple of Khafre at Giza.*

c.2181–c.2055 BC
First Intermediate Period

Herakleopolitan and Theban dynasties control Egypt.

c.2055–c.1650 BC
Middle Kingdom

Egypt conquers Nubia, trades with Syria and Palestine.

Mudbrick pyramids built in Middle Egypt and at Dahshur.

Rock-cut tombs constructed in Middle Egypt.

c.1650–c.1550 BC
Second Intermediate Period

c.1600 BC

The horse is introduced into Egypt.

Hyksos claim control in Delta.

c.1550–c.1069 BC
New Kingdom

c.1550–c.1069 BC

Royal tombs built in the Valley of the Kings.

c.1348 BC

Akhenaten introduces worship of Aten, the sun disc, in place of established religion, and establishes a new capital, Akhetaten.

c.1336 BC

Capital moves back to Memphis.

c. 1327 BC

Burial of King Tutankhamun in Valley of the Kings.

c.1250 BC

Ramesses II decorates the Hypostyle Hall at Karnak.

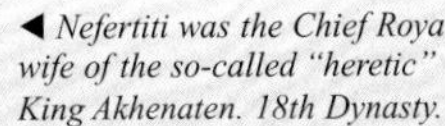

◀ *Nefertiti was the Chief Royal wife of the so-called "heretic" King Akhenaten. 18th Dynasty.*

c.1274 BC

Battle of Qadesh against the Hittites.

c.1209 BC

Egypt attacked by Mediterranean Sea Peoples.

c.1176 BC

Sea Peoples defeated by Ramesses III.

c.1069–c.747 BC
Third Intermediate Period

Egypt becomes politically divided.

c.747–c.332 BC
Late Period

671 BC

Assyrians invade Egypt and reach Memphis.

525 BC

Egypt becomes part of the Persian Empire.

332BC–AD395
Ptolemaic and Roman Periods

332 BC

Egypt invaded by Alexander the Great, bringing it under Macedonian Greek rule. Alexandria founded.

305 BC

Ptolemy assumes power after death of Alexander.

30 BC

Egypt becomes part of the Roman Empire.

AD 324

Egypt adopts Christianity.

AD 395

End of Roman rule in Egypt.

The Land of Egypt

▲ *For most of the length of the Nile Valley, strips of fertile land border either side of the river, and the dividing line between desert and cultivation is clear-cut, as here at Tell el-Amarna.*

Ancient Egypt existed in a landscape of extremes, with vast expanses of arid desert bordering a narrow ribbon of wonderfully fertile land – and very little has changed to this day.

The Nile is Egypt's lifeblood. North of Aswan it flows for 900km (560 miles) through the Nile Valley until it reaches the Delta, which it traverses in a number of branches (five during the pharaonic period) before feeding its muddy water into the Mediterranean Sea. The silt it deposits is thick and black, inspiring the ancient Egyptians' name for their country, *Kemet* ('Black Land'). In contrast, the barren desert cliffs were seen to glow pink at dawn, so the desert was described as *Deshret* ('Red Land').

In ancient times, the Egyptian name for the summer season was *Akhet*, or Inundation. It was equivalent to the four months from July to October, when the great river overflowed its banks and flooded the Nile Valley and the Delta. The huge volumes of water originated as rain that fell in central Sudan, raising the level of the White Nile. A few weeks later the summer monsoon rain falling over the Ethiopian highlands caused a very rapid swelling of the Blue Nile, and its tributary, the Atbara. All of these sources of water combined, reaching Egypt in a great swollen rush at the end of July.

Only in 1968 were the waters of the River Nile finally tamed, by the construction of the Aswan Dam. The Nile Valley is no longer flooded every year, and this has made a huge difference to Egypt's natural environment and way of life.

◀ *Scenes of agricultural life were commonly painted on the walls of private tombs. Here in their Theban tomb Sennedjem and his wife harvest their bountiful crops. c.1200 BC.*

As well as providing ancient Egypt with, usually, two healthy harvests a year, the Nile was the principal means of transportation. It supplied much of the protein in the people's diet (in the form of fish and water birds). Ivory came from the tusks of the hippopotami that lived in the river, and papyrus was made from reeds that grew along its banks. Finally, the river was the source of mud, the chief ingredient of the most widely used building material – mudbricks. At the same time, the river could be treacherous: hippopotami, crocodiles, winds, currents, shallow waters and cataracts were all hazards that had to be taken seriously by the people whose lives depended on the Nile.

The Longest River

The Nile is the longest river in the world, flowing 6,741km (4,189 miles) from its source in the East African highlands to the Delta, a fertile area of about 22,000sq km (8,500sq miles). The Delta, named by the Greeks because it resembled the shape of the fourth letter of their alphabet, lies 17m (57ft) above sea level. Here the Nile once split into several channels before emerging into the Mediterranean Sea: of these only two now remain.

The impregnable desert

The river was not the only place where danger lurked. The ancient Egyptians also particularly feared the desert. It was a place of searing heat by day and freezing cold by night, a waterless place of wild animals, fugitives and nomads. The desert dwellers often turned out to be marauders, and in addition there were countless demons who were supposed to live in the desert.

On the other hand, much of the greatness of the Egyptian civilization came from wealth yielded by the inhospitable desert. Its treasures included amethyst, turquoise, copper, limestone, sandstone, granite and – above all – gold. The desert lands also fulfilled another important function: they helped to make Egypt into an almost impregnable fortress. To either side of the Nile were the wastelands of the Eastern and Western, or Libyan, Deserts, to the north the Mediterranean Sea, and in the south was the first cataract of the Nile, which made the river unnavigable at that point. Egypt was protected from almost any outside threat. This resulted in an exceptionally stable society, and a strong sense of national identity flourished. A fear of the unknown resulted in a common mistrust of outsiders or foreigners (who were often described as *hesy*, meaning 'vile' or 'wretched').

► *The copper inlay around the eyes of this painted statue from the 5th Dynasty represents the green malachite scribes wore to protect their eyes.*

Harnessing nature

The ancient Egyptians were self-sufficient in most things, except for suitable timber for building. The agricultural cycle revolved around the Nile flood, which could usually be depended on. Measuring gauges known as Nilometers were used to record the flood levels, so that suitable precautions might be taken if necessary. Efficient irrigation was crucial to agriculture. Farmers practised basin irrigation: they built earth banks to divide up areas of the flood plain, then led water into these artificial ponds and allowed it to stand before draining it off. The system could be administered on a local level.

The major crops were emmer wheat, barley and flax. Tomb scenes and models illustrate the various stages: ploughing, sowing the seed, harvesting, winnowing, threshing, and so on. Also depicted are the production of food and drink, such as grape-picking, wine pressing, brewing and breadmaking.

The dual benefits of the Nile and the sun made the land of Egypt a flourishing place. But as with all natural elements, there had to be precautions against their dangerous aspects. As protection against the overwhelming heat of the sun, people had to wear headcoverings to guard against sunstroke, and protected their eyes by wearing green malachite (copper) or black galena (lead) eye paints. Rain is not usually associated with Egypt, but it did occur in the north, and sometimes caused floods in the desert wadis; such problems had to be coped with. It therefore becomes clear that the lives of the ancient Egyptians were very much dictated by their natural environment and the climate. ◆

▲ *This Nilometer within the temple complex at Kom Ombo was constructed to gauge the river's rising level during the annual inundation.*

The Beginnings of Egyptian Civilization

Ancient Egypt as people usually imagine it – as the land of the pharaohs, with great temples, cities and burial sites, beautiful art and writing in hieroglyphs – came into being with the formation of a unified and centralized state in c.3100 BC. The factors that led to this development are speculative, but the most momentous changes in Egypt's history took place around 3000 BC.

For the first few hundred-thousand years of human occupation, Egypt was home to stone-age, or palaeolithic, hunting, fishing and food-gathering communities, which lived along the river terraces of the Nile Valley. Then, from c.5500 BC, the earliest agricultural communities emerged. Over the next 2,400 years, the country came to be divided between separate, self-governing communities, which developed at different rates socially, economically, politically and culturally. These early developments can be traced mainly by examining the so-called Predynastic burials, which have been excavated at various sites throughout Egypt.

▲ *The ceremonial limestone 'Scorpion Macehead' from Hierakonpolis, shows King Scorpion of the Protodynastic Period engaged in an activity that may be the ritual cutting of an irrigation channel, or perhaps a foundation trench for a temple.*

Material culture

As the local cultures developed, their craftsmanship increased in quality and sophistication. Pottery was painted and jewellery fashioned; stone-working became more elaborate, with the manufacture of palettes, mace heads, knives and vases; metal-working began with the production of copper tools; and the copper ore malachite was used in the glaze for beads.

A recognizably Egyptian style was already beginning to emerge in the items being produced, and the markets for such goods clearly became wider and more specialized. Desert resources, such as gold from the Eastern Desert, were exploited and we know contact was made with traders from outside Egypt, as lapis lazuli from Badakhshan in north-eastern Afghanistan has been found in Predynastic graves.

The evidence of such artefacts indicates that their makers would have been freed from subsistence farming and that society was becoming differentiated, with the emergence of an elite who could afford luxury goods and who presumably controlled the trade routes, local irrigation systems and more elaborate building projects (especially tombs). Luxury goods may have been specially made to place in graves with the dead, and it seems that funerary customs played a major part in the increasing division of labour and the development of greater social complexity and stratification.

◀ *Celestial and bovine themes figure in what appears to be the earliest recorded religious imagery surviving from Egypt, such as on this Predynastic greywacke (slate) cosmetic palette.*

The exchange of goods would inevitably have been coupled with the exchange of ideas. The contact with Mesopotamia (modern Iraq) appears to have been particularly significant in the early period of Egyptian civilization. It is likely that foreign traders would have been attracted to Egypt by the prospect of purchasing its gold.

A centralized state emerges

By c.3100 BC, Egypt was a highly efficient political state, with an administrative bureaucracy, precisely defined boundaries and elaborate kingship rites relating to a single ruler. So why did the Egyptian state emerge when it did? There have been a number of theories, reflecting various trends in thought. They relate to changes in the physical environment and climate, as well as external stimuli. It is most likely that a variety of factors coincided to create the major changes.

▲ *One of the designs most commonly found on Predynastic painted pots is that of a boat with cabins and banks of oars.*

▶ *The Protodynastic 'Two-dogs' ceremonial greywacke palette from Hierakonpolis is decorated with desert animals and two mythical long-necked beasts in the style of Mesopotamian art. The central circular area was for the grinding of pigments.*

Environmental changes are likely to have been tied in with a growth in the population, increased production, and the freeing of specialists from subsistence farming, resulting in the domination of the poor by an elite. It has been suggested that the growth in population caused the need for increased technology to meet the rising demand, which in turn resulted in the need for central organization. Other theories involve population growth leading to conflict between communities. The increasing aridity of the desert over the millennia would have led to the narrowing of the area of habitable land, thus concentrating the population, and Egypt is known to have experienced a wetter period followed by a drier period around 3300 BC. The movement of people because of climatic changes (especially northwards into the Delta region) may well have caused both alliances and conflicts, resulting in the emergence of chiefdoms. Territorial competition and the merger of local chiefdoms no doubt led to increased power in the hands of fewer people.

Outside influences

Cultural transfer, especially from Mesopotamia and Elam, is often considered to have been the catalyst for Egypt's formation as a unified state, and the simultaneous emergence of a highly developed system of writing (hieroglyphs). But the direction and impact of any contact is still highly contested. Egypt's political superstructure was very likely well under way by the time western Asiatic motifs started to appear in Egyptian art. Examples show that the Egyptians made use of foreign ideas in a very Egyptian manner and soon chose to discard them.

While the development of writing helped to consolidate the unification of the state – aiding administrative efficiency and speeding up the processes of centralization of power – there is no evidence that Egyptian hieroglyphs had their origins in a foreign writing system. The beginnings of Egyptian civilization, often referred to as the Unification of Egypt, remain hazy and speculative. ◆

Part One: State Religion

The key to Egypt's enduring stability and prosperity was the relationship between the pharaoh and the gods. The pharaoh was an absolute monarch who was believed to derive his power from the gods and who formed a link between them and the world of humankind. His mediating role was essential in maintaining the divine order that preserved the universe.

It was the pharaoh's duty to build temples and to ensure that offerings were made to the gods housed within them. In return, the gods would bestow blessings on the people, such as victory in battle, bountiful harvests and recovery from sickness. The Egyptian pantheon contained a vast number of gods and goddesses, each of whom might have several different forms or 'aspects', and the myths that concern them say much about the way in which the Egyptians perceived the divine world.

In his role as king, the pharaoh assumed divinity, but to some extent he was in fact a servant of the gods. It was the high priests who acted on behalf of the ruler in the great state temples erected throughout the country, which played a vital role in the structure of Egyptian civilization.

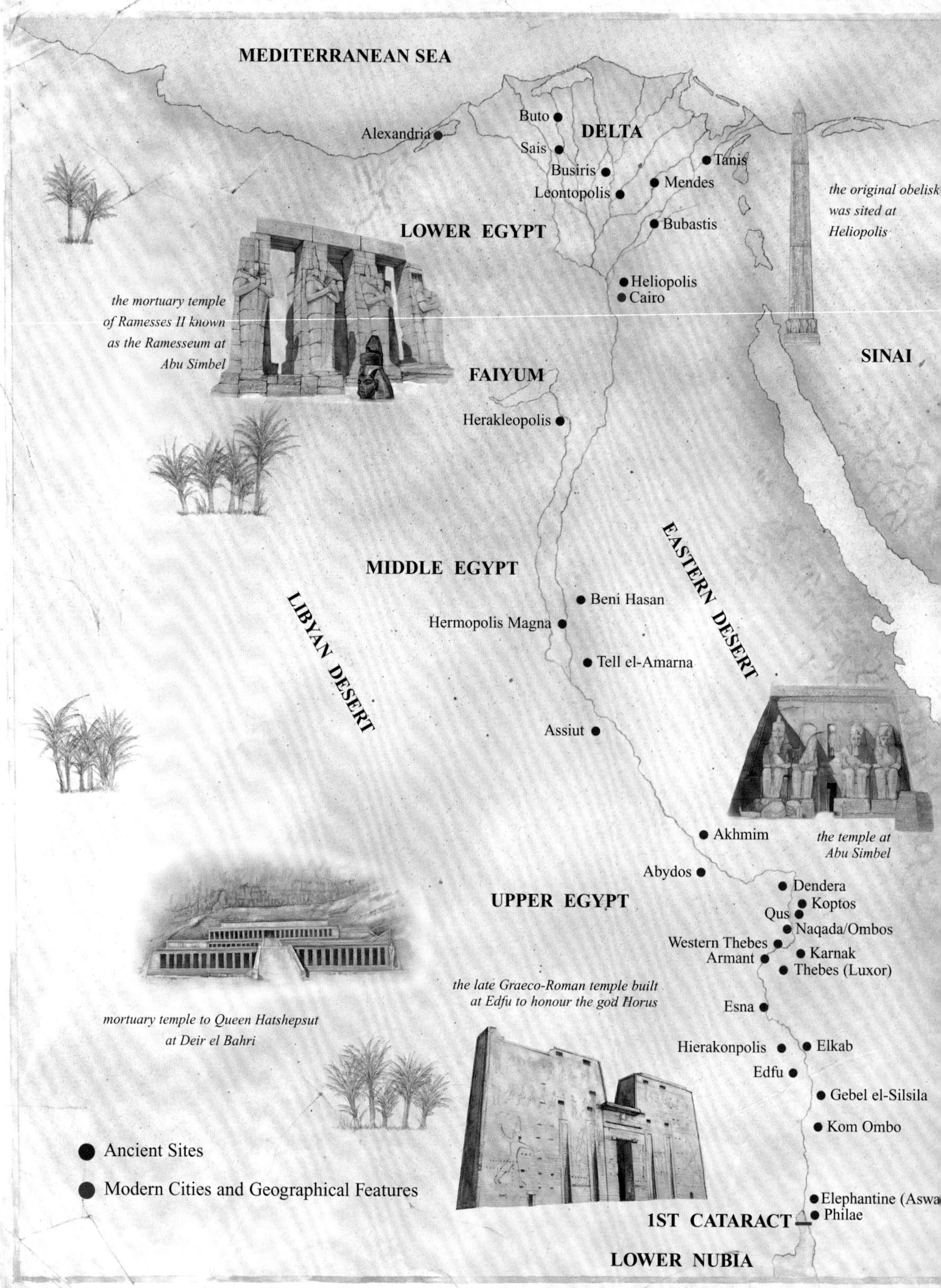
MEDITERRANEAN SEA
Buto
DELTA
Alexandria
Sais
Tanis
Busiris
Mendes
Leontopolis
the original obelisk
was sited at
Heliopolis
Bubastis
LOWER EGYPT
Heliopolis
Cairo
the mortuary temple
of Ramesses II known
as the Ramesseum at
Abu Simbel
SINAI
FAIYUM
Herakleopolis
EASTERN DESERT
MIDDLE EGYPT
Beni Hasan
LIBYAN DESERT
Hermopolis Magna
Tell el-Amarna
Assiut
Akhmim
the temple at
Abu Simbel
Abydos
Dendera
UPPER EGYPT
Koptos
Qus
Naqada/Ombos
Western Thebes
Karnak
Armant
Thebes (Luxor)
the late Graeco-Roman temple built
at Edfu to honour the god Horus
Esna
mortuary temple to Queen Hatshepsut
at Deir el Bahri
Hierakonpolis
Elkab
Edfu
Gebel el-Silsila
Kom Ombo
Ancient Sites
Modern Cities and Geographical Features
Elephantine (Aswa
1ST CATARACT
Philae
LOWER NUBIA

Main Cult Centres

The Nile river and the narrow, fertile band of arable land along its length has always supported the population of Egypt. It was along the banks of the Nile that people first settled. These settlements developed into sophisticated communities, with their own administrative centres, ruling bodies, temples, priesthoods and deities. The gods and goddesses that the local people chose to worship were initially peculiar to each location, although as society evolved and the links between the townships developed, the same gods frequently appear to have been worshipped in more than one centre. The existence of a deity helped to explain the creation of humankind, and other natural phenomena. The gods were beneficent, offering protection against war and famine in return for reverence and worship. The most well-known cult centres are indicated on the map with a red spot.

Gods and Goddesses

The ancient Egyptians worshipped a multitude of gods and goddesses, and an understanding of these is crucial for any enquiry into Egyptian mythology and religion. It is, however, easy to be baffled by the great number of deities, the variety of forms they take and the complexity of the relationships between them.

The Egyptians inhabited a natural environment that could prove hazardous and life was unpredictable. Much of what they encountered in life and the world around them may have seemed mysterious and incomprehensible. The gods and goddesses they conjured up were divine personifications of all that was important to them, particularly in maintaining a sense of order and well-being in this life and the next, ensuring the survival of the next generation and the continued fertility of the soil. So there were, for example, gods of the cosmos, the afterlife, childbirth, grain, even drunkenness and merriment. The stories or myths that evolved around the various gods and goddesses were a means of explaining the unknown, such as why it was dark at night, or the cause of an illness.

Worship often involved making offerings to the gods accompanied by invocation, in order to ensure their continued and benign presence in the lives of the people.

◀ *Ancient Egyptian deities were represented in a variety of forms. Here at Karnak the god Amun appears as ram-headed sphinxes guarding the processional way to his temple.*

Divine Forms

Religion was central to the lives of the ancient Egyptians, and central to their religion were the gods and goddesses they worshipped. They were the protagonists in the religious texts, and in the temple and tomb scenes that survive from Egypt's past. Each had their own distinctive characteristics and identities.

The ancient Egyptians appear to have had no single sacred book into which their ideas and beliefs were consolidated. Among the extant religious treatises there is no one divine explanation as to the origins of humankind and the universe, but several which seem to contradict one another. Each of the main cult centres of Egypt had its own version of the story centred around a different creator god, but it is impossible to know which one was most widely believed at any one time. The diversity of these creation myths serves to emphasize the interconnected and yet seemingly contradictory system of beliefs referred to as ancient Egyptian religion. Various sources reveal the extreme complexity of the representations and interrelationships of the gods and goddesses.

▶ *Bastet was often represented as a cat, but could also appear as a woman with a feline head. Her statues are often adorned with jewellery. The bronze 'Gayer Anderson cat' has silver inlays and gold earrings and nose ring. 30 BC.*

Thoth, for example, was a lunar deity; he was also the god of wisdom and of scribes. He was often represented as a man with the head of an ibis, or entirely in the form of this bird, but he could also be depicted as a baboon. Horus, on the other hand, is always found in partial or complete falcon configuration (not to be confused with the Theban god of warfare Montu, who was also depicted in this way) but on some occasions his mother is said to be the goddess Hathor, whereas at other times she is said to be the goddess Isis. Seemingly distinct deities may actually be incarnations of the same one; for example, Bastet, the mother goddess in cat form, appears to be the more gentle embodiment of the aggressive Sekhmet, the lioness goddess whose name translates as 'the powerful one'.

So we see that in the imaginations of the Egyptians, the gods fused human and animal elements. Greater accessibility might have been achieved by representing deities in male and female human form, but a sense of mystery was instilled by the combination with animal form. It is interesting, however, that divine personifications of the environment or the cosmos, such as Geb, the god of the earth, or Hapy, god of the Nile inundation, tend to be given human form. Even when deities are represented partially or totally as animals, they exhibit human behaviour and express human emotions, haranguing each other in court for example, or getting drunk and falling asleep.

◀ *This scribe from the ancient city of Akhetaten sits cross-legged before Thoth, represented here as a baboon. The god's headdress bears both the full and the crescent moon, indicating his lunar association. 18th Dynasty.*

Gods in animal form

The attributes and behaviour of an animal clearly determined its selection as the representation of a deity. For example, the fierce goddess Sekhmet takes the form of a ferocious lioness and Khepri, god of the sun and creation, is represented as a dung beetle, which has

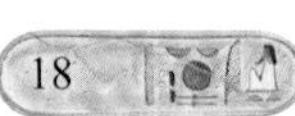

▶ *Taweret's sagging breasts and large rounded stomach identified her with pregnant women and mothers.*

the habit of rolling its eggs in a ball of dung. Another consideration appears to have been that, by depicting a deity in the form of a dangerous animal such as a snake (for example, the fertility goddess Renenutet or Mertseger, the patron deity of the west Theban peak), and then by worshipping that deity, the animal in question might in turn be placated and the hazard allayed.

Sometimes the form particular deities were given must also have been apotropaic (able to ward off harm). Take, for example, the protective goddess of childbirth, Taweret, who is portrayed as a hippopotamus with additional characteristics of a crocodile and a lion. The idea was that such a potentially threatening combination would keep harm away from mother and child.

The concept of a composite animal is most clearly exemplified by the demon deity, Ammit, who was responsible for devouring the hearts of those who had done wrong during their lifetime, thereby denying them a life after death. She was represented as part crocodile, part lion or panther, and part hippopotamus. The ancient Egyptians clearly dreamt up strange combinations of animals in order to represent the more menacing of divine forces.

All the animals in the collective visualization of the divine world were indigenous to the Nile Valley, the marshy Delta region and the desert fringes. Though the giraffe was known to exist, because it had been brought into Egypt as an example of exotica from sub-Saharan Africa; it was never chosen to represent a deity. There is, however, one god whose animal form remains a mystery, and that is Seth. Perhaps due to his association with chaos and infertility, he was depicted as an animal with a forked tail, a greyhound-like body, a long snout and squared-off ears. Either such a beast did not actually exist, or it is long extinct.

The significance of names

Perhaps by visualizing and verbalizing the divine world in terms of customary animals and routine human behaviour, the intention was to demystify and make explicable what was by definition mysterious and incomprehensible. Nevertheless, divinity can never be fully understood and must instil a sense of wonder in the non-divine. In the myth of *Isis and the Sun God's Secret Name*, it is the one unknown name of Re that is the source of his power; the hidden essence is crucial. The names of the deities were decidedly as important as their particular characteristics and the means by which they were represented. Offerings and prayers could be made only to a divine force that had its own name.

Myths served to explain the origins, personalities and relationships of the deities, but it is impossible to know for certain how and when the identities of the gods and goddesses of ancient Egypt evolved. All we can do is identify the earliest known occurrence of the deity in each instance (whether a representation or textual reference). It is likely that the priesthood formulated and developed the various theological ideas associated with the gods and goddesses. ◆

▼ *Hapy, the god of the Nile inundation, was portrayed with rolls of fat and heavy breasts, emphasizing his connection with fecundity. This image, symbolizing the Unification of Egypt exemplifies the ancient Egyptians' love of symmetry in art.*

Deities and Cult Centres

During the Dynastic Period of Egyptian history, from the formation of the state of Egypt in c.3100 BC through to the conquest of Egypt by Alexander the Great in 332 BC, Egypt was divided into administrative districts, called nomes, each with its own capital. There were 22 nomes in the Nile Valley (Upper Egypt) and twenty in the Delta region (Lower Egypt). They probably reflected the composition of the separate chiefdoms of the Predynastic Period, before the unification of Egypt under one king. Each nome had its own cult centre, with a priesthood to service the needs of the local deity (or *njwty*, from the ancient Egyptian *niwt* meaning city), and a temple with a shrine for the residence of the god or goddess.

In fact, each cult centre tended to house not a sole deity but a whole divine family or triad, such as Ptah, Sekhmet and Nefertem at Memphis, or Osiris, Isis and Horus at Abydos. Sometimes, an extended family tree of gods and goddesses can be traced, such as that connected with the cult centre of Heliopolis (see *Creation Myths*). There might also be a mythological link between deities associated with temples some distance apart. For example Hathor of Dendera and Horus of Edfu were united on certain festival days, when Hathor was said to make an annual voyage to Edfu to be united with Horus.

A division of deities into more manageable genealogies would have been necessary for the ordering of such a multitude of divine beings. A survey of these groupings, however, soon reveals overlaps; Amun ('the Hidden One'), for example, occurs in both the triad of Thebes and the Ogdoad (eight gods) of Hermopolis. This does not appear to have troubled the ancient Egyptians. Theirs was an add-on religion, from

Egyptian economy

The administrators of Egypt's forty-two nomes were responsible for the collection of taxes on behalf of the central government. Most people were subsistence farmers and much of the local economy was based on bartering. Taxes were collected in the form of grain, meat, minerals and other goods. The tax system was the responsibility of the king's vizier, or chief minister.

The agrarian system also came under the supervision of the nome administrators, who registered landowners. The total yield of grain in any one year largely depended on the amount of land that could be cultivated as a result of the annual inundation. Irrigation systems were developed to extend this area as far as possible, and it was in the interests of the authorities to see that they were kept in good condition.

◄ *This statue of Horus stands at the entrance to the Hypostyle Hall in the temple of Edfu. As the god of kingship, the falcon deity wears the Double Crown of Upper and Lower Egypt.*

which ideas were never discarded in favour of new ones; instead a cumulative effect can be seen, and in fact the antiquity of any religious element heightened its sacredness.

Politics

The development of the state religion was heavily influenced by political factors. A local deity might rise to national importance because he or she shared a home town with a new ruling family, such as the Eleventh and Eighteenth Dynasties, whose capital was Thebes. Their conquests and claiming of the throne resulted in the prominence of the gods Montu and Amun.

Political motives might also be responsible for the fusion of two deities into one (a process known as syncretism). An example is Amun-Re, head of the pantheon during the New Kingdom (c.1550–c.1069 BC). He was a combination of Amun the patron deity of Thebes, by then the religious capital of the whole of Egypt, and the ancient sun god Re, whose cult at Heliopolis was one of the oldest and whose priesthood had always had particular influence. This union was probably the result of a political alliance.

The degree to which politics and religious belief could interact became even more apparent during the reign of the Eighteenth-Dynasty king Akhenaten (c.1352–c.1336 BC), when he abandoned Thebes to found a new capital, Akhetaten. Here he tried to establish a new religion, erasing the inscriptions to Amun and the other traditional gods and recognizing only one deity, the Aten. Akhenaten's actions may have been an attempt to curb the political power of Amun's priests, but his reforms failed, possibly because they were not welcomed by most Egyptians, who clung to the rich complexity of strongly personalized deities to whom they could relate directly. ◆

◄ *Amun can often be identified by his double-plumed headdress. Here he sits behind a figure of Tutankhamun. 18th Dynasty.*

▲ *Akhenaten attempted to abolish the traditional polytheistic religion. Here he is shown offering lotus flowers to his sole god, Aten, represented as the sun's disc. 18th Dynasty.*

Deification of Mortals

It was rare but not unheard of for the ancient Egyptians to deify eminent individuals from the past. The king himself was considered a god to some extent, particularly after his death, but occasionally a local cult might grow up around a ruler in addition to his official funerary cult, and he would be worshipped as a patron deity in a more unusual way. The most popular was Amenhotep I (c.1525–c.1504 BC), the second ruler of the Eighteenth Dynasty. Together with his mother, Ahmose-Nefertari, he was worshipped as a protective deity and founder of Deir el-Medina, the west Theban village of tomb builders. He was treated like the patron saint of this small workmen's community. There was a shrine dedicated to him, festivals were celebrated in his honour, and sometimes his statue was carried by priests so that his oracle might be consulted.

The best-known non-royal figures who were posthumously honoured with deification were Imhotep and Amenhotep son of Hapu, but from the New Kingdom onwards (c.1550 BC) victims of drowning began to be deified. The River Nile was the lifeline of the ancient Egyptian people and much religious belief surrounded it. By the Late Period a person who had drowned in it might sometimes have a cult established in their honour.

Imhotep's Pyramid

The Step Pyramid at Saqqara was built c.2650 for the burial of the Third-Dynasty king Djoser. The building began as a mastaba tomb (a superstructure named from the Arabic word for 'bench'). This was then extended in size and three further levels were erected over it to form a four-step pyramid. Finally, it was enlarged again and two further steps were added.

The base of the pyramid measures 140 x 118m (459 x 387ft) and it is 60m (197ft) high. At the time of its construction it was by far the largest monument in Egypt, and was also the first to be built from blocks of limestone rather than mudbrick. It was surrounded by a funerary complex for the king, containing mortuary temples and a statue chamber within a walled enclosure.

Imhotep

The great vizier, or chief minister, of the Third-Dynasty king Djoser (c.2667–c.2648 BC), Imhotep was the architect of Egypt's earliest monumental stone structure, the Step Pyramid Complex of Djoser at Saqqara, the chief

◀ *Amenhotep son of Hapu is shown here with his scribal palette hanging over his shoulder, loaded with two circular cakes of red and black ink. 18th Dynasty.*

▲ *Amenhotep I and his mother, Ahmose Nefertari, were worshipped as patron deities of Deir el-Medina long after their deaths. 18th Dynasty.*

burial site at the time for the capital at Memphis. An inscription on a statue of the king honours his vizier as a master carpenter and sculptor, while carvings on stone vessels say that he was a priest.

Imhotep was obviously remembered throughout pharaonic history, but he was not actually deified until the Late Period, some 2,000 years after his death. In fact he was particularly acknowledged during the Ptolemaic Period (332–30 BC), when he was identified with the Greek Asklepios as a god of wisdom and medicine. A reputation for great wisdom does appear to have been a prerequisite for deification, hence the connection between the cults of Imhotep and the Egyptian god of wisdom, Thoth. Healing sanctuaries were dedicated to Imhotep, one of which was built within the confines of the ruler Hatshepsut's Eighteenth-Dynasty mortuary temple at Deir el-Bahri on the west bank of the Nile at Thebes. It was in sanatoriums such as this one that the ancient Egyptians of the first millennium BC indulged in the practice known as incubation. They slept in the sanatorium in the hope of receiving from the deity in question a helpful or healing dream (particularly concerning fertility problems).

Imhotep came to be regarded as the son of the chief god of Memphis, Ptah. Many bronze statuettes represent him wearing a skull cap (like Ptah), and a priest's long linen kilt, seated with a papyrus scroll rolled out across his lap.

Amenhotep son of Hapu

The Deir el-Bahri sanctuary was also dedicated to another god of healing, the second deified sage, Amenhotep son of Hapu, who had been an important official during the reign of the Eighteenth-Dynasty king Amenhotep III (c.1390–c.1352 BC). Like Imhotep he was remembered for his wisdom, and as Director of Royal Works he was also responsible for building a great funerary structure for his king. This was the west Theban mortuary temple of Amenhotep III at Kom el-Heiten. Amenhotep son of Hapu was granted the unique royal favour of his own mortuary temple among those of the kings at Thebes, and statues of him were set up in the largest and most influential temple of the time, that of Amun at Karnak on the east bank at Thebes. ◆

▶ *Imhotep was a favourite subject for bronze figurines during the Late and Graeco-Roman Periods. He sits here with a papyrus scroll stretched across his lap.*

The Deities

The ancient Egyptian gods and goddesses could take many different human and animal forms; Thoth, for example, could be depicted as a baboon, an ibis; or a man with the head of an ibis. Many of the deities would have been worshipped in temples and shrines throughout Egypt, but only their cult centres best known today are listed below. All aspects of life in the human world were reflected in the divine world and the range of associations held by the deities and goddesses listed below show this.

▶ *Hathor was depicted as a cow leaving the desert to come to the papyrus marshes. 19th Dynasty.*

GOD/GODDESS	APPEARANCE	MAIN CULT CENTRE(S)	ASSOCIATION(S)/ROLE
Aker (god)	Two lions back-to-back; tract of land with lion or human heads at either end		Earth; east & west horizons in Underworld
Amaunet (goddess)	Snake-headed	Hermopolis Magna	Primeval; hidden power
Amenhotep Son of Hapu (god)	Man	Thebes	Healing
Ammit (goddess)	Head of crocodile; front part of panther or lion; rear of hippopotamus	Thebes	Devourer of heart at Judgement
Amun (god)	Man with double-plumed headdress; ram or ram-headed; goose; frog-headed	Thebes; Hermopolis Magna	'King of gods'; primeval; hidden power
Anat (goddess)	Woman with lance, axe & shield		War; Syria-Palestinian
Anubis (god)	Jackal or jackal-headed		Cemeteries; embalming
Anuket/Anukis (goddess)	Woman with tall plumed headdress & papyrus sceptre	Elephantine	Cataracts; huntress
Apis (god)	Bull	Memphis	Manifestation of Ptah
Apophis (god)	Snake		Underworld; chaos; enemy of sun god
Arensnuphis (god)	Man with plumed crown	includ. Philae	Nubian
Astarte (goddess)	Naked woman with *Atef*-crown or bull's horns, riding horse		War; Syrian
Aten (god)	Sun disc	Akhetaten	Solar
Atum (god)	Man with *Nemes* headdress or Double Crown; snake	Heliopolis	'Totality'; creator; solar
Baal (god)	Man with pointed beard & horned helmet, holding a cedar tree, club or spear		Sky; storms; Syrian (Ugaritic)
Baba (god)	Baboon		Aggression; virility; penis = bolt of heaven's doors or mast of Underworld boat

GOD/GODDESS	APPEARANCE	MAIN CULT CENTRE(S)	ASSOCIATION(S)/ROLE
Banebdjedet (god)	Ram	Mendes	Virility; sky
Bastet (goddess)	Cat or cat-headed	Bubastis	Daughter; 'Eye of Re'
Bat (goddess)	Human head with cow's ears & horns, & body in shape of necklace counterpoise	Upper Egypt	Celestial; fertility
Benu (god)	Heron	Heliopolis	Solar; rebirth
Bes (god)	Leonine dwarf		Household; childbirth
Buchis (god)	Bull	Armant	Manifestation of Re & Osiris
Duamutef (god)	Jackal-headed		Canopic; stomach & upper intestines; east
Geb (god)	Man (smtms ithyphallic), smtms with goose on head or Red Crown	Heliopolis	Earth; fertility
Hapy (god)	Man with pendulous breasts & aquatic plants headdress	Gebel el-Silsila; Aswan	Nile inundation
Hapy (god)	Baboon-headed		Canopic; lungs; north
Hathor (goddess)	Cow; woman with cow ears, or horns and sun disc on head, or falcon on perch on head	Dendera; Deir el-Bahri	Mother (esp. of king); love; fertility; sexuality; music; dance; alcohol; sky; Byblos; turquoise; faience
Hatmehyt (goddess)	Lepidotus fish	Mendes	
Hauhet (goddess)	Snake-headed	Hermopolis Magna	Primeval; formlessness; flood force
Heket (goddess)	Frog or frog-headed	Qus	Childbirth
Herishef (god)	Long-horned ram with *Atef*-crown & sun-disc headdress	Herakleopolis	Primeval force; creator; solar
Horus (god)	Falcon or falcon-headed	Edfu; Hierakonpolis; Behdet	Sky; kingship
Hu (god)	Man		Divine utterance; authority
Huh/Heh (god)	Frog-headed; man holding notched palm-rib	Hermopolis Magna	Primeval; formlessness; flood force; infinity
Ihy (god)	Child	Dendera	Sistrum (rattle)
Imhotep (god)	Seated man with skull cap & papyrus roll	Memphis; Thebes	Wisdom; medicine
Ipy/Ipet (goddess)	Hippopotamus	Thebes	Magical protection
Ishtar (goddess)	Woman		Astral; 'lady of battle'; sexuality; fertility; healing; Assyrian
Isis (goddess)	Woman with throne headdress	includ. Philae	Mother (of king); magic
Imsety (god)	Human-headed		Canopic; liver; south
Kauket (goddess)	Snake-headed	Hermopolis Magna	Primeval; darkness
Khepri (god)	Scarab beetle or man with scarab beetle for head		Creator; solar
Khnum (god)	Ram or ram-headed	Elephantine; Esna	Creator; potter; cataract; fertile soil
Khons(u) (god)	Child with headdress of full and crescent moon	Thebes	Moon
Kuk (god)	Frog-headed	Hermopolis Magna	Primeval; darkness
Maat (goddess)	Woman with single feather headdress		Order, truth, justice
Mafdet (goddess)	Woman; panther		Protector against snakes & scorpions
Mandulis (god)	Man with headdress of ram horns, plumes, sun-discs & cobras	Kalabsha; Philae	Solar; Lower Nubian
Mehen (god)	Coiled serpent		Protector of sun god

GOD/GODDESS	APPEARANCE	MAIN CULT CENTRE(S)	ASSOCIATION(S)/ROLE
Mehet-Weret (goddess)	Cow		Sky; primordial waters; 'great flood'
Mer(e)tseger (goddess)	Cobra	Western Thebes	'Peak of the West'; 'she who loves silence'
Meskhen(e)t (goddess)	Brick with human head; woman with bicornate uterus headdress		Childbirth; destiny
Mihos (god)	Lion	Leontopolis; Bubastis	
Min (god)	Man with erect phallus, & double-plumed headdress	Koptos; Akhmim	Fertility; mining regions in Eastern Desert
Mnevis (god)	Bull	Heliopolis	Sacred bull of sun god; oracles
Montu (god)	Falcon or falcon-headed, with sun disc & double-plumed headdress	Thebes	War
Mut (goddess)	Vulture	Thebes	Motherhood
Naunet (goddess)	Snake-headed	Hermopolis Magna	Primordial waters
Nefertem (god)	Man with lotus headdress; lion-headed	Memphis; Buto	Primeval lotus blossom
Neith (goddess)	Woman with Red Crown of Lower Egypt holding shield & crossed arrows	Sais	Creator-goddess; warfare; weaving
Nekhbet (goddess)	Vulture	el-Kab	Tutelary goddess of Upper Egypt
Neper (god)	Man		Grain
Nephthys (goddess)	Woman with headdress of a basket & enclosure		Funerary; protective
Nun (god)	Man; holding solar barque above head; frog-headed; baboon	Heliopolis; Hermopolis Magna	Primordial waters
Nut (goddess)	Woman; cow	Heliopolis	Sky; sarcophagus
Onuris (god)	Man; beard; four plume headdress;	This	Warrior/hunter carrying spear
Osiris (god)	Mummified man with *Atef*-crown, holding crook & flail	Abydos; Busiris	Death; Afterlife; rebirth; fertility; agriculture
Pakhet (goddess)	Lioness	Includ. entrance to wadi in E. desert nr Beni Hasan	
Ptah (god)	Semi-mummified man with skull cap and *was-djed-ankh* sceptre	Memphis	Creator; craftsmen
Qadesh (goddess)	Naked woman standing on lion		Sacred ecstasy; sexual pleasure; Middle Eastern
Qebehsenuef (god)	Falcon-headed		Canopic; lower intestines; west
Re/Ra (god)	Ram- or falcon-headed with sun disc & cobra headdress	Heliopolis	Creator; solar
Renenutet (goddess)	Cobra	Faiyum	Harvest; nursing
Reshef/Reshep (god)	Man with beard & White Crown with gazelle head at front & ribbon behind		War; Syrian (Amorite)
Sah (god)	Man		Orion
Satet/Satis (goddess)	Woman with White Crown & antelope horns	Elephantine	Protectoress of southern border; fertility
Sekhmet (goddess)	Lioness or lioness-headed	Memphis	'Powerful'; daughter of Re; healing
Selket/Serket (goddess)	Woman with scorpion headdress		Funerary; protective
Seshat (goddess)	Woman with panther-skin robe, & seven-pointed star on head		Writing

GOD/GODDESS	APPEARANCE	MAIN CULT CENTRE(S)	ASSOCIATION(S)/ROLE
Seth (god)	Unidentified quadruped or 'Seth-animal' headed	Ombos Naqada	Chaos; infertility; desert; storm
Shay (god)	Man		Destiny
Shezmu (god)	Man	Faiyum	Underworld demon; wine & unguent-oil presses
Shu (god)	Man with feather on head; lion-headed	Heliopolis; Leontopolis	Air; 'Eye of Re'
Sia (god)	Man		Divine knowledge; intellectual achievement
Sobek (god)	Crocodile or crocodile-headed	Kom Ombo; Faiyum	Pharaonic might
Sokar (god)	Mummified man with crown of horns, cobras, *atef*, & sun disc; hawk-headed	Memphis	Funerary
Sopdet/Sothis (goddess)	Woman with star on head		'Dog star' Sirius
Tatenen (god)	Man with double-plumed crown & ram's horns	Memphis	Emerging Nile silt from receding flood waters; vegetation
Taweret (goddess)	Hippopotamus (with lion & crocodile parts)		Household; childbirth
Tayet (goddess)	Woman		Weaving
Tefnut (goddess)	Woman; lioness-headed; cobra	Heliopolis; Leontopolis	Moisture; 'Eye of Re'; *uraeus*
Thoth/Djehuty (god)	Baboon; ibis or ibis-headed	Hermopolis Magna	Moon; knowledge; scribes
Wadjet/Edjo (goddess)	Cobra; lioness	Buto	Tutelary goddess of Lower Egypt; *uraeus*
Wepwawet (god)	Jackal or jackal-headed	Assiut	'Opener of the Ways'

▲ *The goddess Neith was associated with warfare. 25th Dynasty.*

▲ *The goddess Nut continued to be represented inside coffins well into the Roman period in Egypt. Early 2nd century AD.*

▲ *The goddess Maat, the divine personification of truth, order and justice, wore an ostrich feather on her head. 19th Dynasty.*

Headdresses and Crowns

An incredible variety of crowns and headdresses are represented in the art of ancient Egypt. For those who are unable to read the hieroglyphic inscriptions which often accompany the depictions of gods and goddesses, the headdress can be crucial for identifying a particular deity. Some of the characteristics of divine headdresses include: feathers; horns, lunar and solar discs; various birds, insects and other creatures; stars; a notched palm frond; a pot; a lotus flower; a shield with crossed arrows; a throne; and so on. The king might be depicted wearing one of several different crowns, although he was often shown wearing the simple linen *nemes* (headcloth). Various deities could also be portrayed wearing a royal headdress, for example Osiris who often sported the *Atef*-crown. The Blue Crown was especially associated with warfare.

▲ *Identification of this Nile deity by its headdress is especially useful when late period bronze figurines such as this one are uninscribed.*

Selket/Serket

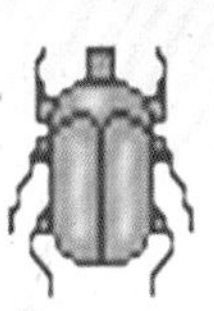

Khepri

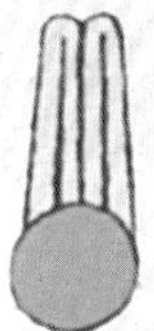

Montu

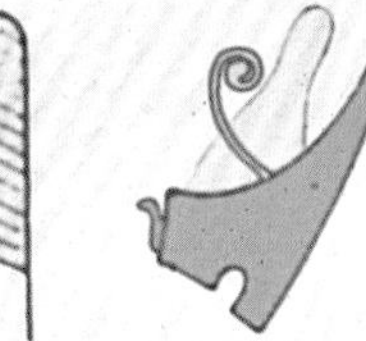

Maat, Shu

Atum, Horus

▲ *The elongated headdress is characteristic of 'Amarna Art'. Here Akhenaten's headdress is surmounted by ram's horns, a sun disc, and the tall plumes. 18th Dynasty.*

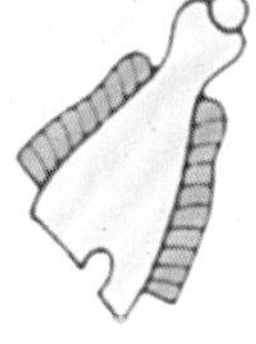

Osiris

Neith

Nekhbet, Mut, Isis

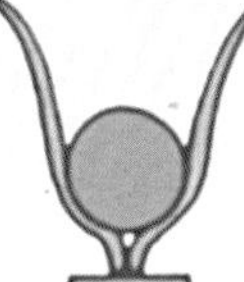

Hathor, Isis, Ipy/Ipet

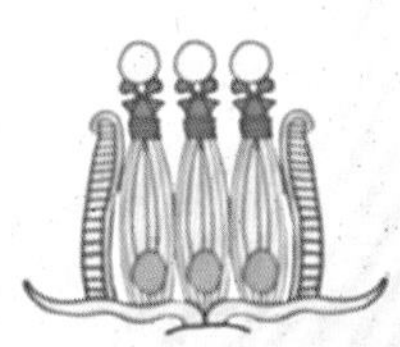

Mandulis

Seshat

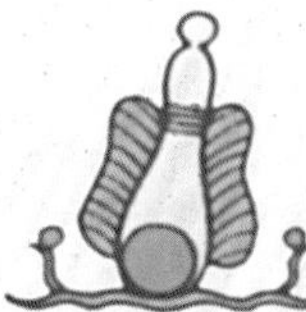

Khnum

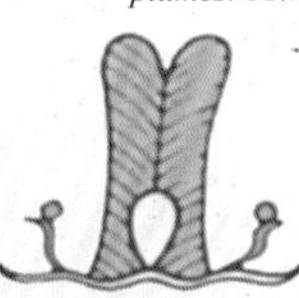

Sobek

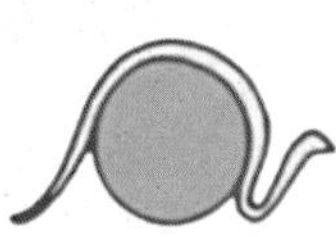

Re-Horakhty, Sekhmet, Sokar

▲ *Osorkon II as Osiris, flanked by Horus and Isis, wear characteristic headdresses. Isis is also often shown with a throne on her head. 22nd Dynasty.*

Geb

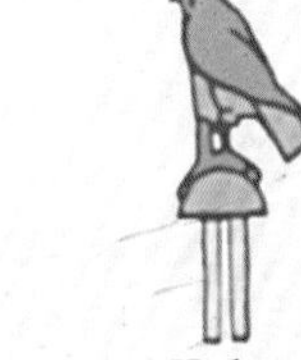

Hathor

Khons

Satet/Satis

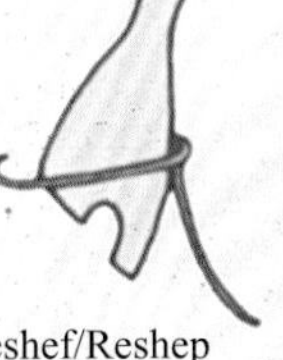

Reshef/Reshep

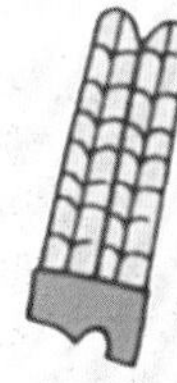

Amun, Horus, Min

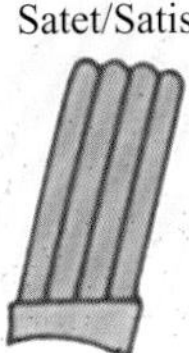

Onuris

Anuket/Anukis

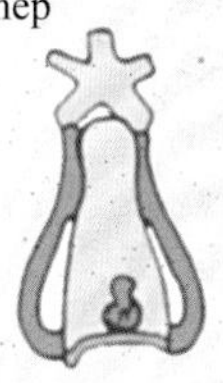

Sopdet/Sothis

Geb

Gods and Goddesses

The Egyptian pantheon included hundreds of deities: many originated as local gods who became the focus of important cults, while some were borrowed from other cultures. Some deities were merged, or 'syncretized' with each other, blending their attributes, sometimes allowing a lesser god to take on the distinction and importance of a greater one. Most of the major, or universal, deities represented cosmic forces, such as the sun or the flood, or were associated with the mysteries of human life, such as birth and death.

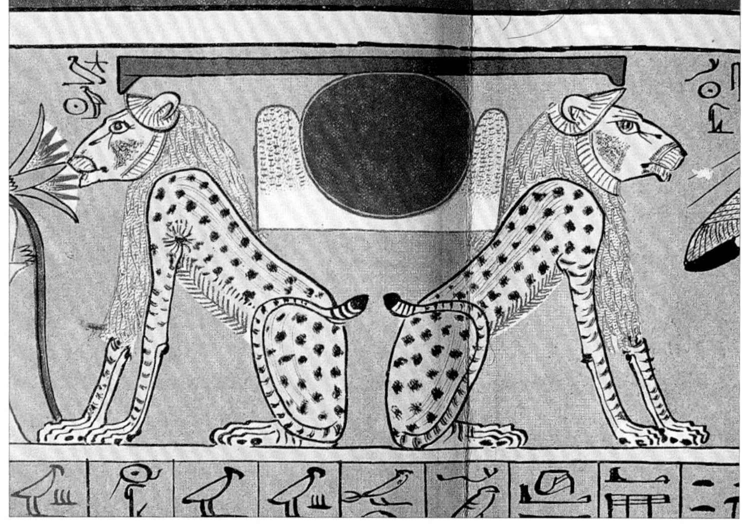

▲ *Above the backs of the two lions representing Aker, the artist of this papyrus Book of the Dead of Ani has painted the hieroglyphic signs for 'horizon' (*akhet*) and 'sky' (*pet*).*

Aker

The earth god Aker was the divine personification of the eastern and western horizons, which signified the entrance and exit into and out of the Netherworld, Aker was important in funerary texts and imagery. He was represented as two lions sitting back to back, or as a piece of land with a lion or a human head at each end (one facing east and one facing west).

Amun

By the New Kingdom (c.1550–c.1069 BC) Amun had achieved the position of head of the state pantheon. His national significance was due to the emergence of local Theban rulers who were successful in reuniting and ruling the whole of Egypt after a period of disruption. An early Twelfth-Dynasty inscription in the jubilee chapel of King Senusret I (c.1965–c.1920 BC) at Karnak describes Amun as 'the king of the gods'. His pre-eminence also had much to do with his amalgamation with Re, the ancient sun god of Heliopolis, to create the deity Amun-Re. He was also combined with the fertility god Min, to form the god Amun-Min or Amun Kamutef ('Bull of his Mother').

Amun's name means 'the Hidden One' and one of his epithets was 'mysterious of form', although he was usually represented in human form wearing a tall double-plumed headdress. He could also be envisaged as a ram – *Ovis platyra* – with horns curving inwards close to the head. In a hymn on Papyrus Leiden 1,350, he is described as the 'Great Honker' – a primeval goose.

From at least as early as the Eleventh Dynasty (c.2055–c.1985 BC) Amun's chief cult centre was the temple at Karnak in Thebes, where he was worshipped with his consort, the vulture mother-goddess Mut, and their child the lunar deity Khonsu. As early as the Fifth Dynasty (c.2350–c.2345 BC) he appeared in the Pyramid Texts accompanied by a consort named as Amaunet.

▼ *In reliefs at Luxor the supreme god Amun takes an ithyphallic form as Amun Kamutef.*

Anat

As a goddess of war, Anat was believed to protect the king in battle. Thus she was often depicted with a lance, axe and shield. She also wore a tall crown surmounted by feathers.

Anat is an excellent example of the Egyptian acceptance of foreign deities into their pantheon of gods, because she actually originated in Syria-Palestine as

▲ *These ram-headed sphinxes (criosphinxes) originally formed part of the avenue between the temples of Luxor and Karnak. Both were dedicated to the god Amun, who was sometimes represented as a ram.*

a deity of the Canaanites and Phoenicians. She was said to be the sister, or sometimes the consort, of Baal. There is evidence of a cult dedicated to her in Egypt from at least the late Middle Kingdom (c.1800 BC).

Like other more benign goddesses, Anat held the titles 'Mother of All the Gods' and 'Mistress of the Sky'. At various times she was regarded as the consort of Seth or the fertility god Min.

Anubis

The god of embalming and cemeteries, Anubis was an ancient deity to whom prayers for the survival of the deceased in the Afterlife were addressed during the early Old Kingdom before Osiris rose to prominence as the god of the dead. Anubis continued to assist in the judgement of the dead and accompanied the deceased to the throne of Osiris for the ritual of the Weighing of the Heart. He was also the patron of embalmers. Anubis had several epithets including 'foremost of the westerners' (i.e the dead buried on the west bank of the Nile); 'he who is upon his mountain' (i.e the desert cliffs overlooking the cemeteries); 'Lord of the Sacred land' (i.e the desert in which the burials were located); 'the one presiding over the god's pavillion' (i.e the place where embalming took place, or the burial chamber); and 'he who is in the place of embalming'.

Anubis was depicted as a jackal or as a man with the head of a jackal. Priests who prepared bodies for burial and conducted burial ceremonies are thought to have impersonated the god by wearing jackal masks. Since jackals were common scavengers in Egyptian burial sites, the honouring of Anubis in this guise may have represented a way of protecting the dead from molestation.

▲ *As a funerary deity, Atum's presence is significant on the walls of non-royal Theban tombs of the New Kingdom (c.1550–c.1069 BC) such as that of Sennedjem. c.1300 BC.*

Astarte

This goddess appears to have been almost interchangeable with Anat. She was also associated with war (particularly with horses and chariots), and was thought to protect the king in battle. She was of Syrian origin, and there is no evidence for her cult in Egypt before the Eighteenth Dynasty (c.1150–c.1295 BC).

She was usually represented as a naked woman riding a horse and wearing the *atef*-crown or bull's horns on her head. She was variously regarded as the daughter of Re or of Ptah, and was thought to be one of Seth's consorts.

Atum

Atum ('the All') was the self-engendered creator god who arose from the primordial waters of chaos, Nun, in order to form the primeval mound and to bring the elements of the cosmos into being. As the head of the so-called Ennead (or nine gods), he held the title 'Lord to the Limits of the Sky'. His cult centre was at Heliopolis, and he was regarded very much as a solar deity (at some stage he was syncretized with the pre-eminent sun god, Re, in order to form the combined deity Re-Atum).

Atum was very much associated with kingship, and was believed to lift the dead king from his pyramid to the stars. Later, as a result of the gradual democratization of funerary religion, he came to be regarded as the protector not only of the king but of all dead people on their way into the Afterlife.

Atum was usually represented as a man wearing the Double Crown of Upper and Lower Egypt, although he could also be portrayed as a snake. Additional animals were deemed sacred to him, including the lion, bull, mongoose, lizard and dung beetle.

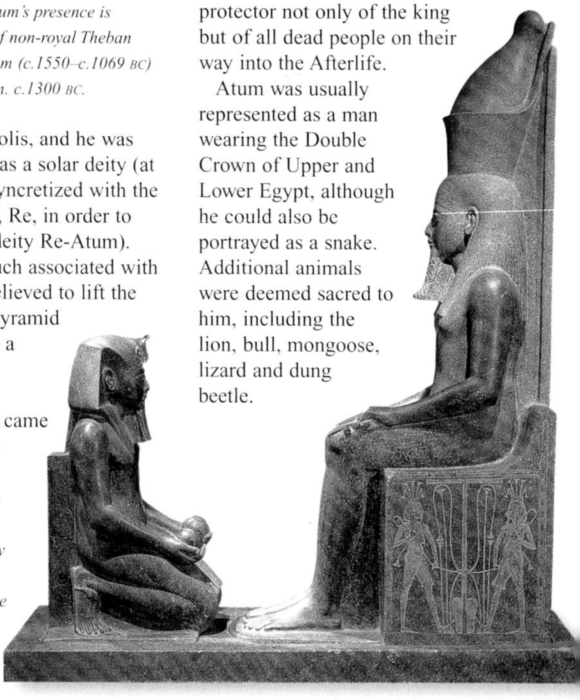

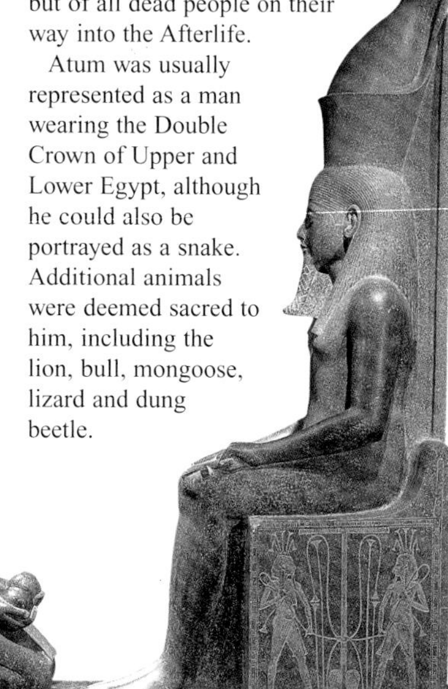

▶ *Relative size is used to denote importance in Egyptian art, as shown by this diorite statue of Horemheb kneeling before the seated figure of Atum. c.1300 BC.*

Baba

At his most dangerous, Baba was believed to murder humans and feed on their entrails. He was associated with aggression and virility – especially those of the king. Sometimes his penis was said to be the bolt on the doors of heaven, and at other times it was the mast on the ferry in the Netherworld. He was believed to be able to ward off snakes and to control darkness and turbulent waters. He was represented as a baboon.

Eye of Re

According to this strange concept, the eye of the sun god was in fact separate from him and could act independently. In the myth of *The Destruction of Humankind* it manifested itself first as Hathor and then as the more ferocious divine female force, Sekhmet.

The Eye was also identified with the cobra goddess Wadjet, one of the protective female deities of kingship, who appears rearing up at the front of the royal headdress, ready to spit poison at the king's enemies. This rearing snake is known as the uraeus.

Geb

As the divine personification of the earth, Geb was a god of fertility. For this reason, he was sometimes coloured green and was visualized with plants growing out of him. He was often depicted reclining beneath the arched body of his sister-consort, the sky goddess Nut. In *The Creation Myth of Heliopolis*, Geb and Nut were the two children of Shu and Tefnut. They were lovers, but were forcibly separated by their father Shu, the god of air.

Geb was always represented in human form, sometimes with an erect penis. He occasionally wore the Red Crown of Lower Egypt, but more often had a white-fronted goose on his head. Thus, his daughter Isis could be described as the 'Egg of the Goose'. Like his father Shu, he had a dark side to him, which was expressed in funerary religion: he was considered able to trap the dead in his body. Earthquakes were described as the 'laughter of Geb'.

◀ The sistrum was shaken like a rattle by priestesses of Hathor. Late Period.

◀ The influence of the Near Eastern goddess Astarte was widespread in the ancient world. This pectoral plaque depicting the goddess was found in the Camirus cemetery on Rhodes. Early Greek.

Hathor

A mother goddess, Hathor was associated with love, fertility, sexuality, music, dance and alcohol. She was sometimes represented entirely anthropomorphically, in the form of a cow, or as a woman with cow's ears. When in human form, her headdress could be one of cow's horns with a solar disc, or a falcon on a perch. She was also a sky goddess, and was regarded as a vast cow who straddled the heavens, with her four legs marking the four cardinal points.

◀ *The cow-goddess Hathor was often depicted with a human face but with cow's ears on column capitals, such as this one at Dendera, site of the most famous of her temples. Hathor's representation as a cow identified her as the great mother, symbolizing fertility, motherhood and nurture.*

▼ *The favourable support and protection bestowed on the king by the whole of the divine world is epitomized by the image of the cow goddess Hathor suckling the adult ruler (in this case Amenhotep II). 18th Dynasty.*

In various contexts she was honoured as 'Lady of the West' or 'Lady of the Western Mountain', 'Lady of Byblos', 'Lady of Turquoise' and 'Lady of Faience'. The 'west' or 'western mountain' refers to the place of the setting sun and thus, by analogy, the realm of the dead. Byblos was a port on the Lebanese coast, important for Egyptian trade and particularly in the importing of cedar wood, since Egypt had no native timber for the construction of boats or large buildings. Egypt exploited turquoise mines from Predynastic times, especially in the Sinai Peninsula (a temple to Hathor has been found at the mining site of Serabit el-Khadim). Faience was a much-used glazed ceramic material composed primarily of crushed quartz or quartz sand, and usually a blue or green colour (perhaps a cheap imitation of turquoise).

Like Isis, Hathor was considered to be the mother of the falcon deity Horus, and thus of the king (who was closely identified with Horus). Her name means 'the House of Horus'. However, inscriptions on the temple of Horus at Edfu refer to Hathor marrying this deity. The king was sometimes depicted being suckled by the goddess in cow form, as shown by a wonderful statue in the Cairo Museum from Deir el-Bahri of the Eighteenth-Dynasty pharaoh Amenhotep II (c.1427–c.1400 BC) enjoying just such sustenance. Although she was sometimes identified with the Eye of Re, she appeared on other occasions as the sun god's daughter.

From the Old Kingdom (c.2686–c.2181 BC) Hathor's chief cult centre was at Dendera. Her festivities appear to have been suitably debauched. An emblem of her cult was the sistrum (or rattle), which would have been shaken as part of the ritual proceedings. The existing temple on this site dates to the Graeco-Roman Period, and is dedicated to the triad Hathor, Horus and Ihy, Hathor's son, who played the sistrum in her honour.

Horus

The king of Egypt was closely identified with Horus from the beginning of Dynastic history (c.3100 BC). The god was represented as a falcon, or with the head of a falcon, and one of his most ubiquitous symbols was the 'Eye of Horus' (the *udjat-* or *wadjat*-eye). In one version of the myth of *The Contendings of Horus and Seth*, Horus had both his eyes gouged out. In other versions he lost (and then regained) only his left eye. As the weaker of the two, it came to be associated with the moon while the right eye was associated with the sun. Because in both instances his eyesight was eventually cured, his eye came to symbolize healing (*udjat* literally means 'sound'). It was used as a protective amulet, symbolizing strength and perfection, and also represented the waxing and waning moon.

◀ *As the god of kingship, Horus was often shown wearing the combined Red and White Crowns of Lower and Upper Egypt, as on this column at the temple of Kom Ombo.*

▲ *The 'Eye of Horus' is a ubiquitous emblem in ancient Egyptian art. It symbolized healing, wholeness, strength and perfection. New Kingdom.*

Horus's name means 'He Who is Above', and is probably linked to his status as a god of the sky and to the high soaring of the falcon. As 'Horus in the Horizon' he was called a Horemakhet and in this capacity he was amalgamated with the solar deity Re to become Re-Horakhty.

From the Late Period (c.747 BC) he appeared in his child form, Hor-pa-khered (whom the Greeks called Harpocrates) on a form of stela known as a *cippus* of Horus. He was usually depicted treading crocodiles underfoot and grasping snakes, scorpions and other such dangerous creatures. It is always clear that he was intended to be a child because he was pictured naked, sporting a particular hairstyle known as the 'side-lock of youth'. The idea behind this aspect of the god was that since Horus as a young boy had managed to survive certain dangers, a ritual could be performed using his image to protect children from similar threats (or perhaps to cure snake bites and scorpion stings). Water was poured over the *cippi* (which were covered in spells), causing the liquid to be imbued with their magical potency, so it could be ritually imbibed or applied.

Horus was honoured as an element of the divine triad at the cult centre of Abydos, but he is most associated with the temple at Edfu (ancient Mesen), where he was worshipped as part of a triad with his consort Hathor and their child Harsomtus. He was also closely associated with Hierakonpolis ('Town of the Hawk', ancient Nekhen) in the south and a town called Behdet in the Delta. As 'Horus of Behdet' he was represented as a winged sun disc.

▲ *On the back of one of Tutankhamun's thrones, the god Heh kneels on the hieroglyphic sign for gold, and clutches notched palm branches, symbolizing the passing of time. 18th Dynasty.*

▼ *Khepri is depicted here in the tomb of Seti I on a boat on the waters of Nun. The wish is expressed in the early royal funerary texts that the sun should come into being in its name of Khepri. 19th Dynasty.*

Huh/Heh

The frog-headed god Huh was the personification of formlessness and infinity. His consort was the snake-headed goddess Hauhet. He was often represented anthropomorphically holding in each hand a palm-rib (the hieroglyph for 'year').

Isis

Like Hathor, Isis was a mother goddess and was identified more specifically as the mother of Horus, and thus of the king. The image of her suckling Horus (especially found in the form of numerous bronze figurines dating to the Late and Graeco-Roman Periods) is reminiscent of the Christian mother-and-child icon.

Isis tended to be represented as a woman with a throne, or solar disc between cow's horns, on her head. She was sometimes regarded as the personification of the throne: the hieroglyph for her name is the image of a throne, and her lap came to be seen as the throne of Egypt. She was also frequently depicted with huge, sheltering wings. She was part of the Ennead of Heliopolis, and as consort to Osiris and mother of Horus, she appeared in the triad of deities worshipped at Abydos. Her best-known cult centre was on the island of Philae, on the southern border of Egypt, near Aswan. She was particularly closely associated with magic. Her ability to heal and to transform herself into any guise she desired are evident in the myths about her. Two important manifestations of this goddess were the 'Great White Sow of Heliopolis' and the Isis-cow which gave birth to the sacred Apis Bull of Memphis. Her following eventually spread beyond Egypt, to Syria, Palestine, Greece and throughout the whole Roman Empire, and she was worshipped until well into Christian times.

▶ *Several species of dung beetle are found in Egypt, but the large sacred scarab,* Scarabeus sacer, *is the one most commonly represented in ancient Egyptian art.*

Khepri

The god Khepri (which literally means 'He who is Coming into Being') was a creator and solar deity. He was represented as a scarab or dung beetle, or as a beetle-headed man. The choice of a dung beetle to portray a creator god and the manifestation of the rising sun is significant because of the activities of such a beetle. It was observed to roll its eggs in a ball of dung along the ground, and the ball was identified with the sun. The baby beetles were seen to emerge from the dung, as if life was emerging from the primeval mound, and so dung beetles were thought capable of spontaneous creation.

From the Middle Kingdom (c.2055–c.1650 BC) onwards the scarab-form amulet was very popular, and was worn in bracelets and necklaces. Scarabs were used as funerary talismans, and were placed over the heart of the deceased to keep it from confessing sins during its interrogation.

Khnum

Khnum was an ancient deity represented as a man with the head of a ram, or in entirely ram form. The type of ram used to portray him was the earliest one to be domesticated in Egypt – the *Ovis longipes* – which had curly horns extending horizontally from the head. The ancient Egyptian for 'ram' was *ba*, which was also the word for a concept akin to our 'personality' (possibly those non-physical attributes which make any one human being unique, or perhaps the moral essence of a person's motivation and movement). It may well then have been thanks to the ancient Egyptian love of puns that Khnum came to be regarded as the *ba* of the sun god Re, and so this deity was represented with a ram's head while passing through the Netherworld in his solar barque. Certainly the *ba* of the dead appeared to be more mobile than their *ka* ('spirit').

Connected with Khnum's capacity as a creator god was his role as patron deity of potters, and his association with the fertile soil, the annual inundation and the Nile cataracts. His chief cult centre was situated on the island of Elephantine, at the first cataract at the southern border of Egypt. Another important temple to Khnum was located at Esna. Here his consort was the lioness-goddess Menhyt. And it was here that the Festival of the Potter's Wheel was celebrated each year.

▼ *The ram was a symbol of fertility and male virility. It was used to represent the creator god Khnum, who fashioned the universe out of clay.*

◀ *Khonsu was depicted as a young man usually wrapped in the bandages of a mummy or other tight-fitting garment and carrying the royal crook, flail and sceptre.*

Khonsu

The son of Amun and Mut, Khonsu's name means 'wanderer', which probably refers to the passage of the moon across the sky, as he was a lunar deity. In the late period, he was also considered an important god of healing. His chief cult centre was at Thebes.

Kuk

The frog-headed god Kuk was the personification of darkness. His consort was the snake-headed Kauket.

Min

As a god of fertility, Min was represented in semi-mummified human form, his left hand holding his erect phallus and his right arm raised. The key feature of his headdress was two tall plumes. The emblems of his cult were the lettuce and an unidentified shape which could possibly be a door-bolt, a barbed arrow, a lightning bolt or a pair of fossil shells. He was a particularly ancient deity, and was also regarded as a protector of the mining regions in the Eastern Desert.

His main cult centres were at Koptos and Akhmim (which the Greeks called Panopolis because they identified their god Pan with Min). He was sometimes described as the son of Isis, but on other occasions he was said to be her consort, with Horus as their son. By the New Kingdom (c.1550–c.1069 BC) he had merged with the Theban deity Amun.

Nefertem

This deity was associated with the lotus blossom, and was represented in male human form with the blue lotus (*Nymphaea caerulea*) on his head (see *Plants and Flowers in Mythology*). His headdress sometimes also incorporated two plumes and two necklace counterpoises.

The *Creation Myth of Hermopolis Magna* states that the sun rose from the primeval lotus flower, and Nefertem was

▶ *Ramesses I is depicted on the wall of his tomb face to face with Nefertem, the divine personification of the lotus blossom.*

◀ *In this scene from the New Kingdom papyrus Book of the Dead of Ani, the sister goddesses Isis and Nephthys kneel with their arms raised in the posture of worship and adoration. c.1400* BC.

closely linked with the sun god. The Pyramid Texts of the Old Kingdom refer to Nefertem as 'the lotus blossom which is before the nose of Re' (Utterance 266). His universal importance is expressed in his title 'Protector of the Two Lands' (*khener tawy*), referring to Upper and Lower Egypt.

Nefertem was worshipped at Memphis as the son of god Ptah and the lioness-goddess Sekhmet, so he was sometimes depicted as lion-headed. He was also occasionally referred to as the son of the cat-goddess Bastet or, to complicate matters further, as the son of the cobra-goddess Wadjet at Buto.

Neith

A particularly ancient goddess whose main cult centre was at Sais in the Delta, Neith rose to particular prominence during the Twenty-sixth Dynasty (664–525 BC), when Sais was the home of the ruling family and the capital of Egypt. Her emblem was a shield with crossed arrows, emphasizing her association with warfare (the Greeks later identified her with their goddess Athena). This symbol has been found on objects dating all the way back to the First Dynasty (c.3100–c.2890 BC). She is usually depicted wearing the Red Crown of Lower Egypt. Neith formed a triad with her consort Seth and their child Sobek, the crocodile god. As a mother goddess she was given the epithet 'Great Cow' (as were the goddesses Nut and Hathor). She was also considered a creator goddess and as such was equated with the primordial waters of chaos, Nun.

Together with Isis, Nephthys and the scorpion goddess, Selket, she was a funerary goddess: they each protected one of the 'Four Sons of Horus' who in turn looked after the internal organs of the deceased. Neith was specifically associated with the jackal-headed Duamutef who protected the stomach and upper intestines. She was also linked with the linen mummy bandages because she was believed to have invented weaving.

Nephthys

In later mythology, Nephthys was regarded as the mother of the jackal-headed god of embalming, Anubis, as a result of a union with Osiris. She was the sister of Isis, Osiris and Seth (of whom she was also thought to be a consort). She appears to have been an aide to her better-known sister Isis. Like her, Nephthys was usually depicted in human form, but could also be represented as a kite. Her name means 'Lady of the Mansion', and her headdress consisted of the hieroglyphs for this epithet (a basket on top of the enclosure wall of a grand house).

Nephthys was associated with the head of the deceased or the coffin (in collaboration with Isis at the foot). She was also one of the protective canopic deities: she protected the baboon-headed son of Horus, Hapy, who in turn guarded the lungs of the deceased.

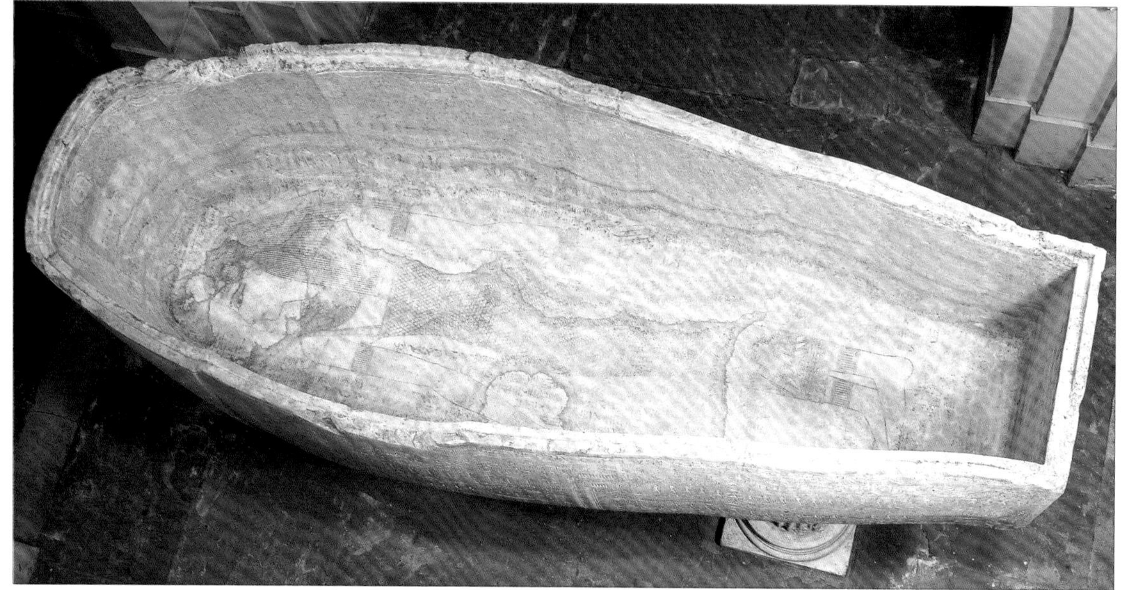

▲ *In the Pyramid Texts of the Old Kingdom (c.2686–c.2181 BC), the sky goddess Nut, painted inside this coffin of Seti I, is variously described as the king's coffin, sarcophagus and tomb. 19th Dynasty.*

▼ *In illustrations of the Heliopolitan creation myth, as here on the papyrus of Nespakashuty, Nut arches naked over her consort Geb, the earth god.*

Nun

Nun was the divine personification of the primordial waters of chaos, which preceded creation. He was described as the 'eldest father' and 'maker of humankind'. After creation had taken place, chaos was believed to continue to exist beyond the edges of the universe, and in the Netherworld, and was the place of social outcasts and demons.

The mudbrick enclosure walls of temples were sometimes constructed in curved courses (pan bedding), which resulted in a wavy effect. This was possibly meant to imitate the waters of Nun, the temple itself symbolizing the universe (see *Temple Architecture*). Nun was also thought to be present within the context of the temple, in the form of the sacred lake.

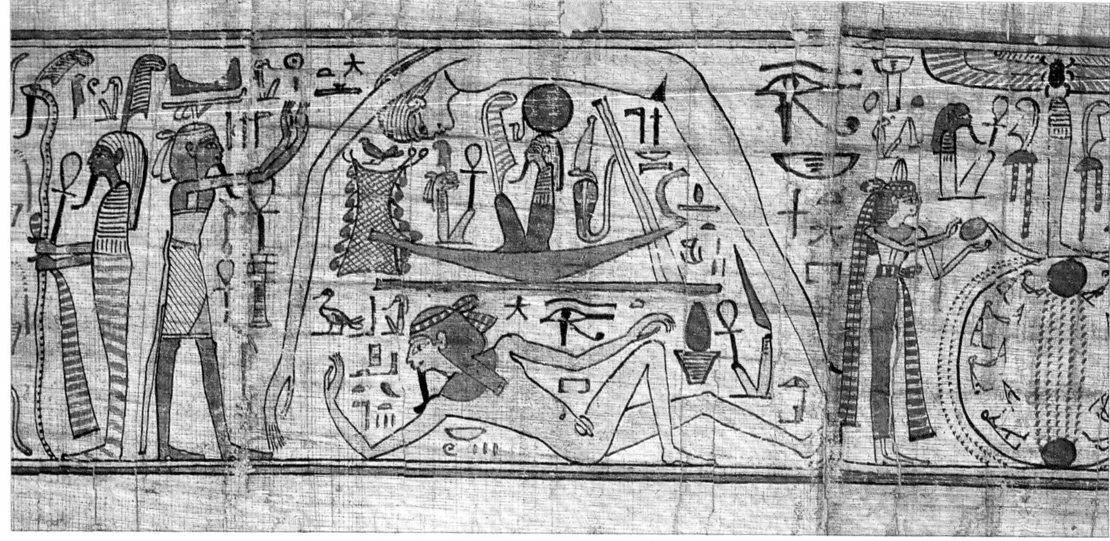

Nun could be represented as a baboon, or with a frog's head, or in an entirely human form, with a beard. In the latter guise he was often depicted holding the solar barque aloft. His consort was the snake-headed goddess Naunet.

▶ *In the papyrus Book of the Dead of the priest of Amun-Re, Chensumose, the* djed-*pillar, considered to be the embodiment of Osiris's backbone, is semi-personified:* ankhs *hang from its arms and it holds aloft an encircled snake. 21st Dynasty.*

Nut

The goddess Nut was the divine personification of the sky. According to the Heliopolitan creation myth, she was one of the children of Shu and Tefnut, and the sister and consort of Geb, the earth god. The darkness at night was explained by the belief that Nut swallowed the sun in the evening and gave birth to it at dawn, so it spent the night hours travelling through her body. This image was often depicted on the ceilings of tombs and on the undersides of sarcophagus lids, expressing the belief that Nut divinely personified the coffin and burial chamber. Because the sun was said to be born from her each morning, the deceased might be reborn from her into the Afterlife.

She was usually shown as a woman arching over the earth, but could also be represented as a cow. The 'Divine Cow' was believed to carry Re, the sun god, on her back each morning.

Osiris

God of the dead and the Afterlife (as well as of rebirth and fertility), Osiris was represented in a mummified anthropomorphic form, often holding a crook and flail, and with the *atef*-crown (described as 'sky piercing') on his head. His skin could be green or black (signifying fertility or the thick black Nile silt), or white (the colour of the linen mummy bandages). One of his emblems was the *djed*-pillar, a symbol of stability, which was equated with his backbone and was particularly revered at his cult centre of Busiris (ancient Djedu) in the Delta.

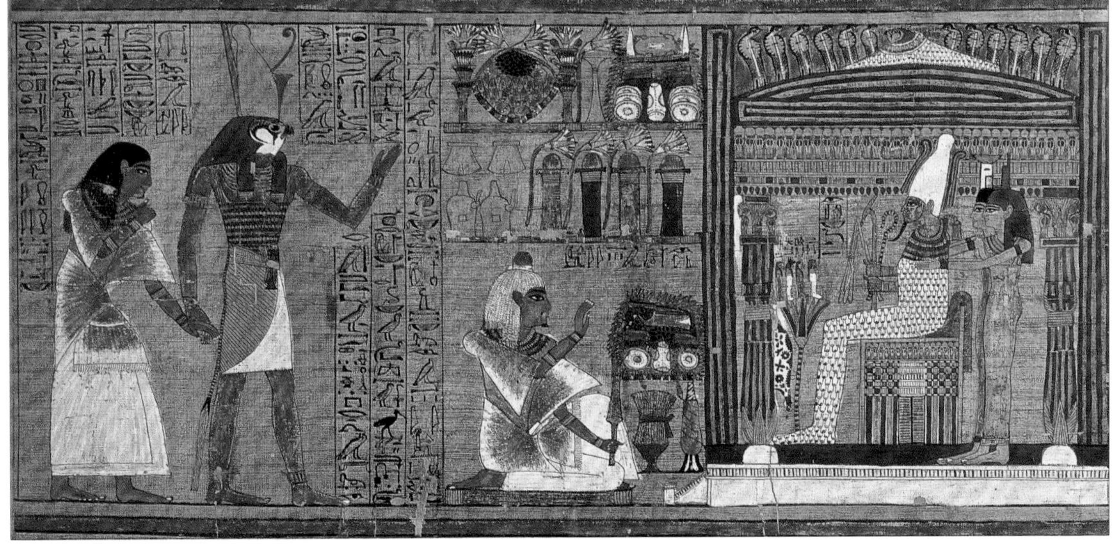

▼ *Ani's Book of the Dead shows the dead man being led by Horus to the enthroned Osiris, who is attended by his sisters Isis and Nephthys.*

▲ *The Theban tomb-builders' village of Deir el-Medina, located in the desert about 2km (1 mile) west of the Nile Valley, consists of about 70 limestone and mudbrick houses of uniform size.*

The chief cult centre of Osiris was his legendary burial place (and consequently an important pilgrims' destination) Abydos (ancient Abdjw), where he was worshipped together with his sister-consort Isis and their son Horus, and where an annual festival was held in his honour. He was a member of the important Ennead (nine gods) of Heliopolis (see *Creation Myths*), a genealogy that appears for the first time in the Pyramid Texts of the Fifth Dynasty. These were found – as the name implies – on the interior walls of certain pyramids.

Epithets applied to Osiris included 'eternally good' and 'foremost of the westerners' (that is the dead, who were thought, like the sun, to enter the Netherworld in the west). He was assimilated with two Memphite deities, the creator god Ptah, and the hawk-headed funerary deity Sokar, forming the syncretized funerary god Ptah-Sokar-Osiris.

The deceased king of Egypt was identified with Osiris from at least the Fifth Dynasty (c.2494–c.2345 BC). By about 2000 BC, a democratization of funerary religion had begun to take place, and dead people other than the king were also identified with Osiris.

Ptah

Recognized as the chief deity of the city of Memphis, Ptah was worshipped as part of a triad with his consort the lioness-goddess Sekhmet and the lotus-god Nefertem. At a later stage, Imhotep, the deified architect of Djoser's Step Pyramid Complex at Saqqara, was regarded as a son of Ptah (see *Deification of Mortals*). As chief creator god, Ptah was regarded as the patron deity of craftsmen, and so was an important figure at Deir el-Medina, the village of craftsmen who were responsible for the tombs in the Valley of the Kings. At Memphis, the High Priest of his cult held the title 'Great Over-seer of Craftsmen' (*wer kherep hemw*).

◀ *Wooden figures of Ptah-Sokar-Osiris were part of a wealthy Egyptian's funerary equipment. Miniature rolls of papyrus might be deposited in a compartment in the base. Late Period.*

Ptah was represented in human, semi-mummified form, wearing a skullcap and holding a staff which combined the *was*-sceptre of power, the *djed*-pillar of stability and the *ankh*-sign for life. From the Middle Kingdom (c.2055–c.1650 BC) onwards he was depicted with a straight beard.

During the Old Kingdom (c.2686–c.2181 BC) Ptah was merged with the Memphite hawk-headed funerary deity Sokar, creating the god Ptah-Sokar. This composite deity went on to become Ptah-Sokar-Osiris in the Late Period. Wooden, mummiform, hawk-headed figures of this god were often placed in tombs as part of the funerary equipment.

Re

With good reason, the ancient Egyptians considered the sun to be a potent life force; together with the annual inundation of the Nile, it was responsible for their successful harvests. Re was the pre-eminent solar deity.

His cult centre was at Heliopolis (called Iunu by the ancient Egyptians and now a suburb of modern Cairo) where an extremely powerful priesthood officiated. From the Fourth-Dynasty reign of Djedefre (c.2566–c.2558 BC) onwards, one of the king's five names was introduced with the epithet 'Son of Re', emphasizing the association of the king with the god. The focal point of Re's cult was the obelisk, or *benben* stone (deriving from the verb *weben,* 'to shine forth').

In the myth of the Destruction of Humankind, Re is described as having the bones, flesh and hair of an old man, but his divinity is evident because they are of silver, gold and lapis lazuli (the last was considered especially valuable by the ancient Egyptians because it had to be imported from as far away as Badakhshan in north-eastern Afghanistan). This description may be that of a cult statue, such as would be found in the *naos* or shrine of each temple, housing the very essence or potency of the deity in question. The myth also states that he was self-created, coming into being in Nun, the primordial waters.

Re was frequently represented anthropomorphically, but with the head of a ram or a hawk wearing a sun-disc headdress. As the sun god, he was thought to voyage across the sky in a boat during the twelve hours of daylight, and through the Netherworld during the hours of darkness. In another version of the myth of his nightly journey, he was swallowed by Nut, the sky goddess, and

▼ *The royal title 'Son of Re' is written with the hieroglyphic signs of a duck (meaning 'son') and a solar disc. Karnak.*

travelled through her body to be reborn each morning.

The sun god was ubiquitous and powerful. By the process of syncretism, Re was amalgamated with other deities such as Amun, becoming Amun-Re, and Horus, becoming Re-Horakhty ('Horus of the Two Horizons'). Or he might be identified with other gods; one of the texts inscribed on the walls of some tombs in the Valley of the Kings during the New Kingdom (c.1550–c.1069 BC) is the 'Litany of Re', in which Re is identified with Osiris, god of the dead.

Sekhmet

The goddess Sekhmet was the ferocious aspect of female divinity, whether of Hathor, Bastet (the cat goddess of Bubastis in the Delta) or the mother goddess Mut whose temple at Karnak was filled with statues of Sekhmet by the Eighteenth-Dynasty king Amenhotep III (c.1390–1352 BC): it is thought that there was one for each day of the year. She was associated with war and battle, and helped the king to vanquish his enemies. Her name literally means 'the Powerful One', and she was visualized, appropriately, as a lioness, or at least as a woman with the head of a lioness. She wore a sun disc identifying her as the daughter of Re.

Sekhmet played an important role in the capital city of Memphis, as the consort of the creator god Ptah and the mother of Nefertem.

Seth

Seth was Osiris's 'wicked' brother and, as such, was a member of the Heliopolitan family of gods and goddesses. He was associated with chaos, infertility and the desert, but in certain geographical areas (such as the north-eastern Delta) and at certain times in Egyptian history, he was highly honoured. There were kings of the Nineteenth and Twentieth Dynasties, for example, whose names derived from his, such as Seti and Sethnakhte. His worship recognized that chaos had to be acknowledged before order could be seen to exist, and though the desert was an arid and dangerous place it was also of enormous value to the Egyptians (particularly for its natural resources such as gold, amethyst and turquoise). The god had an important cult centre at Naqada in Upper Egypt. Tradition maintained this had been the place of his violent birth from the sky goddess Nut.

Seth was represented in the form of an animal that cannot be conclusively identified: it had a long curved snout, pricked, flat-topped ears, a canine body and a forked tail. He was sometimes shown as a man with this animal's head. It is possible that this animal may have belonged to a species that is now extinct, but it is more likely to have been fabricated to produce a disconcerting appearance for a deity associated with trouble and barrenness. Seth could also be represented as a pig, a donkey or a hippopotamus (see *The Contendings of Horus and Seth*).

▲ *The bizarre Seth animal, with its long snout and pricked, blunt-ended ears, often appeared on magical objects, such as wands designed to protect against harm.*

Shu

The divine personification of air as well as sunlight, Shu's name probably means 'He who Rises Up'. Although he was thought to bring the sun to life each morning and to protect it against the serpent demon Apophis in the Netherworld, he was also often associated with the lunar deities Thoth and Khonsu. Perhaps improbably, he was additionally thought to be the leader of a pack of demons that threatened to torture the deceased.

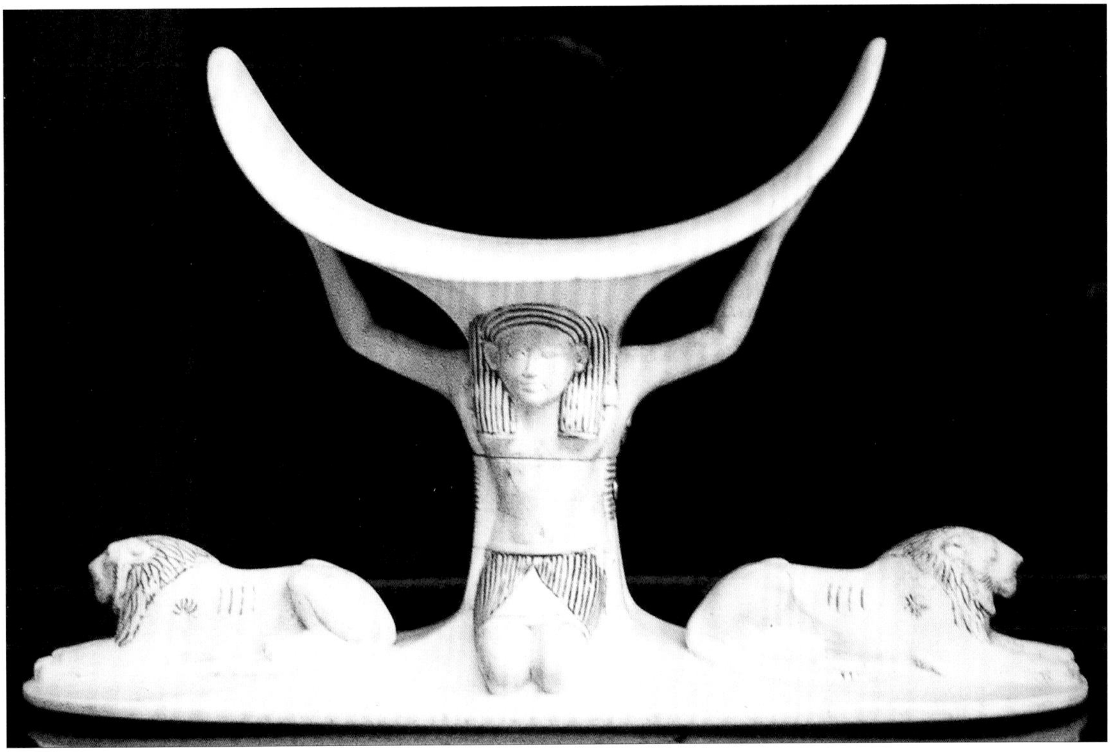

He was represented in human form with a feather on his head, and was often depicted standing between his offspring, Geb (the earth god) and Nut (the sky goddess), supporting the latter. He could also be visualized with the head of a lion, and it was in this guise that he was referred to as an 'Eye of Re', and was worshipped at Leontopolis (Tell el-Muqdam) in the Delta.

Sobek

The crocodile god was represented either as the reptile itself or as a man with the head of a crocodile. Sobek was worshipped in the Faiyum and at the temple of Kom Ombo. Sobek was associated with the might of the Pharaoh, and in the form of Sobek-Re he was worshipped as a manifestation of the Solar diety. His consort was Hathor and Khonsu, elsewhere said to be the son of Amun and Mut, was regarded as their child.

▲ *Incorporated into the design of this ivory headrest found in the tomb of Tutankhamun is Shu, the god of air, who here supports the head of the sleeper rather than his usual load, his daughter Nut, the sky goddess.*

▼ *The ancient Egyptians worshipped Sobek in the form of a crocodile, or with the head of a crocodile, in the hope that this would help to protect them from the hidden dangers of the River Nile. Kom Ombo.*

Sokar

This god was associated with the earth and fertility, but particularly with death and the cemetery of the capital city of Memphis. His funerary association led him to be syncretized with Osiris, and his Memphite importance resulted in his syncretism with the chief deity there, Ptah – hence the invention of the god Ptah-Sokar-Osiris. Sokar's association with Ptah also meant they shared the same consort, the lioness goddess Sekhmet.

▶ *In his role as scribe and messenger of the gods, Thoth was usually represented as a man with the head of an ibis. 19th Dynasty. Valley of the Kings.*

▼ *One of two colossal granite statues of Thoth, the god of wisdom and writing, represented as a baboon. They are all that remains of the once great temple at Hermopolis Magna. 18th Dynasty.*

In the Pyramid Texts, Sokar is described as the maker of 'royal bones'. He was represented as a mummified man, sometimes with the head of a hawk. Wooden statuettes of him were placed in tombs together with a host of other funerary equipment. He could also be portrayed as a mound of earth surmounted by a boat containing the head of a hawk.

Sokar's chief cult centre was at Memphis. During the festival held there in his honour, his devotees wore strings of onions around their necks. Onions were certainly used in the embalming process – their skins or whole bulbs were placed over the eyes or stuffed into the ears or the body cavity. Today onion is used to disguise nasty smells, and in folklore it is believed to combat infection.

Tefnut

As one of the cosmic deities of the Ennead, Tefnut was the divine personification of moisture.To tie in with the imagery of symmetrical pairs, when her brother-consort Shu was associated with sunlight, Tefnut was associated with the moon.

Like Shu, Tefnut could be regarded as an 'Eye of Re', and as such was represented with a lioness head (and was worshipped at Leontopolis). She also appeared in the form of a rearing cobra, in which case she was identified with the *uraeus* on the front of the royal headdress. When depicted in human form, she wore a sun disc encircled by a cobra on her head.

▲ *The vulture head and cobra on the brow of Tutankhamun's solid-gold mummy mask are decorated with glass and faience, with quartz, carnelian, lapis lazuli and obsidian inlay. The uraeus, or rearing snake, was poised to protect the king from attack by his enemies.*

▼ *The Eye of Horus, flanked by Nekhbet, the vulture goddess of Upper Egypt, and Wadjet, the cobra goddess of Lower Egypt, adorns this pectoral pendant found wrapped under the twelfth layer of linen bandages on Tutankhamun's mummy.*

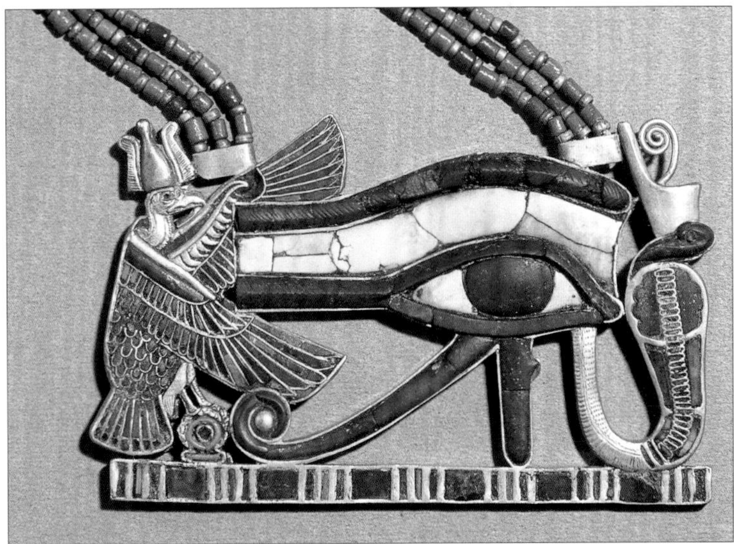

Thoth

The god of wisdom and the scribal profession, Thoth manifested himself as a baboon, an ibis or a man with the head of an ibis. He was frequently represented recording important proceedings, such as at the 'Weighing of the Heart' ceremony which was believed to take place after death. He was also closely associated with the moon, so was often depicted wearing a lunar disc and crescent on his head.

His chief cult centre was that of Hermopolis Magna (ancient Khmun; modern el-Ashmunein) in Middle Egypt, where all that remains today are two huge statues of baboons erected by the Eighteenth-Dynasty king Amenhotep III (c.1390–c.1352 BC). These statues are extremely impressive; they are sculpted from great blocks of quartzite, are about 4.5m (15ft) tall (excluding the bases), and weigh about 35 tons each.

During the Ptolemaic Period (332–30 BC) Thoth was identified with the Greek god Hermes; for this reason the city of Khmun became known as Hermopolis ('the city of Hermes').

Wadjet

The ancient goddess Wadjet was nearly always portrayed in the form of a cobra wearing the Red Crown of Lower Egypt. The Egyptians regarded the cobra as a symbol of sovereignty. Wadjet had her cult centre at Buto in the Delta. Her name means 'the Green One' or 'She of the Papyrus'. Together with the vulture goddess Nekhbet (whose cult was based at El-Kab in Upper Egypt) she was believed to protect the king. One of the ruler's five names was his *nebty* or 'two ladies' name, referring to these two particular goddesses. Wadjet appeared as the *uraeus* ('she who rears up') on the king's forehead, poised to spit venom at an unsuspecting enemy. She was also sometimes represented as a lioness. ◆

Myths and their Settings

Stories or myths evolved in all cultures in order to provide a divine explanation for the fundamentals of human existence. In ancient Egypt the realm of the gods was clearly envisaged to reflect that of mortals, as a means of bringing the divine world to life and furnishing the gods and goddesses with a certain accessibility.

Surprisingly few myths actually survive considering the vast time-span of the Egyptian culture and the huge number of its deities, as well as the cult centres with accompanying priesthoods that might have been expected to generate such literature. It is likely that there was a strong oral tradition and that many stories have been lost, but those to which we do still have access were inscribed in hieroglyphs on the walls of temples and tombs, or written on papyrus in the more cursive hieratic and demotic scripts.

The myths that follow have been selected to show how the Egyptians assimilated the mysteries of creation, life and death into their world-view, and to illustrate the recognizably human characters of the major deities, their displays of emotion and the relationships between them. Each myth is accompanied by explanatory details which help to set it in a historical and sociological context.

◄ *The creation myth of Heliopolis envisaged the sky and earth as anthropomorphic deities: Nut the sky goddess and Geb the god of the earth.*

Creation Myths

Several explanations as to how the universe came into being survive from ancient Egypt. Each major centre of religious belief had its own version of the myth of creation, with a different main creator deity who was self-engendered and who went on to generate the other gods and goddesses before creating humankind. The particular deities mentioned in each of the stories relate to the geographical areas where the myths originated. It is impossible to say which of the myths was the most widely accepted at any one time.

The Creation Myth of Memphis

Ptah was the self-engendered creator god who was referred to as the 'father of the gods from whom all life emerged'. He brought the universe into being by conceiving all aspects of it in his heart, then speaking his thoughts out loud. First he created the other deities, and then towns with shrines in which to house them. He provided wood, clay and stone statues to act as bodies for the spirits or divine power (*ka*) of the deities, and offerings to be made to them forever. All things, including all people and animals, were brought into being by Ptah declaring their names.

▲ *Ptah's role as a creator god made him the ideal candidate for patron deity of craftsmen. His high priest was given the title of 'Lord of the Master Craftsmen'. Kom Ombo.*

The Creation Myth of Elephantine

The creator god of this cult centre was the ram-headed deity of the southern cataract region, Khnum. He created the universe by modelling the other gods, as well as humankind (both Egyptians and all those who spoke other languages), animals, birds, fish, reptiles and plants out of clay on his potter's wheel. He paid particular attention to the moulding of the human body, getting the blood to flow over the bones and stretching the skin carefully over the body. He took special care with the installation of the respiratory and digestive systems, the vertebrae, and the reproductive organs. Afterwards, he ensured the continuation of the human race by watching over conception and labour.

The Creation Myth of Hermopolis Magna

This myth begins by concentrating on the elements that were necessary for creation to take place. The fundamental factors were arranged in four male-female pairs: primordial water (Nun and Naunet); air or hidden power (Amun and Amaunet); darkness (Kuk and Kauket); and formlessness or infinity, otherwise interpreted as flood force (Huh and Hauhet). These divine personifications

◀ *Thoth had several guises, including that of a man with the head of an ibis, as shown here in a wooden figure with a bronze head dating to the Late Period.*

of the basic elements of the cosmos are referred to as the Ogdoad (Greek for 'group of eight'; in Egyptian, *khmun*). The four male gods were all frog-headed, and the four goddesses were snake-headed. At some point the eight elements interacted to create a burst of energy, allowing creation to take place.

There are two versions of the events that followed in this creation myth. In one version a primeval mound of earth described as the Isle of Flame rose up out of the primordial water. The god Thoth, in the form of an ibis, placed a cosmic egg on the mound of earth. The egg cracked, hatching the sun, which immediately rose up into the sky.

According to the alternative version, a lotus flower (divinely personified as the deity Nefertem) was bobbing on the surface of the primordial waters when the petals opened and the sun rose out of it. On this occasion the sun was identified as Horus.

The Creation Myth of Heliopolis

Before anything existed or creation had taken place, there was darkness and endless, lifeless water, divinely personified as Nun. A mound of fertile silt emerged from this watery chaos. The self-engendered solar creator god Atum ('the All' or 'the Complete One') appeared upon the mound. By masturbating (or sneezing, according to other versions of the myth) he was able to spit out the deities Shu (the divine personification of air) and Tefnut (moisture). Now that a male-female pair existed, they were able to procreate more conventionally. The results of their sexual union were Geb (the earth) and Nut (the sky). These two were forcibly separated by their father Shu, who lifted Nut up to her place above the earth.

The so-called Ennead (Greek for 'group of nine'; in Egyptian *pesedjet*) of Heliopolis includes these deities: Atum ('the Bull of the Ennead'), Shu, Tefnut, Geb and Nut, and is completed by the offspring of the latter two gods – Osiris, Isis, Seth and Nephthys. ◆

▼ *This papyrus scene, from the Third Intermediate Period Book of the Dead of Tameniu, shows the sky goddess Nut arching over her prostrate consort, the earth deity Geb. The fertility of the earth is clearly indicated, and as was usual, the cosmological deities are represented in entirely human form.*

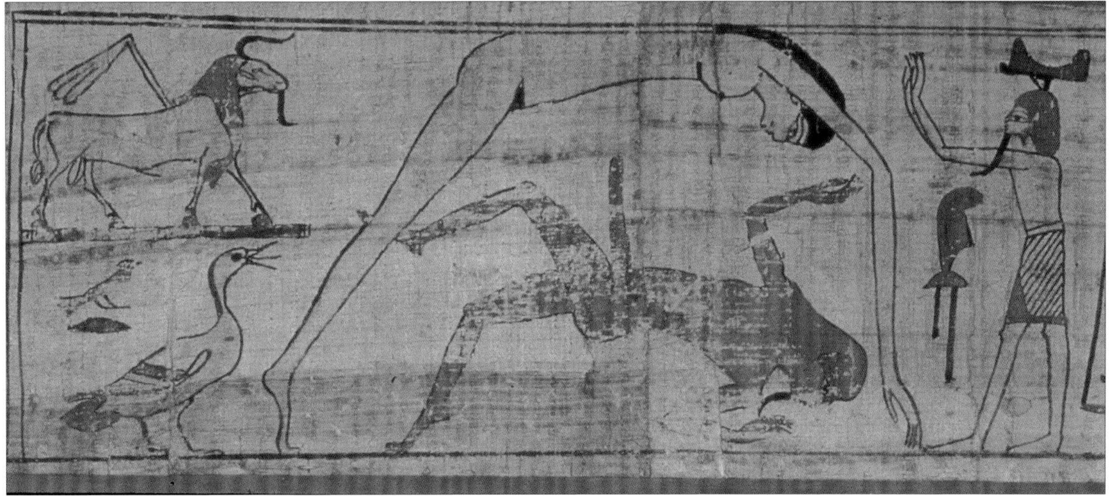

The Creation Myths in Context

The principle underlying all the different creation myths is that of order being established out of chaos. A state of primordial wateriness is used to represent chaos, out of which emerges a mound, and on it a solar deity. This mythological chain of events clearly reflects the annual flooding of the Nile and the subsiding of the water to reveal deposits of thick black silt, which were incredibly fertile but which required the sun for growth to take place.

All the explanations tend to hinge on the fertility of the land (thanks to the Nile inundation) and the heat of the sun. However, at Memphis the priests devised a myth centred around their supreme deity Ptah, which was decidedly less earthy and rather more metaphysical. Instead of relying on solar energy for creation to take place, the Memphite explanation depended upon the harnessing of three abstract catalysts: *heka* (magic or divine energy), *sia* (divine knowledge) and *hu* (divine utterance). This is similar to the 'logos' doctrine of the biblical New Testament, according to which the word of God became incarnate in the body of Jesus, the second person of the trinity.

▲ *The Shabaqo Stone bears a hieroglyphic inscription which is partially obscured by the slab's subsequent use as a mill stone.*

▼ *From the Middle Kingdom Period, the god Ptah was portrayed wearing a strap-on beard like that of the living king.*

The Background to the Creation Myth of Memphis

Memphis (ancient Men-nefer) is about 24km (15 miles) south of modern Cairo in the area of the modern village of Mit Rahina. It was founded as the administrative capital of Egypt at the beginning of the First Dynasty (c.3100 BC), but very little of this ancient capital survives today, mainly because its ruins were quarried during the medieval period for stone to use in the building of Cairo's churches and mosques.

The Memphis creation myth has survived inscribed on a rectangular slab of black granite measuring 92 x 137cm

◄ *The water table is so high in the region of Memphis that the ancient administrative capital is all but submerged. Preservation of this great city is extremely poor.*

(36 x 54in) now in the British Museum in London. The inscription was commissioned by the Twenty-fifth Dynasty king Shabaqo (c.716–c.702 BC), who ordered it to be set up in the temple of Ptah at Memphis.

The introduction explains that the king ordered the story to be copied on to stone because the original was written on a material which was becoming very worm-eaten (presumably papyrus or leather), and thus difficult to read.

It was once thought that the language used in the inscription was typical of the Old Kingdom (c.2686–c.2181 BC), and that the original must date to this period. It is now agreed that the original was probably of the late Ramesside Period (c.1100 BC), or possibly even later, although Ptah was clearly regarded as a creator god as early as the Old Kingdom. In the Coffin Texts of the Middle Kingdom (c.2055–c.1650 BC), as well as in later Ramesside texts (c.1200 BC), he is deemed responsible for fashioning the gods and the sun, and for ripening the crops.

The thinking heart

In this myth it is clear that the heart is regarded as the organ for thinking. The ancient Egyptians were not aware of the function of the brain, and instead believed the heart to be the seat of both wisdom and emotion (the idea of thinking with the heart appears frequently). The fact that the brain was considered to be mere stuffing in the head is particularly well exemplified by ancient Egyptian funerary practices. During the embalming process the brain was removed through the nose and discarded as if a waste product, while the heart was always left safely inside the body. The belief was that the dead person required his or her body and – even more importantly – heart in order to be reborn into the Afterlife. The dead person was judged by weighing his or her heart in a balance against the feather of Maat, the goddess of truth.

Order and chaos

The Egyptians had a high regard for order, as is evident from their carefully regulated social structure and intricately documented ritual procedures. Yet their lives were governed by a natural phenomenon which was beyond their control and was not entirely predictable – the inundation of the Nile. This was an event that tended not to be depicted: pictures of the landscape invariably showed the orderly state of the countryside once the river had returned to its normal course.

The creation myths envisaged the beginning of the world as the imposition of order on primeval chaos. The primordial waters of Nun symbolized chaos, while a sense of order was associated with the agricultural cycle and the passage of the sun. Maat, the goddess of truth and justice, also represented social and religious order, which maintained the equilibrium of the Egyptian world.

◄ *Horus performs the Opening of the Mouth ceremony on the mummified body, restoring Sennedjem's senses and enabling him to be reborn into the Afterlife. From the tomb of Sennedjem, Deir el-Medina, 13th century BC.*

The potency of names

The idea of naming something in order to give it a life force is apparent here, as elsewhere in ancient Egyptian thought. The belief that the name was the essence of a deity's potency is clearly illustrated in the myth of *Isis and the Sun God's Secret Name*. In the world of mortals, 'Execration Texts' show that if the ancient Egyptians knew an enemy's name they believed that they could magically destroy him by writing it in a curse on a clay bowl or figurine in the form of a bound captive, which could be smashed as part of an execration ritual.

In the Memphite creation myth the initial concept of a god coupled with the uttering of his or her name caused his or her vital force (*ka*) to come into being; this then required a vessel in which to reside. Most usefully the vessel would be a statue, because this could then act as the icon or focus of the cult.

Human beings were each believed to have their own *ka* which was represented in art as a person's double. On death it was thought necessary to preserve the body so that the *ka* (often translated as 'spirit') could survive. A similar ritual was performed on statues of gods and kings destined for the shrines and temples as was performed on mummified bodies before burial. In the 'Opening of the Mouth' ceremony, the last rite before emtombment, various ritual instruments were held up to the mouth and nose of the statue or dead body in order to ignite the senses and breathe life into the vessels for the *kas*. Ptah, the creator god of Memphis, was credited with having invented this particular ritual.

The modern name 'Egypt' derives from the Greek word for the country, *Aiguptos*, and it has been suggested that this in turn derived from the name of one of Ptah's temples at Memphis, *Hwt-ka-Ptah* (which means 'The Mansion for the *ka* of Ptah').

▼ *Figures of bound captives were used in execration rituals. The potency of the magic was heightened by inscribing the name of the enemy (potential or actual) on the figurine. It is unusual for an execration figure to be female.*

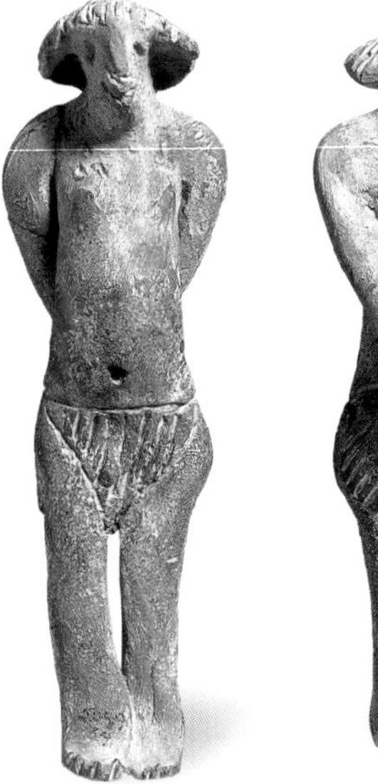

▲ *The cataract region of Aswan looks idyllic, but the granite rocks over which the river flows here can make navigation treacherous.*

The Background to the Creation Myth of Elephantine

Elephantine is an island in the centre of the River Nile opposite the modern town of Aswan, in the area of the first cataract at the southern border of Egypt. Archaeological excavations since the 1970s have established that it was the site of a large urban settlement, by at least the Roman period.

The city of Elephantine was the chief cult centre of Khnum, the ram-headed god. Here he was worshipped as part of a triad with his consort Satet (usually depicted as a woman wearing the white crown of Upper Egypt with antelope horns on each side) and their daughter Anuket (normally represented as a woman wearing a tall plumed crown and holding a papyrus sceptre), who was the goddess of the first cataract. Khnum's female counterpart was the frog goddess Heket, who was regarded chiefly as a goddess of childbirth, acting as a divine midwife at royal births. Just as Khnum fashioned the first humans on his potter's wheel, so Heket gave life to the unborn child by fashioning it inside the mother.

The Elephantine version of the creation myth appears on the walls of the Graeco-Roman temple at Esna in Upper Egypt. This temple survives only in the form of one hypostyle hall. Hymns dedicated to Khnum by his priests relay the premiss of the myth. The same theme can be found in the myth of the divine birth of the ruler, in which Khnum fashions the ruler and his or her *ka* from clay on his potter's wheel (see *The Divine Birth of the Egyptian King*).

Deities of the Nile

The creative force of the Nile was acknowledged in the worship of deities associated with the river. While Khnum was revered at Elephantine as a creator god, his consort Satet was associated with the annual flood, and daughter Anuket with the cataracts. Goddesses of fertility and childbirth were portrayed as Nile creatures, such as Heket, the frog-goddess and Taweret, the hippopotamus goddess. The chief deity of the Nile inundation was Hapy who was thought to live in the caverns of the cataract presided over by Khnum. Hapy was depicted as a man with a paunch and pendulous breasts. He often wore aquatic plants on his head.

▲ *The sacred lake in a temple complex such as Karnak would have been the source of water for libations and purification rituals.*

The Background to the Creation Myth of Hermopolis Magna

Hermopolis Magna (modern el-Ashmunein; ancient Khmun) is situated on the west bank of the Nile in Middle Egypt, close to the modern town of Mallawi. It was the chief cult centre of the god Thoth, identified by the Greeks with their god Hermes.

The earliest known version of this myth dates to the Middle Kingdom (c.2055–c.1650 BC). It offers a perfect example of the way a local deity associated with a specific theology could rise to national prominence when the centre of his cult grew in importance. In this case the god was Amun, who occurs in this myth as Amun Kematef ('he who has completed his moment'). At Thebes, Amun came to be considered as the supreme creator god, and his priesthood was able to surpass the king in power in that region (see *The High Priests*).

Elsewhere, in representations of the sun god coming into being, the eight primordial deities mentioned in this myth are sometimes depicted as baboons in the posture of greeting the rising sun. This is a fine example of the way in which the ancient Egyptians made observations of the natural world and then incorporated them into the iconography of their religious beliefs. At dawn, baboons have a habit of sitting up on their hind legs with their front paws raised, in order to warm their undersides in the morning rays of the sun. This upright posture, with arms and hands raised in front of the face, was adopted as the posture of adoration by humans before the gods.

The numbers four and eight were considered magically significant by the ancient Egyptians. Both numbers were associated with totality, and so the creation of eight deities, in four pairs, makes sense within the context of the Hermopolitan idea of the cosmos.

The city of Thoth

Thoth, the god of wisdom and writing, was the scribe to the gods and also their messenger. Because of this latter role, the Greeks identified him with Hermes. His city, Khmun, was therefore renamed Hermopolis ('City of Hermes') during the Graeco-Roman period.

Thoth was worshipped in this period under the name of Hermes Trismegistos ('Thrice-great Hermes'). He was believed to command 'the sacred books in the house of life', i.e papyrus rolls housed in temple libraries, inscribed with medical treatise, mathematical problems, etc.

▲ *When David Roberts drew the Colossi of Memnon in the 1838, the Nile still flooded annually, as it had done in ancient times. These two giant statues of Amenhotep III originally flanked the gateway to his mortuary temple in western Thebes.*

The Background to the Creation Myth of Heliopolis

Heliopolis is a Greek name meaning 'City of the Sun'. The ancient Egyptians called the city Yunu or On; it is now known as Tell Hisn. It lies a short distance north of the ancient capital at Memphis, and today the site is built over as the area forms part of the north-eastern suburbs of Cairo.

The Ennead (nine gods) of the Heliopolitan myth occur for the first time in the Pyramid Texts of the Old Kingdom (c.2350 BC). Elsewhere the word ennead sometimes serves as a collective noun for gods. In the Pyramid Texts for example, all the gods of the Egyptian pantheon are described as the 'Two Enneads'.

The idea of the primeval mound emerging from the watery chaos is quite clearly an image borrowed from the natural environment – that of the floodwaters subsiding to reveal the deposits of fertile Nile silt. The ancient Egyptians built their settlements on the highest possible ground in order to avoid the damaging inundation. When the Greek historian Strabo (c.63 BC– c.AD 21) visited Egypt during the reign of the Roman emperor Augustus (30 BC–AD 14), he commented that as a result of the annual flooding of the Nile, 'the whole country is under water and becomes a lake, except the settlements, and those are situated on natural hills or on artificial mounds and contain cities of considerable size and villages which, even when viewed from afar, resemble islands' (*Geography* 17.1.4).

Once Atum has sparked off the process of creation, the myth hinges on the existence of male-female partnerships, and sexual intercourse is the catalyst for continued creation. It is interesting that the divine personification of earth (Geb) is male whereas in most other cultures earth is considered to be female. It is also noteworthy that all the procreative couples have brother-sister relationships, thereby providing divine stereotypes for childbearing marriages within the royal family, especially in the case of Osiris and Isis who were regarded as the archetypal royal couple. However, this incestuous arrangement seems to have been confined to royal couples, stressing their divinity and separating them from ordinary people: when non-royal husbands and wives (both lovers and married couples) referred to each other as 'brother' and 'sister', they appear to have been using these terms as expressions of affection rather than describing actual familial relationships. ◆

The Death of Osiris

▲ *It is appropriate that this shrine of Osiris should resemble a coffin, as he was god of the dead and the Afterlife. In his myth he dies when he is confined in a chest by his brother Seth.*

During a time beset by turmoil, the birth of the god Osiris was heralded by an array of good omens and positive signs. Before his appearance, war and cannibalism appear to have been the order of the day – the people were said to be barbarians. Osiris became king of the Delta town of Busiris, but it was not long before he was made king of all Egypt. His skill lay in his ability to teach the unruly population to farm the land successfully and to lead law-abiding lives and worship the gods. Order had quite clearly been restored to the country when Osiris decided to go away on a journey and his wicked brother Seth seized the opportunity to gather together 72 conspirators. They hatched a treacherous plot.

On Osiris's return they threw a party and, following an enormous banquet, Seth suggested that the revellers should play a game (devised by him of course). A chest was laid out in the great hall and the game was to see who could fit inside it. When Osiris's turn came, he climbed into the chest, and – not surprisingly – it was the perfect-sized coffin for him.

One of the conspirators leapt forward and slammed down the lid, trapping Osiris inside. Unable to free himself, Osiris died and thus became ruler of the dead in the Afterlife.

This is by no means the end of the myth, however, because Osiris's dead body, still inside the chest, was disposed of in the Tanitic branch of the Nile. Its journey had only just begun, for instead of sinking to the murky depths as Seth had hoped, it floated with the current northwards towards the coast, and then out into the Mediterranean Sea. As if that was not far enough, it proceeded to bob all the way to the busy Lebanese port of Byblos, and finally came to rest in the entangled roots of a tree. Engulfed by the tree, the chest became part of its trunk. In due course the tree was cut down and turned into a pillar. Soon, Osiris's body was helping to support the roof of the palace of Byblos's ruler.

▼ *In the funerary art, Isis (here on the left) and her sister Nephthys are often shown as kites.*

The quest of Isis

Meanwhile, Osiris's sister and consort Isis had set her heart on retrieving the body of her husband, in order to give it a proper burial in accordance with Egyptian customs. To make her searching easier, and fearful of her brother Seth's intentions, she hid her young child Horus in the Delta marshes, under the watchful eye of the protective cobra-form goddess Wadjet, who had her cult centre at Buto (ancient Pe).

Isis followed a tip-off to Byblos, where she befriended a group of the queen's maids and thereby gained access to the

◀ *In addition to faience examples such as this one, an enormous number of bronze figures of Isis suckling the infant Horus have survived from the Late Period of ancient Egyptian history.*

▲ *This papyrus illustration from the Book of the Dead of Lady Cheritwebeshet shows Seth protecting the sun god from the threat of the serpent-demon Apophis. 21st Dynasty.*

temple. Her magical powers (including turning herself into a swallow, and performing rituals to make the dead Osiris immortal) became known to the king and queen, who offered the goddess anything they might be able to give her. They presumably hid their surprise when she requested a certain column in the royal house.

Osiris's burial

Thus in possession of the chest, Isis returned to Egypt with it, and hid it in the marshy Delta while she went to collect her son. This proved to be unwise, because Seth happened to be out hunting that night in that particular vicinity, and no doubt could not believe his luck when he happened upon the chest. He proceeded gleefully to hack Osiris's body into 14 pieces (or more, according to inscriptions at the temples of Dendera and Edfu), scattering them far and wide.

It seemed as though Osiris's body was destined not to receive the burial it deserved, but Isis refused to give up and began her search for the strewn pieces. At each place that she found a missing piece, she conducted a burial ceremony (thus explaining the claim made by several of the ancient Egyptian temples that they housed the tomb of Osiris). Only one part of his body was never found, and that was his penis, which had been swallowed by a fish. In order to ensure the correct burial of Osiris's entire body, his dutiful wife made him an artificial penis.

So Isis was able to work her magic, not to bring her husband back from the dead, but finally to bury his dismembered remains. Meanwhile Osiris had taken up the position of king of the dead in the Afterlife. ◆

Osiris's gifts to humankind

As the son of Geb, the earth, and Nut, the sky, Osiris probably originated as a fertility god of earth and underworld. During his reign as king of Egypt, he taught his subjects how to make bread and wine, and oversaw the building of the first temples and statues to the gods. He built towns and set just and fair laws. Having civilized Egypt, Osiris embarked on a journey to repeat the process in neighbouring countries.

The Death of Osiris in Context

This version of the myth of Osiris is the one recorded by the Greek writer Plutarch (c.AD 46–c.126). He visited Egypt and was inspired to write an account of this age-old story (albeit with a Greek slant). He called it *Peri Isidos kai Osiridos*. There is no doubt that Plutarch was relating a truly Egyptian tale, but a survey of the various accounts of Osiris's death reveals a number of variations.

The legend of Osiris's rule over Predynastic Egypt was being written down from as early as the Fifth Dynasty (c.2494–c.2345 BC), but those references that survive in the Pyramid Texts really give very little detail. The king dies 'falling on his side' on the riverbank at Abydos (or Nedjet) but no cause of death is given. Early accounts do not mention the dismemberment of Osiris's body but they do tell us that Isis has to search for the body and, finding it, she 'gathers up his flesh' so that it can be embalmed at Abydos. The mention of this temple site is significant because throughout pharaonic history it was believed to be the burial place of Osiris.

The Coffin Texts of the Middle Kingdom (c.2055–c.1650 BC) inscribed, as the name implies, on coffins of this period embellish the story. They say that it was indeed Seth who killed Osiris at Nedjet, and Isis (together with her sister Nephthys) is said to have mummified the dead body.

Osiris's penis

A major variation on Plutarch's telling of the myth can be found in the Chapel of Sokar, in the temple built by the Nineteenth-Dynasty king Seti I (c.1294–c.1279 BC) at Abydos. It contains reliefs indicating that Horus

▶ *Osiris's false curled beard, as illustrated here in the tomb of Nefertari in the Valley of the Queens, is distinct from the false straight beards worn by the living pharaohs. 19th Dynasty.*

▲ *This Roman period gilt coffin shows Isis and Nephthys mourning the death of Osiris. Isis is also portrayed as a kite hovering over the mummified body.*

had not been born before Osiris's death. In one scene Osiris is lying on an embalming table manually stimulating his penis. The relief on the opposite wall displays Isis in the guise of a sparrow-hawk hovering over Osiris's erect penis so as to be impregnated by him. Unlike Plutarch's version, in the pharaonic tradition Osiris's penis was not swallowed by a fish, but was laid to rest in the capital of Memphis (close to modern-day Cairo).

▼ *The fish motif, used in this glass vessel from Amarna, was common in ancient Egyptian art. 18th Dynasty.*

The idea of Horus as a young boy being hidden away in the marshes is evident in the pharaonic tradition because he is thought to have survived a scorpion sting while hiding. The ancient Egyptians believed that if children were stung by a scorpion they must identify them in spells with the child Horus, and this, it was hoped, would cure them.

Mummification

In the myth of Osiris, the belief, is evident that the gods ruled over the Egyptian people before the advent of the mortal dynasties.

This myth is, however, particularly important because it provides a divine prototype for the practice of mummification, and for the concept of rebirth into the Afterlife. It was believed that Osiris's body was the first to be mummified, and the lengths to which Isis went in order to retrieve the various parts of Osiris's body and to give them a proper burial, weaving lengths of linen for the wrapping of the body, reflects the ancient Egyptian fear of dying in the desert or abroad in case this meant that they would not be buried in accordance with traditional funerary rituals.

The ancient Egyptians believed that in order to be granted a place in the Afterlife a person needed his or her body to be buried intact and should also have a suitable funeral, including all the correct spells and rituals. So this myth provides a model for ancient Egyptian funerary beliefs as well as for the concept of the deceased king of Egypt being identified with the god Osiris. It is also the prototype for brother-sister marriages within the royal family. ◆

Dying and rising gods

Osiris's death and the story of his grieving consort Isis contain elements common to myths about dying and rising gods in other cultures. All were associated with vegetation, fertility and the harvest, offering reassurance that their worshippers could rely on bountiful crops. They underlined the regenerative powers of nature, suggesting the continuance of future generations and, above all, the annual rebirth of the natural world.

Isis and the Seven Scorpions

▲ *It has been calculated that a mummy might be wrapped in up to 375sq m (450sq yd) of linen bandaging. This bandage bears a vignette from the 'Book of the Dead'.*

The tale begins with Isis busily weaving the linen mummy wrappings for the body of her dead husband Osiris, who had been murdered by their brother Seth. She was interrupted by the god of wisdom and writing, Thoth, who advised her to take her young son Horus into hiding, in order to protect him from his uncle Seth.

Isis took heed of Thoth's words, and that evening she set off with an escort of seven scorpions. In order that Seth should not learn of their absence, Isis instructed the scorpions to be vigilant, and on no account to talk to any strangers on the way. Travelling through the Delta, they arrived at a place called the Town of the Two Sisters. There, rather than being welcomed by the local prosperous family, they had the front door slammed in their faces by the lady of the house. The scorpions were riled and vowed to wreak revenge. Six of them added their own personal supplies of poison to the sting of the seventh, who crawled under the rich woman's door and stung her young son almost to death. Beside herself, the woman rushed around the town desperately seeking help, but nobody responded to her cries.

A happy ending

Just as the boy was about to die, Isis intervened. She had been given lodgings by a peasant girl, and would not tolerate the death of this innocent child. To cure him, she held him and uttered a magic spell that involved naming each of the scorpions in turn, thus allowing her to control them. The event was to be life-changing for the boy's mother, who offered Isis and the peasant girl all her worldly possessions.

◀ *Egypt is home to two types of scorpion, the darker, relatively harmless* Scorpioniae, *and the paler, more poisonous* Buthridae. *The goddess Selket, shown here, took the form of a scorpion, and guarded the canopic jar containing the intestines.*

Isis and the Seven Scorpions in Context

This story about the magical powers of Isis offered a means of curing, or protecting against the possibility of, scorpion stings. The same purpose is served by the myth of *Isis and the Sun God's Secret Name*.

The myth of Isis and the Seven Scorpions is found inscribed on the Metternich Stela, which is now in the Metropolitan Museum of Art in New York. This stone stela is a *cippus*, which means that it resembles a gravestone in shape, and has a central image of Horus as a child standing on a crocodile, clutching scorpions, snakes and other threatening creatures. Within this particular vignette the child Horus (Hor-pa-khered) is protected not only by the presence of the spirit deity Bes, but also by other deities and *udjat*-eyes, since the Eye of Horus was used as a protective amulet. A number of spells are also inscribed on the *cippus*, for use in a ritual in which water became imbued with magical potency when it was poured over the *cippus*. The liquid could then be ritually drunk or applied.

The recitation of the spell used by Isis in this myth was to be accompanied by a prescription of barley-bread, garlic and salt. Cereals, bread and salt are still used in Egyptian rituals today to appease and ward off evil influences. A poultice of barley-bread is also still used to draw out the poison when someone has been stung by a scorpion. The idea of sympathetic magic is very much apparent on the Metternich Stela: by identifying any child suffering from a scorpion sting with the young boy in the myth, they too could be healed.

Knowledge is power

As in the myth of *Isis and the Sun God's Secret Name*, the belief in the knowledge of a name giving control is an extremely important element. Isis can exert power over the scorpions only by naming them in her spell. The fact that there are seven scorpions is also significant, because the number seven was deemed to be magically potent and was used in various spells, particularly one involving the ritual tying and untying of seven knots.

Although healing spells derived from myths like this one often dealt with the most commonplace of problems, some of the most important of the Egyptian deities were involved in their solutions and remedies. So even the most superior of the gods and goddesses might play a part in the daily lives of the Egyptians, indicating how closely state and popular religion were interwoven. ◆

Horus and the scorpion

Although Isis's magic was effective in counteracting the poison of the seven scorpions, she seems not to have had the power to cure her own small son, Horus. Having hidden him in the marshes at Khemmis in the Delta while she went to find food for herself, she returned to find that he had been stung. Her screams reached the ears of the sun god, Re, and caused him to bring his solar boat to a halt so that the earth was plunged into darkness.

Thoth left Re's boat and uttered a spell to cure Horus, threatening that the earth would remain dark until the poison left him. Horus was restored to health and Thoth charged the people of Khemmis with his care. Then he returned to Re's boat, which set sail again.

► *The magical potency of a Cippus of Horus was no doubt strengthened if it was held by a statue of a priest.*

The Contendings of Horus and Seth

The myth opens with a courtroom scene and plunges straight into the deliberations of a trial that had already been dragging on for 80 years. This was, of course, no ordinary courtroom, but that of the gods, presided over by the sun god Re, and centre stage were Horus and Seth, who were there to contest the rightful claim to the throne of Egypt.

This long episode follows the death of the reigning king Osiris. The murder of this god, who had been maintaining a stable and prosperous rule over Egypt, was clearly the first step in a plan by his brother Seth to usurp the throne, but Osiris had died leaving a son and heir, Horus, who, it might be assumed, would have inherited the throne.

▲ *Neith wears the Red Crown of Lower Egypt. She was revered as 'mistress of the bow...ruler of the arrows'.*

▲ *Kharga is the southernmost and largest of the major Egyptian oases in the Western Desert.*

The indecision of the jury

The gods presiding in the court were by no means unanimous in their opinion. Some considered Horus too young to rule, and they believed Seth's strength would make him a more successful ruler. They were swayed by the fact that Seth travelled in Re's boat and repulsed the sun god's enemies, especially the serpent demon Apophis (see *The Journey of the Sun through the Netherworld*).

The divine court decided to turn to the advice and wisdom of the ancient goddess of warfare, Neith, who resided at Sais in the Delta. She was adamantly in favour of Horus, but was a fair arbiter and believed that Seth should be compensated with treasure and two Syrian goddesses, Anat and Astarte (described as Re's daughters). Her decision was coupled with a threat not to be taken lightly: if Horus were not allowed to succeed to the throne, the sky would fall down on the Egyptian people.

The gods appeared not to take this threat seriously because they still refused to agree on a final outcome. The argument was starting to get heated, especially when the deity Baba dared to insult Re by telling him his shrine was empty. The great sun god left sulking and returned only when he had been cheered up by his daughter Hathor, who made him laugh by exposing her genitalia to him.

A change of scene

The gods were beginning to get bored by the proceedings, so they decided on a change of scene. They relocated to an island, but Horus's mother Isis, who was particularly concerned that her son should inherit his father's throne, was believed to have a biased view, so the ferryman Nemty was forbidden to take her across the water from the mainland. But this goddess was a mistress of disguise and, transforming herself into an old hag, she fooled the ferryman into transporting her to the island. Once there she turned herself into a beautiful young woman and proceeded to seduce the unsuspecting Seth. She claimed to have been married to a cattle herder who had died, leaving her with a young son. She spun the piteous yarn further by telling him that a stranger had turned up and

► *The hippopotamus hunt depicted on the wall of the tomb of Mereruka at Saqqara symbolizes the victory of good, or order, over evil, or chaos, epitomized by the triumph of Horus over Seth. Old Kingdom.*

Courts of law

The administration of justice was not dealt with by specialized lawyers, but by general tribunals, consisting of local officials and respected citizens, which met when the need arose. The site of Deir el-Medina has yielded information on these courts. From the time of the New Kingdom (c.1550–c.1069 BC), oracles were sometimes consulted to help settle legal arguments.

Punishments for crimes included beatings and enforced labour, and the death penalty was used in serious cases such as treason.

had tried to steal their cattle and throw her son out of their house. As Isis had hoped, Seth condemned the behaviour of this stranger, and in so doing, passed judgement on himself for his attempt to confiscate Horus's inheritance.

Horus was awarded the throne, but just as the matter seemed to have been decided, the proceedings became still more complicated and ambiguous.

Seth appealed and challenged Horus to an underwater contest, with both gods taking the form of hippopotami: if either of them was to surface before the end of three months he would lose his claim to the throne. Isis of course wanted to help her son as much as possible, so she decided to kill Seth and hurled a copper harpoon into the water. But the result was not as planned, for it accidentally embedded itself in Horus's flesh. Isis panicked, but was able to withdraw the weapon using magic, and threw it again. This time it hit Seth, but Seth reminded Isis that he was her brother and a pang of guilt caused her to withdraw the harpoon a second time.

Events grew stranger still when Horus rose out of the water, and in a fit of rage cut off his mother's head. She turned into a flint statue and he realized that he had overreacted. Fearing punishment he fled with his mother's head to the area of the Kharga and Dakhla oases in the Western Desert. But Seth was out to avenge his sister's decapitation. He tracked down his nephew lying under a tree, and gouged out his eyes (which, when buried, grew back as lotus flowers). It was left to the cow goddess Hathor to cure Horus's sight, which she did using gazelle milk.

The gods realized that things were getting out of control, so they summoned Horus and Seth back to court. But nobody could have predicted what would happen next.

A banquet was thrown during which Seth sexually assaulted Horus in order to humiliate him publicly,

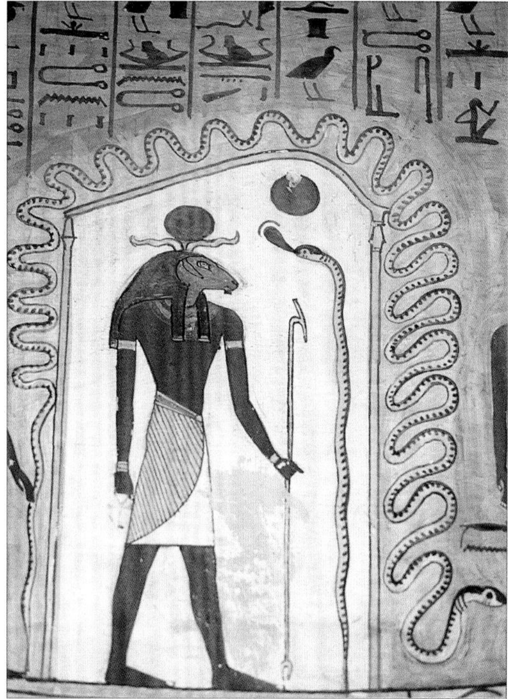

► *Re, the sun god, was often depicted in his solar boat with a ram's head, wearing a sun disc on his head.*

and to display his own strength and superiority. The incident did not go as Seth had planned, however, because Horus managed to catch Seth's semen in his carefully positioned hands before it could enter him. He went running to his mother (whose head had been magically restored) with the rogue ejaculate. Shocked, she cut off her son's hand, disposing of it (and thus the semen) in the marshes. She realized that to foil Seth's plan completely he must now be tricked into ingesting Horus's semen, so Horus obliged (having had his hand magically replaced by Isis) and she spread some on Seth's favourite food, lettuce. Seth duly tucked into his doctored snack.

Back in the courtroom, the semen of the two gods was asked to speak out in order to ascertain its whereabouts and prove Seth's story about the assault. But instead of speaking from inside Horus, Seth's semen spoke out from the marshes, while Horus's identified itself inside Seth and emerged as a gold sun disc (indicating its divine origins) from the top of his head.

The final outcome

Seth was, of course, livid and challenged Horus to a boat race. Extraordinarily (although by now little should surprise us), it was decided that the boats must be made of stone. Horus craftily built his using pine painted to look like stone; Seth's (which was made out of a mountain peak) sank. Enraged, Seth turned himself into a hippopotamus and smashed up Horus's boat.

Enough was enough. Osiris sent a threatening message from the Netherworld and Horus was at last confirmed as the rightful heir to the throne. Seth's strength was not to be overlooked, however; he was employed by the sun god to thunder in the sky and to keep evil at bay.

Egyptian morality

The episode of Seth's homosexual assault on Horus seems to show him in a bad light, yet he had planned the whole episode to expose Horus by proclaiming the act himself before the gods' tribunal to help him win his case. The story would have been understood by the Egyptians in terms of the humiliating treatment of a defeated enemy.

Thus, when Horus's semen spoke from inside Seth, the general mockery was turned on him and he was seen as the defeated adversary. The New Kingdom Book of the Dead implies that homosexuality was condemned, but earlier texts suggest that homosexual relations were not considered morally wrong so long as there was mutual consent.

▼ *Wooden model boats were commonly placed in tombs of the Middle Kingdom Period. They might have oarsmen for heading north with the current, or sails when their journey was southwards with the wind.*

The Contendings of Horus and Seth in Context

This detailed version of the myth is found on a papyrus roll that has come to be known as Papyrus Chester Beatty number one (now in the Dublin Museum). It covers almost sixteen pages, and is written in hieratic script (the cursive form of hieroglyphs) by a scribe who had very fine handwriting. It comes from Thebes and dates to the Twentieth-Dynasty reign of Ramesses V (c.1147–c.1143 BC).

The Edfu reliefs

A more combative version of the myth appears on the walls of the Ptolemaic temple at Edfu, which is dedicated to Horus. In this series of text and relief it was Horus who, in the form of a winged disc, accompanied the sun god Re in his solar boat, and protected the sun against its enemies (which appear mainly as hippopotami and crocodiles, two animals that regularly threatened the safety of the ancient Egyptians).

In this version Seth was the leader of the pack of enemies, so he and Horus repeatedly came up against each other, taking various forms; for example, Seth was a cheetah or a snake while Horus was a lion. In the final showdown, Seth turned himself into a red hippopotamus. The battle took place at Elephantine, at the southern boundary of Egypt, and is said to have happened during a wild storm which churned up the river. In this way, an explanation is provided for the cataract at Elephantine – a granite outcrop under the water that turns that particular stretch of the river into a series of unnegotiable rapids. Horus triumphed by killing Seth with his harpoon. As Seth was dismembered, Isis decided that his bones should be fed to the cats and his fat to the worms.

The principal point made in this myth is that the son of the king should inherit the throne. The story provided a model for the smooth succession of the royal line. The aim was to protect the son and heir by providing a divine prototype – the living king would be identified with Horus, and the deceased king with Osiris. Seth played the possible usurper, who in reality may or may not have been a member of the royal family. The royal office was especially vulnerable when the son and heir was a minor on his father's death, as in the case of Horus, and when the alternative claimant was supported by a powerful court faction.

▲ *The gods in the reliefs in the temple at Edfu, as elsewhere, were considered pagan by the Christians and were vigorously excised. Graeco-Roman Period.*

▶ *On the walls of the temple at Edfu, Horus wears the double crown of the pharaoh and harpoons Seth as a hippopotamus. Graeco-Roman Period.*

▲ *Temple reliefs and religious texts make clear the divine or magical properties believed to be held by breast milk.*

Courts of justice

The ancient Egyptians clearly believed that the divine world reflected that of mortals, and gods and goddesses behaved in much the same way as humans, for example in taking their disputes to court.

The important role of the court in ancient Egyptian society is well documented, particularly at the site of Deir el-Medina, the village on the west bank at Thebes inhabited during the New Kingdom (c.1550–c.1069 BC) by the tomb builders and their families. The local court was called the *kenbet* and its members were respected villagers joined by government officials connected with the community, such as a scribe from the vizier's office, which was based across the river in the main city of Thebes. The *kenbet* was mainly concerned with civil disputes between private individuals, especially over property and arising from economic transactions.

The vizier, who was the king's chief minister, presided over the 'Great Kenbet' or 'Supreme Court'. This was not a permanent assembly, but a selection of between eight and fourteen Theban VIPs who gathered when necessary to preside over the prosecution of particularly serious crimes, such as the tomb robberies of the late Ramesside Period (c.1100 BC).

Milk and lettuce

Both milk and lettuce have an interesting significance in this myth: Horus's eyes are said to be cured by the application of gazelle's milk, and it is said that Seth's favourite food, which is consequently drizzled with Horus's semen, is lettuce.

The milk used in the myth is that of a gazelle, but it is also true that human breast milk was considered an effective ingredient in medical prescriptions and magical rituals (although distinct in modern minds, the two were closely related according to the ancient Egyptian magico-medical texts). The milk of a mother who had given birth to a male child was considered especially useful for remedying colds, burns and eye diseases.

Similar cures continued to appear in the work of Hippocrates and of other classical writers such as Pliny and Dioscorides, as well as in Coptic medical texts and in European medical treatises up until the seventeenth

Sons and heirs

The throne of Egypt, having been granted to Horus, was thereafter known as the Horus Throne. Each successive king was identified with Horus while he lived and with Osiris, perceived as Horus's dead father, after his death.

The act of burying his predecessor, reflecting the service performed by Horus for Osiris, was enough to fulfil the new king's role as Horus and legitimize his position as son and heir to the throne. This could hold true even if the old king had not actually been his real father. If a king died without having produced a son, a successor – who might not necessarily be of royal blood – could validate his claim to the throne by burying the dead king. According to ritual, seventy days should elapse between the king's death and his burial, to allow for the funeral preparations.

◄ *The tall lettuces behind the ancient god Min, on this fragment of relief from Koptos, were symbols of his cult and of fertility and sexuality.*

century. Even today, in Britain and other Western countries, mothers are commonly advised to treat their babies' eye infections with breast milk.

Some ancient Egyptian pots have been discovered that may well have been designed to hold breast milk. They are modelled in the shape of a breast-feeding woman or Taweret, the hippopotamus goddess of pregnancy and childbirth. Occasionally the pot has a hole in place of one of the nipples, which would presumably have acted as a spout. It has been calculated that each pot holds just over 100ml (4fl oz), roughly equivalent to the amount of milk produced by one breast at one feed. Perhaps the ancient Egyptians believed that when they put an animal's milk in such a pot, it magically became (or at least took on the therapeutic properties of) a woman's milk.

Lactating women were obviously considered in some way special in religious terms, because they were credited with *heka* or magic. A wet nurse might bear the title *Sau*, implying that she had a protective, safeguarding role, as *sa* was the word for 'protection' and also for 'amulet'.

The type of lettuce referred to in the myth is *Lactuca sativa longifolia*, which grew tall and straight like a modern cos lettuce and emitted a milky-white liquid when pressed. This fluid was presumably thought to resemble semen because the lettuce was closely associated with the fertility god Min, and the Egyptians considered it to be an aphrodisiac. Thus the choice of this particular vegetable in the context of this myth becomes more understandable.

In Egyptian folklore today, the lettuce is still considered an aphrodisiac. But classical writers had very different views on the effect the lettuce might have. Athenaeus stated that lettuce caused impotence; Pliny wrote that one particular sort of lettuce was called 'the anti-aphrodisiac' or 'the eunuch's lettuce' because it was 'an extremely potent check to amorous propensities' (instead, he recommended leeks as a sexual stimulant). Lettuce must have had a similar reputation in the seventeenth century as it was 'commended for Monkes, Nunnes, and the like sort of people to eate'. ◆

The Destruction of Humankind

▲ *This gold statuette of Amun-Re holds an ankh, symbolizing the giving of life, in one hand, and the scimitar, a symbol of strength, power and foreign conquest, in the other.*

The events of this myth took place when the sun god Re was king of both the divine and the mortal worlds. He is described as elderly, with bones made of silver, flesh of gold, and hair of lapis lazuli.

The king learnt that humankind was plotting a rebellion against him. His immediate reaction was to destroy the race, but he felt he ought first to seek advice. He summoned his followers and ordered them to bring a number of deities to his court. Among them were to be Shu, Tefnut, Geb, Nut, Nun and, most crucially, a goddess he referred to as his 'Eye': this turned out to be Hathor in her peaceful manifestation, turning into Sekhmet when she became savage. The gods had to arrive secretly so that the human beings would not discover that their plot was being foiled.

The Eye of Re

The gods arrived at the palace and bowed before the king, who asked for their opinion on the matter in hand. Their unanimous suggestion was that he should send his Eye to slaughter the humans as they tried to escape into the desert. Re adopted their recommendation and the goddess readily obliged. However, after a day of massacre, Re was compassionate and felt that enough had been done to show humankind who was in charge. But the Eye of Re, as Sekhmet, was bloodthirsty and out of control: she was ready to wipe out the human race.

Now that the malevolent force of the goddess had been unleashed, Re had to find a way to restrain her. He sent swift-footed messengers to Aswan in the south to fetch a large amount of red ochre (a fine earth containing iron oxide,

▲ *This limestone statuette of a buxom brewer was placed in the tomb of Meresankh at Saqqara to ensure the production of beer for him in the Afterlife. 5th Dynasty.*

◀ *One of the black granite statues of Sekhmet placed by Amenhotep III in the temple of Mut at Karnak. 18th Dynasty.*

or haematite) and take it to his temple at Heliopolis, where the high priest was instructed to grind up the haematite. Maid servants were ordered to crush enough barley to make 7,000 jars of beer. This was to be no ordinary beer, but was to have the red ochre mixed in with it, so that it looked like blood. Work began immediately and continued throughout the night.

Could the human race be saved? Re rose early and ordered the fields where Sekhmet was due to resume her massacre to be flooded with the red beer. The goddess was ecstatic when she saw it, thinking she had happened upon a sea of human blood, and she gulped it down greedily. This had the desired result, and in her drunken state she did not even notice the people of Egypt, let alone continue to kill them off.

▲ *Hathor's customary headdress was a sun disc sitting between cow's horns, but she was also shown wearing a falcon on a perch, as in this painted relief in the tomb of Horemheb in the Valley of the Kings, Thebes.*

Re's abdication

Re had saved his people, and the frenzied goddess was once again peaceful. But the experience had been too much for the king. He decided he had had enough and abdicated, leaving the responsibilities of government to Thoth, the god of wisdom and writing. Re left Thoth to teach humankind the skill of literacy, and ascended into the sky on the back of the Divine Cow for a spell of peace and quiet.

The Destruction of Humankind in Context

▲ *The sky goddess could also be represented as a sow. A comparison was being made between a sow eating her young and Nut swallowing the sun and stars.*

Sections of this myth have been found in five of the tombs in the Valley of the Kings, on the west bank at Thebes. This particular royal burial site was employed by rulers of the New Kingdom (c.1550–c.1069 BC). The earliest example of the myth occurs on the interior of the outermost of the four gilded shrines that were found by Howard Carter in 1922 over the sarcophagus of the Eighteenth-Dynasty king Tutankhamun, (c.1336–c.1327 BC). The contents of this tomb are now in the Cairo Museum. There is a longer version of the text in a side-room off the burial chamber of the tomb of the Nineteenth-Dynasty ruler Seti I (c.1294–c.1279 BC), as well as variations of the text in the tombs of his successor Ramesses II (c.1279–c.1213 BC), and two of the Twentieth-Dynasty kings, Ramesses III (c.1184–c.1153 BC) and VI (c.1143–c.1136 BC).

Although all the known copies of the myth date to this particular period of Egyptian history, the style of writing is in fact that of the Middle Kingdom (c.2055–c.1650 BC), and so it is likely that it was originally written down at that time.

The myth is actually part of a longer religious text known as 'The Book of the Divine Cow', incorporating spells to protect the body of the king and to ensure his safe ascension to the heavens. This was done by identifying him with the sun god, who rises successfully into the sky at the end of the myth.

The wrath of the gods

The main theme of the myth is, of course, the divine punishment of the human race, a theme which also occurs in the Mesopotamian and Biblical stories of the Flood. The significance of the image of a flood for the ancient Egyptians cannot be underestimated, but in this myth they are saved by it; their lives would have revolved around, and even depended upon, the annual flooding of the Nile that took place between July and October.

It is known from other sources that the ancient Egyptian gods were believed capable of meting out punishment to

◀ *The cobra goddess Mertseger ('she who loves silence') was known as the Goddess of the Peak. She commanded fear and respect among the villagers of Deir el-Medina, especially as she was believed able to cause blindness and venomous stings.*

◀ *The original obelisk was the sacred* benben *stone at Heliopolis on which the first rays of the sun were said to have shone.*

individuals for wrongdoings. The offences might be against specific deities (as witnessed by various penitential hymns found inscribed on stelae from Deir el-Medina), or they might be more general offences, such as the long list of wrongdoings that the dead had to be able to swear they had not committed in order to be granted a place in the Afterlife.

Born of the gods

But the gods were quite clearly merciful because it was perceived that their own existence was ultimately dependent upon the existence of mortals. The gods required the ancient Egyptian people to tend to them, provide them offerings of food, and build temples for them. A marked interdependence was evident – the gods were worshipped in exchange for their benefice.

Another reason why Re might well have had a change of heart when it came to wiping out all human beings was the fact that humankind had emanated from the sun god himself, that is to say from his tears, when he created the world. The ancient Egyptian love of wordplay and punning is conspicuous here, considering the similarity between the ancient Egyptian words for people (*remetch*) and tear (*remyt*). The magical association of similar-sounding words also occurs in the texts known as Dream Papyri. These were collections of dream scenarios that were thought useful for predicting the future.

The idea of the gods ruling over humankind is certainly not unique to this myth (see also *The Death of Osiris*), and was quite clearly crucial to the ancient Egyptians' understanding of their own past. In the early third century BC an Egyptian priest named Manetho was commissioned to write a history of Egypt by the Ptolemaic ruler of Egypt Ptolemy II (285–246 BC). Although he wrote his *Aegyptiaca* in Greek, he would presumably have had access to earlier Egyptian lists of kings, temple archives, and popular tales. Before dividing the rulers up into thirty-one dynasties, beginning with a king named Menes and ending with Alexander the Great, he described a period when gods had ruled over the Egyptian people. ◆

Flood myths

A limitless ocean featured in the creation myths of many cultures as the primeval state of the world. A flood of global proportions was also a common theme, in which an inundation was sent to wipe out sinful humankind and restore the world to its pristine original state. The Egyptians believed that Re might well one day tire of humanity and that he had the capacity to return the world to the watery abyss of Nun.

Myths about overwhelming floods reflected the ambiguous nature of humanity's relationship with water, which was vital to life but also carried the threat of violence and devastation. In Mesopotamia, the Rivers Tigris and Euphrates flooded unpredictably, and their fearsome character was expressed in several versions of a flood myth which eventually found its way into the Hebraic tradition as the story of Noah's ark.

Isis and the Sun God's Secret Name

The sun god Re had many different names, but the one that held the key to his supreme power was a secret one that only he knew. Anyone lucky enough to discover the secret would be able to claim a position next to Re at the head of the pantheon of gods and goddesses.

Isis, who was very clever, was determined to discover this secret name so she hatched a plan. As an old man, Re drooled, and Isis collected some of his saliva and mixed it with earth to conjure a demon in the form of a snake, symbolizing Re's own strength.

Isis knew that Re was partial to a daily stroll outside his palace, so she familiarized herself with his usual route, and left the snake at the crossroads he was likely to pass. Of course he did walk this way, and the snake bit him, as Isis had intended.

The snake's venom entered Re and he became overwhelmed by a terrible fever. Because he had not created the snake, Re had no idea how to cure himself of the effects of its bite. He cried out in agony and the other gods came running but were unable to help him in his distress. His future was looking bleak, when Isis arrived. She offered to cure him on condition that he told her his secret name.

The sun god is cured

As well as being considered 'great in magic', Isis was known to have impressive medical skills, so Re was tempted, but he knew that having someone else in possession of his secret identity could put him in a vulnerable position. He tried to pull the wool over Isis's eyes by reeling off a long list of his other names, such as 'Moulder of the Mountains' and 'Maker of the Bull for the Cow in order to bring Sexual Pleasure into Being'.

But Isis could not be duped, and Re's symptoms grew even worse – he was sweating, shivering and losing his sight. In desperation, he agreed to Isis's bargain. He told her his secret name, but knowing that she would not be able to resist passing it on to her son, he insisted that she promise to make Horus swear an oath that he would keep the secret.

In receipt of this arcane knowledge, Isis became known as the 'Mistress of the Gods who knows Re by his own name', and recited a spell to cure the sun god's ailment.

▲ *Atum and Re appear as cats on this stela from Deir el-Medina. Below them, a married couple recite a hymn to the 'great cat' and the sun god. 19th Dynasty.*

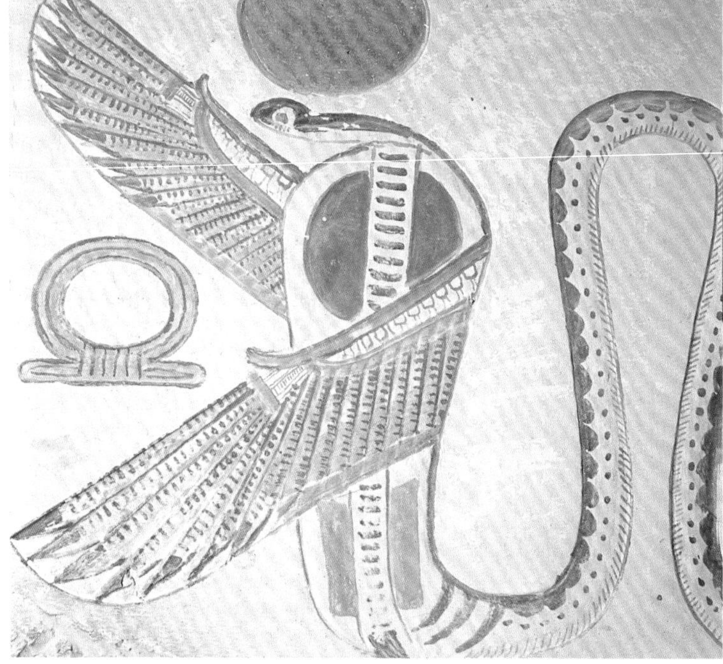

▶ *The circular motif in front of this winged snake is a* shen, *the ancient Egyptian symbol of eternity. Valley of the Queens.*

Isis and the Sun God's Secret Name in Context

This myth survives on a papyrus dating from the Nineteenth Dynasty (c.1200 BC) which is now in the Turin Museum in Italy; a version of it can also be found in a more fragmentary state on another papyrus, Papyrus Chester Beatty XI, in the British Museum, London.

The main point of the myth was to emphasize the significance of a name, and the fact that knowledge of a name was equated with power. The ancient Egyptians believed the name to be very much part of the personality of an individual or the nature of an object. Generally, the myths served to provide the deities with their names and identities. It was not until a force had a name that offerings and prayers could be made to it by worshippers. But to know a name was to be able to exercise a certain degree of control over the deity (or person or thing) to which it belonged. Knowing the relevant names was particularly crucial in spells and their accompanying rituals (see *Isis and the Seven Scorpions*).

Mystery of the divine

It is significant that, in this myth, although Isis eventually managed to learn the sun god's secret name, the reader (or listener) never does. It was important to the ancient Egyptians that they could, to a certain extent, make sense of, and even identify with, their gods and goddesses, but by its very nature the divine world could not be completely familiar: it always retained a degree of mystery. The gods had to be believed to have their own secrets in order to inspire awe.

Magic and medicine

In this myth, Horus became party to the secret of the source of the sun god's power, so if the king was identified with Horus, he would presumably have been considered to be the only mortal with possession of this hidden knowledge, the key to certain powers.

The myth was obviously used in a ritual 'to ward off poison'. It includes the words of the spell with which Isis cured Re. Because she was successful in her combination of magic and medicine, it was thought that anyone suffering from a poisonous sting could be similarly cured.

As far as the ancient Egyptians were concerned, magic and medicine were not two distinct fields. The ten or so magico-medical texts that have survived show that spells and the use of amulets and other ritual objects were regularly combined with clinical observation and carefully worked-out prescriptions. This particular text stipulates that recitation of the spell is to be accompanied by a remedy of 'scorpion herb' mixed with beer or wine. ◆

Names

Egyptian names were chosen with care as they were considered to be an important aspect of a person's character. They might be derived from words indicating desirable qualities, such as beauty or wisdom, or from the names or attributes of gods to show devotion. Others associate the individual with the king.

From the Old Kingdom (c.2686–c.2181 BC) the king took five names, the first four of which he acquired when he came to the throne. The first was the Horus-name, or chief name. The second was the 'Two Ladies' name, giving him the protection of the goddesses Nekhbet and Wadjet. The third name, the Golden Horus name, referred to his divinity and the fourth, his throne name, introduced by the epithet 'He of the Sedge and the Bee' to his role as ruler. His last name, called the nomen, was the name given to him at birth and was preceded by the title 'Son of Re'.

▲ *The ideogram of a scorpion is one of the earliest known hieroglyphs; amulets in this form exist from the Old Kingdom.*

The Journey of the Sun Through the Netherworld

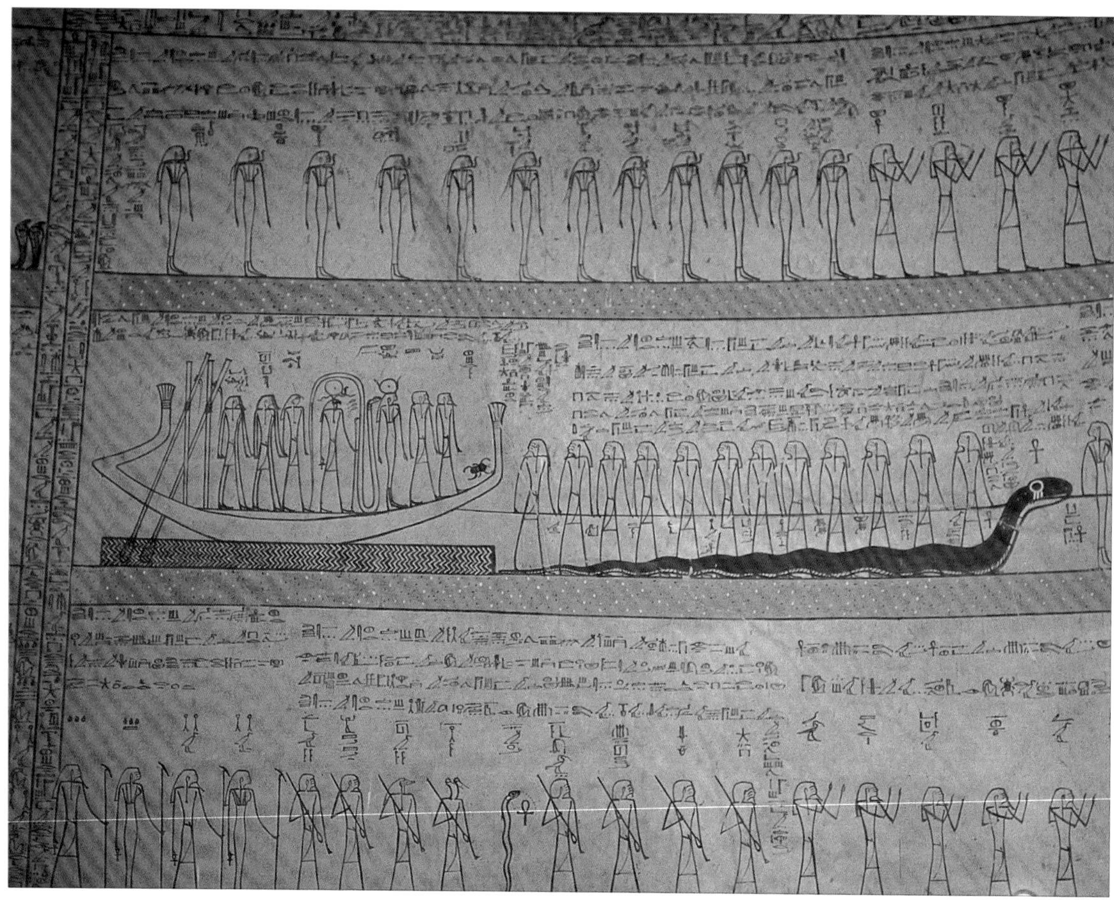

The sun god Re arose each day and, having bathed and fed, began his journey across the sky in his solar day boat. On the way, he spent one of the 12 hours of the day inspecting each of his 12 provinces, as he made a serene progression from east to west. During the night, however, he had to make a perilous voyage through the Netherworld while the land was left in darkness awaiting his return the following morning. The myth that describes his ordeal begins just as night falls.

The sun god had reached the western horizon, ready to begin his nightly journey through the Netherworld. He was all set to travel along the River of Wernes, a journey that would take him 12 hours.

In the first hour of the night he embarked on his journey in his night-boat with a crew of deities, including 'Path-opener' and 'Guide of the Boat'. He was also accompanied by two sets of nine baboons, who sang to Re as he entered the Netherworld and were there to open doors for him, as well as 12

▲ *The tomb of Tuthmosis III is painted with scenes from the Am Duat, 'The Book of that which is in the Netherworld'. Valley of the Kings.*

snake goddesses whose job it was to light up the darkness. In the second hour Re sailed on to the region of Wernes, where he granted land rights to the grain gods. In the third hour, he performed an important ritual act: he revived the god of the Netherworld, Osiris, by bestowing on him two divine forces described as 'Will' and 'Mind'. In the fourth hour, he reached a passage which was the way to

► *The fourth and fifth hours of night (the realm of Sokar) are shown on this sarcophagus. 30th Dynasty.*

the underworld from the Gate of the Passageways, the entrance taken by the dead, and the route to the body of the hawk-headed Memphite funerary deity Sokar and the tomb of Osiris. The passage was guarded by a number of fantastic snakes with human heads and several short legs, or with wings and multiple snakes' heads.

The hazards of the journey

In the fifth hour, Re's solar boat was towed across a mound referred to as the Mound of Sokar, but in fact representing the tomb of Osiris and therefore flanked by his two sisters Isis and Nephthys in the form of kites. The tow-rope of the boat was held by a scarab beetle, symbolizing the coming emergence of Re from the night in the form of the scarab beetle deity Khepri. The entrance to the mound was guarded by four heads spurting flames, and even more extraordinary was a primeval embodiment of Re which appeared at this stage of his journey: Sokar balancing on a snake with a human head at one end and three snakes' heads at the other, emerging out of a mound of sand on the back of Aker, the double-headed leonine earth god. In the sixth hour, Re visited Thoth, the god of the moon, wisdom and writing, who appeared in the form of a baboon, but holding his other manifestation, an ibis. Thoth's role in this myth was to found a city for the gods and rulers of Egypt. Re also encountered an image of himself – the dung-beetle, in death

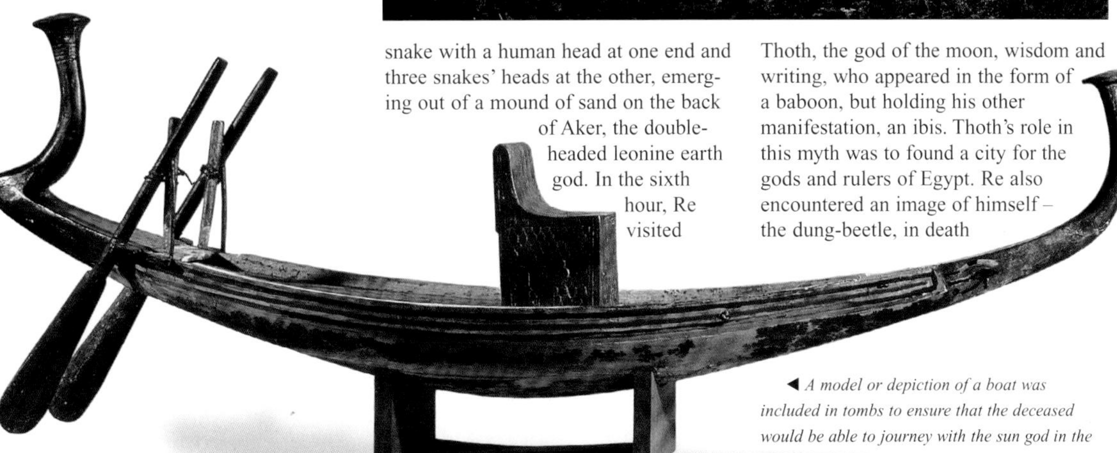

◄ *A model or depiction of a boat was included in tombs to ensure that the deceased would be able to journey with the sun god in the Afterlife. 18th Dynasty.*

the body of Khepri enveloped in the body of a five-headed snake.

In the seventh hour, Re sailed past enemies of Osiris (who his protectors were busily decapitating and lassoing with a rope) before coming face to face with his most terrible of enemies, the serpent demon Apophis, whose main aim was to swallow the sun. Re's magical protection allowed him to come into close contact with Apophis only if the demon was disabled in some way. Apophis had knives sticking into him, and in case this was not adequate disablement, the scorpion-goddess Selket held his head, and the 'Director of Knives' held his tail.

In the eighth hour, Re had to face further enemies, but luckily he had an entourage of human-headed staffs, each of which had a knife with which to destroy Re's demons. A variety of deities, including gods with the heads of rats and mongooses, called out to Re as he passed their caverns. In the ninth hour, Re met the 12 alarming guardians of Osiris, fire-breathing cobras who lived on the blood of their captives. Decidedly less intimidating were the deities Re sailed past, who were responsible for carving trees and plants, and who held nothing more threatening than palm branches.

▼ *This bejewelled winged scarab beetle rolling the sun with its forelegs, and resting its hindlegs on a basket, is the hieroglyphic representation of Tutankhamun's throne name Neb-Kheperu-Re, 'Lord of the manifestations of Re'. 18th Dynasty.*

▲ *In this wall-painting in the Theban tomb of Inherkha, a knife-wielding cat slays the serpent-demon Apophis near the* ished*-tree. 19th Dynasty.*

The end in sight

In the tenth hour, Re was beginning to prepare for dawn; he ordered his armed escort of 12 gods to seek out the last of his enemies, as he revealed himself as a scarab beetle, the manifestation of the sun god at dawn. In the eleventh hour, the hawk-god Horus presided over the final slaughter of the enemies of the sun god, which took place in pits of fire and was distinctly gory.

Re had survived the perils of the Netherworld, and the final hour before dawn had arrived. In the twelfth hour, the solar boat was towed into the body of an enormous snake, and the sun god emerged from its mouth as the scarab-beetle deity Khepri. Shu, the god of air, sealed the exit to the Netherworld behind him, and the sun god proceeded on his way in his daytime vessel.

The Journey of the Sun Through the Netherworld in Context

This particular myth of the nightly journey of the sun god is found in the 'Book of Am-Duat', or 'Book of What is in the Netherworld'. It is recorded in its most complete form in the Eighteenth-Dynasty tombs of the kings Tuthmosis III (c.1479–c.1425 BC) and Amenhotep II (c.1427–c.1400 BC), both of which are in the Valley of the Kings, the burial ground of the rulers of the New Kingdom (c.1550–c.1069 BC) on the west bank of the Nile at Thebes. In each instance the text is accompanied by a series of weird and wonderful painted images.

Similar, detailed descriptions of the journey of the sun god through the Netherworld are to be found in compositions entitled the 'Book of Gates' and the 'Book of Caverns'. The former can be found in its fullest version on the walls of the tomb of the Twentieth-Dynasty king, Ramesses VI (c.1143–c.1136 BC) in the Valley of the Kings, and inscribed on the sarcophagus of the Nineteenth-Dynasty ruler Seti I (c.1294–c.1279 BC), which was originally in his tomb in the Valley of the Kings but is now in the Sir John Soane Museum in London. The 'Book of Caverns' is the rarest and latest of the three funerary compositions, and it also occurs in its complete form in the tomb of Ramesses VI.

▲ *The Valley of the Kings actually consists of two separate valleys: the eastern valley is the main royal cemetery of the New Kingdom, while the western one contains only four tombs.*

Darkness and death

The story identifies the journey of the sun during the hours of darkness with the passage of the dead (especially the king) into the Afterlife. Sunset is equated with death, and sunrise with rebirth. By recording the successful journey of the sun god in the tomb of the king, it was believed that the king would in turn be reborn without mishap. His enemies were regarded as the same as those of the sun god, and so it was important that they – especially Apophis – should be symbolically destroyed.

The myth also serves to explain the hours of darkness, so it is an alternative to the idea of the sun being swallowed by the sky goddess Nut in the evening, passing through her body during the night, and being given birth to by her in the morning. Other myths include the idea that the earth god Geb grew angry with his consort Nut for swallowing her 'children'. In the temple at Abydos, Nut is compared to a sow which eats its piglets.

The ancient Egyptians believed the Sun god to assume different manifestations at different times in the day. The most commonly occurring solar deity was Re, who tended to be associated with the midday sun. Atum was associated with the setting sun, and the scarab-beetle deity Khepri was the form taken by the rising sun. The fact that the sun god is imagined travelling in a boat should not surprise us because the chief means of transport both for people and goods would certainly have been by river. ◆

The Days Upon the Year

The myth is set at the time of creation, when the cosmological deities were coming into being. The sky goddess Nut was pregnant (following an illicit sexual encounter with the earth god Geb), but the supreme solar deity Re felt threatened by the prospect of the arrival of more gods and goddesses on the scene. He had convinced himself that his supremacy would be at risk if he did not take precautions, so he cursed Nut, preventing her from giving birth on any day of the year (which at this time still totalled 360 days).

As a result, Osiris, Isis, Seth and Nephthys would never have been born if Re had had his way. Luckily for them and humankind, the lunar deity Thoth decided to intervene. By beating the Moon in a board game, he managed to win enough light to create an additional five days each year (referred to by the ancient Egyptians as 'days upon the year' and as 'epagomenal days' by the Greeks). On each of these days, Nut was able to produce one of her offspring. To explain the existence of the fifth day, in this particular myth Nut is also said to be the mother of 'Horus the Elder' (Har-wer; Haroeris in Greek).

▲ *A scene from the Satirical Papyrus, showing a lion and an antelope playing* senet, *the best-known board game from ancient Egypt. Late New Kingdom.*

▼ *This cosmological vignette of Shu separating Nut from Geb comes from the Book of the Dead belonging to Nesitanebeteshru, a 21st Dynasty priestess.*

The civil year

Even after the addition of the days upon the year, the Egyptian calendar did not coincide precisely with the solar year, which is 365 1/4 days long. The civil year gradually fell behind the solar year, moving backwards by one month every 120 years and only coming into alignment again after 1,460 years. As the civil calendar fell out of step with the seasons, festivals associated with the natural cycle (such as harvest) continued to be held in their correct season.

The Days Upon the Year in Context

This myth has survived in the work of the Greek writer Plutarch (c. AD 46–c.126), in a volume called *Peri Isidos kai Osiridos*. It was obviously originally devised as a means of explaining the five days which were added to the calendar in order to match it more closely to the solar year. The ancient Egyptians were in fact the earliest people to adjust their calendar to a length of 365 days.

Watching the stars

The New Year (*Wep Renpet*, literally 'the Opening of the Year') was celebrated when the dog star Sirius, the brightest star in the sky, was sighted on its heliacal rising. The Egyptians noticed that there was a 70-day period when the dog star could not be seen. During this time the earth, the sun and the dog star are so nearly in line that the light of the star is swallowed up in the sun's brightness and becomes invisible. At the end of this period is a night when, just before dawn, the dog star is momentarily visible just above the eastern horizon, an astronomical event known as its heliacal rising. It so happened that this usually took place at the time when the period of low water was coming to end, and it appeared to herald the inundation.

The Egyptians divinely personified Sirius as a goddess, Sopdet, depicted as a woman with a star on her head. They also created a god of the main southern constellation Orion, named Sah. Stars in general were often depicted as gods sailing on crescent-shaped barques through the body of the goddess Nut.

The calender

Initially, the Egyptian calendar was based on the agricultural cycle, which in turn revolved around the flooding of the Nile. The year was divided into three seasons, each of four months (each month averaged thirty days and was named after an important religious festival that took place during that period). The first season was that of the flood (*Akhet*), the second of planting and growth (*Peret*), and the last of the harvest and low water (*Shomu*). All three seasons were divinely personified as male deities.

▲ *The three seasons were divinely personified. Mereruka, the vizier of the 6th-Dynasty king Teti, is shown at the entrance to his mastaba seated before the seasons. Each is accompanied by four crescent moons symbolizing the four lunar months of each season. Old Kingdom.*

The days of the demons

In the Calendars of Lucky and Unlucky Days, days were categorized according to the mythical events said to have taken place on them, and they would have been consulted in order to decide whether an activity should or should not be carried out on a particular day. The calendars made it clear that nothing of any consequence should be done on any of the 'days upon the year'. These extra days were added to the end of the calendar and did not form part of any month: all the months continued to be thirty days long. Of the five days upon the year, the one on which Seth was supposed to have been born was considered to be particularly dangerous, but all were collectively known as 'the days of the demons'. ◆

Trees in Egyptian Mythology

The shade of trees afforded the ancient Egyptian people welcome respite from the searing heat of the sun, so it is hardly surprising that sites associated with cults were often situated in groves. Soon the groves themselves came to be regarded as sacred and, according to various local traditions, gods were believed to shelter under, or even live in, particular trees. Trees were also important in the cemetery regions on the edge of the desert. But trees were relatively rare in ancient Egypt and this fact presumably heightened the respect in which they were held. There were no trees native to Egypt that could yield timber suitable for building work, so cedar had to be imported from the Lebanon for such uses as constructing ships and making roof beams.

There are two ways of finding out which trees were considered sacred in each of the nomes (or districts) of ancient Egypt. First, the emblems adopted by the nomes often include trees, and second, there are lists inscribed on the walls of Ptolemaic temples that describe the trees in each of the sacred groves around the country. The most common appear to have been the sycamore, persea (a sacred fruit-bearing tree), date palm and acacia.

Tallying the days

The hieroglyphic sign for 'year' (*renpet*) was a branch from a date palm with all the leaves stripped off (the notches left by the leaves were thought to indicate the passing of time). The presentation of a symbolic palm branch to the king was an important part of his jubilee festival, (see *Royal Jubilee Festivals*). Heh, the god of eternity, was depicted wearing a notched palm branch on his head or holding one in each hand.

▲ *Nespawershefi, the 21st-Dynasty Chief of all the Scribes at Karnak Temple, is depicted making offerings before Nut, the sycamore tree goddess, on the side of his coffin. His* ba *is shown drinking the liquid poured by the goddess.*

Tree deities

Presumably because of the shade and the fruit provided by them, goddesses associated with protection, mothering and nurturing were closely associated with them. Hathor, Nut and Isis appear frequently in the religious imagery and literature. Any of these goddesses might be represented as a woman with a tree on her head, as a tree with the upper half of a woman growing out of it, or as a semi-personified tree with arms. In the tomb of the Eighteenth-Dynasty king Tuthmosis III (c.1479–c.1425 BC), a goddess (probably Isis) is depicted as a sycamore tree with a breast.

Hathor was sometimes referred to as 'Mistress of the Date Palm' (this refers to the male palm, *imaw*), and in the Book of the Dead the goddess was occasionally depicted in front of this kind of tree. She could also be called 'The Lady of the Sycamore' (the *nehet*, which also means 'refuge'), or more specifically, 'The Lady of the Southern Sycamore' – an actual tree that grew at the temple of Ptah in Memphis during the Old Kingdom (c.2686–c.2181 BC).

According to the Book of the Dead, two 'sycamores of turquoise' grew on the eastern horizon at the place where the sun rises each morning, so the sycamore also had a male aspect as a manifestation of the solar deity Re-Horakhty. According to the Pyramid Texts, gods were thought to live in the branches of the sycamores on the eastern horizon.

In a funerary context, the goddesses Hathor and Nut occurred as sycamore tree goddesses, offering shade, food and water to the souls of the dead who, in the form of human-headed birds (*bas*), enjoyed the sustenance. The *bas* of the dead might be visualized sitting on the branches of a tree, rather as the gods were imagined on the eastern horizon. Sycamores were often planted near tombs, and models of leaves of this tree were used as funerary amulets.

▲ *This semi-personified tree with a breast, suckling Tuthmosis III, is probably intended to be identified as the mother goddess Isis. Valley of the Kings.*

The sacred ished

A tree that grew in the sacred groves of 17 of the nomes was the *ished*, a fruit-bearing, deciduous tree that was probably the same as the persea. Like the sycamore, it was associated with the rising sun and the horizon. And like the sun god, it was protected from the serpent demon Apophis by the 'great cat of Heliopolis'. According to the Book of the Dead, the cat that was said to sit in the shade of the *ished* tree was in fact Re himself. An inscription on the Heliopolitan obelisk known as Cleopatra's Needle in London records that a sacred *ished* grew at Heliopolis from the Old Kingdom through to the Graeco-Roman Period. (There were also *ished* trees at Herakleopolis, Memphis and Edfu.)

From the Eighteenth Dynasty (c.1550 BC), reliefs show Amun-Re, Thoth, the god of scribes, and Seshat, the goddess of writing, inscribing the leaves of the *ished* with the names and titles of the king and the number of years in his reign, so this kind of tree was associated with royal annals. The Egyptian word for 'records' or 'annals' was *genut*, from *genu*, meaning 'branch'.

Trees and rituals

The willow (*tcheret*), often identified as tamarisk, was sacred to Osiris. It was believed to have sheltered his dead body, while his *ba*, in the form of a bird, was said to sit in it. Those towns (including Memphis, Heliopolis and Herakleopolis) where part of Osiris was said to have been buried by Isis (see *The Death of Osiris*) had willow groves, and an annual festival called 'Raising the Willow' was celebrated to ensure the fertility of the land. Representations of the tomb of Osiris sometimes showed a tomb-chamber covered by a mound with trees growing on top of it or beside it.

Inscriptions at Philae record that milk was poured at the foot of trees at what was believed to be the sacred tomb of Osiris. These libations were thought to revive the god so that he might be reborn into the Afterlife. The reliefs show Osiris standing in a tree growing out of a small pool. An inscription at Philae describes Osiris's *ba* as living in the branches of a cedar tree while, according to Plutarch, a tamarisk shaded Osiris's tomb.

Deities were also associated with several other types of trees. The jackal-god Wepwawet was said in the Pyramid Texts to have 'emerged from a tamarisk bush', while Horus was believed to have come forth from an acacia (*shened*). In another myth, Horus was said to have taken refuge under an acacia tree as a child. A sacred acacia appears to have grown at Heliopolis. The crocodile god Sobek was associated with the *kesbet* tree and the moringa tree. Cypresses were deemed sacred to Min, and he was often worshipped under them.

Sacred trees are still important in Egypt. They are usually connected with the tombs of famous sheikhs, whose spirits are thought to dwell in them. They are believed to be able to cure problems such as infertility, and gratitude may be expressed by hanging votive gifts on their trunks. ◆

▼ *Another semi-personified tree offers food and drink to Sekeh, the deceased mayor of Memphis, and his* ba, *or soul.*

Plants and Flowers in Mythology

The papyrus plant (*Cyperus papyrus*) played a key role in the rise of the ancient Egyptian civilization because of the high-quality writing material that could be produced from it. The papyrus reed is a member of the sedge family and needs to grow in soft, easily penetrable soil, with its roots completely submerged in water. For this reason, the Faiyum and Delta districts were ideal habitats, and papyrus thickets were abundant in ancient times. As well as the fine sheets manufactured using strips of its juicy, starchy pith, the outer fibres of the papyrus plant were turned into boats, sandals, basketry, matting, boxes, ropes, jar stoppers and even building materials.

It is not surprising that the papyrus plant was highly prized. It was so closely associated with the northern region, that it came to be regarded as a heraldic emblem of Lower Egypt. In the iconography of the 'Unification of the Two Lands', a Nile deity or the god Horus might be depicted holding (or even wearing) this plant (see *The Concept of Duality*). Because it symbolized Lower Egypt and was believed to have grown on the primordial mound of creation, and in the belief that papyrus 'pillars' held up the sky, temple complexes usually included limestone or sandstone columns carved to represent single or composite papyrus stems, with capitals in the form of open umbels or closed buds.

For the ancient Egyptians, the papyrus plant also symbolized freshness, flourishing, youth and joy. To ensure the presence of these attributes in their lives, they would wear or carry a tiny amulet in the shape of a single stem and umbel of papyrus. It was stipulated that this should be made of green or blue-green faience, and it was referred to as *wadj* (literally 'green'). Goddesses such as Hathor, Bastet and Neith were often depicted holding a papyriform sceptre.

▲ *These two red granite pillars form part of the barque sanctuary of Tuthmosis III at Karnak. The pillar in the foreground depicts the lotus/lily and the other the papyrus plant.*

Lotus or lily?

The symbol of the South (Upper Egypt) is generally referred to as the lotus, but was actually the water lily (sometimes called the 'southern plant'). There were two species of lotus or water lily that grew in ancient Egypt, the white *Nymphaea lotus*, and the blue *Nymphaea caerulea*. It was the latter species that was most commonly depicted and was usually described as the sacred lotus. It too occurs in the imagery of the 'Unification of the Two Lands', held (or worn) by a Nile deity or by Seth. Because of its significance, the sacred lotus was also an important element in the design of temple columns.

Flowers of life and death

During the New Kingdom the flowers of the *ished* tree were considered life-giving and were called 'flowers of life'. Together with the lotus blossom they were used at funerals for decorating the coffins and statues of the deceased.

▶ *This wooden sculpture of Tutankhamun's head emerging from a lotus blossom has been plastered and then painted. The image likens the boy king to the sun god rising out of a lotus, in accordance with the mythology of creation.*

The ancient Egyptians observed that the lily flower closed for the night and sank under the water, rising and reopening as the sun rose, and for this reason it was associated with the night-time journey of the sun god Re and his 'rebirth' at dawn. In time it came to be associated with creation and rebirth in general. One version of the creation myth of Hermopolis Magna tells us that the sun rose for the first time out of a primordial lotus bobbing on the waters of chaos (see *Creation Myths*).

Throughout Egyptian history images were created of figures rising out of lotus blossoms, such as the wonderful painted wooden head of Tutankhamun found in his tomb and now in the Cairo Museum. The lotus became so important in ancient Egyptian religion that it was divinely personified in the form of the god Nefertem, 'Lord of Perfumes', who was portrayed anthropomorphically with a lotus growing out of his head (sometimes with two tall plumes extending upwards out of the flower). In the Pyramid Texts of the Old Kingdom Nefertem is described as 'the lotus at the nose of Re', and gods and goddesses are often depicted sniffing lotus blossoms.

Gods and flowers

Deities as well as people were thought to love the pleasurable stimulation of their senses, and flowers were considered to be important offerings to the gods.

We know that the sense of smell was highly regarded by the ancient Egyptians – the nose was the hieroglyphic sign used as a determinative in the writing of the verbs 'to enjoy' and 'to take pleasure in'. Flowers are ubiquitous in the scenes of festivity on the walls of Theban private tombs of the New Kingdom (c.1550–c.1069 BC). They are shown as festoons and garlands worn by the merry-makers, but are also depicted being held to the nose for the pleasure of their scent. It is likely that when added to alcohol they would have released psychoactive properties.

Certain plants were particularly associated with certain deities. The lettuce (*Lactuca sativa longifolia*) was, for example, an emblem of the cult of the fertility god Min at Koptos. This association may have arisen from the resemblance of the milky juice of the lettuce to semen (see *The Contendings of Horus and Seth*). ◆

◀ *The heavy black wigs and fine white linen dresses of these women, together with an abundance of flowers, are typical of the banqueting scenes on the walls of non-royal Theban tombs of the New Kingdom.*

The Concept of Duality

The crux of the ancient Egyptian system of beliefs was the relationship between order (*maat*) and chaos (*isfet*). Although a state of order was considered to be the ideal, it was acknowledged that an opposing yet interdependent state of chaos must exist in order for equilibrium to be achieved. For the ancient Egyptians, a state of order (or harmony or balance) was of such vital significance in their lives that they divinely personified the abstract concept of order in the form of the goddess Maat. She was represented as a woman wearing an ostrich feather, which represented truth, on her head.

A sense of unity was created by the existence of a duality, which was expressed clearly in religious iconography. The god Horus was associated with all that was right and ordered, whereas the god Seth was linked with chaos, as well as with infertility and aridity (see *The Contendings of Horus and Seth*). The presence of both of these deities indicated an idea of completeness. In the Cairo Museum there is an impressive triad statue which was found at Medinet Habu, the mortuary temple of the Twentieth-Dynasty king Ramesses III (c.1184–c.1153 BC). The king is shown flanked by Horus on one side and Seth on the other – the two gods together constituting a wholeness.

The ancient Egyptians believed that the fertile part of Egypt (the Nile Valley and the Delta) in which they lived was a place of order with a reliable pattern to it – particularly the agricultural cycle hingeing on the annual flooding of the Nile. Maat was present in this, the 'Black Land' (*Kemet*). On the other hand, the desert or 'Red Land' (*Deshret*) was considered to be a place of chaos. A precarious, yet highly important, relationship existed between the two.

▶ *Maat, the goddess of order, wearing an ostrich feather on her head, is characteristically shown seated on a plinth. The symbol of the plinth is included in the hieroglyphic writing of her name and represents the primeval mound of creation.*

Unification

The conventions of Egyptian art were perfect for illustrating the concept of duality, because symmetry was frequently used to create a balanced design. This is best exemplified by the artistic representation of the fundamentally important idea of the 'Unification of the Two Lands' (*sema tawy*). The ancient Egyptians viewed their country as consisting of two distinct parts: Upper Egypt (*Shemau*) and Lower Egypt (*Ta-Mehu*). These correspond to the South (the Nile Valley from the first cataract north to just south of Memphis) and the North (the Delta), respectively. The people believed that the origins of the state of Egypt could be traced to an act of unification of these two regions by a ruler named Menes (for whom there is no actual archaeological evidence) at the beginning of the early Dynastic Period (c.3100 BC).

The hieroglyphic sign used to express the notion of this unification was a stylized rendering of a pair of lungs, with a windpipe extending straight upwards out of the middle of them. In art this emblem might be flanked by two deities, sometimes Horus and Seth, on other occasions two Nile gods, one with papyrus on his head and the other with the lotus (or water lily) plant (see *Plants and Flowers in Mythology*). The figures on each side are often depicted tying the papyrus and lotus stems in a knot around the hieroglyph. This is further symbolic of the unity of Egypt because the papyrus plant was a heraldic emblem of the Delta, and the lotus was a heraldic emblem of the Nile Valley.

The two crowns

The Red Crown of Lower Egypt had a tall, thin back and a narrow coil that protruded at the front. It was the customary headdress of the northern goddess Neith, and its earliest known appearance is on a Predynastic pot from Naqada.

The White Crown of Upper Egypt was shaped like a tall cone with a bulbous tip. It was sometimes adorned with two plumes in a form called the *atef*-crown, which was associated with the god Osiris. It was placed inside the Red Crown to form the Double Crown.

▶ *Snofru sits beneath his cartouche wearing the Double Crown of Upper and Lower Egypt. One of his chief titles, 'He of the Sedge and the Bee', is easily identifiable, and beneath this is his 'Two Ladies' epithet.*

Lord of the two lands

This particular aspect of the notion of duality manifested itself very clearly in the royal titles. The king's chief titles were 'Lord of the Two Lands' (*Neb Tawy*) and 'King of Upper and Lower Egypt' (*Nesw Bity*), which translates literally as 'He of the Sedge and the Bee'. The sedge plant was an emblem of the Nile Valley, and the bee was an emblem of the Delta. Another of his titles was 'He of the Two Ladies' (*Nebty*), which referred to the two goddesses who were thought to protect him: the vulture goddess, Nekhbet, who had her main cult centre at el-Kab in the South, and the cobra goddess, Wadjet, whose principal cult centre was at Buto in the North.

The regalia of kingship also reflected the idea of duality. The king might be depicted wearing the White Crown (*Hedjet*) associated with Upper Egypt, the Red Crown (*Deshret*) of Lower Egypt, or sometimes the Double Crown (*Pschent* or *Sekhemty*), which incorporated the crowns of both regions.

So north and south were distinct but both were necessary to create a whole. Similarly east and west were opposing and yet interdependent. The places of the rising and setting sun resulted in the east being associated with the living, and the west being associated with the dead. But as the sun rose again each morning, so the dead were believed to be reborn into the Afterlife. ◆

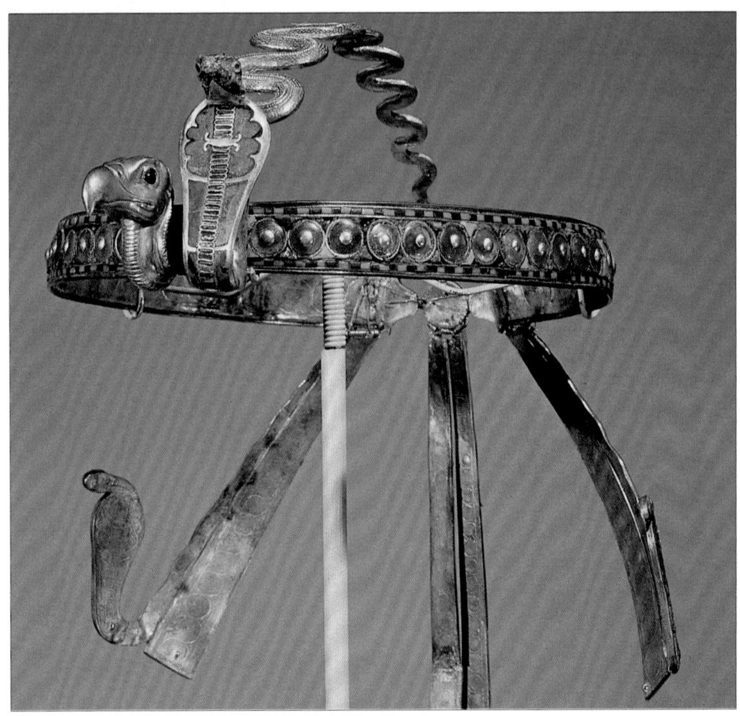

▶ *This diadem was found under the bandaging on Tutankhamun's mummy. For safekeeping, the cobra had been detached and placed on Tutankhamun's left thigh, and the vulture on his right thigh.*

Kingship and the Gods

Did the ancient Egyptian people believe that their king was a god? The extent to which they did seems to have varied according to the period of Egyptian history, and also to have depended on context. The king could be regarded as a god, or as somewhere between the divine and mortal world, or as a mere human being. It is safe to say, however, that the concept of kingship – the office, rather than the man himself – was considered divine. It was felt that the king could relate to the gods in a way that none of his subjects would have been able to, which must have enhanced the nature of kingship and inspired respect, if not awe, in the people.

Many sources reveal that the king was identified with a god, both in life and after death. Myths, inscriptions and royal titles all stress the reigning king's identification with the falcon-god Horus. After death, the king was identified with Osiris. The divinity of a dead king was less ambiguous than that of a living one, and is well attested throughout Egyptian history. By the New Kingdom (c.1550–c.1069 BC), the royal mortuary temples were on a par (in terms of size, wealth and administration) with the cult temples of the deities.

◀ *On the wall of a corridor in the temple of Seti I at Abydos, this king and his son, Ramesses II, stand before a list of cartouches representing their royal predecessors.*

Kings of Egypt

All dates are BC unless stated otherwise

Early Dynastic Period c.3100–c.2686

FIRST DYNASTY	c.3100–c.2890
Narmer	c.3100
Aha	c.3100
Djer	c.3000
Djet	c.2980
Den	c.2950
[Queen Merneith	c.2950]
Anedjib	c.2925
Semerkhet	c.2900
Qa'a	c.2890
SECOND DYNASTY	c.2890–c.2686
Hetepsekhemwy	c.2890
Raneb	c.2865
Nynetjer	
Weneg	
Sened	
Peribsen	c.2700
Khasekhemwy	c.2686

Old Kingdom c.2686–c.2181

THIRD DYNASTY	c.2686–c.2613
Sanakht (= Nebka?)	c.2686–c.2667
Djoser (Netjerikhet)	c.2667–c.2648
Sekhemkhet	c.2648–c.2640
Khaba	c.2640–c.2637
Huni	c.2637–c.2613
FOURTH DYNASTY	c.2613–c.2494
Sneferu	c.2613–c.2589
Khufu (Cheops)	c.2589–c.2566
Djedefre (Radjedef)	c.2566–c.2558
Khafre (Chephren)	c.2558–c.2532
Menkaure (Mycerinus)	c.2532–c.2503
Shepseskaf	c.2503–c.2494
FIFTH DYNASTY	c.2494–c.2345
Userkaf	c.2494–c.2487
Sahure	c.2487–c.2475
Neferirkare	c.2475–c.2455
Shepseskare	c.2455–c.2448
Raneferef	c.2448–c.2445
Niuserre	c.2445–c.2421
Menkauhor	c.2421–c.2414
Djedkare	c.2414–c.2375
Unas (Wenis)	c.2375–c.2345
SIXTH DYNASTY	c.2345–c.2181
Teti	c.2345–c.2323
Userkare	c.2323–c.2321
Pepi I (Meryre)	c.2321–c.2287
Merenre	c.2287–c.2278
Pepi II (Neferkare)	c.2278–c.2184
Nitiqret	c.2184–c.2181

First Intermediate Period c.2181–c.2055

SEVENTH AND EIGHTH DYNASTIES	c.2181–c.2125
Numerous short reigns	
NINTH AND TENTH DYNASTIES (HERAKLEOPOLITAN)	c.2160–c.2025
Khety (Meryibre)	
Khety (Wahkare)	
Merykare	
Ity	
ELEVENTH DYNASTY (THEBES)	c.2125–c.2055
[Mentuhotep I ('Tepy-aa')]	
Intef I (Sehertawy)	c.2125–c.2112
Intef II (Wahankh)	c.2112–c.2063
Intef III (Nakhtnebtepnefer)	c.2063–c.2055

Middle Kingdom c.2055–c.1650

ELEVENTH DYNASTY (ALL EGYPT)	c.2055–c.1985
Mentuhotep II (Nebhepetre)	c.2055–c.2004
Mentuhotep III (Sankhkare)	c.2004–c.1992
Mentuhotep IV (Nebtawyre)	c.1992–c.1985
TWELFTH DYNASTY	c.1985–c.1795
Amenemhat I (Sehetepibre)	c.1985–c.1955
Senusret I (Kheperkare)	c.1965–c.1920
Amenemhat II (Nubkaure)	c.1922–c.1878
Senusret II (Khakheperre)	c.1880–c.1874
Senusret III (Khakaure)	c.1874–c.1855
Amenemhat III (Nimaatre)	c.1855–c.1808
Amenemhat IV (Maakherure)	c.1808–c.1799
Queen Sobekneferu (Sobekkare)	c.1799–c.1795
THIRTEENTH DYNASTY	1795–after 1650
About 70 rulers, of whom the most frequently mentioned are listed below	
Hor (Awibre)	
Khendjer (Userkare)	
Sobekhotep III (Sekhemrasewadjtawy)	
Neferhotep I (Khasekhemre)	
Sobekhotep IV (Khaneferre)	c.1725
FOURTEENTH DYNASTY	c.1750–c.1650
Series of minor rulers, probably contemporary with the kings of the Thirteenth Dynasty	

Second Intermediate Period c.1650–c.1550

FIFTEENTH DYNASTY (HYKSOS)	c.1650–c.1550
Salitis	
Khyan (Seuserenre)	c.1600
Apepi (Aauserre)	c.1555
Khamudi	
SIXTEENTH DYNASTY	c.1650–c.1550
Minor Hyksos rulers, contemporary with the kings of the Fifteenth Dynasty	
SEVENTEENTH DYNASTY	c.1650–c.1550
Several rulers based in Thebes, of whom the most prominent are listed below	
Intef (Nubkheperre)	
Taa I (Senakhtenre)	
Taa II (Seqenenre)	c.1560
Kamose (Wadjkheperre)	c.1555–c.1550

New Kingdom c.1550–c.1069

EIGHTEENTH DYNASTY	c.1550–c.1295
Ahmose (Nebpehtyre)	c.1550–c.1525
Amenhotep I (Djeserkare)	c.1525–c.1504
Tuthmosis I (Aakheperkare)	c.1504–c.1492
Tuthmosis II (Aakheperenre)	c.1492–c.1479
Tuthmosis III (Menkhpererre)	c.1479–c.1425
Hatshepsut (Maatkare)	c.1473–c.1458
Amenhotep II (Aakheperure)	c.1427–c.1400

Tuthmosis IV (Menkheperure)	c.1400–c.1390
Amenhotep III (Nebmaatre)	c.1390–c.1352
Amenhotep IV/Akhenaten (Neferkheperurawaenre)	c.1352–c.1336
Nefernefruaten (Smenkhkare)	c.1338–c.1336
Tutankhamun (Nebkheperure)	c.1336–c.1327
Ay (Kheperkheperure)	c.1327–c.1323
Horemheb (Djeserkheperure)	c.1323–c.1295
NINETEENTH DYNASTY	c.1295–c.1186
Ramesses I (Menpehtyre)	c.1295–c.1294
Seti I (Menmaatre)	c.1294–c.1279
Ramesses II (Usermaatra Setepenre)	c.1279–c.1213
Merenptah (Baenre)	c.1213–c.1203
Amenmessu (Menmire)	c.1203–c.1200
Seti II (Userkheperur Setepenre)	c.1200–c.1194
Saptah (Akhenra Setepenre)	c.1194–c.1188
Tausret (Sitrameritamun)	c.1188–c.1186
TWENTIETH DYNASTY	c.1186–c.1069
Sethnakhte (Userkhaure Meryamun)	c.1186–c.1184
Ramesses III (Usermaatre Meryamun)	c.1184–c.1153
Ramesses IV (Hekamaatre Setepenamun)	c.1153–c.1147
Ramesses V (Usermaatre Sekheperenre)	c.1147–c.1143
Ramesses VI (Nebmaatre Meryamun)	c.1143–c.1136
Ramesses VII (Usermaatre Setepenre Meryamun)	c.1136–c.1129
Ramesses VIII (Usermaatre Akhenamun)	c.1129–c.1126
Ramesses IX (Neferkare Setepenre)	c.1126–c.1108
Ramesses X (Khepermaatre Setepenre)	c.1108–c.1099
Ramesses XI (Menmaatre Setepenptah)	c.1099–c.1069

Third Intermediate Period c.1069–c.747

TWENTY-FIRST DYNASTY (TANITE)	c.1069–c.945
Smendes (Hedjkheperre Setepenre)	c.1069–c.1043
Amenemnisu (Neferkare)	c.1043–c.1039
Psusennes I [Pasebakhaenniut] (Aakheperre Setepenamun)	c.1039–c.991
Amenemope (Usermaatre Setepenamun)	c.993–c.984
Osorkon the Elder (Aakheperre Setepenre)	c.984–c.978
Siamun (Netjrkheperre Setepenamun)	c.978–c.959
Psusennes II [Pasebakhaennuit] (Titkheperure Setepenre)	c.959–c.945
TWENTY-SECOND DYNASTY (BUBASTITE/LIBYAN)	c.945–c.715
Sheshonq I (Hedjkheperre Setepenre)	c.945–c.924
Osorkon I (Sekhemkheperre)	c.924–c.889
Sheshonq II (Hekakheperre Setepenre)	c.890
Takelot I	c.889–c.874
Osorkon II (Usermaatre Setepnamun)	c.874–c.850
Takelot II (Hedjkheperre Setepenre amun)	c.850–c.825
Sheshonq II (Usermaatre)	c.825–c.773
Pimay (Usermaatre)	c.773–c.767
Sheshonq V (Aakheperre)	c.767–c.730
Osorkon IV (Aakheperre Setepenamun)	c.730–c.715
TWENTY-THIRD DYNASTY (TANITE/LIBYAN)	c.818–c.715

Several contemporary lines of rulers at Herakleopolis Magna, Hermopolis Magna, Leontopolis and Tanis, three of whom are listed below

Pedubastis I (Usermaatre)	c.818–c.793
Sheshonq IV	c.780
Osorkon III (Usermaatre Setepenamun)	c.777–c.749
TWENTY-FOURTH DYNASTY	c.727–c.715
Bakenrenef (Bocchoris)	c.727–c.715

Late Period c.747–332

TWENTY-FIFTH DYNASTY (KUSHITE)	c.747–c.656
Piy (Piankhy)	c.747–c.716
Shabaqo (Neferkare)	c.716–c.702
Shabitqo (Djedkaure)	c.702–690
Taharqo (Khunefertemre)	690–664
Tanutamani (Bakare)	664–656
TWENTY-SIXTH DYNASTY (SAITE)	664–525
[Nekau I	672–664]
Psamtek I (Wahinre)	664–610
Nekau II (Wehemibre)	610–595
Psamtek II (Neferibre)	595–589
Apries (Haaibre)	589–570
Ahmose II (Khnemibre)	570–526
Psamtek III (Ankhkaenre)	526–525
TWENTY-SEVENTH DYNASTY (FIRST PERSIAN PERIOD)	525–404
Cambyses	525–522
Darius I	522–486
Xerxes I	486–465
Artaxerxes I	465–424
Darius II	424–405
Artaxerxes II	405–359
TWENTY-EIGHTH DYNASTY	404–399
Amyrtaios	404–399
TWENTY-NINTH DYNASTY	399–380
Nepherites I	399–393
Hakor (Khnemmaatre)	393–380
Nepherites II	c.380
THIRTIETH DYNASTY	380–343
Nectanebo I (Kheperkare)	380–362
Teos (Irmaatenre)	362–360
Nectanebo II (Senedjemibre Setepenanhur)	360–343
SECOND PERSIAN PERIOD	343–332
Artaxerxes III Ochus	343–338
Arses	338–336
Darius III Codoman	336–332

Ptolemaic Period 332–30

MACEDONIAN DYNASTY	332–305
Alexander the Great	332–323
Philip Arrhidaeus	323–317
Alexander IV	317–310
PTOLEMAIC DYNASTY	
Ptolemy I Soter I	305–285
Ptolemy II Philadelphus	285–246
Ptolemy III Euergetes I	246–221
Ptolemy IV Philopator	221–205
Ptolemy V Epiphanes	205–180
Ptolemy VI Philometor	180–145
Ptolemy VII Neos Philopator	145
Ptolemy VIII Euergetes II	170–116
Ptolemy IX Soter II	116–107
Ptolemy X Alexander I	107–88
Ptolemy IX Soter II (restored)	88–80
Ptolemy XI Alexander II	80
Ptolemy XII Neos Dionysus (Auletes)	80–51
Cleopatra VII Philopater	51–30
Ptolemy XIII	51–47
Ptolemy XIV	47–44
Ptolemy XV Caesarion	44–30

After the chronology in the British Museum Dictionary of Ancient Egypt *by Ian Shaw and Paul Nicholson*

Was the King Really Divine?

The belief in the divine nature of the position of pharaoh was central to the ideology of kingship in ancient Egypt. The term 'pharaoh' (*per-aa*) actually means 'great house' and it was not used to describe the ruler himself until the New Kingdom period (c.1550–c.1069 BC); before that time it was used to refer to the king's palace or the royal court.

The divinity of kingship was an important part of the Egyptian system of beliefs and social structure from the very beginning of the pharaonic period (c.3100 BC). Some very early inscriptions have been found that describe the king as *netjer* ('god') or, more usually, *nefer netjer* ('good god'), which may in fact indicate a lesser or minor god. Several inscriptions are also known in which the king is referred to as *aa netjer* ('great god').

▼ *Wings were a symbol of protection: Horus protected the king and the earth with his wings, as did the vulture mother and funerary goddesses.*

More is known about the ruler's identification with the god Horus: for example, that the falcon was a symbol of kingship from the Protodynastic Period. On the Narmer Palette, a falcon holds a rope in its talons which is attached to a ring through the nose of a semi-personified papyrus marsh. The falcon presumably symbolizes Narmer, whose victories are commemorated on this schist ceremonial palette, which was found in the 'Main Deposit' at Hierakonpolis and is now in the Cairo Museum.

Royal titles

From the Old Kingdom (c.2686–c.2181 BC), each king had five names, which were each introduced by an important title. Only one name was given to him at birth; the other four were bestowed when he was crowned king. They encapsulated the ideology of kingship. Two of the names were introduced by titles that stressed the rule of the king over two lands that had been united: 'He of the Sedge and the Bee' (*Nesw Bity*) and 'He of the Two Ladies' (*Nebty*) (see *The Concept of Duality*). The other two names – 'Horus' (*Hor*) and 'Golden Horus' (*Hor Nebw*) – could not have more clearly emphasized his identification with the god.

The office of kingship was decidedly male, and during the 3,000 or so years of pharaonic history female pharaohs were few and far between. The best known is probably Hatshepsut (c.1473–c.1458 BC), who necessarily had to make use of the masculine royal titles and regalia. She was even referred to as 'he' in the inscriptions on the walls of her mortuary temple at Deir el-Bahri on the west bank at Thebes. This is not to underestimate the political and religious importance of female members of the royal family – in particular the king's mother and wives (especially the 'Chief Royal Wife').

▲ *In the Hypostyle Hall at Abydos the royal Horus image surmounts one of the king's titles, 'Mighty Bull', common during the New Kingdom.*

In the ruler's succession and coronation he re-created the myth (parts of which were recorded as early as the Pyramid Texts) of Horus rightfully ascending to the throne of his deceased father Osiris (see *The Death of Osiris* and *The Contendings of Horus and Seth*). On his accession the king was crowned with the Double Crown, which Horus is often depicted wearing in temple and tomb reliefs. The king would also have performed rituals identifying

himself with the falcon god. Of particular significance would have been the symbolic triumph over the god Seth.

Festival of victory

Inscriptions and reliefs on the walls of the temple dedicated to Horus at Edfu describe the events of the annual Festival of Victory. Although these scenes date to the reign of Ptolemy IX (116–107 BC), rituals of this kind were probably being enacted as early as the New Kingdom (c.1550–c.1069 BC). The aim of the ritual drama was the annihilation of Seth. The king, identified as Horus, had to pierce Seth with ten harpoons. Seth took the form of a hippopotamus, and it is likely that a model hippopotamus would have been made for the festival; the final ritual certainly involved the eating of a cake in the shape of a hippopotamus. The act of harpooning this wild animal, whether symbolic or actual, was an ancient royal ritual that symbolized the triumph of order over the forces of chaos.

Royal regalia

At the front of his crown, the king wore the *uraeus*, the image of a rearing cobra poised ready to strike down any potential opponent of the ruler, and therefore any threat to the order of the state.

The royal insignia included various sceptres. Two of the most important were the 'crook' symbolising government and the flail, perhaps deriving from a fly whisk. The king might also be represented holding various weapons, such as the mace and the scimitar, to signify his role in the defence of order.

A false beard was another mark of royalty, tied under the chin by a cloth strap.

The king is also seen to play the part of Horus in the Ramesseum Dramatic Papyrus, which is now in the British Museum, London. This document dates to the reign of the Twelfth-Dynasty king Amenemhat III (c.1855–c.1808 BC), although the drama had originally been written down for the Jubilee Festival of king Senusret III (c.1874–c.1855 BC). The king, as Horus, had a conversation with the other gods; he received the 'Sacred Eye' (a powerful protective amulet); he ordered oxen to refrain from trampling on barley because it symbolized his father Osiris, the god of vegetation; and he engaged in mock battle with Seth.

It is clear that in such rituals the king was identified with Horus, but he was also believed to come under his protection. The magnificent diorite seated statue of the Fourth-Dynasty king Khafre (c.2558– c.2532 BC) has a beautifully sculpted Horus falcon on the back of the king's head, with the wings in a protective posture around it. In the Ramesside Period (c.1295–c.1069 BC), the figure of Horus became part of the royal headdress, with his outstretched wings wrapped around the crown.

Son of Re

In accordance with the mythology of kingship, the king's father (and thus by definition the deceased king) was identified with the god of the dead,

▲ *Seti I is depicted at Abydos wearing the Blue Crown* (Khepresh) *and burning incense before a seated deity.*

rebirth and vegetation, Osiris. But the divine parentage of the ruler differed according to the context. In the fivefold titles mentioned earlier, the king's birth name was introduced by the title 'Son of Re' (*Sa Re*) – that is, son of the sun god, whom the king was thought to join on his death. This title was first used by the Fourth-Dynasty king Djedefre (c.2566–c.2558 BC). The birth name (called the nomen) and the throne name (the prenomen), introduced by the titulary 'He of the Sedge and the Bee', were the two names that appeared in the royal cartouche (ancient Egyptian *shenu*). This oval outline represented an encircling rope with knotted ends, and was believed to have protective properties.

▲ *Hatshepsut, represented here as a sphinx, wore the false beard of the pharaoh despite the fact that she was a woman.*

In the New Kingdom Period (c.1550–c.1069 BC), rulers claimed to be the offspring of Amun, the 'king of the gods'. The 'divine births' of the Eighteenth-Dynasty rulers Hatshepsut (c.1473–c.1458 BC) and Amenhotep III (c.1390–c.1352 BC) were documented on the walls of Hatshepsut's mortuary temple at Deir el-Bahri and the temple of Luxor respectively (see *The Divine Birth of the Egyptian King*). These kings continued to use the title 'Son of Re', but this would not have appeared contradictory to the ancient Egyptians because Re, the supreme solar deity, had by this time been merged with Amun to become the principal deity Amun-Re.

A variety of religious texts show that the king might be identified with a range of deities, depending on the context. He was often referred to as being 'like' (*mi*) a particular god. A marvellous example of the comparisons made between a particular ruler and the divine world is the cycle of hymns composed in honour of the Twelfth-Dynasty king Senusret III (c.1874–c.1855 BC) (see *Temple Literature*). The status accorded to kingship is exemplified by the occasional reference to the ruler as a creator god. For example, in the Twelfth-Dynasty tomb inscription of Khnumhotep at Beni Hasan, the king is referred to as Atum. In fact, throughout the Old Kingdom (c.2686–c.2181 BC), the king was said to have the divine powers of Sia (divine knowledge), Hu (divine utterance) and Heka (divine magic), which were usually attributed to the creator gods.

Inescapable mortality

In the eyes of the Egyptian people there must have been strict limitations on the living king's divinity, and clear distinctions were made in references to the king and the gods. During the Middle Kingdom (c.2055–c.1650 BC), the mortality of the man who held the divine office of king was acknowledged for the first time in some of the texts, such as *The Instruction of King Amenemhat I for his Son Senusret I*, the theme of which is regicide. Although written as if it were the advice of the Twelfth-Dynasty king Amenemhat I (c.1985–c.1955 BC) to his son and successor Senusret I (c.1965–c.1920 BC), it must have been composed during the latter's reign because it refers to the assassination of the older king. The tone of the piece is rational, personal and bitter, dealing as it does with the dangers of political office. The new king is warned about the treachery of his subjects in a manner that appears realistic and in conflict with the dogma of divine kingship.

The decision to emphasize the humanity as well as the divinity of the king can be seen in the art as well as the literature of this period. The statues of Senusret III (c.1874–c.1855 BC) and Amenemhat III (c.1855–c.1808 BC) of the Twelfth Dynasty, portray a sense of weariness in the faces, which are lined with age. These are a far cry from the typically stylized features of earlier Egyptian kings who, in representation, always had to appear youthful and vigorous. The fact that being pharaoh was a tough job was publicly acknowledged for the first time. In cases where the king was assassinated in a palace conspiracy, or if several kings died in quick succession, the mortality of the ruler would have been evident to all. Jubilee festivals were celebrated with the emphasis on the revivification of the king (see *Royal Jubilee Festivals*).

▼ *The large ears on this black granite statue of Senusret III might indicate the all-hearing capacity of the king. The more realistic royal portraiture of this era is also apparent.*

Glorification of the king

By the early New Kingdom (from c.1550 BC), the Old Kingdom (c.2686–c.2181 BC) was regarded as the glorious past, and the rulers emulated the heightened status of kingship of the Old Kingdom (whose pharaohs had certainly left their mark in the form of enormous pyramids). The king could be worshipped and supplicated for aid as a god. The Eighteenth-Dynasty king Akhenaten (c.1352–c.1336 BC) elevated himself and his family to the status of a divine royal family, whose members were then worshipped at shrines in households throughout his capital city of Akhetaten (see *Akhenaten's New Religion*). The Nineteenth-Dynasty king Ramesses II (c.1279–c.1213 BC) built throughout Egypt on an incredible scale and covered the country with large images of himself, including four statues 21m (69ft) high fronting his temple at Abu Simbel in Lower Nubia, seemingly attesting to his divinity. He even had a cult worshipping him.

▲ *Tutankhamun probably never went into battle but, as this decorated chest reveals, by his reign it had become standard practice to represent the king conquering his enemies, because the triumphant imagery had symbolic value.*

▼ *The wild bull hunt of Ramesses III, illustrated on the temple pylon at Medinet Habu, symbolized the king's control over chaos and potential danger to the Egyptian state. 20th Dynasty.*

The king as high priest

Throughout Egyptian history the pharaoh was nominally the high priest of every god in every temple throughout the country. (In practice high priests had to be appointed in each of the temples to function on behalf of the king.) In this way, the pharaoh stood as the intermediary between every god and the human world. Reliefs on the walls of the temples showed the king making offerings to the gods, and performing the required rituals before them (see *Temple Rites and Offerings*). It was considered of prime importance that he should be portrayed as the one who presented *maat* (translated as 'truth', 'order' or 'justice') to the gods, because this was what the Egyptian gods lived on. It was the role of the king to ensure the beneficence of the gods and thereby ensure peace, harmony, and prosperity in Egypt.

The king was essential to universal order, and it was his duty to maintain *maat* at all times. This function also involved quelling chaos, which was believed to manifest itself in wild animals and foreigners. Even if the king never actually involved himself in wild bull hunts and military campaigns abroad, the convention was for him to be depicted on temple walls engaged in such activities. In this way the king was symbolically subduing chaos and ensuring order. A common motif was the king smiting the enemy or a bound captive. It was essential for the dogma of divine kingship that the Egyptian ruler should always be portrayed as triumphant. The king's victories in battle were not, however, put down to the fact that he was a god, but that he had been granted them by the divine world, after the appropriate offerings and prayers.

It was traditional for a new pharaoh to have texts composed claiming that the land had been in a state of disorder prior to his ascent to the throne, and that, thanks to his greatness, he had restored it to its former balance and glory. Sometimes these texts did follow a period of upheaval, but they tend to be formulaic and together form a genre of literature that glorified the new king and legitimated his right to rule. ◆

The Divine Birth of the Egyptian King

The reliefs are fading fast in the colonnades of the west Theban mortuary temple at Deir el-Bahri, built in honour of the deceased Eighteenth-Dynasty ruler Hatshepsut (c.1473–c.1458 BC). But it is just possible to make out a series of scenes that tell an interesting story concerning ancient Egyptian ideas about kingship and their gods – the so-called 'divine birth' of their pharaoh.

Amun, the 'king of the gods' in the New Kingdom Period (c.1550–c.1069 BC), is shown being led by the hand to a queen's bedchamber by the ibis-headed Thoth, the 'messenger of the gods'. Amun is depicted in human form wearing the curled beard that was associated with divinity. He wears a tall, double-plumed headdress and holds a *was*-sceptre (associated with divinity, power, well being and prosperity) in his free hand. The queen in question is Ahmose Nefertari, the wife of the Eighteenth-Dynasty king Tuthmosis I (c.1504–c.1492 BC).

The next scene is a wonderfully modest portrayal of the sexual union between the queen and Amun. They are shown fully dressed, seated upright together on a bed which is supported on the heads of two goddesses. Amun and the queen have their knees entwined and he holds an *ankh* (the sign of life) up to her nose: thus she takes in his vitality and procreative force.

Following this night of passion, in the next scene Amun passes on his instructions to Khnum, the ram-headed creator god. They both hold *was*-sceptres and *ankhs*. As a result of this meeting, Khnum fashions Ahmose Nefertari's

▲ *The 'messenger of the gods' Thoth accompanies the 'king of the gods' Amun.*

▼ *Amun, wearing the characteristic double-plumed headdress, is seated together with Queen Ahmose Nefertan in a euphemistic portrayal of sexual union.*

▼ *The goddess of childbirth, Heket attends the creation of Hatshepsut on Khnum's potter's wheel.*

daughter and the ruler-to-be, Hatshepsut, on his potter's wheel (see *Creation Myths*). Alongside the tiny figure of Hatshepsut on the wheel is an identical figure, representing her *ka* or 'spirit'. Heket, the frog-headed protective goddess of childbirth, is also present at this creation of the ruler.

Idealism in art

Ancient Egyptian art is highly stylized and idealized. Women are depicted as slender young beauties regardless of their actual age and looks, and it is almost unheard-of to find a representation of a pregnant woman. The scene of the pregnant queen being led to the birthing chamber by Khnum and Heket is one such rare example, although you have to look very closely to detect any sign of pregnancy – the queen's abdomen is only very slightly rounded. Like the sexual intercourse, the scene of the birth is entirely euphemistic. A goddess, presumably acting as midwife, kneels before the seated queen and hands her the newborn child. Kneeling behind the queen is Meskhent, the goddess of the birthing bricks. Finally, Hatshepsut is presented before the gods, the most important of whom is of course her 'father', Amun.

▼ *Hatshepsut is presented before Amun, who holds an ankh in his right hand.*

Divine parentage

The idea of Amun being the father of the monarch was not particular to Hatshepsut, but as a woman, she might have felt it necessary to emphasize her legitimacy in this way. On the other hand she may well have felt no need for 'propaganda' of this kind, and in commissioning these reliefs she was merely doing what was expected of her as an Eighteenth-Dynasty ruler, emphasizing an aspect of the divinity of kingship. Amenhotep III (c.1390– c.1352 BC) had a similar series of reliefs carved in the temple of Luxor on the east bank at Thebes. In this case the queen was Mutemwia, and although Amun was represented in his usual way (as at Deir el-Bahri), the hieroglyphs indicate that he took the guise of her husband Tuthmosis IV (c.1400–c.1390 BC) for the purpose of this ceremonial sexual union (perhaps to put the queen at ease). ◆

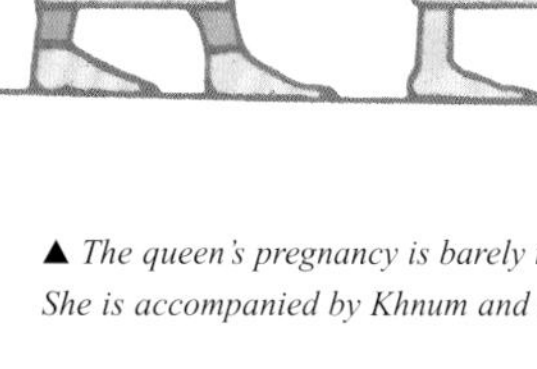

▲ *The queen's pregnancy is barely noticeable. She is accompanied by Khnum and Heket.*

Goddesses of childbirth

Women in ancient Egypt appear to have given birth in a crouching position supported on 'birthing bricks'. Because infant mortality was high and the Egyptians were well aware of the dangers of childbirth, they sought as much divine assistance and protection as possible, and the bricks were divinely personified as the deity Meskhent, one of the goddesses of fate who governed the future of newly born children.

The frog goddess Heket, at one time regarded as the consort of the creator god Khnum, acted as the divine midwife and was said to attend royal births. The protection of the hippopotamus goddess, Taweret, extended to all pregnant women.

Royal Jubilee Festivals

It was important for the king to remain strong and agile in the eyes of his people. This must have been very difficult if the king had been ruling for any length of time and had become noticeably stooped and wrinkly. The Sixth-Dynasty king Pepi II (c.2278–c.2184 BC), for example, supposedly reigned for around 94 years, so towards the end of his reign he can hardly have looked spry at public appearances.

It was traditional to celebrate a royal jubilee festival (*heb sed*) 30 years into the reign, but sometimes a king might choose to hold such a celebration at another time. Amenhotep III (c.1390–c.1352 BC), for example, is said to have ruled for 38 years and yet he celebrated three *heb seds*.

The festival consisted of a number of rituals which were intended to rejuvenate the king, to display his fitness to continue ruling, to consolidate his claim to the land over which he ruled, and to ensure the fertility of the land. Reliefs depicting the events of such a festival emphasize the honouring of the enthroned king, who is often shown wearing a very particular short cloak and sitting in a pavilion special to the occasion. He is also depicted ceremonially running (often holding ritual implements) between markers which may well have symbolized the borders of Egypt, thereby staking his claim to the whole territory.

Royal athleticism

A very early depiction of a *sed*-festival can be seen on an ebony label in the British Museum, London. It was found at Abydos in the tomb of the First-Dynasty king Den (c.2950 BC). An illustration carved on the label shows Den wearing a Double Crown, sitting on his throne in a special festival pavilion. He is also shown running between two sets of three boundary markers – an image that crops up throughout pharaonic history.

The Third-Dynasty ruler Djoser (c.2667–c.2648 BC), for example, is portrayed running on a relief found in the underground chambers of his Step Pyramid complex at Saqqara. In fact various structures in this king's mortuary complex were dedicated to his

The Step Pyramid complex

It is still possible to visit the *heb sed* court to the south-east of Djoser's Step Pyramid. This open court is home to a number of 'dummy' shrines representing the ancient chapels of local gods of the nomes of Egypt. At its southern end is the base of what would originally have been a double festival pavilion containing two thrones, one to symbolize the king's rule over Upper Egypt, and the other to symbolize his rule over Lower Egypt.

▼ *This limestone fragment shows two figures of Akhenaten wearing the traditional short cloak of the sed-festival. On the right he is accompanied by his Chief Prophet, who carries the king's sandals. 18th Dynasty.*

▶ *Dummy chapels such as this one were stone replicas of those built for the celebration of the* sed*-festival. Their presence in Djoser's Step Pyramid complex was intended to ensure that the king would be able to celebrate jubilee festivals throughout eternity. Old Kingdom.*

enactment of the *sed*-festival. The Step Pyramid does not stand alone, but is surrounded by a series of courts, temples, and other important buildings. In the large court to the south of the pyramid there are the traces of boundary markers, so perhaps this was where the king performed his ceremonial display of athleticism.

Commemorative buildings

Important religious buildings were still being built and decorated in connection with the royal jubilee festivals very much later in Egyptian history. Examples include the mortuary temple of the Eighteenth-Dynasty king Amenhotep III (c.1390–c.1352 BC) on the west bank at Thebes (of which only the two statues known as the Colossi of Memnon survive), as well as the temple to the Aten at east Karnak built by his successor Akhenaten (c.1352–c.1336 BC) and the *sed*-festival court at Bubastis built by the Twenty-second-Dynasty king Osorkon II (c.874–c.850 BC).

The large lake to the east of Amenhotep III's palace at Malkata on the west bank at Thebes appears to have been the setting for one of this king's splendid jubilee festivals, during which he was rowed in a boat in a ceremony reminiscent of the sun god's night-time journey through the Netherworld. The rejuvenation of the king reflected the rising of the sun (see *The Journey of the Sun through the Netherworld*). ◆

▶ *This false door stela in the South Tomb of Djoser's Step Pyramid Complex, shows the king performing the ceremonial* heb sed *run.*

Temples and Priests

The temples of ancient Egypt have inspired awe throughout the ages. The modern visitor still marvels at their magnificence – their huge size and the beauty and detail of the reliefs on their walls.

To ensure their survival, these grand structures, mostly of stone, were built in the desert fringes, just beyond the reaches of the Nile flood. It is, of course, the most recent structure at any one site that still stands today, and most surviving temples are not pharaonic at all, but date to the Ptolemaic and Roman Periods (332 BC–AD 395). They do, however, comply with the ancient conventions of temple-building. It was possible for a cult centre to have been dedicated to a particular deity for centuries, while the temple itself was rebuilt, perhaps more than once.

The architectural splendour of the great religious buildings is impossible to overlook, but finding out what actually went on inside them involves closer scrutiny. As well as inscriptions on temple walls, hymns, prayers and records of administration and offerings were kept on papyri. Many votive offerings have also survived. From such sources it is possible to build up a picture of the roles of the various priests, and to begin to fathom the rituals of the High Priest, who enjoyed a more intimate interaction with the resident deity of the temple.

◄ *Colossal statues of rulers and elaborately decorated columns were key features of the great temples of Egypt.*

Temple Architecture

The temples that survive in Egypt today tend to date from the New Kingdom onwards (c.1550 BC). They may have varied in size depending on the importance of a particular deity, but whether they were dedicated to gods or kings (living or dead), all Egyptian temples had essential architectural features in common.

The grand approach

Each temple was approached by a processional way or avenue, often flanked by rows of statues. The approach to Karnak Temple is typical, lined on each side by stone sphinxes with ram's heads (the ram was one of the guises of Amun, who was worshipped at this temple). It once connected the great complex at Karnak with Luxor Temple, about 2km (1 mile) to the south.

The processional way led to the main gateway, known as the first pylon (the ancient Greek word for 'gate') of the temple. This consisted of two enormous tapering towers of masonry with an opening between them. Flags on long poles projected outwards from the front of the temple on each side of the entrance. These flags, flying majestically, would have been visible from a long way off and would have been an image closely associated with the temple. It is therefore interesting that the hieroglyphic sign used to write the ancient Egyptian word *netjer*, which means 'god', was possibly intended to represent a flag on a pole. The onlooker would also have been struck by the size of the statues of the king which flanked the gateway, such as those of Ramesses II (c.1279–c.1213 BC) at Luxor Temple. It would certainly have heightened the people's belief in the divinity of kingship to witness these statues of the ruler in such a hallowed setting, and being so colossal they must have seemed like gods. Sometimes an obelisk, or a pair of obelisks, also marked the entrance to the temple.

▲ *There were originally two obelisks in front of the First Pylon at Luxor Temple, but the other is now in the Place de la Concorde in Paris.*

▼ *The roof of the great hypostyle hall at Karnak Temple was originally supported by 134 massive stone columns.*

▶ *Plant-life is a common theme of temple decoration, and is seen here at Kom Ombo.*

Inside the great entrance was the peristyle court, a large, open square surrounded by a colonnade. It is likely that some of the population (at least in the later periods of Egyptian history) would have been allowed at certain times into this 'public' area of the temple, although all who entered the temple's confines would have had to comply with the criteria of ritual purity (see *The Temple Complex*).

The temple lay on a straight axis. On the other side of the great court, opposite the back of the first pylon, was a smaller gateway known as the second pylon. Access through this inner entrance was restricted to those with priestly titles, and the rooms within were used for storing cult equipment and for performing the secret rituals of the temple (see *Temple Rites and Offerings*).

The inner sanctum

On the other side of the second pylon was the hypostyle hall, with a roof supported by rows of columns. This was usually broader than it was deep. To walk through it was like wandering through a forest. Gaps at the top of the outer walls provided clerestory lighting – shafts of light piercing the mysterious darkness. It would have been only just possible to make out the painted reliefs and inscriptions on the walls and columns. The gloom and the dense columns formed a perfect screen between the outside world and the secluded dwelling-place of the god.

The number of peristyle courts and hypostyle halls depended on the size of the temple, as did the number of storerooms, antechambers, vestibules, offering halls and shrines which led off the inner hypostyle hall. But deep within every temple lay the 'holy of holies' – the sanctuary where the god lived. The god or goddess resided in a cult statue, which stood in a raised shrine or *naos* (the ancient Greek word for the innermost part of a temple or shrine), usually of stone or wood with wooden doors. From the New Kingdom onwards (c.1550 BC) the shrine often took the form of a boat, as at the temple of Horus at Edfu, and was known as a barque shrine. Only the High Priest could enter the presence of the god.

The god's home

The temple was very much the house of the god. The ancient Egyptian for 'temple' was *hwt netjer*, 'the god's mansion', or *per netjer*, 'the god's house'. The temple was also regarded as a model of the place where creation was believed to have taken place. The floor level rose gradually from the temple entrance to the shrine in the innermost sanctuary, and the *naos* was thought to reflect the mound projecting from the primordial waters, with the deity standing on it as the creator god had first done.

The primordial waters (Nun) were symbolized by a 'sacred lake', such as at Karnak, where the priests made their ablutions. The Victory Stela of Piy (c.747–c.716 BC) in the Cairo Museum records that when this Twenty-fifth-Dynasty king visited Heliopolis and ritually cleansed himself in the sacred lake there, he claimed that he had washed his face in 'the river of Nun', as the sun god was believed to do each day before dawn. It is also possible that the undulating mudbrick wall surrounding some of the temple enclosures was meant to represent the waters of chaos.

The cosmological theme was extended elsewhere inside the temple. A marsh was evoked by the halls with their rows of papyrus- and lotus-form columns. The flat ceilings were often painted dark blue and covered with yellow stars. The hieroglyphic sign for 'horizon' was a tract of land with the sun rising between two mountains, and it is possible that the great pylon forming the entrance to the temple was meant to represent this. ◆

▲ *The monolithic* naos *of highly polished syenite in the sanctuary at Edfu Temple is the oldest part of the building, dating to the 30th-Dynasty reign of Nectanebo II.*

Different Types of Temples

There were two main types of temple: cult temples dedicated to deities, and mortuary temples built in honour of dead kings. Both were very similar in design and function: offerings were made to the gods in the former, to ensure the beneficence of the divine world; and to the spirits (*kas*) of the deceased kings in the latter, ensuring their continued existence in the Afterlife. Both procedures were seen as crucial to the maintenance of order and peace (see *Temple Rites and Offerings*).

Cult temples were usually dedicated to a triad of deities, whereas mortuary temples were concerned with the deceased king and his identification with a number of gods. A king's mortuary temple was clearly also intended to be used for ceremonies during his lifetime, and provided the focal point for a complex of buildings built in celebration of divine kingship, including a royal palace which could go on to serve as a dummy palace for the dead king's spirit.

▲ *The columns in this colonnade at Karnak are papyriform: their capitals resemble stylized papyrus buds.*

▲ *Statues of Ramesses II in the form of Osiris stand before pillars in this king's mortuary temple, the Ramesseum.*

In all temples, priests officiated (see *The Role of Priests*), offerings were made and rituals performed. The focal point of any cult temple was the statue of a god, whereas in a royal mortuary temple it was the statue of a king.

Cult temples

Very little has survived of cult temples built before the New Kingdom (c.1550 BC). During the Old Kingdom (c.2686–c.2181 BC) it is likely that temples to the deities were built of mudbrick, which is obviously a less durable building material than stone. (Today, Egyptian farmers make use of the ancient mudbrick as a fertilizer, called *sebakh* in Arabic.) During the Middle Kingdom (c.2055–c.1650 BC) cult temples were apparently built of stone, but little has survived. Usually the stone from these structures was re-used in the buildings of the New Kingdom (c.1550–c.1069 BC) and later temples located on the same sites as the earlier ones. The ancient Egyptians were great recyclers, as modern Egyptians are today. Why go to the bother of quarrying in the searing heat of the desert, transporting heavy loads across vast distances and working stone with stone and bronze tools, when ready-dressed blocks were available on the site from an earlier structure that had perhaps fallen into disrepair? A good example of such re-use is a stunning relief of the Twelfth-Dynasty king Senusret I (c.1965–c.1920 BC) and the god Min which presumably once graced the walls of an important Middle Kingdom temple. Now in the Petrie Museum of Egyptian Archaeology, it was discovered by the 'Father of Egyptian archaeology', William Matthew Flinders Petrie (1853–1942), turned face down and re-used as a paving slab in a much later Ptolemaic temple at the site of Koptos.

Mortuary temples

Royal mortuary temples (referred to in the ancient texts as 'mansions of millions of years') have survived from

▲ *The cenotaph temple of Seti I at Abydos has an unusual L-shaped plan.*

the Early Dynastic Period onwards (c.3100 BC). They became larger and grander as time went on. The earliest examples are simple offering chambers adjoining the earliest royal tombs, called mastabas (Arabic for 'bench') at the royal burial sites of Abydos and Saqqara. By the Third Dynasty they were more complex. The mortuary temple in the burial complex of King Djoser (c.2667–c.2648 BC) was attached to the north face of his pyramid. It was made of stone and consisted of two courts, one of which was presumably dedicated to Djoser as king of Upper Egypt, and one to him as king of Lower Egypt. By the Fourth Dynasty, the mortuary temple had been shifted to the east face of the pyramid, so that it could be joined via a straight causeway to a 'valley temple' at the edge of the cultivation, usually at a quay on a canal. The best preserved mortuary temples from the Old Kingdom (c.2686–c.2181 BC) are those of king Khafre (c.2558–c.2532 BC) at Giza.

By the New Kingdom (c.1550–c.1069 BC), the mortuary temples were separate from the tombs of the kings. The tombs were in the Valley of the Kings on the west bank at Thebes, whereas their accompanying temples were some distance away on the desert fringes, more conveniently sited close to the cultivation and the river. They were imposing structures, elaborately decorated and on a par with the contemporary state cult temples.

A variation on the theme of the mortuary temple were the 'cenotaph temples' at Abydos, the legendary burial place of Osiris, god of the dead, rebirth and vegetation. These temples were closely associated with the cult of Osiris, and their function was to associate the dead king with various gods. The earliest royal cenotaph at Abydos was built by the Twelfth-Dynasty king Senusret III (c.1874–c.1855 BC), but by far the best preserved and thus best known is that of the Nineteenth-Dynasty ruler Seti I (c.1294–c.1279 BC).

▼ *The unusual altar in the sun temple of Niuserre at Abu Gurab is sculpted out of calcite and is some 6m (20ft) in diameter. 5th Dynasty.*

Sun temples

The remains of stone sun temples date from the Fifth Dynasty (c.2494–c.2345 BC). They were dedicated to the sun god Re, but were also closely associated with royal burials. They were built by the first six rulers of this dynasty and were connected with their pyramids (which, like the obelisk, were presumably solar symbols) and with the cult of the sun god at Heliopolis. Six sun temples are known from inscriptions, but only two have actually been discovered; they are those of Userkaf (c.2494–c.2487 BC) and Niuserre (c.2445–c.2421 BC), and are both situated at Abu Gurab, north of Abusir (part of the necropolis of ancient Memphis). The sun temple of Niuserre houses the remains of an enormous squat stone obelisk, and a gigantic altar in the form of four hieroglyphic signs for 'offering' (*hetep*). ◆

The Temple Complex

The purpose of the ancient Egyptian temple was to reflect and maintain the divine order of creation. It was not a place of organized public worship, comparable with a mosque, synagogue or church. No form of service was held, and rather than everyone being welcomed into the temple, the public were generally excluded from it. A large number of priests was employed by each temple but very few of them actually performed religious rituals.

The temple was rather like a medieval European monastery, in that it was a great landowning institution and functioned very much as the hub of the local economy, and as a place of learning. It was run by a large and complex bureaucracy, and temple workers included farmers, builders and scribes as well as priests.

▲ *The ears on this painted stela were included to ensure that the god would hear the prayer.*

Ritual purity

All who entered the confines of the temple had to comply with the strict rules regarding ritual purity. According to inscriptions on the walls of the temple at Esna, all those entering temples from the Late Period (c.747 BC) were expected at least to have cut their fingernails and toenails, shaved their heads and removed other body hair, washed their hands with natron (a naturally occurring salt), be dressed in linen (they were forbidden from wearing wool), and to have not had sexual intercourse for several days. Priests were not required to remain celibate outside the temple.

Much ritual purification would subsequently have gone on inside the temple, making use of ablution tanks and the Sacred Lake.

Public access to the deity

During much of Egyptian history most people would have been allowed only as far as the gateway of the temple complex. They did, however, come to the outer precincts of the temple to say prayers and enlist the help of the gods. At the mortuary temple of Ramesses III (c.1184–c.1153 BC) at Medinet Habu, for example, the corridor inside the entrance gateway had an image of 'Ptah who hears prayers' on its wall. In this way, people who would only ever be granted access to this part of the temple could petition, or give thanks to, the god. No member of the public would ever have laid eyes on the cult statue of the god housed in the inner shrine. However, by the later period of Egyptian history, the peristyle court (see *Temple Architecture*) appears to have become available to a certain degree of public access, and was a place where offerings and supplications could be made before statues of gods and kings (see *Temple Rites and Offerings*). The emphasis was on the gods hearing the prayers of the people, so stelae, statues and even walls might be inscribed with numerous ears in order to ensure this would happen. Sometimes stelae and statues set up in the outer parts of the temple were covered in hieroglyphs. These were often spells to help to cure, or protect against, scorpion stings, snake bites, and other such hazards and illnesses. Today these stelae are known as *cippi* of Horus (see *Isis and the Seven Scorpions*) and the statues as 'healing statues'.

▲ *Musical instruments of all kinds were played in the temples. Paintings and reliefs reveal that male harpists were often blind. 18th Dynasty. Tomb of Nakht, west Thebes.*

Festivals

At all times of the year singing, chanting and the playing of musical instruments would have taken place in the temples – the gods were thought to enjoy such aural delights at all times, but never more so than at the festivals, the most joyous occasions in the lives of the temples. It was at these celebrations that the statue of the deity emerged from his or her secluded shrine, carried on the shoulders of priests, but always still concealed from the eyes of the masses, sometimes in a carrying shrine in the form of a boat (known as a barque shrine). The oracle of the god could then be consulted. His or her answer might be sought to questions such as whether it was sensible to make a difficult journey north, or who, out of a list of suspects, was responsible for stealing an article of clothing.

◀ *This basalt 'healing statue' of the priest Djedhor is covered in hieroglyphs of incantatory texts. The priest sits behind a* cippus *of Horus, and the basin in the plinth is for the collection of water which was ritually poured over the statue to be imbued with the potency of the magic spells. 30th Dynasty.*

▲ *The foreleg of the ox was the choice cut of meat for offering to the gods and to the dead. 6th Dynasty. Tomb of Idut, Saqqara.*

The god's needs

The daily rituals of the temple took place in the darker, more secluded parts of the building on the far side of the hypostyle hall (see *Temple Architecture* and *Temple Rites and Offerings*). Every need of the deity was tended to, directly by a minority of the priesthood and indirectly by a large number of temple workers. According to the longest known papyrus from ancient Egypt, Papyrus Harris (40.5m or 133ft long), which dates to the day the Twentieth-Dynasty king Ramesses III died

► *The migdol gateway of Ramesses III's mortuary temple at Medinet Habu was a quasi-defensive feature borrowed from the design of Syrian fortresses.*

▲ *Windows in the inner parts of temples were usually clerestory, allowing shafts of light to filter down from the tops of the walls, as here in the hypostyle hall at Edfu.*

(c.1153 BC), the estate of Karnak Temple employed a total labour force of 81,322 people (see *The Role of Priests*). The papyrus also records that this great temple of Amun exercised control over 2393sq km (924sq miles) of arable land, 433 orchards, 421,362 head of livestock, 65 villages, 83 ships and 46 workshops.

Temple economy

The ancient Egyptian temple was the economic hub of the locality. The temple complex would have had its own landing quay, giving it easy access to the river for transporting produce. In the larger temple complexes, food production would have taken place on a grand scale in the temple butcheries, breweries and bakeries.

By a process known as the 'reversion of offerings', a large proportion of the population could in practice be fed via the temple. Much of the produce of Egypt passed, by various requirements, to the temples throughout the country, especially in the big cities such as Thebes and Memphis where there were huge temple complexes, each with a number of different deities to be offered to on a daily basis. The greater the quantity of offerings, it was hoped, the greater the beneficence of the gods. Food offerings of all kinds were made to the gods, but most of what was offered eventually reverted to the priests. From them it was passed to their families and to the many workers and dependents of the temple and temple estates, not to mention the poor at the temple gate (see *Temple Rites and Offerings*).

A place of scholarship

The temple was also a place of learning, providing education for those boys who would go on to hold administrative or priestly positions. During the New Kingdom (c.1550–c.1069 BC), it is known from texts that there were at least two schools in Thebes, one in the temple of the goddess Mut at Karnak, and one behind the Ramesseum, the mortuary complex of the Nineteenth-Dynasty king Ramesses II (c.1279–c.1213 BC), although no excavated structure has been found which can be identified as having been used as a school.

The local temple was the storehouse for local records, which were written on papyrus rolls kept in locked chests. In general, the temple, with its high surrounding walls and massive gateway, would have functioned as the local safe place. The temple at Medinet Habu, for instance, was one of the most defensible places in western Thebes. The east gate was fortified with guardhouses flanking the entrance, and in the late Twentieth Dynasty, when the people of the west Theban workmen's village of Deir el-Medina felt threatened by marauding foreigners, they hid themselves in the precincts of the temple. ◆

The Role of Priests

If, as is stated in Papyrus Harris (c.1153 BC), the temple of Amun at Karnak employed 81,322 people towards the end of the New Kingdom, it is clear that the temples must have been the chief places of employment in the country. There is no implication that those 81,322 individuals could possibly all have been priests. In fact it is a matter of dispute whether any of these temple employees would actually have been priests in the modern sense of the term.

The conventional translations of ancient Egyptian terms can be misleading when they employ words that have very specific meanings and associations for us today. The ancient Egyptian term *hem netjer* is normally translated as 'priest', but it literally means 'servant of the god' and not all those described in this way were necessarily trained in theology. They certainly would not have conducted the kind of worship or services performed by priests in any of the religious traditions that are familiar today. It is possible that most of those described as 'servants of the god' would not have performed any kind of ritual in the temple.

▲ *Tuthmosis III wears a leopardskin to identify his role as High Priest.*

Priestly garments

Apart from the obligation to be clean shaven, priests of lower ranks who are depicted in reliefs and paintings are indistinguishable from ordinary people. However, some priests did wear distinctive clothing as a sign of their office. The *sem*-priests who performed the final purification and revivification rites at funerals, wore cloaks made of leopardskin. When the king was portrayed officiating in his priestly role he was sometimes shown wearing this form of dress.

A priestly rota

The number of temple employees depended on the size of the temple, which in turn depended on the status of the deity to whom it was dedicated and the size of the town or city. Throughout Egyptian history, the main body of priests was made up of people who spent much of the year engaged in their own, different, occupations. A rota system was devised whereby the priests of each temple were divided into four groups (usually referred to today by the Greek word *phyle*). The members of each group performed their temple

▲ *A libation of water (indicated by a zig-zag line, the hieroglyphic sign for water) is poured from a* heset-*jar on to a heaped offering table in this relief at the temple of Kom Ombo.*

▼ *An enormous variety of foods, including beef, fish, duck, bread, fruit and vegetables, were offered to the gods and to the spirits of the dead. Tomb of Horemheb, Saqqara.*

duties for one month, then returned to their own jobs for three months, so that they worked for the temple for a total of three months in every year. At the end of each month-long shift, a stock taking was carried out, and records were made on papyri or wooden boards.

For most members of the community, it would have been well worth their while to perform this temple service because the priests received a proportion of the temple revenue (this would have been given in kind, because there was no coinage in ancient Egypt). The ancient Egyptians believed that the deity consumed the essence of the food given to him or her as an offering, and it could then be passed on to the priests. This system was known as the 'reversion of offerings' (see *The Temple Complex*). The practice could at times prove lucrative – as it did during the New Kingdom (c.1550–c.1069 BC) when tithes and war booty created huge temple incomes – to the extent that it was sometimes even considered worth purchasing a priestly office.

Priests were also exempted from some taxes, and could often avoid undertaking state labour that was otherwise a compulsory service, such as the digging of irrigation systems.

The purified ones

Most of the priests had very little contact with the cult statue of the deity, the focal point of any temple, although tending the statue was the most important temple rite and would have been carried out by the most senior priests. The reliefs on temple walls can be misleading because it was believed that it was only the king who was worthy of being depicted standing opposite a deity, so priests are never shown making offerings to the gods.

All those working in the temple had to be considered ritually pure in order to do so. In fact the majority of the priests

▲ *The calendars of festivals carved on the walls of temples such as this one at Kom Ombo, were based on the lunar months, stellar sightings and the annual inundation of the Nile.*

◀ *The 18th-Dynasty king Ay (c.1327– c.1323* BC*) is depicted on the north wall of Tutankhamun's burial chamber wearing the leopardskin of a priest and performing the ritual of the Opening of the Mouth on the mummy of the dead king; thus Ay legitimized his accession to the throne as Tutankhamun's heir.*

were called *wab* ('purifier' or 'purified') priests. The Greek historian Herodotus, writing in the fifth century BC, stated that Egyptian priests washed twice daily and twice nightly, that they were clean-shaven, had no body hair, were circumcised, abstained from sexual intercourse for several days before entering the temple, wore no wool or leather clothing, and had sandals made of papyrus. In addition, priests seem to have had to rinse out their mouths with a solution of natron (a natural compound of sodium carbonate and bicarbonate, found as crystals at the edges of certain lakes) and rub their bodies with oil. A judicial document now in the Turin Museum tells us that a *wab* priest of Khnum was brought to justice because he had sworn not to enter the temple at Elephantine until he had spent ten days drinking natron, but in fact he had entered after only seven days and was considered ritually impure.

A variety of jobs

Most priests would not have come into direct contact with the divine cult image, so although their job might have been to see to the needs of the god, it would have been only by indirect means. The man who was able to interact most closely with the god was the High Priest (see *The High Priests*). His deputy was the Second Prophet, who was in charge of the economic organization of the temple. He oversaw its provisioning from estates and endowments, and he made sure that the right amount of offerings were delivered each day. He would have had a host of administrators working with him.

The majority of the priests were occupied with ensuring the maintenance and security of the temple. They ran the workshops, storerooms, libraries and other affiliated buildings, as well as acting as doorkeepers and porters. The daily tasks of washing, dressing and feeding the cult statue of the deity appear to have been carried out by Stolist Priests (see *Temple Rites and Offerings*). They would have worked closely with the Lector Priests, whose job it was to recite the words of the god. They chanted magic spells while important rituals were carried out; for example, they would recite spells from the Book of the Dead while a dead body was being embalmed and mummified.

The *sem*-priest, who can be distinguished in images by the leopardskin he wears, was also very important at death. This priest's function developed in the New Kingdom out of the duties performed by the first-born son at his father's funeral. These included the final rites of purification and the Opening of the Mouth ceremony, which was performed on the mummified body to revive its senses, so that the deceased could be reborn.

All those people who worked in the temple confines had to swear not to spread the secrets or mysteries of the temple, and were considered to occupy a privileged position. ◆

Special skills

Many priests with specialist knowledge worked in the temples. Examples include the Hour Priests, who were perhaps astronomers responsible for compiling the calendars of festivals – occasions when the priests carried the cult statue of the deity into the local community, and manipulated the divine oracle. Scholarly priests, who worked in the House of Life (*Per Ankh*), taught reading and writing to the elite local boys, and copied out manuscripts for the temple library or record office. Many of them would have functioned as scribes in the local community, being called upon to write up documents such as wills or divorce settlements. Some priests were considered able to interpret dreams, and thereby provide a form of guidance and prophesy. Others would have been cult singers and temple musicians.

◀ *This priest has a figure of the god Amun tattooed on his upper arm. He kneels behind an image of the god. As is often the case, an inscription accompanies the statue.*

The High Priests

The king was nominally High Priest of every cult in Egypt, but basic logistics clearly prevented him from performing the daily rituals in many places at once, and so in practice he had to delegate the day-to-day duties of High Priest to men stationed at temples throughout the country. Thus the position of High Priest (or Chief Priest or First Prophet) was by royal appointment and was a highly esteemed title, both religiously and politically.

▲ *The ruler Hatshepsut wears a false beard, the* nemes *headdress – a striped linen headcloth – and a* uraeus *on her brow. She holds two* nw *pots, characteristically used for offering wine and milk to the gods. 18th Dynasty.*

Acting on behalf of the king, the High Priest had closer contact with the cult statue of the god than anyone else in the temple complex. It is likely that only the High Priest would have been allowed to stand before the image of the god in the shrine. Temple reliefs illustrate what was expected of the High Priest, but because the presence of the king was still considered necessary in the temples, even if only symbolically, it was the ruler who was shown performing the rituals in the various reliefs and statuary (see *Temple Rites and Offerings*). Superb reliefs on the walls of the sanctuaries in the temple at Abydos, for example, depict the Nineteenth-Dynasty king Seti I (c.1294–c.1279 BC) carrying out his priestly duties.

Nepotism

In the Old Kingdom (c.2686–c.2181 BC) all senior positions, whether in the temples, the administrative system or the army, were held by the same small group of people, more specifically members of the royal family – especially brothers, sons and uncles of the reigning monarch – who held multiple honorary titles, each accompanied by privileges granted by the king. As priests these men would certainly have played a role in the temple structure, but would probably not have worked full-time within the temple confines. During the Middle Kingdom (c.2055–c.1650 BC) these three sources of employment for the élite became more distinct, but the highest ranking priests continued also to sit on councils of state in the royal palace, and clearly had political influence.

▲ *The leopardskin was a priestly robe usually associated with the sem-priest.*

During the Eighteenth Dynasty (c.1550–c.1295 BC) the wealth of the largest temples grew dramatically, mainly augmented by booty and tribute resulting from successful military campaigning in Syria-Palestine. The Temple of Amun at Karnak received the bulk of this new source of income, and its High Priest became more and more powerful, thanks to the wealth and manpower under his control. According to Papyrus Harris, by the end of Ramesses III's reign (c.1153 BC) the king had relinquished control over the finances of the estate of Amun. The Wilbour Papyrus, dating to the reign of Ramesses V (c.1147–c.1143 BC), records that this land was not subject to royal taxation, and that its dependents

▲ *In the cenotaph temple of Seti I at Abydos, the king burns incense before a seated figure of Horus. The god holds an* ankh *in his left hand and a crook, flail and* was*-sceptre in his right.*

were exempt from compulsory military service and state labour.

Priestly power

If the reigning king was strong and successful, the excessive power of the High Priest of Amun at Karnak did not necessarily cause any real problems. But if a weak and ineffective king succeeded to the throne there was likely to be trouble, and this is exactly what happened towards the end of the Twentieth Dynasty (c.1186– c.1069 BC). Because of the exceptionally long reign of Ramesses II (c.1279–c.1213 BC), many of the last kings of the New Kingdom succeeded to the throne when they were already elderly and feeble. They chose to pass their days in their palace at Per-Ramesses in the Delta, thus distancing themselves from their people and, more significantly, from the Theban region. Generally their reigns appear to have been fairly ineffectual. But the people of the south of Egypt needed a strong leader, and rather than look to the king they decided it would be most sensible to show allegiance to the High Priest of Amun at Thebes.

At the end of the Twentieth Dynasty, a High Priest of Amun named Herihor was able to get away with claiming royal titles even though Ramesses XI (c.1099–c.1069 BC) was still on the throne. There are inscriptions in the Temple of Khonsu at Karnak which show Herihor's name written in royal cartouches, and his adoption of the full regal titles, including the royal epithet 'Victorious Bull', the rare title 'Great Ruler of Egypt' and even 'Son of Amun', thereby claiming divine descent (see *The Divine Birth of the Egyptian King*). This High Priest was militarily and economically incredibly powerful, and during Ramesses XI's reign he effectively controlled Egypt from its southern border at Aswan north to Herakleopolis near the Faiyum. Despite this, at no time did Herihor claim complete royal power. ◆

▲ *It was unheard of for a high priest to have himself represented with royal titles and his name in cartouches, face-to-face with the god Amun, until Herihor brazenly usurped these royal prerogatives here at Karnak.*

The Role of Women in the Temples

◀ *The design of the hooped* sistrum, *or ceremonial rattle, often incorporated the face of Hathor with her cow ears. Tomb of Sennefer.*

There were far fewer women than men working in the temples of ancient Egypt, but the title 'priestess' (*hemet netjer*, literally 'wife of the god') certainly existed. These women, who functioned in the temple cults, tended to be from the upper echelons of society and were usually married to priests, and as a result their position relied heavily upon the status of their husbands. During the Old and Middle Kingdoms (c.2686–c.1650 BC), the title *hemet netjer* was most usually associated with the cult of Hathor, the goddess of fertility. It was a priestess who was in charge of the management of the estates of this goddess, and even some of the High Priests were women. We also know of female High Priests serving the cults of the goddesses Neith and Pakhet, and during the Old Kingdom a certain queen Meresankh held the office of High Priestess of the god Thoth.

Music and dance

An important part of the cult of Hathor was music and dance – the priestesses accompanied ceremonial dances and rituals by shaking their *sistra* (rattles), instruments whose handles were often decorated with the carved head of Hathor, and rattling their broad, beaded necklaces with long counterpoises, called *menat* necklaces.

From the Old Kingdom onwards, women often functioned as the cult singers, dancers and musicians, playing instruments such as harps, tambourines and clappers in the temples of both

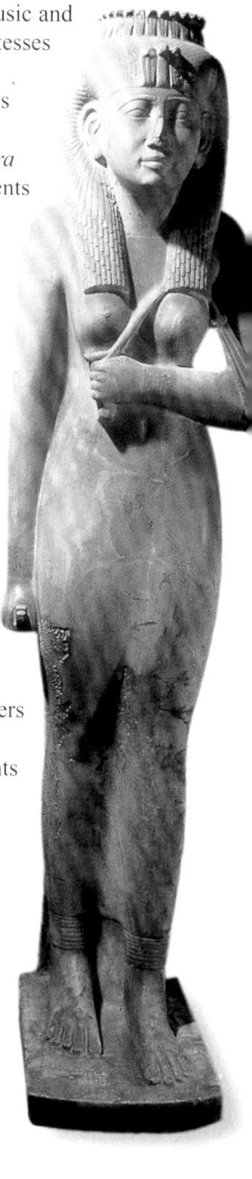

▶ *Amenirdis, the daughter of the Kushite ruler Kashta, was adopted as 'God's Wife of Amun' at Thebes.*

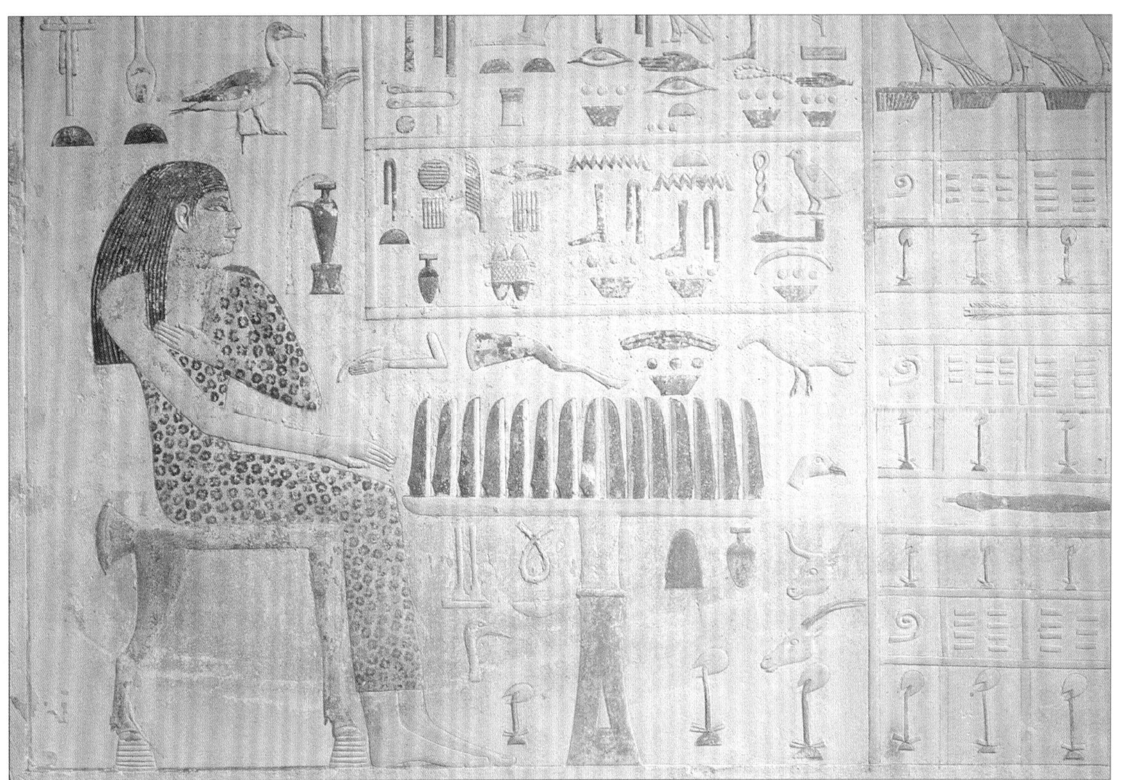

▲ *This painted limestone stela depicts Nefretiabet seated before an offering table laden with bread and surrounded by other commodities such as oil, incense and meat. A list of types of linen appears on the right. 4th Dynasty.*

The Chief Concubine

The Ramesside sources tell us that the wife of the High Priest of Amun-Re at Karnak held the title 'Chief Concubine of Amun-Re'. She had ritual responsibilities, such as leading the female musicians of the temple, and seems to have wielded a certain amount of power. One record mentions that the Chief Concubine acted to ensure the prompt delivery of overdue rations to the protesting necropolis workers of Deir el-Medina. On another occasion a Chief Concubine arranged for the murder of a troublesome policeman.

gods and goddesses. By the beginning of the New Kingdom (c.1550 BC) the title 'Chantress of Amun' was in fairly common use – once again it was usually the wives of priests who gained positions of this kind.

Funerals

Women played an important role at funerals and, during the Old Kingdom (c.2686–c.2181 BC), in the rituals of the mortuary cults of the deceased. Two of the female mourners took the titles 'Great Kite' and 'Little Kite' and impersonated the goddesses Isis and Nephthys. According to the myth of Osiris, these goddesses had taken the guise of kites as they pieced together the body of the god in order to mummify him (see *The Death of Osiris*). At least during the Old Kingdom, priestesses could hold the title '*Ka*-servant' (*hemet-ka*). It was their responsibility to perform rituals in the tomb-chapels of the deceased.

The most prestigious religious title held by a woman was 'God's Wife of Amun', which was also, from the Eighteenth Dynasty, a position of great political significance. This office was based at Thebes, and was held by a daughter of the king in order to ensure royal control of the Theban area. From the reign of the Twenty-third Dynasty king Osorkon III (c.777–c.749 BC), the 'God's Wife of Amun' was expected to remain celibate, so she had to adopt a daughter and successor. She was also given the second title 'Hand of the God', possibly giving her a symbolic role in the act of creation. According to one version of the creation myth of Heliopolis, the god Atum had brought the gods Shu and Tefnut into existence by masturbating.

By the Late Period the God's Wife was more important than the High Priest. She controlled the vast estates of Amun, employed huge numbers of people, and had access to great wealth. ◆

Temple Rites and Offerings

Temple rites revolved around the cult statue of the deity, which resided in each temple shrine. We can guess that these cult statues would often have been made of precious materials such as gold and silver, because very few have survived to this day, at least not in situ. Each statue was believed to house the very essence of the deity in question. A ritual ceremony known as the Opening of the Mouth had been performed on every statue in order to animate it symbolically. As a result, the god, together with his or her family, was believed to live in the temple which was regarded as his or her house (*hwt netjer*, 'the god's mansion' or *per netjer*, 'the god's house').

King lists

In a royal mortuary temple, offerings of food were made to the deceased ruler. The accompanying rituals included prayers that it was believed would allow the king's *ka* or spirit to be nourished by the food. Endowments of land to the temple enabled these rituals to continue for generations after the death of the king to whom it was dedicated.

Some cenotaph temples, including those of the Nineteenth-Dynasty kings Ramesses II and Seti I at Abydos, contained kinglists recording almost all the rulers of Egypt, as well as shrines to various deities. After an offering of food had been made to a deity or the king and he was judged to have finished with it, it would be placed on an altar set before the kinglist so that it could also nourish all the previous kings. Once they were deemed to have been satisfied by the offering, it would be removed and given to the priests serving in the temple.

▲ *Reliefs on the walls of Hatshepsut's mortuary temple at Deir el-Bahri show incense and other exotic goods being imported by boat from Punt. 18th Dynasty.*

Tending the god

The most important temple rites were concerned with the washing and feeding of the god in the form of his statue. Every morning at dawn, the clay seal on the shrine was broken, and the door opened. Two purification rituals were performed before the god: incense was burnt and a libation of water was poured. He was believed to need a good breakfast, so food was brought to him as an offering. The ancient Egyptians would certainly have agreed with the saying that cleanliness is next to godliness. The next stage of the proceedings was to remove the god so that his shrine could be cleaned. The

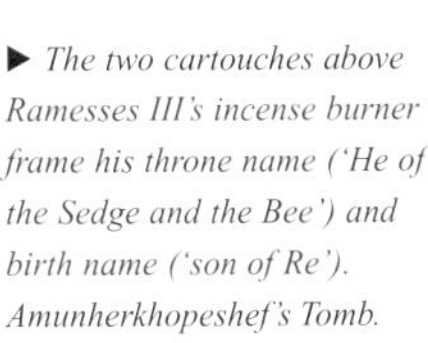

▶ *The two cartouches above Ramesses III's incense burner frame his throne name ('He of the Sedge and the Bee') and birth name ('son of Re'). Amunherkhopeshef's Tomb.*

statue was then undressed, cleansed with incense and water, re-dressed in clean linen, and adorned with jewellery, before being returned to his shrine. The rituals were accompanied by chanting and singing. Similar but less elaborate rituals were carried out at midday and in the evening. The rites were depicted on temple walls in the hope that even if the priesthood failed to perform them, the service would be guaranteed for eternity.

The god's shrine

The Greek word *naos* is generally used to refer to the shrine of the god. It was a rectangular box carved from a single block of wood or stone (often basalt or granite), with wooden doors. If the god needed to leave his *naos* to travel to a particular ceremony or festival, he would be carried on the shoulders of priests in a divine boat (a model of a real Nile vessel). If he needed to travel, his barque was placed on an actual boat. Amun, for example, crossed the river at Thebes to the west bank for the Valley Festival, and Hathor travelled from her temple at Dendera to that of Horus at Edfu for the Feast of the Beautiful Meeting. Very often these barques had an *aegis* (a broad necklace surmounted with the head of the deity in question) attached to the prow and stern. The barque of Amun, for example, was adorned with the head of a ram at each end. At the temple of Edfu the sacred barque stood on a plinth in front of the *naos*, while at the temples of Luxor and Karnak the gods had their own barque shrines.

▶ *Pediu-Imenet is depicted in his Book of the Dead making an offering of incense to Osiris. The fine quality of the dead man's linen clothing is indicated by its transparency. 21st–22nd Dynasty.*

Incense and water

Rites of purification would have been among the most important of the temple rituals. These included the burning of incense and the pouring of libations of water to the gods. The ancient Egyptians burnt a variety of aromatic substances, made from herbs, spices and resins, which were particularly highly prized because they had to be imported. The incenses were brought from the Mediterranean, and also from an east African land which the Egyptians called Punt (thought to be either modern day Eritrea or Somalia). Reliefs on the walls of Hatshepsut's mortuary temple at Deir el-Bahri show balls of a sweet-scented gum resin being brought by boat from Punt to Egypt. The trees from which this resin was tapped were called *antyw*-trees, which is often translated as 'myrrh'. The most common word for incense in general was *senetjer*, which is translated as 'to make divine', emphasizing its importance in religious ritual.

▶ *The animal's legs were usually extended to fit neatly alongside the body which was stretched, treated with resin and wrapped in natron-soaked linen bandages.*

◀ *A series of vaulted mudbrick cat cemeteries has been excavated at the site of Tell Basta (Bubastis), the cult centre of the goddess Bastet. Late Period.*

Pure water was also considered sacred by the ancient Egyptians, explaining the importance of the sacred lake within the temple complex (see *Temple Architecture*). The most common type of lake was called *she netjeri* ('divine pool'). It was a rectangular, stone-lined reservoir filled by groundwater, and examples have been found at temples such as Karnak, Dendera, and Medinet Habu. The remains of ablution tanks have also been discovered in temple confines, such as in the first court (now ruined) at Abydos; and near to chapels, such as the T-shaped pools close to the chapels in the workmen's village at Tell el-Amarna. Water drawn from the lake was used in the temple both for purification and as offering.

▶ *Not only might a dead animal be intricately mummified, but it might also be placed in a plastered and painted wooden coffin imitating the shape of the animal.*

Everlasting offerings

The ancient Egyptian word for 'offering', *hetep* was also their word for 'satisfaction'. The idea was that the gods and spirits of the dead were satisfied by the offerings of food and drink (and other things such as linen) that would be made to them.

The hieroglyphic sign for an offering, and an altar, was a mat (the forerunner to the more sophisticated offering table of stone) with a loaf of bread placed on it. In addition to the actual offerings that would have been placed on these tables, representations of them were carved on the stone surface – these were seen as magical substitutes for the real thing, thereby ensuring an eternal supply of symbolic sustenance for the gods.

The offerings that were depicted on the altar tables include jars of water, beer, wine and milk, trussed ducks and loaves of bread. Grooves that had been cut into the surface of the offering tables were intended to receive the libations that were poured from ceremonial vases. The most highly prized offerings made in the temples and tomb chapels consisted of the meat of oxen, the choice cut being the foreleg. It is clear that the animal itself was not sacrificed in the temple before the god, but was butchered in the temple butchery, and then the choice piece of meat was offered to the god (or the deceased person). The ritual significance of the ox's foreleg is emphasized by the fact that the oxon was also used as a symbol of royal and divine strength or power. ◆

Mummified animals

From the Late Period (c.747 BC) pilgrims to certain temples could purchase a mummified animal to offer to the gods. The animals were bred specially for this purpose, and were considered sacred. Having been dedicated to the particular deity, they were ritually buried at the cult centres, where they have been discovered literally in their millions. Subterranean chambers at Saqqara, for example, have yielded an estimated four million embalmed ibises. Today these animal mummies are scientifically studied, but as recently as the nineteenth century hundreds of tons of mummified cats were shipped from Egypt to the English port of Liverpool to be turned into fertilizer.

Temple Literature

We know that hymns, prayers, and incantations were sung, chanted or recited in the temples. These have been found inscribed on temple walls and on stone stelae erected in temple and burial complexes, as well as written on papyrus. It is most likely that they were composed and copied by the priesthood in a temple room such as the House of Life, where the most able scholars studied texts in all fields of knowledge, from funerary rituals to astronomy.

Ancient Egyptian prayers commonly took the form of a bargain made between the priest, deputizing for the king, and the god. The deal was that offerings were made to the deity in return for the granting of tangible favours or rewards, such as victory in battle or a long life.

Some ancient musical instruments have survived, together with representations of musicians. The title 'Temple Musician' is also found in texts, so hymns were presumably sung with an accompaniment, but no musical notation has survived from ancient Egypt – although we know the words we can have no idea of the kind of tunes to which they were set.

Hymns provide us with a great deal of information concerning the ancient Egyptian perception of the divine world – including the names, titles and epithets of gods and goddesses. In fact, some of the mythological details referred to in them add to our understanding of the myths themselves.

A huge number of funerary stelae have been found inscribed with a hymn to Osiris, the god of the dead and the Afterlife; many of the Nineteenth- and Twentieth-Dynasty royal tombs in the Valley of the Kings have inscribed on their walls a hymn to the sun god, known as the *Litany of Re*, which refers to the king as the son of the god.

▲ *The royal scribe Nebmertef writes on a papyrus roll under the auspices of the god Thoth, the patron deity of scribes, in the form of a baboon. New Kingdom.*

▼ *Granite statues of Senusret III from Deir el-Bahri display youthful, athletic bodies typical of royal statues, but the realistic portraiture of the aging faces is unusual.*

▶ *Offering bearers process with an array of offerings that include the foreleg of a ceremonially slaughtered ox, fish, and the spoils of desert hunting. 18th Dynasty.*

The Abusir Papyri

Of the more secular temple documents that have survived, perhaps the most informative are those known as the Abusir Papyri. These were the administrative documents of the mortuary cult of the Fifth-Dynasty king Neferirkare (c.2475–c.2455 BC), so they would have formed part of an archive housed in the funerary temple complex associated with this ruler's pyramid at Abusir, which was part of the necropolis of Memphis. The documents provide many details of the daily routine and organization of a mortuary temple, which would have continued for generations after the death of the king.

The numerous fragments that have been discovered feature lists of temple staff and their duties, including guard duties, corresponding to the regular daily and monthly rituals as well as the special arrangements for festivals. They outline the general organization of the temple workforce, and stipulate the offerings to be made. They also include inventories of the temple furnishings and cult objects, such as knives, vessels, boxes and jewellery, as well as records of the daily income and expenditure of the temple – accounts of all produce and materials arriving at the temple, their use or storage, and any financial transactions made. They record the quantity and variety of goods that poured into the temple from the royal estates and other institutions. There are also records of temple inspections, including checking for any damage to the stonework. ◆

Hymns to the king

A particularly splendid example of a collection of hymns is the cycle of six hymns sung in honour of the Twelfth-Dynasty king Senusret III (c.1874–c.1855 BC). All six hymns were written on one side of a large sheet of papyrus measuring 114cm (45in) across, discovered at the town of Kahun, which was home to those who worked on the pyramid construction and for the mortuary cult of Senusret III at el-Lahun. They were probably composed to be sung on the occasion of a royal visit, or perhaps they formed part of the service of the cult at the pyramid complex. The ruler was eulogized in poetic and – as one might expect – exaggerated, terms. He was identified with the supreme solar deity, Re:

He is Re, little are a thousand other men!

and with the ferocious lioness goddess Sekhmet:

He is Sekhmet to foes who tread on his frontier!

Scribes and Writing

Most scribes (*sesh*) were educated in schools housed in the temple complexes. They played an important role in the daily life of the temples, and their work involved the composition and copying of literary texts, as well as record-keeping on a grand scale, particularly at the larger complexes. There is a statue of an official and high priest named Bekenkhons in the Staatliche Sammlung Agyptischer Kunst in Munich that has his life story and route to success inscribed on it. He lived during the reign of the Nineteenth-Dynasty king Ramesses II (c.1279–c.1213 BC), and we learn that he spent four years at a school in the temple of Mut at Karnak before spending 11 years as an apprentice scribe in the royal stables. He went on to become a priest of Amun at Karnak for four years, finally achieving the exalted position of High Priest.

► *The 'block statue' provided a useful surface area for inscriptions. Details of Bekenkhons' life are revealed by the hieroglyphs on his statue.*

Patron deities

The patron deity of scribes was the baboon or ibis deity Thoth, who was also considered the god of wisdom. There was also a goddess associated with writing. She was called Seshat, and was depicted as a woman wearing a pantherskin dress and with a seven-pointed star and a bow on her head. She was also associated with measurement. Temple reliefs of the Old and Middle Kingdoms (c.2686–c.1650 BC) show her recording numbers of foreign captives and quantities of booty taken after battles and raids. New Kingdom (c.1550–c.1069 BC) reliefs depict her in a more peaceful environment, that of the *sed*-festival (see *Royal Jubilee Festivals*), where she is shown holding the notched palm rib that symbolized the passing of time or sometimes writing the names of the king on the leaves of the *ished* tree (see *Trees in Egyptian Mythology*).

Tools of the trade

A scribe was typically portrayed in statue form seated cross-legged on the ground, holding a papyrus roll in his left hand, stretched across his lap on his starched kilt, and writing with his right hand from right to left. Scribes wrote with a fine brush made from the stem of a rush (*Juncus maritimus*): the end was cut at a slant and the fibres split. The reed pen was not used in Egypt until it was introduced by the Greeks at the end of the third century BC. The stem of the reed (*Phragmites aegyptiaca*) was cut to a point and split in two like a quill. The scribal palette contained two cakes of ink, one of red

► *Seshat was venerated under the epithets 'She who is Foremost in the House of Books' and 'Lady of Builders'. Late Period.*

▲ *Hesire was Chief of Dentists and Physicians, but on this panel from his tomb at Saqqara he is portrayed not with the tools of his trade, but with staffs of office and a writing kit over his shoulder. 3rd Dynasty.*

(finely ground red ochre, usually from the Aswan region) and one of black (carbon, often the fine soot from cooking pots). These pigments were mixed with a solution of gum and were applied with water.

Writing had a sacred quality for the ancient Egyptians, and this is clearly indicated by their phrase for hieroglyphs: *medw netjer*, 'the god's words'. We use the word 'hieroglyphs', from the Greek words *hieros* ('sacred') and *glypho* ('carved'), because, in the Graeco-Roman Period at least, this form of writing was almost exclusively used for religious inscriptions on temple walls or public monuments. Throughout Egyptian history, hieroglyphs were used for religious and royal or monumental purposes, so they were often carved in stone, whether on temple or tomb walls, or on stelae or the sides of sarcophagi, for example. But they could also be found on other surfaces, such as wooden coffins, gold jewellery, calcite vessels and papyrus. Whatever the material or context, they were usually highly detailed and elaborate.

From as early as the First Dynasty (c.3100 BC), a method of writing cursive or simplified hieroglyphs was used by the scribes for writing more easily and speedily in ink on papyrus or *ostraca* (flakes of limestone and sherds of pottery). This cursive script is known as hieratic (from the Greek, *hieratika*, 'sacred') because it was the script used by the Egyptian priests during the Graeco-Roman Period. During the Dynastic Period, it was the script used for all administrative and literary documents up until the Twenty-sixth Dynasty (664–525 BC), when an even more cursive script was devised, known as demotic (from the Greek *demotika*, 'popular') or as *sekh shat*, ('writing for documents') to the ancient Egyptians. ◆

Papyrus

Papyrus grew in abundance in the marshes of the Faiyum and Delta regions. The inner pith of the stems was used to make fine quality, light-coloured sheets for writing.

Although the word 'papyrus' is the root of our word 'paper', papyrus sheets were made using a different method. One layer of stems was arranged side by side horizontally and a second layer was laid vertically on top. The two layers were then beaten together until the juice that was released bonded the fibres of the stems. A typical sheet measured about 25 x 40cm (10 x 16in), but many sheets could be joined together to create long rolls.

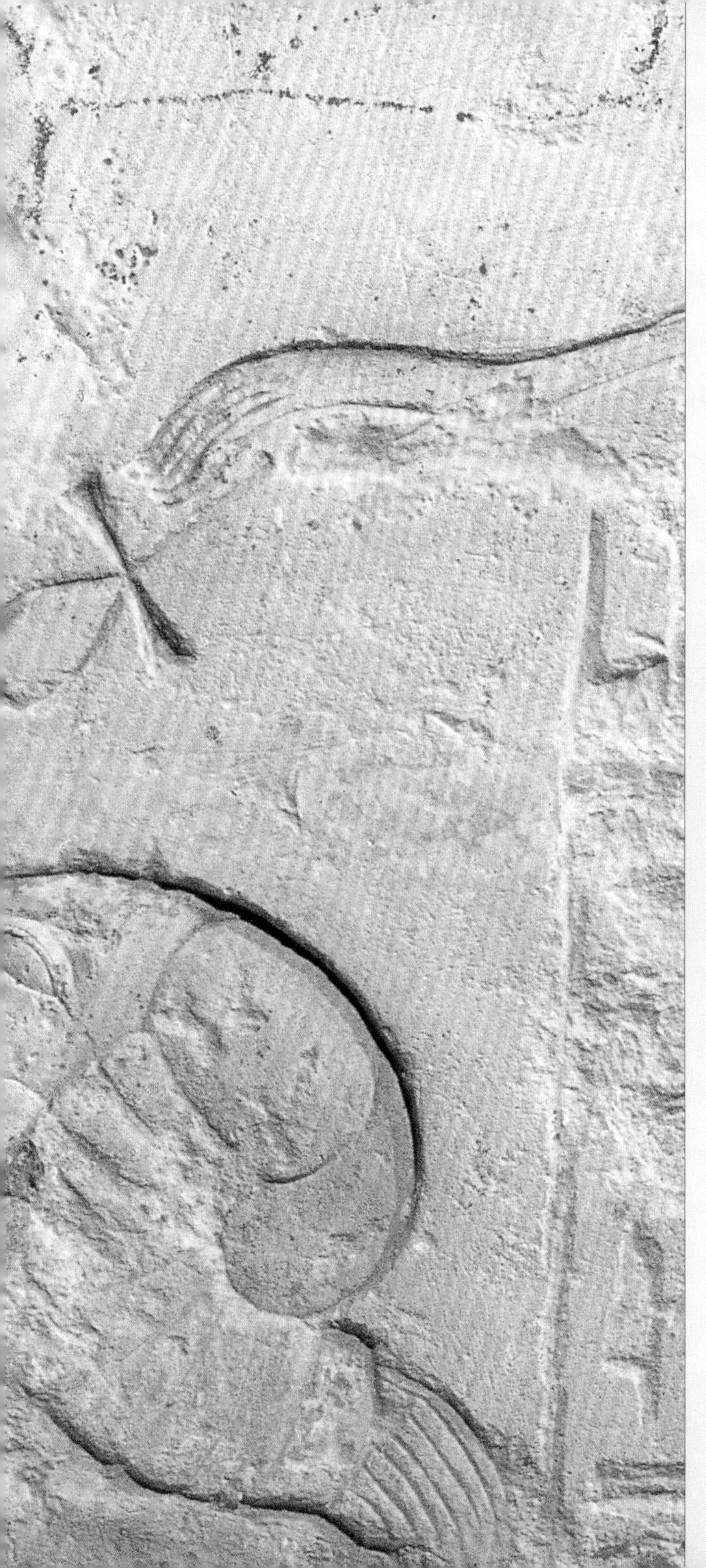

Akhenaten's Religious Revolution

Akhenaten (c.1352–c.1336 BC) was the tenth ruler of the Eighteenth Dynasty. His wife was the beautiful Queen Nefertiti. Akhenaten's reign saw enormous innovation and change. He chose to alter the state religion and mode of worship, and changed the style and content of art and temple architecture to such an extreme that his actions and beliefs have been heralded as revolutionary (he was considered heretical by later rulers).

He began his reign as Amenhotep IV – with the same name as his father, which meant 'Amun is Satisfied', but five years later he had changed his name to Akhenaten ('Beneficence of the Aten'), had extended the name of his wife to Neferneferuaten ('Fair is the beauty of the Aten'), and had founded a new capital called Akhetaten ('Horizon of the Aten'). At the centre of all this innovation and upheaval was the Aten (a manifestation of the solar deity, represented as the sun's disc) which Akhenaten elevated to the status of sole god in an attempt to eliminate the traditional pantheon. The plethora of gods and goddesses, with all the myths, festivals and rituals associated with them, were set aside for the duration of one king's reign. Or were they?

◀ *Nefertiti kisses her daughter. The art of the Amarna Period is characterized by a more intimate portrayal of the royal family than is found at any other time in ancient Egypt. 18th Dynasty.*

Akhenaten's New City

When Akhenaten began his reign, the administrative capital was Memphis and the greatest religious centre was Thebes, which was the home town of the ruling family of the Eighteenth Dynasty. Thebes was also home to the largest and wealthiest temple complex and the most powerful priesthood in the country – that of Amun at Karnak. It had benefited enormously from royal favours, vast quantities of tithes and the booty of war, especially resulting from the military campaigns of Tuthmosis III (c.1479–c.1425 BC) in Syria-Palestine. Because its might had consequently become overwhelming, it was in the interest of the status of kingship for Akhenaten to remove power from the temple of Amun and its High Priest. He achieved this by elevating a deity named the Aten to a position of supremacy and excluding from the state religion all other deities, including (and perhaps especially) Amun (see *Akhenaten's New Religion*). He also founded a new religious centre of Egypt, which became his administrative capital and the site of his royal palace.

In the fifth year of his reign, Akhenaten founded his new capital at the border between Middle and Upper Egypt, on the east bank of the Nile, about 280km (175 miles) south of Cairo. His decision to move the capital was probably politically motivated, but the site he chose was a virgin one, which meant that it had no existing religious associations. It was a wide plain approximately 10km (6 miles) long and a maximum of 5km (3 miles) wide, with perfect natural boundaries: the river lay to the west and desert cliffs formed a semicircular bay to the north, east and south (almost descending into the river at each end). Akhenaten had boundary

▶ *The ancient city of Akhetaten once stood on this desert plain on the east bank of the Nile, sheltered by a bay of cliffs.*

◀ *This vignette at the top of one of the boundary stelae at Tell el-Amarna illustrates that the Aten was worshipped in the open air in broad daylight, rather than within darkened temple sanctuaries as was the custom with other cults.*

▶ *The remains of this house in the central city exemplify the perennial problem of windswept sand in Egypt.*

stelae erected to designate the site of his city-to-be. The inscriptions on them dedicated all the buildings and their inhabitants to the Aten.

A large city, including housing of all sizes, palaces, temples, workshops, factories, bakeries and administrative buildings, was swiftly erected on the site. Many of the structures were enormous, elaborate and highly decorated, but because of the speed with which they had to be built, they were largely of mudbrick, and consequently very little has survived. The buildings were decorated using sunk relief, rather than the favoured, but incredibly time-consuming, raised relief.

The horizon of the Aten

Akhenaten called this city, with its columned halls, lush gardens, painted pavements and open courts, Akhetaten, 'The Horizon of the Aten'. Today the site is known as Tell el-Amarna, a name fabricated by nineteenth-century European visitors to the area. It is a misnomer because the site is not on a *tell* (Arabic for 'mound') created by successive building, as is usually the case with ancient settlement sites. Not only was Akhetaten built on virgin soil, but when the city was abandoned not long after Akhenaten's death it was never again built on or inhabited. The name Tell el-Amarna was probably derived from the names of the modern village of et-Till (and possibly the village of el-Amariya), and an Arab tribe called the Beni Amran, which had settled and given its name to the district and a town on the west bank that belonged to it. The name Amarna has come to be used to refer to this particular period of Egyptian history.

Estimates of the ancient city's population range between 20,000 and 50,000, but it is usually said to have been about 30,000. (It has been worked out that the agricultural land at the city's disposal could have supported a population of 45,000.) As well as the city itself, archaeology at the site has revealed a walled village in the desert, about 1.2km (3/4 mile) east of the main city, today known as the Workmen's Village. Further east still there is a collection of drystone housing, as yet unexcavated, called the Stone Village.

Akhenaten was not to know that his new capital would be abandoned after his death, and so provisions were made for the burial of the royal family and high officials in the desert cliffs surrounding the city. Two sets of rock-cut tombs, one to the north and one to the south, have been discovered, as has the royal tomb complex a short distance to the east of the desert cliffs. Most of the tombs were never finished. ◆

Excavating the site

Archaeologists have been working at the site of Tell el-Amarna pretty much systematically and continuously for the last century. The first significant excavations of the city were carried out by Sir William Matthew Flinders Petrie during the 1891/92 season. In 1911 a German team went on to gain the concession at the site for four seasons, under the direction of Ludwig Borchardt. The concession was regained by the British Egypt Exploration Society in 1921, and its excavations continued until 1936 (under the direction of Eric Peet, Leonard Woolley, Henri Frankfort and, lastly, John Pendlebury). In the 1960s the Egyptian Antiquities Organization carried out some work. But the most accurate and scientific archaeological excavation of the site and analysis of the material has been carried out on behalf of the Egypt Exploration Society by Barry Kemp and his colleagues since 1977.

Akhenaten's New Religion

▲ *In exchange for the offerings made by the royal family, the hands at the ends of the Aten's rays hold* ankhs *to the noses of the king and queen on this sculpted block from the Great Palace at Tell el-Amarna.*

▲ *High officials were usually represented as proud and upright in Egyptian art, but during the Amarna Period they were shown bowing before the king. 18th Dynasty. Tomb of Ramose, Thebes.*

The imagery and inscriptions of Akhenaten's reign reveal that he elevated one god to the unique position of sole deity, and instituted measures to eliminate all other deities. The emphasis on the importance of the sun god was not new, but his sole worship was unprecedented. Later in his reign, Akhenaten sent agents throughout Egypt to destroy the cult statues of other deities and excise their names (even that of Amun in his father's cartouche). By dispensing with the representations of a multitude of deities as weird and wonderful combinations of humans and animals, and with the myths associated with them, Akhenaten seems to have been attempting the creation of a purer and simpler religious doctrine, void of mysticism.

There was nothing innovative about the expression of devotion to the sun god, but Akhenaten took the age-old solar worship to an extreme never before experienced in Egypt. The sun, in the divine personification of Re, had been associated with kingship from at least as early as the Fourth Dynasty (c.2500 BC), when the king first took the epithet 'Son of Re' (see *Was the King Really Divine?*).

The Aten

Akhenaten chose to worship the simplest manifestation of the sun – the disc of the sun itself – the Aten. The Aten was not new; in fact, one of the best-known pieces of Egyptian literature, the Twelfth-Dynasty *Tale of Sinuhe* (c.1900 BC), tells us that when Amenemhat I died he ascended to join the Aten in the heavens. The popularity of the Aten had been growing since the beginning of the New Kingdom: Tuthmosis I (c.1504–c.1492 BC), for example, had taken the title, 'Horus-Re who comes from the Aten', and Amenhotep III (c.1390–c.1352 BC) had named his royal boat 'Glorious is the Aten'. There was certainly a temple to the Aten at Karnak by the reign of Amenhotep III.

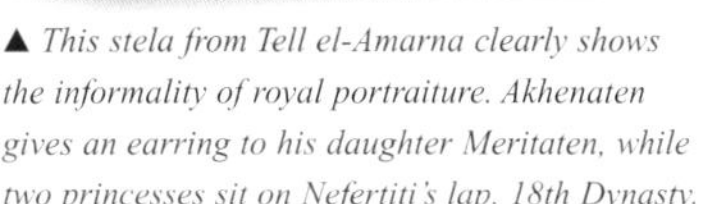

▲ *This stela from Tell el-Amarna clearly shows the informality of royal portraiture. Akhenaten gives an earring to his daughter Meritaten, while two princesses sit on Nefertiti's lap. 18th Dynasty.*

▶ *This colossal sandstone statue of Akhenaten from the site of the Gempaaten temple at Karnak shows the unorthodox representation of the king (a style that was more exaggerated at the beginning of his reign). 18th Dynasty.*

The Aten had come to be represented as the solar deity Re-Horakhty – a hawk-headed man with a sun disc on his head – but early in his reign, Akhenaten put an end to this, and the Aten was to be represented purely as a sun disc. However, the disc did have some of the attributes of the deities that had been rejected. Its rays ended in hands, some of which held *ankhs* (the sign of life). Like the king, the disc wore a *uraeus* (a rearing cobra ready to spit venom at the king or god's enemies), had its names written in cartouches, and a pharaonic titulary. In fact it could be said that the focus of Akhenaten's new religion was really the royal family, whose divine status he stressed. In art, the Aten was depicted holding out *ankhs* only to the mouths and nostrils of immediate members of the royal family. It appears that only the royal family was believed to benefit from the life-giving powers of the sun, and only they might worship the sun directly. Families throughout the city of Akhetaten had household shrines, not with a stela or figurine depicting one of the traditional deities, or one of their ancestors, as we might expect, but a stela or figure of the king and/or his wife and children. They, in turn, were shown interacting with the Aten. The focus of these shrine images was quite clearly the royal family, and there is no expression of an individual's direct relationship with the god.

▲ *The two princesses sitting at the feet of their mother Nefertiti in this wall painting display the extended skull characteristic of Amarna-period portraiture.*

Bizarre bodies

Akhenaten claimed to 'live on *maat*' ('truth', 'order', 'justice') as previously only the gods had been said to. He also chose to have himself (and members of his family) depicted in a decidedly unconventional and distinctive character – with full lips, snake eyes, a long neck, pendulous breasts, a paunch, spindly limbs and swollen hips, buttocks and thighs – a far cry from the strong athletic bodies of the traditional depictions of kings. We do not know why Akhenaten chose to have himself represented in this way, but it may have been an attempt to conjure up a divine persona for himself.

His reign also saw the construction of temples of a new design. We must forget the characteristic style of Egyptian temples – the dark inner sanctuary and cult statue – and must imagine instead large open courts with innumerable altars, so that the Aten was very much worshipped in the open air. The shadowy mystery of the traditional temple had gone. Temples dedicated to the traditional deities were closed down throughout Egypt, and as the temple would have been the centre of the local economy it can be assumed that this heavy-handed policy would have resulted in a certain amount of social unrest and hardship.

King of the Afterlife

Because Akhenaten had done away with the traditional funerary deities, and the myths associated with them, the concept of the Afterlife had to be cast aside (at least at an official level). With Osiris abandoned, Akhenaten claimed to be the ruler not only of the living, but also of the dead. The funerary rites previously deemed necessary for entrance into the Afterlife no longer applied, and the rock-cut desert tombs at Amarna for the administrative elite were very differently decorated to those at Thebes. The private individual was no longer the protagonist in his own tomb. There were no more scenes of funerary rituals, or the Afterlife, or of daily life in the Nile Valley, or of the tomb owner in the presence of the deities. Now Akhenaten and his family were the centre of attention in every tomb, in scenes illustrating their daily activities, and the tomb owner himself was depicted tiny and humble before the king.

Realistically there is no way that Akhenaten could have obliterated the religious beliefs and superstitions of his people. Despite the dogma issued by the government, and the public displays of devotion to the royal family and acknowledgement of the supremacy of the Aten, in private the people of Egypt must have continued to worship the traditional deities, particularly the household gods and goddesses to whom they felt able to relate directly. In fact many amulets, stelae, rings, pendants and other objects representing the traditional deities of Egypt have been found at Tell el-Amarna dating from this period. How could a pregnant woman forget Taweret, for example, when this goddess might be able to help her through a difficult birth? ◆

Thutmose the sculptor

The prize possession of the Egyptian museum collection in Berlin is a painted limestone bust of Queen Nefertiti wearing a tall blue crown (48cm [19in] high), which was found at Akhetaten. It is the work of a sculptor called Thutmose and was found in his studio, close to his house in a part of the south suburb of the city where other sculptors lived and had their workshops.

The Restoration of Traditional Religion

There is archaeological evidence for the increasing importance of the Aten, and interesting changes in artistic style, during the reign of Akhenaten's predecessor Amenhotep III (c.1390– c.1352 BC) – whether or not the two shared a co-regency is still disputed. But it is Akhenaten (c.1352–1336 BC) who was – and still is – regarded as the innovator, if not revolutionary. Soon after his death he was branded a heretic and his ideas and style were quashed.

On Akhenaten's death, he was succeeded by an ephemeral ruler named Smenkhkare (c.1338–c.1336 BC) who, it has been argued, might actually have been Nefertiti, and who was probably sole ruler for only a few months. Smenkhkare's successor probably grew up at Akhetaten, and began his life as Tutankhaten ('Living Image of the Aten'). He was, of course, Tutankhamun (c.1336–c.1327 BC), whose name means 'Living Image of Amun'. He must have changed his name to distance himself from the Atenist cult and the heretical practices of Akhenaten, who was quite possibly his father (his mother being a minor wife, Kiya). Tutankhamun had married one of Akhenaten's daughters by Nefertiti, Ankhsenpaaten, who in turn changed her name to Ankhsenamun.

▲ *Gold necklaces were bestowed as rewards by the king on his loyal entourage. Here Horemheb receives such a gift in his post as Tutankhamun's Commander of the Army and King's Deputy.*

Tutankhamun's reign witnessed the reinstallation of the traditional religion of Egypt. Akhetaten was abandoned and Memphis once again became the administrative capital of Egypt, with Thebes as the main religious centre. Tutankhamun issued a decree regarding the return to polytheism; his reforms have been found inscribed on a stela at Karnak temple. This is known as the Restoration Stela and is now in the Cairo Museum.

It was not until the reign of Horemheb (c.1323–c.1295 BC), who had been the Great Commander of the army under Akhenaten but became the last ruler of the Eighteenth Dynasty, that Egypt experienced a violent backlash to the Amarna Period. The eradication of Akhetaten began, and the cartouches and images of Akhenaten and Nefertiti were defaced. The aim was to remove all traces of the cult of the Aten, to the extent that Akhenaten's name was missed out of later New Kingdom lists of kings (together with those of Smenkhkare, and even Tutankhamun and Ay, his successor). When Akhenaten's name did come up, he was referred to as 'the heretic' or 'the rebel').

Ironically, the demolished stone blocks, or *talata* (from the Arabic 'three hand-breadths', describing their dimensions) from Akhenaten's temples did survive. They were used as rubble infill in the walls and pylons of later temples dedicated to traditional deities, such as Horemheb's ninth and tenth pylons at the temple of Amun at Karnak. ◆

◀ *Tutankhamun and his wife are depicted seated beneath the rays of the Aten on the back of this gold-plated and inlaid wooden throne. 18th Dynasty.*

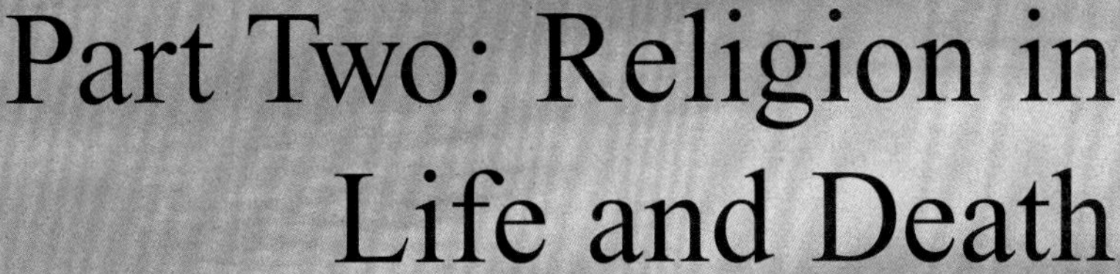

Part Two: Religion in Life and Death

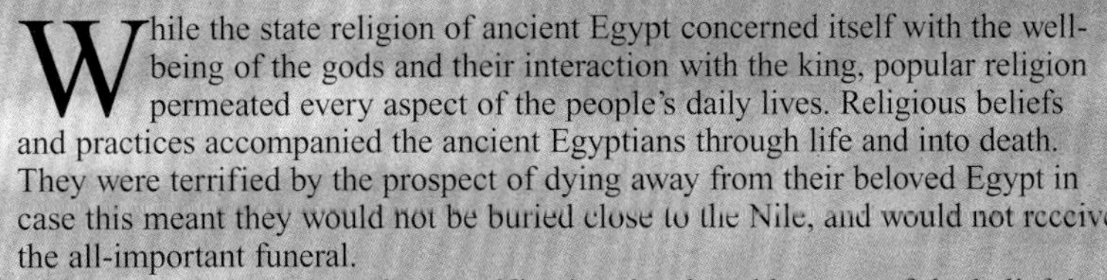

While the state religion of ancient Egypt concerned itself with the well-being of the gods and their interaction with the king, popular religion permeated every aspect of the people's daily lives. Religious beliefs and practices accompanied the ancient Egyptians through life and into death. They were terrified by the prospect of dying away from their beloved Egypt in case this meant they would not be buried close to the Nile, and would not receive the all-important funeral.

The intriguing process of mummification developed because of the belief that the survival of the body was necessary in order to be reborn into the Afterlife. Many other beliefs concerning spiritual life after death influenced Egyptian funeral rites. Mummified bodies have been found in a wide variety of tombs, with elaborate funerary equipment.

The importance of religion in day-to-day existence sheds light on many details of Egyptian life, and evidence remains of all manner of popular beliefs and rituals, as well as moral values and social etiquette.

Modern myths have also developed about ancient Egypt. Is there really a Curse of Tutankhamun? And can one gain immortality by sleeping in the burial chamber of the Great Pyramid? Such legends underline our ongoing fascination with ancient Egypt.

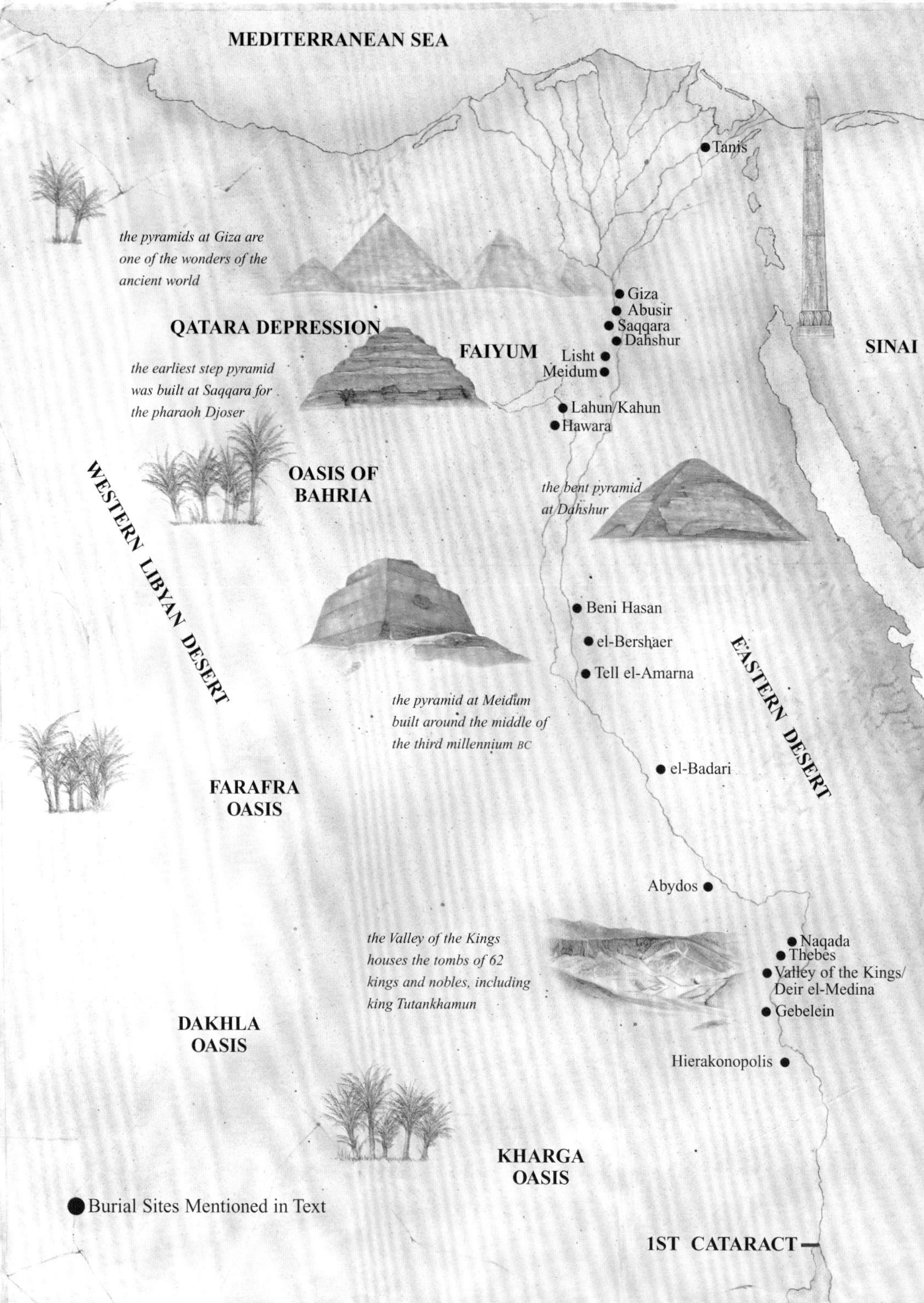
MEDITERRANEAN SEA
Tanis
the pyramids at Giza are one of the wonders of the ancient world
Giza
Abusir
Saqqara
Dahshur
QATARA DEPRESSION
FAIYUM
Lisht
Meidum
SINAI
the earliest step pyramid was built at Saqqara for the pharaoh Djoser
Lahun/Kahun
Hawara
WESTERN LIBYAN DESERT
OASIS OF BAHRIA
the bent pyramid at Dahshur
Beni Hasan
el-Bershaer
Tell el-Amarna
EASTERN DESERT
the pyramid at Meidum built around the middle of the third millennium BC
el-Badari
FARAFRA OASIS
Abydos
the Valley of the Kings houses the tombs of 62 kings and nobles, including king Tutankhamun
Naqada
Thebes
Valley of the Kings/ Deir el-Medina
Gebelein
DAKHLA OASIS
Hierakonopolis
KHARGA OASIS
Burial Sites Mentioned in Text
1ST CATARACT

Burial Sites

The pyramids of Egypt are one of the seven wonders of the ancient world. Each was built as a mortuary – the eternal resting place of a monarch. Such magnificent monuments stand testament to the unwavering belief of the ancient peoples in a life after death. Later kings were buried below ground in tombs no less grand, which were cut into the surface of rock faces. These mortuaries, like the pyramids, housed precious treasures as well as everyday items that would help the monarch assume his rightful role in the Afterlife.

Yet only the very wealthy could afford grand funerals, and mummification did not exist for the masses. For the ordinary people, a burial alongside the Nile river would ensure that they obtained a place in the Afterlife. Here they would assume a more prosperous and bountiful lifestyle than that which they held on earth.

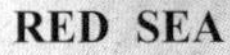

PALESTINE

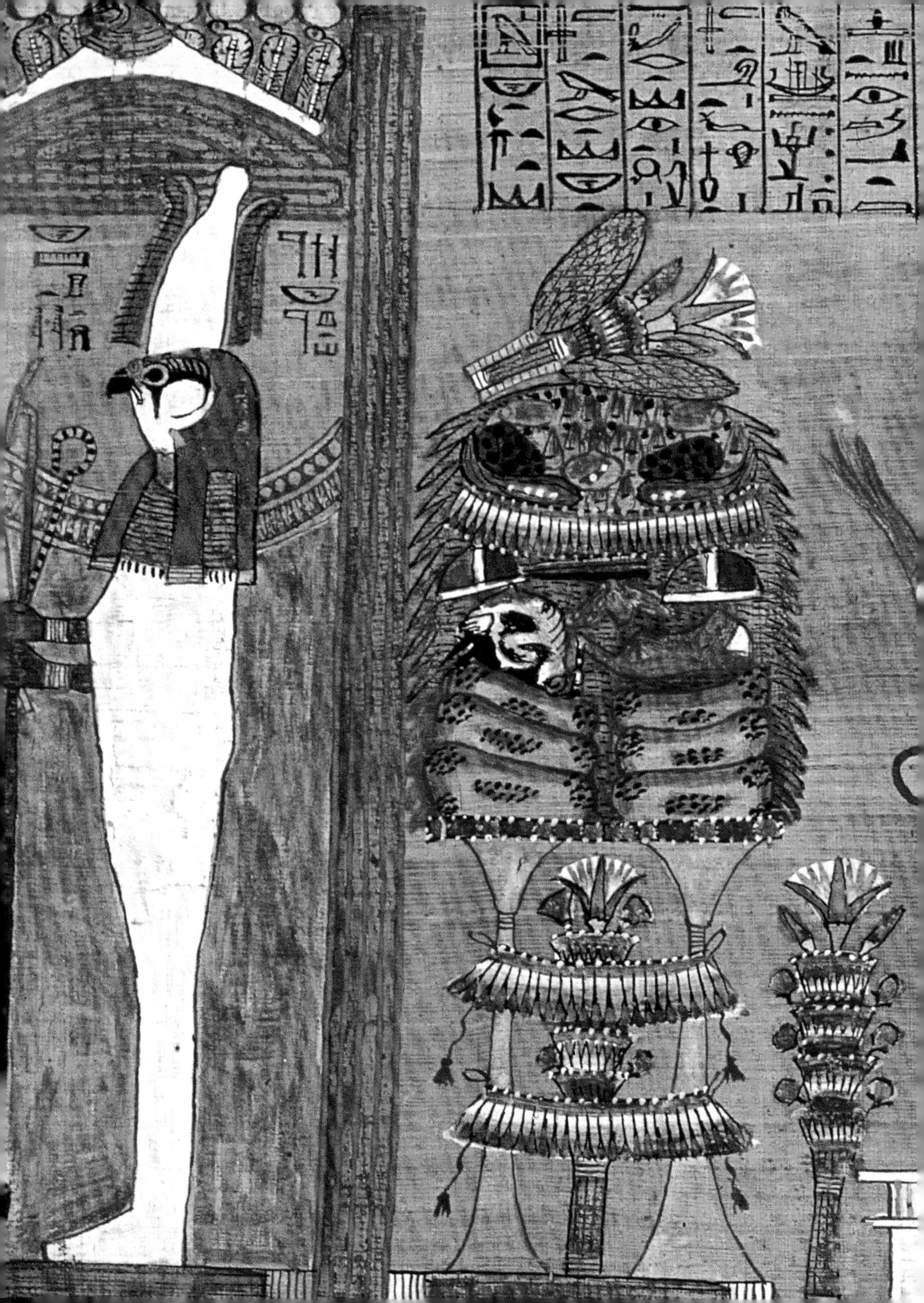

Funerary Religion

The ancient Egyptians clearly believed in an Afterlife long before the advent of writing and a formalized state religion. Burials dating from the Predynastic Period (c.5500–c.3100 BC) contain a range of objects of daily use, such as storage jars, flint knives, ivory combs and slate palettes. Their presence suggests the belief that such 'funerary equipment' was required for the Afterlife.

These excavated burials reveal that the bodies were buried in shallow oval graves at the edge of the desert. The hot dry sand rapidly absorbed moisture, so that bacteria could not breed and cause decay. The body in the British Museum, London, now known as 'Ginger', was buried in the sand at Gebelein in c.3200 BC, and survived intact for more than 5,000 years.

With the emergence of a social élite demanding grander burials, bodies began to be buried in coffins and underground chambers lined with wood, mudbrick or even stone, and they quickly began to rot. Mummification was developed and continued in use until the rise of Christianity in the early fourth century AD. But an elaborate burial was a luxury – although a belief in the Afterlife was no doubt universal, the people of Egypt were equipped for it to varying degrees.

◄ *From the New Kingdom (c.1550–c.1069 BC) it was customary for wealthy Egyptians to include a papyrus roll inscribed with spells and vignettes from the Book of the Dead in their tombs.*

Beliefs About the Afterlife

The preparations that accompanied burials from as early as Predynastic times (c.5500–c.3100 BC) reveal that the ancient Egyptians must have had beliefs about the existence of an Afterlife from very early on. These ideas were certainly formed well before the emergence of Pharaonic Egypt as we know it; that is, before the country was unified into an influential state with a sole ruler and an efficient, centralized government. Pre-dating any evidence for social stratification and the existence of a wealthy minority, there is evidence for burials involving the deposit of funerary goods in the grave alongside the body.

These items were not elaborate or specially crafted ceremonial artefacts, but basic objects of daily life, such as pots, tools and weapons. Presumably the people buried with these things believed that they would need them in a practical way after death. After all, a simple pot is unlikely to have been a token of sentiment or a prized possession; its presence in a tomb must have been considered functional.

▲ *In a land of extreme heat and vast desert expanses, a pool and the cool shade of a date palm were heavenly. By depicting them on the wall of his tomb, Pashedu hoped to enjoy their benefits in the Afterlife. 19th Dynasty. Thebes.*

▼ *An Egyptian lady would have been buried with a selection of objects intended to ensure that she would be able to eat, adorn herself with jewellery, cosmetics and perfumed unguents, and perform rituals in the Afterlife. New Kingdom.*

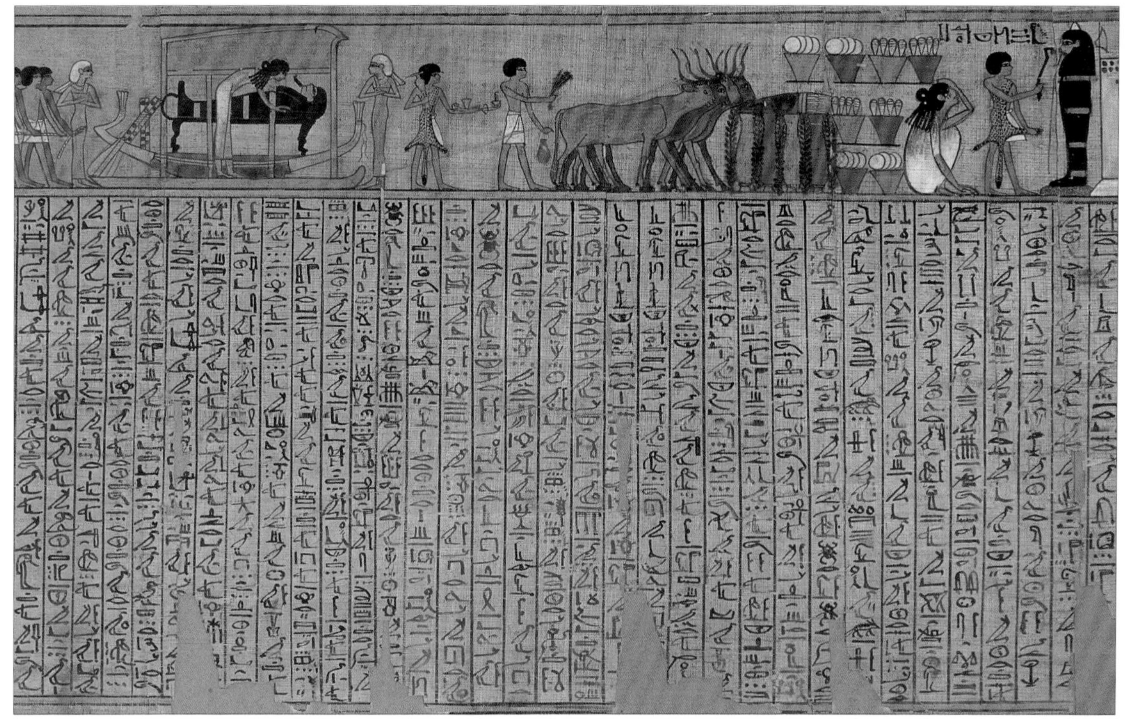

Journeying into the Afterlife

The predynastic custom of burying dead bodies in the foetal position may suggest a belief in the concept of rebirth. Also, the accidental or deliberate unearthing of perfectly preserved bodies may have led the early Egyptians to believe that the dead were living on in some way. The emergence of the practice of mummification early in the Dynastic Period reveals the strongly held belief that the body was required to be intact for the Afterlife.

We can have no idea of what the ancient Egyptians imagined the Afterlife to be until they were able to write down a description of it. The funerary texts that were buried with the dead tell us that they ascended to the Afterlife and that it was located in the heavens – the realm of the sun. Several methods of ascent appear to have been possible. These included riding on the back of a falcon, goose or other bird; being wafted upwards with burning incense; climbing up a ladder formed by the outstretched arms of the gods; or travelling on a reed float or barque that was sailed, rowed or towed. The journey into the Afterlife was no mean feat – all manner of demons and other hazardous obstacles had to be bypassed and overcome. The funerary texts provided guidelines and directions for the routes to be taken, and certain spells and recitations to be uttered at the appropriate time.

Domains of the dead

The ancient Egyptians imagined the Afterlife as a perfect version of life as they knew it in the Nile Valley, with a constant superabundance of produce. The vignettes on papyrus that accompany the text in the Book of the Dead, and the scenes painted on the walls of non-royal tombs, also provide us with a picture of the Afterlife. They tend to show the tomb owner and his wife toiling in the fields, which they did not for one moment expect actually to do (or at least they hoped not to). They certainly would have taken precautions to safeguard against the possibility of any hard work (see *Shabtis*).

▲ *The Book of the Dead includes illustrations of the final procession of the mummified body to the tomb and the last rites before burial, such as the Opening of the Mouth ceremony. The chain of events is depicted here on the papyrus of the high official Nebqed. New Kingdom.*

Egyptian paradise

The Egyptian paradise was called the Field of *Hetep* ('satisfaction' or 'offerings') – the land of Osiris, the god of the dead. The Coffin Texts (spells 464–468) and Chapter 110 of the Book of the Dead describe this land. It was associated with the western horizon (the place of the setting sun) and was imagined as a luscious place. Its fields were irrigated by channels full of water; its crops of emmer wheat, barley and flax grew tall and strong; its fruit trees were heavy with their loads of ripe dates and figs.

▶ *Sennedjem is depicted standing at the gate of the other world. A similar illustration was used to represent the vertical tomb shaft that separated the tomb chapel from the subterranean burial chamber below. 19th Dynasty. Thebes.*

The iconography of the ancient Egyptian religious belief system was strongly influenced by an underlying concept of duality – the importance of opposite but interdependent entities. The two horizons occurred frequently in both the solar and funerary aspects of the religion. Coupled with the Field of *Hetep*, which was associated with the western horizon, was the Field of *Iaru* ('reeds'), a place of purification that was associated with the eastern horizon, the site of the purification and 'rebirth' of the sun each dawn. Two other names that crop up in the funerary texts are '*Duat*' and '*Imhet*'. They were identified as separate locations in the sky: *Duat* referred to the eastern horizon, and *Imhet* to the western one. These terms might best be translated as 'Afterworld'. They are often rendered as 'Underworld' or 'Netherworld', but these translations can be misleading because the deceased appears to have ascended to them. Another name that came to be used as a general term for the Afterworld was *Rosetau* (literally, 'passage of dragging'). It originally referred to the sloping entranceway of a tomb; it was later used as the name for the necropolis of Memphis, and afterwards of Abydos.

Coming closer to the gods

The ancient Egyptians used strong visual images to illustrate, and even animate, their beliefs. The Afterworld was divinely personified as Aker. This was an earth divinity represented as a narrow tract of land with a human or lion head at each end, or sometimes in the form of two lions seated back to back, one facing east and one west (sometimes with the symbol for the horizon between them). These two creatures were thought to guard the entrance and exit to the Afterworld.

There is also evidence that the ancient Egyptians had a concept of an 'undersky' (*Nenet*) and an underworld where demons lived upside-down. As a result, because their mouths were where their anuses should have been, they had to eat their own faeces. Luckily, spells existed to avoid having to face what this place had to offer.

By dying and passing into the Afterlife, an individual was thought to become closer to the gods, and perhaps even influence the divine world. There is evidence to show that the dead were believed to possess supernatural powers that could solve various problems for the living. However, as well as proving helpful, the dead could cause serious disturbances for the living. The unsettled dead were often blamed for causing all kinds of distress, including illness. ◆

Ka, *Ba* and *Akh*

There are three important words which crop up repeatedly in the ancient Egyptian funerary texts, and which are variously translated as 'spirit' and 'soul'. It is probably best to leave them untranslated, because it is very difficult to be sure exactly what these terms meant to the ancient Egyptians, and a word such as 'soul' has connotations that would have been unfamiliar to them.

The hieroglyph used to write *ka* was a pair of arms, but in art the *ka* was represented as an individual's slightly smaller double. For example, in the 'divine birth' scenes on the walls of Hatshepsut's mortuary temple at Deir el-Bahri, two small and identical figures are depicted on a potter's wheel. These are the Eighteenth-Dynasty ruler Hatshepsut (c.1473–c.1458 BC) and her *ka* being created by the ram-headed creator god Khnum.

The *ka* was thought to come into being at the birth of an individual. Dying was sometimes described as 'joining one's *ka*'. The *ka* was intimately linked with the physical body, which was regarded as the vessel for the *ka* after death. This explains the belief in the need for the survival of the body, and the measures taken to preserve it whenever possible. *Ka* is often translated as 'spirit' or 'vital force', as in the creative life force of an individual that enabled the generations to continue through the ages. It was believed that the *ka* required food and drink, so offerings were made to it for as long as possible after death. In fact the word *ka* sometimes means 'sustenance', depending on the context.

▼ *The* ba*-bird not only represented the concept of the 'soul', but also anonymous gods or powers, and as such was present on the walls of New Kingdom royal tombs.*

The hieroglyph used to write *ba* was a Jabiru stork, while in funerary art it was represented as a bird with a human head, and sometimes with human arms. The ancient Egyptian idea of the *ba* appears to have been similar to our concept of personality, that is the non-physical attributes that make any human being unique. It is possible that it also implied the moral essence of a person's motivation and movement. It was considered more mobile than the *ka* and it enabled the dead person to move about in the Afterlife. The ancient Egyptian word for 'ram' was also *ba*, and it was probably for this reason that the ram-headed deity Khnum was regarded as the *ba* of Re, the sun god.

The hieroglyph used to write *akh* was a crested ibis, although it was often portrayed as a *shabti*-like mummiform figure (see *Shabtis*). It may well have been considered the result of the successful reunion at death of the *ba* and the *ka*, and it is sometimes translated as 'transfigured spirit'. Those who failed to achieve this transfiguration were condemned to eternal death.

Together with the *ka, ba,* and *akh*, two other important elements of a person's being, in both life and death, were their name and their shadow. It was believed vital to ensure that these two elements were remembered and protected after death in order that the deceased should survive in the Afterlife.

▲ *Funerary statues were seen as images of the* ka *of the dead, and might incorporate the* ka *symbol on their head, as in the case of this statue of Awibre Hor.*

▼ *The crested ibis symbolizing the* akh *is distinguished by its characteristic ruff of head feathers. 19th Dynasty. Luxor.*

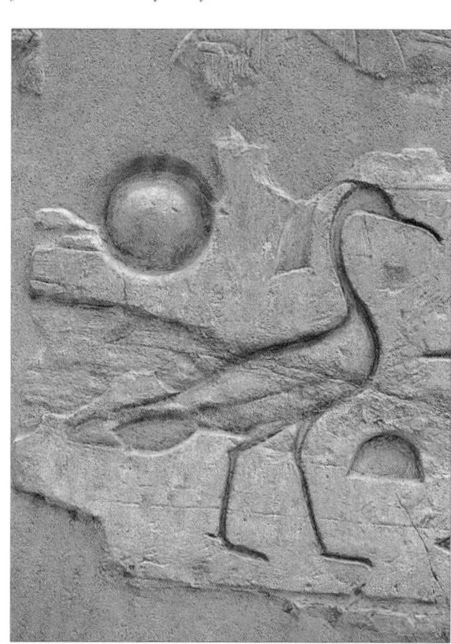

The Weighing of the Heart

The ancient Egyptians believed that, when they died, they would be judged on their behaviour during their lifetime before they could be granted a place in the Afterlife. This judgment ceremony was called the Weighing of the Heart, and was recorded in Chapter 125 of the funerary text known as the Book of the Dead. For this reason it is most commonly recorded and illustrated on papyrus.

The ceremony was believed to take place before Osiris, the chief god of the dead and the Afterlife, and a tribunal of 42 deities. Standing before the tribunal, the deceased was asked to name each of the divine judges and swear that he or she had not committed any of a long list of possible offences, ranging from raising the voice to stealing. This was the 'negative confession'. If found innocent, the deceased was declared 'true of voice' and was allowed to proceed into the Afterlife. The proceedings were recorded by Thoth, the scribe of the gods, and the deity of wisdom and the scribal profession. He was often depicted with an ibis head, writing on a roll of papyrus. His other animal form – the baboon – was sometimes depicted sitting on the pivot of the scales of justice.

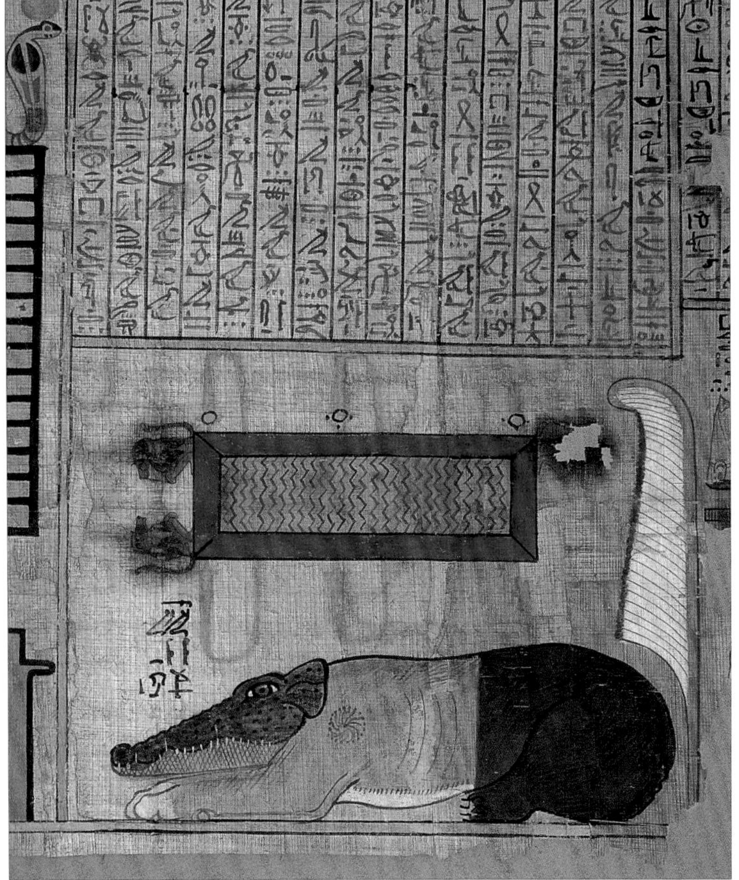

Gobbling the heart

The symbolic ritual that accompanied this trial was the weighing of the heart of the deceased on a pair of enormous scales. It was weighed against the principle of truth and justice (*maat*), represented by a feather, the symbol of the goddess of truth, order and justice, Maat. If the heart balanced against the feather then the deceased would be granted a place in the Fields of *Hetep* and *Iaru* (see *Beliefs about the Afterlife*). If it was heavy with the weight of wrongdoings, the balance would sink, and the heart would be grabbed and devoured by a terrifying beast that sat ready and waiting by the scales. This beast was Ammit ('the gobbler'), a composite animal with the head of a crocodile, the front legs and body of a lion or leopard, and the back legs of a hippopotamus.

Ensuring success

The ancient Egyptians considered the heart to be the centre of thought, memory and emotion. It was thus associated with intellect and personality and was considered the most important organ in the body. It was deemed to be essential for rebirth into the Afterlife. Unlike the other internal organs, it was never removed and embalmed separately, because its presence in the body was crucial.

If the deceased was found to have done wrong and the heart weighed down

◀ *The Book of the Dead of Nebqed includes one of the earliest depictions of the composite beast Ammit, part crocodile, part lion and part hippopotamus. 18th Dynasty.*

▲ *The Weighing of the Heart took place in the Hall of Double Maat. In this scene from the Book of the Dead of Hunefer a lotus flower grows out of a pool beneath Osiris's throne, and on it stand the Four Sons of Horus.*

the scales, he or she was not thought to enter a place of torment like hell, but to cease to exist at all. This idea would have terrified the ancient Egyptians. However, for those who could afford to include Chapter 125 of the Book of the Dead in their tombs, it was almost guaranteed that they would pass successfully into the Afterlife. This is because the ancient Egyptians believed in the magical qualities of the actual writings and illustrations in funerary texts. By depicting the heart balancing in the scales against the feather of Maat (sometimes with the aid of a little adjusting on the part of Anubis, the jackal-headed god of cemeteries and embalming), they ensured that would be the favourable outcome. The entire ceremony was, after all, symbolic.

Following the Weighing of the Heart, the organ was returned to its owner. To make quite sure that this did happen, Chapters 26–29 of the Book of the Dead were spells to ensure that the heart was returned and that it could never be removed again.

▼ *'Heart scarabs' were important protective amulets placed on the mummy to prevent the heart from bearing witness against the deceased. New Kingdom.*

Heart scarabs

Those ancient Egyptians who could afford the luxury of extensive funerary equipment took every precaution possible to ensure their survival through the judgment ceremony. A particularly useful addition to the burial would have been a large 'heart scarab' wrapped up in the bandaging (see *Funerary Amulets*). This form of protection was invented at least as early as the Thirteenth Dynasty and, according to the Book of the Dead, should be made of a specific green stone (*nemehef*), which has not been identified with certainty.

The scarab was inscribed on the underside with Chapter 30 of the Book of the Dead, a short text which was thought to prevent the heart from owning up to any crimes the person had committed in life:

> *O my heart which I had upon earth...do not speak against me concerning what I have done...*

Mummification

The ancient Egyptians mummified the dead bodies of those who could afford such an elaborate and costly procedure. It is important to remember that this was a practice followed only by the royal family and the wealthier classes of Egyptian society. The word used to describe an embalmed and wrapped body is of course 'mummy', but this is in fact a misnomer because it comes from the Arabic *mummiya,* meaning pitch or bitumen, neither of which were actually used in Egyptian mummification. However, bodies mummified during the Late Period (c.747–332 BC) were often so badly embalmed that they were blackened and brittle, and as they were found to burn well it was assumed that they had been dipped in bitumen.

The Greek writer Herodotus made a slightly erroneous account of the mummification process in c.450 BC, and two damaged papyri have survived from the first century AD outlining the final stages of the process. Unfortunately no embalmer's handbook has survived from the Pharaonic Period. Consequently, our understanding of the procedure, and how it developed, is based mainly on examination of the bodies themselves.

In the Early Dynastic Period (c.3100–c.2686 BC) dead bodies were tightly wrapped in strips of resin-soaked linen. This did not prove to be wholly successful, because although the bandages hardened in the form of the body, the body itself decayed, so during the Third Dynasty (c.2686–c.2613 BC) methods of preserving the body itself were explored. The ancient Egyptians came to realize that if they wanted the body to survive they had to dehydrate it from the inside and the outside at the same time, and that to do this effectively they had to remove the internal organs. Up until this time, the dead had been buried in a contracted foetal position, but it was found to be easier to reach the internal organs if the body was stretched out, so the dead came to be buried in this position.

The oldest surviving mummy dates to the late Fifth Dynasty (c.2400 BC), but it is known that the ancient Egyptians were removing the internal organs, and embalming and burying them separately, at least as early as the Fourth Dynasty, because the internal organs of Queen Hetepheres, the mother of the Great Pyramid builder, Khufu (c.2589–c.2566 BC), were found in a canopic chest.

▼ *The standing lion was a symbol of protection and defence, and so embalming tables such as this one painted on the wall of Sennedjem's tomb were carved in this way.*

Purifying the body

Once a successful procedure was arrived at, it appears to have been as follows.

The body was taken to a 'place of purification' (*ibu*). This would probably have been located on the west bank of the Nile, the bank associated with the setting sun and thus the place of the dead. It would need to be sited close to the river for easy access to a good water supply, and undoubtedly as far away as possible from populated sites owing to the nature of its business.

The initial washing of the naked corpse had both a ritual and a practical importance. The body was washed, as was the cult statue in a temple each morning, and as was the sun god Re in the waters of Nun each morning before

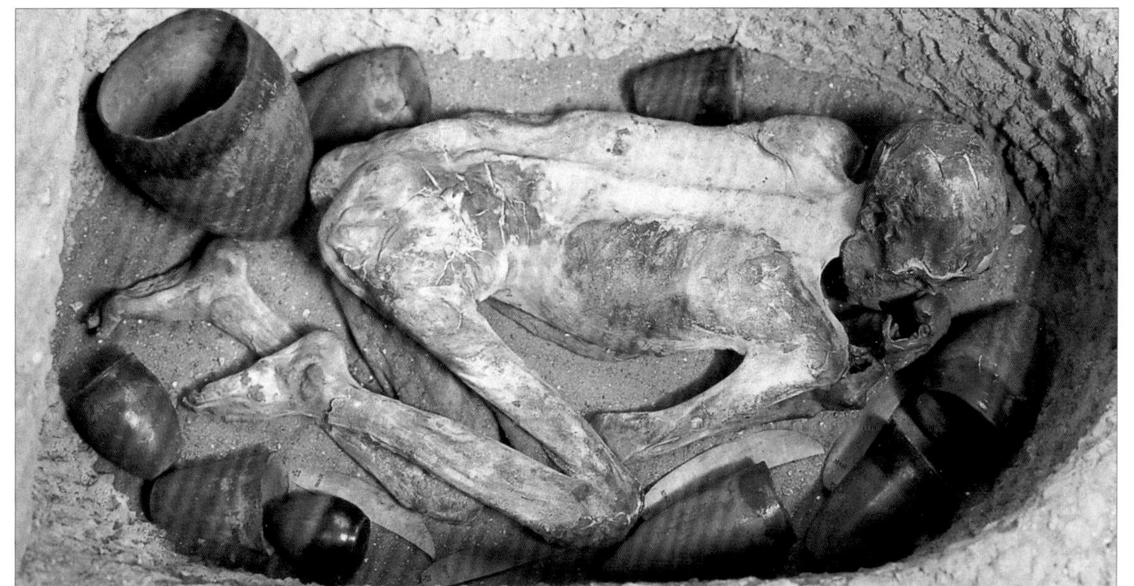

▲ *This man was not mummified but thanks to his body's direct contact with the hot, dry sand it has survived since c.3200 BC, intact but for the top of one of the forefingers.*

▲ *It is uncertain whether depictions of jackal-headed men in the funerary art represent the god Anubis himself, or priests wearing masks in order to represent the deity.*

being 'reborn' at dawn. The washing was done using a solution of natron, so it would have aided the first stage of preservation. Natron is a salt (a natural compound of sodium carbonate and bicarbonate) that the ancient Egyptians found as crystals along the edges of lakes in the Wadi Natrun, 65km (40 miles) north-west of Cairo. One of the ancient Egyptian names for natron was *neteryt* ('belonging to the god'), presumably because of its use in ritual purification. It was particularly useful in the embalming process because it is a mild antiseptic as well as being an effective dehydrating agent (it absorbs water, thus drying out the body but leaving it flexible).

Preparing the body

The purified body was then removed to the actual place of embalmment (*wabt* or *per nefer*), which was originally an enclosure containing a tent or booth. By the Late Period (c.747–c.332 BC)far more bodies were being embalmed than ever before, so for the first time permanent embalming houses were built of mudbrick. The chief embalmer was known as 'He who Controls the Mysteries' (*hery seshta*), and it is very likely that he would have worn a jackal mask during the rituals accompanying the embalming process in order to imitate the jackal-headed god of embalming, Anubis. His deputy bore the title 'God's Seal-Bearer' (*hetemu netjer*), which had originally been a title held by priests of Osiris, the god of the dead and the Afterlife. According to ancient Egyptian mythology, Osiris had been the first person to be mummified, after his death at the hands of his brother Seth.

Once in the embalming house, the body was stretched out on four wooden blocks on a wooden board (an example of which was found at Thebes). The first priority was to preserve the face, and so the head was probably coated with molten resin. From the Eighteenth Dynasty (c.1550 BC) the brain was removed and discarded, because it was considered to be merely stuffing for the head. Sawdust, resin or resin-soaked linen was pushed inside the skull to ensure that it kept its shape. The ancient Egyptians really had no idea about the function of the brain; they thought that the heart was the seat of thought and emotion in the human body.

▲ *Roman encaustic portraits were combined with the Egyptian tradition of mummification in Egypt for about 200 years from the middle of the 1st century AD. In this portrait of Artemidorus he wears a wreath of leaves and berries applied in gold leaf.*

Consequently they never deliberately removed the heart from the body because they believed its presence was crucial at all times and it played a vital part in the judgment of the deceased before he or she was able to pass into the Afterlife.

The major internal organs were removed, but they were embalmed separately and kept safely because the Egyptians believed they were necessary for the continued functioning of the body in the Afterlife. The stomach and intestines were removed through an incision in the lower abdomen (usually on the left side), then the diaphragm was punctured so that the lungs and liver could also be extracted. According to Herodotus and the Sicilian-born historian Diodorus Siculus (c.40 BC), a knife of Ethiopian stone or obsidian was used to make the incision.

Once removed, the internal organs were dried out in crystalline natron, rubbed with sweet-smelling unguents, coated in molten resin and wrapped in linen bandages in four separate packages. These packages were usually then placed in special jars that accompanied the body to the tomb (see *Canopic Jars*), but from the Twenty-first Dynasty (c.1069 BC) they were often placed back in the original positions of the internal organs inside the body. During the Ptolemaic Period (332–30 BC) they were usually placed between the corpse's legs before wrapping.

Embalming

The body, without its internal organs, was packed with temporary stuffing, and covered over with natron for forty days, after which time it would have turned a much darker colour and have become as much as 75% lighter in weight. The temporary stuffing was removed, and the corpse was rinsed out, washed down, dried to prevent mould forming and re-stuffed with wads of linen, linen soaked with resin, bags of natron crystals, sawdust and other materials to help the body keep its shape. During the Late Period (c.747–c.332) bodies were often filled completely with resin.

For both ritual and functional reasons, the body was anointed again, this time with juniper oil, beeswax, natron, spices, milk and wine. The abdominal incision was stitched up, and often covered with gold foil or wax. It was adorned with a protective 'Eye of Horus' – the *udjat* or

▼ *Networks of beads arranged over the entire body of the mummy are typical of the end of the Third Intermediate Period and Saite Era. Images such as winged pectoral scarabs and the Four Sons of Horus were often woven into them. 25th Dynasty.*

wadjat-eye (see *Funerary Amulets*). The nostrils, ears, and mouth were usually plugged with linen, wax, or sometimes onion skins or whole bulbs. Today people use onion to soak up nasty smells, and in folklore it is believed to help combat infection. In ancient Memphis, during the festival of the hawk-headed funerary deity Sokar, his devotees were accustomed to wearing strings of onions. Depending on the wealth and extravagance of the deceased's family, a piece of gold leaf might be placed over the tongue. The whole body was then coated with resin in order to toughen it and make it waterproof.

As well as the practical measures taken, at all times the emphasis was also very much on creating a pleasing appearance to the body. The soles of the feet and palms of the hands might be stained with henna; the cheeks might be rouged; and the lips and the eyebrows might be painted. Sometimes the body was dressed in clothes, sandals and a wig. The bodies of men were often painted with red ochre and that of women with yellow ochre, because these were the standard pigments used to create the skin colour of men and women in art. The bodies of wealthier people were covered in jewellery before the bandaging began. Mummies have been found, dating to the Graeco-Roman Period, with gold leaf on their faces, chests and nails.

▲ *Anthropoid coffins of the 21st Dynasty often incorporate a pair of crossed red 'braces', over an enlarged collar, in their design. Thebes.*

Bandaging the body

At last the body was ready for bandaging. This intricate process was carried out by the bandagers (*wetyw*) and took 15 days, beginning with the fingers and toes. It was accompanied by the recitation of magical spells by a Lector Priest (*hery heb*). The bandages were linen and were often made out of old clothes, towels, and so on. The most sought-after bandages would have been recycled from the cast-off garments worn by divine statues in the temples and shrines. A vast quantity of linen – up to 375sq m (450sq yd) – was used to wrap one body.

The embalmed body was enveloped in a yellow shroud before being bandaged. Each stage was painted with melted resin. Every attempt was made to ensure that the body looked as perfect as possible so if, for example, a hand was missing, an artificial hand would be inserted into the bandaging. Men were usually wrapped with their arms extended and their hands crossed over their genitals, whereas women's hands were usually placed on their thighs. From the early New Kingdom (c.1550 BC) onwards, kings were wrapped with their arms crossed over their chest, in the manner of Osiris, the god of the Afterlife.

The bandaged body was then inserted into one or more shrouds (usually dyed red), which were knotted at the top and bottom and held in place by several more bandages. An interesting feature can be found on top of the bandaging (or just below the surface) of mummies dating to the Twenty-first and Twenty-second Dynasties (c.1069–c.715 BC): two red leather straps crossed over the chest, resembling a pair of braces. A peculiarity of many of the mummies dating to the Twenty-fifth Dynasty (c.747–656 BC) and later is a shroud of blue faience beads, very like the Fifth-Dynasty bead net dress from Qau, now in the Petrie Museum of Egyptian Archaeology, London.

Finally, a mummy mask was fitted over the head and shoulders of the body. The mask was usually made of cartonnage – linen or papyrus stiffened with plaster. In the case of royalty it would have been made of gold, and the upper classes sometimes imitated the costliest of masks by having their cartonnage ones gilded. ◆

Funeral preparations

The entire, complicated process of mummification, from the arrival of the corpse at the *ibu*, lasted 70 days. This was the time permitted for the funeral preparation.

It is likely that a period of 70 days was chosen deliberately in connection with the 70 days when the dog star Sirius (divinely personified as the goddess Sopdet) could not be seen because of its alignment with the earth and the sun prior to its heliacal rising. This annual astronomical occurrence heralded the inundation of the Nile and marked the start of the ancient Egyptian New Year (*wep renpet*).

Pyramid Texts

The oldest surviving funerary texts – collections of spells or 'utterances' that accompanied a burial – are those known today as the Pyramid Texts. These were exclusively the prerogative of the king during the Old Kingdom and First Intermediate Period (c.2686–c.2055 BC). They dealt with his protection while he was still alive (particularly against dangerous animals), but were mainly concerned with his death and what was believed to happen to him afterwards. Later versions of funerary texts – known as the Coffin Texts and the Book of the Dead – were not confined to royal burials, and demonstrate the gradual democratization of funerary religion.

Written in hieroglyphs, the earliest appearance of the Pyramid Texts is as inscriptions on the inner walls of the corridors and chambers of the pyramid of Unas (c.2375– c.2345 BC), the last ruler of the Fifth Dynasty. It was built at Saqqara, one of the great cemeteries of the capital city of Memphis. A further eight pyramids of the Sixth Dynasty and early First Intermediate Period (c.2345–c.2125 BC) have been found to contain very similar inscriptions. Five of these pyramids belonged to kings, and the other three to wives of the Sixth-Dynasty ruler Pepi II (c.2278–c.2184 BC). The Pyramid Texts totalled some eight hundred spells, but no one pyramid was inscribed with all of them, the largest collection being the 675 texts found in the pyramid of Pepi II.

The funeral of the king

It has been suggested that the sequence of the spells relates to the funeral of the king, and the procession of his mummified body from the Valley Temple connected with his pyramid to his burial chamber within the pyramid. The king is identified with Osiris, the god of the dead and the Afterlife, and many of the spells in the burial chamber

◀ *By the 5th Dynasty the emphasis was no longer on enormous grandeur but on the hieroglyphic inscriptions within pyramids such as that of Teti, and the reliefs on the walls of the associated mortuary temples. Saqqara.*

would probably have been recited by the Lector Priest at the funeral. The earliest known recording of the Opening of the Mouth ceremony and early offering rituals are to be found in these texts. The purpose of many of the spells was to protect the dead king in the Afterlife. Because the language in which they are written is archaic in places, it is likely that these were in fact very ancient spells, recorded for the first time in the Old Kingdom.

The emphasis on the cult of the sun god in the texts implies that perhaps they were composed by the priests at Heliopolis, the cult centre of Re. This temple and its priesthood had had close associations with the king since at least the Fourth Dynasty. Utterance 264 is one of many spells that refer to the king's ascension to the realm of the sun. It ends:

> *The Nurse Canal is opened, the Winding Waterway is flooded, the Fields of Reeds are filled with water, so that the king is ferried over on it to that eastern side of the sky, to the place where the gods fashion him, where he is born again new and young.*

The idea was that when the king died he went to join the sun god on his journey through the sky by day and the Netherworld by night. This journey was thought to be made by boat, and it was believed that when the sun god reached

◀ *The behaviour attributed to Nut of swallowing and giving birth to the sun – depicted here in Ramesses IX's burial chamber – was ultimately an enigma, as indicated by her epithet* shetayit, *which means 'mysterious one'.*

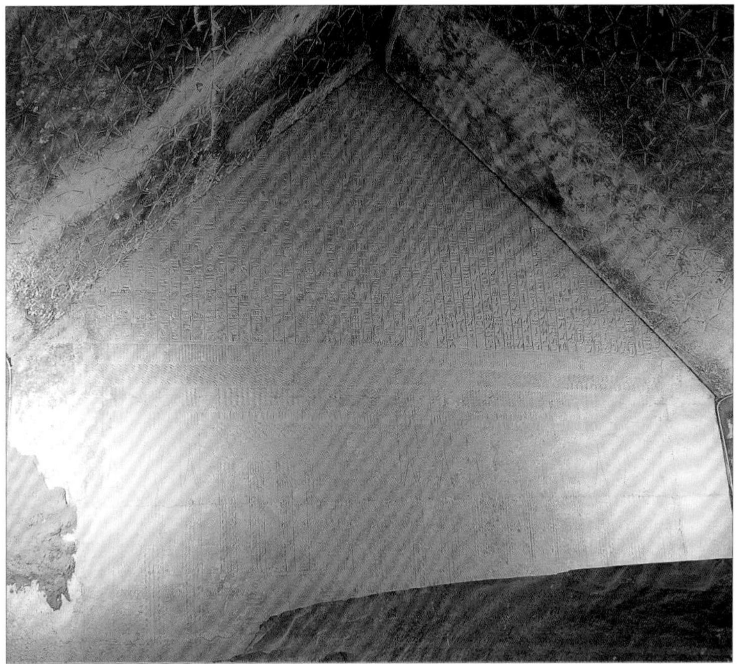

▲ *The ceiling of the burial chamber in the pyramid of Teti is a vault of stars. The Pyramid Texts are inscribed in columns of hieroglyphs on the chamber walls.*

the eastern horizon, just before dawn, he was purified in Nun, the waters of creation. The rising of the sun was identified with the dead king's rebirth.

Rebirth of the king

It has been suggested that names such as the 'Nurse Canal', 'Winding Waterway' and 'Field of Reeds' found in the Pyramid Texts refer to parts of the sky goddess Nut's anatomy. One mythological explanation as to where the sun went at night described it as being swallowed by the sky goddess in the evening, and being given birth to by her at dawn. Nut was often depicted on the ceiling of burial chambers and inside the lid of sarcophagi, displaying the idea that the dead person, like the sun, would be reborn. It may be that, in the Pyramid Texts, the idea of the dead king passing through the body of the goddess is being expressed in metaphorical terms.

The imperishable stars

The Pyramid Texts imply that the king was believed to join the circumpolar stars in the northern sky – the 'imperishable stars' that never disappear from view. In this way these early royal funerary texts equate the dead king with Osiris, the sun and the stars. They also include hymns to the gods and a long list of offerings of food, drink and clothing. These were to be made at the time of the burial and renewed after the king's death, ideally for eternity, because it was believed that they would sustain the king in the Afterlife. ◆

Fifth-Dynasty pyramids

Instead of the solid limestone blocks used for the great monuments erected during the Fourth Dynasty, the pyramids of the Fifth Dynasty were built from small, roughly-dressed stones, but the inner decoration of their burial chambers and funerary complexes was more lavish than ever before.

Coffin Texts

By the Middle Kingdom (c.2055 BC), it was not only kings and queens who were thought to benefit from having funerary texts included in their burials, but also members of the administrative élite. This fortunate minority was not buried in pyramids but in rock-cut tombs. The spells to aid their transition into the Afterlife were recorded in cursive hieroglyphs on the interior walls of their wooden coffins. This accounts for the origin of the modern term 'Coffin Texts' – although they have also been found on tomb walls, sarcophagi, statues and stelae in offering chapels.

▼ *Vignettes in the* Book of Two Ways *show that features of the waterway and landway were guarded by demons brandishing knives. This coffin belonged to Gua, Chief of Physicians. 12th Dynasty.*

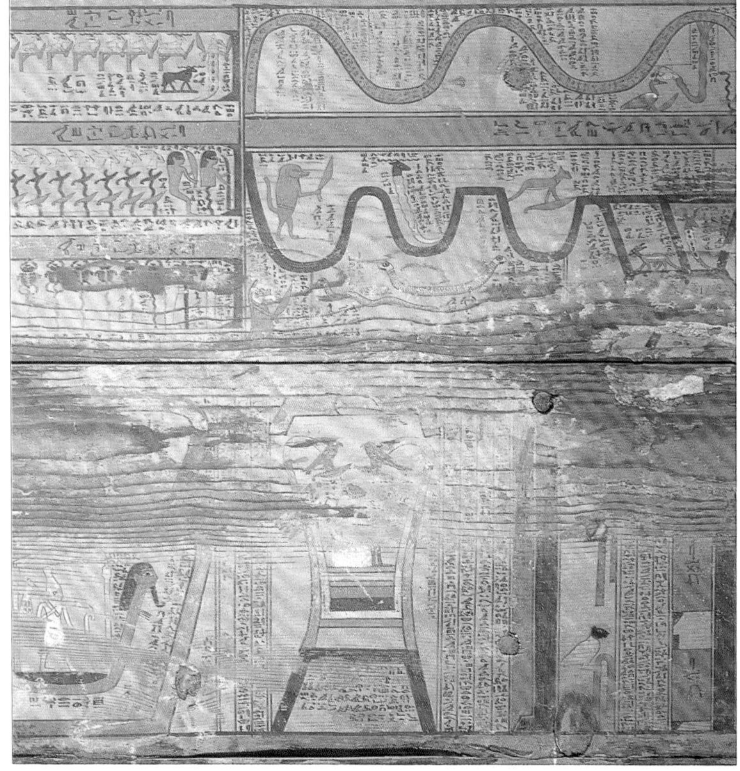

The Book of Two Ways

More than 1,000 Coffin Texts have been collected. They are derived from the body of royal funerary texts known as the Pyramid Texts, with some careful editing and important additions. The chief component of the Coffin Texts is a detailed guidebook to the Afterlife, known as the *Book of Two Ways*. It has been found drawn inside the bottoms of wooden coffins discovered at el-Bersher, the cemetery of Hermopolis Magna, and the cult centre of Thoth, the lunar deity of scribes and wisdom. The occupant of the coffin was promised an Afterlife like that of the deceased king, and the chance to travel in the sun god's solar barque. But there was a condition: he had to be able to reel off the right spells and a brief rendition of the theology of the sun god Re. At the end of the *Book of Two Ways* we find the pledge:

> *As for any person who knows this spell, he will be like Re in the east of the sky, like Osiris in the midst of Duat.*

Like the king in the Pyramid Texts, the dead person was assured that he would be reborn into the Afterlife, just as the sun rose at dawn above the eastern horizon, and he would become one not only with the sun god but also with Osiris, god of the dead. It would have been a useful *aide-mémoire* for the deceased to have the words of the spells (which he was expected to know by heart) written on the inside of his coffin.

Map of the Afterlife

There are two versions of the *Book of Two Ways*, and both are thought to have been composed at Hermopolis Magna. Both include references to the non-royal deceased becoming stars in the sky, alongside Thoth. The Coffin Texts were accompanied by the earliest known map of the Afterlife, and on it the Mansion of Thoth is located in the Place of Maat. This map was specifically designed to guide the spirit of the deceased on its journey into the Afterlife. Knowledge of the spells and possession of the map meant that the deceased might become an *akh aper* ('equipped spirit').

The map located the Mansion of Osiris and the Field of *Hetep* (the Egyptian paradise), where the deceased might continue to serve Osiris. However, as in the Pyramid Texts, the Heliopolitan influence is unmistakable because the largest part of the plan indicated the path followed by the sun god on his voyage. First it moved from east to west along a blue waterway through the inner sky, then it went back again from west to east on a black landway through the outer sky. As in the myth of *The Journey of the Sun through the Netherworld*, found on the walls of royal tombs in the Valley of the Kings dating from the New Kingdom (c.1550–c.1069 BC), the Coffin Texts described the path of the sun god (and thus the deceased) as beset by demons, often wielding knives, throw sticks, spears or nets. If trapped by a demon, it was believed that the dead person might be beheaded, hacked to pieces or burned to death. The most dangerous was the giant serpent Apophis, who threatened to devour the sun every day before dawn, and so had to be symbolically destroyed by the sun's entourage every 24 hours. The only way for the spirit of the deceased to safely pass these obstacles (and others such as mounds, rivers, and gates of fire) was by learning their names and characteristics beforehand.

▲ *Eyes painted on the coffin wall allowed the deceased to see out. Middle Kingdom.*

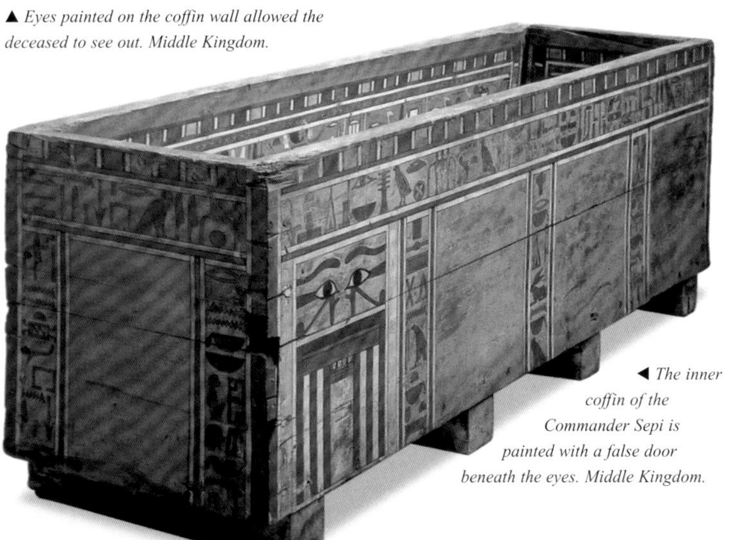

◀ *The inner coffin of the Commander Sepi is painted with a false door beneath the eyes. Middle Kingdom.*

Seeing eyes

Rectangular coffins of the Middle Kingdom were oriented in the tomb with the head to the north. Eyes were painted on the side of the coffin so that the mummy, whose face was positioned behind them, could see out. The body was therefore laid on its left side, facing east towards the rising sun.

Often the eyes were painted above a niched palace façade (*serekh*) design, or a false door, through which the spirit could pass in and out of the coffin.

The Book of the Dead

The end of the Second Intermediate Period (c.1550 BC) witnessed still further democratization of the Afterlife (see *Coffin Texts*), with the emergence of a collection of nearly 200 spells (or chapters). Today these are known as the Book of the Dead, but they were known to the ancient Egyptians as the '*Formulae for Going Forth by Day*'. These funerary texts came to accompany more people to the grave than ever did the Pyramid Texts (a purely royal prerogative) or Coffin Texts, since they were available to anyone who could afford to have them copied. The text was in fact an edited and supplemented version of the Coffin Texts (as the Coffin Texts had been of the Pyramid Texts), which continued to be included in the burials of wealthy people well into the Graeco-Roman Period (332 BC–AD 395).

Although there were 200 or so spells altogether, each burial contained only as many as the deceased or his family chose (or could afford) to have copied. They have mainly been discovered written on papyrus rolls, although certain spells have also been found recorded on coffins, amulets (such as Chapter 30A inscribed on heart scarabs – see *Funerary Amulets*), tomb walls, figurines (for example Chapter 6 on *shabtis* – see *Shabtis*) and statuary.

The papyrus rolls were often placed in the coffin alongside the body, or they might be wrapped up in the mummy bandaging or inserted into a hollowed-out statuette of Ptah-Sokar-Osiris, the Memphite funerary deity, which was then deposited in the tomb along with a range of other funerary goods. These funerary texts were usually written in hieroglyphs, but Books of the Dead in the more cursive scripts, hieratic and demotic, have also survived. The texts were usually accompanied by brightly coloured illustrations or vignettes, ranging from depictions of the amulets to be included in the mummy wrappings to detailed scenes of the Afterlife.

The form of the book

No one copy of the Book of the Dead contained all the spells that were available, although by the Late Period the sequence had become relatively fixed. Egyptologists refer to the spells as numbered 'chapters', following the system imposed in 1842 by Karl Richard Lepsius (1810–84), when he edited the text of the Book of the Dead of Iufankh from the Ptolemaic Period. This example contained 165 chapters. The most significant texts, such as that concerned with the Weighing of the Heart ceremony, were the most lavishly illustrated.

Towards the end of the Ptolemaic Period, the funerary texts grew shorter and the Book of the Dead tended to be replaced by the Book for Breathing or the Book for Outlasting Eternity. These short compositions could be written on single sheets, to be placed at the head and feet of the deceased. They still provided safeguards for his or her passage into the Afterlife, such as the requisite denial of short-comings for the deceased to present at the Weighing of the Heart ceremony.

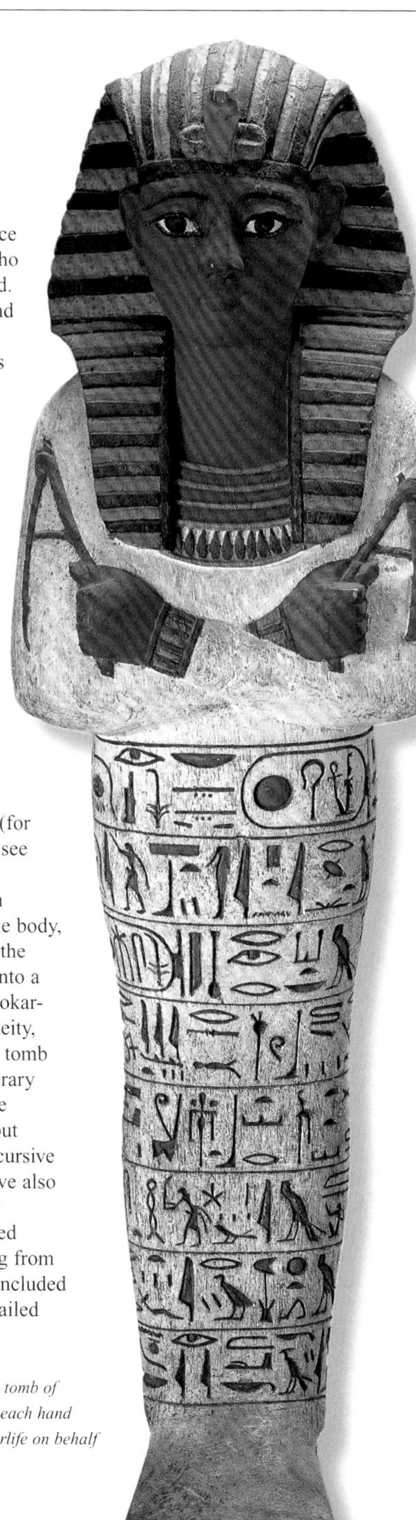

► *This painted wooden* shabti *from the tomb of Ramesses IV is equipped with a hoe in each hand ready to break up heavy soil in the Afterlife on behalf of the deceased king. 20th Dynasty.*

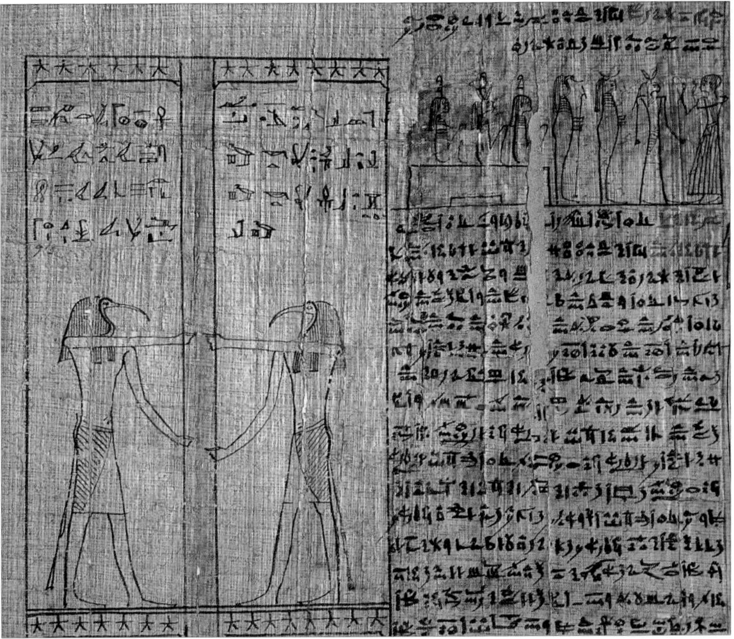

◀ *In the funerary and other religious texts, it is rare to find lines or columns of writing without illustrations alongside. Vignettes tend to accompany the spells throughout the Book of the Dead. These spells in Kahapa's Book of the Dead are written in hieratic, a cursive form of hieroglyphs. Late Period.*

Becoming Osiris

Like the Pyramid Texts of the Old Kingdom (c.2686–c.2181 BC) and the Coffin Texts of the Middle Kingdom (c.2055–c.1650 BC), the main purpose of the Book of the Dead was to provide the deceased person with a collection of spells that would ensure his or her safe passage into the Afterlife. But, unlike the earlier texts, the spells included in the Book of the Dead were dominated by the cult of Osiris, the god of the dead and the Afterlife, rather than that of the sun god Re. Dead people came to be referred to as Osiris, and identification with this god was clearly considered to be the desired goal. It was also Osiris who sat in supreme judgment over the dead, determining their fitness for acceptance into the Afterlife.

Amulets and demons

The texts and their accompanying illustrations provide information on where and when amulets or papyri were to be placed on the body during embalming. Some objects were to be wrapped up in the bandaging, others were to be only temporarily brought into contact with the body. The texts also convey an idea of how the ancient Egyptians imagined the Afterlife they hoped to enter (see *Beliefs about the Afterlife*). As recorded in the Coffin Texts, there were a whole host of threatening demons and other obstacles that stood between the deceased and his or her arrival in 'paradise'. Probably the most crucial section of the Book of the Dead was Chapter 125, which described the final judgment of the dead person before Osiris. His or her lifetime was assessed to check that he or she had behaved well enough to be reborn into the Afterlife (see *The Weighing of the Heart*). If an ancient Egyptian could afford the inclusion of only one chapter of the Book of the Dead in the burial, he or she would have been well advised to choose this one.

Wherever possible, the ancient Egyptians took as many precautions as they could to ensure the comfort of their spirits after death (and who would blame them?). Just one example of this, from an incredible variety of spells, is Chapter 162, the purpose of which was to ensure that the deceased would be kept warm in the next life.

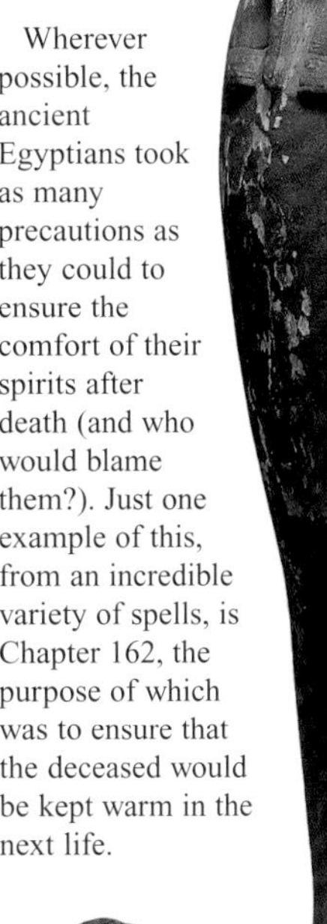

▶ *By the Middle Kingdom, Sokar had been syncretized with the gods Ptah and Osiris, and prayers were being addressed to him as a funerary deity. Here, he is accompanied by the Horus falcon. Ptolemaic Period.*

Funerary Equipment

From Predynastic times (c.5500 BC), the ancient Egyptians chose to include in their burials as much funerary equipment as they could afford. From the Dynastic Period (c.3100 BC), this equipment included the dead person's personal possessions, items made especially for the tomb, ritual objects linked specifically with the funeral and burial, funerary texts (often on papyrus rolls), figurines, statues, coffins, sarcophagi, amulets, food and drink. If the individual concerned was wealthy, as much as possible was included in his or her tomb.

A variety of goods

We know from several sources what was included in burials. First, the objects themselves have been discovered during the excavation of tombs; second, information about the goods to be buried with the dead is provided by the funerary texts; and third, scenes of funeral processions painted on the walls of non-royal tombs, especially during the New Kingdom (c.1550–c.1069 BC), include people carrying a range of goods to the burial.

▶ *Osiris boxes (or beds) were planted with grain intended to grow in the tomb. Only seven are known, but associated with them are Osiris bricks and corn mummies.*

A selection of funerary goods to accompany the deceased into the Afterlife might have included: a bed with a mattress and a headrest; a couple of chairs and stools with cushions; tables and stands (together with the wine jars to stand in them); boxes and chests; linen clothing, wigs, sandals, walking-sticks and staffs of office; draw-neck bags; stone vessels; jewellery; mirrors; fans; and boardgames. In some cases, equipment related to the dead person's profession was included. For example, a scribe might be buried with his scribal equipment; a painter with his brushes, paints and the string he used to mark out a grid with which to proportion figures; and a soldier with his weapons, shield, horse and chariot.

◀ *The circular end of the funerary cones found in New Kingdom tombs may have represented the sun as part of the solar iconography of rebirth.*

Magical paraphernalia

Much of the equipment placed in the tomb would have been objects of daily use, still familiar to us all. But there would also have been a considerable number of magical and ritual items, some of which would have been inscribed with spells or details about the deceased. From the Late Period (c.747 BC), a flat disc made of bronze or cartonnage (plaster-stiffened linen), known as a *hypocephalus*, was placed under the head of the mummy. It was inscribed with vignettes of various gods and the text of Chapter 162 of the Book of the

▲ *About 30 'reserve heads' have been found, all from private mastaba-tombs in the Memphite necropolis (mainly at Giza), and primarily from the reigns of Khufu and Khafre. 4th Dynasty.*

Dead, the purpose of which was to ensure that the deceased would be kept warm in the Afterlife.

Some New Kingdom tombs in the Theban area had as many as 300 'funerary cones' at their entrances. These were made of clay, and measured 10–15cm (4–6in) in length. Their flat circular end was usually stamped with the name, title, and sometimes a short inscription or genealogy of the tomb owner, in hieroglyphs. Although these were not necessarily found *in situ*, their tapering ends were probably set in plaster, with only their broad ends visible.

Symbols and amulets

Some types of funerary equipment have been found in tombs from a particular period of Egyptian history. During the Old Kingdom (c.2686–c.2181 BC), for example, a roughly life-sized model stone head, referred to as a 'reserve head', was placed near the entrance to the burial chamber. Its function was probably to serve as a substitute head for the deceased in the event of his or her actual one being destroyed after burial (perhaps by tomb robbers). During the New Kingdom, an Osiris-shaped box might be deposited in the burial chamber. This was filled with Nile silt and planted with grain, which was watered and was intended to sprout in the darkness of the tomb. This 'Osiris box' would have emphasized the role of Osiris as god of the dead, rebirth and vegetation, and the sprouting of the grain would have symbolized the rebirth of the deceased into the Afterlife.

Also during this period of Egyptian history, four 'magic bricks' of unbaked mud were set on the four sides of the tomb. Each brick had an amulet inserted in it: the one beside the western wall had a faience *djed*-pillar (see *Funerary Amulets*); the one by the eastern wall incorporated an unfired clay figure of the god Anubis; the one by the southern wall contained a reed with a wick, resembling a torch; and the one by the northern wall contained a mummiform *shabti*-like figure. The bricks were inscribed with sections of Chapter 151 of the Book of the Dead, which described the role they played in protecting the dead person against the evil enemies of Osiris. Their positions guarded against such an approach from any of the four cardinal directions.

Imiut

Certain objects that were placed in the tomb were closely associated with a particular deity. One example is the model of an *imiut*, discovered in the tomb of the Eighteenth-Dynasty ruler Tutankhamun (c.1336–c.1327 BC). The *imiut* was a fetish of the cult of Anubis, the jackal-headed god of embalming and cemeteries. It consisted of the headless skin of an animal (usually a feline), which was inflated or stuffed and tied to a pole in a pot.

Funerary Amulets

Amulets were positioned in specific places on the dead body, held in place by the mummy wrappings. Their function was to protect the dead person, and it appears that the greater the number included in the bandaging, the greater the degree of protection they afforded. Often, as many as several hundred amulets have been found on one body. A list of 104 funerary amulets can be found on a doorway in a complex of rooms dedicated to Osiris, in the Temple of Hathor at Dendera.

Sections of both the Coffin Texts and the Book of the Dead are concerned with instructions detailing where and when amulets or papyri should be placed on the body during the embalming process. Some of these objects were to be wrapped up in the bandaging, while others were to be brought into contact with the body temporarily to enable their magical properties to take effect. Pictures of certain amulets might also be drawn on the bandaging.

The ideal, for those who could afford it, was to have a huge variety of different amulets made of precious stones and metals. Amulets that had been worn during life incorporated in items of jewellery were often included in the burial. Of particular importance were the golden vulture collar, the scarab worn over the heart and the Eye of Horus. Chapter 157 of the Book of the Dead was the 'spell for the vulture of gold placed at the throat of the deceased'. The vulture was an incarnation of the protective mother goddess Isis, who kept her son Horus safe within her large encircling wings.

▶ *Four ancient Egyptian words are translated as 'amulet':* meket, nehet *and* sa *derive from verbs meaning 'to guard' or 'to protect', and* wedja *has the same sound as the word meaning 'wellbeing'.*

▶ *The protective Eye of Horus amulet was probably used in greater numbers on mummies than any other amulet. It is first found in the late Old Kingdom, and continued in use until the Roman Period. This glazed-composition example dates from c.600* BC.

The scarab beetle

The protective amulet for the heart was in the form of the scarab beetle, the manifestation of the creator and solar deity Khepri. It was a symbol of new life and resurrection. The scarab beetle was seen to push a ball of mud along the ground, and from this came the idea of the beetle rolling the sun across the sky. Subsequently, the young beetles were observed to hatch from their eggs inside the ball of mud, hence the idea of creation: life springing forth from primordial mud.

The heart scarab was a large scarab amulet which was wrapped in the mummy bandaging over the deceased's heart. It was made out of a range of green and dark-coloured materials, including glazed stearite, schist, feldspar, haematite and obsidian. It was inscribed with Chapter 30 of the Book of the Dead. The gist of the inscription was an instruction from the dead person to his or her heart that, when it was brought before the tribunal of the gods led by Osiris for judgment, it should not confess to any of the wrongs that the dead person might have committed during his or her lifetime (see *The Weighing of the Heart*). As a further precaution, heart-shaped amulets might also be included in the bandaging, to ensure that the heart remained at all times in the body (except during the actual Weighing of the Heart ceremony). Chapter 29B of the Book of the Dead stated that these amulets should be made of cornelian, but they have also been found made of other materials, such as glass.

The sign of the embalmer

An amulet in the shape of two fingers was placed on the left side of the mummy's pelvis, and it is possible that it symbolized the two fingers of the chief embalmer.

Amulets and the gods

The Eye of Horus (the *udjat-* or *wadjat*-eye, literally 'the eye which is whole or sound') was an amulet in the shape of an eye. It was placed over the incision usually cut in the left side of the abdomen of a dead body for the removal of the internal organs. In one version of the myth of Osiris, his son Horus offered his healed eye to his dead father, and it was such a powerful charm that it brought Osiris back to life. The myth of *The Contendings of Horus and Seth* tells us that Horus had his eyesight cured, and so his eye symbolized healing and the process of making whole. The Eye of Horus was used as a protective amulet, symbolizing in particular strength and perfection.

A whole range of other amulets were also included in burials. The detailed instructions accompanying the spells in the Book of the Dead often specified the material out of which the amulet should be made, whether or not it should be strung, and if so the type of stringing to be used. They also specified exactly where on the

◀ *The* djed-*pillar may originally have represented a stylized tree-trunk with the branches lopped off. It is first known to have been used as an amulet in the late Old Kingdom. Ptolemaic Period.*

▲ *Amulets such as the* djed*-pillar,* ankh *and heart amulet, as well as figures of deities, were included in the decoration of coffins.*

body the amulet should be placed, and at which stage of the mummification process this should be done.

The *djed*-pillar amulet was associated with Osiris, god of the dead and the Afterlife (it has been interpreted as his backbone), and was thought to symbolize stability. Chapter 155 of the Book of the Dead contains:

> *...words to be spoken over a* djed-*pillar of gold, strung upon a fibre of sycamore...and placed at the throat of the deceased on the day of burial.*

Another amulet associated with Osiris was the staircase amulet, which represented the stepped dais where his throne stood.

The *tyet*-amulet was a protective amulet associated with the goddess Isis. It was knot-shaped and may have represented the knotted girdle of the goddess, or perhaps a tampon inserted into Isis when she was pregnant. This was done so that she would not miscarry or so that her wicked brother Seth could not harm the son she was carrying. Chapter 156 of the Book of the Dead specified that the *tyet*-amulet should be made of red jasper (the colour of the blood of Isis).

Chapters 159 and 160 were to be said over a *wadj*-amulet made of green feldspar. The ancient Egyptian word for 'green' was in fact *wadj*, and this amulet was in the shape of a single stem and flower of papyrus. In a funerary context its purpose was to ensure that the deceased enjoyed eternal youth.

Models and tiny figures

Other amulets included the headrest amulet, to ensure the head of the deceased would be eternally raised up (like the sun that rose each day); the animal-headed *was*-sceptre amulet, which granted well being and prosperity; the mason's plummet amulet, which guaranteed perpetual equilibrium; and the carpenter's square amulet, which guaranteed eternal rectitude.

Amulets of small figures of deities such as the scorpion-goddess Selket and the jackal-god Anubis, were also included for protection. Tiny models of parts of the body seem to have endowed the deceased with their properties – such as action, movement or use of the senses – and could act as substitutes if the real parts went missing. Models of animals were also considered of magical use for granting the deceased the particular characteristics associated with them: for example, the virility of a bull or ram, the speed of a hare or the fertility of a cow, cat or frog. More enigmatically, a serpent's head made out of a red material was believed to ensure cool refreshment for the throat.

Shabtis

From the Middle Kingdom (c.2055 BC), the ancient Egyptians were buried with small human statuettes known as *shabti*-figures, an incredible number of which have come to light over the years. They were usually mummiform, and were made out of faience, stone, wood, pottery, bronze, wax or glass. They were inscribed with Chapter 6 of the Book of the Dead. This was a spell to ensure that the *shabti*, and not the deceased, would end up doing any hard work that he or she might be called upon to do in the Afterlife:

O shabti, *if the deceased is called upon to do any of the work required there in the necropolis at any time…you shall say, 'Here I am. I will do it.'*

By the Late Period (c.747 BC), the term *shabti* (and the variant *shawabti*) had been largely replaced by the word *ushabti*, meaning 'answerer'. Now the emphasis in the spell was very much on the role of the figure to answer instead of the dead person when his or her name was called. The hard toil anticipated was that of food production – the funerary text specifies the preparation of the land ready for cultivation, the irrigation of the fields, and the clearing of sand from east to west. To ensure the efficiency of these figurines, during the early New Kingdom (c.1550 BC), they were sometimes equipped with a model hoe and basket, and later on they were modelled holding these tools.

By the New Kingdom a person might be buried with as many as 365 *shabtis* – one for every day of the year – accompanied by a further 36 'overseers'. From the Third Intermediate Period (c.1069 BC), these 'overseer figures' were sometimes equipped with whips to make absolutely sure that the workers performed their tasks quickly and satisfactorily. The growing numbers of *shabtis* made it necessary for them to be stored in special *shabti*-boxes.

▼ *One type of* shabti-*box had a vaulted lid and raised ends. During the 19th Dynasty a multiple form appeared with a dividing partition.*

▶ *During the Ramesside and Third Intermediate Periods the overseer* (reis) shabtis, *who were sometimes referred to as 'chiefs of ten', were represented in living form, as in this faience figure from Memphis, while their workforce were represented as mummiform. 22nd Dynasty.*

Canopic Jars

Canopic jars were the containers used to hold the internal organs that were removed from the body before mummification and embalmed separately. During the Old Kingdom (c.2686–c.2181 BC), when mummification was in its infancy, the jars that served this purpose were stone vessels with flat lids. It was not until the First Intermediate Period (c.2181–c.2055 BC) that the four jars each acquired a human-headed

▲ *By the New Kingdom (c.1550–c.1069 BC) the Four Sons of Horus had become members of the group known as the 'seven blessed ones' who were said to guard Osiris's coffin in the northern sky. They are shown here on the wall of Queen Nefertari's tomb in west Thebes. 19th Dynasty.*

◀ *The use of stone and ceramic canopic jars seems to have come to an end around the beginning of the Ptolemaic Period (332 BC). This limestone jar belonged to Prince Hornakht (c.850–c.825 BC) of the 22nd Dynasty.*

stopper. From this time, too, the packages of viscera placed inside them were sometimes decorated with human-faced masks. Then from the late Eighteenth Dynasty onwards, the stoppers of the jars were each shaped like the head of one of the minor funerary deities known as the 'Four Sons of Horus'. These were the baboon-headed Hapy, the human-headed Imsety, the jackal-headed Duamutef, and the falcon-headed Qebehsenuef.

The Sons of Horus

It was the job of these four deities to protect the internal organs of the deceased. These would have been removed from the body, embalmed, anointed and wrapped in linen ready to be placed in the jars for safe keeping, because the ancient Egyptians firmly believed that the deceased required his or her organs in order to be reborn into the Afterlife. Hapy guarded the lungs, Imsety the liver, Duamutef the stomach and upper intestines, and Qebehsenuef the lower intestines.

The ancient Egyptians went to such great lengths to ensure the preservation of the entire body for the Afterlife that each of the four organs, together with the Son of Horus who was its particular guardian deity, was under the further protection of four of the most important of the Egyptian goddesses, who guarded the jars themselves: Nephthys protected the jar containing the lungs, Isis the jar containing the liver, Neith the jar containing the stomach and upper

▲ *By the late Middle Kingdom (c.1650 BC), a set of canopic equipment might consist of a carved stone outer chest and a wooden inner one holding the four jars. This jar stopper belonged to the canopic equipment of Nefertari. 19th Dynasty.*

intestines, and Selket the jar containing the lower intestines. These four goddesses were also associated with the four cardinal points: north, south, east and west, respectively.

In the Pyramid Texts of the Old Kingdom, the Four Sons of Horus were described as the 'friends of the king' because they were said to assist him in his ascent into the sky. In funerary art, for example in tomb paintings and vignettes of the Book of the Dead on papyrus, the Four Sons of Horus occurred as small mummified human figures with their respective heads. They were often depicted close to Osiris, sometimes standing on an open lotus blossom. They might also be included as amulets in the burial – these took the form of small modelled figures of mummified human bodies, again with their respective heads.

Empty jars

By the late Middle Kingdom (c.1650 BC), the set of four canopic jars were commonly stored in a wooden chest which in turn was placed inside a stone outer chest. The whole ensemble was placed in a niche in the burial chamber, close to the coffin.

The ancient Egyptians upheld their longstanding funerary traditions and continued to include canopic jars in their burials, but from the Twenty-first Dynasty (c.1069 BC) the jars were no longer functioning receptacles, in that they were left empty, or were not hollowed out, so their presence in the tomb became purely symbolic. Although the internal organs were still removed for the actual embalming of the body, they were no longer entombed separately but were packaged and returned to the body for burial. The Four Sons of Horus, in the amuletic form of wax figures, were also often inserted into the body together with the packaged organs.

Canopus of Osiris

The term 'canopic jar' is actually a misnomer arrived at by early Egyptologists. They considered that the jars resembled the form in which Osiris, the god of the dead and the Afterlife, was worshipped in the Delta city of Canopus – a port on the Mediterranean coast. The city is said to have been named after the pilot of the ship belonging to the Greek hero Menelaus. According to Homer, Menelaus died on the Egyptian coast after a storm wrecked his ship on his way home after the Trojan wars.

This manifestation of Osiris as a human-headed jar with a foot and a swollen belly was referred to as the 'Canopus of Osiris'. The form has been found on some Roman coins minted at Alexandria, so it must have been a fairly well-known image during at least the Roman period of Egyptian history.

Coffins and Sarcophagi

During the Early Dynastic period, (c.3100–c.2686), if the ancient Egyptians did not bury their dead in direct contact with the sand they used baskets, large pots or square crates. This did not interfere with the age-old tradition of burying the dead in the foetal position. But with the advent of effective artificial preservation of dead bodies, the corpses had to be stretched out to facilitate the removal of the internal organs, and so wooden coffins became full-length and rectangular in shape. By the end of the Old Kingdom (c.2181 BC), food offerings were often painted on the inside of the coffin, in order to provide symbolic sustenance for the *ka* of the deceased (see *Tomb Scenes and Models*). Two eyes were painted or carved on one of the longer sides of the coffin at the head end so that the deceased might magically be able to look out through them. This followed from the ancient Egyptian belief that the dead had their faculties returned to them at the 'Opening of the Mouth' ceremonies (see *Funerals*). The coffin was positioned in the tomb so that the eyes faced east – the place of the living and the rising Sun. These eyes were *udjat*-eyes (or Eyes of Horus), so they symbolized completeness, well being, strength and perfection.

Decoration and design

Royalty and the wealthiest people were buried in sarcophagi of granite, basalt, limestone or calcite, some of which were carved with a design known as a *serekh*. This was a pattern of recessed panelling thought perhaps to imitate the architecture of the earliest royal palaces. The design can also be found painted on wooden coffins.

By the beginning of the Middle Kingdom (c.2055) the key features of the coffins of the higher echelons of society were the Coffin Texts and maps of the Afterlife which were painted on the interior walls and bases (see *Coffin*

◀ *The* rishi *coffin of Nubkheperre Intef was made from a hollowed-out log overlaid with gilded gesso. 17th Dynasty.*

▼ *The stone sarcophagus of King Amenhotep II, carved in the shape of a cartouche, decorated with divine figures and an eye-panel. 18th Dynasty.*

▲ *Many coffins and sarcophagi of later periods, such as that of the priest Ken-Hor (c.750 BC) were made in the shape of the* Per-nu *or Lower Egyptian shrine.*

Texts). Those who could afford it were buried in an inner rectangular coffin placed inside an outer one, both of which would have been made from well-cut planks of imported timber. Anything imported was regarded as a luxury item and thus an indicator of wealth and a symbol of status. The timber native to Egypt was decidedly more flimsy than, for example, the cedarwood that could be imported from the Lebanon. Poorer people naturally had no choice but to use the local timber, such as sycamore or tamarisk, in their burials, and it was often roughly cut with attempts made to disguise it using a coating of plaster.

The Middle Kingdom also saw the emergence of the anthropoid coffin. This appears to have been regarded as a substitute for the body itself, in case the body was destroyed at some stage after burial. Anthropoid coffins were usually made of cartonnage (layers of linen stiffened with plaster) rather than wood, but were placed inside a rectangular wooden outer coffin.

A rather beautiful type of anthropoid coffin appeared at Thebes late in the Second Intermediate Period (c.1650–c.1550 BC). The surface was covered in a pattern of feathers (hence the name *rishi,* from the Arabic word for 'feathered'). This was possibly to indicate that the body was being protected by the enveloping wings of a vulture – a manifestation of the mother goddesses Mut and Isis. Alternatively, it may have been intended to represent the *ba* – the personality or moral essence – of the deceased, which was symbolized as a bird with a human head.

The anthropoid coffins of the Eighteenth Dynasty (c.1550–c.1295 BC) displayed another new feature – the arms on the coffins were carved in high relief. They were usually depicted crossed over the chest like those of the god Osiris, and some coffins had modelled beards like Osiris. These coffins tended to be covered in depictions of deities, with bands of hieroglyphic extracts from the funerary texts. By the Ramesside Period (the Nineteenth and Twentieth Dynasties, c.1295–c.1069 BC), the fashion was to bury the dead inside a nest of anthropoid wooden coffins, which for royalty and noblemen might sit inside an outermost stone sarcophagus. Then by the Twenty-second Dynasty (c.945–c.715 BC) it became usual for the innermost of the coffins to be made of cartonnage with a wooden footboard.

The goddess Nut

Nut, the sky goddess, was closely associated with coffins and sarcophagi. From the late New Kingdom onwards this goddess was often depicted stretched out inside the lid. She was believed to swallow the sun in the evening and give birth to it at dawn. In keeping with the solar aspect of funerary religion, the deceased was believed to be reborn from her (and thus the coffin or sarcophagus) into the Afterlife.

Sarcophagi

The term 'sarcophagus' is derived from the Greek word for 'flesh-eater'. This reflects the Hellenic belief that the type of stone used to make coffins actually consumed their contents.

Tomb Scenes and Models

For the ancient Egyptians, two- and three-dimensional representation and the written word were charged with magical potency, especially within the context of the tomb and temple or chapel. They believed that by depicting something they might magically animate it and make it happen, at least in symbolic terms. But the ancient Egyptians were also a rational and realistic people. They knew that family, friends and passers-by (or the priesthoods of funerary cults if they were particularly important members of society), would eventually give up leaving food offerings at the tombs or associated funerary chapels, so they took further precautions to provide magical substitutes for the actual food supplies. Tomb reliefs, paintings and models representing agriculture and food production served to ensure an adequate and eternal supply of food and drink for the *ka* of the deceased in the Afterlife. The images were expected to work their magic in conjunction with the '*hetep-di-nesw* ('an offering which the king gives') formula'. This was a prayer inscribed on funerary furniture such as coffins, stelae and the false doors in tombs which served as a link between the worlds of the living and the dead. It asked for the king to placate the funerary deity Osiris or Anubis with gifts on behalf of the deceased, and then for offerings such as bread, beer and linen to be made to the *ka* of the dead person. During the First Intermediate Period and Middle Kingdom (c.2181–c.1650 BC), 'soul houses' were often included in the burials of less wealthy people. These were pottery houses (often quite crudely modelled), with courtyards covered in models of food offerings.

▼ *'Soul houses' (symbolic homes for the* kas *of the dead) were placed beside the mouths of shaft-burials. Middle Kingdom.*

▲ *The hieroglyphs beneath Nebamun's raised arm in this fragment of wall painting from his tomb describe him as 'taking recreation and seeing what is good in the place of eternity'. 18th Dynasty.*

Scenes of daily activity, agriculture and food production occurred on the walls of non-royal tombs throughout Egyptian history. Painted limestone figurines of servants brewing beer, grinding corn and so on, have been found in burials dating to the late Old Kingdom (c.2686–c.2181 BC). Of particular note, because of their superb craftsmanship and the incredible number that have survived, are the wooden tomb models of the Middle Kingdom (c.2055 – c.1650 BC). The most famous of these models were discovered in the tomb of the Eleventh-Dynasty chancellor Meketre (c.2000 BC) at Deir el-Bahri. They are now in the Cairo Museum and include absolutely exquisite models of a weavers' and a carpenters' workshop, a butcher, a bakery, boats, a cattle count, and two models of Meketre's house and garden with trees and a pool.

Imagining the Afterlife

The people who were able to afford the extreme luxury of a decorated tomb were highly unlikely ever to have actually toiled on the land. But in a funerary context they were depicted ploughing the land, sowing seeds and reaping the harvest. The emphasis was clearly on the fundamental principle of the importance of an individual's relationship with, and acknowledgement of, his dependence on the fertile silt of the Nile Valley. To ensure that the deceased would not really have to perform these tasks in the Afterlife, they included *shabti*-figures in their burials to do the work for them.

The hope appears to have been that the Afterlife was like this life, but free from worry and hard work. Paintings and reliefs portrayed the tomb owner and his wife, family and friends enjoying themselves at parties and various leisure activities, such as hunting hippopotami or waterfowl. Such scenes were laden with symbolism, particularly connected with fertility and the suppression of evil or chaos. Symbols of sexuality and fertility (the two being considered far more interconnected by the ancient Egyptians than by us today) such as ducks, monkeys, cats, heavy wigs, almost transparent clothing, and vegetation crop up in the scenes. The ancient Egyptian terms for some of the activities portrayed are also worth considering in this context, for the verb 'to throw a throwstick' (*qema*) is the same as that for 'to father a child' or 'to create', and the verb 'to harpoon' (*seti*) is the same as that for 'to impregnate'.

▶ *Models showed the production of food, such as this woman grinding barley, using a saddle quern and rubbing stone, to make bread and beer.*

▶ *The false door was a stone or wooden imitation doorway which first appeared in tombs of the Old Kingdom. It was usually carved with a figure of the deceased seated before an offering table. Here the dead man is Sheshi.*

Idealized portrayals

The portrayal of the tomb owner hunting birds, hippopotami and crocodiles (or wild bulls and lions in the case of kings) showed him taking part in activities that he had probably enjoyed during his lifetime and hoped to enjoy in the Afterlife. But it was also the display of the deceased as a good man who had been assessed as 'true of voice' at the divine tribunal (see *The Weighing of the Heart*), overcoming symbols of evil or chaos, as Horus had conquered Seth in *The Contendings of Horus and Seth*.

At all times, the style and content of the artistic representation was extremely idealized. The tomb owner was always shown as strong and athletic, even if he had died in extreme old age, and his wife was always young and slender despite the fact that giving birth to many children had no doubt wreaked havoc with her body. But anyone who could afford such scenes in their tombs chose to be depicted in this idealized way in the hope that this would indeed be how they might look in the Afterlife.

The Book of the Dead

From the New Kingdom (c.1550 BC) onwards, scenes from the Book of the Dead also appeared. By depicting the funerary rituals taking place it was hoped that they would happen after death. When representing the dead person's heart balancing against the feather of Maat at the Weighing of the Heart ceremony, it was believed that, magically, this would occur. It was as though portraying the deceased and his family in the Afterlife would guarantee entry into paradise.

Funerals

We know how the ancient Egyptians conducted their funerals because they depicted the proceedings on the walls of their tombs during the New Kingdom (c.1550–c.1069 BC). The most detailed portrayals of events are to be found in non-royal tombs.

The mummy passed in procession from the embalming house to the tomb, the attendant grandeur depending on the wealth and status of the individual concerned. The mummy usually lay in an open booth shaped like a shrine and bedecked with funerary bouquets. This was mounted on a boat-shaped bier which in turn sat on a sled drawn by oxen. A priest walked in front of the bier, sprinkling milk and burning incense. The canopic chest was dragged or carried behind the bier. All manner of funerary goods and food offerings were also carried in the procession, destined for burial alongside the body. One of the more enigmatic components of the procession was the *tekenu*, a human-headed sack-like object usually depicted in wall paintings and reliefs being drawn by cattle on a sled. Its significance is very uncertain but it has been suggested that this was a sack containing those parts of the body that were not actually mummified or placed in the canopic jars, but were nevertheless regarded as essential for the rebirth of the deceased into the Afterlife.

Mourning the deceased

Professional female mourners dressed in pale blue were an important presence at every funeral. They let down their hair and tore at it, bared and beat their breasts, wept, wailed and threw dirt from the ground over themselves. The two chief mourners were often identified with the goddesses Isis and Nephthys who, according to mythology, had pieced together the body of their brother Osiris (whose dead body had been hacked apart by their wicked brother Seth), mummified it, and mourned his death. Just as Osiris had been mummified in order to preserve his body and had then been reborn, it was expected that the deceased and mummified person would be reborn into the Afterlife. Dancers also accompanied the procession. These were the *muu*-dancers, who wore kilts and tall white headdresses, rather like the White

▲ *The strict conventions of Egyptian art allowed women to be depicted displaying hysterical behaviour, such as these mourners in the tomb of Ramose, but men had at all times to be portrayed as upright and in control. 18th Dynasty.*

▼ *This vignette from the Book of the Dead of Ani is one of a series of scenes illustrating the role of the* ba *after death. Here the* ba *is united with the body of the deceased.*

▲ *A number of different ritual implements were used in the Opening of the Mouth ceremony (shown here on the papyrus Book of the Dead of Hunefer). Their use was believed to restore the dead person's ability to see, breathe, eat and drink. 19th Dynasty.*

Crown of Upper Egypt. There were also priests, distinguished by their shaven heads.

The key rituals performed at the funeral were the final act of purifying the mummified body with water (probably a natron solution) and incense; the anointing of the mummy with sacred oils; and the ceremony known as the Opening of the Mouth. This was considered vital for restoring the senses to the dead person so he or she could be reborn into the Afterlife, and so the body could become the vessel for the *ka* (spirit) of the deceased. This rite was also performed on any statues of the deceased, as well as the cult statues placed in shrines and temples throughout Egypt, thereby animating the statues as vessels for the divine presence of the various deities. It was originally the eldest son's responsibility to carry out this act so that his parent could live on after death, which explains why the ancient Egyptians considered infertility such a desperate problem. However, during the New Kingdom a new priestly function developed – that of the *sem*-priest, who is depicted in the tomb paintings and vignettes from the Book of the Dead wearing a leopardskin, and performing the Opening of the Mouth ceremony. In the tomb of the Eighteenth-Dynasty king Tutankhamun (c.1336–c.1327 BC) there is a depiction on the wall of the Opening of the Mouth of the deceased pharaoh. It is being performed by his chief official, the vizier Ay, who had himself portrayed in the role of the king's heir in order to legitimize his unlawful claim to the throne. Ay did indeed succeed to the throne and ruled Egypt for about four years (c.1327–c.1323 BC).

It is known that during the New Kingdom this ceremony consisted of 75 separate acts, involving the touching of the mouth, eyes, ears, nose and other parts of the body with a variety of different ritual implements. These included a *pesesh-kaf* (a fishtail-shaped flint knife), a chisel, an adze, a *netjeri*-blade (usually made of meteoric iron), a rod ending in a snake's head, and the right leg of an ox which would have been specially butchered for the occasion.

Interring the body

All stages of the funeral were accompanied by recitation from the funerary texts (especially the Book of the Dead) by a Lector Priest (who would also have recited the spells during the embalming and mummification of the body). The gist of these utterances was the successful rebirth of the dead person and his or her continued and comfortable existence in the Afterlife. The final offerings made to the spirit of the deceased included natron, incense, eye-paint (malachite or galena), linen, food and drink, as well as the foreleg and heart of a bull.

The mummy was placed inside its coffin, often part of a nest of coffins, which was deposited in the burial chamber together with the canopic chest, food supplies for the deceased and other funerary equipment. Magic bricks (see *Funerary Equipment*) were positioned around the coffin or sarcophagus, and after these extensive and elaborate proceedings the body was left in peace as the tomb was sealed. The waste material from the embalming process was not considered pure enough to bury with the body, but it was still thought to be important to the deceased's existence in the Afterlife, so it was buried nearby.

After the burial, the family and guests sat down at portable tables set up outside the tomb to enjoy a feast of all kinds of food, wine and beer.

Tombs

The ancient Egyptian tomb, whether a pyramid or a shallow pit, was considered the eternal resting-place for the body and funerary goods, both of which were believed vital for rebirth and survival in the Afterlife.

Because towns and villages were built of mudbrick and were situated within the floodplain, very few have survived. Our understanding of ancient Egypt thus relies heavily on the information gleaned from tombs, which were built to last for eternity. Wherever possible they were built of stone or were cut into the natural rock, and they were located on the desert fringes, where they avoided the ravages of the Nile flood. In this hot, dry setting they have survived to this day, and often the painted decoration on their walls still looks fresh and vibrant.

The most splendid monuments were luxuries that only the king, his family and officials, and the wealthiest members of society could afford. Each tomb had a burial chamber, but of equal if not greater importance was the associated 'offering chapel', where it was hoped food offerings would continue to be left for the deceased to ensure a continued existence in the Afterlife. By the New Kingdom (c.1550 BC), the tombs of the pharaohs in the Valley of the Kings each had a mortuary temple as grand as any of the temples dedicated to the most eminent of Egyptian deities.

◄ *The Step Pyramid Complex of King Djoser is Egypt's earliest monumental stone structure.*

Mastabas

Important early royal tombs have been discovered at the cemetery sites of Abydos and Saqqara. These were the burials of the rulers of the First and Second Dynasties (c.3100–c.2686 BC), and those of members of their family and administration. The size and complexity of some of these tombs indicates the increased wealth, control of manpower and organization of the Early Dynastic kings and their governments. They provide us with evidence for the initial stages of building on a monumental scale, and the emergence of a distinct architectural symbolism, especially regarding funerary beliefs and kingship.

Because of their shape, these early tombs are called mastabas, from the Arabic word for 'bench'. They consisted of brick chambers (the central one being the burial chamber) in pits dug in the desert or – by the end of the Second Dynasty – excavated out of the actual bedrock. The pit was covered by a simple superstructure in the form of a plain square or rectangular enclosure, its outer wall often recessed in imitation of a palace façade. This enclosure was filled with sand and gravel, or sometimes contained storage chambers or magazines, covering an area of up to 340sq m (410sq yd).

The evidence concerning exactly which of the kings was buried at which of the two sites is a little shaky, and disagreement continues. But it is generally held today that all the kings of the First Dynasty and the last two of the Second Dynasty (Peribsen and Khasekhemwy) were laid to rest at Abydos. Their tombs were marked by pairs of free-standing stone stelae similar to gravestones, bearing the name of the king in a *serekh* design, usually surmounted by the image of the god Horus in falcon form. The other Second Dynasty rulers were buried at Saqqara, on the northern spur of the desert plateau there. This was the cemetery of the administrative capital, Memphis, and so it makes sense that the great administrators were also buried there, in a manner similar to that of the kings.

Osiris's burial place

Later in Egyptian history Abydos became the chief cult centre of Osiris, the deity most associated with the dead and the Afterlife, and according to legend it was his burial place. The early dynastic cemetery at Abydos was situated in the desert at a site now known as Umm el Qa'ab or 'Mother of Pots'. It is so-called because of the vast quantity of pots and sherds that have been found there. These are the remains of offerings made mainly during the New Kingdom (c.1550– c.1069 BC).

Funerary palaces

The subterranean chambers of these early tombs were often lined with wooden panelling – a clear indication of long-distance trade, because the ancient Egyptians had no native timber suitable for such a purpose. From the mid-First Dynasty (c.2950 BC), a stairway paved with blocks of granite led to the burial chamber, providing evidence for quarrying in the region of Aswan in the far south of Egypt. At the same time, fine quality limestone was being used in the tombs at Saqqara, quarried across the river at Tura. The threat of tomb robbers was obviously already a concern, even at this very early stage of Egyptian history, because security measures such as portcullises were already in place.

At Abydos each tomb was associated with a separate building, sometimes referred to as a funerary palace, which was situated closer to the cultivation and water supplies. It is very likely that these buildings served a purpose similar to that of the later mortuary chapels and temples. They housed the *ka* of the deceased in a statue and were the focus of the dead person's funerary cult. As such, offerings and votive material such as stelae inscribed with offering formulae (see *Tomb Scenes and Models*) were placed in them. The best-preserved of these structures belonged to the last ruler of the Second Dynasty, Khasekhemwy (c.2686 BC). It is now called Shunet ez-Zebib ('Storehouse of Raisins'), so it has obviously served a more secular function in its time. It appears to have been enormous: its outer

▲ *While the* serekh *of King Djet (shown here on a stela from his tomb at Abydos) was surmounted by the falcon Horus, the* serekh *of Peribsen was surmounted by the Seth animal, and that of Khasekhemwy by both Horus and Seth. Early Dynastic Period.*

▲ *Djoser's Step Pyramid began life as an almost square mastaba (the outline of which is still visible). This was extended to provide a superstructure for a further eleven burial shafts. A four-stepped pyramid and then a final six steps were added over this structure.*

enclosure measured 54 x 113m (177 x 370 ft) and the inner wall still stands 11m (36ft) high in places and is 5.5m (18ft) thick.

At Saqqara, by the end of the First Dynasty (c.2890 BC), the architects chose to combine the two elements of a tomb and a funerary palace in a single structure, with a mortuary chapel on the north side. This feature continued into the Third Dynasty (c.2686–c.2613 BC) on the north face of the earliest pyramid, the Step Pyramid of King Djoser (c.2667–c.2648 BC).

Both the royal tombs and the funerary palaces were surrounded by rows of simple graves. These were marked by stelae, which tell us that these dead people had been members of the royal entourage. Many were women, but there were also minor palace staff, craftsmen, court dwarfs and the king's favourite dogs. It is impossible to be absolutely certain, but it does seem that some of these retainers died just before the royal tomb was closed, raising the question of human sacrifice. In the case of the First Dynasty king Djer, as many as 580 retainers were buried around his tomb. Were these people killed to accompany and serve the king after his death? If so, this custom did not survive into the Old Kingdom (c.2686–c.2181 BC), when the royal entourage was replaced by models of servants performing tasks, and later by *shabti* figures.

Boat burials and bulls' heads

The mastabas at Saqqara have survived much better than those at Abydos, and they display some interesting features. Three of the tombs had an associated mudbrick boat burial on their north side (see *Boats in Egyptian Religion*). One of these tombs also had an estate modelled in mud-covered rubble on its north side. Another tomb had a tree plantation on its east side, the purpose of which was probably to provide cool shade for the *ba* of the deceased. A particularly fascinating feature was a raised platform with bulls' heads sitting on it, which ran around some of the mastabas. The heads were modelled out of mud but the horns were real, and it has been estimated that a tomb might be surrounded by up to three hundred of them. Throughout Egyptian history the bull was closely associated with kingship. The pharaoh was referred to as 'Mighty Bull', in the belief that he could assimilate the strength and virility of the animal.

Towards the end of the Early Dynastic Period, the mound-like superstructures of the mastabas at Saqqara were being constructed in the shape of a low stepped pyramid, and so it is possible to trace the development of the early royal tomb from the mastaba to the pyramid. By the Old Kingdom (c.2686 BC), the king was no longer buried in a mastaba, but his high officials continued to be buried in them.

▼ *A recessed outer wall like a palace façade and bulls horns on a surrounding platform have been excavated at tomb 3504 at Saqqara.*

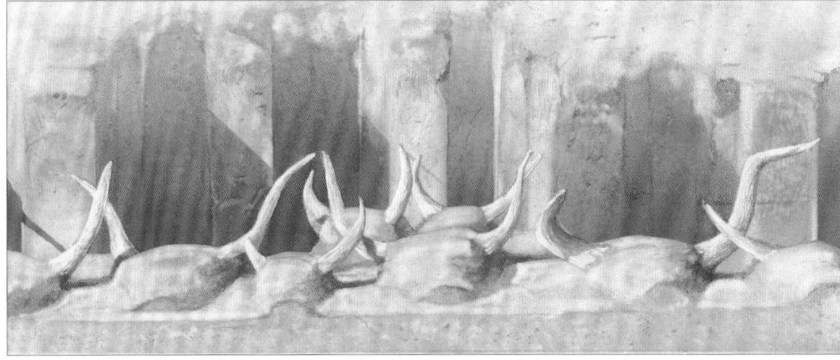

Pyramids

▲ *Djoser's Step Pyramid complex at Saqqara measures over 500 x 250m (547 x 273yd).*

The word 'pyramid' (ancient Egyptian *mer*) comes from the Greek word *pyramis* meaning 'wheat cake' (presumably because such a cake resembled a pyramid in shape). The humble origin of the name belies the sheer magnificence of many of the ancient Egyptian pyramids, some of which, many would argue, are the most stupendous structures ever built.

Djoser's Step Pyramid

The earliest pyramid was not quite the type we usually picture, but rather a large stepped structure – hence its name, the Step Pyramid. It was built at Saqqara to house the burial of the Third-Dynasty king, Djoser (c.2667–c.2648 BC), and it is the earliest known monumental stone building. The idea of a stepped superstructure for a tomb was not new, (see *Mastabas*), but much about the Step Pyramid and its surrounding complex of courts, temples and other buildings was truly innovative.

The later Pyramid Texts emphasized the ascent of the dead king to the heavens, so perhaps the concept behind the Step Pyramid was to provide a giant ladder for the king to reach his heavenly destination. It has also been suggested that the pyramid might have represented the primordial mound that was believed to have risen out of the waters of chaos at the time of creation (an image also closely associated with the solar deity). Djoser's pyramid was the masterpiece of his great vizier and architect, Imhotep. The structure developed in stages. It began as an almost square mastaba tomb; it was then extended on all four sides; next a four-stepped pyramid was added over this structure; and finally it was converted into a six-stepped pyramid. It was built out of local limestone and cased in the better quality Tura limestone from the quarries across the river. The shaft to the burial chamber beneath the pyramid was plugged with a granite boulder weighing three tons.

The architects and builders of the time were experimenters – they made use of smaller and more easily portable stone blocks than were used in the later pyramids. The columns they built were engaged rather than free-standing, and they were built up from segments of stone rather than being carved from single blocks. The builders worked the stone in a way that imitated earlier, more organic building materials. The ceiling blocks and columns in the processional way, for example, were carved to look like bundles of reeds. If the tomb itself imitated a ladder to the Afterlife, perhaps the entrance colonnade was designed to symbolize the Field of Reeds – the place of purification for both the sun and the dead king.

The Meidum Pyramid

The next great achievement in the development of tomb building was the pyramid at Meidum. This was the earliest occurrence of a stepped pyramid with the steps filled in and cased to form a smooth-sided, geometrically true pyramid. The monument may well have been begun by Huni (c.2637–c.2613 BC), the last ruler of the Third Dynasty, and it was completed by Sneferu (c.2613–c.2589 BC), the first ruler of the Fourth Dynasty. It began life as a seven-stepped pyramid, which was cased in Tura limestone. It was later enlarged to become an eight-stepped structure and the steps were cased again. Finally the steps were filled in and cased a final time. It is possible that the smooth sides of the pyramid were thought to symbolize the rays of the sun.

▶ *Today the pyramid at Meidum stands as a three-step tower rising from a mound of debris, probably the result of collapse and quarrying.*

◀ *The pyramids at Giza are one of the seven wonders of the ancient world.*

Khufu's Great Pyramid

The pyramid was an icon of the cult of the sun god Re, which increased in importance during the Fourth Dynasty (c.2613–c.2494 BC). It was the most magnificent of status symbols – an unmistakable expression of the might of kingship and the success of the particular ruler buried in it. The most enormous of these structures was the Great Pyramid of the Fourth-Dynasty king Khufu (c.2589–c.2566 BC), built on the desert plateau at Giza. Its complete height would originally have been 146m (479ft). One of its greatest architectural features and feats of engineering is the 'Grand Gallery', which leads to the burial chamber. This is 46m (150ft) long and over 8m (26ft) high, with a huge corbelled vault constructed with its roofing slabs laid at an angle steeper than the slope of the gallery, in order to prevent a build-up of pressure at any one point. Similar precautions were taken in the granite burial chamber, where five compartments were built above the flat ceiling to minimize any risk of collapse.

The sun and the stars

The construction of the pyramids shows that the ancient Egyptians were incredibly successful engineers. They were also very much concerned with the rituals and beliefs surrounding death. It is clear from the Pyramid Texts that there was a fundamental solar element to their funerary religion, but there was also an important stellar one. In the Great Pyramid, two shafts running from the burial chamber were aligned with various stars, including the constellation of Orion (divinely personified by the Egyptians as the god Sah). Orion was possibly intended as the destination of the king's *ba* when he ascended to take his place among the circumpolar stars. In this and similar ways the ancient Egyptians incorporated the stars into their religious beliefs as well as using a certain amount of astronomical observation in the building of the pyramids, especially in the precise alignment of the tomb with the four cardinal points.

It was not until the reign of King Unas (c.2375–c.2345 BC) at the end of the Fifth Dynasty that the ancient Egyptians began to inscribe funerary texts on the interior walls of their kings' pyramids (see *Pyramid Texts*). From these we can begin to get a clearer idea of how the ancient Egyptians envisaged the rebirth of the king and his survival in the Afterlife. Rulers continued to be buried in pyramids right up until the Second Intermediate Period (c.1650–c.1550 BC). After this, Thebes became the royal burial site, where tombs were cut into the desert cliffs. Meanwhile, non-royals could choose to incorporate a small mudbrick or stone model of a pyramid, known as a pyramidion, into the design of their tombs. This ties in with the notion of the democratization of funerary religion.

▼ *The 'Bent Pyramid' at Dahshur was built, together with the neighbouring 'Red Pyramid' by King Sneferu.*

Benben Stones and Obelisks

Each of the pyramids would originally have sported a gilded pyramidion (a mini-pyramid) at its pinnacle, which would have glinted strikingly in the sunlight. This feature, together with the sloping sides of the entire structure resembling the rays of the sun as they are seen to jut through the clouds, would have made the pyramid an appropriate icon of solar religion. This was also an important aspect of funerary religion, especially of the king, and especially during the Old Kingdom (c.2686–c.2181 BC).

The sun cult at Heliopolis

The heyday of the pyramid was during the Old Kingdom, a time when the cult of the sun god Re at Heliopolis rose to the forefront of Egyptian state religion, and one of the king's five names came to be introduced by the title 'Son of Re'. The prototype for the true pyramid may well have been the focal point of the cult at Heliopolis. This was a squat standing stone, pointed at its apex, known as a *benben* (from the verb *weben*, 'to rise', which also provides the origins of the ancient Egyptian word for the cap-stone or pyramidion at the top of a pyramid – a *benbenet*). This monument, the original and most sacred of the *benbens*, was erected at Heliopolis at least as early as the First Dynasty. It may well have symbolized the primordial mound that appeared out of the watery chaos of Nun, whence the sun rose for the first time and creation began. It was certainly believed to have been the first point hit by the rays of the rising sun. It is also possible that this stone symbolized the petrified semen of Atum, the creator god of Heliopolis, whose act of masturbation played a key role in the creation of the divine personifications of air and moisture, Shu and Tefnut.

During the Fifth Dynasty, the structure was imitated in sun temples, which were associated with royal pyramid burials, but were also clearly dedicated to the sun god Re. The sun temple of Niuserre

▼ The obelisks of Tuthmosis I and Hatshepsut at Karnak temple. There is a description of the quarrying and transport of two granite obelisks to Karnak on the walls of Hatshepsut's mortuary temple at Deir el-Bahri.

◀ *This obelisk from Luxor Temple was erected in the Place de la Concorde in Paris in 1836 using ropes and pulleys.*

(c.2445–c.2421 BC) at Abu Gurab, north of Abusir (part of the necropolis of the ancient capital at Memphis), was named 'Delight of Re'. It would originally have been dominated by an enormous limestone *benben*, 36m (118ft) in height. This sacred stone would have stood on a pedestal in the form of a limestone truncated pyramid, 20m (66ft) high, with red granite around the base.

▼ *If the 'unfinished obelisk' in the Aswan granite quarries had been successfully removed from the rock it would have been 42m (138ft) tall and weighed 1197 tons.*

Gold-tipped obelisks

Throughout history, the ancient Egyptians also incorporated a more tapering, needle-like version of the *benben* into the design of their tombs and temple complexes. Today we call these sacred stones obelisks. The ancient Egyptians called them *tekhen*, a word that might also relate to the verb *weben*. They too would originally have had gilded tips, which were also referred to as *benbenet*, and would have reflected the sun's rays majestically. The solar imagery was often extended to the designs carved on the obelisks, such as figures of baboons. These animals were observed to greet the rising sun with great excitement each morning, and to sit on their hind legs, their front paws raised at dawn in order to warm their undersides (hence the ancient Egyptian posture for worship and adoration). The splendour and elegance of the obelisk has continued to command respect, not only in Egypt but throughout the world, and obelisks have been removed from Egypt and re-erected in cities such as Rome, Paris, London and New York.

The *benu*

Like the Greek phoenix, the Egyptian *benu*-bird was connected with the sun and rebirth. As a sacred bird of Heliopolis, the benu was closely associated with the solar deities Re and Atum, and with the obelisk and *benben* stone.

In the Pyramid Texts, the *benu*-bird appears as a yellow wagtail, but by the advent of the Book of the Dead, it was being represented as a kind of grey heron with a long, straight beak, and a two-feathered crest.

Chapter 83 of the Book of the Dead was the 'spell for being transformed into a *benu*-bird'.

The Great Sphinx

When we speak of the Sphinx, we are referring to the earliest colossal statue in Egypt. It is 73m (240ft) long, with a maximum height of 20m (66ft), and is probably a statue of the Fourth-Dynasty king Khafre (c.2558–c.2532 BC). His head, wearing a pleated linen *nemes*-headdress and a *uraeus*, is superimposed on the body of a lion – an animal closely associated with kingship due to its great power and might. In connection with the solar iconography of the pyramid, benben stone and obelisk, the lion was also regarded as a solar symbol in ancient Near Eastern cultures.

The word 'sphinx' comes from the Greek and means 'the strangler', but this implies that the statue had a terrifying aspect, and this was not an idea shared by the ancient Egyptians. It is possible that 'sphinx' was a distortion of the Egyptian *shesep ankh*, meaning 'living image'. Vast numbers of considerably smaller sphinxes have also survived from ancient Egypt. These include not only statues of rulers in sphinx form, but also gods, such as the avenue of ram-headed sphinxes (manifestations of the god Amun) that run between Karnak and Luxor temples.

Khafre's temples

The Sphinx was carved out of a natural outcrop of the limestone rock alongside Khafre's valley temple at Giza. The valley temple was the king's funerary temple, built on a quay at the edge of the Nile Valley and linked by means of a causeway to the smaller mortuary temple adjoining the eastern face of the pyramid. It is possible that the sphinx was intended to serve as a guardian for Khafre's splendid valley temple. But there was another temple, more closely associated with the great statue, located beneath its front paws. Referred to as the Sphinx temple, it appears to have been specifically dedicated to the Sphinx. It is impossible to be certain about the architectural symbolism and functioning of this temple, because no Old Kingdom texts have survived that refer to it, and none of the Old Kingdom

▲ *The head of the Sphinx was carved from a much better building stone than the soft layers of the body, which have been severely eroded, while the base is carved from a petrified hard shoal and coral reef.*

▲ *Several New Kingdom stelae commemorating visits made to the restored Sphinx show a royal statue behind the Dream Stela.*

tombs at Giza belonged to priests or priestesses of its cult. Much about the temple remains a mystery, but it does seem that there was an important solar element to it. It has been suggested that its eastern and western sanctuaries were associated with the rising and setting sun, and that the Sphinx symbolized Khafre in the role of making offerings to the sun god in the court of the temple. However, it is also possible that the Sphinx was originally viewed as an image of the sun god himself, because this certainly appears to have been the case over 1,000 years later during the New Kingdom (c.1550– c.1069 BC), when the Sphinx came to be known as Horemakhet, or 'Horus-in-the-Horizon'.

Tuthmosis IV's dream

The Eighteenth-Dynasty king Tuthmosis IV (c.1400–c.1390 BC) was instrumental in restoring the Sphinx and reactivating its cult. He erected a granite stela, weighing 15 tons and 3.6m (12ft) high, made out of a lintel from one of the doorways of Khafre's mortuary temple, between the paws of the Sphinx. The upper part of this stela depicts the king making offerings to the Sphinx, which the hieroglyphs identify as Horus-in-the-Horizon.

It is because of its detailed inscription that the stela has come to be known as the Dream Stela. It recounts the tale of Tuthmosis as a young prince on a hunting expedition at Giza. He fell asleep under the Sphinx and, as he slept, the Sphinx, as the solar and creator deity Khepri-Re-Atum, appeared to him in a dream. He promised Tuthmosis the throne of Egypt if he would repair the giant body of the statue and clear the windswept sand that had accumulated up to its neck. Tuthmosis did just this – he restored the lion body with stone cladding and built an open-air chapel between the paws of the Sphinx, with the stela as its centrepiece.

▶ *The head of a king on the body of a lion, this bronze example depicting Tuthmosis III, was the most common type of sphinx, but sometimes they were ram-headed (criosphinxes) or hawk-headed (hierakosphinxes). 18th Dynasty.*

Boats in Egyptian Funerary Religion

◀ *Khufu's boat is 43m (142ft) long and 6m (19ft) wide; it has a maximum draft of 1.5m (5ft) and a displacement of 45 tons.*

Boat-shaped pits have been excavated alongside royal mastaba and pyramid burials of the Early Dynastic Period and Old Kingdom (c.3100–c.2181 BC), but the most impressive are those associated with the Great Pyramid of Khufu at Giza. Close to the mortuary temple and three subsidiary pyramids just to the east of the Great Pyramid, five boat-shaped pits were found that appear never to have actually housed boats, and were in fact symbolic.

However, just to the south of the pyramid, two more interesting pits were discovered. They are long, narrow and rectangular, but unlike the boat-shaped pits, they were actually intended for the burial of boats. Indeed, the disassembled parts of a real cedar-wood boat have been found in each. The boats were obviously intended to be dismantled because the pits are not large enough to have contained them when assembled. One of them has been pieced together and is on display in a specially built museum near the pyramid. Its 1,224 individual pieces were painstakingly 'stitched' together using vegetable fibre rope, and joined using mortise and tenon joints, to bring to life a breathtaking vessel measuring a magnificent 43m (142ft) long. Its prow and stern are in the form of papyrus stalks, and its design is based on that of a papyrus reed boat. The boat in the other pit has been photographed using a tiny camera inserted through a hole into the pit, but it has not yet been excavated.

Why boat pits?

Because the River Nile was the main thoroughfare through Egypt, boats were essential in Egyptian daily life. They were the only means of transport across the river, and were by far the most sensible means of travelling up and down the country. For this reason, it is not surprising that the boat should be so highly valued and that it was incorporated into the rituals of death and beliefs concerning the Afterlife.

There are several possible reasons for the occurrence of boat-shaped pits and buried boats in the vicinity of the Great Pyramid. The boatless pits must have been purely symbolic, and were presumably connected with the journeying of the king to the heavens after his death. It was believed that he needed to join the circumpolar stars in the northern sky, but he was also thought to voyage with the sun, and according to much mythology the sun god Re passed through the solar cycle

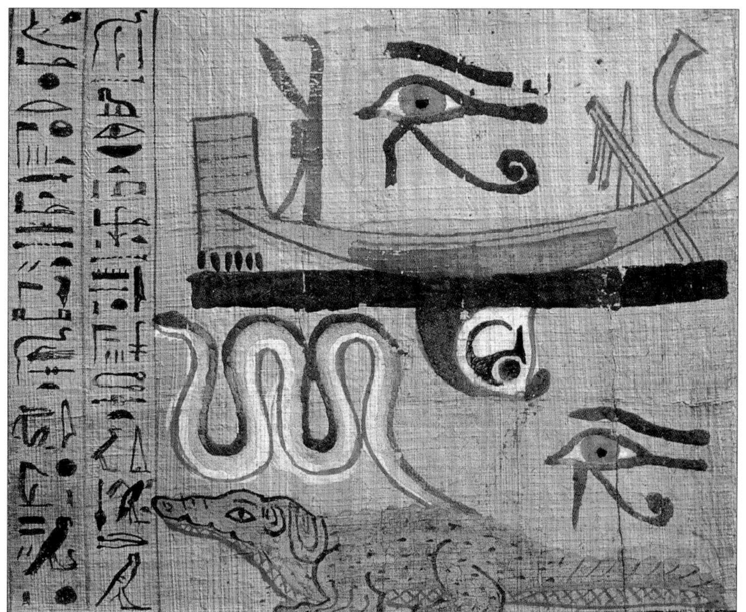

▲ *The hieroglyph for 'follower' (*shemset*) – a crook or staff with a knife and some sort of package lashed to it – is often depicted in representations of the solar barque, such as this one from the Book of the Dead of Heruben. 21st Dynasty.*

by boat. A boat pit might also have been deemed necessary to symbolize the transportation of the king's *ka* statue.

The significance of the real boats is likely to have been somewhat different. The fact that they were deliberately dismantled when they could have been buried whole, and the fact that their burials would have lain just outside the original enclosure wall of the pyramid complex, indicates that they are less likely to have had a symbolic role in the funerary complex. They were probably used in the funeral cortege of the dead king, and having performed their function, they were ritually disposed of close to the royal burial.

Model boats

Throughout Egyptian history boats were depicted on the walls of non-royal tombs, and during the Middle Kingdom (c.2055–c.1650 BC) it was popular to place wooden models of them in the tombs. Because the ancient Egyptians travelled by boat while alive, they expected to do so in the Afterlife. An actual journey that might be depicted in painted or model form was the transport of the dead body from the realm of the living on the east bank to that of the dead on the west bank. A symbolic journey that might also have been represented was the pilgrimage made by the deceased to the cult centre and legendary burial place of Osiris at Abydos.

▲ *A boat pit to the south of the mortuary temple on the east face of Djedefre's pyramid at Abu Roash, recalls the one just outside the entrance to Khufu's temple alongside the Great Pyramid.*

◀ *Relying on oars and the current, this boat would have been heading north against the wind.*

Rock-cut Tombs

Throughout Egyptian history, tombs were cut into the desert rock. Both mastabas and pyramids often had subterranean burial chambers excavated into the rock, but the term 'rock-cut tomb' tends to be used to describe a tomb that has been cut into the desert cliffs, with no superstructure, but very often with a separate funerary chapel or temple.

The best-known rock-cut tombs in Egypt are those located in the area known as the Valley of the Kings, on the west bank of the Nile at Thebes (modern Luxor). It is home to undoubtedly the most famous of the tombs, that of the Eighteenth-Dynasty king Tutankhamun (c.1336–c.1327 BC), which was discovered by the British archaeologist Howard Carter in 1922. The world continues to marvel at the treasure it yielded. Tutankhamun was actually a relatively minor ruler of the New Kingdom (c.1550–c.1069 BC) but, together with the Twenty-first and Twenty-second Dynasty burials excavated at Tanis by the French archaeologist Pierre Montet in 1939, his tomb was by far the best preserved of any royal tomb.

Contrary to popular belief, Tutankhamun's tomb was not intact on discovery – it had been entered, partly robbed, and resealed in antiquity – but the quality and quantity of the funerary equipment found in it were quite stupendous. Many of the objects are made of gold, lapis lazuli, turquoise, amethyst and other precious materials. They include wonderful examples of ancient Egyptian craftsmanship, such as Tutankhamun's mummy mask, coffins, jewellery and shrines, which are now on display in the Egyptian Museum, Cairo.

Despite the richness of its contents, Tutankhamun's tomb was far less grand than others in the Valley of the Kings. It consisted of only four small rooms rather than the usual long corridor-style

▲ *There are 62 tombs in the Valley of the Kings, the most famous being that of the young king Tutankhamun.*

▼ *This was the view of the antechamber of Tutankhamun's tomb that greeted Howard Carter when he first looked into it in 1922.*

tomb, and as such was probably originally intended as a private burial place (perhaps that of his vizier Ay). On Tutankhamun's death, this tomb may have been hastily enlarged to receive a royal burial, but only one of the rooms was ever decorated.

Design features of the tombs

The first king to choose to have his tomb cut in the Valley of the Kings was probably Tuthmosis I (c.1504–c.1492 BC), the third ruler of the Eighteenth Dynasty. The character of the rock is likely to have dictated the somewhat meandering approach corridor to his squarish burial chamber. The tomb of his successor, Tuthmosis II (c.1492–c.1479 BC), appears to have been more carefully planned. It introduced two interesting new features – a bent axis to the approach corridor and an oval burial chamber. The sudden sharp left turn to the corridor may well have been devised to fool any prospective tomb robbers into believing that the blocked corridor continued straight onwards when in fact, behind another blocked wall, it headed off at a right angle. The oval burial chamber reminds us of the cartouche used to surround the king's name, and in a similar way the walls of the chamber would have surrounded and protected the dead body of the king.

▶ *The lotiform chalice found in Tutankhamun's tomb is carved of a single piece of calcite and inlaid with blue pigment.*

Tomb robbery and flooding

The ancient Egyptians had obviously learned by experience that the burial chambers needed to be safeguarded against both robbery and flooding. The unique survival of Tutankhamun's tomb reveals the lack of success the Egyptians had in protecting their dead and the material buried with them. The plunder of tombs continues to be a problem to the present day, as does the disastrous effect caused by occasional torrential rain that results in destructive flash floods racing through desert wadis such as the Valley of the Kings.

Tuthmosis III's architects introduced a deep 'well' into his tomb, perhaps to protect it against flooding or robbers. They also built a pillared antechamber between the well and the burial chamber, and four small rooms were cut into the two long sides of the burial chamber for the storage of funerary equipment.

Innovation also crept into the tomb of Amenhotep II (c.1427–c.1400 BC), which had a rectangular, columned burial chamber with a sunken crypt at the far end. Horemheb's reign (c.1323–c.1295 BC) heralded the use of a tomb with a straight axis. Unique to the tomb of the Nineteenth-Dynasty king Seti I (c.1294–c.1279 BC) was a passage more than 136m (149yd) long below the burial chamber. Its end cannot be reached, but it seems to be approaching the level of the water table, and the idea behind it might have been the linking of the burial chamber to the primordial waters of creation. The last tomb to be cut in the Valley of the Kings was that of the last ruler of the New Kingdom, Ramesses XI, who died c.1069 BC.

Wall decoration

Like most rock-cut tombs throughout Egypt belonging to men of high status from viziers to craftsmen, the tombs in the Valley of the Kings were elaborately decorated. The walls of the royal rock-cut tombs were covered in paintings of detailed funerary scenes relating to the king's Afterlife, and his interaction with the gods and goddesses of the Egyptian pantheon.

▼ *The four canopic coffins containing Tutankhamun's internal organs are miniature replicas of the second of the king's three coffins.*

Tomb-builders' Towns and Villages

◀ *The tools used by the tomb builders included copper and bronze chisels, adzes and spikes, heavy wooden mallets and hammers of hard stone bound into wooden hafts, and heavy wooden-handled bronze hoes.*

A great deal concerning the construction of the tombs of ancient Egypt, especially the pyramids, remains a mystery. But archaeologists have unearthed texts that refer to towns, and the towns that housed the tomb builders and craftsmen, or the priests, officials, guards and other personnel involved in the daily running of the funerary cults and complexes of the dead kings. The remains of such settlements have been discovered at Giza, Il-Lahun, Tell el-Amarna and Deir el-Medina on the Theban west bank.

The Giza settlements

At Giza, home to the magnificent Fourth-Dynasty pyramids of Khufu, Khafre and Menkaure, the names of two settlements are known. They are the southern Tjeniu ('boundary mark' or 'cultivation edge') of Khafre, which was probably to the south of the king's valley temple, and the northern Gerget ('settlement') of Khufu, which may have been situated around this king's valley temple. Mudbrick buildings, broken pottery, bread moulds, cooking pots, animal bones, grinding stones, charcoal and ash have all been discovered in this area. Unfortunately, the ancient settlement appears to extend beneath the modern, ever-growing city of Cairo and its sewers, so further excavation is just about impossible. A community of small mud huts, with storage bins and grain silos, has also been excavated in front of Menkaure's valley temple. This was a random arrangement of slum housing which eventually overtook the front of the valley temple.

The town of Kahun

The pyramid town of Kahun at Il-Lahun, at the eastern edge of the Faiyum some 100km (62 miles) south-east of Cairo, was specially built to house the men (and their families) who built the pyramid of the Twelfth-Dynasty king Senusret II (c.1880–c.1874 BC). It later provided homes for the priests, officials and their families who served the dead king's funerary cult. It was carefully planned and laid out on a grid system.

▼ *Research into the genealogies of the builders at Deir el-Medina has shown that about 25 interrelated families lived in the village.*

Altogether, 220 small houses have been excavated in the western and southern parts of the town. The north-eastern area was the site of nine or ten sizeable urban estates, each with a large house, garden and granary – presumably the occupants of these were the king's highest officials.

Deir el-Medina

The settlement site that has yielded more written and archaeological evidence of daily life than any other is Deir el-Medina. During the New Kingdom (c.1550–c.1069 BC) it was home to the workmen (and their families) who quarried and decorated the rock-cut tombs in the Valley of the Kings on the west bank at Thebes. The small village was specially planned and constructed to serve this purpose. It was situated in a sheltered spot in the desert, between the Ramesseum and Medinet Habu, with relatively easy access to the Valley of the Kings. We know that the original outer enclosure wall of the village was built during the reign of the early Eighteenth-Dynasty king Tuthmosis I (c.1504–c.1492 BC) (probably the first king to be buried in the Valley of the Kings) because his cartouche has been found stamped on some of the bricks. However, throughout the village's lifetime (that is, for the duration of the New Kingdom, while kings were being buried in tombs in the Valley of the Kings), its founding father and patron deity was considered to be Tuthmosis I's father Amenhotep I (c.1525–c.1504 BC). At the end of the Eighteenth Dynasty, with the return to Thebes following the Amarna period (when the ruler Akhenaten overshadowed Thebes by building a new religious and political capital named Akhetaten in Middle Egypt), the village of Deir el-Medina was enlarged to include about 12 new houses.

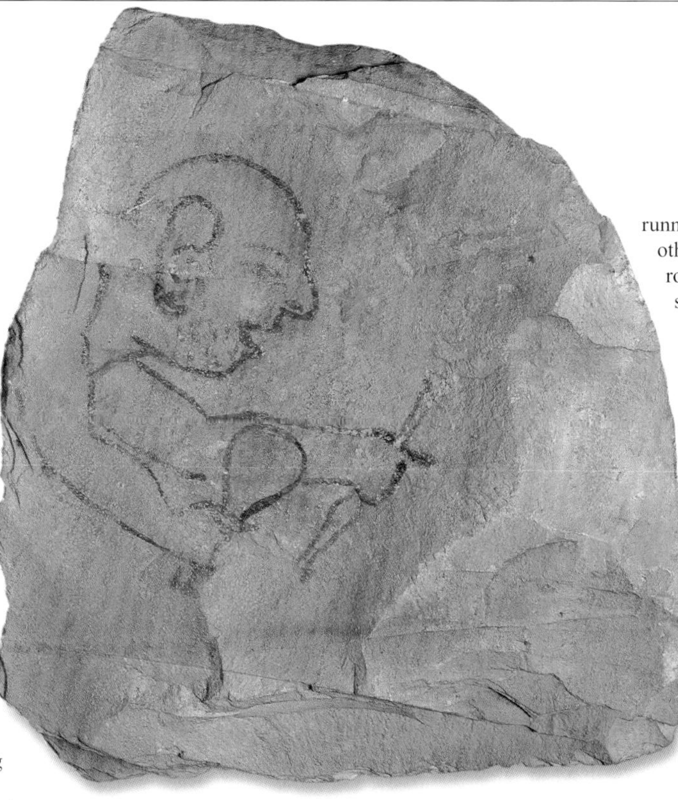

▲ *In addition to their work in the Valley of the Kings, the Deir el-Medina tomb builders such as this stonemason, might take commissions from the wealthy folk of Thebes to quarry and decorate their rock-cut tombs. 19th Dynasty.*

The community was divided into an eastern and western section by a narrow street, which was probably originally roofed over. The 70 or so houses were all similar in design, built in a combination of the usual domestic building material, mudbrick, and rough limestone set in mortar. There were also certain architectural features of stone, such as doorways, and whitewashed walls to reflect the sun. The houses were 5–6m (16–20ft) wide, with four rooms running one behind the other, two large family rooms, followed by a smaller kitchen and storage room. Staircases led to the flat roofs that served as extra living space, and cellars were often cut from the desert rock for cool storage. It has been suggested that at any one time the village housed about 25 interrelated families.

Excavation beyond the confines of the village has revealed shrines – smaller versions of the huge stone temples of state deities such as Hathor – just to the north, stables for cows and donkeys, and a rubbish dump to the south. Most excitingly, on the desert hillside to the west, is the main cemetery, with beautifully decorated tombs of the village's inhabitants. There are tomb shafts, small mudbrick chapels, and miniature pyramids.

During the reign of Akhenaten (c.1352–c.1336 BC), the inhabitants of Deir el-Medina probably moved to the site today known as Tell el-Amarna in order to quarry out and decorate the tombs of the élite and royal family of the new city of Akhetaten. Here, in the desert about 1.2km (3/4 mile) from the main city of Akhetaten, a village has been excavated. It was roughly 70m (77yd) square, with a thick enclosure wall surrounding 73 identically sized houses and one larger one. The whole settlement was divided into two unequal parts by a thick wall. In its environs were buildings such as chapels, pigsties and storehouses.

Tomb Robbery

◀ *Upon death the king was identified with Osiris. Ramesses II's presence in his mortuary temple, the Ramesseum, includes semi-mummiform figures of him as Osiris attached to the columns.*

The plunder of Egyptian tombs is by no means a modern phenomenon. At all periods of ancient Egyptian history the possible threat of tomb robbery had to be guarded against, and precautions – such as stone portcullises, confusing corridors and deep pits – were incorporated into all types of tombs. The prolific ancient evidence for disturbance, destruction and theft from tombs reveals just how unsuccessful these measures tended to be. Of most interest to tomb robbers were goods that could be disposed of easily, such as textiles, perfumes and cosmetics, precious woods and ivory. Also valued were objects made from materials that could be recycled, such as gold and silver.

The most detailed and extensive documentation about tomb (and temple) robbery dates to the end of the New Kingdom, during the reigns of Ramesses IX (c.1126–c.1108 BC) and Ramesses XI (c.1099–c.1069 BC). This was a time of various problems, such as ineffectual rulers, corruption and bribery throughout officialdom, a possible civil war, agricultural failure, inflation and external threats (especially from the Libyans to the west and the Nubians to the south). Compared with these, tomb robbery might have been regarded as a minor trouble, but in fact it was taken extremely seriously. After all, to enter a sealed tomb and remove its contents, destroying – or at least endangering – the mummified body in the process (robbers often burned mummies) would have been considered a threat to the existence of the deceased in the Afterlife. In the case of the king it was even a threat to the stability and well-being of Egypt and its people, since the ancient Egyptians believed that the dead were able to affect the lives of the living.

▼ *In this illustration from Olfert Dapper's* Description de l'Afrique *(1686) the tomb robbers are huddled around an Egyptian mummy.*

▲ *The hypostyle hall at Medinet Habu provided a barrier between the outer courts of the mortuary temple and the mysterious inner sanctuaries.*

The tomb robbery papyri

A number of judicial papyri, known as the 'tomb robbery papyri', tell us how the tomb robbers were dealt with. As they concerned the plunder of royal tombs in the Valley of the Kings, it is not surprising that the king seems to have been personally responsible for setting up a commission to investigate the robberies. A court (*kenbet*) was set up to hear the proceedings at Ramesses III's mortuary temple at Medinet Habu, and scribes were present at all times to record the trials and the confessions. The court records appear to have been hidden for safekeeping in the mortuary temple of Medinet Habu.

The document known as Papyrus Mayer B of Ramesses IX's reign is a detailed account of the theft of bronze and copper vessels, utensils, clothes and textiles from the tomb of Ramesses IX in the Valley of the Kings. Other documents contain references to the theft of objects by the foreman Paneb from the tomb of Seti II, and an attempted entry into the tomb of Ramesses II and his children's tomb in the twenty-ninth year of Ramesses III's reign. (This is the same year as the earliest strike in recorded history, staged by the workman of Deir el-Medina when they did not receive their usual pay.)

The Abbott and Amherst Papyri are dated to the sixteenth year of Ramesses IX's reign. They recount the inspection of both royal and non-royal tombs that it was claimed had been violated, and the beatings and confessions of certain thieves. Other papyri contain accounts of thefts by priests from temple buildings (including Ramesses III's temple at Medinet Habu), and the recovery of gold, silver and copper from tomb thieves, all of whom turned out to be members of the necropolis staff.

Punishment for theft

There is evidence of the guilty being imprisoned in the Temple of Maat at Thebes, threats of mutilation, including having the nose and ears cut off, and of being sent to Ethiopia. But the ultimate punishment for tomb robbery must have been death. Seven men were put to death on the stake following a trial described in three separate papyri.

Royal mummy caches

The tomb robberies in the Valley of the Kings at the end of the New Kingdom seriously threatened the survival of the royal mummies. In about 1000 BC the worried priests made the important decision to transfer the bodies of 56 dead kings and queens to safer hiding places. Forty of these mummies were discovered in a tomb near Deir el-Bahri in 1881. The other 16 were unearthed 17 years later in the tomb of Amenhotep II in the Valley of the Kings.

Popular Religion

Ancient Egyptian life was beset by trials and tribulations. These included dangerous animals such as scorpions, snakes, hippopotami, crocodiles, lions and hyenas; the loss of livestock and crops; famine; infertility; infant mortality and illness. All these had to be contended with, and religious beliefs were often the best way to explain otherwise inexplicable calamities. Rituals could help to solve everyday problems and maintain stability and well being.

'Popular religion' is the term used to describe this day-to-day religion of the people, but the evidence is so biased towards the literate, wealthy minority that it requires careful detective work to glean any information about the ideas and practices of the ordinary person. We can, however, learn about the private aspects of folk religion from finds such as a desperate, childless woman's votive offering of a fertility figurine at the local shrine of Hathor, the cow goddess of fertility; and the more public ones, such as a community's celebration of a divine festival at the local cult temple.

Magic and superstition played a crucial part in daily life, and were by no means considered unorthodox or an alternative to the religion of the state temples. A priest used to performing rituals in the cult of a state deity could also be called upon to carry out what we would term magic or sorcery. State and popular religion were clearly interrelated.

◀ *Crocodiles and hippopotami were among the perils of daily life that needed to be safeguarded against. This Nilotic scene appears on the wall of Meremka's 6th dynasty tomb at Saqqara.*

Magic

Clement of Alexandria, writing in the third century AD, observed that 'Egypt was the mother of magicians', and right up to the present day, Egypt has been viewed by those outside it as a place of magic and mysticism. The ancient Egyptians had a word, *heka*, which we translate as 'magic'. But we must not corrupt its meaning with the modern associations of magic – the idea of magic as non-establishment, or as an alternative to the generally accepted religious norm, would not have applied in ancient Egypt.

Heka, for the ancient Egyptians, conveyed a sense of the catalyst or energy that made creation possible. So every time a ritual was performed involving *heka*, it was as if a further development was thought to have been made in the process of creation. In the mythology of creation, *heka* was associated with *sia*, 'divine knowledge', and *hu*, 'divine utterance'. *Heka* itself was considered to be neither good or bad, but as an energy or power it could be channelled in either direction. The recorded incidents of what might be called antisocial magic in ancient Egypt tend to be fairly rare before the Roman Period, and any instances of unacceptable magic were usually attributed to foreign sorcerers. Similar to *heka* was *akhu*, which tends to be translated as 'sorcery', 'enchantments' or 'spells'. Again, *akhu* was in itself neither a negative nor a positive phenomenon and it could be worked in either direction.

There would have been certain members of each local community who were credited with the ability to perform rituals using *heka*. There were also people who were believed to have an intrinsic possession of the force – either having been born with it, as dwarves were thought to be, or gaining it during certain periods of their life, as was the case with breast-feeding women. All kings, deities and the dead, by their very nature, were thought to have a certain degree of *heka*.

◀ *Seneb, an achondroplastic dwarf, was Chief of all Palace Dwarves, in charge of the royal wardrobe and a priest of the mortuary cults of kings Khufu and Djedefre, so he was clearly highly respected and by no means ostracized.*

Magical cures

Magic aided the search for an answer to the perennial question 'Why me?' If a woman was suffering from a headache and convulsions, she might be visited by a respected member of the community (see *Who Performed Magic?*). He or she might trace the source of the disease to the anger of a particular deity, the magic of a foreign sorcerer, the malevolence of a demon or the ghost of a dead relative (see *The Negative Influence of the Dead*). The solution might then have been the performance of a ritual, including the recitation of a spell, in order to cure the woman. Deities and the dead tended to cause particular problems for the living when their temples or funerary chapels fell into disrepair or their offerings were forgotten.

God of magic

The ancient Egyptians chose to personify divinely all that was crucial to them, including abstract concepts and natural phenomena. In this way they could pay their respects and make offerings to them, in order to ensure their continued and benevolent existence. The magical force of *heka* was divinely personified as the god Heka, who was represented in human form, holding snakes crossed in front of him. Like the household gods and goddesses, no major cult centres dedicated to Heka, or temples built in honour of him. He was worshipped as a secondary deity at Heliopolis, Memphis and Esna, and his

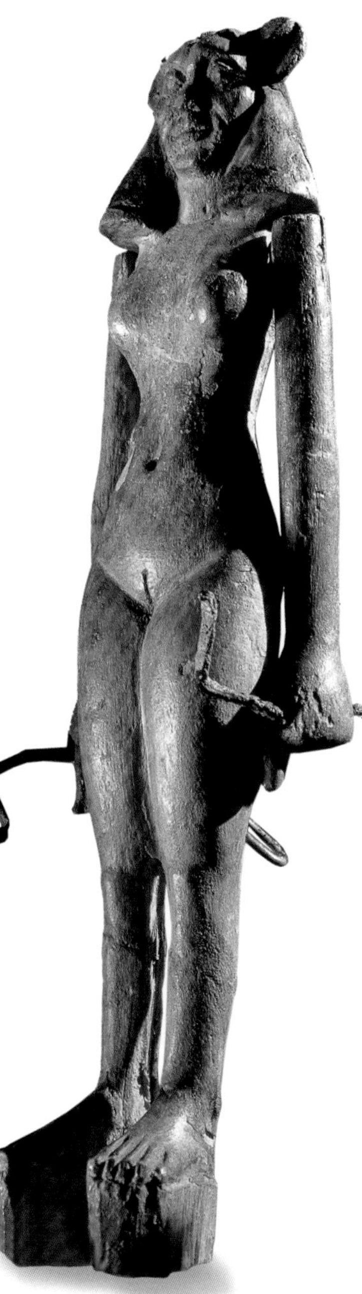

▲ *This wooden female figurine, found in a tomb under the Ramesseum in western Thebes, holds metal snake wands. It is uncertain whether the figure represents a goddess with a leonine head (perhaps Beset) or a woman wearing a mask,*

presence would have been ubiquitous in the temples throughout the country dedicated to other deities. We can discover something of the nature and characteristics of Heka by reading a range of ancient texts from different periods of Egyptian history. The Coffin Texts of the Middle Kingdom (c.2055–c.1650 BC) describe him as 'the unique lord made before duality had yet come into being', while he is referred to as 'Lord of Oracles, Lord of Miracles, who predicts what will happen' in an inscription found on the Graeco-Roman temple at Esna.

We also know of a goddess called Weret Hekau, meaning 'Great of Magic'. She took the form of a cobra, and it is possible that the snake-shaped wands used by those skilled in magic were crafted in this way in order to represent this goddess. The rearing cobra, known as a *uraeus*, on the front of the royal headdress, which was poised ready to spit venom at the king's enemies, was also sometimes described as *weret hekau*.

Wands and spells

A variety of wands and other paraphernalia of popular ritual have survived from ancient Egypt, as have collections of magic spells recorded on papyrus. The aim of these spells tended to be to ward off danger, such as the threats posed by snakes and scorpions, and to prevent or cure illness and particularly problems relating to fertility, pregnancy and birth. As in funerary religion, there was clearly a strongly held belief in the creative power of the words and images used in Egyptian magic. Knowledge of the relevant names was essential for the magic to prove effective.

Another important aspect of ancient Egyptian magic was sympathetic magic. The mythology told that as a young boy, Horus had survived the threat of snakes and scorpions in the marshes of the Delta, and so if children were identified with the young god, they too could be protected from harm. Similarly, the goddess Isis (or Hathor, depending on the text) had successfully given birth to Horus, and so a woman having a difficult labour might transfer the pain by identifying herself with that goddess (see *Rites of Passage*).

▲ *The deity Heka was represented anthropomorphically, sometimes holding two crossed snakes.*

Who Performed Magic?

Every community in Egypt must have had at least one wise person to whom the local people turned in times of need. This person was trusted and believed able to offer advice and perform rituals, using *heka*, or magic, to solve people's problems. Various titles have survived indicating the particular areas of expertise of these people. As was usual with Egyptian professions, it is likely that a father would have handed down his skills and secret knowledge to his son (or a mother to her daughter), and so one family would probably have become well known for practising magic over many generations.

▲ *The lioness goddess Sekhmet, who was feared as the bringer of disease, paradoxically became associated with healing because of the need to appease her wrath. The title 'Priest of Sekhmet' became synonymous with 'doctor'.*

Chiefs of mysteries

The word *hekau* (sometimes translated 'magician') existed as a general term for anyone who used magic, and a title that was obviously associated with magic was that of *Hery Seshta*, 'Chief of Mysteries or Secrets'. This title was found on the lid of a wooden box in a tomb of the late Middle Kingdom found under the Ramesseum in western Thebes. The box was among a selection of objects that had evidently been used for magical purposes. They included spells and religious papyri, a bronze snake wand, a wooden female figure wearing a mask of Beset (the female form of the protective spirit-deity Bes) and holding metal snake wands, a female fertility figurine, an ivory clapper and part of a magic rod.

The owner of this equipment for performing magical rituals was a priest, who would presumably have played an important role in the life of the local temple and that of the community. It may have been the figure known as the Lector Priest, whose job was also an extramural one. It was the Lector Priest who was responsible for reciting the spells in the temple, and during the embalming process and funerals. Among their other special skills, Lector Priests were believed to be able to interpret dreams.

Other temple titles associated with the performance of magical rites were '*Hekau* of the House of Life' and 'Scribe of the House of Life'. There would have been a House of Life in most temple complexes. It was a place of copying, reading and research, rather like a library, scriptorium, school and university rolled into one.

Another important man was the *Sau*. It is uncertain exactly what he did, but the word *sa* is the word for both 'protection' and 'amulet', and so *Sau* tends to be given the rather ambiguous translation, 'amulet man'. Perhaps he was responsible for making the amulets required by the local villagers or townspeople. Or perhaps, once a craftsman had manufactured the amulets, he was able to perform the ritual that would imbue the amulets with magical significance and supernatural

▲ *Selket appears as a protective deity together with Isis, Nephthys and Neith on the four corners of Tutankhamun's golden shrine.*

powers. The records show that the *Sau* could be a woman, especially if she was also a midwife or a nurse.

A more specifically female title was *Rekhet* (literally 'knowing one'), which can probably best be translated 'wise woman'. The *Rekhet* appears to have been a medium, so if someone believed he was suffering because of the anger of one of his deceased relatives, he would consult a Rekhet. She would then liaise with the spirit world to find out which relative required appeasing (see *The Negative Influence of the Dead*).

Warding off crocodiles

Boatmen on the River Nile faced the daily danger of attack by crocodiles. Sanctuaries of the crocodile god Sobek were erected at points on the river where these creatures congregated in the greatest numbers, but extra protection could be gained with the use of spells, amulets, wands and magic rods. Herdsmen protected their cattle against the threat of crocodiles by using a particular hand gesture and reciting spells for 'warding off the crocodile by the herdsmen'.

Scorpion charmers

Someone whose skills would have been much sought after was the *Kherep Selket*, literally, 'the one who has power over the scorpion goddess' – or, the local scorpion charmer (who no doubt also charmed snakes). The enormous numbers of spells to ward off snakes and scorpions, and to cure their bites, indicate the extent of the problem, and one that is still common in Egypt today. Modern snake charmers use practical techniques to ensnare their prey, but they also rely on magical chanting.

In ancient Egypt, a Lector Priest and a doctor could also hold the title *Kherep Selket*. The title *Sunu*, 'doctor' or 'physician', was held by people who prescribed both medical and magical remedies (see *Medicine*). The priests of the lioness goddess Sekhmet specialized in medicine and were closely associated with magic. Because this goddess was feared as the bringer of plague and other disease, magical rituals had to be performed in order to appease her and dissuade her from doing harm.

▲ *Animal figurines (usually turtles, lions and crocodiles) were often attached to the top side of decorated hollow 'magic rods' which were probably used to establish the magician's authority over these various animals.*

Medicine

▲ *This wooden statue represents a doctor who was practising his medical skills as early as the 5th Dynasty.*

As far as the ancient Egyptians were concerned, there was no clear distinction between magic and medicine, and the two were fundamentally interrelated. About ten papyri have survived containing texts that today we call magico-medical texts because they combine the use of various remedies (to be taken internally, applied externally, or administered by fumigation), together with spells to be recited as part of magical rituals incorporating amulets and other such devices. It was crucial that the seemingly rational cures, which clearly influenced Greek medicine, were used in conjunction with spells. A woman suffering from irregular periods, for example, was advised to take a herbal remedy while reciting an incantation.

As already noted, the title *Sunu*, which means 'doctor' or 'physician', was held by people who practised both practical medical and magical techniques. The priests of the goddess Sekhmet would have been involved in temple rituals, but they also specialized in medicine.

Magico-medical papyri

During the third century AD, Clement of Alexandria observed that of the 42 books that comprised the sum total of all Egyptian knowledge, six were devoted to medicine, covering the topics of anatomy, illnesses, surgical instruments, drugs, eye ailments and gynaecology. These books have never been discovered, but various papyri do provide us with interesting information on all these subjects. Diagnosis was clearly based on both clinical examination and empirical knowledge. Pregnancy, for example, was diagnosed by pulse rate, propensity to vomit and internal gas, together with the appearance of the eyes, breasts and skin pigmentation. It appears that the Egyptian approach to medicine was perhaps more 'scientific' than in Babylonia and Assyria, where illness tended to be more readily attributed to possession by demons. The ancient Egyptians accepted that some illnesses were incurable and so did not attempt to treat them. They also realized, for example, the effect of diet on a person's health (a Roman Period papyrus, Papyrus Insinger, blames ailments in the limbs on overeating).

Many of the ingredients for the prescriptions in the magico-medical texts are decidedly unappealing. For example, at least 19 different types of excrement are mentioned, including that

▶ *The medicinal use of onion appears frequently in the magico-medical papyri, for example in remedies for snake bites. This wall painting in the Theban tomb of Nakht shows them being carried. 18th Dynasty.*

of the fly and the ostrich. The logic behind such a peculiar choice of medicine appears to have been the principle of treating like with like. Rotting food trapped in the body was thought to cause a range of problems, and remedies containing faeces were thought to encourage these residues to travel out of the body.

Useful drugs

The Egyptians were the first people to use a number of drugs that modern studies have proved would have been medicinally effective. Honey, for example, was used both for magical and ritual purposes (see *Demons* and *Rites of Passage*), and for medical ones. It is now known to be resistant to bacterial growth, to act as a hypertonic – drawing water from bacterial cells, causing them to shrivel and die – and to exhibit antibiotic action due to a bacterial enzyme called inhibine which is secreted by the pharyngeal glands of the bee. It has proved to be efficacious against staphylococcus, salmonella and candida bacteria, and has been used to treat surgical wounds, ulcers and burns. In the Nineteenth-Dynasty Papyrus Leiden 1,348, the first of the spells prescribed for the cure of burns was to be said over a dressing of honey.

Onion occurs in the ancient texts, and it is now known that onion juice is an antibiotic, a diuretic and an expectorant.

▶ *Only the lower portion survives of this statue of the kneeling figure of the physician Horkheb. Beneath his offering of* hes-*jars is an inscribed 'Appeal to the Living' that priests should make offerings to his spirit now that he is dead, with a curse on those who fail to do so. 26th Dynasty.*

▲ *A number of implements are depicted on an offering table on this wall relief in the temple of Kom Ombo. There is much uncertainty as to their use, but they are probably Roman surgical instruments (the relief dates to the latter half of the 2nd century AD).*

Garlic was also used for medicinal purposes, and its healing properties are generally accepted today. It is said to contain an amino-acid derivative called allium, which releases the enzyme allinase. Its antibacterial qualities (it is an antibiotic exhibiting 1% of the strength of penicillin) are useful for treating wounds, and it is antifungal against candida. Thanks to the presence of methyl allyl trisulphide, which works to dilate the blood-vessel walls, it thins blood, lowers blood pressure and helps to prevent heart attack. It also lowers cholesterol levels, aids digestion and stimulates the immune system.

Ox liver or its juice was employed in ancient Egypt for night blindness, and we now know that animal liver is high in vitamin A and may indeed be effective against some forms of night blindness.

The various prescriptions did not necessarily have to be taken internally, but might be applied to parts of the body – for instance, raw meat used on wounds is very good for stopping bleeding.

The mouse cure

Some outlandish remedies, which we would not expect to find anywhere but in ancient sources, do actually occur much closer to home and almost to the present day. For example, according to the Nineteenth-Dynasty papyrus now known as Berlin 3027, which deals with the illnesses of young children and their mothers, the cure for an uncertain illness called *sesmi* was to eat a cooked mouse. This remedy can be found used in a very similar way in the works of Dioscorides, Pliny, the Algerian physician 'Abd er-Razzak at the end of the seventh century AD, and the Arabic physician Ibn el-Betar in the thirteenth century AD. Mouse also figures in Culpeper's *Pharmacopoeia Londinensis* (1653), and in the *Pharmacopoeia Universalis* (1831). It has been said that in England during the 1920s, mouse was flayed, fried, boiled or made into pie and given to children in order to cure incontinence, dribbling and whooping cough.

Because it was usual for the ingestion of remedies to be accompanied by magic rites, Papyrus Berlin 3027 states that the bones of the mouse should be wrapped in a linen cloth (often stipulated for amuletic devices), knotted with seven knots (a magic number) and worn around the neck. A similar practice has been found among the Tlokwa of Botswana. The magical potency of the mouse may relate to a belief expressed by Pliny, and found in medieval bestiaries, that the mouse spontaneously emerged from the Nile mud after inundation.

Demons

The ancient Egyptians used magic to guard against the possible threat of demons and other malevolent forces, such as evil spirits, ghosts and hostile manifestations of deities. Demons were believed to be able to cause a variety of problems, especially illness. It has already been noted that the ancient Egyptians did not regard magic and medicine as distinct entities, but as very much interrelated (see *Medicine*). Demons were particularly associated with the goddess Sekhmet, who was regarded as the bringer of plague and other serious illness. In fact, there was a class of demon known as the 'Messengers of Sekhmet'. Sekhmet was also associated with fire and heat, so a fever might be blamed on her demons. Headaches and stomach problems were often said to be caused by demons contaminating the ill person's body, and so an emetic might be prescribed in an attempt to rid the person of the demon.

The desert and the netherworld

Demons were thought either to live in the desert, which was barren and associated with Seth, the god of chaos and infertility, or in an inverted netherworld. This meant that they lived upside down, so their mouths were where their anuses should have been, and they were said to eat their own faeces. In direct contrast to humans, for whom honey was sweet and delicious, demons were believed to find it bitter, and even to fear it. For this reason, honey was ideal for use in rituals to ward off demons and evil spirits. After giving birth, a woman might eat a cake made of honey, presumably to give her energy, but also to keep demons at bay at this particularly vulnerable time in her and her newborn baby's life. Garlic was also believed to have an apotropaic effect on demons. It was said to harm them, and so it was used in spells and rituals to protect young children against malevolent spirits.

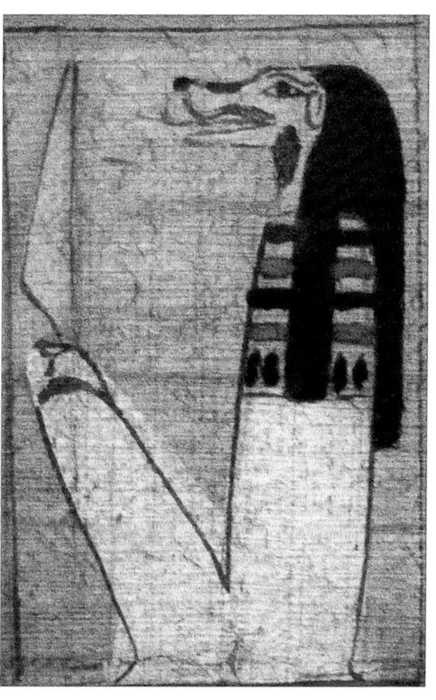

▲ *In ancient Egyptian religion the knife was considered a magic weapon.*

▼ *An important aim of funerary spells was to help the dead person deal with demons in the underworld. The donkey was identified with the demon par excellence, Seth: in the Book of the Dead of Chensumose, it is depicted trussed as a way of controlling its malevolence. 21st Dynasty.*

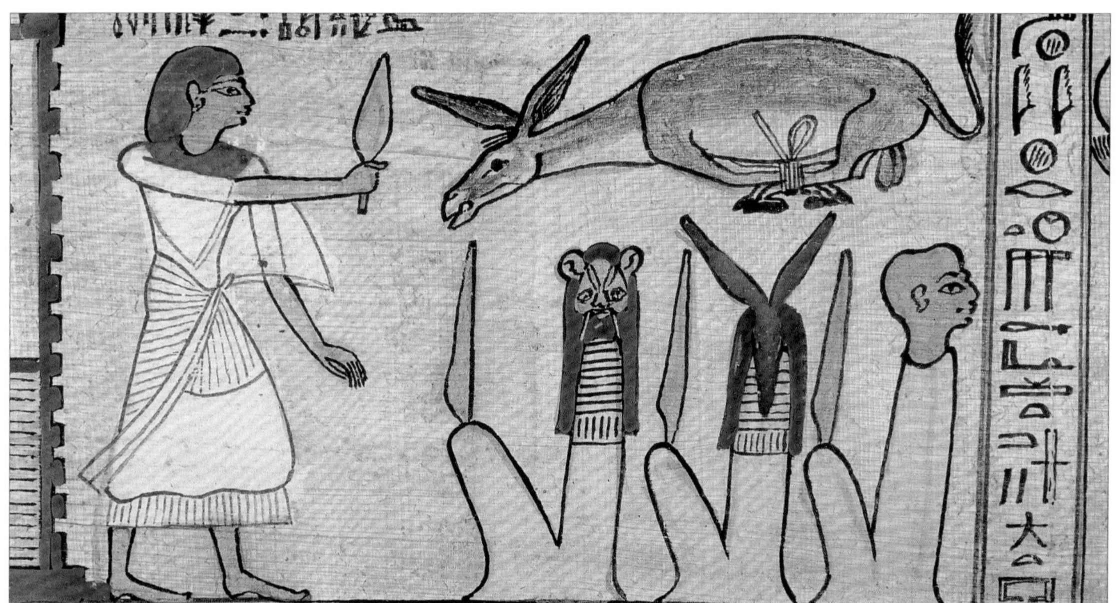

Household Deities

The two deities most closely associated with protection of the household and family life, especially women and children, were Bes and Taweret. They must have been close to the hearts of the ancient Egyptians, as they feature heavily in the various spells associated with illness and the hazards of everyday life. Like Heka (see *Magic*), no cult temple was dedicated to either of these deities, but their presence was ubiquitous in family life. Although they were associated with the relatively peaceful environment of the household, they could certainly be forces to be reckoned with. It was important to stay on the right side of these deities, by invoking them and making offerings to them. Both deities could be depicted looking surprisingly fierce, with teeth bared and tongue sticking out. It is thought that this may well have been for apotropaic reasons – that their aggressive expressions would scare away evil influences – and so their presence at particularly vulnerable times, such as childbirth and childhood, would have been deemed valuable. Bes was also thought to be able to ward off snakes from the house.

◄ *Taweret's name means 'the Great One'. In the magical texts she is sometimes referred to as 'sow'* (reret).

Bes the spirit-deity

It would probably be more correct to refer to Bes as a spirit or a benevolent demon than as a fully fledged deity. In fact, Bes may well have been a generic term for a number of protective demons. He was represented as a rather strange bandy-legged dwarf, with a lion's ears and mane, and a tail. He often wore a feathered headdress and an animal pelt over his back, and held a *sa* amulet of protection. His appearance ranged from jovial to really quite ferocious. He was often depicted playing musical instruments and hopping about, especially in the context of childbirth. His head appears in a protective capacity above the naked figure of the child Horus on the stelae known as *cippi* of Horus (see *Paraphernalia of Ritual*).

▲ *The female musician playing the lute on this faience dish has the image of the protective spirit Bes tattooed on her thigh. 18th Dynasty.*

The hippopotamus goddess

Taweret was portrayed as a hippopotamus standing on her hind legs, with a large stomach and pendulous breasts, so there was a clear visual association with pregnant women, and she could be called on to help every woman, whether royal or commoner, in childbirth. To heighten her apotropaic, or protective, capacity she was made to look more terrifying by having a crocodile tail on her back and a leonine muzzle, arms and legs. The most terrifying guise the ancient Egyptians could give a deity was as a composite animal incorporating elements of dangerous creatures, the prime example of which was the funerary demon Ammit (see *The Weighing of the Heart*). Taweret was often portrayed wearing a headdress composed of a low *modius* (a cylindrical headdress) surmounted by two plumes, sometimes with horns and a disc. She usually clutched a *sa*, *ankh* or *tyet*-amulet (see *Amulets*).

◀ *Cosmetic spoons and dishes were often decorated with the image of a duck, which appears to have had erotic connotations. Bes was also a common motif on toilet objects and other personal possessions.*

Amulets and furniture

An incredible number of amulets in the miniature form of these deities have survived, so their popularity is evident. They were also incorporated into the design of furniture (especially beds), musical instruments, pottery and other vessels. Faience vessels have been found in the form of Taweret with a pouring hole in place of one of her nipples, and it is assumed that these would originally have contained milk. Images of Bes and Taweret on headrests would have been popular because sleep was considered a particularly vulnerable time, not only to actual threats such as scorpions but also to ghosts and nightmares. In keeping with their apotropaic presence, Bes and Taweret were often depicted brandishing knives. The figure of Bes was also used as a tattoo, usually on the upper thigh of female singers and musicians.

The persistence of tradition

The archaeological record at the site of Tell el-Amarna reveals that however radically the Eighteenth-Dynasty 'revolutionary' King Akhenaten (c.1352–c.1336 BC) attempted to change the state religion, there was no way that he was going to succeed in stamping out the traditional popular beliefs of the ancient Egyptian people. The presence of numerous amulets in the form of these domestic deities, and a stela depicting a mother and child worshipping Taweret (found under the stairs in one of the houses in the Main City) are good evidence for the continued reliance of the average person on the deities of most immediate importance in their lives. In the walled village at Tell el-Amarna, as well as in the tomb builders' village at Deir el-Medina, fragments of wall painting have been discovered in the main living rooms of some of the houses, which include Bes and Taweret in their design. Both deities were ever-present in the lives of most ordinary ancient Egyptian people.

Paraphernalia of Ritual

A variety of unusual objects have been discovered whose definite use and symbolic value will probably always remain uncertain. But this leaves us exciting scope for speculation. Rituals pertaining to the trials, tribulations and celebrations of everyday life would have been performed in the home, at shrines and at tombs or graves (especially those of relatives). The 'equipment' of popular ritual and belief included wands, amulets, votive objects, ceremonial vessels and a range of other artefacts, both inscribed and uninscribed.

Figurines

In the early twentieth century, the female figurines that today are called 'fertility figurines' were regarded as symbolic 'concubine figures' placed in tombs to service the sexual needs of the deceased male tomb owner. Closer scrutiny of the archaeological contexts of these objects has revealed that a larger number have actually been found in temple and domestic contexts than in tombs, so they were more frequently a ritual object of the living rather than of the dead.

Most are likely to have been votive offerings to deities such as the goddess of fertility, Hathor, and spirits of the dead particularly fathers, see *The Positive Influence of the Dead*. They may have been offerings from women who were unable to conceive, and who were seeking help from the divine or spirit world to solve their desperate problem. They tended to be made out of clay, wood or faience, and the emphasis in the fashioning of them was quite clearly on the pubic region and, to a lesser extent, the breasts. Sometimes the head was merely a 'pinch' of the clay, and the feet were rarely modelled. It has been suggested that this was a deliberate device to prevent the figurine from

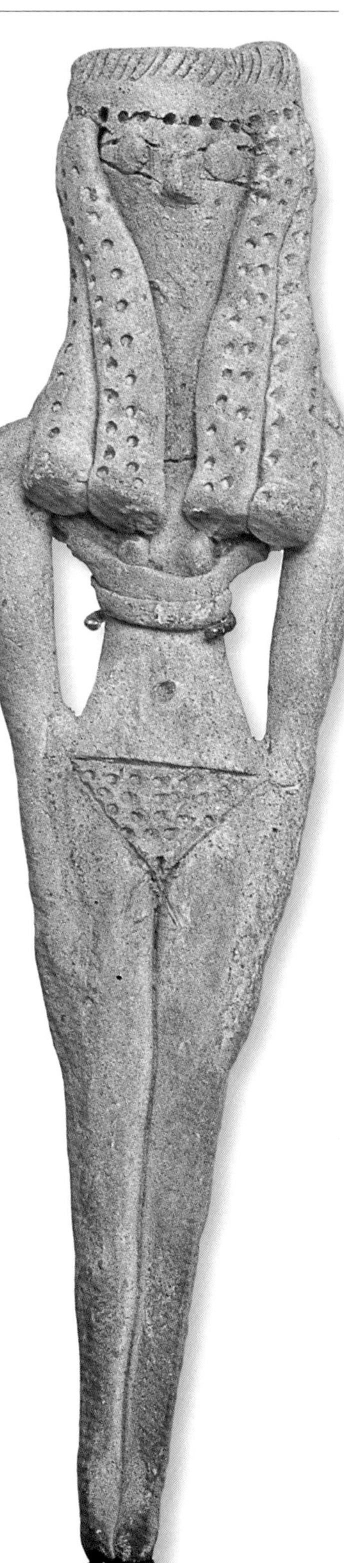

▶ *The patterns on some female fertility figurines are thought to represent tattoos. Middle Kingdom.*

◀ *Over a dozen feminoform vessels have been found, all dating to the Eighteenth and Nineteenth Dynasties, and perhaps made to contain milk. They range from 11–17cm (4½–6½in) in height.*

▲ *By depicting the enemies of Egypt in a subdued state, it was believed this would magically become reality. Tutankhamun's ceremonial stool shows Syrians and Libyans on the top surface, and Nubians and Sudanese on its underside.*

leaving the place where it was deposited, since the ancient Egyptians believed in the magical creative properties of their religious imagery. We can be more certain of the purpose of these figurines when they were inscribed, usually with a woman's plea for a child (infertility was always regarded as a woman's problem).

There is evidence for private fertility cults that would have made use of a selection of ritual paraphernalia. A cache of votive material was discovered under the stairs of a house at the site of Tell el-Amarna, the ancient capital city of Akhetaten. The stash included a stela showing a woman and child worshipping the household goddess Taweret, two broken female figurines, and two model beds. It is impossible to tell whether these objects had been hidden here, were placed here for safekeeping, or whether this was in fact the location of a household shrine.

Another magical type of figurine was the execration figurine – a rough clay figure of a bound captive, often inscribed with a curse against a named foreign ruler, a group of people, or a particular place. The knowledge of a name was of magical significance and allowed the exercise of magical control over the possible threat of the foreigner. Often such a figure would be smashed in an execration ritual to destroy the power of the foreign ruler. Such execration texts were also sometimes inscribed on pottery bowls, which might be similarly ritually smashed and buried.

Ritual vessels

Various types of vessel clearly had a ritual significance, for example those in the form of pregnant and breast feeding women, and the deities Bes and Taweret. Pots have been discovered in the form of pregnant women with their hands rubbing their distended stomachs. These pots often date to the Eighteenth Dynasty (c.1550–c.1295 BC) and tend to be made of calcite (although there is a particularly

fine pottery example from Abydos in the Cairo Museum). The oil they contained would have been used to ease stretch marks and may have had some aromatherapeutic value, but the pots themselves would have also had a sympathetic magical significance. Several pots have been discovered with tampons painted on them. These were used to prevent miscarriage, and so a woman who possessed a feminoform vessel protected in this way would have hoped that she would benefit from the magical security it offered.

Pots dating to the Eighteenth and Nineteenth Dynasties (c.1550–c.1186 BC) have also been found in the form of breast-feeding women, sometimes with a spout in place of a nipple. Breast milk may have been stored in these vessels. Lactating women's milk was an important ingredient in several spells and remedies, indicating belief in its magical potency. It is possible that whatever the type of milk stored in a feminoform jar, it was believed to magically 'become' women's milk, and so might be used for magical purposes.

Cippi of Horus

Spells were often recorded on ritual objects, such as a type of stela known as a *cippus* of Horus. Examples that have survived tend to be made of stone or wood, and range in date from 1400 BC to the second century AD. The focus of each *cippus* was an image of the god Horus as a child (depicted naked and wearing the characteristic hairstyle of childhood, the 'sidelock of youth') triumphing over a selection of dangerous animals such as crocodiles, snakes and scorpions. A representation of the head of the protective spirit-deity Bes tends to figure over Horus. Much of the rest of each *cippus* is covered in spells relating to dangers such as snakes and scorpions. The idea seems to have been that water (perhaps ideally rainwater) was poured over the *cippus* so that it would become magically imbued with the potency of the spells. The water could then be drunk or applied externally as a cure, antidote or preventative against hazards such as scorpion bites. Like breast milk, rainwater was considered to be of particular magical and medicinal effectiveness. For some reason we shall probably never know, it was thought to be especially effective in the healing of leg ailments.

Identical in purpose to the *cippi* were 'healing statues', of which a particularly fine example is that of Djedhor now in the Cairo Museum. He holds a *cippus*, but all the available surfaces of Djedhor, himself, together with the plinth on which he kneels, are also covered in spells. Water was obviously meant to run over the statue because it sits in a collecting trough, and there is at least one channel for draining off the water.

◀ *The protective influence of the spirit-deity Bes was harnessed on the stelae called* cippi *of Horus used in the later period of Egyptian history, and held here by a healing statue inscribed with magical texts. Ptolemaic Period.*

Ritual gestures

A number of symbolic gestures occur repeatedly in illustrations of ancient Egyptian rituals. A magical protective gesture is illustrated in many tomb reliefs of the period c2400–1800BC. This was the pointing of the index finger and thumb at calves being born, for example, or cattle being driven through crocodile-infested water.

A ritual gesture described in magical texts was the placing of a hand on a patient or woman suffering in childbirth (the terminology implies that this was to 'seal' the vulnerable person in order to prevent harmful forces intruding.

Wands

The most treasured possession of a practitioner of magic, such as a *Hery Seshta* ('Chief of Mysteries or Secrets'), would probably have been his wand. Three types have survived from ancient Egypt: the snake-shaped wand, the apotropaic (or protective wand) and the magic rod.

Snake-shaped wands were usually made of bronze. They could either be elongated, such as the Eighteenth-Dynasty example in the British Museum, London, or more coiled, such as the one dating to the First Intermediate Period (c.2181–c.2055 BC) in the Fitzwilliam Museum in Cambridge. It is possible that these wands were believed to represent the cobra-form goddess Weret Hekau ('Great of Magic'). Depictions of the divine personification of magic, Heka, show him holding two crossed snakes, and wooden and ivory figures masked like Bes or Beset, and connected with magic, hold metal snake wands. The Old Testament Book of Exodus records that the magicians attending Pharaoh performed the miracle of turning their wands into serpents.

Apotropaic wands

About 150 curved apotropaic wands have been found, mainly dating to the First Intermediate Period and Middle Kingdom (c.2181– c.1650 BC). They could be made of calcite, faience or ebony, but were usually of hippopotamus ivory. It is therefore possible that a deliberate association was being made with Taweret, the hippopotamus goddess. All manner of weird and wonderful magical imagery decorate these wands, including dancing baboons, snake-breathing lions, winged quadrupeds, human-headed winged snakes and sun discs on legs. More conventional representations of vultures, hippopotami, frogs and crocodiles also appear, as do depictions of protective *sa* and *udjat*-eye amulets and Seth, the god of chaos and infertility, as well as the apotropaic household deities Bes and Taweret, who are often shown wielding knives in a rather threatening fashion. Sometimes the terminal of the wand is adorned with the head of a leopard. When the wands are inscribed, the brief inscriptions are concerned with protection.

The inscriptions and imagery imply that these wands were used to benefit women and children, particularly at times of birth and early childhood. Their exact ritual purpose is uncertain. Perhaps they were placed or touched upon the pregnant woman or newborn child, or used to mark out a magic space in which the pregnant woman or mother and child would be protected from misfortune.

Magic rods

Similar imagery can be found on the magic rods that have survived from the Middle Kingdom and Second Intermediate periods of ancient Egyptian history (c.2055–c.1550 BC). Glazed steatite examples incorporate representations of frogs, turtles, baboons, crocodiles and felines, as well as lamps and amuletic symbols such as *sa*s and *udjat*-eyes. These rods would have had miniature models of the animals attached to them using tiny pegs. We are not certain how they were employed, but they were presumably used to dominate the animals depicted on them, and turn their power into a protective rather than a malignant force. Some magical spells refer to the brandishing of a stick or a branch (the poor man's bronze or ivory wand), particularly in the commanding of malevolent spirits and demons.

▶ *It is possible that the break in this ivory apotropaic wand was done deliberately before it was placed in a tomb. On its other side this wand is inscribed with a promise of protection for the Lady of the House, Seneb.*

◀ *This coiled serpent wand was found in a tomb under the Ramesseum in western Thebes, tangled in a mass of hair.*

Amulets

▲ *The best known of all ancient Egyptian amulets is the scarab, examples of which have been found made of every material known to the Egyptians.*

Amulets were miniature devices believed to endow the owner or wearer with powers or magical protection. The ancient Egyptian words for 'amulet' – *sa*, *meket* and *nehet* – all derived from verbs meaning 'to guard' or 'to protect', while a fourth term – *wedja* – had the same sound as the word meaning 'well being'.

The earliest recognizable amulets date back to the Badarian phase of the Predynastic Period (c.5500–c.4000 BC). They have been found in graves, but it is likely that they were also considered useful to the owners during their lifetimes. We have no texts for the Predynastic Period, so cannot know the significance of these amulets. An amulet of an antelope's or gazelle's head, for example, might have been considered to be able to turn the owner into a successful hunter of the animal; it might have blessed the owner with the swiftness attributed to the animal; or if the animal was associated with evil, as it was later in Pharaonic history, it might have served an apotropaic purpose.

Stringing and knotting

Most amulets had a loop attached so that they could be suspended. Some rare examples of the original stringing have survived – intricately twisted and knotted thread made from flax fibres. The ancient Egyptians may have worn their amulets beautifully strung around their necks for all to see, but the evidence appears to indicate that they were probably knotted and bundled together and secreted somewhere safe on the person. We know that the tying and untying of knots were certainly very important in ancient Egyptian magic. The magico-medical texts record that amuletic images were sometimes painted or drawn on linen placed on the patient's body. Or they could be drawn directly on the patient's hand and then licked off. We also learn from the texts that certain spells were to be recited over very specific amulets. Spell 30 of the magical text on Papyrus Leiden 1,348, had to be recited four times over a 'dwarf of clay' placed on the forehead of a woman suffering from a difficult labour. This would probably have been an amulet of the dwarf spirit-deity Bes.

Miniature representations of deities such as Bes, Taweret and Hathor were acquired to ensure the protection and influences of the divine world. Other popular amulets were the scarab, with its creative and solar associations, the protective *udjat* or Eye of Horus, associated with wholeness and healing, and the *tyet* (see *Funerary Amulets*).

The *tyet*-amulet was particularly important for the protection of women during pregnancy and childbirth, because it was associated with Isis and, more specifically, with her blood. We cannot be certain of its meaning but it is knot shaped. It possibly represented the knotted girdle of the goddess, or it has also been suggested that it represented a tampon inserted into Isis when she was pregnant so that she would not miscarry

▶ *The decoration on Tutankhamun's chest includes the alternation of the* ankh *and the* was-*sceptre (symbolizing power) above the hieroglyphic sign of a basket meaning 'all'.*

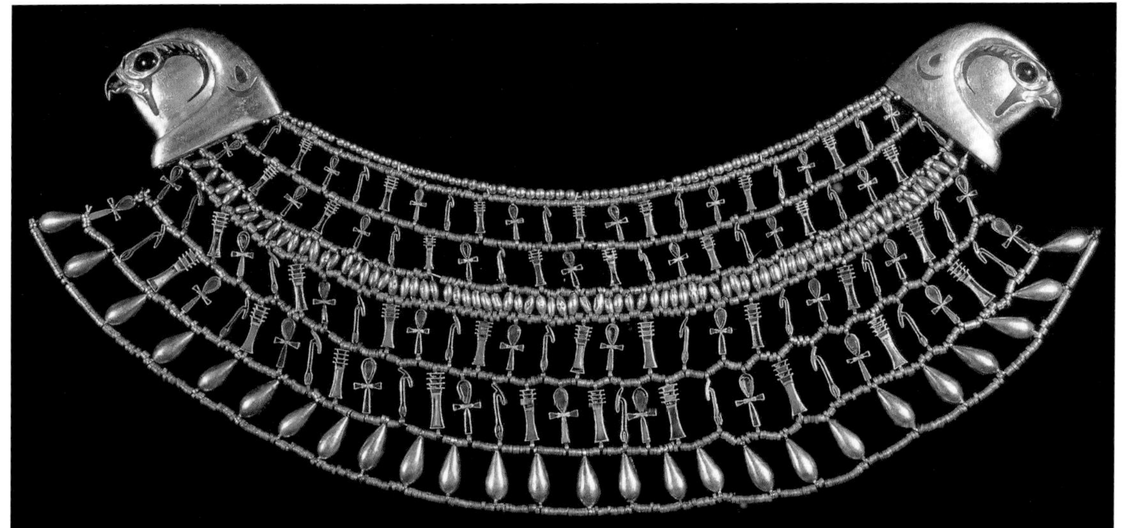

▲ *The* ankh, djed, *and* was *amuletic signs are often found together, with the symbolic meaning of 'life, stability and power'. This collar belonged to Khnumit, daughter of the 12th-Dynasty king Amenemhat II.*

or so that her wicked brother Seth could not harm the son she was carrying. It would therefore have been hoped that by sympathetic magic, the owner or wearer of the amulet would also be protected against miscarriage.

Two other amulets that would have been particularly meaningful in popular religion were the *ankh* and the *sa*. The *ankh* was the hieroglyphic symbol for 'life' (or perhaps, more specifically, the life-giving elements of air and water), and may have represented a sandal strap, or perhaps a more elaborate knot or bow. The *sa* was an amulet of protection, and may have represented a mobile papyrus shelter, tied up for transportation – vital protection against the sun for anyone who worked out in the fields or desert. The household deities Bes and Taweret were often depicted standing, resting their front paws on *sa* amulets.

As might be expected, these amulets were included in the decoration of magical implements such as apotropaic wands and magic rods (see *Wands*), and ceremonial devices such as the sistrum (see *Music and Dance in Religion*). They were also included in the design of more secular objects, such as furniture, musical instruments, vessels, cosmetic spoons and mirrors. Other amulets included cowrie shells (either the actual shells or imitations of them made from other materials), which were often strung to make girdles, worn by women to protect their fertility; parts of animals such as claws and hairs from a cat; and models of parts of the human body, plants or animals.

Oracular amuletic decrees

During the late New Kingdom and Third Intermediate Period (c.1100–c.747 BC), amulets also took the form of short spells written on tiny pieces of papyrus rolled up inside cylindrical tubes, designed so that they could be worn around the neck. The text usually read as if it were a proclamation by a deity or the gods in general, promising to protect the wearer and threatening divine retribution to those who endangered him or her. One Twenty-second Dynasty example of an oracular amuletic decree in the British Museum, London, declares:

> *We shall fill her womb with male and female children. We shall save her...from miscarrying, and from giving birth to twins.*

Often it is obvious that the wearers were children, whose fates were decreed by the gods at birth. They were promised long life, good health, lots of possessions, and protection against demons, foreign sorcerers, the Evil Eye and harmful manifestations of the gods and goddesses.

▶ *The frog was a symbol of creation, fertility, birth and regeneration. This amulet dates to the 1st Dynasty, but much later on, the Christianized Egyptians adopted the frog as a symbol of the resurrection.*

Rites of Passage

In all cultures, the transitional stages of the human life cycle are vulnerable times, coinciding with the fundamental changes from non-pregnant to pregnant, from foetus to child, and from child to adult. The ancient Egyptians believed that rituals were necessary to help them through the precarious phases of pregnancy, childbirth, early childhood and puberty. All of these, if attained without mishap, were marked by celebrations that involved giving thanks to the gods.

Fertility rituals

A woman's ability to conceive was of paramount importance to the security of her marriage, her social standing, and the comfort of her spirit after death. She would not have fulfilled her expected role in society if she died before bearing children. For this reason it is hardly surprising that childless women should turn to the divine or spirit world for a solution to their problem. There is much evidence of fertility rituals, both within the house – involving imagery of Bes and Taweret (see *Household Deities*) – and at sacred places such as tombs, temples and shrines, involving votive offerings such as fertility figurines (see *Paraphernalia of Ritual*).

Both household deities and great state gods and goddesses, such as the cow goddess Hathor and the ithyphallic god Min, were closely associated with fertility (both of the Egyptian people and of the land). During the Graeco-Roman period, if not earlier, women seem to have exposed their genitals before the cult statue of Hathor in an attempt to assimilate the goddess's fertility. Various amulets were worn, or made as votive offerings, to ensure fertility. These included tiny representations of the deities Bes, Taweret and Hathor, as well as model penises, breasts and female genitals.

An absence of menstruation was clearly linked to pregnancy. Both menstrual and birth blood must have been considered to be impure because women were expected to perform purification rituals after both of these events. Pregnant women were thought to be particularly susceptible to the ill effects caused by harmful spirits and demons. Spells were devised to prevent the demon personification of death from having sexual intercourse with a pregnant woman – a violation that would have had adverse effects on the unborn child.

Women in society

The primary role of ancient Egyptian women was to have children and to run the household. Ordinary women did their share of hard physical work, such as gathering in the harvest and grinding the corn. They tended to be responsible for food production and were employed as musicians, dancers, acrobats and mourners, among other jobs. Women did not hold public office and it is unlikely than many of them were literate. A woman's status largely depended on that of her husband, but we do know that women of the higher social class were able to sit on local tribunals; witness documents, execute their own last testament; inherit, buy, administer and sell property; free slaves; adopt children; and sue.

Ensuring a trouble-free birth

Rituals were performed to ensure that the expectant mother had a trouble-free pregnancy and

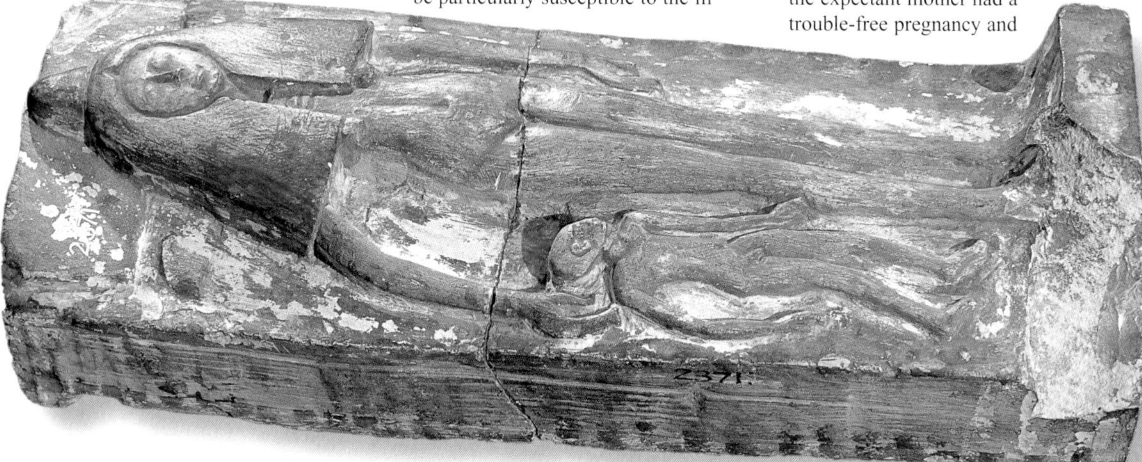

▼ *In addition to free-standing fertility figurines, examples exist of limestone or terracotta figures of naked women lying on model beds (sometimes decorated with convolvulus), often with a child (usually male) beside her thigh or being suckled.*

birth, to speed up the labour, to safeguard the newborn baby, and to guarantee the mother an adequate supply of milk. These often involved reciting a particular spell at the appropriate time. Associated with the significance of knots in ancient Egyptian magic, the woman probably bound up her hair very tightly when the baby was due, so that it could be loosened during labour, thereby sympathetically releasing the baby from the womb. Certain props were also used in the popular ritual at birth, such as amulets and apotropaic wands.

Women had their babies squatting on bricks or sitting on a wooden birthing stool. Like all that was of greatest importance in the lives of the ancient Egyptians, the birth brick was divinely personified as the goddess Meskhent. She was depicted as a brick with a human head, or as a woman wearing a headdress consisting of a brick or a peculiar emblem. This may have represented the forked uterus of a cow (or perhaps two long palm shoots with curved tips), or a *peshesh-kaf* knife (a flint fishtailed knife that was used to cut the umbilical cord). It was thought that the goddess predetermined the lives of newborn babies, and their fates were ritually inscribed or recited over the bricks.

Sympathetic magic was also used during childbirth. Spell 28 of the magical text written on Papyrus Leiden 1,348 declares: 'Hathor, the Lady of Dendera is the one giving birth.' This meant that Hathor would give birth, and in so doing suffer on behalf of the woman who was actually in labour; a transfer of pain was believed to take place. The playing of musical instruments, singing and dancing also appear to have been important at the time of childbirth.

It may be that the fragments of wall painting found in houses at Deir el-Medina and the workmen's village at Tell el-Amarna portray the period of confinement and celebration following a successful birth. The scenes include parts of figures of the household spirit-deity Bes; a dancing female flute player with a Bes tattoo on her thigh and the convolvulus plant (which was associated with fertility) around her; a child; the lower part of a naked kneeling woman with convolvulus and a servant girl. The paintings decorated mudbrick platforms, today referred to as 'box-beds'. It has been suggested that these beds were where women gave birth or nursed their newborn babies, but they may well have

▲ *Hathor, Lady of Dendera, retains a reputation for helping women who have fertility problems to this very day. Egyptian women who want children still visit the crypts of her temple.*

▲ *Rectangular mudbrick 'box-bed' structures (which would originally have been plastered and painted or whitewashed) have been found in the corner of the front room of 28 of the 68 houses excavated at Deir el-Medina.*

▼ *The mother and child on this ostracon have been drawn in a 'confinement pavilion' surrounded by convolvulus.*

been ordinary beds, or altars (or neither). The subjects of the paintings are similar to those found on *ostraca* (inscribed pieces of pottery or limestone flakes) from Deir el-Medina.

We know from one of the *Tales of Wonder*, a collection of stories composed during the Middle Kingdom (c.2055–c.1650 BC) and found on Papyrus Westcar, that beer-drinking was considered to be obligatory after childbirth. But first the mother and child had to undergo a period of confinement or separation from the outside world. The end of this period of 14 days was marked by ritual cleansing and by eating a honey cake that was thought to keep demons at bay and to stabilize and strengthen the mother.

Breast feeding provided essential nourishment for the newborn baby. A lactating woman could ensure or stimulate her milk supply by wearing an amulet in the form of the rising moon. Amulets in the shape of breasts have also been found. Lactating women were credited with *heka* (see *Magic*), and breast milk (especially that of a woman who had given birth to a male child) was considered to be a potent ingredient in a number of the magico-medical texts (especially in remedies for colds, eye problems and burns).

Vulnerability in early childhood

In addition to the predictions made about a baby at his or her birth, it was believed that a baby's viability was indicated by its first utterance. If it was '*ny*' it would live, and if it was '*embi*' it was bound to die. Infant mortality was indeed high in ancient Egypt, and early childhood was a vulnerable time. The texts known as the *Incantations for Mother and Child*, found on Papyrus Berlin 3027, consist of two books of spells and prescriptions for the treatment of infant illnesses, and for the protection of children against demons and the dead. It was feared that female spirits might try to snatch the infant from his or her mother (see *The Negative Influence of the Dead*). One of the spells is intended to cure a child of a fever. It is entitled 'Spell for a Knot' and was to be recited:

> *...over the pellet of gold, the forty bread pellets, and the cornelian sealstone, with the crocodile and the hand. To be strung on a strip of fine linen; made into an amulet; placed on the neck of the child.*

A child's name was vital to his or her personal identity. The names given at birth could reflect several popular religious practices, including the

▲ *The man performing this ritual circumcision operation is identified as a* ka-*priest, but this may well have been an honorary title for élite men of various occupations or official positions.*

celebration of festivals of particular deities, such as *Hathoremheb* ('Hathor is in festival'), and the consultation of oracles during pregnancy, for example *DjedDjehutyiwefankh* ('Thoth says he will live'). Others were devised to protect the child from harm, for instance *Amunhedebirtbint*, which means 'Amun kills the evil eye'.

Rituals of puberty

The ability to produce offspring was presumably the deciding factor in the transition from childhood to adulthood. Rituals probably accompanied a girl's first menstruation, but very little is known about ancient Egyptian puberty rituals. Any symbolic or ritual recognition of attaining adulthood quite possibly involved the cutting off of the 'sidelock' – the hairstyle often worn by young children. There is also some evidence for the circumcision of pubescent boys. The Sixth-Dynasty tomb of Ankhmahor, the 'royal architect', at Saqqara contains what appears to be a scene of a young boy (aged about ten or twelve) being circumcised. The inscription on a stela from Naga ed-Deir, now in the Oriental Institute in Chicago, claims that the owner was circumcised together with 120 others. Another First Intermediate Period inscription (c.2181–c.2055 BC), this time in the tomb of Mereri in Dendera, tells us that Mereri was proud of having circumcised the youths of the town. Certainly by the Twenty-fifth Dynasty (c.747 BC), circumcision was associated with purity.

Marriage would have formalized adulthood because it meant that women could begin to produce children. Consequently marriage, at least for a woman, probably took place in her early teens, so that she could conceive as soon after her first menstruation as possible.

As far as we know there was no religious marriage ceremony, but no doubt a celebration would have accompanied the initiation of a new household, and the first step towards the formation of a new family unit (the basis of the ancient Egyptian social structure). Marriage – at least for those with property and disposable wealth – was marked by the drawing up of a contract, which supplied the woman with a surprising number of rights and benefits. The surviving agreements show that divorce was socially acceptable, that women remained in possession of their dowries, and that divorced women could expect compensation from their ex-husbands.

Taboos

We know of various taboos in ancient Egyptian society, but it would probably be wrong to assume that each one applied to all classes of people living throughout Egypt during all of Pharaonic history. It is more likely that particular taboos corresponded to a certain type of person (for example the priesthood) in a particular geographical area, during a certain period of Egyptian history.

Taboos were particularly associated with ritual cleanliness. For this reason, for example, sexual intercourse was taboo for several days before entry into sacred places such as temples. The eating of certain foods also appears to have been considered taboo (identified as they were as *bwt*, the ancient Egyptian word used to refer to the concept of taboo), especially those relating to demons, specific deities or to a state of purity.

Food

The Calendars of Lucky and Unlucky Days prohibited the eating of certain foods on certain days. The food most frequently prohibited in the most detailed surviving example of such a calendar, called the Cairo Calendar, is fish. Fish appears to have been considered unclean, and it has been suggested that eating fish may have been considered unsuitable for a state of religious purity because it caused the breath to smell. The word for a 'stink' (*henes*) was written with the hieroglyphic sign of a *Petrocephalus bane* fish. The ancient Egyptians also made use of the *Barbus bynni* fish to write the word *bwt*, ('abomination'), and the *Mormyrus kannume* oxyrhynchus fish was used to write the word *hat*, ('corpse'). According to Plutarch's version of the myth of Osiris in the first century AD, Osiris's penis ended up in the river Nile and was eaten by three types of fish: the Nile carp (*Lepidotus*), the oxyrynchus (*Mormyrus*), and the phragus. This did not, however, stop the oxyrynchus fish from being regarded as sacred in the town of that name in the Faiyum region.

Another negative aspect of fish might have been its association with the sea, which was regarded as a place of chaos. The king and priests appear not to have been allowed to eat fish because of its association with Seth, the god of chaos and barrenness. The Twenty-fifth-Dynasty Victory Stela of Piye, now in

▲ *The Turin Erotic Papyrus contains relatively rare examples of depictions of sexual intercourse. Dating from the 19th Dynasty, it seems to portray the adventures of a comic character on a visit to a brothel.*

Epagomenal days

Certain days of the year were considered taboo for performing activities of any consequence. These were especially the 'epagomenal' days, which had been added on to the original calendar of 360 days. According to mythology these five extra days were created in order that the five children of Geb and Nut (Osiris, Isis, Seth, Nephthys and Horus the Elder) could be born. The day of Seth's birth had a particularly evil reputation, but all five were known as 'the days of the demons'.

▶ *The status of the pig was somewhat ambiguous but in the tomb of Kagemni a swineherd is depicted giving milk to a piglet from his own mouth. Saqqara*

the Cairo Museum, tells us that most of the Delta princes were forbidden from entering the palace because they had not been circumcised and because they ate fish, which, according to the inscription, was an 'abomination to the palace'. There is, however, considerable evidence for the consumption of fish in ancient Egypt, so that a fish that was taboo in one area may have been eaten in another. Archaeology has shown that the most numerous of all the food remains found in floor deposits in the main chapel of the Walled Village at Tell el-Amarna are fish bones, so fish was obviously at least prepared in this sacred environment.

Some foods certainly seem to have been considered impure, as is evident from this threat found in a tomb:

> *All who enter my grave in their impurity and who have eaten what an eminent spirit detests...I/shall seize his neck like that of a bird...*

So it was considered blasphemous, or at least disrespectful, to enter a tomb after having eaten certain foods. Inscriptions in the Graeco-Roman temple at Esna inform us that abstinence from certain foods was necessary for a period of about four days before entering the temple or celebrating religious festivals. These might have included certain kinds of fish, pork, beans, salt and onions, all of which were taboo (although by no means universally so).

▶ *The bulti fish* (Tilapia nilotica) *was observed to incubate and hatch its eggs in its mouth, so it came to symbolize the concept of rebirth.*

It may be that any avoidance of pork was due to the association of the pig with the god Seth. The lengthy record of temple offerings written on Papyrus Harris, which dates from the reign of the Nineteenth-Dynasty king Ramesses II (c.1279–c.1213 BC), does not mention pork, but it has been found in other offering lists. Before the Eighteenth Dynasty, pictorial representation of domestic pigs or reference to them in the magico-medical texts was very rare, but pork was clearly eaten throughout Egyptian history (although probably less so than beef, lamb or mutton, and goat, and to a greater extent by the poorer classes). Pig bones have been excavated with butchery marks on them; pigsties and accompanying butchery facilities have been excavated alongside the Workmen's Village at Tell el-Amarna; and pigs are listed among farm products in such texts as *The Tale of the Eloquent Peasant*. A pork taboo might have originated from the severe illness caused by the consumption of pork if it was not eaten or preserved immediately after slaughter.

Aphrodisiacs and alcohol

The aphrodisiac properties credited to a particular foodstuff could have been a reason for prohibiting it to certain members of society. Plutarch, writing in the first century AD, supposed any abstinence from salt in Egypt to be for this reason. According to Herodotus and other classical writers, Egyptian priests did not eat beans. Diodorus Siculus, in the first century BC, explained the bean and lentil taboo of the Egyptian priests by the supposition that if everyone was allowed to eat everything, something would run out. However beans must have been a staple of the Egyptian diet, and it is likely that the classical writers did not always fully understand the circumstances in Egypt. Pliny and Plutarch are unlikely to have been correct, for example, when they wrote that libations of wine were prohibited at the temple of Heliopolis. If a taboo concerning wine did exist at this temple it is more likely to have been one forbidding the priests from drinking it in the sacred enclosure. There may have been rules regulating the daily alcohol consumption of priests, and again it is the classical writers who suggest that similar limits were set for the king.

Maat

Maat was the principle that held ancient Egyptian society together and underpinned religious belief. The word is usually translated as 'truth', 'order', 'justice' or 'balance'. To recognize abstract concepts in their system of beliefs, the ancient Egyptians felt a need to divinely personify them and this they did with *maat*, which was represented as the goddess Maat, a woman with an ostrich feather on her head.

The idea of *maat* as universal order or harmony corresponds with the most fundamental role of the reigning king. This was to maintain *maat* on a national level by building temples and making offering to the gods (in fact, the ancient Egyptian deities were said to live off *maat*) and thereby placating them; by exercising control over the potential enemies of Egypt (which basically amounted to all foreigners); and by controlling nature (especially wild animals). Life in Egypt was thought to be characterized by *maat*, whereas outside its borders *isfet* reigned, that is chaos, epitomized by the desert, wild animals, foreign lands and foreign people.

Wisdom literature

There is a body of surviving literature from ancient Egypt, known today as Instructive or Wisdom Literature. It tended to be written as if by a father for his son, or by a tutor for his pupil, and it tells us how a young boy was expected to lead his life correctly – a code of moral values that would have acted as a check on human behaviour.

The text known as the *Writings of Ptahhotep* was attributed to a vizier of the Fifth Dynasty, but its earliest appearance is in a papyrus dating from the Twelfth Dynasty. It offers a series of maxims to be followed to achieve success in life, based on the ideal of an existence in accordance with the principle of *maat*.

The *Instruction of King Amenemhat I* was written as if the dead king is speaking in a revelation to his son and successor Senusret I. It warns Senusret of disloyalty among the courtiers, and emphasizes the contrast between the divinity of kingship and the limitations of a mortal king, between the ideal – embodied in the concept of *maat* – and the realities of life.

▲ *In a funerary context the goddess Maat was often depicted with large enveloping wings – much associated with protective female deities – as here in the tomb of the 19th-Dynasty king Sethnakhte in west Thebes.*

The moral code

The ideal was to lead a life in accordance with *maat*, corresponding to the socially acceptable or ethical way to behave. The texts of the Wisdom Literature reveal that certain crimes were considered crimes against *maat*. These included disorder, rebellion, envy, deceit, greed, laziness, injustice and ingratitude. The Old Kingdom *Writings of Ptahhotep* declare that 'Maat is great and lasting in effect'.

▲ *In the Middle Kingdom Maat, was described as being at the nostrils of Re, while by the 18th Dynasty she was being called 'daughter of Re'. This tomb scene at Deir el-Medina dates to the 19th Dynasty.*

The emphasis was very much on how people should listen as opposed to being deaf to *maat*, and on the idea that greed destroys social relations. In the Middle Kingdom *Tale of the Eloquent Peasant*, the lazy and the greedy are said to be deaf to *maat*.

If, when he died, a man wanted it known that he had spoken truthfully and had acted in accordance with justice, thus maintaining social harmony, he would have a recurring formula inscribed on his tomb: 'I have spoken *maat*, I have accomplished *maat*.'

The concept of *maat* and the importance of living a just life was central to the beliefs about judgment after death – when the dead person's heart was weighed in the balance against *maat*, symbolized by the feather worn on the head of the goddess Maat.

Justice for all?

The concept of justice for all is apparent in the textual evidence from ancient Egypt and in theory everyone in Egypt had access to a fair hearing. The author of the *Instruction for Merikare,* written during the Middle Kingdom (c.2055–c.1650 BC) advised the new king to 'make no difference between a man of position and a commoner'. Later on, in the New Kingdom (c.1550–c.1069 BC), the viziers were being instructed, 'See equally the man you know and the man you don't know, the man who is near you and the man who is far away.' As overseer of the courts of Egypt, the vizier held the title, 'Priest of Maat'.

Of course, in practice it would be very surprising to find a society in which position, influence and wealth did not count for anything. Bribery was probably common practice, because in another piece of instructive literature dating to the Ramesside period, the author Amenemope felt it necessary to write: 'Do not accept the reward of the powerful man, and persecute the weak for him.'

▼ *The king ('Beloved of Maat') was frequently depicted holding an effigy of Maat out to the gods on the palm of his hand.*

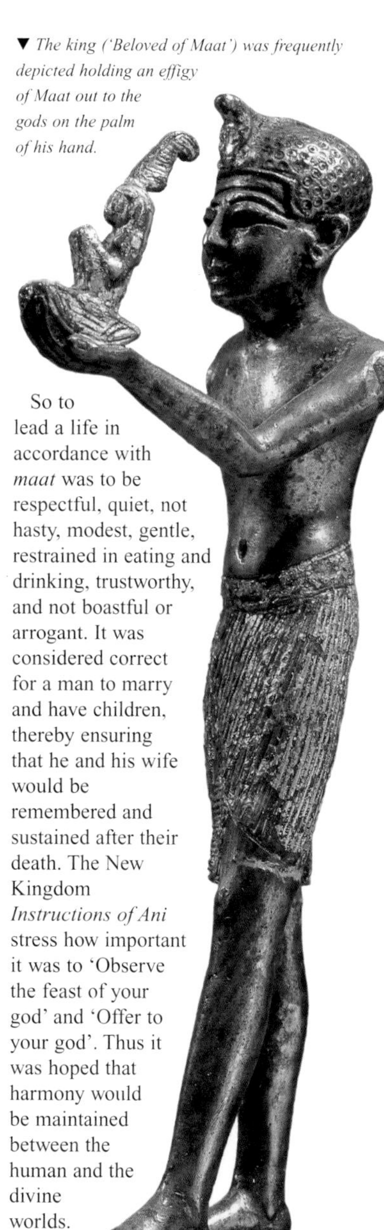

So to lead a life in accordance with *maat* was to be respectful, quiet, not hasty, modest, gentle, restrained in eating and drinking, trustworthy, and not boastful or arrogant. It was considered correct for a man to marry and have children, thereby ensuring that he and his wife would be remembered and sustained after their death. The New Kingdom *Instructions of Ani* stress how important it was to 'Observe the feast of your god' and 'Offer to your god'. Thus it was hoped that harmony would be maintained between the human and the divine worlds.

Purification

▲ *Opinion differs as to whether the nine large calcite basins in Niuserre's solar temple at Abu Gurab were used in the slaughter of animals or the ritual purification of offerings.*

We know that everyone who entered the temples of ancient Egypt was expected to be ritually pure. Most priests were called *wab*, meaning 'purified'. Their daily rituals involved washing themselves and the cult statues of the gods, hence the importance of the sacred lake within each temple complex. Our best evidence for ritual purity dates to the later periods of ancient Egyptian history. Inscriptions tell us that those entering temples were expected to cut their nails, shave the hair on their head and remove other body hair, wash their hands in natron (a naturally occurring salt), dress in a certain kind of linen (they were forbidden from wearing wool), not to have recently had sexual intercourse, and to have abstained from certain foods for about four days.

However, we can assume that similar criteria would have applied throughout Pharaonic history. At the end of the New Kingdom (c.1069 BC), a *wab*-priest of the ram-headed creator god Khnum at Elephantine, having sworn an oath not to enter the temple until he had spent ten days drinking natron, entered after only seven days, and was consequently considered ritually impure. A papyrus document records the charges of ritual impurity and perjury brought against this priest.

Washing facilities

T-shaped and rectangular limestone purification troughs, together with sunken mudbrick plastered basins and rectangular limestone lustration slabs, have been found near the shrines close to the Workmen's Village at Tell el-Amarna. Similar facilities were discovered during excavations in the shrine area to the north of the Ptolemaic temple dedicated to the goddess Hathor at Deir el-Medina. Ritual purity would have been closely linked to the concept of taboo (*bwt*). The ideal state of ritual purity during the New Kingdom is described in Chapter 125 of the Book of the Dead as:

> *...pure, clean, dressed in fresh clothes, shod in white sandals, painted with eye-paint, anointed with the finest oil of myrrh.*

And the image corresponding to the spell was to be drawn:

> *...on a clean surface in red paint mixed with soil on which pigs and goats have not trodden.*

Obligatory ritual purity also applied to entry into tombs, visitors to which were liable to be punished if they caused any damage or did not comply with the conventions of purity.

Purification rituals were also important on a more popular level, for ensuring social acceptance and thus a harmonious, ordered household or community. Within the life cycle of the family, sexual intercourse, menstruation and birth were all considered unclean, requiring subsequent purification rituals in order to allow the individual(s) concerned to be reintegrated into society, especially after a period of confinement or seclusion, for example following childbirth.

The ancient Egyptian word used euphemistically for 'menstruation' and 'to menstruate' is *hesmen*, the same as that for the verb 'to purify oneself', and the purifying agent natron. In the tale of Setne-Khaemwese and Naneferkaptah, written in demotic on a papyrus of the Ptolemaic period, now in the Cairo Museum, a woman named Ahwere reveals her pregnancy by announcing the absence of her menstruation with the words: 'When my time of purification came, I made no purification.'

Cleansing rituals

Bodily fluids, and particularly menstrual and birth blood, do appear to have been considered to be impure. The fear seems to have been that the pollutive blood might attract demons. These demons were thought to be scared of honey, so it was considered sensible for women to eat cakes made of honey after having given birth. In the tale entitled *The Birth of the Royal Children* on the Middle Kingdom Papyrus Westcar, now in the Egyptian Museum, Berlin, we are told that following Ruddedet's giving birth to triplets, she '...cleansed herself in a cleansing of 14 days'. Purification rituals of this kind involved washing and the burning of incense. Scenes of the confinement period, when the mother and baby were kept separate from the rest of society, were illustrated on ostraca (flakes of limestone) and on paintings on the brick platforms in the living rooms of houses at Deir el-Medina and in the Workmen's Village at Tell el-Amarna. These include female serving girls holding mirrors, basins and cosmetic tubes, as well as musical instruments. The required purification was usually followed by celebration. Following Ruddedet's 'cleansing' in Papyrus Westcar, she sends her maid to fetch beer and then '…they sat down to a day of feasting'.

▼ *The blade of this razor from Deir el-Medina is bronze, and the handle is wooden.*

Texts have survived from the tomb-builders' village at Deir el-Medina that reveal that one of the reasons for a man's absence from work in the Valley of the Kings might have been because he was 'making himself pure for Taweret' (or 'Taweret was making him pure'). Taweret was the household goddess associated with pregnancy and childbirth. It may have been expected that a man should miss work and perform a purification ritual if a female member of his family was menstruating or had given birth.

◀ *From the Middle Kingdom onwards, mirrors took the form of a sun disc of polished bronze or copper, with the handle often in the form of a papyrus stalk and/or the goddess Hathor.*

The circumcision of children also seems to have related to purity. Herodotus made this association in the fifth century BC, when he commented that the Egyptians were circumcised as they 'preferred purity above fresh air'. The inscription on the Twenty-fifth-Dynasty Victory Stela of Piye tells us that three local rulers were not granted an audience with the king because they were 'uncircumcised and ate fish'. In contrast Namart, the prince of Hermopolis, was allowed entry because he was 'pure and did not eat fish'.

In the magical texts, such as the Demotic Magical Papyrus of London and Leiden which dates to the beginning of the third century BC, it is made clear that a state of purity is deemed necessary for the efficacy of the particular spell or ritual. The only specified requisite for purification was an abstinence from sexual intercourse (seemingly for three days beforehand), and it was considered ideal to include a young boy in the ritual, specifically because he was a virgin.

The ancient Egyptians also appear to have associated the condition of impurity with the period of mourning, as temple access was denied to people in this state.

Lucky and Unlucky Days

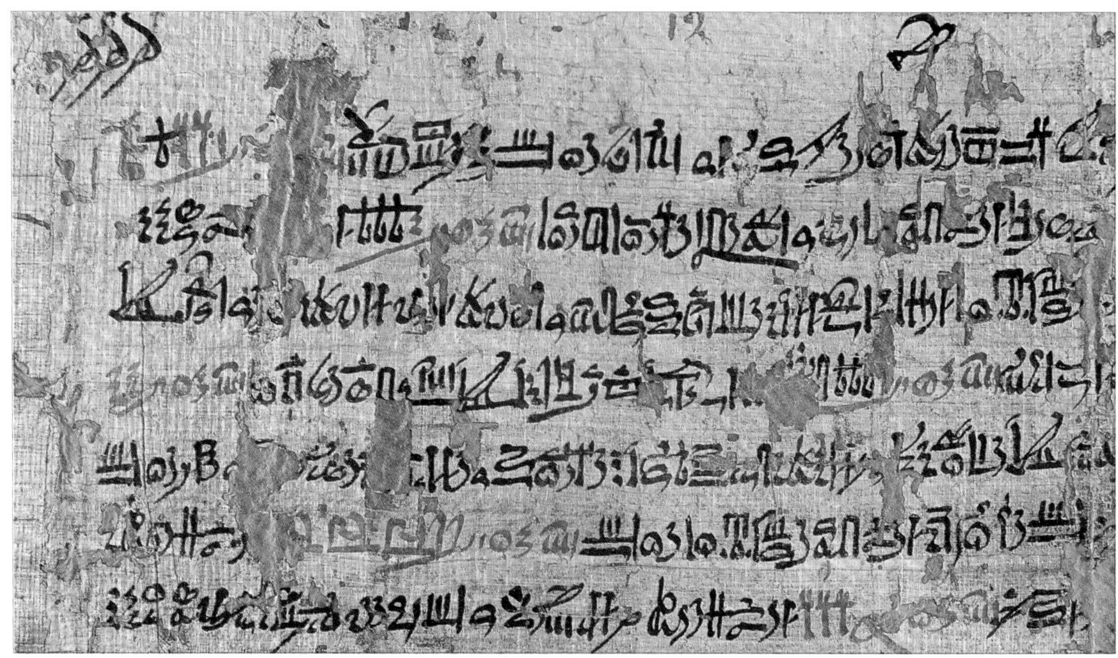

▲ *On this calendar, days described as lucky are written in black, and those described as unlucky in red. 19th Dynasty.*

Calendars that have survived from ancient Egypt categorize each day of the year as either lucky or unlucky. The best known of these is the one known as the Cairo Calendar, which is said to have come from Thebes and to date to the reign of the Nineteenth-Dynasty king Ramesses II (c.1279–c.1213 BC). But the language in it seems earlier than Ramesside, and the text does not mention the Theban triad of deities, Amun, Mut and Khonsu, so the original contents of the calendar were probably earlier in date.

Days seem to have been categorized according to the mythical events that were said to have happened on them. For example, a day on which two gods had fought was considered unlucky, whereas a day on which a god had made a successful journey was regarded as fortunate. By consulting a Calendar of Lucky and Unlucky Days, an ancient Egyptian would know whether or not it would be sensible to carry out a certain activity on a certain day. For example, some days were deemed to be suitable for performing certain rituals in the home, for pacifying the spirits of dead relatives (see *Ancestor Worship*), or for making a votive offering at a local shrine or temple, inscribed or accompanied by an oral request. These calendars may have been consulted to determine the most auspicious day for a magician to work a spell for someone.

Rituals carried out in temples were tied in with the calendar of religious festivals. The basis for the reasoning found in the Calendars of Lucky and Unlucky days seems to have been a religious calendar of the festivals of the various gods and goddesses.

It is possible that the Calendars of Lucky and Unlucky Days were the result of amassing a body of recorded incidents, which were then listed in a calendrical order according to experience. Private individuals must have been able to own their own version of such a calendar, because the scribe Qenherkhepshef, who lived at the tomb-builders' village of Deir el-Medina in the late thirteenth and early twelfth centuries BC, certainly possessed his own copy, which is now in the British Museum, London.

The epagomenal days

The calendars made it clear that nothing of any consequence should be done during the five-day period added on to the original year of 360 days. According to the mythology these five extra days were created in order that the five

▲ *According to Egyptian mythology, Seth and Nephthys were two of Nut's children, and were also thought to be consorts.*

children of Geb and Nut – Osiris, Isis, Seth, Nephthys and Horus the Elder – could be born, and it was considered to be an extremely dangerous period. The day on which Seth was supposed to be born had a particularly evil reputation, but all five were known as 'the days of the demons'.

Directions and predictions

The calendars specified certain activities to be carried out on certain days. For example, it is advised that on the nineteenth day of the second month of the season of *Akhet* ('Inundation'), when, according to myth, the embalming oil was prepared for Osiris, wine should be drunk until sundown instead of beer, the more usual daily drink. The calendars were also used to predict the cause of death if someone died on a certain day. For example, if someone died on the sixth day of the second month of *Akhet*, it was likely to be as a result of intoxication. This must have been considered a favourable way to meet one's end because it coincided with a day of revelry in the divine world.

The calendars were used to predict a child's future, depending on the day on which he or she was born. The fifth day of the second month of *Akhet*, for example, was described as a day of offerings to the deities Montu and Hedjhotep, and it was predicted that a child born on this day would have his or her death caused by copulation. A child born on the tenth day of the fourth month of *Akhet* was destined to die of old age with an offering of beer poured on his face – this may well have been considered an ideal way to end one's life. Herodotus, writing in the fifth century BC, noted:

> *The Egyptians have ascertained the god to whom each month and day is sacred and they can therefore tell, according to the date of the child's birth, what fate is in store for him, how he will end his days, and what sort of person he will become*

The idea of a Calendar of Lucky and Unlucky days persisted in medieval Europe. In the thirteenth century AD astrological calendars were produced in which some days were designated as 'Egyptian Days'. These were considered to be unpropitious for anything except the working of black magic. The observance of such 'Egyptian Days' was one of the charges made against French heretics at the inquisitorial courts in the thirteenth century AD.

▼ *An enormous quantity of written evidence, both on papyrus and on ostraca (flakes of limestone and potsherds), has been discovered at the tomb-builders' village of Deir el-Medina.*

Dreams

The ancient Egyptians believed that what they dreamed had a bearing on their daily lives, and that the interpretation of dreams was a valid means of predicting the future. A collection of texts has survived from ancient Egypt, which are known today as 'Dream Books'. They consist of lists of possible dream scenarios and what the dreams indicate will happen in the life of the dreamer. For example, if

▶ *Hatshepsut's mortuary temple at Deir el-Bahri is set in a deep bay in the desert cliffs which were in turn at the foot of the pyramidal peak sacred to the goddesses Hathor and Mertseger.*

A dream directory

The Dream Book of qenherkhepshef discovered at Deir el-Medina is written in tabular form, with the dreams described in one column of text and interpretation in another:

If a man sees himself in a dream...

...submerging in the river: good: this means purification from all evils.

...eating crocodile: good: this means acting as an official among his people.

...burying an old man: good: this means flourishing.

...seeing his face in a mirror: bad: this means another wife.

...shod with white sandals: bad: this means roaming the earth.

...copulating with a woman: bad: this means mourning.

...his bed catching fire: bad: this means driving away his wife.

someone dreamt that he was drinking warm beer, it was thought to forewarn that the dreamer would soon suffer harm. A careful reading of the texts in the original shows that many of the correlations between the content of the dream and the prophecy are based on the use of puns (a potent form of magic). For instance, to dream about a harp meant that something evil would surely happen to the person in question; whereas to dream about a donkey indicated that the dreamer was soon to be promoted. To get a sense of the magical use of language in these predictions we have to know that the ancient Egyptian word for 'harp' was *benet*, and the word for 'evil' was *bint*; that the word for 'donkey' was *aa* and the word for 'to be promoted' was *saa*.

Who would actually have been in possession of these books? Did certain priests and magicians own them? Or might a family have had its own copy of such a manual in their home, ready to consult whenever they felt the need? We know that the scribe Qenherkhepshef, who was in charge of the administration of Deir el-Medina in the late thirteenth and early twelfth centuries BC, owned one. Today it is known as Papyrus Chester Beatty III. It is written in the hieratic script and is now in the British Museum in London. Although it dates to the Ramesside Period, it has been noticed that the language used is very Middle Kingdom in style, and so perhaps it is a copy of a text originally compiled in the Eleventh or Twelfth Dynasty. The library of this particular scribe was pretty impressive, including as it did, examples of poetry, literature, history, magical spells and a Calendar of Lucky and Unlucky Days.

The Lector Priests would have acted as the link between the temples and the local communities. Their role in the temple was associated with the written and spoken word in the form of spells and incantations, and they were closely associated with magic throughout Egyptian history. Apart from their ritual duties, they had a reputation as interpreters of dreams. They presumably consulted these 'Dream Books'.

▲ *As 'Lady of the West', Hathor was protectress of the west Theban necropolis. She was depicted on stelae and funerary papyri as a cow leaving the desert to come down into the papyrus marshes and she acted as a link between the tombs and life in the Nile Valley.*

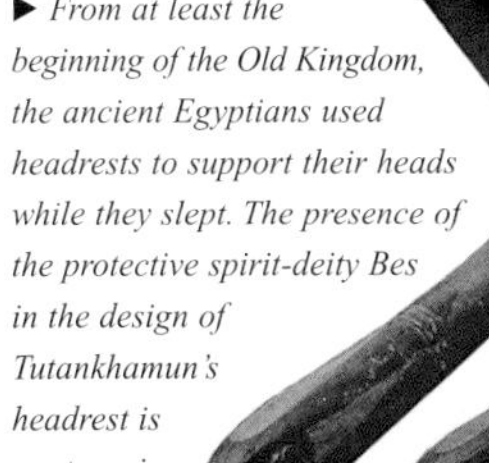

▶ *From at least the beginning of the Old Kingdom, the ancient Egyptians used headrests to support their heads while they slept. The presence of the protective spirit-deity Bes in the design of Tutankhamun's headrest is apotropaic.*

▶ *Tuthmosis IV recorded his dream in which the Great Sphinx appeared to him in all its aspects – Khepri-Re-Atum – on the stela he set up between the paws of the Sphinx.*

◀ *Imhotep, the architect of the Step Pyramid at Saqqara, was deified during the Late Period and was one of the patron deities of the healing sanctuary in Hatshepsut's mortuary temple.*

Fear of nightmares

Because dreams were believed to be of such great significance, it becomes clear why the Egyptians were so concerned about nightmares and attempted to guard against them with spells and apotropaic headrests. Papyrus Chester Beatty III suggests using protective spells on waking from a nightmare, and examples of headrests have been found decorated with images of the protective household deities Bes and Taweret (sometimes brandishing knives against any possible threat to the sleeper).

The magical papyri of the Ptolemaic Period explained to people how they could go about directing the anger of the god Seth against their enemies, causing them nightmares or even death. It was thought possible to cause someone much upset and trauma by sending them dreams of ill omen.

Incubation

During the first millennium BC, a practice known as 'incubation' became popular. People went to sleep in structures known as sanatoria or healing sanctuaries, built specifically for this purpose inside the precincts of temples, in order to have healing or helpful dreams, particularly to help to solve infertility problems. Part of the Eighteenth-Dynasty ruler Hatshepsut's mortuary temple at Deir el-Bahri was converted into one such sanatorium. It was dedicated to the two deified sages Imhotep (the vizier and chief royal architect during the reign of the Third-Dynasty king Djoser (c.2667–c.2648 BC)) and Amenhotep, son of Hapu, a high official during the reign of the Eighteenth-Dynasty king Amenhotep III (c.1390–c.1352 BC).

In the story of Setne Khaemwese and Si-Osire, written in demotic on papyrus and dating to the Roman Period, Mehusekhe, the wife of Setne, seeks a solution to her inability to conceive. She spends a night in a sanctuary where she has a dream in which she is advised to concoct and take a remedy made from the crushed gourds of a melon vine. This she does, but it is also clearly stated that she must have sexual intercourse with her husband and, as a result, she becomes pregnant.

There were some occasions on which gods were said to have appeared to people in dreams and in this way to have affected or sanctioned a particular decision (a form of oracular consultation). During the New Kingdom (c.1550–c.1069 BC), one Theban official was said to have been inspired by the goddess Hathor in a dream to build his tomb in a certain place.

Oracles

The earliest unambiguous evidence that the ancient Egyptians consulted oracles dates from the New Kingdom (c.1550–c.1069 BC). It takes the form of papyri, and – more often – ostraca, the pieces of pottery or limestone on which scribes took notes, from the tomb-builders' village of Deir el-Medina on the west bank of the River Nile at Thebes. At Deir el-Medina it was usually the oracle of the tomb-builders' royal patron deity Amenhotep I that was consulted. His shrine was located just outside the village, to the north.

Oracles tended to be consulted on certain festival days, when the cult statue of the god was carried in procession out of his or her shrine or temple on the shoulders of a number of priests. An expression that regularly occurs in the records as an introduction to a description of the consultation with the deity is the phrase 'As I stood before (him)'. However, although the ordinary person might have come closer to a cult statue during this festival procession than at any time (it was usually in the temple), it was still always concealed from view, often in a barque shrine.

Ostraca now in the British Museum, London, reveal that oracles were used mainly in disputes over property (especially houses and tombs). They might also be consulted to end a disagreement between a buyer and a seller. On Ostracon 576 from Deir el-Medina, it is recorded that the buyer asked the oracle to specify the amount of grain he ought to receive because a certain tradesman had the reputation of sneakily reducing it. Sometimes advice or questions were asked of the oracle. Ostracon 562 records the specific question: 'Should I go North?' In this way we are able to learn something of the mundane problems and indecisions of ordinary life, and the comfort to be gained from having the gods endorse everyday decision-making.

▲ *On festival days the barque shrine of Amun was processed on the shoulders of priests, as shown here in a relief from Hatshepsut's chapel at Karnak. It was on these occasions that the oracle of the god might be consulted.*

Oracular judgement

Oracles were also considered useful for helping to solve crimes, and for bringing the guilty to justice. In the case of a robbery, a list of suspects might be named before the god, and he then had to indicate the guilty suspect. Ostracon 4 from Deir el-Medina records that two articles of clothing had been stolen from a man. The houses of the possible thieves were named in front of the cult statue of Amenhotep I, and when that of the scribe Amen-nakht was named the god made a sign of affirmation. The scribe was summoned to a tribunal (*kenbet*) with his daughter, who was in fact found to be the thief. So the local oracle and the court would have strengthened each other's decision-making in the judicial process.

The ancient texts are ambiguous about the way the oracles gave their answers, but there were various ways in which a god might have made his decisions known: by the priests speaking; by mechanical manipulation inside the statue, such as the movement of the head; by the statue carried by the priests moving forwards or backwards; or by the god approaching an affirmative or negative piece of writing placed on either side of the processional way. In the previously mentioned case of the names of the houses possibly sheltering the thief, the names may have been written on reed strips, with the god then somehow guiding the decision as to which one was drawn.

The word of the oracle does not seem to have necessarily been final (it was obviously not automatically accepted as law). Two separate papyri exist that each refer to the same dispute, with a lapse of three years between them, indicating that it was still being debated. If the response given by one oracle was not what the petitioner wanted to hear, it appears to have been possible for him to go on to consult other deities. Even so, it seems to have been usual for those consulting oracles to be called upon to swear oaths binding them to the oracle's decision: in view of this it may be that the ancient Egyptians were not quite so fearful of their gods as we often assume them to have been.

Oaths

The ancient Egyptian words for 'oath' (*wah* and *ankh*) and 'to swear' (*ankh* and *ark*) were the same as those for 'to endure', 'to live' and 'to wrap or bind'. Oaths tended to be sworn on the life or reign of the ruler, beginning, 'As the Ruler who lives forever endures…' Others were sworn by a god, in which case it could be a specific deity such as Re, Re-Horakhty, Amun or Ptah in his specific role as 'Lord of Truth'; or by the *ka* (or spirit) of a particular deity, such as Thoth; or by the idea of *netjer* – the divine – or gods in general. The Eighteenth-Dynasty ruler Akhenaten (c.1352–c.1336 BC) chose to revolutionize the state religion of ancient Egypt, so that all gods were abolished except for the solar deity Aten, whom he elevated to a supreme position together with himself and his family. In tombs at Tell el-Amarna, the site of Akhenaten's capital city, the inscriptions of oaths begin, 'As the Aten endures and as the Ruler endures...'

▼ *The donkey was the principal load-bearer of the ancient Egyptians, whose word for 'donkey' was the onomatopoeic* aa. *20th century copy of a wall painting from a Theban tomb by Nina de Garis Davies.*

The Oath of the Lord

One particular oath was especially used for legal purposes, and that was the *ankh n neb* or 'Oath of the Lord'. It was a royal oath, because the lord in question was the ruling pharaoh. It is possible that the Egyptians did not want

◀ *The crocodile (*Crocodilus niloticus*) was common and dangerous in the Egyptian environment. Being thrown to the crocodiles was sometimes threatened as an extreme penalty for the breaking of an oath.*

suspected criminals speaking the actual name of the king. Ancient texts inform us of lawsuits, and provide us with lists of witnesses who were called upon to swear an oath such as, 'As Amun endures and as the Ruler endures, we speak in truth.' One of the papyri that deal specifically with the extensive tomb robbery that took place at the end of the Twentieth Dynasty states that, 'The Oath of the Lord was given to him [the foreigner Pai-Kamen] not to speak falsely.' It appears that the defendant or witness might be beaten before even taking the oath; for example, Papyrus Mayer A tells us that, 'The citizeness Ineri was examined by beating with a stick. The Oath of the Lord was given to her not to speak falsely.'

Instances of people swearing falsely are, however, recorded. We learn from Papyrus Salt 124 that a man named Paneb was charged with having stolen a goose, and that 'He took the oath of the Lord about it, saying "I do not have it" (but) they found it in his house.' We know of the penalties threatened for perjury, but there is much less evidence of punishments actually being carried out. Papyrus Mayer A informs us that 'Examination was made of the herdsman of the House of Amun, the thief Pai-Kamen. An oath on penalty of mutilation, not to speak falsely.' On another occasion, outlined in Papyrus Abbott, a coppersmith was taken to the scene of a confessed crime and 'He took the Oath of the Lord on penalty of beating and having his nose and ears cut off, and of being put upon the stake.' Punishments for the breaking of an oath that are referred to in other accounts include being sent to Ethiopia or being thrown to crocodiles.

Oaths might accompany sale contracts. The presence of registered witnesses to an oath seems to have made it legally binding. Sometimes oaths were taken several times to emphasize them. Oaths also accompanied promises, such as the promise to repay borrowed money (a failure to repay could be treated as theft). Oaths were also used in marriage contracts, for example, the marriage agreement in Papyrus Berlin 304, dating from the Twenty-second Dynasty, includes the words, 'He said, "As Amun lives and as Pharaoh lives and as the chief priest of [Amun] lives... If I wish to divorce her and I love another woman, I am the one who must give her the things recorded above".'

A promise and a threat

Sometimes an oath was coupled with a curse. A woman named Rennefer wanted to make her slave foster-children freemen, so they might inherit her property, and she said: 'As Amun endures and as the Ruler endures, may a donkey copulate with him, and a female donkey copulate with his wife, he who shall call one of them slave.'

▲ *Each plume of Amun's headdress was divided into two, reflecting the duality of the Egyptian world view, and each feather was divided into seven horizontal segments (seven being a ritually significant number). 20th Dynasty.*

Breaking an oath

It seems unlikely that the ancient Egyptians would have taken an oath sworn in the name of a deity lightly but, just as the pronouncements of the oracles were not necessarily accepted, oaths do not appear to have carried absolute authority. In a case of sexual misconduct said to have taken place at Deir el-Medina, a man called Mery Sekhmet was found to have broken the oath he had been made to swear. He was not punished for this misdemeanour, however; he was just instructed to swear another one.

Festivals and Pilgrimages

Festivals were occasions of celebration – of music, dancing, eating and drinking. They were also times when ordinary people might benefit from a closer encounter with the cult statue of a deity than was usually possible. For most of the time, the cult statue resided in a shrine in the dimly lit inner sanctuary of a temple – a place forbidden to the impure and uninitiated. But on festival days, the statue was carried in procession out of the temple, accompanied by musicians, singers, dancers, acrobats and incense burners. People might have come close to the statue, but still would not have seen it because it was carefully hidden from the masses. During a festival they might be given the opportunity to commune with the deity by consulting its oracle. This gave them a chance to consult the god for his wisdom on an issue that was important to their daily lives, such as whether it was a good time to make a long and difficult journey. The divine go-ahead was sought. A god might also be asked to settle a dispute or indicate the person responsible for a crime.

Calendars of festivals

The Hour Priests working in the House of Life in each of the temples worked out the annual calendar of festivals around which the temple's year revolved. Some of the calendars have survived; for example, in the Festival Hall of the Eighteenth-Dynasty king Tuthmosis III (c.1479–c.1425 BC) at Karnak temple, 54 feast days are listed for one year. And at Ramesses III's mortuary temple at Medinet Habu, 60 festivals are listed. We learn from this 'calendar of feasts and offerings' that 84 loaves of bread were required for a monthly festival, and almost 4,000 for the national Festival of Sokar, the Memphite funerary deity.

The focus of some festivals was the visitation by one deity on another. The cow goddess Hathor, for example, left her main cult centre at Dendera each year to journey by boat to Edfu, where she was united with the falcon deity Horus. Another annual festival, held from the early Eighteenth Dynasty onwards, was the Festival of Opet, which lasted from two to four weeks. The cult statues of Amun, his consort Mut, and their child Khonsu were carried in procession in barque shrines from their temple complex at Karnak to Luxor temple, along a route lined with ram-headed sphinxes. In the late Eighteenth Dynasty they began to make this journey in ceremonial boats on the River Nile. At Luxor, Amun was

▲ *Many ostraca depicting figures like this female acrobat originate from the tomb-builders' village of Deir el-Medina.*

► *Bread and beer were the staples of the Egyptian diet, and wooden models such as this one were intended to ensure their production for eternity. Middle Kingdom.*

▲ *In this tomb painting the cones balanced on the heavy black wigs of these women revellers at a banquet symbolize sweet-smelling ointments. They also wear jewellery and fine clothing.*

believed to have sexual intercourse with the mother of the reigning king so that she would give birth to the royal *ka*. The king was then united with his *ka* in the sanctuary of the temple, and he was believed to emerge as a god.

The dead were also involved in important festivals such as the Beautiful Festival of the Valley, which lasted 12 days and was celebrated from the early Eighteenth Dynasty onwards. The divine family of Karnak left their east-bank temple and crossed the river to visit Deir el-Bahri, and later, another mortuary temple as well. Ordinary people celebrated this festival at their family burial place by sharing a meal with the spirits of their dead relatives.

Revelry at Bubastis

People made pilgrimages to the more important festivals. Writing in the mid fifth century BC, Herodotus recorded the journeying of pilgrims to the cult site of Bubastis in the eastern Delta, to celebrate the festival of the cat goddess Bastet. He described the trip to Bubastis by boat, during which the women on the river hurled abuse at women on the banks, danced, hitched up their skirts, and exposed their genitals to the world around them. This bawdy behaviour was probably meant to pass fertility from the women to the land (or vice versa). We know that on other occasions women exposed themselves before a statue of the goddess Hathor, hoping to benefit from the goddess's close association with fertility.

Herodotus wrote that 700,000 people (excluding children) attended the festival of Bastet. People sang and musical instruments such as the flute and castanets were played. Sacrifices were made, and more wine was drunk than during all the rest of the year.

Probably the cult centre most commonly visited by pilgrims was Abydos, the legendary burial place and chief temple of Osiris, the god of the dead, the Afterlife, rebirth and vegetation. During the Middle Kingdom (c.2055–c.1650 BC), thousands of people went to Abydos and set up private stelae in cenotaphs and tombs around the temple of Osiris, thereby hoping to ensure a never-ending participation in the festivals of the god. These stelae also functioned as family monuments, and for this reason repeated pilgrimages were made, both to the temple of Osiris and to these memorials to the deceased. Scenes on the walls of New Kingdom private tombs often depict a symbolic pilgrimage being made by the dead person to Abydos.

▶ *A married couple are depicted on this limestone stela from Abydos. The man holds a* sekhem *sceptre in his right hand, denoting 'power' and 'might'.*

Music and Dance in Egyptian Religion

Singers, dancers and musicians were an important part of temple life. People believed that the gods enjoyed, and were pacified by, singing, music and dance. In the New Kingdom *Teachings of Ani*, song, dance and incense are described as the food of the gods. These activities accompanied the daily temple rites, figured highly at festivals and formed a part of more personal religious rituals – during funerals and at childbirth, for example. No musical notation has survived from ancient Egypt, but we do have the words of songs; illustrations of musicians, singers and dancers; the titles of people in these professions; and ancient musical instruments such as the harp, lute, lyre, flute, double reed-pipe, drum, cymbals, tambourine, bells and a form of guitar.

▲ *The double reed-pipe was played by female musicians accompanying dancers at festive occasions. 18th Dynasty.*

Temple musicians

If temple musicians played before the cult statues of the gods, we can assume that they would not have been allowed to lay their eyes upon the statues (because only the king and High Priest were in a position to do this). It has therefore been suggested that any musicians allowed into the inner sanctuary were quite likely to have been blind. Male harpists depicted on the walls of tombs do occasionally appear to be blind, and disability does not seem to have been considered a bar to purity; there is no reason to believe that people with physical disabilities were ostracized by ancient Egyptian society.

At festivals, musicians, singers and dancers walked in procession out of the temple with the shrine housing the cult statue. Often the point was not to produce pleasing music, but a rhythmic sound to create a state of religious ecstasy – or simply a loud noise to scare away harmful spirits, for example at birth. Clappers and *sistra* were the two instruments most useful for these purposes. Clappers were usually made of ivory, which meant that they were curved like apotropaic wands. They often had a design carved into them, such as a shrine, a woman's head or the head of Hathor (some texts describe this goddess as 'Lady of Dance'). *Sistra* were ceremonial rattles, which were

▼ *Hathor was 'Lady of the Vulva' and the 'Hand of Atum': the combination in these clappers probably had sexual connotations.*

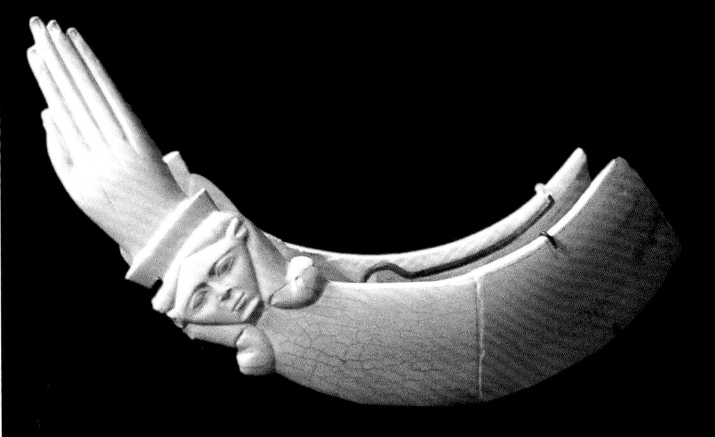

▲ *The ancient Egyptians appear to have made little distinction between dancing and what we would describe as acrobatics, shown in this relief from Hatshepsut's chapel at Karnak.*

most frequently made of bronze. They were very much associated with the goddess Hathor, whose priestesses shook them as part of the rituals they performed. They often had the head of this goddess incorporated in their design, and they may have been thought to stimulate fertility. In her manifestation as Nebethetepet, or 'Lady of the Vulva', Hathor was represented as a *naos sistrum* (a *sistrum* with the design of a shrine incorporated into it). *Menat*-necklaces were also carried and shaken by the priestesses.

The household spirit-deity, Bes, was often depicted playing various musical instruments, especially a drum or tambourine. Bes was closely associated with pregnancy and childbirth, and music was important in the celebration following a successful birth. Several of the fragments of wall painting found in houses at Deir el-Medina show Bes dancing and making music. One fragment reveals a naked, dancing female playing the flute. According to the mythology, Bes appeased the enraged Hathor when she was sulking at Philae by playing the tambourine and harp to her, and he is depicted dancing and playing a tambourine and harp on columns in the Temple of Hathor at Philae.

▲ *Men and women were never shown dancing together. Here men dance on a relief in the tomb of Kagemni at Saqqara.*

Births and deaths

In the tale of *The Birth of the Royal Children* on the Middle-Kingdom Papyrus Westcar, the midwives who arrive at the house of the woman in labour are disguised as dancing girls (they also happen to be goddesses). It may well have been common for female dancers to play a part at the time of birth. A scene in the Sixth-Dynasty tomb of Mereruka at Saqqara depicts a female dancing troupe (a *khener*) before his wife Watekhethor, and the hieroglyphic text reads: 'But see the secret of birth! Oh pull!'

Dancers were also present at funerals to elate the spirit of the dead, and to scare away evil spirits. These were the *muu*-dancers who wore kilts and tall, white reed headdresses. From as early as the Fifth Dynasty (c.2490 BC), lion-masked dwarves appear to have been linked to groups of women employed to sing and dance on religious occasions.

Agricultural rites

Singing was a key element of the rites associated with agriculture. Harvesters might chant a lament, accompanied by a flute, in order to express their sorrow at the first cutting of the crops, which was thought to symbolize the wounding of Osiris, the god of vegetation. Dancing was also related to agricultural rites, both as a means of stimulating growth and and as a form of thanksgiving. A particularly good example of agricultural dances at the time of the harvest can be found in the Theban tomb of Antefoker dating from the Middle Kingdom (c.2055–1650 BC). The dances appear to be measured and fairly sedate. The *keskes*-dance, associated with Hathor, involved holding mirrors and what appear to be wooden or ivory sticks, carved in the shape of a hand at one end; they were probably clappers. The hand-shaped implements may be linked to Hathor in her aspect of Djeritef, 'his hand', that is the hand of Atum, said in the Heliopolitan creation myth, to have created Shu and Tefnut by masturbating.

A limestone relief of c.1400 BC, now in the British Museum, London, includes a male figure with a lion's head (possibly a Bes mask), carrying a staff with a human hand at the tip, in a register labelled 'dancing by children'.

Beer and Wine in Egyptian Religion

Beer and wine – distillation for making spirit drinks was unknown in ancient Egypt – were important in both temple and popular rituals. They were presented as offerings to the gods in the temples and shrines, and to the spirits of the dead in the tombs, funerary chapels and temples. They were also drunk at festivals and other celebrations, and were used in magical rituals and medicine. Together with bread, beer was a staple of the Egyptian diet, and the Wisdom Literature tells us that it was a mother's responsibility to provide these two sources of nutrition for her children. The gods were thought to be pacified and humoured by alcohol. In the myth of *The Destruction of Mankind*, the ferocious lioness goddess Sekhmet is prevented from wiping out humankind altogether by being made drunk on beer dyed red to resemble human blood.

From lists of offerings to the gods compiled during the New Kingdom (c.1550–c.1069 BC), we can learn about the variety, source and quantity of alcohol arriving at the temples. Libation with alcohol played a well-attested role in ancient Egyptian ritual, whether at annual festivals such as the Festival of the Nile and Drunkenness, or at occasional ceremonies, such as the foundation of a new building.

In the Afterlife

Beer- and wine-making depended on successful agriculture and abundant harvests, for which the ancient Egyptians believed they needed the beneficence of certain deities, in honour of whom they held festivals and made offerings. The fundamental need for constant supplies

▶ *Wine and beer figure largely on New Kingdom offering lists. This granite statue of Tuthmosis III holds jars of wine: such offerings were a means of appeasing supernatural forces – both deities and spirits of the dead.*

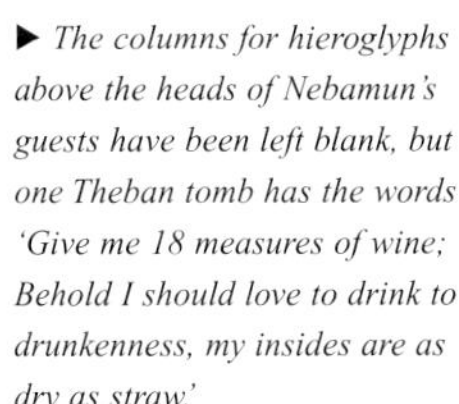

▶ *The columns for hieroglyphs above the heads of Nebamun's guests have been left blank, but one Theban tomb has the words 'Give me 18 measures of wine; Behold I should love to drink to drunkenness, my insides are as dry as straw.'*

of agricultural produce was of crucial importance to the ancient Egyptians, not only on earth but also in the Afterlife. This explains the private tomb scenes of harvesting, brewing, viticulture and winemaking, which represent the hope of having eternal supplies not only for the deceased but also for everyone in Egypt. The practise of depicting particular actions and events was to the Egyptians a means of magically ensuring they would happen in the Afterlife. Thus, by illustrating such scenes of daily life (captioned in hieroglyphs), the basic fundamentals of existence were being recognized and, with hope, laid down for eternity. This preparation for the future ensured the continued smooth running of the natural order of the cosmos, encapsulated in the concept of *maat*.

The patron deity of wine presses was male, Shezmu, but on the whole the female-oriented nature of brewing, from early in Pharaonic history, was closely reflected in the divine world. The presiding deities of beer were the goddesses Menqet and Tenemyt, whose names probably derived from the terms for a type of beer jar and beer, respectively. The equivalent deity of vineyards and wine-making was Renenutet, a cobra-form goddess of harvest and abundance. A number of private New Kingdom Theban tombs contain scenes of viticulture, with the presence of small shrines dedicated to this snake goddess.

Wine had a special significance in the cults of the goddesses Bastet, Sekhmet, Tefnut and particularly Hathor, the goddess most closely associated with alcohol and drunkenness. A song inscribed on a wall of the hypostyle hall of the Temple of Hathor at Philae, tells of a 'festival of intoxication' celebrated in honour of the goddess, and we learn that a perfect year was believed to have its beginnings in drunkenness.

Dance and alcohol were particularly closely related in the cult of Hathor. The spirit-deity Bes, who was associated with music, dance, fertility, sexuality and the protection of the family, was also connected with alcohol. Wine and beer jars were specially made in his form.

Attendance records have survived from the New Kingdom tomb-builders' village of Deir el-Medina in western Thebes. They tell us that it was not unheard of for men to take days off work specially to brew beer for a particular occasion, which was usually religious in nature. An ostracon, or inscribed potsherd, from Deir el-Medina, now in the Cairo Museum, describes the celebration of a festival of the deified king Amenhotep I, who was the patron deity of the tomb builders:

> *The crew* [necropolis workers] *were in jubilation before him* [Amenhotep I] *for four whole days of drinking with their children and their wives.*

Communing with the gods

Drunkenness appears to have gone hand in hand with celebration (inscriptions in the early Eighteenth-Dynasty tomb of Ahmose at El-Kab include the words 'drinking into intoxication and celebrating a festive day'), but it appears also to have been considered beneficial for communing with the gods. Three visiting scribes left a graffito at Abusir, in the fiftieth year of the Nineteenth-Dynasty ruler Ramesses II's reign. It reads: '...It is as we stand drunk before (you) [Sekhmet of Sahure], that we utter our petition.'

▲ *One of the Delta vineyards belonging to the estate of Amun is said to have produced 'wine like drawing water without measure'. Workers tread grapes in this painting from the tomb of Nakht in Thebes. 18th Dynasty.*

The various 'Dream Books' that survive indicate that if an Egyptian dreamt that he or she was drinking beer or wine it was a good omen. Depending on the type of beer being drunk, the dreamer would rejoice, live or be healed. However, if the beer was warm, then it was thought to predict suffering.

Beer and wine figure frequently in the remedies in the magico-medical texts. In many cases, they may well have served only as vehicles for the prescribed ingredients, to improve the taste and consistency. Because beer was probably cheaper and more easily accessible than wine, it is not surprising that it was prescribed more often than the latter. Spell 24 of Papyrus Leiden I, 348 was to be recited while drinking beer, in order to cure stomach troubles. By sympathetic magic, the sufferer was identified with the divine personification of intoxication, Seth, 'in that name of his, "beer",' who '...confuses a heart in order to bear away the heart of the enemy, friend, dead male, dead female...' Other papyri also contain 'spells of the beer', which were similarly intended to drive away the demons thought to be tormenting the patient – a method of exorcism by intoxication. According to Papyrus Berlin 8,278, by drinking wine and beer Seth gained the courage and power to 'take away the heart' of the enemies. For the ancient Egyptians, to remove the heart was to eradicate the being, because this organ was considered the seat of wisdom, emotion and indeed consciousness. In this way, alcohol was deemed capable of the expulsion of a demon from the body.

◀ *It was usual to label wine jars, so we know much about the circulation of wine and that most of it was produced in Lower Egypt. This jar was found in the tomb of Tutankhamun.*

Wine- and beer-making

Vineyards existed in the Delta and in large desert oases such as Kharga and Dakhla. Wine was produced both for ritual use and for consumption in the wealthier households. The juice was extracted by treading the grapes, and tomb paintings show the technique used for wringing the last of the juice from the skins by putting them in a sack tied to two poles and forcing the poles apart. The primary fermentation was in large, unstoppered jars. The wine was then decanted into sealed jars and left on racks to ferment a second time. These wine jars were labelled with the date, the place of origin and the maker's name. Both red and white wines were made.

Beer, the staple drink of the ancient Egyptians, used the same ingredients and similar processes to those involved in bread-making, and these two basic commodities might be produced in the same place. Modern microscopy analysis of dried residues of beer has revealed that it was made by mixing together two parts: one of malted, ground emmer wheat or barley in cool water, with another part of the same in hot water and well heated. The resulting mash was sieved and fermented.

Ancestor Worship

The ancient Egyptians were keen to remember and placate their dead relatives, because of their belief in the effects that the dead could have on their lives (see *The Positive Influence of the Dead* and *The Negative Influence of the Dead*). They worshipped their ancestors on special occasions. These included the annual Beautiful Festival of the Valley, when people visited the tombs of their relatives and commemorated the dead, eating a communal meal with them, and the festivals of Osiris at Abydos, when people visited family memorials erected there in the form of stelae (see *Festivals and Pilgrimages*).

The ancestors were also revered on a more daily basis in family homes. People had shrines to their ancestors in niches in their main living rooms, with special stelae and anthropoid busts providing the focus for worship – the point of contact between the living and their dead relatives. The Calendars of Lucky and Unlucky Days inform us that certain days were considered suitable for 'pacifying your *akhu* [the spirits of the ancestors]', and several texts state specifically that this must take place 'in your house'.

Excellent Spirits of Re

A particular type of ancestor stela has been discovered, mainly at the tomb-builders' village of Deir el-Medina (although six have been discovered elsewhere in the Theban region, and two at Abydos). These are known as *akh iker n Re* stelae ('Excellent Spirits of Re' stelae), 47 of which have been discovered dating to the New Kingdom, but especially to the Nineteenth Dynasty (c.1295–c.1186 BC). The *akhu* to which these stelae were dedicated could be either male or female, and were presumably the spirits of people who had been particularly respected during their lifetime, and after death were

▶ *Most of the surviving 'ancestor busts' are made of limestone or sandstone.*

believed to have particular influence in the divine world. Families seem to have appealed to these ancestors to ensure the continuity of the family line, asking them to act as intermediaries for them in the realm of the gods.

The stelae were fairly standardized, although variations have been found. The dead ancestor tended to be depicted seated before an offering table, smelling a lotus blossom. He or she was often shown holding a cloth, sceptre or *ankh*-sign. Offerings were probably made – and prayers said – before the stela.

Ancestor busts

About 140 'anthropoid busts' are also known from ancient Egypt. They have been found mainly in domestic contexts throughout the country, but again especially at Deir el-Medina. Their significance is uncertain but it is possible that they symbolized a family's ancestors. They range from just over 1cm (½in) to 28cm (11in) in height, and are made of clay, limestone, sandstone, faience or wood, usually painted. They tend to be a single bust, although about five double busts have been discovered.

The bust consists of a human head on a rounded support or base that resembles shoulders. But there is no modelling of the human chest and it is difficult to determine which sex they are meant to be, although the remains of red paint indicates the conventional colour of men's skin in the art of the period. In most cases they wear a collar, some of which have pendant lotus blossoms and buds on the front. Most wear tripartite wigs, but some are bareheaded.

It was always supposed that these objects were associated with ancestor worship in the household, but depictions of them in scenes from the Book of the Dead imply that they served a purpose in a funerary context. The fact that most of them bear no inscriptions makes their interpretation much more difficult.

The Positive Influence of the Dead

The Ancient Egyptians believed that the dead (especially spouses and relatives) possessed supernatural powers that might be called upon to solve various problems in the lives of those still living. The best evidence for this belief comes from the fascinating letters that have survived, written from a living person to a dead one. Today these letters are referred to as Letters to the Dead. The 20 or so that we know of range in date from c.3100–c.1200 BC, but a corresponding oral practice may have been common throughout Egyptian history.

Letters to the Dead

The letters were placed in the tombs of the people to whom they were addressed, probably at the time of the funeral or when the tomb was reopened for later burials. Some were written on pottery dishes, and it is possible that they were left at the tomb full of food offerings, so that as the spirit of the deceased symbolically ate the food the text would reveal itself. One such letter, written in ink in hieratic, can be seen on a shallow pottery dish in the Petrie Museum of Egyptian Archaeology in London. It dates to the First Intermediate Period (c.2181–c.2055 BC) and was discovered at Diospolis in Upper Egypt. The letter is to the dead man Nefersekhi from his 'sister' (probably his widow making use of a term of affection). She tells him that a trustee of the dead man's property is defrauding their daughter of her share of the inheritance, and she is desperately appealing for his intervention.

▶ *A continuous supply of food offerings helped ensure the beneficence of the spirits of the deceased. This wooden model of a female offering bearer is from the tomb of Assiut. Middle Kingdom.*

The content of this letter is typical – it is addressed to a man (usually it was a deceased husband or father who was appealed to in this way), it deals with legal problems (and especially wrangles over inheritance), and it supposes that now that the man is dead he is closer to the divine world – making it easier for him to influence it – and that he himself now has supernatural powers that could be of use to those still alive.

Another similar example, dating to the Old Kingdom (c.2686–c.2181 BC), can be found on a piece of linen in the Cairo Museum. It is addressed to the deceased head of the family by his widow and son. They are distressed because, against their wishes, relatives have come and removed pottery and servants or slaves from their house. The widow is particularly upset and she says that she would rather that either she or her son died (it is not quite clear which one) than she should see her son subordinated to this rogue branch of the family. The letter begins with the widow reminding the dead husband and father that he himself had spoken out against these thieving members of the family on his deathbed. She and her son quote him on the importance of inheritance and of solidarity between the generations.

It is difficult to be certain exactly how the dead man was expected to help the situation. Perhaps the widow had decided to seek help from her husband after her case had failed in the local

◀ *Jewellery and other personal adornment was by no means restricted to women in ancient Egyptian society, as exemplified here by Sennefer's large gold earrings and bracelets in a painting on the wall of his tomb.*

court. It seems that the widow thought that her husband might be able to pursue the case in a kind of parallel divine court. It is possible that the piece of linen was originally wrapped around some kind of votive offering to the spirit of the dead man.

A cure for infertility

In addition to helping out with legal problems, deceased relatives were also appealed to when a woman was having difficulties conceiving a child. Because there were no practical measures to cure infertility, and because a woman's ability to have children was so important to her status and well being, both in this life and the next, childless women would seek help from the divine or spirit world. An Old Kingdom Letter to the Dead on a pot now in the Haskell Oriental Museum of Chicago is a plea to a deceased father from his daughter. It reads: 'Cause now that there be born to me a healthy male child. (For) you are an *akh iker* [excellent spirit].'

Fertility figurines have also survived inscribed with a request to a father to grant his daughter a child. These female figurines, with their exaggerated pubic regions, clearly symbolized fertility and sexuality. There seems little reason to attempt a distinction between the possible erotic and procreative connotations of these figures, for as far as the ancient Egyptians were concerned both concepts united to ensure the continued existence of the people of Egypt. The figurines themselves would have served as votive offerings to the dead. One Middle Kingdom example in the Berlin Museum has a child on the left hip, and an inscription on the right thigh reads: 'May a birth be granted to your daughter Seh.' The ancient Egyptians' belief in the creative and magical potency of the written word was profound. In the inscription on this particular figurine, the quail chick used to write the letter 'w' has been written without legs. Could this have been to safeguard against this hieroglyphic sign coming to life and disappearing? Or perhaps it was intended to reduce the danger such a chick could pose to the crops.

▲ *In a painting on the wall of his tomb in Aswan, Sarenput sits before a table laden with offerings.*

A cure for an illness

The dead were sometimes called upon to help cure illness. The 'Cairo Bowl', which dates to the early Twelfth Dynasty (c.1900 BC), has a letter on it from a woman named Dedi, addressed to her dead husband. It tells him that their servant-girl is ill, and appeals to him to help her to get better.

Ritual objects used in everyday magic, such as apotropaic wands, have been discovered in the accessible outer areas of tombs. They may have been placed there to benefit from the supernatural powers of the dead person. In recent times, village magicians in Egypt and the Sudan are known to have given added power to their magic charms by temporarily burying them in the vicinity of tombs (the most popular tombs being those of people particularly respected in life for their wisdom or piety). Execration figurines have also been found buried near tombs (see *Paraphernalia of Ritual*), perhaps with the intention that the dead would continue the punishment of the enemies of Egypt into the Afterlife.

The Negative Influence of the Dead

The ancient Egyptians believed that unsettled dead people could haunt them and cause them all kinds of distress. These were the spirits of people who had died violently or too young or without a proper burial, or they might have failed to achieve what was expected of them in life, such as the production of children. If an inexplicable disaster struck an Egyptian family, such as a severe illness or the sudden loss of livestock, then a dead person's spirit might be behind it. To forestall such losses and afflictions at the hands of the dead, it was thought a sensible precaution to propitiate their spirits with regular offerings, and to do nothing that might offend them. At all times it was considered that the dead required respect from their families and descendants.

In one story that is partly preserved on several ostraca of the late second millennium BC, the High Priest of Amun-Re confronts an *akh* ('spirit') who has been causing trouble in the Theban necropolis. The ghost admits that it is unhappy because its tomb has fallen into disrepair. In an attempt to settle and appease this restless spirit, the High Priest promises an endowment for cult offerings and a whole new tomb. The ancient Egyptians believed that food offerings and the preservation of the body were crucial for a contented existence in the Afterlife.

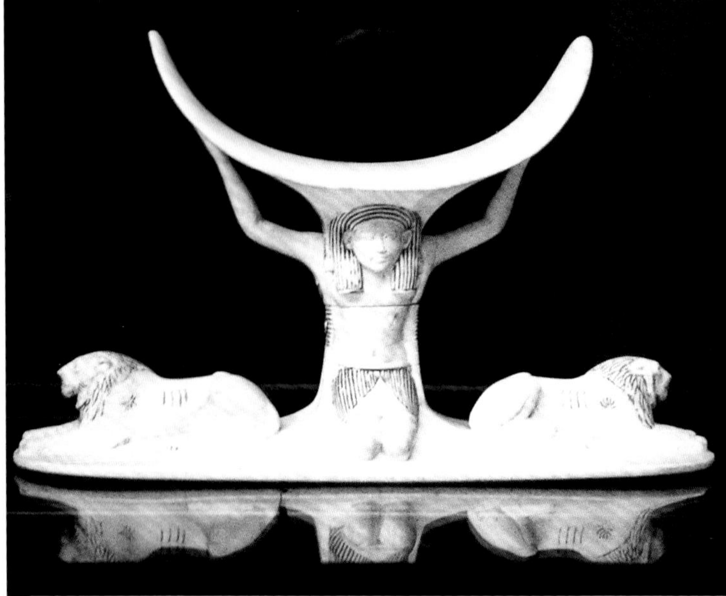

▲ *The recumbent lions on Tutankhamun's headrest were intended to protect the sleeper. Funerary art often shows the crouching lion serving a defensive role.*

Exorcism

The curses known as the Execration Texts were mainly aimed at the destruction of Egypt's enemies, but some were written to exorcise the malignant ghosts of those who had rebelled against the state. By destroying the names of these people, their spirits were considered to have been vanquished, thereby extending their punishment into the Afterlife.

The defacement of images of the dead person also amounted to an attack on his or her spirit in the Afterlife. If the tomb was destroyed, it followed that the spirit would no longer be able to receive sustaining offerings and its power would be correspondingly diminished or eliminated.

Troublesome women

Whereas it was usual to invoke dead husbands and fathers for help and guidance, it tended to be the spirits of dead women who were regarded as troublemakers. In a Letter to the Dead on papyrus which is now in the Rijksmuseum van Oudheden in Leiden, a widowed husband living in Memphis during the Nineteenth Dynasty writes to his wife, who seems to have been dead for about two years. He makes it quite clear that he cared for her during her lifetime and that he has stayed faithful to her after death, and so he does not think it is fair that she should continue to haunt him. Sadly, the letter does not tell us how the hauntings were manifesting themselves, but the man in question had quite clearly had enough and he threatens his deceased wife with some kind of court case before a divine tribunal. A similar letter was written on an ostracon dating to the end of the Twentieth Dynasty, from the Scribe of the Necropolis, Butehamon, to his dead wife Akhtai.

Protection against ghosts

Female ghosts were considered a particular threat to pregnant women and nursing mothers, and to young children, especially if the ghost's antecedent had

▲ *A small pyramidion marked the tomb chapels of the New Kingdom rock-cut tombs at Deir el-Medina, such as this one belonging to the craftsman of the royal tomb, Amennakht, and his wife Nubemsha.*

died before giving birth successfully herself. Many of the oracular amuletic decrees, and the texts in the Brooklyn Magical Papyrus dating to the first millennium BC, mention female ghosts as a dangerous threat against which precautions must be taken.

Another type of harmful spirit was referred to as *mut*, which is often translated as 'dangerous dead'. The texts sometimes classify executed traitors and prisoners of war as *mut*. But in everyday magic, a *mut* seems to have been a ghost who could or would not pass on to the realm of the dead and therefore continued to plague the living.

The ancient Egyptians also used spells to protect themselves against terrifying night-time apparitions (of both male and female ghosts). It was believed that the dead could cause nightmares, and even inflict sickness on the sleeper. In addition to spells to guard against these, they used headrests decorated with apotropaic figures to ward off evil, such as those of the protective household deities Bes and Taweret.

The magico-medical texts quite often cite the malign influence of the dead as a cause of disease, or as a threat to its cure. Even the shadow of a dead person was regarded as a potential source of harm to the medicine prepared by a doctor. Spells were devised to drive the dead out of the limbs of a patient.

Even otherwise benign spirits were considered to be capable of punishing the living if they were roused. The degree of violence that the dead were credited with is exemplified by those tomb inscriptions that warned anyone thinking of robbing the tomb that the dead person was now capable of exacting revenge by killing the robber and ruining his whole family.

Mythologizing Ancient Egypt

Outsiders have always regarded Egypt as an alien place. Its monuments have inspired awe, and the customs of its people have aroused fascination. The civilization of Pharaonic Egypt is so remote that although much evidence has been unearthed we still know relatively little – the scope for misinterpreting or even inventing Egypt's past is huge.

Until the early nineteenth century scientific archaeology was not practised and hieroglyphic script had not been deciphered, so the ancient texts were unfathomable. It is easy to see how 'Egypt of the Pharaohs' came to be mythologized. Scholars of the Western world based their understanding of ancient Egypt on the works of the classical writers, but we now know that these are far from reliable. The Graeco-Roman perception of Egypt was largely created from the legendary poems of Homer and the often inaccurate writings of Herodotus.

Despite great advances in archaeology and philology, the modern age continues to mythologize Egypt's past. Hollywood has helped to foster absurd ideas such as the 'curse of the mummy', and followers of the New Age movement have looked to Egypt as a fount of mysterious knowledge.

◄ *The Great Sphinx, guardian of Khafre's valley temple, has intrigued travellers to Egypt over the centuries. Illustration from* Views in Egypt *by Luigi Mayer (1801)*

The Legacy of the Classical Writers

Until the early nineteenth century, the West's understanding (or misunderstanding) of ancient Egypt had much to do with the works of classical authors, although the seventeenth century did see the first 'archaeological' visits to Egypt. Men such as the English astronomer John Greaves (1602–52) visited Giza twice, measured and examined the pyramids, made a critical analysis of the classical writings about them, and published *Pyramidographia, or a Discourse on the Pyramids in Aegyt* in 1646. Another was the Frenchman Claude Sicard (1677–1726), who visited Upper Egypt four times and was the first modern traveller to identify the sites of Thebes and to ascribe correctly the Colossi of Memnon and the Valley of the Kings on the basis of classical descriptions.

◀ *Serapis was a Ptolemaic invention: a combination of the Egyptian gods Osiris and Apis, represented as a Hellenistic deity (his attributes were those of Zeus, Helios, Hades, Asklepios and Dionysos). Marble sculpture from Pergamon, 2nd century AD.*

▲ *Herodotus was quite clearly mistaken when he wrote, '...they [the Egyptians] have no need to plough or hoe, or to use any other ordinary methods of cultivating their land.' A wall painting from the tomb of Sennedjem shows him farming with his wife. 18th Dynasty.*

The father of history

The greatest influence on the classical writers who documented Egypt was Herodotus (c.490–c.420 BC), who is often referred to as the 'Father of History'. He was certainly the best-known tourist in classical times. He was born in Halicarnassus in Caria on the south-western coast of Asia Minor. He wrote a series of nine books called *The Histories*, whose purpose was to trace the events that brought Greece into conflict with Persia. Within this framework, he also recorded all the information he had been able to collect – and he was undoubtedly an avid collector of information.

Herodotus was probably in Egypt some time between 450 and 430 BC, and it is Book II of his series that describes Egypt. He appears to have gone to some length to collect information in Memphis, which he then sought to have backed up in Thebes and Heliopolis. Wisely, he spoke to priests, who were educated and had access to the nation's archives housed in the temples. But he relied wholly on oral testimony, and he was not familiar with the Egyptian language. He may have misunderstood much of what he was told and, as a foreigner, the Egyptian priests are unlikely to have disclosed much information to him. Quite clearly he did not believe all that he was told, but he chose to record it nonetheless, thereby ensuring the propagation of bizarre stories about ancient Egypt, both via an oral tradition and a written one. For example, after recounting a tale of a phoenix which was said to fly from Arabia to Heliopolis every 500 years, with his dead father in an egg of myrrh, he added, 'I give the story as it was told me...but I don't believe it.'

Herodotus was particularly interested in religion, medicine, mummification, customs and taboos, architecture (especially that of the pyramids) and astronomy; as well as geography (especially the flooding of the Nile), transport, flora, fauna, food, clothing, and historical events. He was intrigued by what he learnt, and had enormous respect for the country and its people:

> *About Egypt I shall have a great deal more to relate because of the number of remarkable things the country contains, and because of the fact that more monuments which beggar description are to be found there than anywhere else in the world.*

▼ *The Palestrina Mosaic formed part of a floor in the Italian town of Praeneste (Palestrina). It probably dates to the early 1st century BC and its subject is a Nilotic landscape, showing the popularity of Egyptian themes in the Roman world.*

▲ *The Rosetta Stone records in Greek, demotic and hieroglyphic scripts the religious ceremonies attending the coronation of Ptolemy V in 205 BC.*

Herodotus felt that he was in a position to compare Egypt with other parts of the ancient world, and the Egyptian people with their neighbours. Because of the stable climate, for example, he wrote, '...next to the Libyans, they are the healthiest people in the world'.

He attempted to explain the inundation of the River Nile, and supplied various theories, such as the occurrence of seasonal winds that checked the flow of the river current towards the sea; the melting of snow in the southern mountains; and the supernatural nature of the river. His own explanation was elaborate, involving the sun, evaporation and winds dispersing the vapours, but the cause of the annual flood was basically deemed a mystery.

Unwittingly, Herodotus laid the foundations for a confused picture of life in Pharaonic Egypt. He wrote:

> *...the Egyptians themselves in their manners and customs seem to have reversed the ordinary practices of mankind.*

He recorded, for instance, that women traded at market while men stayed at home and wove; that women urinated standing up and men sitting down; that they kneaded dough with their feet and clay (and even dung) with their hands. He was fascinated by the Egyptians' relationship with animals, especially the keeping and mummification of sacred animals. His description of their obsession with cats was particularly unreliable:

> *What happens when a house catches fire is most extraordinary: nobody takes the least trouble to put it out, for it is only the cats that matter: everyone stands in a row, a little distance from his neighbour, trying to protect the cats, which nevertheless slip through the line, or jump over it, and hurl themselves into the flames. This causes the Egyptians deep distress.*

▶ *Egyptian scribes wrote using a rush brush. The Greeks introduced reed pens, which were adopted by the Egyptians by the 1st century AD. 25th Dynasty.*

Herodotus's writings on the actual history of Egypt are confused and his chronology is very jumbled. Even for Herodotus, writing in the fifth century BC, the beginnings of Dynastic Egypt were shrouded in the distant past, and the pyramids were already ancient and mysterious tourist attractions. He was, however, in a position to provide relatively accurate information concerning the Twenty-sixth Dynasty (664–525 BC), and the invasion of Egypt by the Persian ruler Cambyses in 525 BC.

Diodorus Siculus

Both the historian Diodorus Siculus (c.40 BC) and the historian and geographer Strabo (c.63 BC–c.AD 24) imitated Herodotus. Diodorus Siculus was born in Agyrium in Sicily. He visited Egypt between c.60 and 56 BC, and described Egypt in the first book of his *Bibliotheca Historica*, which set out to cover the history of the world up to Julius Caesar's conquest of Gaul. He was clearly amazed by some of the customs he believed to be typically Egyptian and, like Herodotus, he included among these

▲ *By the age of 17, Champollion had already learnt to read Arabic, Syrian, Chaldean, Coptic, Latin, Greek, Sanscrit and Persian. Portrait by Léon Cogniet, 1831.*

Champollion

The ancient Egyptian written sources were unintelligible until Jean François Champollion le Jeune (1790–1832) deciphered hieroglyphs. Working on the replicated hieroglyphic and Greek inscriptions on the Rosetta Stone (a priestly decree issued in 196 BC inscribed on a slab of black granite, now in the British Museum), he just beat the English scholar Thomas Young with the publication of his findings in 1822, though he did not achieve his ambition of visiting Egypt until 1828.

Using his knowledge of Coptic, Champollion was able to deduce not only the meaning of hieroglyphs and hieratic text but the structure of ancient Egyptian grammar.

mummification and the excessive treatment and worship of animals. He related the revenge of an Alexandrian mob on a Roman ambassador who had accidentally killed a cat (there is no ancient Egyptian evidence for this kind of behaviour). The pyramids and the Nile also fascinated him.

Strabo

Born in Pontus in north-eastern Asia Minor, Strabo spent several years in Alexandria in about 27 BC, and discussed Egypt in the eighth book of his *Geography*, published in c.23 AD. His descriptions include those of Alexandria, the Faiyum, Theban monuments such as the Colossi of Memnon and the Valley of the Kings, and the Nilometer at Elephantine.

Strabo travelled with the Roman Prefect Aelius Gallus, escorted by priests and guides. In the seventeenth book of *Geography* he claims that tourists continued to be fascinated by the Nile, the monuments, the religion and the funerary customs, the exotic animals and worship of them, and the superior wisdom of the priests. One of his aims seems to have been to verify whether the sites of Egypt were worthy of their reputations. He decided that the following were: the oases; the tombs in the Valley of the Kings; the boating stunts at Philae; the pyramids; and the stone chips around the pyramids, said to be petrified beans that were eaten by the pyramid builders.

Misinterpreting hieroglyphs

None of the classical writers appears to have made any effort to understand hieroglyphs, and until they were deciphered in the early nineteenth century, they tended to be regarded as esoteric and magical. The Renaissance in Europe heralded a keen interest in ancient Egypt, and one of the first classical texts to resurface and be studied in the fifteenth century was Horapollo's *Hieroglyphica*, dating to the fourth century AD. Rather than the true meaning of the ancient inscriptions, this gave symbolic explanations of hieroglyphs, which were believed to encapsulate profound truths.

In the seventeenth century, the Jesuit scholar Athanasius Kircher (1601–1680) published several volumes of entirely fictitious interpretations of hieroglyphic inscriptions, reflecting the theory that hieroglyphic signs were mystical symbols, which could be used to explain the secrets of the Egyptian cosmos.

Misunderstanding the Pyramids

The breathtakingly enormous size of some of the pyramids, their immense antiquity and the fact that it is impossible to know with certainty how they were built (because no texts have been discovered to inform us), have resulted in some wild, unfounded speculation about them. It was Herodotus who first established the mistaken association between the construction of the Great Pyramid and the employment of slave labour, with no mention made of the corvée system. He also propagated the story that Khufu had forced his daughter to prostitute herself in return for blocks of stone, which were then used to build the middle of the three queens' pyramids to the east of the Great Pyramid.

In the first century AD the slave labour myth was augmented by the Jewish historian Josephus, who stated that the Hebrews were worn out during their sojourn in Egypt by, among other great toils, being forced to build pyramids. In fact the pyramids at Giza were constructed over a millennium before the time of the Hebrews.

Building the pyramids

We still do not know exactly how the Pyramids were built. Theories vary, but often include artificial flooding to provide a level, and the construction of earth ramps up which to drag the stone blocks. The enormous labour force needed to erect the pyramids and other great Egyptian monuments was assembled under a regime of obligatory service to the state, known as the corvée system. Each household had to provide food supplies or manpower for the state building projects. An advantage of becoming a priest was the chance of exemption from this conscription.

▲ *Europeans were fascinated by pyramids, which they tended to represent with impossibly steep sides. This scene is from a peepshow box of c.1750 depicting the Seven Wonders of the World.*

Arab legends

When the Arabs conquered Egypt in AD 642, they clearly marvelled at the pyramids and were quick to mythologize them. One popular Arab legend claimed that the great pyramid at Giza was in fact the tomb of Hermes (the Greek deity identified with the Egyptian god of wisdom and the scribal profession, Thoth). The purpose of the pyramid was said to be to conceal the literature and science held within it, well hidden from the eyes of the uninitiated, and to protect them from the flood – seemingly a merging of the catastrophic Biblical flood and the annual inundation of the River Nile. If we were to believe the Yemeni Arabs, the pyramids of Khufu and Khafre on the Giza plateau were actually the tombs of their ancient kings, one of whom was said to have defeated the Egyptians.

According to an early Coptic legend, a certain King Surid was responsible for the construction of the three pyramids at Giza. It tells that he had scientific knowledge recorded on their internal walls; sculptures and treasure placed inside them; and an idol positioned outside each of the pyramids to guard it. Surid was said to have been buried in the 'Eastern Pyramid' (Khufu's), his brother Hujib in the 'Western Pyramid' (Khafre's), and Hujib's son Karuras in the 'Pied Pyramid' (Menkaure's).

Continuing this tradition, the fifteenth-century Arab historian al-Maqrizi recorded that an ancient king named Surid decorated the walls and ceilings of his pyramid chambers with scientific imagery and depictions of stars and planets. He was also supposed to have filled the chambers with hordes of treasure, including miraculous iron weapons that would never rust and glass that could bend without breaking. Al-Maqrizi also stated that when King Surid died, he was buried in the pyramid together with all his possessions. It is possible that the name Surid was a corruption of 'Suphis', the name used by Herodotus in the fifth century BC when referring to Khufu.

▲ *The new entrance to the Louvre Museum in Paris is a high-tech glass pyramid.*

The story of the tremendous treasure buried inside the Great Pyramid can also be found in the tale of *The Thousand and One Nights* (also known as *The Arabian Nights*), along with the description of what is said to be the first ever break-in to the pyramid, in about AD 820, by Caliph al-Mamun, the son of Haroun al-Rashid. His men are said to have used iron picks and crowbars, and to have heated the stones with fire and then poured cold vinegar on them. It is, in fact, highly likely that the first forced entry into the Great Pyramid took place in antiquity, and that al-Mamun's men made use of a passage created by ancient thieves. A man named Denys of Telmahre, the Jacobite Patriarch of Antioch, was present when al-Mamun entered the pyramid, and he states that the pyramid had already been opened before their visit. This particular tale of the alleged earliest break-in was indeed rather too fanciful to be true. The same (albeit tamed) story was recorded by Abu Szalt of Spain. Rather than fabulous treasure, he reports that al-Mamun's men discovered only a sarcophagus with some old bones inside it.

Joseph's granaries

The Coptic and Arab myths were certainly closer to the truth than the explanations of medieval Europeans. Pilgrims to the Holy Land also chose to visit Egypt in order to see sites such as the pyramids, which they believed to be the 'granaries of Joseph' (an idea recorded as early as the fifth century AD in the Latin writings of Julius Honorius and Rufinus). The pyramids were also depicted as granaries in, for example, a mosaic dating to the twelfth century in one of the domes of St Mark's in Venice. Many later fifteenth- and sixteenth-century representations of pyramids were just as inaccurate, even when executed by people who had actually seen them. They tended to be portrayed with much steeper sides than the real things, thereby mirroring more familiar classical monuments.

► *The Freemasons adopted religious imagery for their secret rites, as shown by this nineteenth century Italian design for a Masonic temple. 19th century.*

Mysteries of the pyramids

The seventeenth century saw the advocating, especially by Athanasius Kircher, of the magical and mystical significance of the pyramids - a belief still held by many people today. Modern theories about the pyramids range from the downright silly, such as their construction by aliens, to the less absurd, such as their alignment with the belt of Orion. The weird and wonderful connections made with the pyramids are endless, including their power to achieve immortality and world peace. Even if the ancient pharaohs had not intended any of these associations, they would no doubt be extremely satisfied to find that their pyramids are still inspiring awe and wonder in the twenty-first century AD.

The Curse of the Pharaohs

Everyone loves a good story. Everyone also loves to be scared witless when they can maintain a safe and comfortable distance from the object of their fear. 'Strange and mysterious Egypt', with its dark tombs and ancient mummies, is the perfect setting for terror and intrigue. It is hardly surprising, therefore, that Hollywood was quick to capitalize on the 'Curse of the Mummy'. This idea was, in fact, a popular theme in literature from the mid-nineteenth century onwards. Authors such as Bram Stoker and Arthur Conan Doyle were keen to write about the awful revenge wrought by mummies whose tombs had been disturbed.

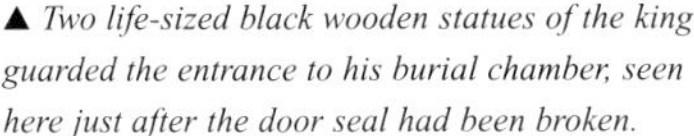

▲ *Two life-sized black wooden statues of the king guarded the entrance to his burial chamber, seen here just after the door seal had been broken.*

Tutankhamun's tomb

It was the discovery of the almost intact tomb of the Eighteenth-Dynasty ruler Tutankhamun (c.1336–c.1327 BC) that resulted in worldwide Egyptomania and an obsession with the ancient curse of the pharaohs. The great discovery was made by the archaeologist Howard Carter (1874–1939) while excavating in the Valley of the Kings, in the employment of the fifth Earl of Carnarvon. On 4th November 1922 he discovered a flight of steps leading down to a blocked door covered in seals bearing the cartouche of Tutankhamun. On entering the tomb on 26th November, 'the day of days', it was found to contain the body of the boy-king and the most incredible quantity of marvellous funerary goods.

Not only was this a discovery of breathtaking gold treasure, but its owner Tutankhamun had been buried in an unusual tomb (see *Rock-cut Tombs*). He had died in his teens, and he was closely connected with the infamous King Akhenaten (c.1352– c.1336 BC), who had made revolutionary changes to the art and religion of Egypt. People's imaginations began to run wild.

▼ *Tutankhamun's mummy lay in a close-fitting nest of three anthropoid coffins (the innermost of solid gold) inside a quartzite sarcophagus.*

▲ *Before removing the contents of Tutankhamun's tomb to Cairo, every object had to be scientifically recorded, photographed and often conserved. The king's body was left in his tomb, inside his outer coffin in the sarcophagus.*

Within six months, on 5th April 1923, Lord Carnarvon died, and in newspapers around the world his unexpected death was instantly blamed on 'the curse'. Conan Doyle declared that it was the result of 'elementals – not souls, not spirits – created by Tutankhamun's priests to guard the tomb'. One newspaper printed the translation of a curse said to be written in hieroglyphs on the door of the second shrine: 'They who enter this sacred tomb shall swift be visited by wings of death.' But this curse was wholly fictitious, as were all the other curses reported to the press, such as the one said by a necromancer to have been found by Carter carved in hieroglyphs on a stone at the entrance of the tomb. It was supposed to have read: 'Let the hand raised against my form be withered! Let them be destroyed who attack my name, my foundation, my effigies, the images like unto me!'

Carnarvon had been a weak man ever since a car accident, and was exhausted by the circumstances surrounding the discovery of Tutankhamun's tomb. He accidentally cut open a mosquito bite while shaving; it became infected, and he ended up with a fever. In this further weakened state, he fell prey to pneumonia. Some of the newspapers suggested that Carnarvon had pricked himself while in the tomb on a sharp object, such as an arrowhead, doctored with a poison so potent that it was still active after 3,000 years. Other articles in the press reported that Carnarvon had become infected by deadly micro-organisms that had laid dormant for millennia.

Rumours spread like wildfire. It was said that at the moment of his death, all the lights went out in Cairo, and his son and heir, Lord Porchester, sixth Earl of Carnarvon, claimed that at their family home in Highclere Castle in England his father's favourite dog howled and dropped down dead at exactly the same moment as the earl passed away.

The newspapers began to report the deaths of anyone who might have had any connection with Carnarvon or the tomb, thereby linking further deaths with 'the curse'. The deaths recorded included those of Carnarvon's younger brother Aubrey Herbert, an X-ray specialist on his way to examine the royal mummy; Carter's right-hand man Arthur Mace (who was in fact already suffering from pleurisy before the tomb was discovered); the American railroad magnate George Jay Gould (who had visited the tomb, but was touring Egypt due to his ill health); an unnamed associate curator in the British Museum (who was said to have been labelling objects from the tomb, although there are no objects from Tutankhamun's tomb in the British Museum); and the French Egyptologist Georges Bénédite (who died as a result of a fall after visiting the tomb). The list of 'victims of the mummy's curse' goes on, but the American Egyptologist Herbert E. Winlock took great pleasure in compiling his own list with the more rational explanations of these people's deaths. Today, the discovery of Tutankhamun's tomb is remembered as much for the 'curse' as for the Egyptological significance of this great archaeological excavation.

▼ *The tombs of Ramesses IX and Tutankhamun at the time of their re-opening in 1922. The Valley of the Kings was known to the ancient Egyptians as* ta set aat, *'the Great Place', or more informally, as* ta int, *'the Valley'.*

Glossary

The word list below is intended as a quick reference for terms that appear frequently throughout the book.

Abusir Papyri: administrative documents of the mortuary cult of the Fifth-Dynasty king Neferirkare (c.2475–c.2455 BC), whose funerary temple complex was associated with his pyramid at Abusir.
aegis: broad necklace surmounted with the head of a deity.
***akh*:** transfigured spirit.
***Akhet*:** four-month season of Inundation, when the River Nile was in flood.
***akhu*:** enchantments/sorcery/spells.
Ammit: 'the gobbler'; composite beast with the head of a crocodile, the front legs and body of a lion or leopard, and the back legs of a hippopotamus; present at the 'Weighing of the Heart' ceremony held after death in order to eat the heart of anyone who was found to have committed wrong during his or her lifetime.
amulet: charm or protective device, usually worn or carried about the person.
***ankh*:** hieroglyphic and amuletic sign for life; it may represent a sandal strap or an elaborate knot.
Apophis: serpent demon who threatened the sun god travelling through the Netherworld at night, and the dead travelling through the Afterlife.
apotropaic: able to ward off harm.
***atef*-crown:** tall white crown with a plume on each side and a small disc at the top.
***ba*:** personality/motivation; portrayed in art as a human-headed bird.
barque shrine: boat-shaped shrine.
***benben*:** squat stone obelisk.
***benbenet*:** gilded cap-stone or pyramidion at the top of a pyramid or obelisk.
Book of the Dead: 'the formulae for going forth by day'; illustrated funerary spells developed in the New Kingdom (c.1550–c.1069 BC), written mainly on papyrus.
Byblos: port on the Lebanese coast, important for the import of cedarwood.
canopic jars: jars used to store the embalmed internal organs following mummification.
cartonnage: plaster (gesso)-stiffened linen.
cartouche: (Egyptian: *shenu)* oval outline around two of the king's five names: his birth name (nomen) introduced by the title 'Son of Re' *(sa Re),* and his throne name (prenomen) introduced by the title 'He of the Sedge and the Bee' *(nesw bity).*
***cippus* of Horus:** stela engraved with the image of the god Horus as a child overcoming creatures such as crocodiles and snakes, and inscribed with spells against scorpions, snakes and so on.
Coffin Texts: funerary texts inscribed mainly on coffins of the Middle Kingdom period (c.2055–c.1650 BC).
Coptic: use of Greek letters to write the Egyptian language; used throughout the Christian Period in Egypt.
Demotic: cursive script derived from hieratic during the Twenty-sixth Dynasty (664–525 BC).
***Deshret*:** (i) 'Red Land'– the desert; (ii) Red Crown of Lower Egypt.
***djed*-pillar:** amulet; symbol of stability; backbone of Osiris.
***Duat*:** the Afterworld, connected with the eastern horizon.
Ennead: (Egyptian: *pesedjet*) group of nine deities associated with Heliopolis.
epagomenal days: 'days upon the year'; five days added to the calendar to make the year up to 365 days.
execration texts: curses naming foreign rulers and places, used to magically destroy the enemies of Egypt, written on bowls, tablets and clay figurines in the form of bound captives, which were then smashed as part of execration rituals.
faience: glazed ceramic material composed primarily of crushed quartz or quartz sand (with added lime and plant ash or natron); usually a blue or green colour.
false door: an inscribed stone or wood architectural feature found in tombs and mortuary temples, in front of which food offerings were placed for the dead.
Fields of *Hetep* *'offering'* and *'satisfaction'*: realm of the Afterlife connected with the western horizon.
Fields of *Iaru* *'reeds'*: realm of the Afterlife connected with purification and the eastern horizon.
healing statue: statue covered with spells to protect against snakes, scorpions, and so on.
heart scarab: large scarab amulet wrapped into the mummy bandages over the heart, inscribed with Chapter 30 of the Book of the Dead.
***heb sed*:** royal jubilee festival usually celebrated by the king after 30 years on the throne.
***Hedjet*:** White Crown of Upper Egypt.
***heka*:** magic/divine energy.
heliacal rising: first sighting of the dog star Sirius on the eastern horizon just before dawn, after a 70-day period when it is invisible due to its alignment with the earth and the sun.
***Hery Seshta*:** 'Chief of Mysteries or Secrets'.
hieratic: cursive form of hieroglyphs.
***hu*:** divine utterance.
***hypocephalus*:** bronze or cartonnage disc inscribed with Chapter 162 of the Book of the Dead; placed under the heads of mummies from the Late Period (c.747–c.332 BC).
hypostyle hall/court: roofed, pillared temple court.
***Imhet*:** the Afterworld; connected with the western horizon.
imiut: fetish of the cult of Anubis; made from the inflated or stuffed headless skin of an animal (usually feline) tied to a pole in a pot.
incubation: practice of sleeping in a temple sanatorium in order to receive helpful or healing dreams from a god or goddess.
***isfet*:** chaos.
***ka*:** spirit/vital force/sustenance; represented pictorially as a person's double.
***Kemet*:** 'Black Land'; Egypt (the Nile Valley and Delta).
***kenbet*:** court/tribunal.
***kherep Selket*:** 'the one who has power over the scorpion goddess'; scorpion and snake charmer.
Lector Priest: priest responsible for reciting spells and ritual texts.

maat: order/truth/justice/harmony.
Mastaba: Arabic word for 'bench'; a tomb with a mound-shaped superstructure and a subterranean burial chamber.
***menat*-necklace:** broad, beaded necklace with long counterpoise.
Metternich Stela: *cippus* of Horus now in the Metropolitan Museum of Art, New York.
***mut*:** 'dangerous dead'/ghost.
***muu*-dancers:** dancers at funerals, who wore kilts and tall hats.
naos: innermost shrine; home to the cult statue in a temple.
Narmer Palette: mudstone ceremonial palette commemorating the victories of the Protodynastic ruler Narmer (c.3100 BC); found in the 'Main Deposit' at Hierakonpolis; now in the Cairo Museum.
natron: naturally occurring salt, a compound of sodium carbonate and bicarbonate.
Neb Tawy: 'Lord of the Two Lands'; royal title.
***Nebty*-name:** 'Two Ladies name'; one of five royal titles, referring to the cobra goddess Wadjet and the vulture goddess Nekhbet.
nemes: simple, pleated linen headdress worn by the king.
Nenet: undersky.
Nesw Bity: 'He of the Sedge and the Bee' (emblems of the Nile Valley and the Delta respectively); King of Upper and Lower Egypt.
Nilometer: measuring gauge used to record flood levels.
nome: administrative district; 22 in Upper Egypt, 20 in Lower Egypt.
obelisk: more tapering, needle-like version of the *benben.*
Ogdoad: (Egyptian: *Khmun)* group of eight deities associated with Hermopolis.
oracular amuletic decree: short spell, in the form of a divine decree, written on a tiny roll of papyrus placed inside a cylindrical tube during the late New Kingdom and Third Intermediate Period (c.1100–c.747 BC).
ostracon: flake of limestone or potsherd used for notes and sketches.
Per Ankh: House of Life in a temple complex; the place for copying, reading and research.
Peret: season of planting and growth.
peristyle court: open, colonnaded temple court.
phyle: one of four groups of priests working in the temple at any one time (on a rota system).
Pschent: Double Crown of Upper and Lower Egypt.
pylon: monumental temple gateway.
Pyramid Texts: funerary texts inscribed on the internal walls of pyramids from the reign of Unas (c.2375–c.2345 BC) at the end of the Fifth Dynasty to the First Intermediate Period (c.2181–c.2055 BC).
rekhet: wise woman.
Restoration Stela: stela from Karnak, now in the Cairo Museum, inscribed with a decree issued during the reign of Tutankhamun (c.1336–c.1327 BC) declaring the state's return to polytheism.
Rishi: Arabic word for 'feathered'; a style of anthropoid coffin decorated with a feathered effect.
Rosetau: 'passage of dragging', entrance to a tomb; necropoles of Memphis and Abydos.
Rosetta Stone: priestly decree issued in 196 BC, inscribed on a black granite slab (British Museum, London).
sa: amulet/protection; mobile papyrus shelter.
Sau: 'amulet man'; title borne by wetnurses and midwives.
scarab: dung beetle; amulet of rebirth/creation/new life.
sebakh: Arabic word for ancient mudbrick and remains of organic refuse used in modern times as a fertilizer.
Sekhemty: Double Crown of Upper and Lower Egypt.
***sem*-priest:** funerary priest who officiated at the 'Opening of the Mouth' ceremony.
sema tawy: 'Unification of the Two Lands'.
serdab: Arabic for 'cellar'; a small room in an Old Kingdom tomb, housing a statue of the deceased, often with eye-holes or a narrow slit in the wall.
serekh: niched/recessed palace façade; copied as a decorative feature on tombs, sarcophagi and coffins; used as a surround to the king's name in the Early Dynastic Period (c.3100–c.2686 BC) prior to the advent of the cartouche.
shabti/shawabti/ushabti: human-form funerary figurine thought to perform hard work for the deceased in the Afterlife; often inscribed with Chapter 6 of the Book of the Dead.
Shemau: Upper Egypt: the Nile Valley from the first cataract north to just south of Memphis.
Shomu: season of harvest and low water.
sia: divine knowledge.
side-lock: hairstyle worn by children.
sistrum: ceremonial rattle.
Sons of Horus: the four deities who guarded the internal organs in the four canopic jars.
soul house: pottery house with courtyard modelled with food offerings; placed in tombs.
sphinx: statue (usually of a king) with a lion's body.
stela: slab of wood or stone, bearing inscriptions, reliefs or paintings.
Sunu: doctor/physician.
syncretism: the fusion of two deities into one; for example, Amun-Re.
talata: demolished stone blocks (maybe from the Arabic for 'three hand breadths', describing their dimensions).
Ta-Mehu: Lower Egypt: from just south of Memphis to the north coast of Egypt.
tekenu: human-headed sack-like object of unknown function, depicted drawn by cattle on a sled in funerary processions.
Tura: limestone quarry on the east bank of the Nile, across the river from Memphis.
tyet: protective amulet; girdle or blood of Isis.
***udjat*-eye:** (or *wadjat*-eye or Eye of Horus) protective amulet; symbolizing healing/making whole/strength/perfection.
uraeus: rearing cobra worn on king's forehead as part of his headdress; poised to spit poison at enemies.
vizier: the highest official, the king's right-hand man.
***wab*-priest:** most common priestly title, indicating that the priest was purified (or perhaps a purifier).
wadj: 'green'; papyrus-form amulet symbolizing freshness/flourishing/youth/joy.
***was*-sceptre:** animal-headed sceptre; amulet of power/divinity/well being/prosperity.
wep renpet: 'opening of the year'; New Year festival.

Museums with Egyptian Collections

Many centuries of plunder, exchange, archaeological excavation and universal fascination with Egyptology have resulted in the dispersal of ancient Egyptian artefacts and the accumulation of important collections throughout the world.

Australia

Melbourne National Gallery of Victoria
Sydney Australian Museum, Nicholson Museum of Antiquities, Ancient History Teaching Collection

Austria

Vienna Kunsthistorisches Museum

Belgium

Antwerp Museum Vleeshuis
Brussels Musées Royaux d'Art et d'Histoire
Liège Musée Curtius
Mariemont Musée de Mariemont

Brazil

Rio de Janeiro Museu Nacional

Canada

Montreal McGill University, Ethnological Museum, Museum of Fine Arts
Toronto Royal Ontario Museum

Cuba

Havana Museo Nacional

Czechoslovakia

Prague Náprstkovo Muzeum

Denmark

Copenhagen Nationalmuseet, Ny Carlsberg Glyptotek, Thorwaldsen Museum

Egypt

Alexandria Graeco-Roman Museum
Aswan Museum on the Island of Elephantine
Cairo Egyptian Museum
Luxor Luxor Museum
Mallawi Mallawi Museum
Minya Minya Museum

France

Avignon Musée Calvet
Grenoble Musée de Peinture et de Sculpture
Limoges Musée Municipal
Lyons Musée des Beaux-Arts, Musée Guimet
Marseilles Musée d'Archéologie
Nantes Musée des Arts Décoratifs
Orléans Musée Historique et d'Archéologie de l'Orléanais
Paris Bibliothèque Nationale, Louvre, Musée du Petit Palais, Musée Rodin
Strasbourg Institut d'Egyptologie
Toulouse Musée Georges Labit

Germany

Berlin Staatliche Museen: Ägyptisches Museum, Staatliche Museen: Papyrussammlung, Staatliche Museen: Preussischer Kulturbesitz,
Dresden Albertinum
Essen Folkwang Museum
Frankfurt-am-Main Liebieghaus
Hamburg Museum für Kunst und Gewerbe, Museum für Völkerkunde
Hanover Kestner-Museum
Heidelberg Ägyptologisches Institut der Universität
Hildesheim Roemer-Pelizaeus-Museum
Karlsruhe Badisches Landesmuseum
Leipzig Ägyptisches Museum
Munich Staatliche Sammlung: Ägyptischer Kunst
Tübingen Ägyptologisches Institut der Universität
Würzburg Martin von Wagner Museum der Universität

Greece

Athens National Museum

Hungary

Budapest Szépmüvészeti Múzeum

Ireland

Dublin National Museum of Ireland

Italy

Bologna Museo Civico
Florence Museo Archeologico
Mantua Museo del Palazzo Ducale
Milan Museo Archeologico
Naples Museo Nazionale
Palermo Museo Nazionale
Parma Museo Nazionale di Antichità
Rome Museo Barracco, Museo Capitolino, Museo Nazionale Romano delle Terme Diocleziane
Rovigo Museo dell'Accademia delle Concordi
Trieste Civico Museo di Storta ed Arte
Turin Museo Egizio

Vatican Museo Gregoriano Egizte
Venice Museo Archeologico del Palazze, Reale di Venezia

Japan
Kyoto University Archaeological Museum

Mexico
Mexico City Museo Nacional de Antropologia

Netherlands
Amsterdam Allard Pierson Museum
Leiden Rijksmuseum van Oudheden
Otterlo Rijksmuseum Kröller-Müller

Poland
Kraków Muzeum Naradowe
Warsaw Muzeum Narodowe

Portugal
Lisbon Fundação Calouste Gulbenkian

Russia
Leningrad State Hermitage Museum
Moscow State Pushkin Museum of Fine Arts

Spain
Madrid Museo Arqueológico Nacional

Sudan
Khartum Sudan Museum

Sweden
Linköping Östergöttlands Museum
Lund Kulturhistoriska Museet
Stockholm Medelhavsmuseet
Uppsala Victoriamuseum

Switzerland
Basel Museum für Völkerkunde
Geneva Musée d'Art et d'Histoire
Lausanne Musée Cantonal d'Archéologie et d'Histoire, Musée Cantonal des Beaux-Arts
Neuchâtel Musée d'Ethnographie
Riggisberg Abegg-Stiftung

United Kingdom
Birmingham Birmingham Museum and Art Gallery
Bolton Bolton Museum and Art Gallery
Bristol City Museum and Art Gallery
Cambridge Fitzwilliam Museum
Dundee Museum and Art Gallery
Durham Durham University Oriental Museum
Edinburgh Royal Museum of Scotland
Glasgow Art Gallery and Museum, Burrell Collection, Hunterian Museum
Leicester Museum and Art Gallery
Liverpool Museum of Archaeology, Classics and Oriental Studies
London British Museum, Horniman Museum, Petrie Museum of Egyptian Archaeology, Victoria and Albert Museum
Manchester Manchester Museum
Norwich Castle Museum
Oxford Ashmolean Museum of Art and Archaeology, Pitt Rivers Museum
Swansea Swansea Museum

United States of America
Baltimore (Md.) Walters Art Gallery
Berkeley (Ca.) Robert H. Lowie Museum of Anthropology
Boston (Mass.) Museum of Fine Arts
Brooklyn (N.Y.) Brooklyn Museum
Cambridge (Mass.) Fogg Art Museum, Harvard University, Semitic Museum, Harvard University
Chicago (Ill.) Field Museum of Natural History, Oriental Institute Museum
Cincinnati (Ohio) Art Museum
Cleveland (Ohio) Museum of Art
Denver (Col.) Art Museum
Detroit (Mich.) Detroit Institute of Arts
Kansas City (Miss.) William Rockhill Nelson Gallery of Art
Los Angeles (Ca.) County Museum of Art
Minneapolis (Minn.) Institute of Arts Museum
New Haven (Conn.) Yale University Art Gallery
New York Metropolitan Museum of Art
Palo Alto (Ca.) Stanford University Museum
Philadelphia (Pa.) Pennsylvania University Museum
Pittsburgh (Pa.) Museum of Art, Carnegie Institute
Princeton (N.J.) University Art Museum
Providence (R.I.) Rhode Island School of Design
Richmond (Va.) Museum of Fine Arts
St Louis (Miss.) Art Museum
San Diego (Ca.) Museum of Man
San Francisco (Ca.) M. H. De Young Memorial Museum
San José (Ca.) Rosicrucian Museum
Seattle (Wash.) Art Museum
Toledo (Ohio) Museum of Art
Washington D.C. Smithsonian Institution
Worcester (Mass.) Art Museum

from the *Atlas of Ancient Egypt* by John Baines and Jaromir Malek

Suggested Further Reading

Adams, B., *Egyptian Mummies* (Shire, 1984)
Allen, J.P. et al., *Religion and Philosophy in Ancient Egypt* (New Haven, 1989)
Andrews, C., *Egyptian Mummies* (British Museum Press, 1984)
Andrews, C., *Amulets of Ancient Egypt* (British Museum Press, 1994)
Baines, J. & **Malek,** J., *Atlas of Ancient Egypt* (Phaidon, 1984)
Bierbrier, M., *The Tomb Builders of the Pharaohs* (British Museum Press, 1982)
Bleeker, C.J., *Egyptian Festivals, Enactments of Religious Renewal* (Leiden, 1967)
Bleeker, C.J., *Hathor and Thoth* (Leiden, 1973)
Borghouts, J.F., *Ancient Egyptian Magical Texts* (E.J. Brill, 1978)
Bowman, A.K., *Egypt after the Pharaohs* (Guild, 1986)
David, A.R., *A Guide to Religious Ritual at Abydos* (Warminster, 1980)
David, R., *The Pyramid Builders of Ancient Egypt* (Routledge and Kegan Paul, 1986)
Dodson, A., *Egyptian Rock-cut Tombs* (Shire, 1991)
Englund, G. (ed.), *The Religion of the Ancient Egyptians: Cognitive Structures and Popular Expressions* (Uppsala, 1989)
Fairman, H.W., *The Triumph of Horus* (Batsford, 1974)
Faulkner, R.O., *The Ancient Egyptian Pyramid Texts* (Oxford University Press, 1969)
Faulkner, R.O., *The Ancient Egyptian Coffin Texts* (2 vols) (Aris and Phillips, 1973, 1977, 1987)
Faulkner, R.O., *The Ancient Egyptian Book of the Dead* (British Museum Press, 1989)
Foster, J.L., *Hymns, Prayers and Songs, An Anthology of Ancient Egyptian Lyric Poetry* (Scholars Press, Atlanta, Georgia, 1995)
Frankfort, H., *Kingship and the Gods, a study of Near Eastern Religion as the Integration of Society and Nature* (University of Chicago Press, 1948)
Ghalioungui, P., *Medicine and Magic in Ancient Egypt* (London, 1963)
Gwyn-Griffiths, J., *Plutarch's De Iside et Osiride* (University of Wales, 1970)
Hart, G., *Egyptian Myths* (British Museum Press, 1990)
Hart, G., *A Dictionary of Egyptian Gods and Goddesses* (Routledge & Kegan Paul, 1986)
Herodotus, *The Histories* (Penguin, 1972)
Hornung, E., *Conceptions of God in Ancient Egypt: The One and the Many* (Routledge & Kegan Paul, 1983)
Iversen, E., *The Myth of Egypt and its Hieroglyphs in European Tradition* (Copenhagen, 1961)
Janssen, R.& J., *Growing Up in Ancient Egypt* (Rubicon, 1990)
Kemp, B.J., *Ancient Egypt: Anatomy of a Civilisation* (Routledge, 1989, reprint 1991)
Lehner, M., *The Complete Pyramids* (Thames & Hudson, 1997)
Lichtheim, M., *Ancient Egyptian Literature Vol. I-III* (University of California, 1973-80)
Meeks, D. & **Favard-Meeks,** C., *Daily Life of the Egyptian Gods* (London, 1996)
Morenz, S., *Egyptian Religion* (Methuen, 1973)
Nunn, J.F., *Ancient Egyptian Medicine* (British Museum Press, 1997)
Pinch, G., *New Kingdom Votive Offerings to Hathor* (Oxford, 1993)
Pinch, G., *Magic in Ancient Egypt* (British Museum Press, 1994)
Quirke, S., *Who were the Pharaohs?* (British Museum Press, 1990)
Quirke, S., *Ancient Egyptian Religion* (British Museum Press, 1992)
Quirke, S., *Hieroglyphs and the Afterlife in Ancient Egypt* (British Museum Press, 1996)
Redford, D.B., *Akhenaten: The Heretic King* (Princeton, 1984)
Reeves, N., *The Complete Tutankhamun* (Thames and Hudson, 1990)
Reeves, N. & **Wilkinson,** R.H., *The Complete Valley of the Kings* (Thames and Hudson, 1996)
Robins, G., *Women in Ancient Egypt* (British Museum Press, 1993)
Romer, J., *Ancient Lives* (Henry Holt and Co., 1984)
Sadek, A.I., *Popular Religion in Egypt during the New Kingdom* (Hildesheim, 1987)
Sauneron, S., *The Priests of Ancient Egypt* (Grove, 1960)
Shafer, B.E., (ed.), *Religion in Ancient Egypt* (Cornell, 1991)
Shaw, I. & **Nicholson,** P., *British Museum Dictionary of Ancient Egypt* (British Museum Press, 1995)
Snape, S. *Egyptian Temples* (Shire, 1996)
Spencer, A.J., *Death in Ancient Egypt* (Penguin, 1982)
Taylor, J.H., *Death and the Afterlife in Ancient Egypt* (British Museum Press, 1999)
Velde, H. te, *Seth, God of Confusion* (2nd edn) (1977)
Watson, P., *Egyptian Pyramids and Mastaba Tombs* (Shire, 1987)
Wildung, D., *Egyptian Saints: Deification in Pharaonic Egypt* (New York University Press, 1977)
Wilkinson, R.H., *Reading Egyptian Art: A Hieroglyphic Guide to Ancient Egyptian Painting and Sculpture* (Thames and Hudson, 1992)

Acknowledgements

AKG Photographic
p7 top (Agyptisches Museum, Berlin), 12–13, 18 bottom (Egyptian Museum, Cairo), 19 left, p28 (Louvre, Paris), p29 bottom (Louvre, Paris), p32 top, p32 bottom (Luxor Museum), p39 (British Museum, London), p41 top (Kunthistorisches Museum, Vienna), p45 bottom, 46 left, p54 top, p66 (National Maritime Museum, Haifa), p77 bottom (Egyptian Museum, Cairo), p83 bottom (Kunthistorisches Museum, Vienna), p88–89, p92 top, p100–101, p114 right, p118, p121 (Roemer-Pelizaeus Museum, Hildesheim), p124 right (Louvre, Paris), p130 left (Egyptian Museum, Cairo), p138–139 (British Museum, London), p145 bottom (Aegyptisches Museum, Berlin), p165 (Aegyptisches Museum, Berlin), p168 top, p175 bottom, p176, p179 right (Louvre, Paris), p186 top and bottom, p195 top, p196, p197 Kunsthistorisches Museum, p212, p217 bottom, p224 bottom (Rijksmuseum van Oudheden), p230 top, p238 top, p241 (Louvre, Paris), p242

A M Dodson
p156 right, p208 top, p231 (Museum of Metropolitan Art, New York)

The Ancient Art & Architecture Collection
p8 bottom, p18 top, 36 bottom, 38 bottom, p58 top, p59 left, p64 left, p65 bottom, p67 top and bottom, p68, p71 right, p78 top, p102 top and bottom, p109, p110, p111 bottom, p112 bottom, p116 left, p119 top and bottom, p128 top, p131 right, p146, p148 bottom, p149, p161 left, p164 right, p169, p182 bottom, p204 top, p209, p213 left, p215 bottom, p218, p219 bottom, p220, p 229

The Ancient Egypt Picture Library
p19 right, p20, p30 top, 38 top (Egyptian Museum, Cairo), p43, 45 top, 47 top, p52 bottom, p56, p58 bottom, p62 bottom (Louvre, Paris), p64 right, p70 left, p80 bottom (British Museum, London), p84, p92 bottom, p94 bottom, p103 bottom, p105 top, p106, p108 bottom, p115 top, p120 right (British Museum, London), p122 bottom (British Museum, London), p133 top, p148 top, p156 left (British Museum, London), p168 bottom (British Museum, London), p175 top, p179 left, p184 bottom, p185 (Fitzwilliam Museum, University of Cambridge), p190, Egyptian Museum, Cairo), p193 top (Egyptian Museum, Cairo), p197 top, p200 left (Louvre, Paris), p204 bottom (Egyptian Museum, Cairo), p207 (Egyptian Museum, Cairo), p211 top, p219 top, p222 top (British Museum, London), p225 top (British Museum, London), p226 bottom (Louvre, Paris), p227 top and bottom, p230 bottom, p232 bottom, p233, p234, p243 top

The Art Archive
p6 bottom, p10 bottom, p21 right (Egyptian Museum, Cairo), p22 (Egyptian Museum, Cairo), p29 top (Egyptian Museum, Cairo), p31, p34 top, 37 top (Egyptian Museum, Cairo), p42 top, p70 right (Egyptian Museum, Cairo), p71 left (Louvre, Paris), p94 top (Egyptian Museum, Cairo), p113, p116 right (Egyptian Museum, Cairo), p120 left (Louvre, Paris), p143top right (Egyptian Museum, Cairo), p145 top (British Museum, London), p150 top, p159 bottom (Louvre, Paris), p163 (Egyptian Museum, Cairo), p166 top (British Museum, London), p174 bottom, p181 top left (Egyptian Museum, Cairo), p184 top (Egyptian Museum, Turin), p187, p194 (Egyptian Museum, Cairo), p199 (British Museum, London), p205, top (Egyptian Museum, Cairo), p213 right (Louvre, Paris), p215 top (British Museum, London), p217 left (Louvre, Paris), p224 bottom (Egyptian Museum, Cairo), p226 top (British Museum, London), p228 (Egyptian Museum, Cairo), p236–237 (Luigi Mayer, 'Views in Egypt', 1801), p238 bottom (Antalya Museum), p240 top (British Museum), p243 bottom (Civic Museum, Turin)

The Bridgeman Art Library
p2 (British Museum, London), p9 left (The Louvre, Paris), p10 top (Ashmolean Museum, Oxford), p21 left (Louvre, Paris), p23 left (Freud Museum, London), p23 right (Ashmolean Museum, Oxford), p33 bottom (British Museum), p35 top (Louvre, Paris), p40 top (Sir John Soane Museum, London), p40 bottom (Louvre, Paris), p41 bottom (British Museum, London), p42 bottom (Louvre, Paris), p46 right, p51 bottom (British Museum, London), p 54 bottom (Fitzwilliam Museum, University of Cambridge), p57 (Stapleton Collection), p61 bottom (British Museum, London), p62 top (Freud Museum, London), p69 (Ashmolean Museum, Oxford), p74 top (Ashmolean Museum, Oxford), p74 bottom, p78 bottom (Giraudon), p80 top (British Museum, London), p82 (Fitzwilliam Museum, Cambridge), p85 bottom (Bode Museum, Berlin), p93, p95 bottom, p98, p99 top, 108 top, p114 left, p122 top (Louvre), p123 (Louvre, Paris), p130 right, p132 (Ashmolean Museum, Oxford), p140 bottom (Fitzwilliam Museum, Cambridge), p141 (Louvre, Paris), p147 top (British Museum, London, p147 bottom (Louvre, Paris), p 153 top (Louvre, Paris), p153 bottom (British Museum, London), p154 (Louvre, Paris), p155 right (Bonhams, London), p158 (Ashmolean Museum, Oxford), p159 top (British Museum, London), p164 left (British Museum, London), p166 bottom (Ashmolean Museum, Oxford), p167 right (Louvre, Paris), p167 left (Ashmolean Museum, Oxford), p170–171, p172 (Louvre, Paris), p181 bottom (Fitzwilliam Museum, University of Cambridge), p202 (Louvre, Paris), p211 bottom (Louvre, Paris), p222 bottom (Ashmolean Museum, Oxford), p224 top (Egyptian Museum, Turin), p232 top (Louvre, Paris), p239 (Museo Archeologico Prenestino, Palestrina), p244 top (The Illustrated London, News Picture Library, London)

C M Dixon
p27 right (National Museum, Florence)

Hulton Getty
p245 top and bottom

The Hutchinson Library
p177 top

Lucia Gahlin
p9 right, p30 bottom, 35 bottom, p50, p87 top, p99 bottom, p103 top, p111 top, p112 top, p128 bottom, p129, p177 bottom, p192, p208 bottom

Michael Holford
p27 left (British Museum, London), p27 middle (British Museum, London), p33 top, p198 left (British Museum, London), p203 top, p216 (British Museum, London), p223 (British Museum, London)

Peter Clayton
p37 bottom, p52 top, p63, p72 top and bottom, p81, p83 top, p115 bottom, p124 left

Robert Harding
p6 top, p36 top (Egyptian Museum, Cairo), p53, p85 top, p87 bottom, p95 top, p133 left, p182 top, p183 top and bottom (both Egyptian Museum, Cairo), p201

Sylvia Cordaiy Photo Library
p8 top, p104 top, p173 top (Guy Marks), p174 top, p178 (Johnathan Smith)

Travel Ink
p16–17, p55, p73, p79, p104 bottom

The Griffith Institute/Ashmolean Museum, Oxford
p244 bottom

Werner Forman Archive
p24 (Egyptian Museum, Cairo), p34 bottom (Egyptian Museum, Cairo), p47 bottom (Egyptian Museum, Cairo), p51 top (Schultz Collection, New York), p59 right (Egyptian Museum), p60, p61 top (courtesy L'Ibis, New York), p65 top, p75 (Archaelological Museum, Khartoum), p76 (E Strouhal), p77 top (Egyptian Museum, Cairo), p86, 105 bottom, p107 top and bottom, p117 (Louvre, Paris), p125 (Egyptian Museum, Cairo), p126–7 (Brooklyn Museum, New York), p131 left (Egyptian Museum, Cairo), p134–135, p140 top, p142 (Dr E Strouhal), p143 bottom left and right, p144 (Louvre, Paris), p150 bottom (E Strouhal), p151, p152 (Egyptian Museum, Cairo), p155 left (private collection), p157 (Egyptian Museum, Cairo), p160 (British Museum, London), p161 right (Egyptian Museum, Cairo), p162 left (Egyptian Museum, Cairo), p162 right (E Strouhal), p180 (Cheops Barque Museum), p181 top right, p188–189, p191 (Manchester Museum), p193 (Metropolitan Museum of Art, New York), p195 bottom (Graeco-Roman Museum, Alexandria), p198 right (Rijksmuseum van Oudeheden, Leiden), p200 right (Aegyptisches Museum, Berlin), p203 bottom (Fitzwilliam Museum, University of Cambridge), p205 (Sold at Christie's, London), p206 (British Museum, London), p210 (Egyptian Museum, Turin), p214, p221, p235, p240 bottom (Egyptian Museum, Cairo)

Index

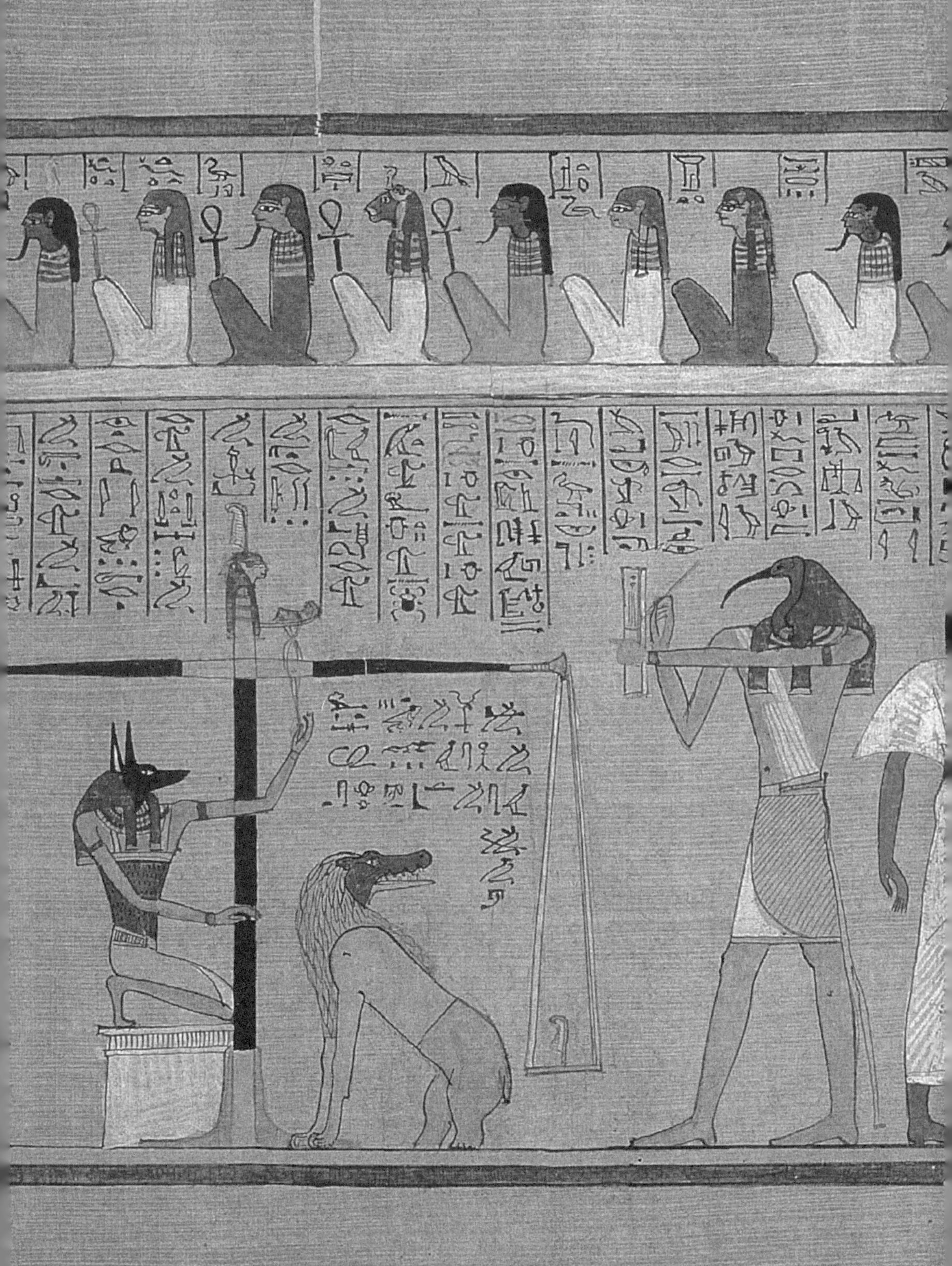